ANNOTATED INSTRUCTOR'S EDITION

TEACHING READING IN THE ELEMENTARY GRADES

ANNOTATED INSTRUCTOR'S EDITION
TEACHING READING IN THE ELEMENTARY GRADES

MARVIN L. KLEIN
Professor of Curriculum & Instruction
Western Washington University

AND
SUSAN PETERSON
Instructional Specialist
Bellingham Public Schools

LINDA SIMINGTON
Director of Instruction
Portland Public Schools

ALLYN AND BACON
Boston • London • Toronto • Sydney • Tokyo • Singapore

Series Editor: Sean W. Wakely
Series Editorial Assistant: Carol L. Chernaik
Production Administrator: Peter Petraitis
Editorial-Production Service: York Production Services
Design: York Production Services
Photo Research: Lisa Feder
Composition Buyer: Linda Cox
Cover Administrator: Linda Dickinson
Manufacturing Buyer: Louise Richardson

Copyright ©1991, Allyn and Bacon
A Division of Simon & Schuster, Inc.
160 Gould Street
Needham Heights, MA 02194

ISBN 0-205-12847-5

Printed in the United States of America

10 9 8 7 6 5 4 3 2 1   96 95 94 93 92 91 90

IS-iv

BRIEF CONTENTS

Contents of Instructor's Section

Introduction to Instructor's Section   IS-vii

Instructor's Section   IS-1

Contents of Student Text

Preface   xv

Chapter 1:   Introduction to Reading and Reading Instruction   1

Chapter 2:   Early Literacy Acquisition and Development   3

Chapter 3:   Literacy Instruction in the Kindergarten   5

Chapter 4:   Teaching and Mentoring the Apprentice Reader   7

Chapter 5:   Planning and Organizing Instruction for the Primary Grades   9

Chapter 6:   The Essential Elements of Reading and Reading Instruction   12

Chapter 7:   Developing Reading Comprehension in the Elementary Grades   14

Chapter 8:   Teaching Reading Vocabulary Throughout the Elementary Grades   16

Chapter 9:   Teaching Study Skills Throughout the Elementary Grades   18

Chapter 10:   Monitoring and Organizing for Reading Instruction and Learning Throughout the Grades   20

Chapter 11:   Reading and the Middle-School Learner   22

Chapter 12:   Teaching the Novel in the Middle Grades   23

Chapter 13:   The Foundations of Children's Literature   25

Chapter 14:   Teaching Reading to the Student with Reading Difficulties   27

Introduction to
Teaching Reading in the Elementary Grades

This comprehensive reading methods text is designed for undergraduate and graduate elementary reading methods courses. We have attempted to make this book not only readable but also valuable for the "soon-to-be" elementary teacher of reading. In fact, our goal was to create a book so rich with ideas for teaching reading effectively it would become an essential professional reference throughout many years of teaching.

Teaching Reading in the Elementary Grades reflects a solid base of reading theory and research. Yet, we do not let theoretical issues dominate the more important mission of providing prospective new teachers with practical and workable ideas for teaching reading effectively throughout the K-8 grade range.

We have also tried to make this book unique in a number of respects, all of which are important to a new teacher of reading. Some of these features are described later in this preface. First, however, we want you to know our philosophy so that you can see why some of these features were created.

Philosophy

This book is based upon the following fundamental beliefs about reading and reading instruction:

1. Young children bring to the beginning school years a rich and vital linguistic literacy that has emerged from a wealth of language-using contexts. That natural

Offers excellent coverage of planning and organizing reading instruction

CHAPTER 5

PLANNING AND ORGANIZING INSTRUCTION FOR THE PRIMARY GRADES

There are only two qualities in the world, efficiency and inefficiency; and only two sorts of people, the efficient and inefficient.

George Bernard Shaw, *John Bull's Other Island*, 1904

PREVIEW

FOCUS QUESTIONS

130

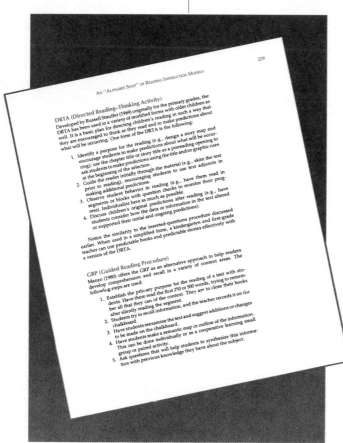

evolving literacy in children provides the fundamental base on which an effective teacher of reading builds to help children become effective and efficient readers. That means that in the early school years, the teacher accepts the language the children bring to the classroom and uses that language ability and their prior experiences to build a more powerful literacy.

2. Language develops naturally when children live and learn in meaningful language-using contexts where they are encouraged to explore talking, reading, and writing, and to see language as both a powerful tool and an enjoyable and exciting part of themselves.

Demonstrates ways of grouping children and organizing for instruction and thoroughly covers a wide variety of reading instruction models.

3. Learners throughout the elementary grades learn to read most effectively when they are in classrooms where teachers teach reading, writing, speaking, and listening in an integrated fashion, and where students are encouraged to view reading as a vital part of an integrated language-using whole rather than as a separate set of isolated skills.

4. The effective teacher of reading functions as an orchestrator of instruction. Children and teacher are partners in a classroom that is a literacy community, with all sharing in the growth of reading, writing, and speaking skills.

5. The classroom teacher maintains balanced instruction in strategies, techniques, and activities. The needs of the learner determine context, timing, and instruction type. The teacher of reading exploits that natural language ability of children in teaching children to be good readers. She or he does not assume that reading ability evolves without instruction. If learners are to reach their greatest potential reading proficiency, then teachers must provide professional instruction.

How the Philosophy is Reflected in this Text

ORGANIZATION OF THE TEXT

The authors recognize the unique nature of learners in the primary grades, intermediate grades, and middle-school grades. The instructional strategies and techniques reflect the needs of learners at these different stages of their development.

Chapter 1 provides a background for the remainder of the text, with an examination of literacy generally and reading in particular. Differing definitions of reading and reading instruction are reviewed.

Chapters 2 through 5 focus on the primary grades, with specific attention to needs of kindergartners and first and second graders.

Chapters 6 through 10 focus on reading instruction through the intermediate grades, with suggested instructional adjustments for teaching comprehension, vocabulary, and study skills across all of the elementary grades range.

Chapters 11 and 12 focus directly on the middle-school grades, with examination of the middle-school learner and consideration of the unique demands of teaching narrative to these students.

Chapter 13 specially treats children's literature across the curriculum and across the grades. Chapter 14 is also cross-curricular and cross-grade as it addresses the instructional needs of special populations of learners.

FOCUS QUESTIONS

Each chapter begins with a brief introduction and several focus questions to help

Reinforcement Activities extend students' thinking and provide helpful suggestions and internal cross-referencing for the instructor.

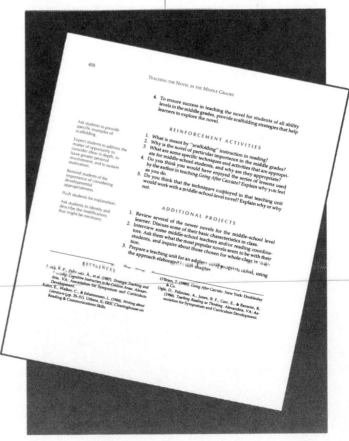

Page from the Annotated Instructor's Edition showing annotations.

the reader establish some important mental benchmarks (advance organizers) for reading the chapter.

HIGHLIGHTS

In addition, each chapter concludes with a "Highlights" section, which summarizes key ideas presented in the chapter. These offer a quick review and refer back to the focus questions.

ADDITIONAL PROJECTS

Finally, each chapter includes suggested additional activities or projects that provide opportunities to extend the learning in a variety of ways.

Chapter 1 provides an insightful treatment of metacognition

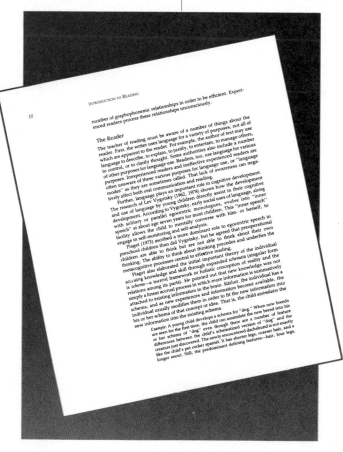

Integrated Approach

This text provides instructional models that consistently capitalize on relationships among elements and features of language. For example, oral language and writing are viewed as integral features of literacy development. The oral language base is emphasized in the instructional strategies and techniques offered for the primary grades. The reading-writing connection is emphasized throughout all of the text for all of the grades, K-8. Also, though children's literature receives a separate focused chapter, both children's literature and content-related subject-matter are used throughout all of the instructional approaches presented in this book.

DIRECT INSTRUCTION

We define <u>direct instruction</u> as the approach to teaching that moves from objectives to orchestrated instructional events to the learning outcomes that occur in the learner. This does not mean, however, that we advocate a particular learning theory (e.g., behaviorism); nor does it mean that we advocate a particular program or skill sequence for instruction. It particularly does not mean that we believe in teaching skills in drill-like isolated lessons.

It does mean that we believe that the teacher of reading is responsible for designing instruction that is organized and coherent so that children can see why they are doing what they are doing in learning to read. The teacher, as orchestrator of learning, creates and adapts the learning environment through careful selection of instructional strategies and techniques that make sense both to the teacher and to the learners.

To orchestrate effective learning, the teacher must engage in an ongoing self-monitoring of the relationship between objectives and instructional events.

Provides practical and workable ideas for prospective teachers — it's a book your students will value and keep.

MONITORING AND EVALUATING READING APPROACH

Monitoring and evaluating reading performance is an important component of reading instruction. The concept of the assessment portfolio, presented in this text, is intended to assist the teacher in a variety of ways. Information accumulated in the portfolio assists the teacher in diagnosing learner strengths and weaknesses in reading and reading-related areas and in designing instruction for meeting individual student needs. In addition, it can serve as a conferencing tool to use with children, parents, and/or supervisor or principal.

GROUPING AND MANAGING FOR INSTRUCTION

The models presented in this text for grouping children and organizing for instruction allow the teacher to choose from different configurations for different purposes. The approaches offered are selected to reflect the integrated philoso-

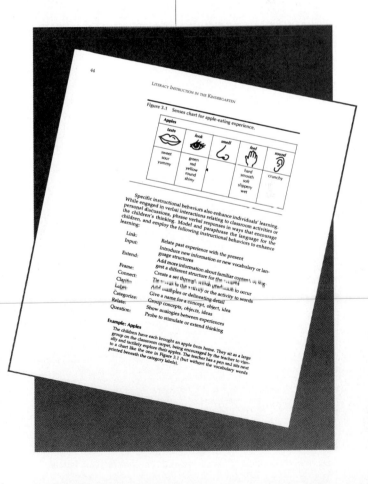

phy of instruction suggested in the various instructional strategies and techniques offered throughout the book.

Acknowledgments

Any book project such as this requires immense support and assistance. Many of those who provide it are behind the scenes — editors, typesetters, printers, marketing and sales people, and so on. Thanks to all of you unknown folks.

Others are easier to identify:

Thank you, Karen, Terry, Burl, and other members of our families for being patient, caring, and always supportive when our work took valuable family time from you. Thank you, Carol Chernaik, Sean Wakely, and others at Allyn & Bacon who have been so patient and helpful along the way. Your confidence in the worth of this project has yielded dividends not possible without your efforts.

Thanks to all of the many reviewers who reviewed with great care and detailed attention to the various stages of manuscript development.

All have our thanks and appreciation. We know this book is better for your help.

REVIEWERS

Carmella Abbruzzese
Regis College

Jack Bagford
University of Iowa

Sandra Hollingsworth
University of California, Berkeley

Susan Daniels
University of Akron

Jill Fitzgerald
University of North Carolina, Chapel Hill

The Annotated Instuctor's Edition — it's an Instructor's Section and fully annotated text bound in one volume working together to provide you with the most complete teaching resource available for the elementary reading methods course.

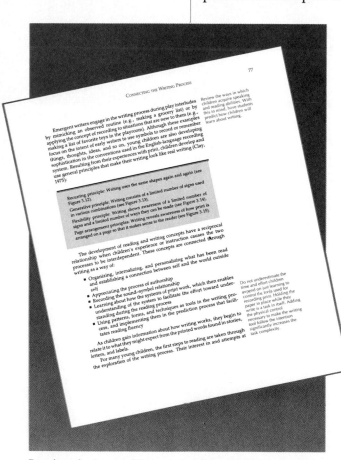

Page from the Annotated Instructor's Edition showing annotations.

Judith Meagher
University of Connecticut

Fred Maclaren
Eastern Illinois University

Leo Schell
Kansas State University

Martha McKnight
University of Louisville

Darlene Michener
California State University, Los Angeles

Marie Eaton
Fairhaven College

Richard Chambers
Boston University

Victoria Hare
University of Illinois

John Beach
University of Maine

Last, but not least, thank you to the hundreds of reading researchers at work every day to advance the development of literacy in the world, to the thousands of classroom teachers, and to the millions of children who make it all worth the effort!

Marv Klein
Susan Peterson
Linda Simington

A Test Bank with 237 items and an IBM Compterized Test Bank complete the teaching materials.

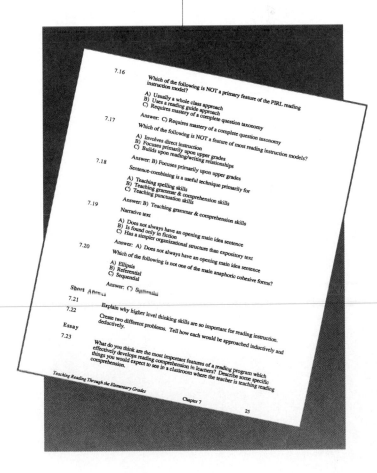

1 ▶ INTRODUCTION TO READING AND READING INSTRUCTION

Chapter Objectives

1. To provide a brief historical overview of educators' conceptions of *reading*

2. To describe and explain different contemporary beliefs about reading and about the reading act

3. To define *reading* as an interactive process

Chapter Overview

Chapter 1 provides a historical and philosophical foundation for the development of a personal definition of reading and of the teaching of reading to children. The chapter is introduced with a historical overview of reading and of historical changes in perspective about how best to teach it. Factors in the 1960s and 1970s that affected reading instruction are discussed. Also examined is the dominant contemporary view of reading as an interactive process. The importance of *process, strategic approach, interactions among reading elements,* and *reading-teacher-as-orchestrator* is emphasized.

The psycholinguistic elements of reading are presented. The text—the semantic, syntactic, and graphophonemic systems—are described. The role of the reader and schema theory are examined, with special emphasis on the notion of how meaning is generated by the reader. Also discussed is the element of "context" and how it interacts with the other elements.

The final portion of this chapter deals with the "Bottom-Up" and the "Top-Down" models of reading, including discussion of how each has dominated at different times since the 1960s. Brief summaries of the specific tenets of each model are provided for the reader.

Key Concepts and Ideas in the Chapter

- Reading as an interrelated component of the language arts
- Relationships between reading and language
- Reading as a skill
- Reading as a process
- Reading as a strategic endeavor
- Reading as an interactive activity
- Psycholinguistic elements of reading
- Schema theory
- Bottom-Up reading models
- Top-Down reading models

Teaching Ideas

1. Ask students to interview their parents, grandparents, or other mature adults, asking them to recall how they learned to read. Have students discuss the results of their interviews in class.

INSTRUCTORS' SECTION

2. Organize students into pairs or small groups, and ask them to examine selected popular basal reading programs from the 1950s, 1960s, 1970s, and 1980s. Ask the pairs or groups to formulate several important general differences and several important similarities that hold over the past several decades of basal reader production.

3. Assign students to several teams. Ask half of the teams to prepare "Top-Down" lesson plans for a first-grade beginning reading class. Ask the others to prepare "Bottom-Up" lesson plans. Have the groups teach their lessons to the rest of the class, which role-plays being first graders. Discuss with students the practical teaching differences in the various lessons.

4. Have students compare different reading programs or approaches within the same reading "camp" (i.e., Top-Down or Bottom-Up). For example, they might compare the McCrackens' conception of the Language-Experience approach to reading instruction with the approach of Jeanette Veach or Roach Van Allen. Alternatively, they might examine commercial basal programs that are still premised on a "phonics-first" philosophy. Also discuss the differences that exist within the same philosophical camps.

2 ▶
EARLY LITERACY ACQUISITION AND DEVELOPMENT

Chapter Objectives

1. To provide an overview of the development of oral language in young children
2. To provide an overview of the development of print awareness in children through the early years
3. To provide a set of guidelines regarding curriculum and instructional design for literacy development

Chapter Overview

This chapter is designed to provide a brief overview of the development of language and literacy in young children. It assumes limited, if any, background in developmental psycholinguistics on the part of the student. Language and literacy development are examined as naturally developing processes in the young child.

Oral language development occurs in stages, each of which is characterized by key features that are generalizable to all normally developing children. The authors' position is that teachers should be open, objective, and respectful regarding the oral language of children. The chapter emphasizes the importance of the home environment, the role of oral language as a communication tool for the developing child, and the differing purposes and forms of oral language, depending on context.

The development of meaning receives special attention because of its importance, while its inseparability from both oral language and print is high-lighted. The chapter also addresses the difference between *concrete meanings* and *abstract meanings,* both of which are necessary for literacy instruction generally and for reading instruction in particular.

Developing print awareness in children is also treated as a naturally developing process in consonance with the development of oral language. The abstract character of print and the crucial importance of understanding the concept of *symbol* for the developing child are emphasized because the discovery of print as being symbolic must precede reading acquisition. Children's awareness of print's symbolic character is an important factor for the teacher of young children to consider when selecting and designing instruction and instructional materials.

Finally, the chapter presents a set of guidelines on literacy development, which bear directly on the design of instruction and the design and selection of instructional materials and contexts.

Key Concepts and Ideas in the Chapter

* "Literacy" as mental set
* Language as developmental process
* Language functions
* Language through developmental stages
* Oral language base

* *Meaning*—concrete and abstract
* Print awareness
* *Symbol* as a concept
* Reading aloud
* Early writing

Teaching Ideas

1. Have students visit a preschool where they can observe young children in a variety of different contexts (e.g., on the playground, in problem-solving situations [working alone and working with another child], in large group learning situations with the teacher directing the context). Discuss the differences in the language used by the children in these different contexts: What are the vocabulary differences, differences in tone of voice (pitch and stress), and differences in the balance of social versus egocentric speech?

2. Ask students to collect samples of early "writing" from children (i.e., from earliest stages of scribble writing to more advanced stages of invented spelling). Have students, working in pairs, generate a set of generalizations that describe the key features or attributes of the different stages of early writing development.

3. Invite a kindergarten teacher to make a presentation to class, discussing the pros and cons of scribble writing and invented spelling as encouraged components of an early literacy development program.

4. Have students find examples of what they think are the best and the worst of instructional materials for use in kindergarten/first-grade curriculum.

3 ▶
LITERACY INSTRUCTION IN THE KINDERGARTEN

Chapter Objectives

1. To develop a knowledge of the elements of a developmentally appropriate reading program
2. To describe the role of the teacher in creating an integrated literacy curriculum
3. To delineate instructional strategies that facilitate language development
4. To provide models for children's active participation in the reading-writing process

Chapter Overview

Based on the learning characteristics of young children, the integrated literacy program described in this chapter is founded on three assumptions:

1. Children seek knowledge and understanding of themselves, others, and their world.
2. Children learn through a process of interaction and reconstruction.
3. Children reference and cross-reference experiences in order to create and test concepts and to build generalizations.

The value of play and the role of the teacher in creating an environment in which children are encouraged to learn through that process is structured using child-centered and teacher-directed instruction.

Child-centered instruction provides opportunities for exploration, application, and practice of new concepts through the manipulation of materials, interaction with peers, and guidance by the teacher. As the children work individually or in small groups in play centers, emphasis is on personal responsibility, decision making, and problem solving.

Teacher-directed instructional opportunities are developed from an objective and move from the children's prior knowledge to the new information or skill and then on to apply to new situations. These instructional steps include

1. Involvement—Linking past experience and knowledge with the instruction that is going to occur
2. Instruction—Modeling with manipulatives or actual materials what is to be learned; instructing

by demonstrating, "this is how you do it"; applying skills or information to the children's daily life and providing opportunities for the children to practice using the skills or the knowledge
3. Expansion—Linking the new concept or skill with other learning

Language learning is the foundation for literacy instruction. The teacher develops lessons, activities, and environments that encourage children to have meaningful oral interaction with adults and peers in both formal and informal settings.

Reading comprehension is the child's ability to make meaning from print. It is a function of the child's ability to predict what will come next, to check to see whether the prediction was correct, and then to analyze why it was or was not accurate. Questioning, summarizing, and story retelling are three strategies that children can experience that will facilitate their comprehension. Learning to comprehend is an activity that takes place within the context of the reading process (i.e., children learn to make meaning from print by actively engaging in the process of meaningful reading).

Children are encouraged to engage in the literacy process through reading big books, little books, charts, trade books, and environmental print. They are also engaged in the process through print experiences such as journal writing, bookmaking, letter writing, and dictation. This chapter provides strategies for engaging children in these processes.

Key Concepts and Ideas in the Chapter

- Developmentally appropriate reading instruction
- Literacy development from integrated language experiences
- Role of the teacher in developing formal and informal environments
- Writing process
- Comprehension as a function of the reading process

Teaching Ideas

1. Present the students with three elements of the instructional process: (a) classroom environment, (b) teacher philosophy, and (c) instruction materials. Ask them to select one and defend it as the most important element in the instructional process.

2. Working in teams, have the students create a collage, mural, or poster representing their philosophy of literacy instruction for the young child. Challenge them to address as many areas as they believe affects the reading process.

3. Ask the students to review several articles from periodicals such as *Young Children, Childhood Education,* or *The Reading Teacher,* which focus on the emergent reader. Have the class members create an annotated bibliography to use as a reference for topic discussions.

4. Have the students select one of the language arts areas—listening, speaking, reading, or writing—and have them work in groups to create menus of activities to share with the other group members.

4 ▶ TEACHING AND MENTORING THE APPRENTICE READER

Chapter Objectives

1. To describe strategies that foster the development of work acquisition and comprehension
2. To define instructional, practice, and independent reading practices
3. To outline writing opportunities that support the reading process
4. To provide an overview of reading methods

Chapter Overview

This chapter deals specifically with the instructional needs of apprentice readers and with the instructional processes that support their apprenticeship.

Instruction is organized into three types of reading that facilitate reading acquisition. The first, instructional reading, features word acquisition and comprehension as it is developed within meaningful text. Word acquisition is treated as a developmental process dependent on a child's recognition and application of semantic, structural, and phonetic cuing systems. The authors discuss an initial sight vocabulary as a basis for phonics instruction, with an emphasis on instruction emerging from text in which the children are engaged. Suggested strategies also include both inductive and deductive instructional models.

The development of reading comprehension is an extension of the suggested strategies mentioned in the previous chapter. Based on the theory that children construct meaning from the text, the suggested strategies are to be used in connection with the stories the children are reading or are having read to them. This chapter includes examples of (a) meeting the developmental needs of the learner, (b) questioning, (c) story mapping, and (d) sociograms.

This chapter also includes effective practices for providing and supporting opportunities for children's practice reading and independent reading. Grouping configurations and strategies that most effectively support these reading activities are highlighted.

The final section of this chapter reviews a menu of several reading methods. These overviews are intended to provide beginning teachers with a way to categorize materials in terms of the basic philosophy on which they are developed and to begin forming initial criteria for program evaluation.

Key Concepts and Ideas in the Chapter

- Vocabulary acquisition
- Semantic and structural cuing
- Phonics
- Comprehension development
- Story maps and sociograms
- Continuous and culminating questions
- Grouping practices
- Integrated reading and writing
- Transition to independent reading
- Reading methods

INSTRUCTOR'S SECTION

Teaching Ideas

1. Have the students review several articles from professional journals, such as *Young Children* and *The Reading Teacher,* related to the strategies presented in this chapter.
2. Ask the students to select a language arts activity and develop a *task analysis* for it (i.e., the skill and knowledge a child must have in order to achieve success at the task).
3. Present teams of four to six students with children's work from a classroom assignment. Ask the students to rate the work, using a scale, and to justify the criteria they used.
4. Have students investigate the concept of *readers' theater* and plan a lesson using selected literature.
5. Discuss the needs of students from a variety of cultural backgrounds. Explore stories, poems, songs, and chants that may facilitate instruction. Investigate the community resources available to assist both the child and the teacher.

5 ▶
PLANNING AND ORGANIZING INSTRUCTION FOR THE PRIMARY GRADES

Chapter Objectives

1. To provide knowledge of the necessary considerations in designing a positive classroom learning environment

2. To introduce and develop organizational and management systems that facilitate instruction
3. To offer models for integrating language arts using literary and content themes

Chapter Overview

This chapter presents systems and strategies for planning an instructional environment that encourages children's literacy development in the classroom setting. The information is presented in two sections:
1. Organizing and managing the instructional setting

2. Planning and implementing the instructional process

Each of these sections offers models that can be implemented in a primary classroom as well as rationales for their use.

Organizing and Managing the Instructional Setting

The instructional setting is organized by planning the physical environment to accommodate large group, small group, and individual work areas. Planning also takes into consideration easy access to all work areas and to supplies and materials.

Planning the daily schedule maximizes the use of time and organizes it into routines that encourage the children to plan their own use of time and that encourage a sense of expectancy and consistency. The design of the daily schedule is based on the developmental needs of the children, physically, emotionally, socially, and intellectually.

Within the daily routine, children can be grouped for instruction as a whole group, as a series of small groups, as peer partners, or as individuals working independently. The selection of these groupings are the result of teacher analysis of the objective of instruction, the time allocated, the materials involved, and the background knowledge and

developmental level of the children. The students participate in the management of the groupings (a) through the use of teacher-made charts designating the time and the task to be accomplished and (b) by learning and practicing study habits taught by the teacher.

This chapter describes two categories of school work habits. The first category is called "group work skills" and is related to those abilities that enable the child to function as a positive group member. These skills typically include
• Participation in group activity
• Following directions
• Attention to discussion
• Attention to task
• Maintenance of work area
• Conformity to rules

The second category includes personal or individual work skills, such as

- Maintenance of personal work area
- Care of personal belongings
- Independence
- Decision making and problem solving
- Appropriate use of time
- Attention to task
- Initiation of work

The authors suggest the direct instruction of the basic work routine to give children a foundation for systematic and consistent use of their time. A typical work routine includes the following:

Get a job.
Go to work.
Complete the work.
Clean up where you were working.
Get another job.

The study habits and work routines included are not intended to suit every classroom situation but to give beginning teachers a springboard for developing their own guidelines, using their own language. Using their own language is an important point because whatever phrases are selected must come naturally to the speaker. The phrases will be repeated many times within each instructional interlude within the day, both formally and informally. In order for the teacher to be effective, these phrases must flow naturally, almost automatically, before the need for them arises.

Planning and Implementing the Instructional Process

The intent of this section is to put the initiate teachers in the situation of thinking over what it is they expect the children to be doing on their own during instruction. It is not unusual for beginning teachers to focus on the instructional plan of the content they are teaching before they have taught their students to behave appropriately during that instruction. Some discussion on what these behaviors are and how to teach them will offer both teacher and student increased success.

Because many of the students in college today are of the age to have received reading instruction that was segmented in terms of listening, speaking, and writing, as well as in the content areas, the concept of integration can be both intriguing and frustrating. It is intriguing because it is new to them and holds a promise of being creative, natural, and enjoyable. It is frustrating because these student teachers have not had the necessary background experiences in integrated literacy curriculum and instruction.

Planning for and delivering instruction requires the students to focus not only on an understanding of the task or knowledge being taught and the background needed to learn it but also on the processes available through which to facilitate the instruction most effectively. The authors focus on the necessity of an organic integration of the language arts, as well as its integration with other content areas. The three strategies suggested for integration—linking, pairing, and combining—provide models for planning based on defined instructional objectives and learners' needs. The intention is to help the students develop abilities in terms of subject or content-area knowledge and skills, as well as in terms of their articulation of that knowledge.

Key Concepts and Ideas in the Chapter

- Organizing the instructional environment
- Instructional management
- Grouping for instruction
- Group management systems
- Work and study habits

- Integrating the language arts
- Integrated instructional planning
- Literary and content themes
- Short- and long-term planning

Teaching Ideas

1. Invite the students to examine school equipment and materials catalogues, with language arts instruction as a focus. Give each student a budget with which to purchase materials to build a balanced reading program for their classroom. Let them report to group members their choices and how they will be used for instruction.

2. Collect daily and weekly schedules from several teachers, and have the students critique them in terms of grouping practices and integration techniques.

3. Invite a Chapter I (Program funded in public schools by federal monies to assist education of disadvantaged learners) teacher to the class to give an overview of the program and to discuss how he/she selects and schedules students for reading instruction.

4. Present the students with selected unit plans from a teachers' edition of a basal text. In teams, have them assess the time it would take to do the selected unit by developing daily and weekly plans for their unit.

6 ▶

THE ESSENTIAL ELEMENTS OF READING AND READING INSTRUCTION

Chapter Objectives

1. To provide an overview of factors in cognitive development, which affect the reading program and reading instruction

2. To provide a working definition of reading by identifying key characteristics of effective readers

3. To describe the essential elements of effective reading instruction

Chapter Overview

This chapter's intent is specifically stated in its title—to elaborate the essential elements of effective reading and the essential elements of effective reading instruction.

It opens with a brief overview of cognitive development in children through the elementary grades. The authors assume that students taking this reading methods course have completed at least one course in developmental psychology and are familiar with the basic features and content of Piaget's framework for cognitive development (i.e., preoperational to concrete operations to formal reasoning). The brief overview highlights only those factors that seem to relate most directly to reading and to reading instruction.

A working definition of "reading comprehension" is provided, and the abilities associated with effective reading and effective readers are elaborated. The authors present these "essential elements" NOT as criteria for testing mastery of reading, but rather as handles for determining effectiveness of materials and instruction. They also provide a generalized framework of objectives that a beginning teacher of reading needs to have. Although they are not intended to be exhaustive, these 11 elements are inclu-

sive enough to provide a solid overview of what reading includes.

The chapter then presents what the authors see as the most important elements of effective reading instruction. Effective reading instruction does the following:

- Teaches reading as a strategic process
- Incorporates development of high-level thinking skills into the selection and design of the lesson and the materials
- Recognizes questioning and its employment as central to all teaching
- Perceives teaching strategies and teaching techniques and activities as related but different concepts that work in relation to each other
- Considers quality lesson plan design as a critical factor
- Recognizes the importance of metacognition for effective reading
- Approaches reading instruction within the larger context of all of the language arts and capitalizes on the natural relationships among them (i.e., oral language–writing–reading ties).

Guidelines for use of effective instructional elements are presented and discussed in terms of their practical applications.

Key Concepts and Ideas in the Chapter

- Relationships between cognitive development and reading
- Working definition of *reading comprehension*
- Critical reading abilities
- Strategic reading
- High-level thinking skills (HLTS)

- Questioning
- Strategy versus technique versus activity
- Strategy types
- Metacognition
- Integrated language arts

Teaching Ideas

1. Ask students to consider additions to, deletions from, or changes in the list of 11 essential elements of reading. Have them discuss the reasons for the changes and/or justification for new elements.
2. Ask students to do the same thing with the questioning and self-monitoring checklist. What can be added or changed? Why?
3. Divide the class into small-group teams or pairs. Ask them to develop a lesson plan with an over-all teaching strategy, within which techniques and activities are embedded. Discuss the different plans and the relationship of strategy as a concept to technique or activity.
4. Have the same groups generate a few specific teaching activities that are premised on an integrated language arts approach. Ask them to explain the interrelationships among the language areas in their individual activities.

7 ▶
DEVELOPING READING COMPREHENSION IN THE ELEMENTARY GRADES

Chapter Objectives

1. To provide an overview of reading comprehension based on an integrated instructional approach
2. To present contemporary models of reading comprehension instruction with relevance for the classroom teacher

3. To describe a variety of instructional strategies, techniques, and activities for teaching reading comprehension
4. To elaborate the importance of high-level thinking skills and their relationship to reading comprehension and reading comprehension instruction

Chapter Overview

This chapter is one of the most comprehensive in this textbook, for it covers the major elements of reading comprehension throughout the grades and how to most effectively develop reading comprehension skills and processes in learners.

The first part of the chapter focuses on the development and use of effective reading instruction lesson plans. A teacher-designed plan is described and compared to a more comprehensive plan, such as the plans typical of basal reading programs. The strengths and weaknesses of each are discussed.

The second, and most comprehensive, of the three chapter parts present a number of instructional models for developing reading comprehension. The importance of approaching reading from a strategic point of view is discussed, with examples demonstrating reading strategies at work. Direct instruction models are presented for use in the prereading phase of the lesson, during the reading stage, and for reading follow-up or the postreading stage.

The models presented incorporate oral language and writing as fundamental components in most cases. Question glossing, story mapping, and other expository and narrative instruction models illustrate how the language arts may be integrated for optimally effective learning of reading.

A special section of Part II is devoted to techniques and strategies that are designed to encourage self-monitoring abilities in developing readers.

All of the models presented are seen as adaptable to a variety of instructional settings and school-district philosophies that may surround the beginning teacher.

The most popular reading instruction models that have held sway over the past several years are also summarized (e.g., DRTA, ReQuest, PReP).

Part III addresses high-level thinking skills (HLTS) and processes and suggests how they can and should be incorporated into the reading instruction program. Six categories of foundation skills are presented as the basis for all high-level thinking development, which is critical for reading comprehension. Problem solving is then discussed in the context of reading comprehension. Formal reasoning—inductive and deductive reasoning—is defined, and its strengths and limitations for reading instruction are addressed.

Finally, selected examples of reading techniques and activities are offered, which can be incorporated into any reading program. These techniques and activities simultaneously serve both to develop high-level thinking and to apply high-level thinking to reading comprehension processes.

Key Concepts and Ideas in the Chapter

- Teacher-designed lesson plans versus basal reading text lesson plans
- Direct instruction strategies
- Question insertion
- Expository text structure instruction
- Story grammars
- Self-monitoring for comprehension
- Reading instruction models (DRTA, PReP, etc.)

- Reading–writing connections
- Narrative text
- Text cohesion
- HLTS
- Foundation skills of HLTS
- Problem solving
- Formal reasoning: inductive–deductive

Teaching Ideas

1. Divide students into "reading philosophy" teams (e.g., basal instruction, Whole Language). Have them prepare a formal debate (informally following debate rules). Discuss the strengths and limitations of the arguments of each.
2. Ask students to select a short story and a passage from a social studies text suitable for use at one of the intermediate or middle-school grades. Have them develop a question insertion sample similar to the one presented in this chapter. Discuss the difficulties of doing such a task.
3. Have students review some of the recent literature on metacognition and present ideas regarding its importance in teaching reading comprehension.

4. Select a specific lesson from a basal reading program, which is designed to teach reading comprehension skills. Ask students to improve it in some way (e.g., incorporating writing, oral language, or literature more effectively). Discuss the differences in learning that are likely to result.
5. Have students select one or more of the reading instruction models presented in the "alphabet soup" section of this chapter. Ask them to review the research literature and to reach some conclusions about what that literature says.
6. Ask students to examine some of the models for developing high-level thinking skills. Ask them to describe the merits and limitations of each.

8 ▶
TEACHING READING VOCABULARY THROUGHOUT THE ELEMENTARY GRADES

Chapter Objectives

1. To develop an understanding of a *mental dictionaries* concept
2. To understand differences among levels of these dictionaries

3. To provide model examples of strategies, techniques, and activities for teaching vocabulary in the elementary grades

Chapter Overview

This chapter is intended to help the prospective teacher develop a conceptual model of how learners learn new vocabulary and how to design and/or select ideas for teaching vocabulary according to that model. The model is premised on the notion that learners make use of "mental dictionaries" in developing and using vocabulary. Language users have a mental "full-ownership dictionary," which houses words that are "owned," in the sense that the dictionary user can use the words readily in daily speaking and writing discourse, as well as being able to comprehend them in reading. Some words in this dictionary are used only in specialized contexts (i.e., *pecuniary* or *fiduciary* might not be used often, even though a person might feel quite confident in the knowledge of them and of how to use them).

A "midrange dictionary" includes those words that a person can comfortably read by inferring the appropriate meaning from the text, but that the person cannot comfortably use in daily oral and written discourse. This is an important dictionary for reading effectively.

The "low-level dictionary" is a marginal one. This dictionary includes those words that have been seen or heard before in one context or another, but that are still questionable or only vaguely understood, yielding little confidence in terms of using them in speech or in writing. By using context and effective inferential processes, a person can often infer a meaning close enough to provide basic comprehension of text. Words in this dictionary will usually work their way into the more advanced dictionaries.

This chapter presents a variety of teaching strategies, techniques, and activities for instruction, according to which dictionary the teacher is expecting students to use. It is important that students in your reading methods class understand this concept, for it bears directly on the effectiveness of their teaching of reading.

Notice, also, that teaching ideas include examples of both direct and indirect instruction. It is important to note that direct instruction strategies are more commonly employed when teaching to the full-ownership dictionary.

Key Concepts and Ideas in the Chapter

- Instrumental versus knowledge hypotheses
- Mental dictionaries

- Learning new words versus learning how to learn new words

- Metacognitive modeling

- Role of language-using classroom context for vocabulary development

Teaching Ideas

1. Ask students to review instructional materials (e.g., basal programs or supplementary books for teaching vocabulary, such as those published by many of the smaller educational publishing houses). Challenge them to find examples of teaching techniques and activities that are suitable for teaching to each of the different dictionaries described in this chapter. Have them explain justifications for using given instructional examples for teaching to a given mental dictionary.

2. Place students in pairs or small groups. Ask them to design instructional ideas for teaching to each of the dictionaries.

3. Have students research alternative approaches to teaching reading vocabulary. Discuss these in class, or ask student teams to present their findings as a symposium or panel.

4. Ask students to examine ideas suggested by the Whole-Language approach, and discuss the place of vocabulary development and instruction in terms of that philosophy.

9 ▶
TEACHING STUDY SKILLS THROUGHOUT THE ELEMENTARY GRADES

Chapter Objectives

1. To establish the importance of study skills as an important component of the reading program
2. To provide an understanding of the roles of both study skills and study tools
3. To present a selection of instructional ideas as models for teaching study skills

Chapter Overview

The chapter opens with a brief discussion of the importance of study skills in the life of the reader. This is followed with an elaboration of basic assumptions the authors make about this important area of study. Primary among these is making a distinction between *study skills* and *study tools*. This distinction is helpful for organizing instruction in both areas. Another basic assumption presented is that self-monitoring is a critical foundation for study skill utilization. Finally, the authors believe that study skills and study tools are most effectively taught in contexts where students can see their practical value and therefore have some motivation to acquire facility in using them.

The key study skills addressed in the chapter are mental set, adjustment of reading rate, previewing, skimming, outlining, note-taking, interpreting graphics and other visuals, assessing information importance, and summarizing.

Key study tools included are dictionaries, thesauruses, encyclopedias, library tools, and computers.

Key Concepts and Ideas in the Chapter

- Study skills versus study tools
- Self-monitoring as a study skill
- Mental set
- Adjustments in reading rate
- Previewing
- Skimming
- Outlining
- Note-taking
- Nonprint visuals and graphics
- Summarizing

Teaching Ideas

1. Have students review elementary curriculum in the content areas (e.g., social studies, science, and math). Ask them to identify the kinds of study skills required for each. Also have them review the extent to which the materials attempt to incorporate study skills instruction within each content area.

2. Ask students to review computer software for programs that teach study skills in the elementary grades. Discuss them in class.

3. Ask your students to visit elementary school learning resources centers and libraries. How has technology (e.g., computers) entered into these areas?

4. Have students design lesson plans for which instruction in the various study skills are integrated into the concepts and skills being taught in a given subject or content area. Discuss the strengths and limitations of such an approach.

INSTRUCTOR'S SECTION

10 ▶
MONITORING AND ORGANIZING FOR READING INSTRUCTION AND LEARNING THROUGHOUT THE GRADES

Chapter Objectives

1. To provide an overview of reading assessment and monitoring
2. To explain the role and components of an assessment portfolio

3. To develop an understanding of how to group and manage the classroom for reading instruction

Chapter Overview

This chapter focuses on the nature and functions of assessment, classroom organization, and classroom management. A brief discussion of the role of assessment in the reading program is followed with an elaboration of a model reading assessment portfolio.

The *assessment portfolio* concept is presented as a workable way for the teacher of reading to organize his or her approach to teaching with a system of performance monitoring that provides information for multiple purposes. Data for use in diagnosing for instruction, for communicating to supervisors and parents, and for student use in self-analysis can all come from an assessment portfolio.

Included in the chapter are details and directions for conducting a number of literacy measures—col-

lecting and analyzing writing samples, designing and using readability measures, cloze tests, and miscue analysis. The role of each is discussed in terms of the assessment portfolio context.

Classroom organization and management as important parts of an effective reading program are also presented. Alternative grouping systems are discussed, and examples are provided. The student will find descriptions of instructional settings for individual, small-group, and large-group instruction.

Essential guidelines for use in decision making for organization and classroom management are also provided.

Key Concepts and Ideas in the Chapter

- Standardized testing—roles and limitations
- Assessment portfolio—nature and roles
- Formal assessment
- Informal assessment
- Cloze

- T–unit analysis
- Miscue analysis
- IRI
- Student learning contracts
- Grouping models

Teaching Ideas

1. Have students examine different standardized tests. Discuss in class the nature of the tests—their strengths and limitations.
2. Invite an elementary school principal to visit your class and discuss with student teachers the role of assessment in the elementary curriculum.
3. Discuss the role of assessment in different instructional philosophies and programs (e.g., a basal reading approach and a Whole-Language approach).
4. Select videotapes from a curriculum library source, which show different instructional configurations in the same or similar classrooms. Discuss the grouping techniques used.

11 ▶
READING AND THE MIDDLE-SCHOOL LEARNER

Chapter Objectives

1. To provide an overview of characteristics of middle-school learners
2. To describe the learning conditions and demands of the middle school
3. To discuss the particular needs at the middle-school level for reading instruction and content

Chapter Overview

This chapter provides essential background on the nature of the middle-school learner. Various developmental characteristics are considered. Physical development, intellectual development, and social–emotional development are described. Attention is also given to the unique nature of peer pressure and attitude development during this time in the life of the learner.

Attention is given to the learning demands placed on learners in the middle grades. The focus on academic subject areas and an increase in departmentalized organization of instruction are described. Teacher expectations in view of this content and organizational change are presented. The chapter also elaborates the particular reading needs that face learners in a middle-school environment.

Finally, specific implications for the teacher of reading in the middle school are discussed in light of the unique nature and particular demands of the middle-school learning context.

Key Concepts and Ideas in the Chapter

- Adolescence
- Physical development
- Intellectual development

- Learner diversity
- Middle-school learning context
- Middle-school teaching characteristics

Teaching Ideas

1. Select a social studies text at the middle-school level. Compare it with an intermediate-grade text in the same subject area. Consider readability level, concept level, and quantity of information.
2. Talk with seventh- and eighth-grade learners. Ask them what they found as the major differences between middle school and their early elementary-grade experiences.
3. Review the extracurricular programs at middle schools and at K–5 or –6 grades. How are they alike? How do they differ? What implications are there for the teacher and student?
4. Prepare a short teaching unit for the middle grades, using a content area such as history, geography, or science. Incorporate ideas for developing reading comprehension and vocabulary in your lessons.

12 ▶
TEACHING THE NOVEL IN THE MIDDLE GRADES

Chapter Objectives

1. To provide an overview of the major story-grammar elements that are important to the understanding of a novel

2. To describe an array of effective strategies and techniques for teaching the novel and its components

3. To provide an elaborated guided response model for teaching a novel in the middle grades

Chapter Overview

This chapter is intended to help the beginning teacher in the middle grades develop effective strategies and techniques for teaching the novel.

The chapter opens with a detailed elaboration of the various story-grammar elements that underpin the novel. The treatment of these elements in this chapter builds on the basic frameworks provided for use in teaching reading comprehension in the earlier elementary grades. Specific ideas, techniques, activities, and projects are offered for each of the important story grammar elements.

Questioning strategies are offered, which provide the teacher with ideas for helping students to understand the nature of the story-grammar elements and, in addition, to see how these elements work together to form cohesive fictional text.

Criteria for selecting a novel for use in the middle grades are presented, with suggested reasons for selecting a novel to teach in the first place. Also presented are guidelines for teaching the novel in such a way as to (a) develop comprehension of its critical elements, and (b) understand the relationships of the elements to each other and to the novel as a whole.

Finally, an elaborated guided response model is described, using the novel *Going after Cacciatto* by Tim O'Brien. The model is intended to illustrate a way in which developmentally appropriate adolescent novels can be taught.

Key Concepts and Ideas in the Chapter

- Scaffolding of instruction
- Support–model–adjust–monitor instruction
- Antagonist
- Symbol
- Mood

- Setting
- Plot
- Character
- Theme
- Guided response instruction

Teaching Ideas

1. Prepare an annotated bibliography of novels suitable for teaching in the middle school. Include a variety of genre types (e.g., adventure, mystery, science fiction).
2. Observe the teaching of a novel in a middle school. In your reading methods class, discuss the strategies and techniques used by the middle-school teacher.
3. Discuss the guided response model presented in this chapter.
4. Select an adolescent novel for teaching in the middle grades. Use the guided response model, and prepare a teaching unit for the novel.

13 ▶
THE FOUNDATIONS OF CHILDREN'S LITERATURE

Chapter Objectives

1. To develop an understanding of the significance of the role of children's literature in the teaching of reading and related language arts
2. To expose students to the language and content of children's books
3. To provide examples of worthwhile activities that bring children *into* the literature, *through* the stories, and *beyond* literature selections
4. This chapter also provides a brief annotated bibliography of quality children's literature selections

Chapter Overview

This chapter is provided as an overview of the use of children's literature in the teaching of reading. It is not intended to replace a course in children's literature, but rather to give students in reading methods classes the tools and knowledge necessary to use children's literature as either the core of a reading–language arts program or to supplement an existing reading program. For the instructor, this chapter offers flexibility in the breadth and the depth of the material on this topic that the instructor may wish to cover, in light of his or her institution's other teacher preparation curriculum requirements and/or the experiences of students in the reading methods class.

Children's literature is becoming an increasingly important component of the reading program. Research has shown that although many methods of teaching reading work if the teacher really believes in the method and in his or her students, none are more effective than using children's literature for the creation of lifelong readers. Children's literature plays an important role in the total educational curriculum by providing
- Worthwhile and motivating reading materials
- A wealth of vicarious experiences that enhance children's experiential backgrounds and, in turn, reading comprehension
- Excellent written language models for children to emulate in their own writings

Children's literature is used in schools in a variety of ways. Whole-Language classrooms use children's literature at the core of their curriculum to drive skill instruction in reading and language arts and to enhance instruction in other curricular areas. Non-Whole-Language classrooms incorporate children's literature to other extents, such as for practice and extension in the more skill-driven reading and language arts programs, or to enhance reading programs through reading aloud and storytelling as motivational devices. Suggestions are offered to guide teachers in setting up a conducive learning environment that includes children's literature.

Because there is such a wide variety of children's literature to choose from, guidelines are included to help students choose high-quality children's literature selections for use in their reading and language arts curriculum. Note the brief annotated bibliography of literature selections for children at various stages of their reading development. A brief reference list is included of additional resources to aid teachers in locating specific children's books. Similarly, guidelines are provided for assistance in choosing literature-based reading–language arts textbooks and materials.

The language and content of children's literature is also discussed. Students in the reading methods class are exposed to the variety of book formats, genres (such as realistic fiction or fantasy), and story grammar (such as plot, setting, or theme). Notice the list of generic questions relative to story grammar applicable to almost any literature selection. Because another value of teaching with literature is the incorporation of literature across the curriculum, an overview of generic cross-curricular activities applicable to most children's literature selections is also provided, along with an example of how this can be done with a specific literature selection.

Children's literature is meant to be shared. Reading aloud to students is one important way to do so. By regularly reading aloud to their students, teachers impart a love for reading as well as a plethora of specific reading–writing awarenesses and skills, as the chapter explains. Storytelling is another valuable technique for sharing quality literature with students who may not have the skills or the desire to read an abundance of quality children's literature selections on their own. Literacy and the development of a lifelong love of reading do not happen overnight, nor do they happen in just one school year. Parents play an important role in sharing high-quality literature with children, and the chapter offers suggestions for soliciting parents' help in this endeavor.

Key Concepts and Ideas in the Chapter

- Awareness of story grammar as a helpful aid in reading and writing skill
- Availability of children's literature in a wide variety of formats and styles
- Extending literature across the curriculum—an important component of an effective reading program

- The important role of literature in the reading curriculum
- Quality, interests, and self-selection—essential elements of using literature in the reading–language arts program
- Effective literature sharing techniques—reading aloud to students, and storytelling by teachers and parents

Teaching Ideas

1. Ask students to read an article about using children's literature in the reading program. Have students personally react to some of the ideas by sharing them in class.
2. Hold a class discussion on differences between literature-based and skill-based reading programs. Ask students "What are some necessary changes in choosing appropriate reading strategies and classroom groupings? For example, which program would be more conducive to individualization, variety of decoding strategies used by students, and so forth?" Ask students to explain their answers.
3. Ask students to bring to class their favorite children's literature selection and to share these in class in small read-around groups.

4. Read aloud one children's literature selection at the beginning (or immediately following the return from a break) of each reading methods class session.
5. Bring in samples of literature-based and skill-based reading textbooks and materials for students to compare. (Most publishers are willing to send college instructors sample materials at no cost, for use in their teaching methods classes.)
6. Allow students to work in cooperative groups to develop units on selected literature selections (for reading–language arts skills and for use across the curriculum), using the generic ideas suggested in the chapter, along with the students' own creative ideas.

14 ▶
TEACHING READING TO THE STUDENT WITH READING DIFFICULTIES

Chapter Objectives

1. To provide an overview of the characteristics of learners who have reading difficulties
2. To present the characteristics of an effective learning environment for the learner with reading difficulties
3. To present an array of teaching strategies and techniques for use with learners who have reading difficulties
4. To present an overview of various special learning populations

Chapter Overview

This chapter describes in some detail the nature of the learner with reading difficulties and the features of the classroom environment that allow for most effective reading instruction for such learners. The chapter elaborates in some detail the particular kind of language learning difficulties poor readers and special learners reflect in their literacy acts and their learning behaviors.

The general features of an effective learning classroom for these learners are presented, along with suggestions on how to create such a learning environment. These suggestions are cast in the framework of classroom teacher needs.

Some attention is given to basic instructional strategies and techniques that are important to consider with students who have learning difficulties. Included are strategies for monitoring student performance, plans for organizing and grouping students for instruction, and modeling techniques, all of which are so important for special learners and special learning populations.

The strategies and techniques offered are those in consonance with a variety of different teaching methodologies and curricula without endorsing one over the other.

Finally, attention is given to special learner populations, including the visually impaired, hearing impaired, bilingual, and gifted learners.

Key Concepts and Ideas in the Chapter

- Learning disabled
- Underachievers
- Remedial readers
- Mildly retarded
- Learner profiles
- Visual discrimination
- Learning patterns
- Attention deficits
- Peer tutoring
- Effective learning environments
- Reading in context
- Reading strategies
- Direct explanation
- Question modeling
- Correction strategies

Teaching Ideas

1. Review reading curriculum that is designed for special learners, such as the curriculum materials discussed in this chapter. Compare and discuss them (e.g., philosophy, learning theory, reading instruction theories present).

2. Discuss the differences and similarities in teaching strategies and techniques suggested in this chapter for special learners with those presented in other parts of this book. What conclusions can you infer?

3. Prepare a teaching unit for a selected grade and for a special learning population (e.g., bilingual, gifted). Discuss how your unit differs from others you might prepare for mainstream classes.

4. What role might contemporary instructional theories (such as the value of cooperative learning) play in the design of a program in literacy for special learners?

NOTES

NOTES

NOTES

NOTES

NOTES

NOTES

TEACHING READING IN THE ELEMENTARY GRADES

TEACHING READING IN THE ELEMENTARY GRADES

BY
MARVIN L. KLEIN
Professor of Curriculum & Instruction
Western Washington University

AND
SUSAN PETERSON
Instructional Specialist
Bellingham Public Schools

LINDA SIMINGTON
Director of Instruction
Portland Public Schools

ALLYN AND BACON
Boston • London • Toronto • Sydney • Tokyo • Singapore

Series Editor: Sean W. Wakely
Series Editorial Assistant: Carol L. Chernaik
Production Administrator: Peter Petraitis
Editorial-Production Service: York Production Services
Design: York Production Services
Photo Research: Lisa Feder
Composition Buyer: Linda Cox
Cover Administrator: Linda K. Dickinson
Manufacturing Buyer: Louise Richardson

Copyright ©1991 by Allyn and Bacon
A Division of Simon & Schuster, Inc.
160 Gould Street
Needham Heights, MA 02194

Klein, Marvin L., 1938–
    Teaching reading in the elementary grades / by Marvin L. Klein and Susan Peterson, Linda Simington.
        p.   cm.
    Includes bibliographical references and index.
    ISBN 0-205-12846-7
    1. Reading (Elementary)   2. Content area reading.   3. Language arts (Elementary)   4. Interdisciplinary approach in education.
I. Peterson, Susan, 1946–   . II. Simington, Linda.   III. Title.
LB1573.K62   1991
372.4—dc20   90-49141
                                                                    CIP

ISBN 0-205-12846-7

Printed in the United States of America

10 9 8 7 6 5 4 3 2 1   96 95 94 93 92 91 90

Photo Credits
All photos by Frank Siteman © 1990 except p. 20 photo by Cynthia A. Orlandi; p. 25 UNICEF photo by Tom Marotta; p. 80 photo by Talbot D. Lovering; pp. 410, 411, 415, 418, 419, 428, 430, 433 photos courtesy of Darlene Michener.

TABLE OF CONTENTS

Preface xv

CHAPTER 1

Introduction to Reading and Reading Instruction 1
Preview 1
Focus Questions 2
Broadening the Definitions of Literacy 2
    Cultural Literacy 3
    Language Literacy 4

Environment for Literacy 4
What is Reading 5
Concepts of the Reading Process 7
The Psycholinguistic Elements of Reading 9
    The Text 9
    The Reader 10
    The Context 12

Views and Models of the Reading Process 12
    The "Bottom-Up" Model of Reading 13
    The "Top-Down" Model of Reading 14
    Eclectic Models of Reading 15

Other Shaping Events 15
Highlights 17
Reinforcement Activities 18
Additional Projects 18
References 19
Additional Resources 19

CHAPTER 2

Early Literacy Acquisition and Development 20
Preview 20
Focus Questions 21
Research in Developmental Psycholinguistics 21
Development of Oral Language 22
    Normal Sequence of Stages 22
    Developmental Interaction of Child and Environment 23

Development of Meaning 24
    Functions of Oral Language 24
    Concrete Versus Abstract Usage of Language 26

Emerging Awareness of Print 27
    Early Awareness of Print Characteristics 27
    Luria's Discovery 27

Guidelines for Early Literacy Development 28
    Early Experiences with Reading 28
    Early Experiences with Conversing 29
    Early Experiences with Writing 30

Highlights 31
Reinforcement Activities 32
Additional Projects 32
References 33
Additional Resources 33

Chapter 3
Literacy Instruction in the Kindergarten 34
Preview 34
Focus Questions 34
Selecting and Providing Instructional Opportunities 35
    Reading for Instruction 35
    Elements of an Early Literacy Program 35
    Creating the Instructional Environment 38
    Applying Instruction to the Elements of Literacy 41

Foundations for Literacy 41
    Integrated Approaches to New Vocabulary,
        Language Structures, and Concepts 41
    Three Strategies for Learning Language 42
    Reading Aloud to Children 47

Strategies for Direct Instruction in Learning to Read 49
    Large Group Read-Aloud Experiences 50
    Making Books 52
    Using Charts 58
    Developing Reading Comprehension:
        Comprehending the Written Language 64
    Using Predictable Language for Instruction 70

Connecting the Writing Process 76
    Developing Concepts of Print 76
    Encouraging Writing in the Classroom 79

Highlights 85
Reinforcement Activities 86
Additional Projects 86

References 87
Additional Resources 87

Chapter 4

Teaching and Mentoring the Apprentice Reader 88
Preview 88
Focus Questions 88
Part I: Reading Program in the Primary Grades 89

Instructional Reading 89
Supported Practice Reading 106
Becoming an Independent Reader 113

Part II: Integrating Reading and Writing 119

Writing As an Integrative Activity 119
Journal Writing 119
Adaptations for Models 120
Posters 121

Part III: A Menu of Reading Methods 121

Basal Reader Approach 121
Language-Experience Approach (LEA) 122
Literature-Based Approach 124
Whole-Language Approach 125
Summary of Reading Methods 126
Highlights 127
Reinforcement Activities 128
Additional Projects 128
References 129
Additional Resources 129

Chapter 5

Planning and Organizing Instruction for the Primary Grades 130
Preview 130
Focus Questions 130
Organizing and Managing the Instructional Setting 131

Organizing the Environment 131
Planning the Daily Schedule 133
Grouping Primary Children for Instruction 139
Teaching Work and Study Habits 147

Planning and Implementing the Instructional Process 150

Integrating the Language Arts 150
Providing Instruction 153

Highlights 159
Reinforcement Activities 160
Additional Projects 160
References 160
Additional Resources 161

Chapter 6

The Essential Elements of Reading and Reading Instruction 162
Preview 162
Focus Questions 162
Cognitive Development 163

Developmental Changes 163
Different Stories for Different Stages of Development 164
Differences in Instruction in Response
  to Developmental Differences 165

Essential Reading Abilities 165

Reading Comprehension 165
Essential Indications of Reading Ability 166

The Essential Elements of Literacy and
  Strategic Reading Instruction 171

Key Features of Strategic Reading
  and of Strategic Reading Instruction 172
Questioning 174
From Strategies to Techniques to Activities 175
Effective Lesson Design 183
Developing Metacognitive Abilities 183
Integration of Language Arts 186

Highlights 189
Reinforcement Activities 190
Additional Projects 190
References 191
Additional Resources 192

Chapter 7

Developing Reading Comprehension in the Elementary Grades . . 193
Preview 193
Focus Questions 193
Part I: Designing an Effective Reading Lesson Plan 194

Four Key Features of a Lesson Plan 194
The Teacher's Edition Lesson Plan versus
  the Teacher's Self-Designed Lesson Plan 196
Plan #1: The Teacher-Designed Lesson Plan 196
Plan #2: The Commercially Developed Lesson Plan 197
Comparison and Contrast of the Two Plans 209
Using the Advantages of Each Plan 210

Part II: Strategic Reading 211

Direct Instruction in Strategic Reading by Modeling 211
Additional Ideas for Developing Self-Monitoring Skills 224
An "Alphabet Soup" of Reading Instruction Models 228
Building Text Structure Knowledge Through Reading
  and Through Reading-Writing Connections 236

Part III: High-Level Thinking Skills (HLTS) 246

   HLTS: Definition and Objectives 247
   HLT Foundation Skills 247
   Applied HLTS: Problem Solving 252
   Formal Reasoning: Inductive and Deductive Reasoning 255
   Some Techniques for Developing HLTS in Reading 257

Highlights 260
Reinforcement Activities 261
Additional Projects 262
References 263
Additional Resources 264

Chapter 8

Teaching Reading Vocabulary Throughout
   the Elementary Grades 265
Preview 265
Focus Questions 266
Benefits of and Approaches to Vocabulary Instruction 266
Some Basic Guidelines for Vocabulary Instruction 268
Selecting the "Dictionary" to which to Teach New Vocabulary . . . 269
Teaching to the Full-Ownership Dictionary 271

   Five-Step Direct-Instruction Model 271
   Topic-Centered Model for Direct Instruction 272

Teaching to the Midrange Dictionary 273

   Teaching Students to Infer Meaning
    of New Vocabulary from Context 274
   Teaching the Use of Inference and
    Context for Acquiring New Vocabulary 276
   Using Cloze to Teach New Vocabulary 276
   Using New Vocabulary to Generalize Inference 278
   Using Mapping and Webbing Techniques 279
   Using Feature Analysis Techniques 280

Teaching New Vocabulary to the Low-Range Dictionary 283

   Language Play 283
   Etymology (Word History) 284
   Dialect Study Projects 284

Highlights 285
Reinforcement Activities 286
Additional Projects 286
References 287
Additional Resources 287

Chapter 9

Teaching Study Skills Throughout the Elementary Grades 288
Preview 288

Focus Questions 289
Introduction and Definition 289
Basic Assumptions 290
The Important Study Skills 291

    Establishing a Mental Set for Studying 291
    Adjusting Reading Rate for Different
      Reading Tasks, Types, and Purposes 292
    Previewing Text 293
    Skimming 294
    Note-taking and Outlining 295
    Mapping, Clustering, and Other Graphics 299
    Other Study Skills .302

Study Tools 302

    Charts, Tables, and Graphs 303
    Maps and Globes 307
    Dictionary and Thesaurus: Tools for Word Usage 313
    Encylopedias 314
    Card Catalog 315

Summary: Other Resources for Learners 315
Highlights 316
Reinforcement Activities 316
Additional Projects 317
References 317
Additional Resources 317

Chapter 10
Monitoring and Organizing for Reading Instruction
    and Learning Throughout the Grades 318

Preview 318
Focus Question 318
Part I: Some Problems with the Measurement of Reading Ability . . 319

    Difficulties and Trends in the Measurement of Reading Ability 319
    Some Changes in the Measurement of Reading Ability 320

Part II: Use of the Reading Assessment Portfolio Overview 321

    How to Set Up and Use an Assessment Portfolio 322
    How to Generate Assessment Portfolio Data 322

Part III: Classroom Grouping Models for Reading Instruction . . . 342

    Planning and Initiating Instruction 343
    Considerations for Instructional Groupings 343
    Coordinating the Options 354

Highlights 354
Reinforcement Activities 357
Additional Projects 357
References 357

Additional Resources 358

Chapter 11

Reading and the Middle-School Learner 359
Preview 359
Focus Questions 359
Developmental Characteristics of Middle-School Learners 360

Physical Development 360
Intellectual Development 360
Social-Emotional Development 361
Diversity in Developmental Characteristics 363

Other Learner Characteristics:
   Prior Knowledge, Skills and Attitudes 364
Learning Demands of the Middle School 368
Factors Affecting Middle-School Learners 370
Middle-School Learner's Reading Needs 371
Implications of Learners' Needs for Teachers of Reading 372
Highlights 374
Reinforcement Activities 374
Additional Projects 374
References 375

Chapter 12

Teaching the Novel in the Middle Grades 376
Preview 376
Focus Questions 376
Instructional Scaffolding 377
Story Elements at the Middle-School Level 378

Story Elements: Understanding the Role of "Setting" 378
Story Elements: Understanding the Role of Plot 382
Story Elements: Understanding the Role of Character 384
Story Elements: Understanding Theme 389

Selecting a Novel for Whole-Group Study 391
A Model for Integrating and Applying Reading Strategies 392

The Complexities of Integration 392
Criteria for an Instructional Model for Teaching a Novel 394
The Key Criterion of Instruction on Novels:
   Students' Understanding and Enjoyment 394
A Model for Exploring the Novel: *Going After Cacciato* 395
Going After Cacciato: Scenario for Teaching a Novel 396
Going After Cacciato: Questions and Activities 399

Highlights 407
Reinforcement Activities 408
Additional Projects 408
References 408

Chapter 13

The Foundations of Children's Literature 409
Preview 409
Focus Questions 410
The Role of Children's Literature 412

Literary Experiences 412
Literature as a Springboard to Literacy 413

The Language and Content of Children's Literature 415

Book Formats 415
Literature Genres 416
Literary Aspects of Literature 417

Using Children's Literature in the Reading Program 419

Selecting Literature 419
Annotated Sampling of High-Quality Children's Literature 423
Additional Resources for Locating High-Quality Children's Literature . . .429
Sharing Children's Literature with Students 429

Follow Through: Incorporating Literature Across the Curriculum . 432

Reading 433
Other Language Arts 434
Math 435
Social Studies 435
Science 435
Art, Music, and Physical Education 436
An Example of Integrating Children's Literature
    Across the Curriculum: The Jolly Postman 436

Parent Involvement 438
Highlights 439
Reinforcement Activities 440
Additional Projects 441
Reference 441
Additional Resources 442

Chapter 14

Teaching Reading to the Student with Reading Difficulties 443
Preview 443
Focus Questions 444
Characteristics of the Student with Reading Difficulties 445

Limited, Delayed, or Different Language Experiences 445
Inconsistent Learning Profiles 446
Difficulty Following Directions 446
Difficulty in Discrimination 447
Inefficient Learning Patterns 447
Attention Deficits 448
Lack of a Variety of Successful Learning
    Strategies Teacher Dependency 449

Characteristics of Effective Learning Environments 450

Consultation and Support for the Classroom Teacher 451
Clearly Stated Expectations for Students 451
Careful and Frequent Assessment of Student Performance 452
Reading Activities Founded on Basic Skills 453
Development of Fluency, as Well as Accuracy 454
Instruction in Reading Comprehension 456
Provision of Sufficient Practice .462
Active Involvement and Engagement in Learning 462
Appropriate Combination of Whole-Group,
    Small-Group, and Individualized Instruction 463
Instruction in Strategies for Learning 465
Use of Flexible Models of Instruction 468

Characteristics of Other Special Students Populations
    and Appropriate Learning Environments 470

Visually Impaired 470
Hearing Impaired 470
English as a Second Language (ESL) or Limited English 471

Appendix A:
Linguistics Terminology Often Used in Reading Instruction 476

Appendix B:
Question Taxonomies 480
Synopsis of a Taxonomy of Questions 480
Underlying Ideas 480
Memory Questions 481
Translation Question 481
Interpretation Question 482
Application Question 483
Analysis Questions 484
Synthesis Questions 484
Evaluation Questions 485
Practice in Classifying Questions 486
Sample Question Taxonomy Tailored to Social Studies 486
The Language of Questions 488
Descriptions Versus Explanations 488
Question Words and Question Categories 488
Basic Guidelines for Using a Question Taxonomy 489
Some Dos 489
Some Don'ts 490
References 490
Additional Resources 490

Index 493

PREFACE

Teaching Reading Through the Elementary Grades: Building, Developing, and Extending Reading, Grades K–8 is a comprehensive reading methods text designed for undergraduate elementary reading methods courses. The authors have attempted to make this book not only readable but also valuable for the soon-to-be elementary teacher of reading. In fact, we have attempted to write a book that will be seen as a valuable professional resource with enough rich ideas for teaching reading effectively to make the book an essential reference through many years of teaching.

The book reflects a solid base of reading theory and research, but the authors do not let theoretical issues dominate the more important mission of providing prospective new teachers with practical and workable ideas for teaching reading effectively throughout the K–8 grade range.

We have also tried to make this book unique in a number of respects important to a new teacher of reading. Some of these features are described later in this preface. First, however, we want you to know our philosophy so that you can see why some of these features are built in.

PHILOSOPHY

This book is premised on the following fundamental beliefs about reading and reading instruction:

1. Young children bring to the beginning school years a rich and vital linguistic literacy that has emerged from a wealth of language-using contexts. That natural evolving literacy in children provides the fundamental base on which an effective teacher of reading builds to help children become effective and efficient readers. Thus in the early school years, the teacher accepts the language the children bring to the classroom and uses that language ability and their prior experiences to build a more powerful literacy.
2. Language develops naturally when children live and learn in meaningful language-using contexts where they are encouraged to explore talking, reading, and writing, and to see language as both a powerful tool and an enjoyable and exciting part of themselves.

3. Learners throughout the elementary grades learn to read most effectively when they are in classrooms where teachers teach reading, writing, speaking, and listening in an integrated fashion, and where students are encouraged to view reading as a vital part of an integrated language-using whole rather than as a separate set of isolated skills.

4. The effective teacher of reading functions as an orchestrator of instruction. Children and teacher are partners in a classroom that is a literacy community, with all sharing in the growth of reading, writing, and speaking skills.

5. The classroom teacher maintains balanced instruction in strategies, techniques, and activities. The needs of the learner determine context, timing, and instruction type. The teacher of reading exploits that natural language ability of children in teaching children to be good readers. She or he does not assume that reading ability evolves without instruction. If learners are to reach their greatest potential of reading proficiency, then teachers must provide professional instruction.

How the Philosophy Is Reflected in This Text

Organization of the Text

The authors recognize the unique nature of learners in the primary grades, intermediate grades, and middle-school grades. The instructional strategies and techniques reflect the needs of learners at these different stages of their development.

Chapter 1 provides a background for the remainder of the text, with an examination of literacy generally and reading in particular. Differing definitions of reading and reading instruction are reviewed.

Chapters 2 through 5 focus on the primary grades, with specific attention to needs of kindergartners and first and second graders.

Chapters 6 through 10 focus on reading instruction through the intermediate and middle grades, with suggested instructional adjustments for teaching comprehension, vocabulary, and study skills across all of the elementary grades range.

Chapters 11 and 12 focus directly on the middle-school grades, with examination of the middle-school learner and consideration of the unique demands of teaching narrative to these students.

Chapter 13 specially treats children's literature across the curriculum and across the grades. Chapter 14 is also cross-curricular and cross-grade as it addresses the instructional needs of special populations of learners.

Focus Questions, Highlights, and Additional Projects

Each chapter begins with a brief introduction and several focus questions to help the reader establish some important mental benchmarks (advance organizers) for reading the chapter. In addition, each chapter concludes with a "Highlights" section, which summarizes key ideas presented in the chapter. These offer a quick review, and refer back to the focus questions. Also, each chapter includes suggested additional activities or projects that provide opportunities to extend the learning in a variety of ways.

Integrated Approach

This text provides instructional models that consistently capitalize on relationships among elements and features of language; for example, oral language and writing are viewed as integral features of literacy development. The oral language base is emphasized in the instructional strategies and techniques offered for the primary grades. The reading–writing connection is emphasized throughout all of the text for all of the grades, K–8. Also, though children's literature receives a separate focused chapter, both children's literature and content-related (subject-matter) text are used throughout all of the instructional approaches presented in this book.

Direct Instruction

We define *direct instruction* as the approach to teaching that moves from objectives to orchestrated instructional events to the learning outcomes that occur in the learner. This does not mean, however, that we advocate a particular learning theory (e.g., behaviorism); nor does it mean that we advocate a particular program or skill sequence for instruction. It particularly does not mean that we believe in teaching skills in drill-like isolated lessons.

It does mean that we believe the teacher of reading is responsible for designing instruction that is organized and coherent so that children can see why they are doing what they are doing in learning to read. The teacher, as orchestrator of learning, creates and adapts the learning environment through careful selection of instructional strategies and techniques that make sense both to the teacher and to the learners. To orchestrate effective learning, the teacher must engage in an ongoing self-monitoring of the relationship between objectives and instructional events.

Monitoring and Evaluating Reading Approach

Monitoring and evaluating reading performance is an important component of reading instruction. The concept of the assessment portfolio, presented in this text, is intended to assist the teacher in a variety of ways. Information accumulated in the portfolio assists the teacher in diagnosing learner strengths and weaknessess in reading and reading-related areas and in designing instruction for meeting individual student needs. In addition, it can serve as a conferencing tool to use with children, parents, and/or supervisor or principal.

Grouping and Managing for Instruction

The models presented in this text for grouping children and organizing for instruction allow the teacher to choose from different configurations for different purposes. The approaches offered are selected to reflect the integrated philosophy of instruction suggested in the various instructional strategies and techniques offered throughout the book.

ACKNOWLEDGMENTS

Any book project such as this requires immense support and assistance. Many of those who provide it are behind the scenes—editors, typesetters, printers, marketing and sales people, and so on. Thanks to all of you folks.
    Others are easier to identify:

Thank you, Karen, Terry, Burl, and other members of our families for being patient, caring, and always supportive when our work took valuable family time from you. Thank you, Carol Chernaik, Sean Wakely, and others at Allyn & Bacon who have been so patient and helpful along the way. Your confidence in the worth of this project has yielded dividends not possible without your efforts.

Thanks to all of the many reviewers who reviewed with great care and detailed attention to the various stages of manuscript development:

Judith Meagher
University of Connecticut

Marie Eaton
Fairhaven College

Fred MacLaren
Eastern Illinois University

Richard Chambers
Boston University

Leo Schell
Kansas State University

Victoria Hare
University of Illinois

Martha McKnight
University of Louisville

John Beach
University of Maine

Jack Bagford
University of Iowa

Carmella Abbruzzese
Regis College

Susan Daniels
University of Akron

Sandra Hollingsworth
University of California, Berkeley

Jill Fitzgerald,
University of North Carolina

Darlene Michener
California State University,
Los Angeles

All have our thanks and appreciation. We know this book is better for your having helped. And, we also acknowledge any remaining deficiences as our own.

Finally, last, but not least, thank you to the hundreds of reading researchers at work every day to advance the development of literacy in the world, to the thousands of classroom teachers, and to the millions of children who make it all worth the effort!

Marv Klein
Susan Peterson
Linda Simington

TEACHING READING IN THE ELEMENTARY GRADES

CHAPTER 1

INTRODUCTION TO READING AND READING INSTRUCTION

They know enough who know how to learn.
Henry Brooks Adams, *The Education of Henry Adams,* **1918**

PREVIEW

Learning how to speak, read, and write are probably the most important skills acquired during a lifetime. The ability to use language competently—to speak fluently, to read, and to write in a variety of forms and for a variety of purposes—provides economic opportunity, social status, and personal pleasure, not to mention self-respect.

Given the importance of knowing how to read, write, and speak well, the profession that teaches children these skills is among the most powerful and rewarding in American society. Those who have chosen to become elementary-school teachers have the remarkable opportunity to play a major role in determining the future of hundreds of human beings. The opportunity to influence profoundly the lives of many others can be a heady experience, but it also implies a heavy responsibility. The challenge of teaching hundreds of students to read, write, and speak well should not be taken lightly.

It is our view (i.e., that of the authors) that reading, writing, and speaking are closely interrelated skills. Nonetheless, it would be tedious to mention reading, writing, and speaking separately each time these skills were mentioned. Therefore, "reading instruction" and "reading skills" are often used as encompassing terms to include reading, writing, and speaking skills. Reading is highlighted as the central skill both because it is the subject of this text and because it is the key to literacy and to most other learning.

Teachers of reading in the elementary grades must thoroughly prepare for all aspects of the teaching of reading. This requires knowing the answers to many questions about how to teach reading, such as "What is literacy?" "How do children best learn to read, write, and speak well?" "What are the most effective strategies, techniques, and activities to use in classroom instruction?" This book offers the answers to these and many other questions.

Before moving to methodological issues and strategies for teaching reading, some background information may prove helpful. This introductory chapter describes key issues and concepts of reading instruction.

The organizational format of this chapter is repeated throughout this book. A brief introduction, with "Focus Questions," is followed by the major contents of the chapter.

You can open this chapter with a discussion of America's ongoing battle with illiteracy. Why do some nations have a lower rate of illiteracy in their country (e.g., Japan)? A few contributing factors are economics, television viewing habits, public attitudes toward literacy, and cultural history. Ask students to suggest additional possibilities.

1

Each chapter then concludes with a "Highlights" listing of key ideas and concepts covered in the chapter. "Reinforcement Activities" and "Additional Projects" help in reviewing and applying what was learned.

FOCUS QUESTIONS

Think about the following questions when reading this chapter:

1. What is meant by *literacy?*
2. How has the definition of *reading* changed over the years, and what have been some of the factors shaping this change?
3. What are the key elements of reading?
4. What are some different approaches to reading instruction?

In the later 1960s, the U.S. Office of Education, which later became the U.S. Department of Education, proclaimed a need for serious attention to illiteracy in the United States. It was asserted that well over 25 million American adults were *illiterate*—they could not read well enough to comprehend text considered essential to fulfilling adult responsibilities. They could not read well enough to fill out application forms for jobs, for Social Security, or even for driver's licenses. They could not read simple manuals and therefore could not perform fundamental social or occupational tasks that require them to read instructions, warnings, or guidelines.

The efforts of the "Right to Read" movement of the 1970s notwithstanding, the problems of illiteracy continue. Millions still cannot read, and even more millions *choose* not to read—the "aliterates." Though aliterates can read, they have neither the desire nor willingness to read anything not essential to their survival.

BROADENING THE DEFINITION OF LITERACY

Current emphasis on the interrelated nature of the language-producing and language-consuming skills and processes fits with the current more comprehensive definition of literacy.

Literacy instruction has always been important in schools, and it is even more so now. Since the 1970s, a more comprehensive definition of literacy has been developed. *Literacy* now encompasses the following abilities:

- The ability to read words in print
- The ability to speak with clarity, conciseness, and cogency
- The ability to write easily and comfortably
- The ability to communicate essential ideas via the written word
- The ability to understand oral messages, attending both to the stated meaning of utterances and to the implied meanings reflected in word choice, sentence structure, and the stress and juncture patterns of speech
- The ability to find satisfaction, purpose, and achievement through the various acts of literacy, thereby making aliteracy less likely

This elaborated range of abilities in all language domains defines the contemporary character of literacy instruction. This perspective is not new. Many reading educators have long believed in and espoused methodologies intended to develop reading, writing, speaking, and listening abilities in concert. Unfortunately, however, in past decades, many did not support an integrated, broad-range approach to literacy. For many years, the dominant operational paradigm approached reading instruction as a discrete set of skills. This has changed; reading is no longer seen as a distinctly separate body of skills and processes divorced from the other literacy domains. What was formerly a minority viewpoint is now a majority one. Further, this broader recognition of the interrelatedness of the language skills does not preclude roles for direct instruction in the skills and processes of reading.

This is a good place to discuss the complexity of the reading act and how teachers can use this knowledge in discussions with parents and others interested in the school reading program.

Cultural Literacy

Since the mid-1970s, the definition of *literacy* has broadened still further. A "literate" person not only possesses and uses reading, writing, speaking, and thinking skills, but also fully participates in the culture of the country and is immersed in all of the processes, forms, and purposes of language and language use.

This broader definition of literacy has been translated into different approaches to teaching reading. Full literacy now requires both the development of skills and the effective utilization of those skills in daily living. Not only have literate individuals mastered the skills and processes of language development and use; literate individuals also can and do use those abilities to acquire and incorporate structures of knowledge about the world into their daily lives. Literate persons are able to share common cultural knowledge—knowledge about American history (e.g., the Civil War and the American Revolution) and about contemporary American culture (e.g., sports events, key political leaders, and rock music). That is, fully literate persons are aware of people and events that shape the quality of our lives in significant ways.

Hirsch's *Cultural Literacy* has raised serious questions about how we define *literacy*. Although his work has been criticized as being "elitist," simplistic, unrealistic, and so on, it certainly has caused reexamination of educators' conception of *literacy*. How important is it for students to understand historical or literary allusions? You might want to ask students in your methods class to formulate their own definition of *literacy*. What does that definition have to say about their approach to teaching reading?

Language Literacy

Literate persons process this shared knowledge through language. We hear, speak, read, write, and think in language. A British philosopher once observed, "Language is the house in which we live." Language dominates our physical and psychological being. It is often impossible to separate reactions to an individual from reactions to that person's ability to use language effectively: "She expresses herself well." "He is very articulate." "Joe is a nice person, but he doesn't know how to get his ideas across when you talk with him." A person's facility with oral language determines in large measure her or his role in society.

Ironically, contemporary research in developmental psycholinguistics (language development in children) indicates that by the time children enter school, most of them have already mastered an extensive vocabulary and are capable of expressing themselves with the majority of the basic sentence patterns they will use in their lifetime. How we, as teachers, capitalize on that knowledge and ability determines significantly the extent to which the individual child will be fully literate.

The ability to use oral language forms the linguistic base for reading. Oral language shapes the development of reading abilities, which makes oral language very important for the teacher of reading. Thus, the roots of reading are in oral language. The importance of reading itself should not, however, be underestimated. The development and maintenance of literacy is articulated through reading and reading is a key component of any definition of literacy.

In addition, a literate person must be able to write comfortably. Ability to communicate through writing is a necessity of contemporary society. The obvious connections between writing and reading have been established by a number of authorities over the years (Klein, 1985; Loban, 1976; Mosenthal, Tamor, & Walmsley, 1983). Learners who write well tend to read well, and good readers tend to be good writers. The continuing expansion of service occupations suggests that the demand for writing skills will continue.

Emphasize the importance of accepting the language children bring to the classroom as a critical aspect of beginning instruction in reading.

ENVIRONMENT FOR LITERACY

It is important for teachers to note that much of the knowledge and many of the skills necessary for literacy depend on experiences well beyond the boundaries of the school, and far beyond the reach of children's teachers. Many children are fortunate enough to be born into families and homes where literacy and cultural awareness and knowledge are respected. These children have a far greater range of experiential opportunities for literacy than do their less fortunate counterparts who come from families without a history of involvement with experiences normally associated

The home environment is recognized increasingly to be crucial in the development of background knowledge, linguistic knowledge, and learner attitudes toward reading. Ask students, "What can the classroom teacher do to assist parents in providing a rich early literacy environment for their children?"

with literacy. For example, children who have visited museums, historical sites, and different regions of the country clearly have a broader experience base and greater background knowledge, both of which are crucial to all domains of literacy, especially reading. For teachers, this difference in learners represents an important challenge.

The literacy requirements of children reflect rapidly changing societal demands for more information, more rapidly processed. Even the kinds of questions reading educators ask themselves have changed in recent decades. Educators now ask questions such as, "What kinds of cultural experiences are critical to literacy acquisition?" "What are the mitigating sociolinguistic factors of an effective reading learning environment?" "How does language acquisition and development affect reading development?" "What is the relationship between reading and writing acquisition and development?" "In what important mental processes is the reader engaged?" A few decades ago, educators asked primarily methodological questions, specific only to direct instruction in reading, such as "What is the best way to teach phonics?" "Must children be taught decoding skills before they can be taught comprehension skills?"

Therefore, before embarking on an investigation of the most effective ways to teach reading, this chapter briefly notes the evolution of the contemporary concept of reading.

WHAT IS READING?

In 1917, Thorndike defined *reading* as

a very complex procedure involving a weighing of each of many elements in a sentence, their organization in the proper relations to one another, the selection of certain of their connotations and the rejection of others, and the cooperation of many forces to produce the final response.

This definition of reading is fairly typical of those that emerged through the first 60–70 years of this century. However, by the early 1970s, definitions of reading moved increasingly toward operationalism. There was greater disenchantment with conceptual definitions of reading. Instead, reading educators selected descriptions of the observable characteristics or behaviors of an acknowledged effective reader. For example, "an effective reader is one who is able to paraphrase correctly, summarize concisely, infer conclusions, detect specious logic, identify cause–effect relationships," and so on.

The advantage of this approach to reading instruction is obvious. Instead of addressing the nature of the reading process itself (i.e., what goes on in the head of the reader during the reading act), educators can go directly to the hierarchies of skills and subskills associated with effective reading performance. The identified reading skills have dominated

Where do contemporary commercially developed reading programs stand on "reading-as-skill"? Remember that the K–8 scope and sequence in the elementary school has a long tradition. Prospective elementary teachers need to be aware of the importance of knowing what is expected of the teachers in the grades both below and above theirs for a variety of reasons. What are some of those?

the scope-and-sequence charts of basal reading programs since the 1970s, and they generally continue to do so now.

In fact, most teachers agree that teaching important reading skills both directly and indirectly is necessary for developing effective readers. Skill frameworks, such as those accompanying basal readers and locally developed curricula, continue to be important. It is important for teachers of reading to know the skills and processes exhibited by effective readers in order to make effective decisions regarding reading instruction. Unfortunately, although such lists indicate fairly accurately the performance outcomes of good readers, they cannot explain how those outcomes are reached. For example, knowing that readers can infer proper conclusions when reading a text fails to indicate *how* readers infer those conclusions. This knowledge does not reveal what mental processes are being employed, how they are being employed, or how best to teach learners to employ them.

Indeed, research into identifying skills and creating hierarchies of skills that must be mastered in order to read effectively has proven disappointing. Thus far, no substantial evidence has shown support for any major skill group or skill hierarchy as being critical to effective reading (Rosenshine, 1980). If no single group of skills or single hierarchy of skills is critical to reading, the usefulness of such groupings and hierarchies for the teaching of reading seems questionable.

Recent definitions of reading have returned to conceptual formulations of reading as a process. Typical of this newer approach is the definition offered by Bloome and Green (1984): the act of reading is a "cognitive activity embedded in social and linguistic contexts."

Most of the contemporary definitions of reading include the following: (1) Reading is a process, (2) reading is strategic, (3) reading is interactive, and (4) reading instruction requires orchestration.

1. Reading Is a Process.

Reading is a process in which information from the text and the knowledge possessed by the reader act together to produce meaning.

Anderson, Hiebert, Scott, & Wilkinson
(*Becoming a Nation of Readers*, 1985)

This is a good spot to discuss whether meaning resides in text, in the reader, in the context, or in some sort of interaction among these.

Notice that this definition argues that meaning resides both in the text and in the reader. It is the interaction of the two that determines the success or failure of the reading act. The reader is *not* a passive participant in the reading act. While the reader must use his or her knowledge of the structures of text and vocabulary, the reader must also work to *impose* experiential and content-based knowledge and meaning onto the text.

2. Reading Is Strategic. Effective readers employ reading strategies appropriate both to the text and to the context in order to construct meaning when reading (Garner, 1987). These strategies vary according to the type of text, the purpose for reading, and so on. One critical aspect of all reading strategies is the ability to "self-monitor" the reading process; all effective readers think about their own thinking—commonly referred to as "metacognition." Less-effective readers not only do not think about their own thinking, but in many instances, they do not even know that they should!

3. Reading Is Interactive. Engagement of the reader's involvement with the text takes place within a particular context. The reader must feel comfortable and must be reading a text that he or she finds worthwhile, serving some purpose to the reader. That is, the text must be both readable and functional. The context must be conducive to reading and supportive of instruction that builds reading skills.

4. Reading Instruction Requires Orchestration. The teacher of reading must orchestrate the content and the conditions of instruction in a way that optimally brings the learner, the text, and the instructional setting into consonance. When that happens, children learn to read as effectively as their individual abilities permit. Effective instruction in reading directly helps the learner to do the following:
   a. Develop the skills necessary for applying existing knowledge to the reading process
   b. Develop the skills necessary for processing language structures and for deriving language meanings that are used in the text
   c. Refine the mental processes and strategies used in the process of reading.

This book is designed to help teachers provide such instruction for children in the elementary grades. However, before considering the most effective means for helping learners to achieve the development and refinement steps "a" through "c," this chapter must address the larger question of "What is reading?" in more detail.

CONCEPTS OF THE READING PROCESS

A child can read if he or she can decode the words.

You know how to read if you can get meaning from printed words.

You know how to read if you can tell what you just read.

The best way to teach children to read is to teach them phonics first.

Because the concept of *metacognition* is elaborated in a number of places throughout the remainder of this text, you might want to take some time here to talk about the larger conception of "metas" that are important for the reader—metalinguistic awareness, metalinguistic sensitivity, metacomprehension, and so on.

The difference between "teacher-as-director" and "teacher-as-orchestrator" is important. You might ask students to observe classes or videos of examples of both and then formulate sets of generalizations that describe the key teacher attributes of each type.

Have students interview children preschool through the upper elementary grades, asking each interviewee the question, "What does *reading* mean?" Discuss the changing conception of reading that children have through the years.

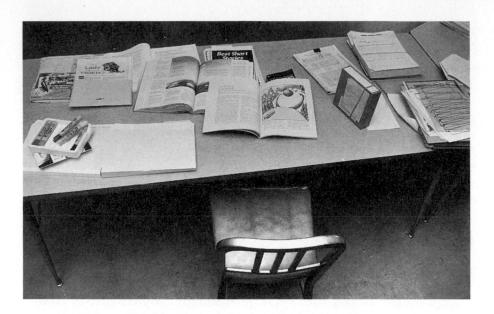

It is important to have a wide variety of quality reading materials in the classroom to encourage learners to value literacy in all print forms and types.

The best way to teach kids to read is by focusing on their language and not on the language of basal textbooks.

Reading is thinking. The best way to teach reading is to teach thinking.

Talk here about the importance of establishing a "literacy community" in the classroom, where everyone, including the teacher takes part and contributes. What would such a classroom look like? How would the instruction differ from instruction in a classroom where such a philosophy did not hold?

All of the preceding observations have been made at one time or another by authorities on reading, including teachers. In fact, in spite of the growth in knowledge about reading and about the reading process, there continues to be major disagreement about two fundamental issues: (1) What is the reading process? and (2) how should beginning and developing readers be taught to read?

Before exploring some of these differing perspectives on reading and the teaching of reading, it is important to remember that children throughout the United States and the rest of the world learn to read through a variety of instructional approaches and with a variety of materials. The famous "First Grade Studies" of the 1960s (Bond & Dykstra, 1967) pointed out that after accounting for the range of variables in different approaches to reading instruction, a single factor proved to be the most important: the classroom teacher. The teacher's rapport with the learners, the comfort level of the classroom, the enthusiasm shown for reading, and the respect and enjoyment shown for the language and its power determine in large measure the success or failure of any and all approaches to reading instruction.

Also, though rapport is certainly important for the teaching of reading, effective teachers of reading must also be knowledgeable. Teachers have a responsibility to know many things about reading, such as its content, structure, process, and pedagogy. To understand how to teach reading, the effective reading teacher must understand the psycholinguistic elements of reading and how they fit into the reading process.

THE PSYCHOLINGUISTIC ELEMENTS OF READING

All accepted models of the reading process recognize at least three critical factors in the act of reading: (1) the text being read, (2) the reader, and (3) the context for reading. A sociolinguist would argue that the interaction of the three—text, reader, and context—must also be considered.

The Text

The Semantic System

Lev Vygotsky, noted Russian developmental psychologist of the 1920s, whose work has only recently become accessible to a wide range of reading scholars, argued that the basis of meaning in language is the word (Vygotsky, 1962, 1978). Whether meaning is vested primarily in the individual words of the language or in larger linguistic or sociolinguistic structures, one thing is certain: Words and word meanings are crucial for effective reading. The structural features of words (i.e., prefixes, suffixes, roots, etc.) and word connotations and denotations play important roles in text.

The Syntactic System

In addition to the semantic system in text, language has a syntactic system or structure. *Syntax* normally refers to the grammar of sentences—clauses and phrases, how they are generated, and how they combine in systematic ways to produce the variety of sentence structures possible in a language. The reader must know (a) the varieties of structural patterns possible in sentences, (b) how those patterns are produced, and (c) how those patterns can be combined and transformed.

Some authorities argue that there are also larger units of grammar in text that the reader must access. For example, some suggest a grammar of paragraphs (e.g., discursive grammar). More recently, reading authorities have described the elements of "story grammars" or story structure. These larger units of grammatical structures are described in more detail in Chapter 2.

The Graphophonemic System

The graphophonemic system is the system of symbol–sound relationships that operate in the language—that is, which letters or combinations of letters represent which meaningful sounds? The reader must master a

In Vygotsky's *Mind in Society* (1978), there is excellent treatment of the importance of play as an early activity in which children begin to form the important concept of "symbol" (e.g., a broomstick comes to symbolize a horse). Ask students, "Why is that conceptualization important for beginning reading instruction?"

He also discusses "the zone of proximal development" as a critical cognitive transition point between the stages of cognitive development elaborated by Piaget. You might ask students to read the specific chapters that deal with these ideas in Vygotsky's book and present them to the class for discussion.

Many college students dislike grammar and believe that it has no place in the elementary curriculum. Also, most authorities now agree that teaching traditional grammar in the elementary grades has limited value in helping children write or read more proficiently. However, teachers of reading need to know the structure of their language in order to know how to teach the structural features that are important to the reader. Clearly, knowledge of language structure is important for both reading and writing. What is at issue is how best to help developing readers and writers acquire this structure.

number of graphophonemic relationships in order to be efficient. Experienced readers process these relationships unconsciously.

The Reader

Chapter 8 elaborates on the treatment of differences in structure and design of different forms of text (e.g., narrative and expository), and relationship to purpose. You may wish to glance over that material there in order to amplify the discussion here.

The teacher of reading must be aware of a number of things about the reader. First, the writer uses language for a variety of purposes, not all of which are apparent to the reader. For example, the author of text may use language to describe, to explain, to justify, to entertain, to manage others, to control, or to clarify thought. Some authorities also include a number of other purposes for language use. Readers, too, use language for various purposes. Inexperienced readers and ineffective experienced readers are often unaware of these various purposes for language use, or "language modes" as they are sometimes called. That lack of awareness can negatively affect both oral communication and reading.

Further, language plays an important role in cognitive development. The research of Lev Vygotsky (1962, 1978) shows how the development and use of language by young children directly assist in their cognitive development. According to Vygotsky, early social uses of language, along with solitary or parallel egocentric monologues, evolve into "inner speech" at about age seven years for most children. This "inner speech" facility allows the child to mentally converse with him- or herself, to engage in self-monitoring and self-analysis.

Notice that there is a logical relationship between mastery of inner speech and ability to self-monitor one's reading, writing, and speaking.

Piaget (1973) ascribed a more dominant role to egocentric speech in preschool children than did Vygotsky, but he agreed that preoperational children are able to think but are not able to think about their own thinking. The ability to think about thinking precedes and underlies the metacognitive processes central to effective reading.

Piaget also elaborated the initial important theory of the individual accruing knowledge and skill through expanded *schemata* (singular form is *schema*—a mental framework or holistic conception of reality and the relations among its parts). He pointed out that new knowledge was not simply a linear accrual process in which more information is summatively attached to existing information in the brain. Rather, the individual has a schema, and as new experiences and information become available, the individual usually modifies them in order to fit the new information into his or her schema of that concept or idea. That is, the child *assimilates* the new information into the existing schema.

> *Example:* A young child develops a schema for "dog." When new breeds are seen for the first time, the child can assimilate the new breed into his or her schema of "dog" even though there are a number of feature differences between the child's schematized version of "dog" and the creature just discovered. The newly encountered dachshund is not exactly like the child's pet cocker spaniel. It has shorter legs, coarser hair, and a longer snout. Still, the predominant defining features—hair, four legs,

barks, and so on—enable the child to fit the dachshund into her schema of "dog."

Suppose, however, the child now sees a Mexican hairless dog. Now the child's schema starts to break down. In order to fit that dog into the "dog" schema, the child must modify the schema to accommodate the information provided by the new experience. The child must modify the critical features rather dramatically.

Whenever possible, people fit new information into existing schema via assimilation; when necessary, however, people adapt schema to incorporate new information via accommodation. Each new experience offers knowledge that redefines the previous conception of reality.

The concept of *schema* is important in reading because the schemata the reader brings to a specific piece of text determine in large measure the meaning that will be derived from the reading. The meaning of the text, conveyed through the text's structure, interacts with the reader's schemata to generate a new unique meaning of the text. The following passage of text demonstrates the importance of the interaction between reader schemata and text structure. While reading it, try to think of a good title for it.

> *The procedure is quite simple. First you arrange things into different groups. Of course, one pile may be sufficient depending on how much there is to do. If you have to go somewhere else due to lack of facilities that is the next step, otherwise you are pretty well set. It is important not to overdo things. That is, it is better to do too few things at once than too many. In the short run this may not seem important but complications can easily arise. A mistake can be expensive as well. At first, the whole procedure will seem complicated. Soon, however, it will become just another facet of life. It is difficult to foresee any end to the necessity for this task in the immediate future, but then one can never tell. After the procedure is completed one arranges the materials into different groups again. They can be put into their appropriate places. Eventually they will be used once more, and the whole cycle will then have to be repeated. However, this is part of life.*

Bransford & Johnson, 1973

Observe that you probably know all of the individual vocabulary meanings, but you may have some difficulty identifying the topic specifically enough to make it all fit together.

If you are told that the article is about washing clothes, notice that it now makes better sense. Your schema of "doing laundry" has components, features, perimeters, and a central organizing structure. When you bring that schema to bear on the reading, the text becomes more meaningful for you. The same is true for the reading of any text. Activating schema is instrumental to any instructional approach to reading.

In many undergraduate teacher education programs, students will have taken a course in developmental psychology prior to their reading methods course. If your students have not taken such a course prior to this class, you may wish to spend some time elaborating the importance of schema to contemporary reading instruction theory (e.g., importance to the prereading phase of instruction and to building/activating background knowledge).

The Context

The context within which the reading takes place determines in important ways the meaning derived from the reading experience (Harste & Burke, 1977; Hickman, 1983; Holdaway, 1982). The "Effective Schooling" research accumulated through the 1970s and early 1980s reinforces the findings cited earlier in the "First Grade Studies" by Bond and Dykstra (1983). The classroom teacher and the learning environment significantly determine the reading achievement that occurs.

An appropriate context for reading implies more than being a sympathetic, understanding, and encouraging teacher—and these are all very important! The teacher of reading must be cognizant of the following:

- The developmental stages of the child
- Appropriate literature and its suitability to the child's stage of development
- The array of opportunities to capitalize on the "teachable moment" for integrating reading instruction with the natural language of the classroom
- The ways in which reading instruction integrates with the subject matter content of the learning settings of the elementary grades.

Beginning teachers must learn how to successfully time their instruction to capitalize on the "teachable moment." You might also want to talk about the importance of having a repertoire of instructional activities appropriate to teaching the same skill or concept so that if one does not work, it is easy to shift rapidly to another. Discuss, also, the importance of ongoing informal monitoring during instruction. (Note: these ideas are presented more fully in Chapter 10.

VIEWS AND MODELS OF THE READING PROCESS

All teachers of reading teach based on an underlying theory of how children learn to read and how best to approach instruction in reading. This is true regardless of whether they can or do articulate their beliefs!

All instructional approaches are rooted in some theory about the reading process. The preceding text examined the elements that must be considered in developing such a theory. This chapter now considers how these elements figure into a mental picture of how readers process text. An exhaustive listing of theories and hypotheses would be impossible. Instead, this chapter examines a limited number of views of reading; these views account for the majority of commonly employed approaches to reading instruction in the schools.

One way to conceptualize these views is on a continuum moving from left to right, where the extreme left is the domain of text-driven views and the extreme right is represented by schema-driven (i.e., readers' schemata) views.

Many undergraduates, anxious to begin their teaching experiences, have little patience with theory and research. This might be a good point at which to talk about how all teachers have theories about how learners learn and how best to teach. Offer some examples of these less-formalized theories that student teachers can observe in an elementary classroom.

Text-driven ——— Text–schema interaction ——— Schema-driven

At the risk of oversimplification, the extreme text-driven approaches perceive meaning as residing in the text. Meaning is to be derived entirely from the text by the reader. Schema-driven approaches, on the other hand, assert that meaning resides in the reader and is then imposed onto the text. As with most other things in life, few reading scholars or teachers advocate extremist positions on either end of the continuum. Instead, most prefer to be somewhere in the middle of the continuum between the extremes.

The "Bottom-Up" Model of Reading

The "Bottom-Up" model of reading is, in its most extreme form, a text-driven approach. The basic tenets of the Bottom-Up model of reading follow:

1. The learner reads text by building from sound–symbol units to words to meaning. Advocates of this model believe that students must be able to decode words accurately before developing comprehension skills in reading. Also, facility and unself-conscious automaticity in decoding are central.
2. The ultimate goal of effective reading is to assist the learner in acquiring near total automaticity in decoding words.
3. Learners use word-identification skills to unlock words not in their "ownership"* or "sight" vocabularies.
4. Word-identification facility is a function of mastery of a discrete set of word-identification skills and subskills.
5. A hierarchy of skills and subskills is amenable to direct instruction for word-identification mastery.
6. Word-recognition accuracy is important for comprehension.
7. The most effective instructional materials are phonics oriented.
8. The various components of reading—decoding, vocabulary, comprehension, study skills, literary appreciation—are discrete components that lend themselves to skill analysis and instruction.

It might be a good idea to discuss the underlying assumptions of this metaphor. The authors have discovered that it is not uncommon to find students in reading methods classes who do not know why "Top-Down" and "Bottom-Up" are used to describe different models of reading.

Ask students to identify and list additional attributes of this model.

The Bottom-Up model dominated much of the 1970s and the late 1960s. Three important factors contributed to the popularity of the Bottom-Up model and the variety of instructional approaches it spawned. First was the advent of linguistics on the pedagogical scene. In particular, *structural linguistics,* the science of the structure of language, became newly popular in education, although it was already a traditional academic area of scientific study. Reading authorities turned to its knowledge base and what that had to say about how the sound system of the language could be described in a scientifically tidy manner.

*Reading authorities often refer to vocabulary that the reader can readily retrieve for use at will as "full ownership" vocabulary—the reader literally owns the word. Another term for this is *sight vocabulary* because readers are able to recognize these words "on sight," without having to decode them or to work to recall their meanings.

So-called linguistic readers and linguistic reading series were published during the 1960s and the 1970s, which focused on initial concentrated study of sound–symbol relationships. Controlled approaches to instruction called for limited vocabulary in beginning instructional materials with all phonological elements being tightly controlled. Texts such as

Dan can fan.
Jan can fan.
Man can fan.

It might be interesting to have students try to write simple stories that use only limited phoneme and morpheme options.

appeared. Note that all sound–symbol combinations are kept constant with the exception of the initial sounds. Some linguistic reader advocates also recommended avoidance of any pictures or artwork that might divert attention from the language itself. (Continuing research on the role of picture adjuncts, however, suggests that pictures or graphics related to the content of the text can be valuable assists in comprehension of the text [Rich & Levin, 1977]).

A second factor supporting the Bottom-Up model was the advent of management-by-objectives (MBO), systems approaches to curricula. During that period, a predominant notion was that management of the curriculum by identifying behavioral objectives in varying increments and measuring individual student achievement by such objectives was the most effective way to improve reading. In 1975, for example, Scott-Foresman published a reading program called Reading Systems. Other reading programs of the 1960s and 1970s also focused on developing management systems by objectives that schools could use to organize, manage, and assess their reading programs. (During that same period, however, little attention was given to effectiveness of instruction in reading.)

Ask students, "Do children need direct instruction in phonics (i.e., synthetic- and/or analytic-based approaches)?" Although this is too early in the course to probe this question in depth, it might be a good point at which to introduce it and discuss it briefly. It can then become sort of a "long-range advance organizer" question.

In 1967, J. Chall published *Learning to Read: The Great Debate*, a review, synthesis, and reanalysis of significant research in reading and reading instruction. Chall concluded that strong reading programs included strong components in decoding instruction. Many inferred from her work that reading authorities advocated a Bottom-Up phonics-based approach to beginning reading instruction.

Since the 1970s, Bottom-Up models of reading instruction continue to be advocated. Many reading programs continue to design their instructional approaches around such models. However, it is probably fair to say that Bottom-Up models of reading instruction are not common among those that are currently espoused as strong models for design of effective approaches to reading instruction in the elementary grades.

The "Top-Down" Model of Reading

The "Top-Down" model of reading is the opposite of the Bottom-Up model. Its fundamental feature is that it is at the schema-driven end of the continuum. The following are among its primary tenets:

1. Meaning is vested in the reader and not in the text per se.
2. The reader imposes meaning onto the text instead of deriving it directly from the text.
3. Comprehension and meaning precede decoding and word attack.
4. What the learner brings to the reading act in the way of background information, elaborated schemata, and literacy knowledge generally determine what is taken away from the reading act.
5. Initial instruction should build from the language of the child and the child's world.
6. Learning proceeds basically from the whole to its parts and not from parts to a whole.
7. Partial cues in the key words and grammar of the sentence are adequate for effective comprehension of text. Perfect word-identification accuracy is not critical in all cases.
8. Instruction should focus on meaning rather than on text structure.
9. The various domains of literacy contribute individually and in concert to the acquisition and development of reading.

After reviewing and discussing this list, ask students to suggest additional attributes of the Top-Down model.

A Top-Down model of reading views the reader as the dominant factor in determining meaning during the reading process. The reader is the center of instructional activity, with instruction building from the child's experiences. Advocates of "Whole Language" approaches to reading instruction, most of the "Language-Experience" approaches to instruction, and other alternative approaches often described as "psycholinguistic" are derived, in most instances, from a Top-Down model of reading and reading instruction.

Eclectic Models of Reading

In reality, good classroom teachers of reading are not theorists or researchers. They know what works without having to conform to a single theoretical perspective. Their teaching reveals that they pick and choose from the best of all that is available to them, including theoretical views and models of reading and reading instruction. Parts of both Bottom-Up and Top-Down models of reading are found in nearly all reading classes.

Philosophically, these classes can probably be aligned with one theoretical camp or model or another. However, the specifics of day-to-day instruction are culled from both extremes, as well as from the middle.

OTHER SHAPING EVENTS

During the 1970s, Piaget had a significant impact on education generally and on educators' views on cognitive processes more specifically. By the late 1970s, a number of researchers working in the reading field—most were psychologists or linguists by training—became interested in applying Piagetian ideas to reading research. Versions of Piaget's schema elaboration (with attendant concepts of assimilation and accommodation) were used in exploring the reader's processing of text in print (e.g., by Bransford & Johnson, Anderson).

In addition, in the 1970s and early 1980s, data from the National Assessment of Educational Progress (NAEP) showed that since assessments of reading achievement had begun in the later 1960s, basic skills in reading (defined as word attack or decoding) had improved in the slower learners. However, inferential and other comprehension abilities had declined, especially in the higher achievers (NAEP, 1980). This suggested to some that the phonics-intensive programs achieved improved word attack skills at the expense of the critical higher-level comprehension skills.

Also, by this time, most publishers of basal reading programs had moved to publish more eclectic programs. The new programs attempted to balance the instruction across a variety of components (including comprehension, vocabulary, study skills, and literary appreciation), instead of focusing primarily on decoding.

When considering the contemporary scene in literacy instruction, in many respects, things have not changed. Good teachers have known for many years that effective literacy instruction must include more than reading, writing, and speaking. Effective literacy development occurs most successfully in the classroom where these language use elements are exploited together in mutually reinforcing ways and in ways that are tied to the accrual and integration of content knowledge.

In addition, however, contemporary educators know a great deal more than was known in the past, particularly in regard to how learners learn, how learners use language to facilitate literacy development, and what kinds of things must exist in a teaching context to assure the most effective literacy instruction.

There seems to be a new boldness among researchers and teachers. Researchers are willing to pull from fields of study and from theoretical models that fall outside the traditional aegis of "reading" and "reading instruction." Linguists, psychologists, developmental psycholinguists—even anthropologists and sociologists—now are exploring the reading process. Teachers, as a group, also appear to be exhibiting a new willingness to try new ideas and approaches. Interest in ideas such as "Whole Language" and "Integrated Language Arts" instruction are, in some respects, excellent indicators of this. Many classroom teachers are trying out pioneering instructional strategies and techniques.

Instructional materials being published by commercial publishers—reading programs, language arts programs, integrated reading and language arts programs, and a large selection of various supplementary materials—are improving in quality. New ideas and established research

Elaborate on the differences among basal reading programs of the 1950s, 1960s, 1970s, 1980s, and 1990s.

appear to be moving more quickly into classroom materials, and critics of the older traditional reading programs are having a more profound impact on new programs.

This is not to say that all reading educators concur about the quality of commercially published programs or that the newer programs are as good as they could or should be. Most educators agree that room for improvement remains. However, a historical perspective would suggest that some important improvements have been made, especially in the past decade.

Supportive curriculum materials, strong administrative support at the local school level, and community support are important for a high-quality reading program. However, the major force and the most important persons in any reading program are the classroom teacher and the children. They ultimately determine the effectiveness of the reading program.

Teachers are the persons for whom this book is written. The remainder of this book is designed to help teachers master the knowledge and skills that assure facile and professional teaching of literacy generally and of reading specifically.

Note also that professional organizations such as the International Reading Association (IRA), National Council of Teachers of English (NCTE), and Association for Supervision and Curriculum Development (ASCD) publish a variety of materials (e.g., videos), which are excellent teacher resources.

What do locally developed curriculum guides in reading look like? What is the relationship between a locally developed curriculum scope and sequence and one that accompanies a commercially prepared reading basal?

HIGHLIGHTS

1. In recent decades, the definition of literacy has broadened to include all of the language abilities associated with effective reading, writing, and speaking, as well as acquisition and integration of the basic structures of knowledge associated with American culture.
2. Contemporary reading educators are more interested in the reading process than were their predecessors. They believe that effective instruction must capitalize on what is known about how learners acquire and develop literacy from the earliest years through adulthood.
3. An effective teacher of reading is aware of the importance of the reader, the text, and the context, as well as the interaction among them. Effective instruction takes what is known about each and brings these factors together so that they are mutually reinforcing.
4. All teachers of reading base their instruction on a personal schema of the reading process. Most of the more commonly espoused models can be categorized as Top-Down or as Bottom-Up.
5. Most Top-Down models approach literacy instruction in a holistic fashion. They assume that it is better to learn the particulars when they are couched within the context of the larger pattern or of the whole process.
6. Most Bottom-Up models view literacy development as one of building from particular basic skills through direct instruction until the whole is mastered.

7. Although it is easy to oversimplify, advocates of direct early and concentrated phonics instruction generally derive their approaches from a Bottom-Up model. On the other hand, proponents of Whole Language and Language-Experience approaches are usually viewed as advocating Top-Down models.
8. Most teachers pick and choose ideas from both Top-Down and Bottom-Up perspectives.

REINFORCEMENT ACTIVITIES

1. How has the definition of "literacy" changed over recent years?
2. How has the definition of reading changed over recent years?
3. What are the four key psycholinguistic elements of most contemporary definitions of reading?
4. Explain the difference between a Top-Down and a Bottom-Up model of reading instruction.
5. Describe the general philosophical characteristics of the ideal reading program that you would prefer to use as a classroom teacher, based on your beliefs about the reading elements and processes described in this chapter. Identify the key characteristics and features that would make your program readily identifiable.

ADDITIONAL PROJECTS

1. Review a number of commercially developed reading programs, and identify them as Top-Down or Bottom-Up in character. Give reasons for your classification of the programs.
2. Visit some elementary classrooms, and observe classes in which reading instruction is taking place. Describe the class activities, and conclude whether the teacher and the program primarily use the Top-Down or the Bottom-Up approach.
3. Interview a number of reading teachers. Ask them about their beliefs about how best to teach reading to children.
4. Prepare a brief paper arguing for either a Top-Down or a Bottom-Up model for developing your reading program. Work with others in your class to arrange for a debate between the Top-Downers and the Bottom-Uppers.
5. Read the monograph *Becoming a Nation of Readers* (Anderson et al., 1985). Discuss in class the approach to reading instruction advocated in this publication. Try to decide whether their position is Top-Down or Bottom-Up.

---

1. It is hoped that students will point out (a) the move to include writing and oral language abilities and (b) the move away from a simplified skills-based definition to contemporary reading-as-process and interactive concept.

2. Again, the move from a strict skills orientation to a process view should be noted.

3. Expect students to address practical instructional implications of these four elements. Ask students "How should these elements guide the design of reading instruction?"

4. Ask students "What are strengths and weaknesses of the extreme interpretations of either position?"

5. Ask students to support their choices theoretically, based on research, or in terms of practical possibilities.

REFERENCES

Anderson, R., Hiebert, E., Scott, J. & Wilkinson, I. (1985). *Becoming a Nation of Readers.* Urbana, IL: The Center for the Study of Reading.

Bloome, D., & Green, J. (1984). Directions in the socio-linguistic study of reading. In P. D. Pearson et al., (Eds.), *Handbook of Reading Research.* New York: Longman.

Bond, G., & Dykstra, R. (1967). The cooperative research program in first grade reading instruction. *Reading Research Quarterly, 2,* 1–142.

Bransford, J. D., & Heidmeyer, K. (1983). Learning from children learning. In J. Bisanz, G. L. Bisanz, and R. Kail, (Eds.), *Learning in Children: Progress in Cognitive Development Research.* New York: Springer-Verlag.

Bransford, J. D., & Johnson, M. K. (1973). Considerations of some problems of comprehension. In W. C. Chase (Ed.), *Visual Information Process.* New York: Academic Press.

Chall, J. (1967). *Learning to Read: The Great Debate.* New York: McGraw-Hill.

Garner, R. (1987). *Metacognition and Reading Comprehension,* Norwood, NJ: Ablex.

Harste, J. C., & Burke, C. L. (1977). A new hypothesis for reading teacher research. In P. D. Pearson & J. Hansen (Eds.), *Reading, Theory, Research, and Practice.* Clemson, SC: National Reading Conference.

Hickman, J. (1983). Classrooms that help children like books. In N. Roser & M. Frith (Eds.), *Children's Choices.* Newark, DE: International Reading Association.

Holdaway, D. (1982). Shared book experience: Teaching reading using favorite books. *Theory into Practice, 23,* 293–300.

Klein, M. (1985). *The Development of Writing in Children: Pre-K through Grade Eight.* Englewood Cliffs, NJ: Prentice-Hall.

Loban, W. (1976). *Language Development: Kindergarten through Grade 12.* Champaign, IL: National Council of Teachers of English.

Mosenthal, P., Tamor, L., & Walmsley, S. (Eds.) (1983). *Research on Writing: Principles and Methods,* New York: Longman

National Assessment of Educational Progress. (1980). *Summary Report.*

Piaget, J. (1973). *The Language and Thought of the Child.* New York: World.

Rich, M. D., & Levin, J. R. (1977). Pictorial organization versus verbal repetition of children's prose: Evidence for processing differences. *AV Communication Review, 25,* 269–280.

Rosenshine, B. (1980). Skill hierarchies in reading comprehension. In R. Spiro, B. Bruce, & W. Brewer (Eds.), *Theoretical Issues in Reading Comprehension.* Hillsdale, NJ: Erlbaum.

Thorndike, E. L. (1917). Reading as reasoning: A study of mistakes in paragraph reading. *Journal of Educational Psychology, 8,* 323–332.

Vygotsky, L. (1962). *Thought and Language.* Cambridge: M.I.T. Press.

Vygotsky, L. (1978). *Mind in Society.* Cambridge: Harvard University Press.

ADDITIONAL RESOURCES

Brown, A. L. (1981). Metacognition: The development of selective attention strategies for learning from texts. In M. L. Kamil (Ed.), *Directions in Reading: Research and Instruction.* Washington, DC: National Reading Conference.

Harris, T., & Cooper, E. (Eds.). (1985). *Reading, Thinking, and Concept Development.* New York: College Entrance Examination Board.

Holdaway, D. (1979). *The Foundations of Literacy.* New York: Ashton Scholastic.

Mason, J., & Osborn, J. *When Do Children Begin "Reading to Learn?": A Survey of Classroom Reading Instruction Practices in Grades Two Through Five* (Tech. Rep. No. 261). (September, 1982). Urbana: University of Illinois, Center for the Study of Reading.

Smith, F. (1988). *Understanding Reading* (4th ed.). Hillsdale, NJ: Erlbaum.

CHAPTER 2

Developmental psycho-linguistics is a relatively new science focusing on language acquisition and development. Prior to its conception, most studies of children's language focused on word counts and measures of sentence length only. Recent discoveries have led to a renewed emphasis on the importance of the preschool home environment and the approaches taken to early literacy instruction.

EARLY LITERACY ACQUISITION AND DEVELOPMENT

I got into my bones the essential structure of the ordinary British sentence—which is a noble thing.
Winston Churchill, *My Early Life,* **1935**

PREVIEW

Of all the things that have been recently discovered about children's development of reading ability, the single most important thing may be the critical importance of development during the early years—birth through the preschool years and into kindergarten. Since the late 1960s and early 1970s, research and study of the developing child and of evolving literacy have provided a picture of emerging literacy in young children. Previously, such a picture either was unimagined or was drawn experientially, without supporting research-based evidence.

For example, many educators thought that early readers represented a small minority of especially gifted children and that most children entered the school years with extremely naïve conceptions of and perceptions about reading and writing. A popular reading text, in fact, included in its opening remarks to teachers the observation that an adult looking at a totally unfamiliar language, such as Japanese, was like a beginning reader looking at the print in preprimers and primers. According to this view, what the child sees is an array of unfamiliar marks and squiggles that bear no connection to reality or any contexts with which the child is familiar.

However, more recent research has shown that preschool children are bombarded with oral language and print in all aspects of their daily lives. Even children reared in homes with minimal reading materials and activities are awash in print—at grocery stores, shopping malls, and fast-food restaurants; on television and billboard advertising; and so on. Children are attuned to the nature and functions of literacy long before they enter first grade (Klein, 1985).

This chapter considers some of the key features of this literacy development in the preschool child, and it considers the implications of that development for the teacher of reading in the beginning school years.

20

FOCUS QUESTIONS

Think about the following questions when reading this chapter:

1. How does literacy develop in young children—from preschool through the primary grades?
2. What are the factors in the home that contribute most positively to developing reading competence in the elementary grades?
3. What can the teacher of reading do to facilitate children's reading development in kindergarten through grade two (K–2)?

These important questions are addressed in this chapter on literacy development. This chapter examines the research in these important areas and considers its implications for the teacher of beginning reading in the earliest grades.

Ask students to identify the most likely printed-language-oriented objects to which young children are exposed (e.g., labels on milk cartons, fast food signs, service station signs).

RESEARCH IN DEVELOPMENTAL PSYCHOLINGUISTICS

Of the many areas of study in reading acquisition and development that have been examined during the past several decades, perhaps none has received more attention than study of general literacy development in young children. The study of early readers and their development has always fascinated reading researchers. More recently, however, two other topics of study have emerged. For one, interest has expanded to include broader literacy issues: What are the stages of normal oral language development? How does written literacy progress in young children? In regard to reading development, what is the role of oral reading to children in the home?

On the other hand, interest has also narrowed to focus on more specific matters of literacy development in young children: In what order do children acquire (i.e., understand and use) different question types? How do young children develop verb-phrase mastery? How do acquisition and mastery of given modes of expression in writing correspond to comprehension of those same modes in reading?

During the 1960s, developmental psycholinguists, armed with newly developed tools in linguistics and developmental psychology, began seri-

Point out here the difference between the concept of "adult grammar" and "child grammar." (In the past, the adult grammar model was used as a benchmark for measuring the "correctness" or "incorrectness" of a child's speech.) The perception of child language as a sequence of normal stages of progression for children (in grammar, vocabulary, meaning, functional uses and purposes, etc.) implies a different teaching attitude as well as a different approach to the design and selection of instructional materials.

ous study of language development in children from the earliest ages through the primary grades of elementary school, and to a more limited extent, beyond into the secondary years. This research supplied a wealth of knowledge about early literacy development in children. That research revealed a great deal about how children acquire the *grammar system* of their language (i.e., the particular grammatical constructs, such as clauses and phrases, questions and question types, etc.).

More recently, study has focused on issues surrounding children's *functional* uses of language (i.e., how children use language in various situational contexts for different purposes). For example, when and how do children develop facility with the various paralinguistic skills necessary for oral communication? What are the linguistic and sociolinguistic factors that affect this development? What kinds of classroom learning environments foster the most effective development of these abilities?

As mentioned earlier, this research has also demonstrated the extreme importance of the earliest learning environments of children—primarily the home—and the importance of involving children in conversations in the home, as well as the importance of reading aloud to preschool-aged children.

This chapter reviews several of the important discoveries about early literacy development in children, specifically in relation to oral language development, the development of meaning, and an emerging awareness of print.

DEVELOPMENT OF ORAL LANGUAGE

Normal Sequence of Stages

> Language develops naturally in children, and it advances through a series of stages. Each stage of language development has distinguishing attributes, and each stage is common to all normally developing children.

Children share the same basic steps in developing their comprehension and use of questions, verb phrases, and so on. Many presumed "language use errors" in children's speech are now known to be attributes of language development in all normal children. For example, overextension of the "-ed" ending to irregular verbs is common in the grammar of children through the kindergarten and first-grade years. ("I falled down" or "I hurted my knee" are normal language utterances at this stage of language development.) The word *because* is used as a coordinating conjunction rather than as a cause–effect term by children through the second grade (Cazden, 1972; Dale, 1976; Klein, 1981). Throughout the primary grades,

Some debate continues regarding the amount of egocentric speech versus the amount of social speech in preoperational children. Most authorities now concur that children use speech for social functions early on and in sophisticated fashion (Piaget suggested that even at first grade, children engaged in extensive amounts of egocentric speech). You might wish to discuss the instructional implications of the speech functions during beginning reading instruction.

Point out the dangers of being too eager to "correct" children's grammar, particularly when persons have mistakenly assumed that this kind of language use is not adultlike.

animistic verbs are often used with inanimate nouns—"The sun *chases* the clouds," and "the boat *wants* to go on the lake" (Piaget, 1959).

Despite these language usage errors, by the age of five, most normally developing children have mastered *all* of the critical features of language structure needed for initial instruction in reading. They can employ all of the basic sentence patterns. What's more, their comprehension vocabulary is about twice the size of their production vocabulary during the first year of school (Dale, 1976).

Developmental Interaction of Child and Environment

How does this language development occur? Does it directly result from instruction they receive from their parents? Do children learn by literally imitating the language used by people around them? How can oral language development be enhanced by the adults who care for children?

Language develops naturally for all normal children. This does not mean that language is strictly a function of innate endowment. If children were isolated from a language-using society—separated from people who use language—they would not learn to speak. However, children do innately possess the capacity for language use, the sense of structure and form in language use, and the drive to use language for communication, for enjoyment, and for a sense of self.

Children do not learn language solely by directly imitating their parents and other language users who share their environment. If that were the case, young children would speak exactly as adults do. Clearly, they do not, though they master the sound system of the adults' language quite early—with but few exceptions. Thus, being able to sound out the same words and sentences that adults do would be theoretically possible. Children do not, however, use the identical language patterns and vocabulary of adults, as was illustrated earlier by children's usage errors.

Children's acquisition and development of vocabulary and sentence structures progresses systematically through developmental stages. These language form and structure patterns correspond to those of the more sophisticated adult language user only in general contour in the early stages. At first, children progress from one-word and two-word utterances to simple assertions.

Complex structures include the following:

- Extended noun phrases and clauses
- Relative clauses
- Subordinate clauses (sentences beginning with words such as "if," "although," "since")
- Passive voice (e.g., "The boy hit the ball" is active voice; "The ball was hit by the boy" is passive voice)

Many students may not be aware of the old controversy between the "innatist hypothesis"—usually attributed to Noam Chomsky's critique of Skinner's work on language learning—and the "behaviorist hypothesis." Some discussion of the implications of these two positions might be helpful here.

Most students are aware of the long-standing research indicating virtually no correlation between traditional grammar instruction and improved writing or reading. Many then mistakenly infer that as elementary teachers, they need not know formal grammar. Some discussion of the difference between "know-that" knowledge and "know-how" knowledge might be helpful here. Even if educators were to assume that no formal grammar instruction should take place in the elementary grades—and that is not a given by any means—there might still be a need for the teacher of children to know a basic amount of "know-that" information about the structure of language and text, which is important for instructional decision making.

These constructions develop gradually. Most children do not comprehend passive-voice sentence structure until some time between the end of first grade and the end of second grade. Mastery of subordinate clauses (both the comprehension and the production of them) develops much later. In fact, many juveniles in middle school and high school have difficulty with comprehending sentences with subordinate clauses.

> *In brief, when it comes to oral language, children through the normal preschool range (through five years or so) are reasonable masters of the language structure, sound system, meaning and meaning formation system, and the varieties of purposes to which language may be put. More importantly, children have become relatively sophisticated hypothesizers, testers, explorers of and with language. Not only do they possess a great deal of language knowledge and skill in its use, but in addition they have developed the critical strategies and processes necessary for developing new language knowledge and new, more sophisticated skills in its employment.*

> **Klein, 1985**

Perhaps most important, the teacher of young children should remember that

> *Oral language is the base from which all literacy develops. Reading and writing receive their initial impetus in oral language. Oral language represents a bridge potential between the two. And, oral language continues throughout the school years, and, indeed, our lives to provide the essential means for reading and writing development.*

Ask students, "What does this quotation imply regarding how to design curriculum for kindergarten, for first grade, and for later grades?"

DEVELOPMENT OF MEANING

Functions of Oral Language

Idea-Oriented Uses of Language
Oral language serves a variety of functions. An obvious function is as an essential means of communication. However, oral language serves other purposes as well. Talking aids in the discovery and generation of new ideas. Communication, discovery of ideas, and generation of ideas are all oral language functions that are central to the development of reading and writing.

In addition to these three different purposes for talk, what do students know about different forms of talk for different contexts (e.g., formal, informal, intimate, ritual)? Ask students what they infer about reading instruction when they consider the different forms and uses of talk. You may wish to mention here that these context-related forms of talk are called "registers," to prepare them for the idea of an "instructional register," mentioned later in this chapter.

Social Uses of Language
Research (Fillion, Smith, & Swain, 1976; Halliday, 1973, 1975; Tough, 1973, 1977) has shown that children from ages 3 to 6 years have a sensible grasp of the following language concepts:

Children talk for different purposes and in different situations that require them to think about meaning. So, it is easy to make links between talking and reading.

- The grammatical structures of language
- The various functions of language
- The meaning of what language is
- The reason that language is used

Prior to the 1970s, most authorities assumed that young children, especially prior to the first grade or so, used language largely for egocentric purposes. Piaget even suggested that as much as 40–50% of a first-grade child's language use was "egocentric"—used primarily for nonsocial communication purposes (Piaget, 1959). Since the later 1970s, however, the work by Joan Tough (cited earlier) and others has established that preschool children use language for a variety of social communication purposes—to describe, to explain, to entertain, and even to manage and control the behavior of others!

The meaning of *meaning* has been an ongoing philosophical argument for years. Many experts today continue to disagree on what constitutes an acceptable definition of *meaning* or *meaningful*. Little wonder then that educators continue to disagree about what is reading comprehension, much less how best to teach it!

Researchers have also discovered many ways in which situational contexts and language-using purposes shape children's choices and modes of expression (Horowitz & Samuels, 1987; Teale & Sulsby, 1986). By the early school years, children ply the entire range of language-use modes, including the use of language to persuade and control. Younger children are not distinguished from their older counterparts by differences in their knowledge about modes of discourse as much as by differences in their degree of sophistication in the use of that knowledge.

Persuasive discourse, and its comprehension and production in writing, remains one of the most difficult text forms for learners to master. Since the early 1970s, national reading and writing assessments of student performance at a number of different ages and grade levels suggest that comprehension scores and writing scores in this mode of discourse are lower than in most other modes. Ask students ''What are some ways in which teachers can improve and increase instruction in this form of text at different grade levels and for different learning abilities?''

Example: Five-year-old Lincoln Hartoonian, when presented with two different souvenir gifts from the author, was asked to make his choice first so that the one left could be given to his older sister. He reacted with an extended discourse on why he should have both gifts because his sister not only did not need a gift, but in all likelihood, probably would not even want one!

Lincoln had a very firm grasp of the persuasive function of language. He lacked some sophistication in the logic he employed when using the persuasive mode, but even his logical skills were marked. His ability to use language is typical of children this age.

Concrete Versus Abstract Usage of Language

Concrete Usage

Children ages 3–6 years use language primarily to achieve concrete goals: "I want a banana." "I want to go to grandma's house for Christmas." "Jimmy broke my bike." "I don't like beans." When they do use language to express abstract ideas or notions, those are typically specifically directed toward concrete objects—"I love you, mommy," or "I don't like Billy."

Abstract Usage

The instructional register is a critical concept for the beginning teacher to grasp—especially for kindergarten, first grade, and even second grade teachers. The language of instruction is both abstract and complex and assumes significant metacognitive abilities for children of this age. Ask students, ''What are some ways in which teachers can design their instruction to help overcome the problems implicit in the instructional register?''

However, when children enter kindergarten and first grade, they are introduced to a new dimension and meaning for language use. At this time, children are introduced to language as an instrument of instruction. This language, used by the teacher in the classroom, is often referred to as the "instructional register" or more commonly the "language of instruction." It is also referred to as "the metalanguage of teaching." The typical kindergarten or first-grade teacher uses terms such as *word*, *sentence*, and *letter* throughout the day. In this way, the teacher uses *language* to tell about or describe *language*. Once introduced, the new abstractive level of language usually dominates the instructional scene. The instructional language of primary-grade teachers adds a new level of complexity for comprehension. This factor in beginning reading instruction must be recognized and considered by the teacher.

EMERGING AWARENESS OF PRINT

Early Awareness of Print Characteristics

In order for children to be able to read or write, they must be aware of the nature and function of print. They must know that the marks and squiggles on paper can represent value and meaning for both the reader and the writer. Most children develop this *metalinguistic awareness* quite early—and usually without the benefit of direct formal instruction on the nature of print. Over the years, researchers have discovered that long before beginning school, most children have such awareness. Harste, Klein, et al. have found that children 3 and 4 years of age are typically aware that writing proceeds from left to right and from top to bottom in the English language. Early scribble writing by children of these ages provides insights into their literacy knowledge.

You might want to point out that the concept of "emergent literacy" is a relatively new one. Work by Jerome Harste and by William Teale and Elizabeth Sulsby might be assigned as additional readings here. (See "References" section for suggested readings.)

Luria's Discovery

This is not to say that children in these preschool years understand the difficult abstractive character of letters of the alphabet. As early as the 1920s and 1930s, the Russian researcher, Alexander Luria discovered that children proceed through a series of early stages of print awareness. They move from "undifferentiated" stages in which print or marks on paper play no meaningful symbolic role through a series of "differentiated" stages in which they understand that there is some connection between the marks and the reader's interpretation of them.

> *Example:* Luria cites a case of a child who uses pictographs as mnemonic cues to verbal descriptions provided by the researcher. The child depicted "a star in the sky" with a mark vaguely resembling a star. Luria then said, "A thousand stars in the sky." The child was temporarily astounded and puzzled. "Oh, I can't do that," she said. "I do not have enough room on the paper." After a few moments, she said, "Wait! I know! I'll make this kind of mark [different from her one star mark], and I'll just remember that it means a thousand stars!" (Luria, 1977–1978).

Contemporary work in children's language development owes a lot to much of the earlier work by Vygotsky and by Luria. Vygotsky's *Mind in Society* (1978; see reference in Chapter 1), in particular, addresses the role of play in symbol acquisition. Alexander Luria's "The Development of Writing in the Child" (1977–1978) provides insight into children's acquisition of the concept of *symbol* (based on work he completed well over half a century ago).

Discovery!

Luria's subject made the incredible breakthrough with language that must be made in order to be able to read and write, as society defines these literacy acts. She already knew that her "one-star" symbol could present a simple reality to her that she could remember; she could use the star that she had drawn as a mnemonic cue to recall a verbal picture. She already had a simplified pictographic alphabet of sorts. However, her alphabet had only presentational potential. It did not have representational potential. Letters in our alphabet do not present but instead represent reality.

The reader must make a major step in abstracting from the symbol to the ideas signified by the symbol.

> The concept of *symbol* must be established before reading acquisition and development can take place.

Contemporary researchers in emerging literacy have found that most children discover this important concept of abstract representation through many varied experiences. They do not grasp this concept overnight or as the result of a single experiment with a researcher. Knowledge of the symbolic character of language and of the abstracting processes necessary for engaging in the higher forms of literacy (i.e., reading and writing) is an evolutionary process. Most people gradually acquire the knowledge, skill, and linguistic sensitivity that define mastery of the foundation skills of literacy.

Most educators and scholars in the reading field consider the heart of reading and writing to be the understanding and mastery of the abstracting processes of symbolic expression. Because this mastery and understanding occurs during early childhood, the critical importance of parents and teachers of young children must be acknowledged. Further, teachers of children in the primary grades bear the major added responsibility to compensate as much as possible for inadequate early home-based literacy environments.

Guidelines for Early Literacy Development

The following basic guidelines offer direction for providing appropriate early literacy experiences and opportunities to young children.

Early Experiences with Reading

Appreciation of Reading

We have known for many years that when children come from homes where they are read to regularly, they develop into more proficient readers than when they do not come from such environments (Holdaway, 1979; Taylor, 1983). A few years ago, it was assumed that the major reason for reading to children in the home and in the primary grades was to help establish a positive attitude toward reading and to establish an early pattern of reading high-quality literature. These remain important reasons

Reading aloud is receiving a major new emphasis, based on research regarding its role in the home and its role in assisting metacognitive growth, as well as from a renewed interest in and accentuation of the importance of children's literature. Remind students that teachers must maintain a balanced approach to oral reading. Effective oral reading helps get children hooked on books. However, teachers must also encourage children to read aloud; if the teacher's polished readings intimidate children who can't read aloud that well, oral readings can produce an unwanted result. It requires work and commitment in order to maintain the classroom literacy community concept.

for reading aloud to children. Recent discoveries, however, have provided additional powerful reasons for this activity.

Knowledge about Literary Forms

Reading aloud to children helps them acquire fundamental knowledge about literature (stories, poems, fables, fairy tales, myths, etc.) that they are going to meet throughout their reading years. This fundamental knowledge facilitates effective reading comprehension.

Knowledge about Literary Structures

Reading aloud to children helps them develop a sense of *story grammar*— the basic structure that all stories possess, which serves as the essential framework around which the content of stories is developed. Setting, plot, character development, climax, denouement, and so on become better understood as children hear more stories built on these structures.

Awareness of Aural Aesthetics

Reading aloud to children provides the reader an opportunity to demonstrate the rhythm and flow of language. Sentence structure, pitch, stress, and juncture in language are part of story content and are necessary elements of language structure and use. Children must be attuned to these aural features of language and literature in order to develop literacy skills.

Early Experiences with Conversing

Adults must talk with children more than to them. Children should be included in normal conversations involving exchanges of ideas on an equal basis with adults. Mealtime conversations in many homes exclude children—probably through oversight more than intent, although some adults still believe that "children are to be seen and not heard." Parents should be encouraged to engage in daily conversations with their children, discussing a variety of topics, and providing adequate feedback. Further, parents should show their children that the children's feelings and opinions are respected and are considered valuable when making decisions that affect them.

Teachers should provide children with opportunities to use language (a) for a variety of purposes, (b) with a variety of audiences, and (c) in a number of different language-using contexts. For example, children should have opportunities to engage in conversational exchanges with peers as individuals and in small-group settings. They should be encouraged to present their ideas and thoughts extemporaneously and informally, as well as to deliver prepared, formal soliloquies to small groups, large groups, or even the whole class. They should use oral language to describe, to explain, to clarify, to inquire, and to persuade or argue for a belief or an idea.

> The most effective instructional techniques and strategies for teaching reading and writing are dominated by speaking and conversing. Both teacher and student rely on oral language as the "coin of the realm" in teaching and learning.

Early Experiences with Writing

Ask students, "What does this first sentence mean? Why is it important?"

Children should begin their experiences with writing in their preschool years (Calkins, 1983; Graves & Stuart, 1985; Harste, Burke, & Woodward, 1984; Klein, 1985). Clearly, these early experiences with writing—versions and varieties of "scribble writing"—will not be the same writing that is viewed in the adult world as constituting composition. Klein defines writing as "the ability to employ pen or pencil and paper to express ideas symbolically so that the representations on the paper reflect meaning and content capable of being communicated to another by the producer using the marks as mnemonic cues." Given Klein's definition (1985), then much of the early writing efforts of preschool and kindergarten children qualify as composition.

What does the sentence highlighted in the box imply for children's daily writing experiences?

> The act of writing generates understanding; understanding does not generate writing.

Children learn to write by writing; they also learn many other concepts and gain many other insights through the process of writing. The act of writing can directly aid cognitive development, especially in relation to reading. The connections of writing to reading and reading development are increasingly well documented (Horowitz & Samuels, 1987; Mason & Au, 1986; Teale & Sulsby, 1986).

The following guidelines may help young children to gain facility with writing, as well as to utilize writing as a cognitive tool for developing full literacy.

- Whenever possible, children should be provided with writing materials and a comfortable place to write at their leisure.
- Parents should be encouraged to develop positive attitudes about their children's writing efforts and to be open and receptive to them. Teachers should praise parents regularly for being open and receptive to their children's writing efforts.
- When appropriate, children's writing efforts in first- through third-grade classrooms should be shared with their parents. Also, parents will be far more understanding of the instruction and evaluation procedures being used if they understand key ideas in the develop-

ment and teaching of writing. For example, parents should be advised of the importance of scribble writing and invented spellings in early writing development. They should also be aware of the important distinctions between teacher responses to children's writing that is done for personal discovery or idea generation and teacher evaluations of children's public writing that is done for sharing with others.

- The primary-grade classroom should have a writing center with writing materials, idea books, cut-and-paste equipment, comfortable seating, and relatively quiet surroundings for children.
- Children should be encouraged to feel comfortable with their writing in the context of reading. Writing on pads or in journals should be a natural part of the reading lesson in the primary grades.
- Children should learn early that much of their writing is personal and is not for display or for sharing unless they choose to do so. They should also have opportunities to share and to publicly display their writing. They should be taught that these two different kinds of writing are treated differently by the teacher and that each kind of writing calls for a different approach by both the writer and the intended audience.
- Oral language, writing, and reading are all closely related literacy acts. They interact with each other, and each builds on the other. Teachers, students, and parents should all act according to this underlying assumption.

The teacher should open communication channels with parents at the beginning of the school year. Ongoing dialogue provides the opportunity for teachers to explain what they are trying to do with children's writing, and it provides parents opportunities to share their concerns. This communication will pay off in dividends for all.

HIGHLIGHTS

1. Literacy development evolves, beginning in the earliest childhood years.
2. Emerging literacy in the preschool child is shaped strongly by both the home and the surrounding social environment.
3. Children have developed substantial oral language abilities by the time they enter school.
4. Children develop language in stages and through a complex array of circumstances and contexts. They do not learn language by simply imitating adults and others in their surroundings.
5. Both talking and writing aid in developing literacy not only by providing means for communication with others, but also by directly facilitating cognitive development, understanding, and generation of knowledge.
6. Writing development should be encouraged in the home during the preschool years. This requires a redefinition of "writing" for many parents and teachers.

7. The natural connections between talking, writing, and reading should be exploited during the school years.

REINFORCEMENT ACTIVITIES

1. Many answers are possible, so ask students to justify their answers.

2. Look for a balanced response. Language and learning are too complex for a simple description.

3. Oral language is the base!

4. Discuss ways in which to overcome the obstacles presented by the language of instruction.

5. Emphasize what contemporary research says about the importance of the home environment. Ask students always to think in terms of how to maintain open communication with parents (e.g., letters, newsletters, conferences).

1. What are some of the factors that affect early literacy development in children?
2. Do children learn language by imitating others? Explain your answer.
3. How does oral language influence the process of learning to write and to read?
4. To what does *instructional register* refer? Why is it important for the primary-grade teacher to be aware of this concept?
5. What are some of the things that should take place in the home and in the primary-grade classroom to insure literacy development in children?

ADDITIONAL PROJECTS

1. Review some of the magazines and journals designed for parents of young children. Evaluate articles on language and literacy in these publications. Discuss them with colleagues in light of the information in this chapter.
2. Prepare a brief newsletter that a kindergarten or first-grade teacher might send home to parents. In the newsletter, outline some interesting literacy-development activities that parents might do with their children.
3. Examine a number of commercially developed kindergarten programs, or examine the kindergarten–first-grade components of contemporary basal reading and language arts programs. Discuss the strengths and/or weaknesses of these programs in class. In addition, look for ideas to share with parents.
4. Arrange to have a preschool child speak into a tape recorder. If the child has not used one before, explain how a tape recorder functions, and remember to make the child feel comfortable. Most young children have fun doing this. You might have the child (a) tell a story that he or she likes; (b) describe an object that you share with the child; (c) talk about a favorite activity, game, or pet; and so on.

   Next, arrange to obtain a similar tape sample from a third- or fourth-grade child talking about the same topic.

   Transcribe both tapes, and compare them for language structure, vocabulary, organization, and other language features. Discuss the differences and similarities with other teachers.

Transcribing audiotapes is a demanding and time-consuming process, so this is a labor-intensive project. Nonetheless, the experience can be valuable for undergraduate students.

REFERENCES

Bond, G., & Dykstra, R. (1967). The Cooperative Research Program in first grade reading instruction. *Reading Research Quarterly, 2,* 1–142.

Calkins, L. (1983). *Lessons from a Child.* Exeter, NH: Heinemann.

Cazden, C. (1972). *Child Language and Education.* New York: Holt, Rinehart and Winston.

Dale, P. (1976). *Language Development: Structure and Function.* New York: Holt, Rinehart and Winston.

Fillion, B., Smith, F., & Swain, M. (1976). Language "basics" for language teachers: Towards a set of universal considerations. *Language Arts, 53,* 740–745.

Graves, D, & Stuart, V. (1985). *Write from the Start.* New York: New American Library.

Halliday, M. A. K. (1973). *Explorations in the Functions of Language.* London: Edward Arnold.

Halliday, M. A. K. (1975). Learning how to mean. In E. H. Lenneberg & E. Lenneberg (Eds.), *Foundations of Language Development* (Vol. 1). New York: Academic Press.

Harste, J., Burke, C., & Woodward, V. (1984). *Language Stories and Literacy Lessons.* Portsmouth, NH: Heinemann.

Holdaway, D. (1979). *The Foundations of Literacy.* New York: Scholastic.

Horowitz, R., & Samuels, S. J. (Eds.). (1987). *Comprehending Oral and Written Language.* New York: Academic Press.

Klein, M. (1981). Language and the child: A few key generalizations. *Educational Leadership,* March, (Vol. 38, pp. 446–448).

Klein, M. (1985). *The Development of Writing in Children: Pre-K through Grade 8.* Englewood Cliffs, NJ: Prentice-Hall.

Luria, A. (1977–1978). The development of writing in the child. *Soviet Psychology, 16,* 65–113.

Mason, J., & Au, K. (1986). *Reading Instruction for Today.* Glenview, IL: Scott, Foresman and Company.

Piaget, J. (1959). *The Language and Thought of the Child.* New York: Humanities Press.

Taylor, D. (1983). *Family Literacy: Young Children Learning to Read and Write.* Exeter, NH: Heinemann.

Teale, W., & Sulsby, E. (1986). *Emergent Literacy: Writing and Reading.* Norwood, NJ: Ablex.

Tough, J. (1973). *Focus on Meaning.* London: George Allen and Unwin Ltd.

Tough, J. (1977). *The Development of Meaning.* New York: Wiley.

ADDITIONAL RESOURCES

Kimmel, M., & Segel, E. (1984). *For Reading Out Loud!* New York: Dell.

Lamme, L. (1984). *Growing Up Writing: Sharing with Your Children the Joys of Good Writing.* Washington, DC: Acropolis Books.

Maguire, J. (1985). *Creative Storytelling: Choosing, Inventing, and Sharing Tales for Children.* New York: McGraw-Hill.

Temple, C., Nathan, R., & Burris, N. (1982). *The Beginnings of Writing.* Boston: Allyn & Bacon.

CHAPTER 3

LITERACY INSTRUCTION IN THE KINDERGARTEN

There is always one moment in childhood when the door opens and lets in the future.

Graham Greene, *The Power and the Glory*, 1940

Ask the students to discuss their own experiences with preschool and childcare before they attended school: How much of the time did they spend in activities that were academic versus social? How has their city changed since they attended elementary school, and what effects do those changes have on younger children? How is school expected to respond to those changes?

PREVIEW

Kindergarten is usually the 5-year-old's first formal experience with literacy instruction. The kindergarten year was initially created to facilitate children's socialization and to provide a transition for children between their home and the school. Instruction was given through directed group experiences and routines, and play was considered the most essential medium for developing socialization.

The role of the kindergarten has changed as society's needs have changed and as research has engendered greater understanding of the younger learner. Instruction now encompasses all the content areas, with objectives for each having been developed to guide the program. Specialized training is advocated for the early childhood teacher, and assessment and evaluation procedures are being refined.

The value of early literacy instruction is now recognized and accepted. Historically, as early childhood programs developed, reading instruction became more isolated from the language arts and more focused on the development of identified sequential skills. However, the influence of contemporary learning theory and research in reading has stimulated the reconnection of reading with the other language arts and has established a more comprehensive approach to the instruction of reading skills and concepts. This linking of reading instruction to the other areas of the language arts has provided to the teacher of young children a new, broader focus on literacy.

FOCUS QUESTIONS

Think about the following questions as you read this chapter on early literacy:

1. How do the developmental characteristics of young children influence the ways in which reading is taught in the kindergarten?

34

2. What are the critical elements of an early literacy program?
3. What are the typical materials that form a foundation for early reading?

Ask students, "Why has early literacy instruction become a focus for teachers in recent years? How does a teacher justify that instruction when considering the drug and other health problems facing young children?"

SELECTING AND PROVIDING INSTRUCTIONAL OPPORTUNITIES

Readiness for Instruction

In the school setting, a child's readiness to learn depends on how closely the content and the processes of instruction match the child's interests and abilities.

Traditionally, if it was anticipated that the child would experience success from the offered instruction, the child was said to be ready for the instruction. Readiness programs were developed for children who did not demonstrate abilities, attitudes, or behaviors believed to be necessary for success. These programs were created based on what the children did not know and/or could not do.

A greater understanding of how children approach the process of learning has affected the way in which the term *readiness* is used. This understanding includes valuing the child as a dynamic thinker who is striving for autonomy and is making meaning from his or her experiences. This insight has refocused the intent of readiness, which should be to create a foundation of support for the efforts of the individual child. Readiness is now a continuous process of helping children use their strengths to foster growth in new areas. A *readiness program* capitalizes on the processes children use for continued learning by helping them to explore concepts, evaluate ideas, and make connections using a variety of methods and materials.

Several readiness programs are available from most basal textbook publishers. Have the students review and compare the content and the objectives of these programs. Ask students, "Do these programs provide opportunities that will facilitate children's thinking, work habits, and self-concepts?"

Elements of an Early Literacy Program

An effective literacy environment fosters the continued development of children's oral language and encourages the acquisition of reading and writing concepts and skills with instruction that most closely matches the way children learn. An appropriate literacy program for young children responds to the developmental needs, abilities, and interests of the children themselves. The program is based on three assumptions, which are described here next:

1. Children seek knowledge and understanding of themselves, others, and their world.
2. Children learn through a process of interaction and reconstruction.
3. Children make connections across and within their experiences in order to create, construct, and test concepts and generalizations.

Children seek knowledge and understanding of themselves, others, and their world.

Children naturally desire to competently control their own destiny. They seek to develop abilities they have seen modeled by older children and adults because they desire the independence that those abilities bring. They are curious, eager, and often unrelenting in their striving for understanding.

Children learn through a process of interaction and reconstruction.

Children learn by doing. They develop meanings for objects, activities, and processes through their personal involvement in a variety of experiences. They learn to represent these developing meanings through their engagement in symbolic play. Symbolic play encourages children both to explore their understandings of the things they have experienced and to practice linking concepts to the language associated with the experience.

Young and inexperienced children learn about things by pretending to be those things. It is not unusual for small children to pretend to be cats, dogs, mommies, or cartoon characters. By going through the actual motions of experiencing the world from alternative viewpoints, they are better able to understand and remember what they are representing (Bruner, 1966). As children gain more experience and knowledge, they become able to use what they know to infer what it may be like to be an animal or an object. By playing with a representation of that object, such as a stuffed rabbit, toy truck, or doll, children can practice using dialogue in the situations that go with the object. The toy is not exactly like the real thing but it is enough like it that children can recognize the characteristics and generalize the discriminating elements that make it a representation.

As children begin to focus on pictures and print, they translate what they know about things in the real world through the pictorial representations of those things (Tough, 1977). The relationship between an object or an action and a printed symbol is the outcome of children's understanding of the concept of *representation*: things can hold meaning for other things. This is an important reason for play in the early curriculum. Children experience symbols in a personal way by using themselves to hold the meaning of a cat when they drink milk from a saucer and by pretending to be a mommy driving a car. They experience it when they discover that the stuffed toy cat is a facsimile of their family pet and when they realize that the picture of the daddy washing the dishes reminds them of the time when Daddy let them help in the kitchen. Though the picture is not exactly like having the experience happen at the moment, it helps the child recall when it was happening. The picture *represents* the event. It facilitates the translation from concrete reality to symbols that represent it.

Printed symbols are a refinement of the concept of representation because, unlike toys or pictures, printed symbols do not look anything like the things they represent. Children become familiar with this more sophisticated understanding of this concept by seeing their names printed on invitations, letters, or belongings, by observing labels on favorite foods or toys, or by noticing the names of family members or pets.

It is important for teachers to know that children's understanding of the concept of *symbol* evolves. Pretending to be an object (e.g., a monster, a snowman, a doll) and using objects for pretend play (e.g., stick horses and other props) both are critical to the child's developing concept of symbol. A child must have an implicit understanding of the concept of symbolization to learn to read. The exposure to printed language in stories helps expand the concept to include groups of words. Through storybooks, children learn that just as spoken words can describe an event or experience, so can printed words.

> Children make connections across and within their experiences in order to create, construct, and test concepts and generalizations.

Because the young learner reaches into every experience to extract meaning from a personal perspective, every instructional encounter holds the potential for providing clues or answers to questions beyond the teacher's immediate instructional objective. When a teacher presents a science lesson with the objective for the children to learn about the properties of water, a child may also see a relationship between the letters at

Ask students "What are some of the cultural and environmental differences a teacher might expect from a diverse kindergarten population? Why would these differences affect the content and style of reading instruction?"

the end of the name of a classroom pet, "Scooter," and the letters at the end of the word "water." A child involved in a mathematics lesson dealing with one-to-one correspondence may go beyond an intuitive grasp of this concept and may put words to the relationship in terms of corresponding sound to a letter or letters.

Adults, in their need to organize for instruction, often separate information by content areas where children pull from different experiences to create patterns of understanding about their world. In fact, children are often busy putting together what we have carefully taken apart.

Creating the Instructional Environment

Because there is such an increasingly diverse kindergarten population in terms of cultural and environmental experiences and because each child is unique in the rate and quality of his or her emotional, social, physical, and intellectual development, the options for instruction must vary as well. In the kindergarten, this diversity and individual responsivity of instruction is achieved by creating two interrelated systems of instruction: the child-centered system and the teacher-directed system. Both of these systems are designed to facilitate learning in developing kindergarten children, who are

- Active, curious, and eager to learn
- Increasingly cooperative and able to develop close relationships
- Proud to take responsibility for themselves as they learn to tie their shoes, put things away, and control their behavior
- Eager to please people who matter to them
- Interested in how they can use words and ideas
- Curious about nature and how things work
- Able to learn best (a) by touching real objects (e.g., blocks, paints, puzzles, animals, sand), (b) by moving around a lot, and (c) by planning and discussing projects with each other

(Peck, McCaig, & Sapp, 1988)

Child-Centered Instruction

This form of instruction is developed by the teacher in response to the developmental and educational needs of the 5-year-old. The child-centered system provides opportunities for exploration, application, and practice of new concepts through manipulation of materials, interaction with peers, and guidance by the teacher. This daily opportunity, often labeled "work time" or "play time," is characterized by

- Children's individual decision-making regarding the activities in which they engage
- Children's development of personal responsibility in managing their learning behavior for themselves and as group members

Assign students to work in groups of four; assign each group a characteristic of a developing kindergartener. Have each group describe an appropriate teacher behavior that would use the assigned characteristic to enhance learning.

- The large amount of verbal interaction of children among themselves and with the teacher

The physical arrangement of the child-centered room is tailored to encourage these characteristics. A typical child-centered kindergarten has small tables, each of which is surrounded by four to six chairs and which are separated by low shelves containing books, toys, and tubs filled with small construction or other manipulative materials. These separated areas create informal work centers ("learning centers") that encourage small groups of children to interact with the grouped materials while interacting with each other.

In this traditional, developmentally appropriate kindergarten, children learn mostly through play and through freely choosing and using a variety of the learning centers throughout the classroom. At the learning centers, children figure out how things work, interact with each other, try out new roles, experiment with their own ideas, build on their experiences, and solve real problems (Fein & Rivkin, 1986).

Within each of the designated centers, materials are carefully organized for clarity of intent of their use and enticingly presented to offer easy access. The centers may focus on a content area (such as science or math), or they may be arranged by different play areas (such as blocks, housekeeping, and construction). Many kindergarten environments offer a selection of both types of centers, so it would not be unusual for a classroom to have an art center, a math center, a block corner, a housekeeping area, a reading corner, and so on. This type of arrangement has more to offer the children for exploration and more to offer the teacher when presenting different types of information in a variety of ways. Sometimes these centers contain references to a central theme the students are experiencing, and at other times, only a few may seem related by topic.

Within these centers, there is a balance of structured and unstructured materials with which the children interact. *Structured materials* are those that encourage a particular activity and are usually unidimensional in their application. Materials such as puzzles, letter templates, and lotto games fall into this category. Their function is to provide opportunities for the child to develop skills and gain information. *Unstructured materials* encourage children to generate what the material will become. These raw materials include construction paper, crayons, scissors, glue, clay, blocks, legos, and dress-up clothes. Unstructured materials demand that children create or recreate emerging concepts and that they apply skills to new situations.

To maximize the use of the child-centered environment, teachers develop instructional interludes that directly provide students with opportunities to learn new information and skills or organize, apply, or extend currently held concepts and skills.

As a whole group, brainstorm the types of furniture and equipment that might be found in a kindergarten. Use this list as a foundation for creating a classroom floor plan. Refer to the examples found in Chapter 5.

Ask students, "How does a teacher organize materials so that it is clear to the students what materials are available, how they are to be used, and how they are to be put away?"

Have the students visit a toy store to see the types of materials that would be appropriate for a kindergarten. Ask each student to select one toy for which she or he will describe the intent of the toy and categorize it as to its structured or unstructured characteristics.

To allow for these whole-class or large-group instructional interludes, such as story time, music and movement activities, discussions, and direct instruction, a large carpeted area faces a chalkboard, pocket chart, and chart rack holding charts of poems and songs. Nearby is a record player to support the group's music experiences. This area is almost always punctuated by a teacher chair, sometimes a rocking chair, sometimes a small child's chair, from which the teacher presents a lesson, directs a group discussion, or shares a story.

Direct Instruction Opportunities

Teacher-directed instructional opportunities are developed based on an objective, and they follow a pattern that bridges from the children's knowledge and interests to the new concept or skill. Directed instruction is organized into three phases: involvement, instruction targeted toward the objective, and expansion. These three phases are designed to guide the children through an expanding circle of learning. Instruction begins with what children know about or what they know how to do, and it builds on this knowledge as the foundation for the new skills or information being developed. After the direct instruction, the children are encouraged to expand that learning by using it in other experiences. Directed instruction can be generated from activities developed in the learning centers, and those same learning centers can provide the opportunities for expanding the learning once instruction has taken place. Thus, the process of involvement, instruction, and expansion gradually increases the child's experiential and knowledge base for further instruction.

The direct instruction model can be seen as cyclical because previous learning forms a foundation for new learning, which, when practiced, becomes a foundation for future new learnings.

1. **Involvement** The children may already have had extensive experience exploring and relating to a concept or materials in the learning centers. Time spent in learning centers helps to link the children's past experience and knowledge with the instruction that is going to occur.

2. **Instruction** Direct instruction itself has three elements: modeling, instructive teaching, and applying.

Modeling Demonstrate with manipulatives or other materials the procedures, skills, and information that supports the instruction. Make clear to the learners, ''This is what we are going to learn about and this is how it holds meaning for you.''

Instructive teaching Use language and models to demonstrate how children can achieve the objective of the instruction. Show the learners, ''This is how you do it.''

Applying Use language and models to demonstrate how the objective of the instruction can be used in the children's daily experience. Provide opportunities to have guided practice in making or using the model. Encourage children to take the opportunity to try applying the new knowledge and skills in supportive contexts and experiences.

3. Expansion Encourage the children to link the new concept or skill with other learning. This phase is a reentry into the child-centered system of instruction as the children internalize and personalize the learning through their independent explorations.

Applying Instruction to the Elements of Literacy

The options available to the teacher in developing the instructional opportunities can be used to enhance literacy learning. Carefully select which objectives would be covered best via the teacher-directed or the child-centered system, and evaluate before instruction which experiences need to be developed in the child-centered system before they become a focus of directed instruction. Particularly, in developing literacy instruction, plan activities and experiences that develop oral language as a foundation for reading and writing concepts and skills.

FOUNDATIONS FOR LITERACY

Literacy instruction in the kindergarten integrates (a) the child's experiences with language development, (b) the reading instruction, and (c) the children's opportunities for writing. Teachers plan lessons based on the interests and the developmental level of the learners, and they generate activities that will extend their current experiences and knowledge.

Integrated Approaches to New Vocabulary, Language Structures, and Concepts

Teachers develop lessons, activities, and environments that encourage children to increase their vocabularies, extend their manipulation of language structures, and develop new concepts. They make these opportunities meaningful by linking them to the children's past experiences, verbally modeling and labeling the processes and concepts being addressed, and making it necessary for the children to recreate or apply the language.

Ask students "What are some of the interests of young children? How do they show their interest, and how can a teacher facilitate sustained interest?"

To increase the meaningfulness of language learning, teachers design lessons so that vocabulary, language structure, and concepts are developed interdependently. The children learn new words and concepts through guided experiences that the teacher demonstrates and describes.

Ask students to select an interest area for young children, develop three concepts about that area, and highlight the vocabulary words that support those concepts.

Instructional strategies involve symbolic or pictorial manipulation, auditory input, and peer interaction, all of which happen simultaneously as a result or condition of the experience. The teacher uses new vocabulary words as labels, in context, as they relate to the progression of the activity. The children, as a part of their experiences, are expected to interact with the teacher, the materials, and their peers in an effort to explore, clarify, practice, extend, and apply new variations of language in familiar or related contexts.

Through the use of language with peers and with adults during an experience and in later applications, children practice (a) the correct pronunciation of new words, (b) the nuances of meanings of the new words in various contexts, and (c) the ways in which the new words can be used to make sense. These same processes apply to new language structures (i.e., syntactic inflection, syntactic differences in meaning, and usage). Having a language model that provides accurate input, various richly labeled experiences, and opportunities for meaningful practice and application of new language is fundamental to these language learning processes.

In the classroom, children learn language by

1. Having experiences that are closely tied to descriptive and/or explanatory language (i.e., demonstrations, field trips, instruction)
2. Having opportunities to discuss, clarify, and practice the language (i.e., working in play centers, playing games, socializing with peers while a task is being attempted)
3. Applying the language to new situations (i.e., interacting in new experiences, learning new information or skills, working in learning centers).

Three Strategies for Learning Language

Children recognize the purpose for learning new language when they have experiences that make the content meaningful to them. In this way, classroom experiences and interactions set the stage for implementing language learning strategies. Three strategies facilitate language learning: (1) Provide opportunities to develop language in context, (2) instigate teacher–student interaction, and (3) encourage peer dialogue.

Contexts for Language Learning

The following example shows how children can develop language meaningfully by participating in an activity.

Example: Corn on the Cob

Setting: As a result of a trip to a garden, the children are preparing corn on the cob to eat for a snack. They picked the corn from the stalks grown in a community garden.

Have students select and develop an experience for a kindergarten group. Outline the main activity, suggested practice situations, and possible extensions.

TEACHER: "Was your *ear* of corn difficult to pull from the *stalk?* Was it high on the *stalk?* Did you pick your *ear* of corn from the *stalks* near the pumpkin *patch?* Those corn *stalks* were so tall I couldn't see which row you were in. I wonder whether the *cornstalks* in our room came from that row."

(These questions and comments from the teacher demonstrate how the new vocabulary words [shown in italic type] are properly pronounced and used structurally to make sense in sentences. The teacher's language also gives children clues to the meaning of the new words. In addition, dialogue with students creates an opportunity for new information to be tied to earlier knowledge, which allows for new learning to occur.)

The teacher guides the children through the preparation of their ears of corn for cooking. By consistently giving verbal descriptions and directions while demonstrating what the language means, the teacher is encouraging the children to make sense of the language without stopping to define each word. The teacher is assuming that the use of language in a meaningful context does this. The children are practicing using context in order to comprehend new vocabulary. Later, they will be able to apply this skill when they read new vocabulary words in meaningful contexts.

TEACHER: "The first thing you do with your *ear* of corn is to *husk* it by pulling these *husks* off and removing the *corn silk* from the top of the *ear*. When you have *husked* your *ear* of corn, pull off the *strands* of *corn silk* stuck between the *kernels* on the *cob*. As soon as you have *husked* your ear of corn, compare it with a partner whose little yellow *kernels* look like yours. What do you think holds them onto the *cob?* Decide which *ear* of corn you think has more *kernels*. Be ready to describe how you were *calculating*. I want to know how you figured out your answer."

Have the students work with partners to list the teacher's objectives from this scenerio. What new vocabulary words might the teacher emphasize? Extend?

Throughout the teacher's verbalizations, the children have models for using the new words in different ways. The children are also encouraged to use the new words with their peers in a task-related application, and there is an indication that a discussion will take place requiring the use of the developing vocabulary.

Further use of the new words can be generated by a class mural recreating the visit to the garden. The language needed to communicate about the materials (e.g., "Who can bring paper bags to twist up for making the stalks of the corn plant?") and about completing the project (e.g., "Rose, how many kernels are you gluing on your corn cob?") will reinforce and extend the learning.

Ask students to listen for the listed instructional behaviors to occur in peer conversations: "See whether you can identify any patterns of their use."

Teacher Interaction

Use various techniques when interacting with students. These techniques are used with the whole group or with individuals during directed or guided experiences. Instruction is set up to connect experience with the language through a natural interaction with words, objects, and actions.

Figure 3.1   Senses chart for apple-eating experience.

Apples				
taste	*look*	*smell*	*feel*	*sound*
sweet sour yummy	green red yellow round shiny		hard smooth soft slippery wet	crunchy

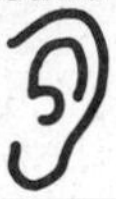

Specific instructional behaviors also enhance individuals' learning. While engaged in verbal interactions relating to classroom activities or personal discussions, phrase verbal responses in ways that encourage the children's thinking. Model and paraphrase the language for the children, and employ the following instructional behaviors to enhance learning:

Link:	Relate past experience with the present
Input:	Introduce new information or new vocabulary or language structures
Extend:	Add more information about familiar content, or suggest a different structure for the content
Frame:	Create a set through which prediction to occur
Connect:	Tie words to the activity or the activity to words
Clarify:	Add examples or delineating detail
Label:	Give a name for a concept, object, idea
Categorize:	Group concepts, objects, ideas
Relate:	Show analogies between experiences
Question:	Probe to stimulate or extend thinking

Example: Apples

The children have each brought an apple from home. They sit as a large group on the classroom carpet, being encouraged by the teacher to visually and tactilely explore their apples. The teacher has a pen and sits next to a chart like the one in Figure 3.1 (but without the vocabulary words printed beneath the category labels).

TEACHER: The apples we ate last week **[link]** provided us with food and a way to practice slicing with a knife and a way to share with a friend. Our apples gave us one other thing. They gave us information **[frame]** about what apples are like. We felt them, looked at them, and tasted them. The apple Maxie shared with me was crisp **[input]**. When I took a bite, there was a sound. Close your eyes and picture yourself biting into a big crunchy apple **[clarify]**. Listen for the sound. What sound do you hear?

CHILD: My apple crunched. My teeth crunched it.

TEACHER: Your apple made a crunching sound when you bit into it **[extend]**.

CHILD: Pop.

TEACHER: You heard a pop when you bit into your apple. Was it a loud pop or a quiet popping sound? **[question]**.

CHILD: A little one.

TEACHER: Make that sound for us. Let us hear what it sounded like.

CHILD: Pop *[barely audible]*

TEACHER: That was a quiet **[label]**, almost silent, pop **[connect]**. Is that a baby-bear pop **[relate]**?

The discussion continues with the teacher asking questions about other ways apples can sound. As the children respond, the teacher begins recording their responses on the senses chart (see Figure 3.1), one category at a time **[categorize]**.

The teacher uses the children's language to **extend** the language of their peers and to **categorize** the words they use. The children eat their apples and add other words to the chart **[connect]**. The chart words can then be retrieved for use in a poem written by the class **[extend]**:

My apple tastes juicy and sweet
It is really good to eat.
My apple looks green and red
I'm going to take it to bed.
My apple sounds. . . .

The words can also be selected and copied for a record of attributes of the apple the child has eaten.

My apple tasted _____ .
My apple felt _____ .

This experience can be **extended** by making another chart of either a similar or a very different type of food and then comparing the charts **[relate]**.

This type of critical analysis not only develops the concepts but also provides descriptive words for remembering the experience. Thus, the language aids in understanding the experience, and the experiential context aids in understanding the language. With reinforcement through repeated use, the new words become part of the child's *ownership vocabulary* (defined in Chapter 1).

Encouragement of Peer Dialogue

Language development is facilitated by modeling dialogue with children: Actively engaging in the reciprocal "I talk, you talk" process demonstrates how conversations work. Both listening and speaking are important to this modeling process. Listening is modeled by giving the child eye contact when he or she is speaking and by responding to statements with body language or gestures such as head nods or smiles. Appropriate verbal responses are modeled by (a) staying on the topic the child is discussing, (b) asking questions to clarify or generate information, and (c) sharing relevant information or making appropriate suggestions. To encourage children to initiate conversations, respond to their approaches with openness and attention and accept their topics as worthy. Valuable and enjoyable teacher–child dialogues lead to rewarding child–child dialogues.

To benefit fully from the teacher's modeling of dialogue, children must have many opportunities for peer dialogue. Peer dialogue supports the children's oral communication efforts by encouraging application of the teacher's modeled behaviors. Therefore, teachers must not only encourage spontaneous peer dialogue, but also establish and monitor specific planned opportunities for peer interaction. These opportunities occur in child-centered experiences, teacher-directed instruction, and daily living interactions.

Child-Centered Experiences

1. The teacher takes a role in the sociodramatic play, modeling dialogue through interaction with students.
2. New props that support play or exploration are periodically added to the center.
3. Children take part in dialogue through the use of puppets or toy characters.
4. Children dress up in hats or clothes representing selected characters in the sociodramatic play centers.
5. The teacher allows children to select a peer group and regularly provides time for them to work together.

Directed Instruction

1. The teacher models dialogue with students during all three phases of instruction (i.e., modeling, instructive teaching, and applying).
2. The teacher models dialogue through reading of stories, teaching of fingerplays, and developing dramatic plays.
3. The teacher instructs the children to discuss with each other responses to questions related to an activity.

Have students observe and record the behavior of listeners when paired with speakers. Ask students "How do the listeners move their bodies, heads, and eyes in response to the speakers? How do the speakers respond to the listeners' movements?"

The teacher also verbalizes to the children the desired behavior while modeling being a good listener and speaker. Such comments as, "I'm going to look right at Sunny's face when he's telling me this story so he know's I'm listening," give some children the added support they need in acquiring these skills.

4. The teacher encourages the children to work in pairs during the exploration or application part of a lesson.

Daily Living

1. The teacher encourages the children to ask each other for assistance.
2. The teacher allows the children to talk quietly with a friend while waiting for the bus.
3. The teacher encourages the children to work together when setting out supplies, preparing class materials, or cleaning up after an activity.
4. The teacher asks the children to explain routines and classroom information to visiting adults or students.

Reading Aloud to Children

In addition to all of the preceding language experiences and activities, one other educational experience uniquely fosters children's literacy: reading books aloud to children.

Why Read Stories?

Story reading offers children the opportunity to hear both how the language sounds and how it is used to share information and ideas. Stories also share the values of our culture and the elements of our humanness. From the foundation of pleasurable story reading, children become interested in learning to control print in order to create this pleasure for themselves. Do not overlook nonfiction work as well, e.g., biography, autobiography, and historical narrative.

Have the students review several children's stories, select one, and present the important learnings available through the reading of the text. Ask students, "Why read this book to a child?"

Reading stories is one of the most important experiences you can offer young learners. Hearing the language of books, observing how the pages are organized, and becoming familiar with the relationship between spoken language and print supports the children's effort to become literate. The enjoyment of reading is shared between the teacher and the children, creating a love for literature and for reading.

Selecting a Story

Children are interested in listening to a variety of printed materials. Content information from children's magazines about animals or events, newspaper articles about other children, or chapters from primary-grade history books are samples of the selections available for reading aloud. Perhaps the favorite read-alouds for both the reader and the listener are make-believe stories written for young children.

Apply the selection criteria to picture books intended for young children. Select a favorite book and give examples from the text showing how it is a good example of each criteria.

In choosing a selection, consider the interests, needs, and developmental levels of the listeners. After prereading the selection, consider the following questions:

1. Is this story interesting to the listener?
2. Will the listener understand the plot? the punch line?
3. Does the text read well out loud?
4. Is the language rich and diverse?
5. Are new vocabulary words too frequent or too difficult?
6. Is the reading time appropriate to the listener?
7. Does this story have value beyond one reading?
8. Will this story provide an enjoyable experience?

The quality of a storybook is also affected by the format of the text and the value of the illustrations. With this in mind, also assess the ability of the listener to visually separate the print from the illustration or to follow it from word to word. The illustrations have an *artistic value* (providing enjoyment and cultivating aesthetic sensibilities), as well as their value in assisting the listener's comprehension.

READ-ALOUDS FOR YOUNG READERS

The following books have offered countless children (and adult readers) immeasurable enjoyment.

Corduroy
by Don Freeman
    A stuffed bear is rescued from the department store shelf by a young girl who takes him home to be her friend.

Goodnight Moon
by Margaret Wise Brown
    Mother Rabbit settles her little one into bed through rhyme by saying goodnight to the things in the great green room.

Ira Sleeps Over
by Bernard Waber
    When he is asked to spend the night at his friend's house, a young boy must decide whether to take along his teddy bear.

Make Way for Ducklings
by Robert McCloskey
    This is a story of the city adventures of Mr. and Mrs. Mallard and their eight ducklings.

Sylvester and the Magic Pebble
by William Steig
    Sylvester makes a wish on a magic pebble and is unable to undo his wish and return home to his family. The story resolves when Sylvester is reunited with his mother and father.

The Very Hungry Caterpillar
by Eric Carle
    The egg hatches into a caterpillar that eats its way through several pages before turning into a beautiful butterfly.

Reading the Story

There are two aspects of story reading to control during story reading. The first focuses on the management of the physical setting, the materials, and the children. The second focuses on the language, the story, and the reading experience.

Before beginning the reading experience, the children should be seated so that they face a minimum of distractions from looking directly at the teacher and the book. For example, the students should not face a door that opens onto a busy hallway. Any story materials or props are within the teacher's reach, but any particularly attractive items should be out of the view of the children until needed.

To further set the stage for reading, the teacher clearly states the rules for the reading. Each story may demand its own set of rules. For some selections, the children might be encouraged to participate as the story is read. Usually, however, the children are to stay where they are seated and to refrain from making sounds or movements that will distract themselves or the other listeners.

Once the ground rules have been established, the story is introduced by creating a link between the children's experiences and the text. Specific vocabulary words may be introduced or defined and a purpose for listening created. During the story reading, the children may be directed to listen silently, listen and participate, or read with the teacher.

Reading Follow-Ups

To exploit the full potential of the reading experience, after reading the story, further develop the story in some of the same ways in which it was introduced. A few of the options for follow-up include reviewing the story, asking questions about the story elements or vocabulary, and engaging the children in a related discussion or activity that enhances comprehension. Another obvious follow-up to reading aloud to children is reading instruction.

Have the students work in partners and bring stories to read to each other. The reader introduces the story by preparing the listener with expectations for their behaviors as the story is being read.

STRATEGIES FOR DIRECT INSTRUCTION IN LEARNING TO READ

For young learners, reading instruction is a natural extension of the reading activity they have enjoyed since infancy—having stories read to them. Just as they have learned to walk, eat, and speak by involving themselves in the processes of imitating, adapting, and re-creating, so do they learn to read. They imitate reading to themselves the stories that have been read to them. Their imitations reveal how much they have learned about reading from these experiences: The book is held upright, pages are turned after the appropriate words have been spoken, and dialogue related to the text is repeated, often with tonal changes to indicate changes in character. The awareness of and interest in the printed symbols is secondary to the process of re-creating the story reading experience. Therefore, beginning reading instruction starts by involving the children in the imitating (i.e., re-creating) process. Many reading models are presented, and opportunities to imitate are encouraged through both teacher-directed and child-centered systems of instruction.

Large-Group Read-Aloud Experiences

Value of Big Books

Clearly, the read-aloud experience is different between parent and child than between teacher and class. The degree of intimacy and responsivity to individual needs must differ, which may affect the selection of stories and topics for stories. Another factor in choosing books for classroom reading is simply the size of the books, of the pictures, and of the print. Small books with small pictures and fine print do not work well in classroom read-aloud experiences. Large books with print easily visible to a child seated in the back of the group have been developed. Often, these class-sized books containing enlarged print are reprints of popular children's literature with original illustrations and text. Recently, as the usefulness of large text in modeling print concepts has been recognized, new titles have been created. Remember, however, that in one-on-one situations, children love tiny books!

Strategies for Using Big Books

The story and the story language presented by the enlarged print is used to teach elements of literature and the skills and concepts of oral and written language. The stages of instruction are organized so that children may move from their own experiences, to the experiences offered in the text, and on to a reconnection of their experience with a new breadth or depth of understanding.

To more clearly demonstrate the usefulness of enlarged or big books in promoting concepts, bring a few to class and use them to model the reading process. Show the students the different ways that they can be held and that their pages can be turned. Include information about the eye level of the students at the front and at the back of the group.

Stage I: The beginning stage puts more emphasis on developing the relationship between what the children know and what the language means.

Stage II: The middle stage emphasizes story comprehension, story grammar (defined in Chapter 2), the specific language of the story.

Stage III: The final stage focuses on how the story and its language can be used as a tool for learning independent reading skills.

Stage I

1. Introduce the story by linking it to some experience with which the children are familiar.
2. Introduce the character(s) and setting, and give an overview of the plot.
3. Read the story all the way through without interruption.
4. Make closing or summary statements that draw conclusions, summarize, or reconnect the story to the children's experiences.
5. Optional: Create an experience or activity for the children that extends their understanding of the events, situations, settings, or characters in the story.

Stage II

1. Reintroduce the story in the same way but more briefly and with a new connection.
2. Review the story's character(s), setting, and plot. Use a questioning technique to encourage participation by the students.
3. Reread the selection, this time pausing to invite recall, prediction, and participation when children can anticipate specific language phrasings or events.
4. Reread again, encouraging the children to read along.
5. After this rereading of the story, focus on comparing, analyzing, or evaluating the character, plot, setting, story sequence, and so on.
6. Optional: Move into a related activity, providing guided practice of a skill or concept or in developing meaning of the language.

Ask students to use these stages as a model for writing a plan for a story. The plans should include samples of their planned dialogue and related activities.

Stage III

1. Guided by teacher questioning, the students review the story and link it to their own experiences.
2. The children read the story to the teacher. The teacher facilitates this reading (a) by reading along with a softer voice in order to give clues when needed, and (b) by ceasing to read when the children can read (repeat the words) confidently. Repeat this step once more.
3. The teacher selects a sight word(s), concept, or skill as the focus of further instruction.
4. The teacher reconnects the content of the focus objective to the language of the story.
5. Optional: The teacher provides an activity related to the instruction.

SELECTING A BIG BOOK

The criteria for evaluating a big book are the same as the criteria used for any children's storybook, with the addition of the following qualities:

1. The book is not so large that it is difficult to hold on your lap with one hand and turn the pages with the other hand.
2. The print is clearly distinguishable from the illustrations. The child will not have to work to visually discriminate the units of print from the illustrations.
3. The story does not need to be long to be effective.
4. The print is placed on the page so that it is visible if the bottom of the book is in your lap or on an easel.
5. There is a strong relationship between the print and the illustrations. Ask, "Do the pictures help tell the story?"
6. The print is large enough to be seen from the back of the group.
7. The text of the book carries some instructional qualities, such as predictability (enhanced by repetitive elements).
8. The binding and paper quality is able to stand up to repeated readings.
9. The binding allows the book to remain open easily.

Because the concept of the big book has become valued by teachers of younger children, publishing companies have been eager to put their own versions on the market. Some examples have used unnatural or contrived text, unrelated illustrations, and poor-quality paper and bindings. Select carefully. Read the book out loud before you purchase it to see that it phrases well, has a rich vocabulary, and offers openings for instruction.

Making Books

Children also learn about books by re-creating the publication process. The bookmaking experience gives children opportunities to develop skills and concepts in all the language arts areas, and it offers them a meaningful product as well. The classroom environment should simultaneously offer opportunities for the children to receive instruction in the bookmaking process while participating in group bookmaking projects that serve as models for constructing books, and to practice bookmaking through the creation of their own books.

Modeling the Bookmaking Process: Models for the Beginning Bookmaker

Provide instruction and models for making books through bookmaking projects. Three general kinds of model bookmaking projects are class books, group big books, and individual small books. The amount of detail and guidance included in the development of the model depends on the level of ability and understanding the children have about the process.

Class Books The contents of these books are illustrated by the children in the class, and they may be written by the children, by the teacher, or by someone else entirely. Their topics are usually a response to questions posed by the teacher, a response to an activity or a common experience, or a response to a familiar poem or song.

Question-Response Books These books generally respond to an open-ended question posed by the teacher, such as,

What is your favorite activity on the playground?

What do you like to do on Saturday?

Where do you find spiders?

What did you see on this morning's walk?

The students respond to the question by recording their thoughts in picture form. Teachers may choose to take dictation from the children regarding the ideas and experiences their pictures represent. Sometimes the front cover of the book contains the beginning of a sentence that forms an answer to the posed question, and either one word or a phrase supplied by the children finishes the sentence.

> *Example:* A teacher demonstrates how a class book, made by assembling student's drawings, could be a way for the children to share information with their parents on visitation night. After exploring the classroom as a group and participating in a related discussion, the students are asked to respond with a picture to the question, "What is your favorite activity in the classroom?" The book title on the cover is *At School, I Like To. . . .*
>
> As each child completes her or his picture, the teacher moves around the room printing the child's response on the picture. Some children give one-word responses, and others give several sentences. When the children meet again as a group, the teacher reviews the topic of the pictures, the title of the cover, and the purpose of the pages. With the children watching, the teacher staples the pages inside the cover and then reads the children the book that they have produced.

Experience Books These are produced in response to an experience in which the class members have participated. Its purpose is to relate the event through the language of the children.

> *Example:* After a trip to the fire station, the teacher engages the children in a discussion, first reviewing the sequence and then filling in the details of the experience. As the children respond, the teacher records their responses on a chalkboard or a large chart. When the discussion ends, the teacher tells the children that they can make a book about their trip by drawing pictures of the things they remember. By referring to the children's recorded responses, the teacher can help the children select topics for their drawings and later organize them in sequence in relation to when they occurred, from first to last.

Ask the students to participate in making a class book by completing the topic frame, "On Saturday, I like to _____ ," and illustrating it on a pieces of photocopy paper. Staple these sheets together with a cover and read them to the class.

When the pictures and dictation have been completed, the teacher gathers the children together to organize the pages for inclusion in the book. Children who have drawings about events or observations during the first part of the trip give their pictures to the teacher, then the teacher refers to the chart to recall the next section of pictures to include in the book. This process continues until all the pictures are collected and the pages can be stapled into the cover. The book is then read to the children.

Literature-Response Books Books, poems, or songs may provide familiar language units that the children enjoy repeating. Select a poem or book, or even a section of a story for the children to respond to, or have the children provide the illustrations for the already created text.

Example: *A Little Mouse*
A little mouse,
A bigger mouse,
A great big mouse
I see.
Now, count the mousies
1 2 3.

Author Unknown

Have the class create several experience books by working in teams of six. Each team defines a common experience and creates a frame to be filled in by each team member. These pages can then be stapled together, with a cover, and read to the other teams.

The children had heard this poem many times and had used their fingers to represent the differently sized mice as they said the words. The teacher had drawn pictures of each mouse on a separate card, as well as preparing a card for the words "I see" and the numerals "1, 2, 3." These cards are held up as the children say the corresponding words. The teacher demonstrates how the cards can be put together to make a book and how the children can make books for the classroom by coloring pictures to go along with the words of different parts of the poem.

As the teacher reads a line of the poem, the teacher helps the children choose which of the lines they want to illustrate. The children who asked to draw an illustration to go with those words are given pieces of drawing paper. As the children complete their drawings, the teacher prints the appropriate words at the bottom and then sorts the pictures so that each book has the pages it needs to make a complete poem. The pages are covered with pieces of construction paper and stapled together down the left side. The title of the book is printed on the cover, and the children whose drawings are inside sign the book.

Have the students share books, poems, or songs that could be used to make big books. Compile a list from their selections, and make copies for each of the students. Note on the list whether the resources are also suitable for copy changes.

Group Big Books These are very similar to class books except that they are intentionally developed with large print and sturdier binding so that they can be used for whole-class or small-group instruction.

Identical Replica Books These are large copies of favorite children's books found in the classroom library. These books usually have brief text

Figure 3.2   Sample class book, based on a mouse poem.

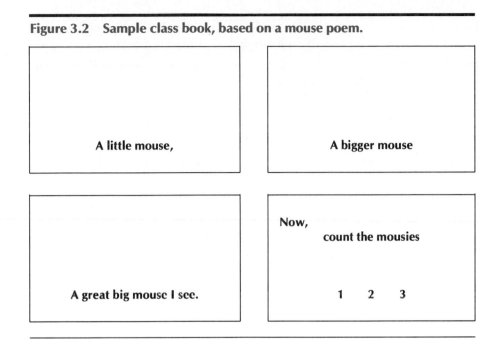

and high predictability. The teacher makes a large replica of the book, copying the text in the same format as in the original. The children are invited to add the illustrations for the text. These illustrations do not have to replicate those from the book; instead, they give the children's interpretation of the text.

Literature-Response Books These story, song, and poem response books are very similar to those described previously except that the print size is larger, and the format is sturdier. Glue the children's illustrations on a larger sheet of paper, with the words of the poem or song written on a separate sheet and glued either above or below the picture. The binding for these pages is still a series of staples down the left side of the book, but a strip of tape is folded over the staples on the left edge, to protect fingers and reinforce the staples. (Figure 3.3 illustrates how this might be done.)

Copy-Change Books These books are developed from familiar poems, stories, or songs. The language in the book follows the original pattern, but the children change the words to adapt it to a new situation. The adaptation is recorded in the big book format.

      Example: What's For Lunch?
               What's for lunch?
               A COCONUT?

Figure 3.3   Sample of a class literature-response book, illustrating large format and reinforced binding of group big books.

Individual replica books can be books the teacher makes for the children by photocopying pages. The children then can move to stapling a few pages together or to adding their own work to already assembled books. The important issues are that the children see the connection between their book and the big book and that they feel some ownership of it. When children can practice reading these books along with the teacher, both goals are facilitated.

No, thank you.
Apples?
No, thank you. . . .
. . . .BANANAS?
Yes, please!
They are my favorites.
Thank you very much.

Eric Carle, 1982, Putnam

The children are assumed to be already very familiar with this predictable text. The teacher discusses what the children like to eat for lunch and then asks what the children often eat for dinner. Using magazines as a source for pictures, the children hunt for representations of the food they eat for dinner. Each child glues a picture on a page of a premade book and gives dictation, as in Figure 3.4. The book is then read and reread to the children.

Individual Small Books These are the children's personal replicas of class-made books or adaptations of classroom big books from which they have been reading in class. Making the big book as a class project can serve as a model for producing their own books, and the familiarity with the language can act as a motivation to make a book that can be read and reread at home. Children may be involved in this process to varying degrees. For less-sophisticated learners, teachers may prepare the books and have the children add the text and/or illustrations, as needed. Stu-

Figure 3.4   Sample of a copy-change kind of group book.

Beans?
Yes, please!

Milk?
Yes, please!

Potatoes?
Yes, please!

dents with more experience are able to become involved in the writing, the illustrating, and the bookmaking process.

Premade Books   These are books assembled before they are given to the children. The pages may also contain the text or parts of the text (see Figure 3.5) of the book. The children are to add the appropriate illustrations and/or a selected word.

Format Books   These books are printed in a particular way on a piece of paper so that the children learn to see the pattern of the story. That is, the story is written on the paper from left to right and from top to bottom, and the children are then taught to cut apart the paper and to reconstruct the sections into a book.

Example: Figure 3.6 represents a printed sheet that is either 8.5 x 11 or 11 x 14 inches.

Directions: Color the pictures that go with the words.
Cut apart the pages of the book.
Say the poem as you put the pages in order.
Staple the pages together.

Creating Books on Their Own: Constructing Self-made Books
Once children discover that making books is within their control, they begin to experiment with the process and with possible materials. Children's first attempts at bookmaking are rough approximations, sometimes motivated by a desire to operate the stapler or to own the paper. It is important to understand that the construction of a book is itself a

There is clearly potential for a lot of wasted paper, tape, staples, and so forth, in this bookmaking process. The use of paper can be minimized by providing the children with smaller pieces of paper for their pages. These will also be easier for their shorter arms to control.

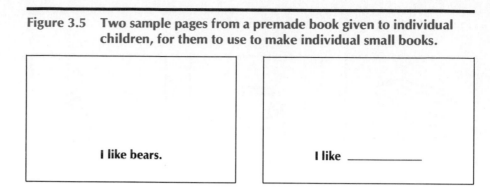

Figure 3.5   Two sample pages from a premade book given to individual children, for them to use to make individual small books.

significant learning and is separate from the knowledge of how information is selected and organized within a book.

Teachers should encourage children to play with the different ways of constructing books by providing (a) a diversity of bookmaking materials that are readily available, (b) many model books to examine, and (c) time to experiment with the process. Books can be constructed at the cut-and-paste table, a writing center, a bookmaking center, or the drawing table. Each of these areas may offer generic bookmaking materials, paper, and writing tools. Working with these materials children develop the following concepts:

> What I think, I can draw.
> What I draw, I can talk about.
> What I talk about, I can write about.
> What I write about, I can put in a book.

Teachers should not expect the children to write in the books they are making: Their goal is to construct not to compose.

Often the children's first books are experiments with ways to make the pages stay together. Staplers, tape, and punched holes with yarn may be made available for the students to manipulate. The teacher's role is to recognize the efforts at attempting to assemble several sheets of paper. The recognition of these approximations will give the students the courage to risk still further bookmaking quests. The contents of the book is the least of the teacher's focus at this initial stage, especially because these books are often made with blank pages!

Using Charts

Charts are large sheets of heavy paper (24- x 36-inch tag or railroad board), on which are printed

Figure 3.6   Sample of a format book, used by individual children, to reinforce left-to-right, top-to-bottom sequencing while making individual small books.

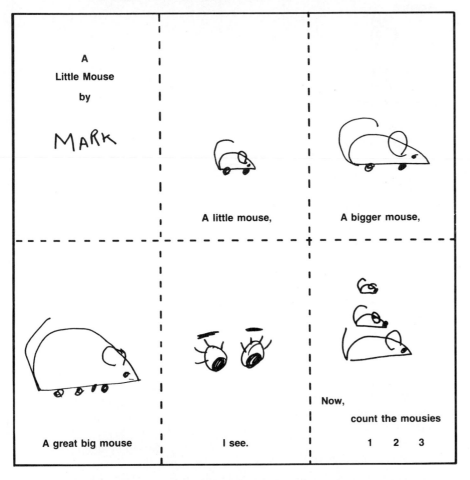

A
Little Mouse
by

MARK

A little mouse,

A bigger mouse,

A great big mouse

I see.

Now,
count the mousies
1   2   3

1. The entire text of poems, songs, fingerplays, stories, or other narratives, or
2. Partial texts of songs or stories, such as the refrain or a repeated pattern component.

This text is printed in large enough letters for the class members to see as they sit within the group. The chart is usually hung from a chart rack or from hooks above the chalkboard. Because the paper tops of these charts wear easily with repeated use, tape the tops of these charts to coat hangers so that they can be hung from hooks quickly and easily.

Ask students, "What are the elements a teacher considers in selecting a text for chart work?"

Figure 3.7   Chart illustrating pictorial cues to words in a poem about apples.

Apples

Apples   *are green.*

Apples   *are red.*
I like to eat them

  under my bed

Cues

To support the children's effort to make meaning from the text, the chart is prepared by arranging and coding the words to provide cues. These cues encourage the children to develop or recognize relationships between what they already know and what is new to them.

Color   Color cues are used to highlight a color word, focus on a word without adding other clues, or to delineate supportive language such as dialogue or text that answers a question.

> **Apples**
> *Apples are green.*
> *Apples are red.*
> *I like to eat them*
> *under my bed.*

Susan Peterson, 1976

The print in books is almost exclusively done in black ink, so a touch of color can be exciting. In this case it could be used to identify the word *green* by printing it in green ink or by underlining the word printed in black with a green line. The same can be done for the word *red*, using red ink. Instead of focusing on the color words, the teacher may select the word *apples* and highlight it with a blue underline whenever it appears. Another option for highlighting with a color are the rhyming words, *red* and *bed*.

Picture   Pictures can be used to identify selected key words in the text, to provide guideposts for following the story sequence, or to emphasize selected sight words. Figure 3.7 shows how the pictures cue the key words and give a visually cued, sequential trip through the language. If students

Figure 3.8 A variation of the apples poem. Children can see the familiar words in a new position on the paper and within new text.

are familiar with the language, the children can just look at the pictures in a top-to-bottom order, say the picture words, and build the rest of the language around them. Sometimes, words that are not nouns can be also symbolized by pictures. For example, a picture of a mouth could represent the word *eat* or *taste*, eyes could represent *see*, and an ear could represent *hear*, such as was done in the apples chart in Figure 3.1. Sometimes, the pictures could be used instead of the words, as shown in Figure 3.8.

Format Format cues are developed by organizing the words on the page in a particular way in relation to each other. Two elements can be manipulated: the placement of a word on a line, and the placement of a line of print on the page (or chart).

The first two sentences of the poem are purposely placed one above the other so that the pattern of the printed language obviously displays its relationship to the pattern of oral language. It is easier for the children to compare the sequence of the letters when they are closely aligned. The last line is indented to signify that the phrase belongs with the part of the sentence preceding it. This also makes this phrase stand out so that it can be a focus for discussion in response to the question, "Where else could you eat apples?"

Combining Cues Combinations of cues can create a set of systems for the children to use as aids in identifying or remembering words in the text. It is important to keep the text clearly visible for the children. Selecting the objectives of the instruction is the first step in deciding what kind of and how many cues to use. It is also possible to laminate the charts with a clear plastic coating. This permits the teacher to add appropriate cues with erasable or wipe-off markers, modifying them for different groups of children, as needed.

Using the Charts with Children

The charts can be used as a way to share printed language with large groups, small groups, or individuals. Build on the strengths of group members by introducing and using the text with oral language support. Recall the three phases of directed instruction: (1) involvement, (2) actual guided instruction in the primary objective(s), and (3) expansion.

Step I: Involvement in the Process As with any language to which they are exposed, the children begin the comprehension process by linking the new language to a part of their past experience or knowledge. By asking, "What do I know that is related to this language?" children become involved with it. Involve children by helping them to develop these links to the language. For example, an activity may precede the introduction of the chart's language, which would provide background information, or previous shared experience might be used as a link to understanding the text.

Sometimes, the text on the chart can be introduced orally without reference to the print, as a way to have the children experience the auditory components of the language. This listening experience could lead to an activity that involves children in linking the language to personal meanings.

Step II: Providing Instruction Once the children have activated their minds to link their experiences to the content of the language, the chart may be used to model the processes of reading. This modeling may take the form of strategies for deriving meaning from the text or making sense from the print.

Ask students, "How will the steps to using charts with children contrast with those of reading a story to them? Why are these different?"

A typical modeling procedure is for the teacher to run a hand in a left-to-right motion under the words as they are read by the teacher. Although the children know the words by heart and are not yet truly reading the words, the use of appropriate actions shows them what reading looks like. The teacher's eyes should be focused on the print, moving left to right in line with the moving hand, so the words being said match the words being looked at. You may additionally engage in self-talk, such as: "I'm getting ready to read. My body is comfortable and my eyes are right up here on the first word of the poem."

In order to demonstrate one way to bring meaning to print, model a read-and-think strategy. While moving the hand from left to right under the print, stop after a segment and become involved in a self-dialogue paraphrasing or interpreting the words. (For example, "When Humpty Dumpty fell, he really hurt himself. It was a great fall. Falling down did a lot of damage.")

Another instructional sequence might focus on the concept that a printed word has a constant letter pattern, which moves the children from linking meaning with the word and observing how the teacher manipulates the print, to a demonstration of how that word is defined in print. Applying the rules of constancy, the teacher demonstrates the matching of one word or letter pattern to another identical printed word.

Instruction of the concept implies that students are taught both that the matching exists and the way in which they can do it for themselves. Break this ability down into smaller tasks (e.g., begin at one end of the group of letters in the word, and match the letters one at a time to see if the patterns are the same; then check to see whether the word makes sense in the language context). For each small subtask, work back and forth demonstrating and watching the students; demonstrate the task again, adjusting, rephrasing, and reinforcing the students' attempts or approximations.

Application of the instruction is the opportunity for the children to use their learned abilities in a situation similar to the one in which instruction was given. Word constancy could be applied in a "Word Concentration" game or a "Word Lotto" game where the children are encouraged to match identical words. A more complex application encourages the children to identify identical words in a context such as cloze reading. In *cloze reading*, children and teacher read a passage together, then the teacher stops reading at the matching word and asks the children to orally fill in the word. Cloze reading could also be used when introducing a new story containing a previously used word; this would give children an opportunity to apply the cloze strategy in figuring out what the word was.

Step III: Expanding the Learning Once the children have become familiar with the oral and written forms of the language, they have a body of background information to further support their efforts at skill and

Ask students to do the following: "Select a text for a chart, state your objectives for using this chart, and outline the instructional steps you'd take."

concept development. It is a natural process for them to find ways to broaden their sense of this learning. Expanding their learning might take the form of seeing relationships between number patterns and the patterns found in words or groups of words. Expanding their learning might mean testing their knowledge of story sequence by dictating the sequence of events from a recent activity. Finding ways to play with the learning in creating variations, drawing analogies, or sharing it with a new person expands learner opportunities further.

Developing Reading Comprehension: Comprehending the Written Language

In addition to read-aloud experiences and bookmaking experiences, children need instruction in comprehending printed language. Children must learn to make meaning via two major interrelated fields of understanding: (1) understanding what the language means, and (2) understanding the individual printed words. For children to develop an understanding of or to create meaning from printed language, they must also understand the individual words. They derive their understanding of new words from the context and from their understanding of *syntax* (how words are structured in sentences to relate meaning). These internalized means for understanding are the basis for making sense of words that are read to them.

Children also develop comprehension of printed language by having experiences that interpret the print, just as oral experiences help children to interpret spoken language. As the children begin to read the print themselves, they use additional systems to assist their efforts in knowing which letter patterns or relationships represent which spoken words. This system for relating sounds to printed symbols to make units of meaning is called "decoding."

Although there are some differences between spoken and written language, many of the same strategies that children use to make sense of spoken language can be adapted to the comprehension of written language. This is especially true of the pre- or emergent readers because they do not depend on themselves for decoding the print but on someone who decodes for them. When children are learning to comprehend printed language, they are frequently involved in using comprehension strategies to develop meaning from the print. It is also important for children to learn why and how to use comprehension strategies independently.

Three main comprehension strategies are discussed in this section: (1) questioning, (2) retelling, and (3) adapting language models. They are not organized in a hierarchy but are interrelated in the sense that skills in one strategy can support or facilitate the development of understanding, which can help to develop skills in using another strategy (Figure 3.9).

Ask students, "How might the children demonstrate the use of these strategies in their play? How do adults use them to facilitate their comprehension?"

Figure 3.9   The interrelated strategies that facilitate reading comprehension.

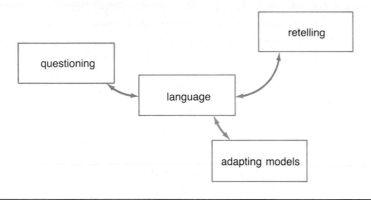

Questioning

This comprehension strategy teaches children to ask themselves questions about the text. Questioning occurs before, during, and after the reading, in order to help stimulate students to

Predict

Determine cause and effect relationships

Infer

Draw conclusions

Distinguish between fantasy and reality.

The most significant process for teaching this behavior is teacher modeling. As parts of the story are read, engage in overt self-questioning, such as, "I wonder what this story is about? Is the elephant going to feel better? Where is the baby's mother? I wonder how I would feel if that happened to me."

Though the teacher does not label these sentences as questions during the dialogue, other contexts offer ways to label them. For example, language games are very useful in drawing the children's attention to the questioning process.

> *Example:* Teacher-made riddles for finding objects around the room
>
> The teacher says, "I am small, red, and live in the blue bucket. What am I? Who can answer that question? Marika, can you answer that question? Juan, do you agree with Marika's answer to the question, 'Who am I?' Once familiar with the game, the teacher encourages the children to play it in small groups or with partners. This strategy can then be adapted to the characters or characteristics of a story, poem, or song.

It is important to note that this questioning of the text does not mean the teacher asks the children questions; instead, the teacher says out loud the kinds of questions and statements that arise while he or she is reading. Answers to these questions are not always necessary.

The questioning strategy is also promoted through the use of songs, poems, or stories that have questions embedded in them. *Whose Mouse Are You?* (Kraus, 1970) uses questions and answers as the text format: Whose mouse are you? Nobody's mouse. Where is your mother? and so on.

Example: Participation poem, *Who Stole the Cookies?*

Here the children actively participate with their peers in asking questions and giving answers. The teacher later transfers the questioning experiences to story comprehension by asking and encouraging the children to ask questions beginning with the key question words: who, what, where, when, why, how.

Who Stole The Cookies from the Cookie Jar

TEACHER TO CLASS: Who stole the cookies from the cookie jar?

CLASS MEMBERS: You stole the cookies from the cookie jar.

TEACHER: Who me?

CLASS MEMBERS: Yes, you.

TEACHER: Not me!

CLASS MEMBERS: Then, who?

TEACHER: Mary stole the cookies from the cookie jar.

MARY: Who, me?

CLASS MEMBERS: Yes, you.

MARY: Not me!

CLASS MEMBERS: Then, who?

MARY: (selects another student and the game continues)

This questioning game can be adapted to stories such as "The Little Red Hen" or "The Three Bears." Have students write an adaptation for one of these or another story.

This game is easily adapted to other situations, such as "Who took the crayons from the crayon box?" or "Who drew the monkey on the coconut tree?" The children naturally respond to the rhythm of this game and begin to fill in their own versions during work time or playground play. It can easily be incorporated into science or social studies units by adapting the word to fit the concepts such as:

CLASS MEMBERS: Who took the garbage to the garbage truck?

CHILD WITH HARD HAT: I took the garbage to the garbage truck.

CLASS MEMBERS: Who, you?

CHILD: Yes, me!

CLASS MEMBERS: Who took the mail to the mailbox?

CHILD WITH MAIL BAG: I took the mail to the mailbox.

CLASS MEMBERS: Who, you?

CHILD: Yes, me!

Retelling

Retelling stories and events encourages the children to establish the main idea with supporting details and to sequence the events. Model this for children when establishing the work routines at the beginning of the school year, by summarizing the children's behavior as they are working:

- Listen to the children describe their play
- Paraphrase the children's comments
- State the main idea, and add relevant supporting details and sequences of events

> *Example:* House Corner Play
>
> CHILD: She's the dog. I'm the daddy. She barked and did this and this. (The child pretends to grab at her arm with her mouth and then at a bowl.)
>
> TEACHER: The dog showed you she was hungry.

When this listening and paraphrasing routine is used after a child has described an event, the teacher reflects the child's talk, repeating back the event in discussion style and using sequence words such as *first, then, next,* and *last.*

Model the retelling of stories when reviewing a favorite story before rereading to the class, when preparing for instruction that follows a story, or when discussing the differences and similarities among books.

Sometimes, picture books may be used to recall story elements and sequence. Children also may participate by using picture sequence cards representing main parts of the story. They tell about the individual pictures, or the pictures are used to develop the story sequence. Children also practice retelling stories to each other during reading time by taking turns telling a favorite tale.

Opportunities for story retelling may be effectively provided in group or individual settings through the use of storyboxes (Peterson, 1982). Using small representational objects that correlate with the key characters and story setting elements, the children are able to play out the story events. Storybox materials encourage the children to use their own language in expressing how the characters take their roles, and they provide visual and tactile reminders of the story sequence. Peterson, in her book, *Storybox: Hands-on Reading–Writing for Young Children,* anecdotally describes three different retelling models children use: approximation, accurate practice, and adaptation.

> **Approximation** *Dylan flips open the storybox of "Ride a Cockhorse to Banbury Cross" and turns the box upside down, emptying it of its contents. Reaching first for the horse, he snatches it up and begins giving it a bucking ride while making appropriate horse noises. Once the horse has settled, Dylan, without moving the objects, begins to chant, "Ride a cockhorse to the cross to see a lady on the horse. She likes music!"*

Ask students, "How is the retelling strategy used in storybook and chart reading with young children? How would you use retelling at each step of retelling chart stories versus retelling stories from books."

Accurate Practice *Dana is now organizing for practice of the rhyme, "The Five Little Pigs." After picking up a pig and placing it on the left side of the mat next to a basket, she proceeds silently through the rhyme, lining up the other pigs and objects in order from left to right. Very methodically, she begins to repeat the rhyme, pointing to the proper pig as she goes along. Dana has had practice and shows confidence in her control of the materials.*

Adaptation *Kate removes the storybox "Baa, Baa, Black Sheep" from the shelf and sits on the davenport, making herself a little work area by arranging the pillows around her. She quietly begins make-believe play with the objects. Inside her work space of pillows she has used the piece of felt from the storybox as a bed and the Master and the Dame have become Mother and Father for the little boy who is sleeping. The sheep sleeping next to the bed is the boy's pet. After a silent work time, Kate begins speaking in conversation form, moving from one character to another.*
Kate (holding the Dame in one hand and the Master in the other):
DAME: Is there enough firewood, Honey?
MASTER: I'll get some in a little while. I don't think it will be too cold tonight.
DAME: Oh, our little boy needs to stay warm. He is so delicate!
MASTER: Oh, my, let's see what the sheep is doing. . . .
Kate reaches for the black sheep and begins baa, baa, sounds.

Children use these same categories of story retelling when using books, pictures, and learning center props. The types of retelling are not hierarchical, but they tend to show differences in the quality of the retelling.

Adapting Models

Through this process, children use language models in new or different ways. The adapting process provides opportunities for the students to create or infer relationships from the information in the text and/or information previously known, to see the information in a new way and to examine the language at a different level of understanding. Three types of adaptations mentioned here are (1) adapting the content, (2) adapting the form, and (3) adapting both the content and the form.

Have students select a story, poem, song, or chant and use it as a foundation for developing their own storyboxes.

Adapting the Content of a Language Unit To adapt the content of a story or poem, simply replace the character, plot, or setting with a new one. The story of "The Three Billy Goats Gruff" can be adapted by substituting the goats with elephants and the troll with an alligator. The children work with the story pattern, adapting and creating language as is appropriate.

The adapting process relates to the specific language in the text. Adapting can initially take place in the play areas of the room, where the children enact the language in a personal adaptation.

Adapting the Form of a Language Unit This provides children with new ways to use the words with which they are working. From the following nursery rhyme,

Rain
Rain on the green grass,
Rain on the tree,
Rain on the housetop,
But not on me!

the children are encouraged to develop sentences about what the rain can be on. These sentences may take the form of filling in sentence frames: "The rain is on the _____ ." It may take the form of dialogue, such as, "I saw the rain on the _____ ." The teacher may also encourage the children to write stories about a day that it rained. The topic of the adaptation is the same, but the form in which the information is given has changed.

Adapting both the Content and the Form Combining the previous two adaptations is the result of using one language unit to promote change in another. Using the story of "The Three Billy Goats Gruff," the teacher applies it to the poem about rain, encouraging the children to use information from the story to make this poem,

Goats
Goats on the green grass,
Goats on the bridge,
Goats on the mountain top,
But not in the frig!

Again, enactment of the adaptation would facilitate the understanding of the adapting process, as well as of the newly created text.

The reverse process would involve substituting the story characters with characters from a poem with which the children are very familiar. The poem could be used to develop characters for the story "The Three Bears."

A Little Mouse (Bear)
A little mouse (bear)
A bigger mouse (bear)
A great big mouse (bear) I see.
Now, count the mousies (bearsies)
  1 2 3.

Most children do not need to be taught to adapt models. Often, teachers need only to take the opportunity to recognize what the children are already doing. They naturally go through this process, and they need only have permission to do it at school, by receiving the time and the materials for exploration. This process can also be fostered by recognizing the children's approximations in creating adaptations and by encouraging them to continue to do so.

Using Predictable Language for Instruction

Benefits of Predictability and Predictable Elements in Literature

Thus far, the reading strategies in this chapter have included experiences with read-aloud stories, bookmaking, and comprehension activities. These experiences show children to appreciate reading, to understand story grammar, and to derive meaning from printed language. Another key to learning to read is the ability to recognize patterns and to use those patterns to anticipate what might come next to fit into the pattern. These language units are currently referred to as "predictable materials or predictable stories." Some songs, stories, and poems are created around a pattern or set of patterns, and they can be used to prompt children to

1. Learn the language through frequent repetition of the pattern
2. Recognize a relationship between sounds and printed symbols
3. Actively interact with the language by being able to confidently predict it
4. Develop a repertoire of patterns available for easy reference
5. Internalize the concept that reading is an ongoing "guessing game" in which the reader is always making predictions or guesses about what will occur next.

Have students work with partners to practice reading pages of text, stopping intermittently to allow the other partner to predict the word that will come next. Ask students to note that the more experience they have with a text, the more accurate their predictions become. Ask students to suggest reasons for this phenomenon.

Stories, poems, and songs foster prediction in children in several ways. The use of rhythm, rhyme, repetition of vocabulary, repetition of story structure, or story patterns (Lynch, 1986) can give a selection increased predictability. Sometimes more than one attribute is used. For example, the folk tale "The Gingerbread Man" uses a repetitive story line and incorporates a refrain that uses rhythm, rhyme, and repetition of vocabulary: "Run, run, as fast as you can! You can't catch me. I'm the Gingerbread Man."

Supporting Predictability Using Sensory Modalities

Each child has a strength or set of strengths he or she uses for acquiring and remembering information orally or in print. Some children are strongly oriented toward learning through the *auditory* sensory modality, which means that they understand and remember information that they hear, such as information given to them orally by someone. Other children learn better from visual presentations of information, and yet others depend primarily on gaining information through their tactile–kinesthetic sense (*tactile:* touch; *kinesthetic:* sensation of the movement of muscles).

Although many children have a preferred modality, most learners use a combination of sensory abilities when they are learning. It is not uncommon for teachers to use a variety of learning modes to present information, with the intent of instructing to each child's strength or set of strengths. An additional benefit of multimodal instruction is to provide opportunities for children to develop learning modes that they

Table 3.1 Three Modes of Instruction

Sensory modality	Auditory	Auditory/visual	Auditory/visual tactile–kinesthetic
Child's involvement	Child listens	Child listens and sees	Child listens, sees, and moves

Instrumental activities	Songs
	Rhymes
	Chants
	Storytelling
		Charts of
		    Poems
		    Songs
		    Rhymes
		    Chants
		Big books
		Story books
		Choral reading
			Fingerplays
			Drama
			Rhythm instrument
			Snap and clap to a
			    beat or a rhyme
			Pocket chart/card
			Puppets
			Action songs

have not yet developed well. Predictable language can be presented in a variety of forms that will meet a range of learner needs. Table 3.1 illustrates some of the possibilities for instruction, and the remainder of this section shows several possible strategies and techniques for each sensory modality. In each of these modalities, children are responding verbally, joining in with the teacher.

> Teaching is not doing something *to* a child but doing something *with* a child.

Strategy I: Sample—Auditory Interaction

Rain
Rain on the green grass.
Rain on the tree.
Rain on the housetop,
But not on me!

                                                          Mother Goose

Technique: linking The teacher builds a readiness in the children to hear the rhyme by relating to a current common experience, such as walking in the rain on the way to school or while coming in from recess. The introduction to the rhyme is prefaced with comments and questions such as, "The rain was getting everything wet. What do you see that is getting wet? Anything else? Would you get wet if you went outside? You wouldn't? Why not? I know a rhyme about rain."

Technique: repeated exposure

TEACHER: (Chants rhyme to children. Repeats the rhyme. Asks children to join in. Repeats this several times over a few days time, with children joining in with the parts they know.)

Technique: completion (cloze)

TEACHER: Rain on the (Teacher pauses expectantly)
CHILDREN: green grass
TEACHER: Rain on the
CHILDREN: tree
TEACHER: Rain on the housetop,
CHILDREN: But not on me!

Technique: verbal cuing

TEACHER: Rain . . .
CHILDREN: (Begin saying as much of the rhyme as they are able to with the teacher providing clue words if there are pauses or the words become confused.)

Technique: connecting

TEACHER: That reminds me of the rhyme we know about rain.

The teacher then waits to see if that stimulates the children to begin repeating the rhyme. This strategy not only prompts repetition but also encourages the development of comprehension because the teacher is relating a new experience to known words.

Strategy II: Sample—Auditory/Visual Interaction The nursery rhyme shown in Figure 3.10 is printed on a large chart so that the words are visible to all the children. It is printed in the format shown in Figure 3.10 so that the children can easily see the similarity between the instances of *Humpty Dumpty* on each of the first two lines, and so that the sequence of events is clearly visible. The key words of the rhyme, *Humpty Dumpty*, *wall*, horses, men, are labeled with picture symbols above them, to act as visual clues for working through the word puzzle.

Some children sit with a group involved in a choral response and do not respond verbally. Ask students, "Why might this occur? When should the teacher intervene? What are some possible interventions?"

Figure 3.10   Illustrated chart of "Humpty Dumpty."

Humpty Dumpty

Humpty Dumpty *sat on a wall.*
Humpty Dumpty had a great fall.

All the king's horses *and*

All the king's men

Couldn't put Humpty Dumpty together again.

Mother Goose

Technique: linking Drawing on the children's past knowledge prepares them to think about the meaning of the language that is being introduced. Linking the meaning of words such as *dropped* to the word *fall* can provide an avenue for entry to the meaning of language in print.

TEACHER: I *dropped* the pencil. It had a *fall* from my hand, but it didn't break. Have you ever seen something have a great fall? Have you ever seen an egg have a great fall? What happened? I know a story about an egg that had a great fall. What do you think will happen? Listen to find out.

Technique: demonstration reading The teacher reads the picture-cued chart to the children, moving a hand from left to right along the words as they are spoken.

TEACHER: (Second and subsequent reading:) My hand moves along the printed words as we say them. Where will I begin reading? Did someone watch my hand last time? Show me where to begin reading. Yes, we begin reading at the top of the page and watch my hand move back and forth like this across the page as we read the words.

Technique: picture cuing—skill focus, sequencing Using the picture-word relationship, the teacher can demonstrate the written sequence of the rhyme. In print, what is said first comes first in a top-to-bottom order. The teacher can walk the beginning reader through the language in this order be referring to the pictures on the chart. Pointing to the top picture on the chart, the first Humpty Dumpty, the teacher says the first line of the rhyme.

TEACHER: What comes next in the rhyme?

CHILDREN: Humpty Dumpty had a great fall.

The children are given the visual cue when the teacher points to the second Humpty Dumpty picture. The teacher's hand moves along the line focusing on the picture as a hint to the correct language.

TEACHER: How did you know what to say?

CHILDREN: Because I remembered it. (or) That's how it goes.

TEACHER: What on the chart shows you what comes next?

CHILDREN: Because of that, (pointing to the picture).

TEACHER: What is that?

CHILDREN: It's Humpty Dumpty. (or) It's a picture of Humpty.

TEACHER: So, this picture can give you a clue to what comes next in the writing. Let's see if that will work for the next part of the rhyme. What is the picture that comes next? Does it match what your ear tells you should come next? How can we check?

The children begin repeating the language out loud, matching the picture symbols with the verbal symbols as they go along. The teacher's hand guides the children's eyes along the print, pausing at the pictures for emphasis.

Technique: independent review The children are given cards that match the pictures on the chart. With these picture cards, many children can individually sequence the rhyme by saying it and laying the cards down in a left-to-right or top-to-bottom order in accord with the lines being spoken. Some children, operating with less sophisticated knowledge of printed language, relate the picture to the spoken word while laying down the correct cards in any spatial order as they repeat the rhyme.

Strategy III: Sample—Auditory/Visual/Tactile–Kinesthetic Interaction Figure 3.11 shows the chart used with this strategy.

Technique: linking The teacher distributes several plastic spiders to the children. The children, handling the spiders as they pass them along, are asked to look at the long, thin legs and the round bodies. Through this guided observation, the children are encouraged to share spider stories with the children sitting near them.

Figure 3.11   Illustrated chart of "Itsy Bitsy Spider."

Itsy Bitsy Spider

Itsy Bitsy Spider

    crawled up the water spout.

Down came the rain

    and washed the spider out.

Out came the sun

    and dried up all the rain.

And Itsy Bitsy Spider

    crawled up the spout again.

Technique: previewing

TEACHER: (Addressing the children) I have a story to share about a very small spider. This spider lived on a house and was very curious. He wanted to see the other side of the house. So one day, he made a plan to crawl up the water spout on the side of the house to the roof. Once he was on the roof, he was going to look over and see the other side of the house. But something happened on his way up the water spout. It began to rain and all the rain that came down on the roof ran into the water spout and washed the spider right out of the spout.

Technique: say and do Once the story has been previewed, the teacher tells the children the poem, using the finger motions as the words are spoken. The teacher repeats the poem several times, using the finger motions and encouraging the children to participate with the motions as well as the words.

Technique: read and do The teacher continues to repeat the poem with the addition of the picture coded chart. The teacher reads the chart, moving a hand across the lines of print, as the children continue saying the words and making the corresponding finger motions.

Technique: drama The teacher encourages a few children to demonstrate how a spider might climb up the water spout and how they would use their bodies to show how the spider was washed from the spout. The teacher reads the poem, and the children act out the words, using their whole bodies.

Assign partners to role-play one of the techniques described in Strategy I, II, or III.

Technique: mime completion (cloze) The teacher reads the chart and instructs the children to make the actions for the word on which his or her hand stops. The teacher begins with the word *spider* and stops on each *spider*, *climbs*, and *sun*.

Summary: Multimodal Instruction Using a multimodal approach to instruction has the most instructional power for the learner. Combining the various learning modes increases the number of ways children can reach into their memory and exploit their background knowledge. It also increases the probability of their relating to the experience in such a way that the children's interests extend beyond the learning of the language unit. Experiences involving moving in some way in response to the language expands the potential for a more complete comprehension of parts or all of the words being presented.

CONNECTING THE WRITING PROCESS

Developing Concepts of Print

Very young children explore print products and the process of producing print in much the same way they learn about speaking and reading. Attending first to the conceptual whole, children discover that written symbols represent thoughts, ideas, and things. After this holistic exploration, they learn to discriminate elements that form the standards or conventions of written communication. Using a process of making and amending rules, early writers depend heavily on writing-rich environments, which include

1. Adults who encourage and include children in the processes of using print in meaningful contexts
2. Numerous diverse opportunities to observe and rehearse the production and uses of print
3. Time to explore and adapt the emerging concepts, using a variety of materials in pretend and real-life situations.

Emergent writers engage in the writing process during play interludes by mimicking an observed routine (e.g., making a grocery list) or by applying the concept of recording to situations that are new to them (e.g., making a list of favorite toys in the playroom). Although these examples focus on the intent of early writers to use symbols to record or remember things, thoughts, ideas, and so on, young children are also developing sophistication in the conventions used in the English-language recording system. Resulting from their experiences with print, children develop and use general principles that make their writing look like real writing (Clay, 1975):

Recurring principle: Writing uses the same shapes again and again (see Figure 3.12).

Generative principle: Writing consists of a limited number of signs used in various combinations (see Figure 3.13).

Flexibility principle: Writing shows awareness of a limited number of signs and a limited number of ways they can be made (see Figure 3.14).

Page arrangement principles: Writing reveals awareness of how print is arranged on a page so that it makes sense to the reader (see Figure 3.15).

The development of reading and writing concepts have a reciprocal relationship when children's experience or instruction causes the two processes to be interdependent. These concepts are connected through writing as a way of:

- Organizing, internalizing, and personalizing what has been read and establishing a connection between self and the world outside self
- Appreciating the process of authorship
- Recording the sound–symbol relationship
- Learning about how the systems of print work, which then enables understanding of the system to facilitate the effort toward understanding during the reading process
- Using patterns, forms, and techniques as tools in the writing process, and implementing them in the prediction process that facilitates reading fluency

As children gain information about how writing works, they begin to relate it to what they might expect from the printed words found in stories, letters, and labels.

For many young children, the first steps to reading are taken through the exploration of the writing process. Their interest in and attempts at

Review the ways in which children acquire speaking and reading abilities. With this in mind, have students predict how children will learn about writing.

Type so it can be put on overhead

Do not underestimate the time and effort children expend on just learning to control the tools used for recording print. Holding the paper in place while they write is a task in itself. Adding the physical control necessary to make the writing tool follow the intention significantly increases the task complexity.

Distribute samples of children's writing to teams of three to four students, and ask them to identify the writing concepts shown in the samples.

Figure 3.12 Kate, age 3, illustrating the recursive principle.

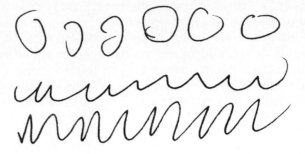

Figure 3.13 Richie, age 3, illustrating the generative principle.

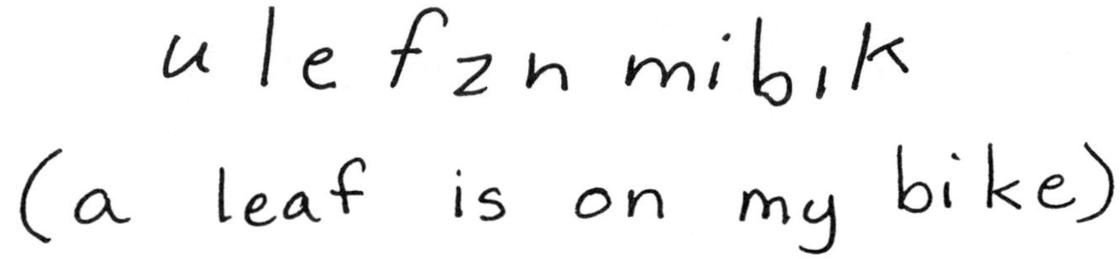

ulefzn mibik
(a leaf is on my bike)

Figure 3.14 Beth, age 6, illustrating the flexibility principle.

I LIKE cats
I Like Dogs
by
BETH

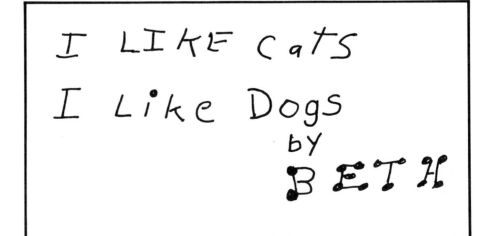

Figure 3.15 Kate, age 6, illustrating the page-arrangement principle.

writing develops a foundation of understanding that print holds meaning and is related to spoken words. Through their manipulation of the tools of print, they become familiar with the patterns and shapes of the symbols used in creating print, as well as developing the concept of themselves as being capable of participating in the two processes of written language: reading and writing.

Encouraging Writing in the Classroom

In the classroom, take advantage of this reciprocal relationship to develop directed and child-centered instruction that induces the continued interest and development of writing abilities. Teachers interact with the children in three ways: as translator, as model, and as facilitator.

As translator, change the children's spoken words into printed words. As model, demonstrate how print is used in many different situations. As facilitator, encourage children's writing attempts by making the time and materials available for the children to explore writing on their own, and support the children with an attitude of acceptance. Interact with the children as a translator, a model, or a facilitator, or in combinations of these roles, while moving through the three phases of instruction (i.e., involvement, directed instruction, and expansion).

Involving Children in Writing

The foundation for involving children in the writing process is the same as for involving them in the reading process—by providing them with language-rich experiences. In the kindergarten, extend children's experiences by making the writing process an ongoing part of the daily schedule.

The teacher uses specific oral language while engaged in each of these roles, to support the children's efforts to gather and make sense of the writing processes.

When composing, children should be encouraged to write for various purposes and with different readers in mind. Connecting their reading and writing will be easier if reading and writing are viewed as related activities.

Writing for Planning, Organizing, and Recording Children enjoy taking part in the procedures teachers use to plan upcoming activities. Participation gives them an opportunity to directly experience the planning process, such as determining the key elements of the plan and organizing the resources that are pertinent to the planned project. Acting as a translator, record the information on a chart, using words keyed with picture symbols to represent the elements and the resources. Verbally translate the word–picture symbols to the children as they are first recorded, and then refer to them by pointing to them as they are brought up in discussion. Your activity demonstrates the reciprocal relationship between the reading and the writing. Upon completion, the chart serves as a reference for remembering the group plan. Model the function of the chart by referring to—or by encouraging the children to refer to—the chart for the information they need.

> *Examples:* Planning a pizza party, organizing for a cookie-making project, rearranging the classroom, getting ready for free work time, having a visitor give a presentation, giving a play to parents or schoolmates, going on a field trip.

Ask students, "What other props could be added to the kindergarten to facilitate the children's interest in or acquisition of the writing process?"

Writing as a Part of Daily Living Because young children form their concepts through personal interaction, the tools, documents, and machinery for writing must be made available for their exploration in the context in which they are used. Adding writing props to the learning centers gives the children this opportunity to use writing materials in conjunction with their play. The following examples illustrate a few possibilities for learning centers.

House Center
Note pad and pencil by the telephone
Pad for grocery list near the refrigerator
Stationery for writing letters
Paper and crayons for drawing
Empty booklets for diaries

Grocery Store
Receipt book for listing purchased items
Note pad and pencil for taking orders or messages
Order book
Accounting sheets for recording money
Chart for checking out videos
Calculator or cash register that prints onto tape

Block Center
Straws, tinker toy circles, tape, paper, and pens for signs
"4 x 6" cards to be folded and used for writing labels
Paper and crayons for drawing maps and making plans
Invoices, receipt books, pens for delivering freight
Large sheets of tagboard for making building and road signs
Typewriter and typing paper for writing business letters

Facilitate children's explorations by encouraging them to use these props. For example, ask questions (e.g., "Did she give you a receipt?"); make suggestions (e.g., "Leave her a note"); provide information (e.g., "One way to tell the drivers what to do is to make a traffic sign"); or recognizing their efforts (e.g., "Mandy, I saw the note you wrote to Sara. Would you like to read it to me?").

Instructing Children in Writing

Writing instruction gives children information to add to their already growing knowledge of how writing works. The first step in this instructional process is to provide models of where print comes from, the different forms it can take, and how it is organized on paper. Children are then given demonstrations of how to use these processes themselves and opportunities to apply and practice the new information with the teacher's guidance.

CONCEPTS
Print is a means for recording what we say.
Printed symbols relate to individual sounds.
There are conventions for recording print.
Individual sound symbols can take many forms.
I (child) can make printed symbols.
Print can help me remember what the symbols represent.
Print can inform and entertain.

Strategies for Instruction Several strategies can be used in the process of instruction in writing. Some are presented to the group as a whole, with application practiced as a whole group; some strategies are presented to the whole group and then children work individually on the guided practice; others demand that the teacher works individually with each child, through the whole instructional process. The three key strategies are using models, taking dictation, and making written records, each of which can be used in various ways.

Using Models Models give children information about the possibilities available to them and give them a framework to use for their practice. As these models are selected and used with the children, it is important to remember that the *process* of learning about the models is as important as the *outcome* of being aware of the models. Provide models in child-centered and directed instruction using:

Copy

Cloze (fill-in-the-blank)

Adaptations and variations of familiar language forms

Letter writing

Class books

Individual books

Several word processing programs are available for young children, which add a new dimension to the reading and writing process. Explore some of these programs, and debate the use of them with very young children.

Taking Dictation Taking dictation is a comprehensive strategy for teaching young children about reading and writing because it includes the attributes of modeling, as well as opportunities for direct instruction during the dictation process. In its simplest form, taking dictation is writing down exactly what the child says. Dictation can take place using the following prompts and activities:

Pictures, stickers

Story retelling

Puppet plays, drama

Events, experiences

Letter writing

Class books

Individual books

The primary purpose for taking dictation is to demonstrate to children that what people say can be recorded in print and that they (children) are capable of participating in this process. If the process is done so that the child can visually observe the recording, the teacher models how print is produced and recorded following print conventions. During the dictation process, teachers have the option of offering instruction about the formation of letters, the initial sounds produced by particular letters, the letter patterns of selected words, or the left-to-right sequence of words, depending on whether this would enhance or detract from the language experience.

It may sometimes seem wise to question the child for clarity or sequence, in order to prompt organized or logical thinking. The teacher may also choose to guide a student in participating in the dictation process by encouraging him or her to print a letter in a word or an entire word that has been spoken. These options are also available once the dictation has been completed. The teacher and the child may also read the selection aloud, either together or independently. This activity provides the child with an opportunity to experience the concept that "what is written can be read." The teacher may encourage the child to select a special word from the dictation, examine its attributes, and perhaps print over or below the word as it occurs in context or put it on a word card to be played with, read, or copied.

The learning that results from the dictation experiences occur only when the students develop a positive attitude toward and a desire to record their oral language. This requires the teacher to accept what the children have to say without criticizing or making fun of it. It also means that the instruction is offered only when the child is interested and only as long as the child is interested.

PHYSICAL SET-UP FOR DICTATION

As mentioned previously, it is important for the child to see the words being printed on the paper. Ideally, seat the child between you and the paper when the printing occurs; in that way, the child's eyes are able to see letter formations and the left-to-right direction of the printing. When that is not possible, in order for the child to see the writing from the writer's perspective, the child's body should be on the opposite side of your writing hand. If you are right-handed, seat the child to your left to view your hand movements. Seat the child to your right if you are left-handed. You may also say the words while recording them so that the child relates the spoken and the written words.

Ask students, "How should a teacher respond to a student who uses language that is socially inappropriate or dictates text that perhaps should be confidential or is offensive to his or her family?"

The dictation process is often initially stimulated by a child's drawing, painting, toy, construction, or personal belonging. Because these things are visual, the child has a prompt for the language, and the teacher has a model for the labels or descriptive language used for extending or supporting the child's efforts. The most common way to introduce taking dictation is to say to a child, "Tell me about your _____ , and I will write what you say on this paper." If the dictation is about a picture or a painting, ask the child whether and where the child would like the writing to be done. Sometimes, it is best to put the words on another sheet of paper and either staple or tape it to the work of art.

Using the preceding list of activities, dictation can be adapted successfully to a variety of writing situations. Selectively apply the instructional objectives to individual children through each personal interaction, or select one objective to develop when taking dictation from every child.

Making Written Records Print can help people to organize and remember information used to get along in daily living. Charts developed and used daily by the children help them to develop these concepts. For example, *word lists* are a type of chart used to organize and remember words that go with a particular theme or topic that has been experienced.

1. Classroom management: lunch, attendance, and helpers charts
2. Information retrieval: concept and attribute charts; word lists

Concept charts contain pictures or objects that relate to an idea or an object. A concept chart relating to the color *red* would depict red objects and pictures of objects that are red. A concept chart relating to birds would show pictures of different kinds of birds; items with birds on them, such as vases or cups; other bird-related items, such as birdfeeders; and different types of real bird feathers.

A *retrieval chart* is a collection of information about one or more topics or objects, with the information organized by subtopic. These charts show children how information can be organized and used for systematic retrieval of data.

Summary: Strategies for Instruction Although each of these strategies has been listed separately, many of them may be used in combination. For instance, you may prepare a letter pattern (model) for the children to follow in writing their own messages and then may write the message (dictation) for students who want the assistance in putting the message on paper.

Expanding the Writing Process: Rationale and Strategies

Because the concepts and skills necessary to the writing process are not arranged in a hierarchial form, the children are constantly using their knowledge of writing in their daily lives, adapting what they do know and creating what they do not. Teachers can facilitate this process by accepting and encouraging the efforts of each child and by making the time and materials available for it to occur, such as in the following examples:

1. A writing center, a bookmaking center, a cut-and-paste table, an easel, or a drawing table are often the places children incorporate the knowledge they have about writing with new content information they have acquired or discovered. Support the children's efforts to put their information into print by reading what others have written during classtime and by asking the writers to share where they did the writing and what materials they used.

2. Journals are booklets containing plain pages. The children are expected to write each day in the booklets. The writing may consist of pretend stories, real events or concerns, content information, or models of other language units, such as copied poems or charts. The recording may be done in pictures, diagrams, or words, whichever the child chooses. The teacher's role is to spend a bit of time with each child during the week and to visit with each regarding the contents of their journals. In these conferences, the teacher may ask the child to tell about his or her drawing, to read a passage, or to retell a story. The child may ask the teacher to take dictation, to spell a particular word, or to give the child more information on a topic about which the child has written or would like to write.

HIGHLIGHTS

1. Children learn to read and write by participating in the processes of reading and writing. The teacher facilitates this process by offering both teacher-directed and child-centered instruction.
2. Child-centered instruction provides young children with daily opportunities for the exploration and application of new concepts and skill. Children's learning is supported through the manipulation of materials, interaction with peers, and guidance given by the teacher.
3. An effective early literacy program enhances the social, emotional, physical, and intellectual development of each child by offering opportunities that promote integrated experiences.
4. Children learn by doing. By becoming actively involved in creating and re-creating the literacy processes, they develop fundamental concepts, skills, and attitudes.
5. Becoming literate is an integrated process building on the child's listening, speaking, reading, and writing strengths.

REINFORCEMENT ACTIVITIES

1. Explain the role the teacher takes in fostering the development of young children during a planned experience, such as a cooking activity, field trip, or art project.
2. Using the model provided in this chapter, develop a directed-instruction lesson for a reading or writing objective.
3. Design an individual or small-group learning center that provides instruction or exploration in the language arts area. Describe the objective, the materials organization, and the instructional procedure you will use.
4. Define three comprehension strategies teachers can use in teaching comprehension of written language. Create and label examples of each strategy.
5. Describe two ways in which language is predictable. Discuss the role that predictable language plays in fostering reading development in young children.
6. Select a story to read to a kindergarten child or to a group of children. Prepare an activity that introduces the story and/or an activity that will expand the story.

ADDITIONAL PROJECTS

1. Visit a children's library, and review several books found in the easy-to-read and picture-book section. Evaluate the selections on their potential for use as big books, as project or activity starters, or as literature lessons.
2. Observe 5- and 6-year-olds at play and interacting with an adult. Record their dialogue, and evaluate it using the 10 teacher interaction techniques provided in this chapter.
3. Make a big book or chart, and use it to teach a selected objective to a small group of kindergarten children.
4. Review commercially published kindergarten language arts/reading programs and evaluate them in terms of their (a) emphasis on integration of language arts instruction, (b) balance of teacher-directed instruction and child-centered instruction, and (c) integration of other content area objectives.
5. Make a booklet or file of a collection of poems, fingerplays, and songs that will serve as your resource for language arts lessons.
6. Invite a kindergarten teacher to your classroom to share his or her reading program, samples of children's work, and his or her views on the needs of the young child.

REFERENCES

Bruner, J. (1966). *Toward a Theory of Instruction*. New York: W. W. Norton.

Carle, E. (1982). *What's For Lunch*. New York: Putnam.

Clay, M. (1975). *What Did I Write?* New Hampshire: Heinemann Educational Books.

Fein, G., & Rivkin, M. (Eds). (1986). *The Young Child at Play: Reviews of Research* (Vol. 4). Washington, DC: National Association for the Education of Young Children.

Kraus, R. (1970). *Whose Mouse Are You?* New York: Scholastic.

Lynch, P. (1986). *Using Big Books and Predictable Books*. New York: Scholastic–TAB Publications.

Peck, J., McCaig, G., & Sapp, M. (1988). *Kindergarten Policies, What Is Best for Children?* Washington, DC: National Association for the Education of Young Children.

Peterson, S. (1982). *Storybox: Hands-on Reading–Writing for Young Children*. Bellingham, WA: Storybox, Inc.

Tough, J. (1977). *The Development of Meaning*. London: George Allen & Unwin.

ADDITIONAL RESOURCES

Barrett, F. (1982). *A Teacher's Guide to Shared Reading*. Ontario, Canada: Scholastic–TAB.

Cohen, D., & Rudolph, M. (1977). *Kindergarten and Early Schooling*. Englewood Cliffs, NJ: Prentice-Hall.

DeHaven, E. (1988). *Teaching and Learning the Language Arts*. Glenview, IL: Scott, Foresman.

Goodman, K. (1986). *What's Whole in Whole Language?* Ontario, Canada: Scholastic–TAB.

Hunter-Grundin, E. (1979). *Literacy: A Systematic Start*. London: Harper & Row.

Klein, M. (1985). *The Development of Writing in Children*. New Jersey: Prentice-Hall.

Ramsey, M., & Bayless, K. (1980). *Kindergarten: Program and Practices*. St. Louis, MO: C. V. Mosby.

Schickedanz, J. (1986). *More Than the ABCs*. Washington, DC: National Association for the Education of Young Children.

Trelease, J. (1982). *The Read-Aloud Handbook*. New York: Penguin Books.

CHAPTER 4

TEACHING AND MENTORING THE APPRENTICE READER

Let's put on our thinking caps shall we and think what flowers
we are going to be. . . . a horse isn't a flower Sidney. . . . No
a carrot isn't a flower Sidney . . . No Sidney you can't be a
super jet—all right you can be a cauliflower, but be it 'gently'

Id., *Flowers*

PREVIEW

Once children (a) recognize that print exists, and (b) become aware of print's role in providing pleasure and independence, the internal motivation for literacy is sparked. Using their thinking abilities to unlock the keys to reading, children explore, hypothesize, test, experiment, create, and re-create generalized rules of reading. As their thinking skills become more sophisticated, so do the complexities of their theories related to reading. It is only through this exploration, practice, and re-creation of the knowledge and skill of reading that children become readers.

The role of the classroom teacher is determined by the needs of the learner. Nurturing and encouraging the apprentice reader is a process that requires an understanding of the learner's needs, the processes of reading, and the available strategies and skills for instruction. The teacher selects the materials, methods, and instructional strategies based on the interests, abilities, and strengths of the students.

FOCUS QUESTIONS

While reading this chapter, keep the following questions in mind:

- How does the teacher develop and maintain an encouraging, nurturing reading environment?
- What is the role of phonics instruction, and how do early readers learn to use it?

- How does the teacher support the child's reading efforts?
- What are the strategies and activities available to the teacher in helping children learn to read?

READING PROGRAM IN THE PRIMARY GRADES

The reading program in the primary grades consists of three general types of reading opportunities: instructional reading, practice reading, and independent reading. Each plays an important role in launching children into a lifetime of reading. One is not exclusive of the other, and the teacher goes to some lengths to promote reciprocal relationships among them. This effort increases the probability that the children will transfer what they learn in instruction to practical applications such as reading independently for information and enjoyment.

INSTRUCTIONAL READING

Instructional reading is the reading a child does while receiving skill or strategy instruction from a teacher. This instruction can occur as a whole-group, small-group, or individualized activity during which the teacher monitors the students. These instructional episodes may last a few moments or for more than 30 minutes. The teacher's responsibility is to apply or control the quantity and quality of instruction according to the needs of the learners.

Planning for instructional reading focuses initially on two main areas: word acquisition and comprehension development. *Word acquisition* includes all of the methods by which children acquire a knowledge and understanding of written words, as well as the skills for continuing to increase their knowledge of words. *Comprehension development* builds on the experiences discussed in the previous chapter (i.e., questioning, retelling, and adapting language models) and is facilitated by continuous and culminating questioning, by story mapping, and by developing sociograms.

The process of constructing meaning from print causes children to think. Ask students, "What types of thinking processes do children engage in when they are constructing their meaning? In what kinds of thinking does good literature cause children to engage? Compare the processes defined in the first question with those of the second question."

Ask the students to predict teacher and student behaviors when they are engaged in instructional reading, practice reading, and independent reading. Note these predictions for confirmation or correction as they continue reading. Discuss with the students the instructional strategy they are employing when doing this, and ask them to evaluate prediction and confirmation as a comprehension tool.

Ask students, "How are listening, speaking, and writing activities supporting the instructional reading process? How is this support influencing other aspects of reading, such as fluency?"

Have the students, working in teams, create a written language with new symbols for their alphabet and new rules for writing and decoding. Ask the students to help another team discover the codes for using the new symbol system in order to make meaning. Let the students evaluate with their team members the intellectual and affective processes they experienced. Relate their experiences to those of an emergent reader.

Word Acquisition: Balancing the Instruction

Ask students, "Did you use letter-by-letter comparison, significant feature comparison, or similar letters strategies in making sense of your classmates' unknown code? What other strategies did you or could you have used?"

Instruction is developed by selecting methods and materials that support the child or the group of children in their effort to derive meaning from print. Because reading requires the use of semantic, structural, and phonetic cuing systems, it is important to recognize and balance the instructional elements of each. This chapter describes word-acquisition instruction in developing sight-word vocabularies, using structural cuing, and applying phonetic information.

Sight Words

Developing a Sight-Word Vocabulary A *sight word* is a word that is immediately identified "on sight." A *sight-word vocabulary* is an individual's complete lexicon of personally recognized sight words. Usually, these words are listed out of context, with no other language around them to help with inferring what they may mean. Lists of sight words grouped by grade level or by the most commonly used are available commercially from many sources, although experts disagree on which of these are really important enough for direct sight-word instruction.

Young children begin building their personal banks of sight words with the first sets of letters that consistently hold a special meaning. These first words are identified by a parent, teacher, sibling, playmate, or other significant person in a context where the learners immediately relate the symbol pattern to the referent for which it stands. Often, this experience is closely tied to the child's attempts at printing the word. It is common for this first sight word to be the most meaningful word in any vocabulary; the child's own name.

Learning to recognize one's own name or any letter pattern is a constant process of discriminating the elements of configuration that make that set of letters unlike any other set of letters. Usually, the child will focus on an attribute of the word and will use that attribute exclusively as the element of comparison. As the child has more experience with printed words, whether presented in the classroom or as a consequence of other interactions with the environment, the child increases the number of words and attributes that can be used for comparisons with new words. The following examples demonstrate four strategies for progressive word comparison: (1) letter-by-letter comparison, (2) significant-feature comparison, (3) similar letters, and (4) similar contexts.

Letter-by-letter comparison Usually, the first letter of the word is recognized and compared with other words with the same first letter. Because both words may not be present for a letter-by-letter analysis, the child is consistently having to go back to the original word, examine it, try to remember some other feature of the word, and remember that feature to use for a second criterion.

Triep	Kara	Billy	Mike	Sarah
tree	Karla	Bobby	milk	salad

Very often, the child remembers the second letter in the word sequence, then the third, and so on until the word is complete.

If the child is unaware that words begin at the left, the ending letter might be chosen as the initial point for comparison.

Significant feature comparison Sometimes, the child keys in on some other feature of the word that makes it memorable (e.g., word shape or letter placement), and the child uses that feature as the point of reference and criterion expansion. For example, consonant pairs:

Kitty	little	Missy
Kettle	letter	Messy

Similar letters Often children recognize a group of letters as representing a word pattern but have not firmly organized the order in which the letters must appear or have not designated correctly the individual letters in order to represent a particular word.

crops	was	Ann	bite	what
coops	saw	and	bike	that

Similar context Sometimes one of the child's first words will be one found in the environment, such as a label or a sign. This can often be misleading and sometimes humorous as the child attaches erroneous but logical meaning to a symbol.

> *Example:* A child lying on the floor in front of the cat's dish points to the letters around the base of the bowl. The child moves his finger back and forth across the letters C-A-T saying "food."

This anecdote shows that the child expects print to

1. have a referent
2. hold meaning
3. relate to its context.

It further demonstrates the beginning reader's need for learning word-attack skills that add clues to confirm the guess.

Learning Sight Words in the Classroom Children in the primary grades show differing degrees of sophistication in identifying, remembering, and using sight words. Activities presented in the classroom can foster this natural developmental process as an integral part of the program. The criteria for planning and instructing are

1. The child has opportunity to explore the sound–symbol–object relationship within meaningful contexts.

When facilitating sight-word acquisition, the teacher must also use specific language in identifying the relationship between the printed and spoken word. The one-to-one correspondence between the verbal and written symbol systems is a developing concept, so the child is dealing with more than a mere memory exercise.

2. The child chooses the words that hold meaning for him or her individually.
3. The words are consistently available for checking and rechecking.
4. The child's opportunities to use chosen sight words are ample and meaningful.

The teacher facilitates the child's effort by providing a wide selection of activities or experiences that are connected with the printed symbols that represent the activities and/or aspects of the experiences. The teacher also provides opportunities to practice using these sight words in a meaningful context for sustained periods of time. Teachers should provide the child with opportunities to

1. Read the child's name on labels for the child's drawings, storage cubbie, work paper, and so on
2. Give dictation about a picture or other work
3. Discuss an opinion or an analysis of a printed word
4. Write stories, plays, notes, and other things
5. Play with words
6. See the teacher use print meaningfully (e.g., class phone book, recipe, notes)
7. Use print as an integral part of the functioning each day—lunch and milk charts, attendance slips, name cards, and so on

Have students review some of the available word lists, analyzing the types of words in terms of their interest to emergent readers and their occurrence in children's literature.

If the children are in an environment where their writing is not only accepted but also encouraged, children often list their increasing sight-word vocabularies in printed form. Figure 4.1 shows how this evidence might appear. Very often, this list begins with names of significant others in the child's environment and may then include other child-selected words.

Teaching Sight-Word Vocabulary Teaching sight words is often one of the first steps in reading instruction for the beginning reader. There are some very important reasons for this.

First, if the child knows even a small number of words that are likely to appear repeatedly in the text, it increases the child's ability to read, even with limited sound–symbol relationship instruction. Thus, the child begins to experience the success of reading with a minimum amount of direct instruction in sound–symbol relationships. From these known whole words, the child has a point of reference for the application of the decoding instruction when it occurs.

Second, children are more interested in words and their meanings than they are in the applications of *phoneme* (meaningful sound units) and *grapheme* (meaning printed units, such as letters and diphthongs) relationships. As for most of us, reading for children has more to do with bringing meaning to words and sentences than with analyzing parts of words. It is

Figure 4.1   Kate, age 5, spontaneously written list of her sight-word vocabulary.

through this immediate process of making meaning that children are motivated to continue their reading efforts.

Interestingly, most words included on word lists play a structural rather than a semantic role in our language. For example, consider prepositions—"in," "on," "out," "of," and so on. These words are critical to comprehension of sentences, yet they are extremely difficult to define in a very telling way. Primary-grade children, especially, would have difficulty dealing with their definitions. This unnecessary complexity can be avoided by teaching these and other words that do not follow conventional phonological patterns as sight words in patterned sentences.

The following example demonstrates a strategy for teaching sight words within a meaningful context.

> *Example:* **Where Have You Been?**
> *Little black bug*
> *Little black bug*
> *Where have you been?*
>
> *"Inside the rug,"*
> *Said Little Black Bug*
> *"That's where I've been."*
>
> **Margaret Wise Brown—an adaptation**

This excerpt is printed on a class chart, a big book page, or an individual worksheet. The children then follow along as the teacher reads the words to the children. The children see the teacher pointing to the words as they are read out loud. The children are encouraged to say the words with the teacher as they are indicated and then to begin to read them independently. After several readings, the teacher highlights individual words to call attention to their configuration and spelling.

When introducing new stories to the children, carefully preread the story to evaluate the number of new words that may be introduced in the selection. If a word is used a number of times and it is clearly a new word for most of the children, it is a good idea to teach it as a sight word prior to the children's reading, even if it is a decodable word for them.

When teaching whole words to the beginning reader, consider the following:

1. Provide opportunities for the children to use the new word in their writing. Provide handouts with cloze sentences into which the word will fit. Have them work independently on this activity.
2. Encourage them to use the word in class in both their oral and written work. This offers opportunity to practice the word in an environment where the effort can be reinforced and monitored for correctness.
3. Provide ample practice in a variety of ways. Have the children develop word-bank cards with the new words. Encourage them to share their words with the other students and then play games telling each other what the words mean. Select new words from upcoming stories, and display them on a special bulletin board for new words, with picture or word clues to their meaning. Encourage students to incorporate their new words into traditional games such as "Word Bingo" and "Concentration."

Have students compare this strategy for teaching a sight word with one found in a selected basal text. Ask students, "How do each of these strategies make the most of the child's motivation to acquire the new word?"

4. Teach a limited number of sight words at one time. Although the quantity can vary, three to four words per lesson should be seen as a maximum for the beginning reader. The more critical the words are for comprehension of the text, the fewer the new words that should be introduced.

5. Use a pocket chart with sentences from stories and other text with which children are likely to be familiar so that they can use their background knowledge and sentence structure to take educated guesses—make predictions—about what the new word will be. For example, use sentence strips.

   Sample sentence strips:

   Red Riding Hood walked into the _____ .

   Grandmother lived in a small _____ .

6. Use a direct and predictable teaching strategy for sight-word instruction. For example, the following Five-Step Strategy (Klein, 1988) is useful not only for teaching whole words in the beginning reading program, but also, in a modified form, for teaching reading vocabulary to older students for their overall vocabulary growth.

Have students select one of the indicated considerations in teaching sight words and describe how they would use it in teaching a sight word.

The five-step strategy applies to all three categories of words that form a child's reading vocabulary: the full ownership dictionary (defined in Chapter 1); the *midlevel dictionary* (accessible with contextual assistance); and the *low-level dictionary* (marginally available; possible, but with increased risk of error). Chapter 8 describes these dictionaries in greater detail.

The "Five-Step" Direct-Instruction Model

1. Look at the word, and say it.
2. Tell the meaning of the word.
3. Analyze the word structurally.
4. Discuss the word.
5. Use the word in context.

Have students plan both an inductive and a deductive introduction to sight-word instruction. Next, have pairs of students work together to select and model one introductory technique.

Look at the word; say the word The word can be presented to students in a variety of ways. It may be viewed directly in the text, or the teacher can write it on the board or on an overhead projector transparency. At least most of the time, the word should be presented within sentence contexts, and these sentences should be dominated by vocabulary that is in the students' full-ownership dictionaries. The word should be highlighted (e.g., underlining, boldface, italics).

Be sure that all students can pronounce the word correctly before moving on to Step 2. If there are questions about why it is pronounced as it is, take some time to discuss the reasons. Step 3 will go more deeply into this area. The primary concern at this first step is for students to be able to pronounce the word correctly, even if that means simply imitating the teacher's pronunciation of it.

To vary this first step, use an *inductive technique* (i.e., showing many specific examples in order to help learners infer a general principle) with related activities. For example, present a sequence of words with similar spelling and structural characteristics. Point out to the students that the meanings of these words (which they already know how to pronounce) are not important. However, they should look at the words' similarities in sound to give them a clue as to how the new word is pronounced.

The decision whether to use an inductive technique in this first step is determined by a couple of factors. Normally, time spent on task is closely correlated with the knowledge acquired. An inductive technique requires more class time, means more discussion and opportunity for new word use, and generally involves the learner to a greater extent. Thus, to be worth this intensive effort, the new word must be important to the reading of the text (or important for some other reason, such as student interest).

Another instructional consideration is that although the strategy should remain consistent and predictable, instruction should also offer enough variety in techniques and activities to keep motivation and interest high. That means that, in some instances at least, inductive approaches should be mixed with *deductive techniques* (i.e., simply presenting the general principle directly to the students, and then supporting it with specific examples).

Tell the meaning of the word Provide a definition of the word that is most appropriate to the meaning or meanings used in the text. This is normally not the time to present alternative definitions unless such definitions are important to the comprehension of this particular text.

Analyze the word structurally This third step involves analyzing in detail the structure of the word. Identify the root word or base *morpheme* (the smallest part of a word that affects the meaning of the word), along with any prefixes or suffixes. Separate the components in writing on the board or on an overhead transparency. Discuss the meanings of each morpheme in the word. (You might have to do some homework on the generic meaning of some prefixes and suffixes prior to the lesson.)

Ask students for related words that have the same structural characteristics or features. For example, what are some words that begin with the same prefix or end with the same suffix? How are their meanings similar because of that structural similarity? Can they find words in their texts that are structurally similar?

Discuss the word The fourth step of this model allows the greatest flexibility in the strategy. The teacher must determine here the amount of

Step 4, "Discuss the word," requires teacher judgment in terms of both the time spent and the selection of technique. Ask students, "What criteria will you use in making your instructional decisions? What will cause you to select particular examples, a specific amount of time, or a necessary technique?"

time warranted, observe carefully the skill and knowledge of each student, and adjust teaching techniques and activities accordingly. This step is critical; here, the student brings together semantic, structural, and contextual information to determine the role of the word in his or her life.

At this step, the teacher would normally present other examples of the word in use, pointing out synonyms, antonyms, homophones, and homographs, if they are of interest or worthy of note. Again, the teacher must decide how much time to commit to this and must determine the role or roles of various inductive and deductive techniques and activities.

Use the word in context The final step of this strategy places function and language context front and center. Although there are opportunities for using sentence contexts throughout the previous steps, in this final step, context becomes even more important. Have available a number of different sentence contexts from different texts in which the word is used. Be sure not to use examples in which different senses of the word are employed—that is, the word in the additional contexts must have the same meaning as in the original context. Despite this, it is important to demonstrate the word's versatility and usefulness in different reading contexts on other occasions.

Have students make up sentences orally and in writing, using the word appropriately. Ask them to exchange papers with a friend and assess each other's use of the word. Discuss the sentences in class.

Ask students, "What are the implications for reading instruction for students who have a limited proficiency with the language used for instruction, or for students who have delayed language development due to environmental deprivation?"

Structural Cuing

Expecting print to make sense is the foundation for using structural cuing effectively. When children are involved in the context of the language in print, they predict what will come next by thinking about what would make sense to come next. This predictive sensibility is developed from experiences with what language should sound like and from the child's increasing mental list of possible words from which to select.

Two types of cuing are helpful to the reader: (1) cues based on an intuitive sense of "how language sounds," and (2) cues based on formal, conscious knowledge of the structure of words and of sentences. The first type of cuing comes from intuitive knowledge of the structure of our language. For example, a child, without instruction, will recognize the inappropriateness of the sentence, "The blue, three flowers are in the vase." Though children are not taught the rule, "Number precedes color when describing a noun," they use that rule effectively in their speech. This ability to intuit the correct sound of the language enables them to make predictions.

Because language contains certain patterns or sets of patterns, a second type of prediction becomes possible, based on the formal structure of words and sentences. Linguists use a shorthand for many of these patterns: "C" designates consonants, "V" designates vowels, and individual letters are indicated by lowercase letters. For example, one elementary pattern of English words is basic syllable patterning, such as long-vowel patterns (CV, CVe, CVVC: "go," "tie," "real"), short vowel patterns (VC, CVC: "in," "can"), "r" patterns (CVr: "car"), and "e" patterns (CVCCe: "judge," CVCe: "cake").

Sentences are also structured around basic grammatical patterns:

Subject + verb phrase	"Joe left."
Subject + verb phrase + direct object	"Joe hit the ball."
Subject + to be verb + predicate adjective	"The dress is blue."
Subject + to be verb + predicate nominative	"Joe is the leader."

These same patterns appear recursively in all sentences and words. After hearing them over and over, children learn these implicitly and begin to use them as clues to language use and meaning.

Phonics

Phonics is a reading strategy that focuses on linking speech sounds to their associated letter symbols and then connecting those symbols with one another, to represent the sounds that make up spoken words. Young children are taught this system of using the sound–symbol relationship as a way that they can read words they may not have seen before or words they have not committed to memory. Phonics instruction is provided to introduce children to the decoding process once they have developed the following:

- Significant skill in discriminating the different sounds
- Relatively large sight-word vocabularies
- Demonstrable interest in the reading process

Building Foundations for Phonics Instruction The foundation for relating different sounds to their designated symbols requires mastery of both the auditory skill of discriminating one sound from another and the visual skill of discriminating the differences among the many symbols. These skills are developed naturally as children interact with their environment. These skills occur in varying levels of refinement in individual children because of congenital, developmental, and environmental differences. Teachers guide the development of these two kinds of skills by providing meaningful opportunities for their use.

Auditory Discrimination Activities Encourage the development of auditory discrimination by carefully planning for an enriched learning environment. The environment includes not only the types of objects and

Some children are capable of acquiring and using large sight-word vocabularies. How might this strength facilitate their reading acquisition? How might this strength inhibit their acquisition of phonics?

experiences in which the children engage, but also the way in which interactions are facilitated. The following examples illustrate facilitative interactions:

1. Practice using language in context. When involved in language learning experiences, listen to individual children repeat the language. Practice with them, taking turns correctly pronouncing the words in appropriate contexts.
2. Listen to the children when they speak. This motivates the children to speak to be understood; also, they will imitate the listening process being modeled.
3. Play listening games. Games such as "Alphabet Bingo" encourage the children to use their eyes to observe the differences they are hearing in the letter names. Learning to attend auditorily is also encouraged by interactive songs such as "Colors" by Hap Palmer, through which the children respond with the actions directed by the singer.
4. Encourage the children to talk to each other. The most important audience a child can have is a friend. Children are motivated by peer speech, and they can support each other as no other teacher can. Play is one of the best opportunities children have for this type of learning. While they are engaged in reciprocal dialogue, the children ask each other for clarification and extension of their ideas and are able to correct each other's pronunciation. Because this interaction occurs within a meaningful context, learning is increased.

Visual Discrimination Activities Visual discrimination activities encourage children to see the similarities and differences between and among things, as well as to gain skill in making qualitative comparisons of attributes. The following activities facilitate visual discrimination

1. Practice looking at things. Focus the children's attention on the visual attributes of related objects being presented.
2. Refer to objects by their shape characteristics and other visual attributes. Incorporate the use of descriptive words in sentences. While interacting with children during individual or group discussions, extend the language used by the children. For example, add descriptions of detail, or create analogies, such as "The end of this fork is like the end of the comb because. . . ."
3. Play games that require visual discrimination skills. Make posters picturing items that have the same basic shape, and encourage the children to describe why the objects are on the poster. Play "Shape Bingo" (children must visually match the selected shape with shapes printed on their playing cards). Let the children play with "Object Lotto" games (pictures are matched to identical pictures).

4. Encourage the children to describe objects when they speak.

By kindergarten or first grade, young children have developed visual discrimination skills, to varying degrees. Some first-grade children may still confuse such different letters as "t" and "z," or "c" and "z," but as they continue their language development, these confusions diminish.

Phonics Instruction in the Classroom Although there are several different theories about how efficient readers process printed language, no one disagrees with the assertion that a reader must be able to decode individual words. Disagreement does exist on the answers to two questions: (1) What are phonics and phonics analysis? and (2) How can teachers optimally ensure that young learners will master what they need to in order to successfully decode words?

Preparation and delivery of phonics instruction requires the consideration of many elements. Several helpful generalizations may facilitate the children's learning:

1. Children learn all oral and written language most effectively and efficiently when the language is meaning based. The implication for phonics instruction is that it must be related to the natural language of the children and must be derived from background experiences and interests of the children.

2. Sound–symbol relationships should be taught in the context of words and sentences that the children already know and can use confidently. In this way, the learner also can use the semantic cues to assist in decoding the word, as well as in making the decoding skills more meaningful. Developing the sound–symbol relationship in context also increases the likelihood of success in the guided and independent practice of those relationships.

   Example:

   Read "Little Red Ridinghood," pausing after each sentence that contains a word that begins with "s" so that children can identify the word. As you read, run one hand under the words from left to right. Once the story is read, list the words that begin with "s" on the chalkboard. Read the completed list, calling on volunteers to underline each initial "s."

3. Because decoding skills are cognitive tools that allow the reader to access the text, the decoding skills in a phonics lesson should not be goals in and of themselves. Mastery of phonics skills for the sake of mastering phonics skills takes away from their application, which is necessary for being an effective reader.

4. Initial phonics instruction does not teach learners how to pronounce words that they do not already know how to pronounce. It teaches them how to decode the written representation of a word with which they are already familiar. In fact, when the reader reaches the stage of needing to apply phonics skill to "sound out"

Many young children spend much of their day watching television. Ask students, "What effects could this have (a) on their ability to interact with other children in play situations, (b) on their listening skills, (c) on their understanding of and ability to engage in dialogue? How might this affect their phonics acquisition?"

an unfamiliar word, additional semantic or word meaning knowledge is required, as well as structural analysis skills, which go beyond much of what is traditionally seen as "basic phonics skills."

5. Decoding instruction that capitalizes on the interrelationships between oral and written language is more productive than instruction that adheres to a single approach or remains isolated from the children's natural language or experience. With this in mind, writing and the reading of the writing should be ingredients of any approach to decoding instruction.

The Deductive and Inductive Instructional Models You can use two general models of direct instruction in presenting decoding information to the children: (1) deductive models, and (2) inductive models.

Deductive Approach The deductive model presents a rule or formulates a generalization about some sound–symbol relationship, which is followed by examples of words that substantiate or illustrate that rule.

Have the students review several basal texts, listing the order of introduction of different consonant, vowel, blends, and so forth. Discuss why the differences exist and the implications of those differences for teaching reading.

Example: Deductive Word Identification Skill

Decoding Skill—Distinguish between voiced and unvoiced 'th" in initial positions of words.

Steps of Instruction:

1. Teacher prints "th" on the board and tells children that this letter combination has two different possible sounds at the beginning of words.
2. Teacher prints the word "this" on the board and pronounces the word.
3. Teacher asks children to pronounce the word with her or him.
4. Teacher uses the word in a sentence and asks the children to join in.
5. Teacher prints the word "that" on the board and repeats Steps 2–4.
6. Teacher sounds out the voiced /th/ sound appearing in both words.
7. Teacher asks children to pronounce the sound with her or him.
8. Teacher prints the word "thin" on the board and pronounces the word.
9. Teacher repeats Steps 3–4.
10. Teacher prints the word "throw" on the board and pronounces the word.
11. Teacher repeats Steps 3–4.
12. Teacher pronounces the two separate voiced and unvoiced sounds and asks the children to note the difference.
13. Teacher has children pronounce the two different sounds.

14. Teacher prints the word "thick" and the word "they" on the board and pronounces them.
15. Teacher asks children which of the words is like "that" and which is like "thin."
16. Teacher indicates that "th" combinations can represent two different sounds in the language.

Ask students, "When do children move from (a) using phonics to decode the written representation of a word they already know to (b) using phonics to pronounce words they have not heard before?"

Inductive Approach The second model for teaching word identification skills, the inductive model, works in reverse. The learners are presented with a series of words that are similar in character and share an important phonetic rule.

Example: Inductive Sound–Symbol Identification Skill
Decoding Skill—Distinguish initial "f."
The children can be presented with the following list of words and encouraged through questioning to reach a conclusion about the sound–symbol characteristic they have in common:

fit
fat
for
far
fin

It would be hoped that students would conclude that a particular sound is represented by the letter "f" when it appears in a word in which the "f" is followed by a vowel.

Example:

Decoding Skill—Distinguish the initial consonant sound "b" preceding a vowel.

Steps of Instruction:

Have the students work with partners to select and develop either an inductive or a deductive model for phonics instruction. Direct the students to take turns teaching each other, using their selected models.

Ask students, "Why could consistent use of teacher-dominated lessons discourage children's involvement in the instruction? What student behaviors might clue the teacher regarding a need for change? How might the teacher feel pressured to ignore these clues? How might a teacher resolve this?"

1. The teacher prints the following series of words on the board: boy, bat, but
2. The teacher asks the children to say the words with her or him. (This step can be modified, depending on whether these words are in the children's sight-word vocabulary.)
3. The teacher asks the children to use the words in sentences.
4. The teacher asks the children, "In what ways do the words sound alike?"
5. The teacher discusses with the children the sound represented by the letter "b."
6. The teacher asks the children to think of words that start with the "buh" sound and writes the words that are volunteered on the board.

7. The children are asked to make up sentences with the volunteered words.
8. The children are asked to identify the letter that represents the "buh" sound.
9. The teacher asks the children to tell what they know about words that begin with "b."

In this type of lesson, the teacher becomes a careful orchestrator of the children's responses and the lesson's goal. For example, if a child volunteers a word such as "broke" in Step 6, the teacher will point out that "broke" will not work because it does not have a vowel immediately after the "b." Throughout the interaction, the teacher structures the context to shape what is inferred by the children.

Comparison of the Models There are advantages and disadvantages to using each model. The deductive model is direct and concise. It is much quicker than the inductive method, and there is less risk of the children being confused or drawing incorrect inferences. The deductive model is also more tightly structured, with less opportunity that irrelevant comments or activity will occur. However, deductive lessons are usually teacher-dominated and if they are used exclusively, they can discourage the children's involvement in instruction.

The inductive model, on the other hand, encourages more active involvement from the children. Higher-level thinking is employed, and the children are more likely to retain the learning because of their participation in the problem-solving activity. However, this model takes more instruction and more teacher skill in questioning and guiding the thinking of the students.

Reading programs that use a phonics approach usually use a balance of inductive and deductive lessons, with some lessons being taught using both models. Lessons that contain more familiar or less complex skills or concepts are taught quickly using the deductive model. Lessons that focus on less familiar, more complex, or more important objectives are taught using the inductive model. As is the case in most instances, the teacher's assessment of the lesson, the students, and the learning environment are the keys to selecting the most effective models for instruction.

Have students examine basal reading texts for the number and types of instructional models used in teaching phonics.

Many parents purchase phonics workbooks for their children to use at home. What advice would you give a parent advocating this approach. Would the advice be the same for all students? All parents?

Extending Comprehension Strategies

The previous chapter covered three general strategies for comprehension development: questioning, retelling, and adapting models. Acquisition of each of these strategies mutually reinforces the others, and together, they support children's efforts to derive meaning from print. As children gain experience in the preschool years, they develop readiness for learning increasingly complex strategies. They are ready to learn new sophisticated strategies, as well as higher-level applications of known strategies. Each

An effective way to help students in reading and writing is through the use of conferencing. A teacher can assist the child and monitor the child's progress in a conference.

It is often a surprise for teachers new to teaching reading to discover that some students appear to read very well out loud but have no sense of meaning for the words they have said. Ask students, "How does this develop in early readers, and how might it be prevented? How can a teacher identify such a student?"

Have students select children's stories to read to or with the children. Have them prepare continuous and culminating questions that encourage children to use high-level thinking skills (i.e., prediction, inference, synthesis, evaluation, etc.).

new strategy is learned in relation to the context in which it is to be used—not in isolation from meaningful text—and is demonstrated and supported by the teacher.

One reason that strategies must be taught in meaningful context is to reinforce the most important concept that children can learn about print:

Printed text is supposed to make sense.

Readers who know this feel required to interact with the words they are reading by thinking about what is being communicated and what they think about what is being communicated. This interaction is fostered when children actively monitor their reading using two self-questioning processes: continuous and culminating. Teachers facilitate children's use of each process by (a) modeling the behavior in relevant situations, (b) demonstrating it in direct instruction, (c) guiding the children as they use it, and then (d) monitoring the children's independent practice.

Continuous Questioning

Continuous questioning takes place during the process of reading a passage. Students monitor their reading by asking themselves questions, by relating what they read to what they already know, or by making predictions, such as the following:

I wonder what this story is about?

I know some things about dogs.

Is that boy going to get that dog?

I think his grandma is going to give it to him.

What did I just read?

Does this make sense according to what I already know?

How does this relate to what I just read?

That dog looks just like Bobby's dog.

Does this go along with what I see in the pictures?

How does the title fit these words?

What is going to happen next? In the end?

I wonder if the character would like my dog?

Where is the mother in this story?

Begin by modeling this process when reading orally to the children. Read for a time, pausing to think and self-questioning, then continue to read the text, letting the children experience what is happening inside the teacher's head during the reading. Next, discuss this process with the children, and have them participate in making up questions to short selections that have been read out loud.

Ask students, "How can the complexity be increased for students who are highly capable learners?"

Follow this with guided practice, allowing the children to read silently and stop themselves every so often to ask a question about the text or about their own thinking. Also, reinforce reading behavior during independent reading time.

Culminating Questioning
Culminating questioning is a method of reviewing the entire selection after it has been read. It encourages the children to ponder more sophisticated questions relating to cause–effect relationships, character interactions, and story sequence.

Story Mapping, Sociograms, and Question Cards
These three activities encourage children to review the stories they have read.

Story Mapping The use of story mapping allows the child to pictorially or diagrammatically review the events of the story. Introduce the children to this strategy through the use of picture cards representing key events in a familiar story. By arranging the cards in a predicted sequence and then comparing that sequence to the one experienced while the story is being read, children learn that the cards have the potential for representing sequential order of the story.

When the children are adept at responding to prepared cards, guide them through the process of developing a class set of cards from a story

For further story mapping models and instructional techniques, see Z. Davis & M. McPherson (1989), "Story Map Instruction: A Road Map for Reading Comprehension." *The Reading Teacher, 43*(3), pp. 232–240.

that has been read previously. "Walk" the children back through the book, recalling the events. As the events are recalled, the teacher or a selected child records the event on a card. When the sequence is complete, the teacher guides the children to practice lining them up, left to right, in the order in which they appeared in the story.

You may choose to have the children create their individual sequence cards on a divided piece of paper. The children enter their representative drawings in a left-to-right, top-to-bottom order as the group agrees on each sequential event.

Stories such as "The Gingerbread Man," in which events follow a linear sequence related to the setting, are well suited to story maps. Organizing class members to make murals or bulletin boards depicting the sequence of the story is one way to show the mapping process. Create a background of sky and grass and let the children work individually or in pairs creating the setting props and the characters. Review the story to help the group to agree on the placement of the items on the board.

Story maps can also be created on overhead projectors and photocopied papers. Figure 4.2 shows an example of a child's map that could be photocopied for class use. As the teacher and the children follow the map, they retell the story. The ultimate outcome of this strategy is to encourage the children to independently develop story maps after reading selections of their choice.

Sociograms A sociogram is a graph of the relationships occurring between a character's personality or behavior and the events in the story. This strategy is very clearly described by Johnson and Louis in *Literacy through Language* (1987). Figure 4.3, from their book, illustrates the use of sociograms.

Question Cards Question cards are culminating questions created by the students when they complete the reading of a selection. The questions can cover several aspects of the reading, such as story elements (plot, character, and setting), story events, or open-ended questions involving evaluation or speculation. These questions can be written on 3- x 5-inch cards and kept in library pockets inside the books. As the children take turns reading the selections, they can select a question or two from the pocket and discuss it with the question's author.

SUPPORTED PRACTICE READING

As children are introduced to new words, they need to practice reading them in new contexts. Practice offers opportunities to use all the skills and concepts necessary for reading, as well as opportunities to enjoy the written word. By using principles of instruction and different types of

Figure 4.2 Mike, age 6, story map of "The Gingerbread Man."

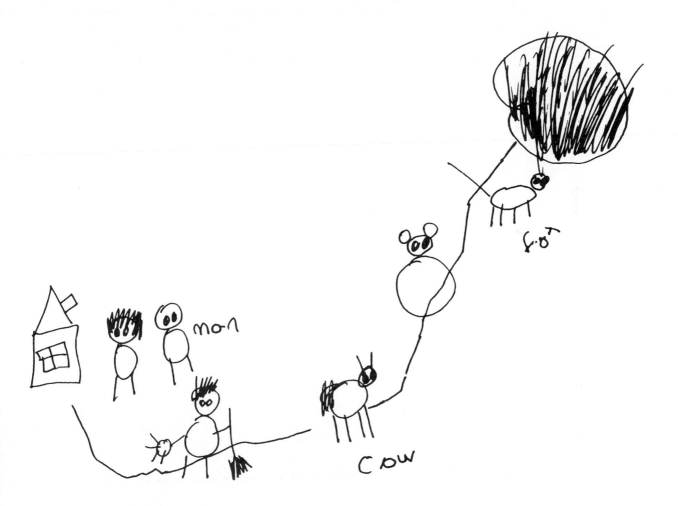

Mike, age 6
The Gingerbread Man

Figure 4.3 Johnson and Louis's description and illustration of sociograms. (a) First the names of the book's characters are arranged around that of the central character. Arrows connecting the characters show the direction of the relationships and brief statements label their nature. (b) Such diagrams can be developed by asking a series of questions and using the answers to fill out the sociogram. As the inner logic of the arrangement becomes apparent the children can suggest suitable placements for each character. (c) The level of generalization used in summarizing relationships will vary with the age of the children. Young children think in very concrete images while older ones are able to express ideas in more abstract terms. Reproduced with the permission of Heinemann Educational Books, Inc. Copyright 1987. All rights reserved.

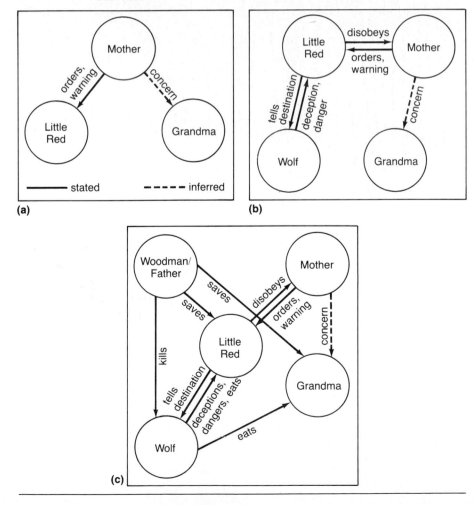

groupings, teachers support the children during these initial attempts at practice reading.

Types of Support

Support does not mean stopping the readers at every miscue and correcting them or filling in every word at which the reader hesitates. In fact, research by Goodman (1976), as well as other researchers, suggests that *all* readers have miscues in reading. Even proficient readers substitute words: for example—a reader might say "big" instead of "large." Some even think that effective readers make more miscues than poor readers. They read faster, know more synonyms for descriptive words, and can substitute freely. It is not the miscue per se that is important; rather, it is the degree or quality of the miscue that matters. Regardless, support for the reader can come in a variety of ways, most of which can be categorized into the following three categories:

1. Emotional
2. Technical
3. Peripheral

Emotional Support

Encouraging the reader to stay at a new and possibly difficult task, to take the risk of trying the unknown and to persist in the effort of learning to read are the types of behaviors to support during practice readings. Recognition and assurance can be shared in very subtle ways, such as eye contact, verbal comments, pats on the shoulder, or just being physically close to the child. It can also be shared in very public ways, such as class charts, notes to parents, or group comments.

Technical Support

Reteaching information, such as decoding, structural analysis, or story grammar, can provide the information needed to analyze, correct, and improve the reading effort. Teachers may also introduce skills or concepts to an individual reader at this time if the situation is appropriate. Technical support also includes recognizing and practicing comprehension strategies and fluency techniques. Questions about the text or discussion of the topic may help to clarify developing concepts.

Peripheral Support

There are many types of assistance children need when they are learning a new and complex task such as reading. Many important kinds of support may be overlooked because they seem so basic to meeting the children's learning needs. Making sure that the room is organized and comfortable and that desks and chairs fit the students exemplify this type of support.

The role of the teacher has changed dramatically since many of the students attended elementary school. Once the boot camp of reading instruction, the primary classroom now takes on a more nurturing, encouraging affect. The assumption is that children want to learn and, in fact, are always in the process of learning. Have the students work in pairs, taking turns role-playing a discouraged reader and a supportive teacher engaged in a reading conference.

Even encouraging parents to provide breakfast to children helps children to be ready for reading. Peripheral support comes in other ways also, such as helping the children to obtain public library cards, to find books of special interest, or to investigate a new word not found in their current reading.

Each type of support involves more than a specific set of teacher behaviors. Support is also provided through the way in which teachers carry out effective reading instruction. Teachers' attitudes of fondness, encouragement, and caring should consistently permeate interactions with children to increase children's trust and to help ensure success.

Classroom Configurations

Supported practice reading can be scheduled into the school day in a variety of classroom configurations. Some of these practice reading routines are more suited to particular times of the year, types of materials, or styles of learners. Analyze the learners' needs, and select the routines or combinations of routines that provide the most successful reading practice.

Whole-Group Practice

Ask students, "Are there other ways the whole group might engage in supported practice reading? Are there circumstances in which whole-group practice might be a disadvantage to the readers? What are they, and what criteria will you use to select this grouping?"

Written language that is familiar to all the class members can be practiced as a whole group. The children, sitting together as a large group, read from the same printed materials. The teacher leads the practice, reading from a large chart, big book, or overhead projector that is easily seen by all. Multiple copies of trade books, student-made books, and photocopied reading material also help to make the reading selection available for each child to have physical contact with the words.

Because the words and context are familiar to them, only a brief reference to the selection is necessary to get the children ready for the reading. By focusing the children's attention on the print, using a pointer, hand, or verbal cue to a picture, letter, or word referent, the teacher begins reading out loud and encourages the children to follow along. The teacher and the children practice reading the words orally together, discussing the meaning of the text and analyzing words or sections that have been a focus of instruction. The selection may be divided into several parts, and different groups within the class may read orally while the other groups follow along silently. Another option is for the teacher to read out loud, stopping intermittently to let the group fill in the next word.

Example: Experiencing the Selection

1. Display the Shared Reading Book. Read the selection aloud to the children.
2. Reread the selection aloud, having the children join in with the train sounds.
3. Read the poem chorally, either

- In unison, or by
- Assigning sections to groups or individuals.

Have the children form a train and move around the room as they read. Increase and decrease the volume of the oral reading as the train approaches and recedes. Add sound effects, such as, whistles, "All aboard," and so on. Have the children use percussion instruments to mark the beat and the rhythm pattern of the poem.

Read the poem in two groups.

One group repeats: *Click-ety-clack.*
                       Click-ety-clack.
                       Click-ety, clack-ety
                       Click-ety
                       Clack.

The other group reads the rest of the poem.

4. Have the children listen to and read along with an audio cassette tape of the poem.
5. Have the children read the selection independently. "All the children should experience the selection in the various ways. Some beginning and developing readers may be able to read the selection independently after doing the other methods" (*Impressions*, 1984, p. 128).

This type of practice has the advantage of giving everyone the opportunity to practice at one time and is, therefore, efficient in giving all the students exposure to the language as well as to the print. Each student responds at the level most beneficial to his or her development during this time. Some students will be recognizing the printed words as they say them, some may be relating the spoken word with the sight word, and others may simply be getting familiar with the oral language before they focus on the print.

Small-Group Practice

Though whole-class practice works well for many situations, there are times when it is better to have groups of only two to eight children come together to practice sharing the reading of one or more identical selections. In this setting, books with enlarged print, charts, sentence strips in pocket charts, and transparencies on the overhead projector may be used. Children can also read from multiple copies of trade books, photocopied poems, and student-made books. Rotate the groups of children so that each group comes together, either routinely or randomly, as time permits. While the teacher meets with the groups, the other students read independently, work on assigned tasks, meet with an instructional aide, or work with a volunteer.

Often, the teacher forms the group, but this does not always need to be the case, as the purpose is to share the reading process, not to go further with instruction. Thus, the groups need not be sorted according to their

Although the disadvantages of rotated groupings are covered in the next chapter, this might be a good time to explore what types of individual work would be meaningful and purposeful for those students who are working independently during small-group reading periods.

skills or knowledge, as perceived by the teacher. Within this group situation, more competent students can provide good models of reading behavior for those who may not yet have experienced a high level of success. Mixing the group membership has many other advantages as well. Much of what people become relates to their beliefs about how others perceive them. If all readers are to become good readers, then it is important that they perceive themselves as capable of becoming good readers. Children of varying reading abilities can read with their friends, can meet new friends, and can thereby avoid pigeonholing themselves as members of high, middle, or low reading groups.

Paired Practice

Children receive a great deal of support from their peers. When two children take turns reading to each other or reading in unison, they release this powerful source of instruction. Depending on the type of material being practiced, the range of students' ability levels, and the personalities of the learners, the paired-practice reading model can be sustained as briefly as a minute or two, or as long as 20 minutes or more.

For an extension of paired reading in the form of peer tutoring, see K. Topping (1989), "Peer Tutoring and Paired Reading: Combining Two Powerful Techniques." *The Reading Teacher, 42*(7), pp. 488–494.

Selection of partners may be done by the teacher or by the students themselves. Partners can practice reading small books that replicate books with enlarged print; self-made books; journals; photocopied experience stories, poems, or songs; trade books; or basal texts. The whole class or small groups may be paired off for practice reading. All pairs may be reading the same selection or a variety of selections.

Ask students, "How will you know whether individual practice reading is an effective strategy to use with a student? How can you encourage a student who finds this type of reading difficult?"

To maximize the potential for partner support, the teacher must instruct and monitor the students regarding their roles in this cooperative effort. Guidelines must be established for emphasizing the task objective, maximizing the time spent on the task, and using appropriate techniques for supporting fellow learners.

Individual Practice Reading

Daily, semiweekly, or weekly, children should spend time by themselves with familiar reading materials. The children may read quietly while looking at library books, self-made books, journals, small books that replicate class big books, or handheld copies of charts, pocket charts, or overhead transparencies, showing stories, poems, or songs. If the whole group is involved in this activity, the teacher moves about the room (a) guiding the selection of materials; (b) discussing and monitoring to check comprehension, interest, or appreciation; (c) reviewing instruction; and (d) reading with or to the children.

Have the students work in teams of four to plan a sequence of instruction that moves children through instructional, practice, and independent reading. Encourage them to use a trade book, poem, song, or traditional folktale.

Often, students practice reading individually while the teacher works with a group of children. The readers, then, are encouraged to solve reading questions on their own, using guides, charts, and resources found in the room. In addition to developing self-reliance, the children are learning to sustain themselves with reading materials, to work without disturbing others, and to read independently from the teacher.

BECOMING AN INDEPENDENT READER

> The goal of reading instruction is to foster the children's growth toward becoming independent readers.

An *independent reader* not only reads with little or no assistance, but also, more significantly, chooses to read because reading offers a source of pleasure. The instructional implications here are that children find the process of reading internally motivating and that frustration involved in learning to read is proportionately less than the rewards of being involved in the process of learning to read. This translates into instructional interludes during which children see the value of their experiences and feel involved meaningfully in the process.

Creating Transitions to Independent Reading

The teacher is constantly connecting reading instruction, practice reading, and independent reading, thereby enabling the children to connect instructional applications of reading to their own enjoyment of their developing reading ability. The transition from one type of reading to the other is facilitated by (a) the careful planning of the content and sequence of instruction, (b) the routine allowance of free time for the children to interact with reading materials, and (c) the variety of materials available for student selection. The planning of the content and sequence of instruction, as well as the scheduling of time for independent reading, is covered elsewhere in this volume. The present section addresses the selection and presentation of independent and transitional reading materials.

Transitional Reading Materials

The reading materials available for the children to read independently are selected on the basis of (a) the students' familiarity with the sight words in the texts, (b) the students' interest in the text content, and (c) the quality of semantic and structural cuing available in the text. In other words, select materials for the emerging independent reader that create the highest probability for the children's success and for their enjoyment of their success.

If the children have been involved in stories and poems relating to the instructional theme of insects, the teacher searches for materials that connect with basic vocabulary experienced in the instructional and practice readings. These selections could take the form of

1. Songs and poems
2. Related nonfiction texts
3. Related storybooks

Songs and Poems Children may be familiar with many poems and songs, either in their present forms (such as "The Ants Go Marching") or in an adapted form (such as "A Little Bug"). These brief verses give the children background knowledge to use as they begin reading on their own. If the sight word fails to come to mind immediately, the context of the language and the memory of the pattern will facilitate the child's reading.

The Ants Go Marching
The ants go marching one by one.
Hurrah! Hurrah!
The ants go marching one by one.
Hurrah! Hurrah!
The little one stopped to suck his thumb
And they all go marching down into the ground
To get out of the rain.

Traditional

A Little Bug
A little bug
A bigger bug
A great big bug I see
Now, count the bugsies,
1, 2, 3.

Traditional

Have students survey a selection of children's books, selecting those that would facilitate a child's move to reading independently. Ask them to include books that offer content-area information.

Related Nonfiction Texts Many easy-to-read books are available to support the children's early desire to read on their own. These books can be fictional or developed from content information. An example of a commercial published series dealing with content information is the "See How It Grows" series by Modern Curriculum Press (Nash, 1983). These child-sized paperbacks cover science topics often presented in the primary grades. In the example of materials relating to the study of insects, the teacher could select one or multiple copies of *The Butterfly* (Nash, 1983). The first page of the book gives a list of the key vocabulary words next to a picture representing that word. The next pages use a simplified text to develop the concept of the life cycle of the butterfly. The text is very simply and accurately reflected in the illustrations (see Figure 4.4).

Figure 4.4 Sample pages from *The Butterfly*, by Pamela Nash, from the "See How It Grows" series, copyright © 1983 by Modern Curriculum Press. Reproduced with the permission of Modern Curriculum Press, Inc.

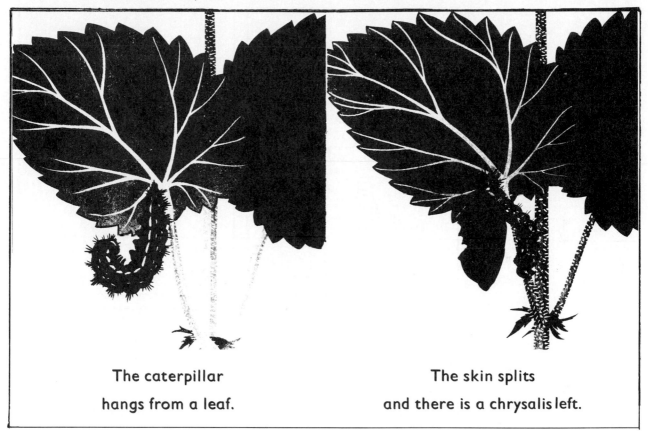

The caterpillar

hangs from a leaf.

The skin splits

and there is a chrysalis left.

The butterfly	Title
See the butterflies.	page 1
The butterfly lays eggs on a leaf.	page 2
Caterpillars hatch from the eggs.	page 3
The little caterpillars eat the leaves. . . .	

Another type of easy-to-read book can be generated from the children's own classroom or home experiences (see Figure 4.5). These books can take the form of framing sentences in which children complete the sentences with words of their choice. Books can be class books, with one sentence coming from each student, or they can be collections of several sentences from one student (e.g., Figure 4.5). The illustrations can be (a) drawings made by the children involved, (b) photographs taken to

Figure 4.5   An easy-to-read book written and illustrated by a child. The child was provided with a series of framing sentences to complete and compile in order to form the book.

represent the text, or (c) magazine pictures cut specifically for this purpose.

Related Storybooks Picture books of normal story-reading length should remain available to the children. Because emerging readers are in transition, they still need to imitate the reading of longer, more complex selections. They may be identifying enough of the words from sight, through context cuing, and from memory if they are familiar with the book that they are actually reading. It is important to keep the children immersed in valuable literature so that as their reading experiences grow, they are encouraged to sustain their efforts.

Have students draw a design for a library corner or center. Ask them to list the furniture, materials, and resources they have included, and write a rationale for their inclusion.

Library Corner

The classroom reading or library corner offers the children an opportunity to select their reading materials in an informal setting. This space in the room should contain comfortable, soft seating areas, stuffed animals, pillows, and a soft floor covering. The walls should be attractively and invitingly decorated with posters, pictures, and student art work. The children should be encouraged to select and read the materials available in this center during regularly scheduled times of the school day.

Avoid having numerous rules and regulations for the library corner. Excessive regulation makes it difficult for children to gain access to it and makes it a less inviting place to be. It is also important to design the school day to make access possible for all students, regardless of whether they have finished assigned work, misbehaved in an unrelated area, or found it difficult to select a book independently. When the rules for the library corner are consistent with other classroom rules, the children are already aware of the consistent expectations and need not learn an additional list of dos and don'ts.

Strategies for Encouraging Independent Reading

While the children are in the process of acquiring sight words and learning word-identification skills, they are also encouraged to model independent reading behavior. Several situations elicit this behavior in a way that the children perceive as rewarding. Three such strategies for encouraging this independent reading behavior are (1) sustained silent reading (SSR), independent classroom reading, and integrated independent reading.

Variations of SSR may include either journal writing that reflects a response to the text or oral retelling or sharing with a partner at the end of the reading.

Sustained Silent Reading—SSR

Planned, whole-group, silent reading periods are the foundation for SSR. The teacher directs this process by introducing the children to this reading routine in small increments of time and gradually increasing the time as the children learn to focus their attention on their reading material for longer periods. After self-selecting a book to "read," younger or inexperienced children are encouraged to attend to that text for about 3–5 minutes. This is expected to be a silent time, with the exception of the quiet reading sounds some children make as they read aloud to themselves. As the children learn to attend, the time is increased. Older or more experienced students may read for 10–15 minutes. Every person in the room is expected to have a book or other reading material to look at and to attend only to that text. Neither teacher nor children interact with each other, and no one moves around the room.

Independent Classroom Reading

There are many times during the day when the children can be responsible for the use of their time; such as (a) between one teacher-directed activity and another, (b) after independent assignments have been completed, or (c) during learning-center or individual work times. Such times offer the children opportunities to self-select their work. Encourage the children to keep selected books in their desks, both for transitions lasting a few minutes, and for independent work time options. Other reading material would be available for the children in the classroom library corner or reading center.

Children in a classroom could be observed performing a variety of tasks during reading time. Some children might be involved in directed activities with the teacher; some children might be working on writing- or learning-center activities, and some may be reading independently from materials they have chosen. The teacher may choose to initiate some controls over the frequency or amount the children read, by using goal setting and reading graphs or other types of motivational activities. The responsibility for the independent reading is shared by the teacher and the students; both have a role in the process.

Integrated Independent Reading

Some classrooms are organized around thematic projects that are initiated by either the teacher or the students. These projects are used to facilitate students' learning and usually follow a problem-solving format. The student selects a project, such as building a model airport, sewing a pillow, constructing a boat, or researching an animal. The teacher acts as a process monitor, coordinator, and facilitator in the children's progress toward their projects' goals. Within this process, the teacher creates and implements ways for children to experience math, reading, writing, science, and social studies in an integrated way related to the projects. Independent reading in this setting usually relates to the children's project goal. This does not preclude reading for entertainment, as either of the two aforementioned independent reading strategies can be supplemental to this one.

This strategy is the most student-driven of the strategies mentioned. It would be typical to observe children involved in integrated independent reading using many different parts of the classroom in a variety of ways. Some children may be at an interest center where an animal is available for observation. Several picture books, easy-to-read books, and science books relating to that animal might be neatly arranged for the children's investigation. Drawing paper, writing paper, and writing tools might suggest recording activity, as well as samples of previous students' work. Clay, construction paper, and other supplies are available in the art area for other types of representation of the students' acquired information. As the project is completed, the students report orally or in writing the process and content of the projects.

Another group of children may be involved in a group process in which their collective goal is to create a farm. Research would be initiated

---

Margin notes:

Have students list the necessary conditions for making this strategy successful. Some children may find it difficult to manage themselves in this setting. Ask students to describe how the teacher can help these children to become successful.

Ask students to develop projects from selected folktales that could be used as model projects for children. Ask students, "What materials do they anticipate the children might need? How would they introduce the concept of a project?"

in the library and continued in the classroom. Key vocabulary words would be listed and defined either by a picture or by other words. Diagrams and processes are recorded, and plans are carried out. The children's goal, to have a farm with which to play, is the main motivating factor for the reading.

Individual children may also select projects. These individual projects may focus on the comparison of characters, plots, or types of writing; puppet plays may be developed, board games created, or murals painted. Options are open, with the specific goal setting and the choice of readings often guided by the teacher acting as a resource person. Independent reading is an expected and necessary outcome of membership in the project-oriented classroom environment.

PART II

Integrating Reading and Writing

Writing as an Integrative Activity

When children write, they call into play all they know or think they know about the language—structurally, phonetically, and semantically. Writing causes them to think, to apply, to synthesize, to evaluate, to create, to problem solve, to integrate all that they know and know how to do with language. They practice constructing words, sentences, paragraphs, and stories, using the models they have acquired, and experimenting with solutions to problems they have yet to experience. Vocabulary, old and new, is worked and reworked to express their ideas and to share the world from their point of view. In terms of offering opportunity for developing the ability to understand written language, student writing is probably the most comprehensive tool teachers have. Journals, adaptations from models, and posters are three avenues of writing that work particularly well with students.

Journal Writing

Journals are booklets of blank paper that the children use for recording their thoughts and ideas. Used on a daily basis, the children go beyond learning the skills of writing to the habit of using writing as tool for organizing and thinking about their experiences. Teachers select one or more of the following instructional uses of student journals:

- *Recording* is the children's activity of writing in the journal what is on their mind. This writing is private. Only the selections the

Adopt a fellow instructor's classroom as pen pals for your students. Have the students keep a journal of the interactions with their pen pal and their insights on the writing process.

student chooses are read by the teacher or by other children. Some children may elect to read their writing to other individuals or to the group. The main teaching role is to motivate the writing and to support it by (a) giving children words, (b) commenting appropriately when asked, and (c) consistently respecting the approximations of the beginning writer.

- *Interactive writing* occurs when the teacher and the student use the journal for communicating with each other. The student writes, and the teacher responds to the writing with thoughts, ideas, and related experiences. Teacher comments do not reflect evaluation of the writing skill, the content, or the quality of the children's thinking. It is a written, nonjudgmental discussion. In later grades, this is referred to as "journal dialoguing," with the teacher carrying on a written dialogue with the student via the journal.

Instructive writing also includes character development, description of setting, and literary techniques such as repetition and so forth.

- *Instructive writing* is another way to use the journal format. As an outcome of instruction, the children use the journal as a collection of their guided and independent practice responses. Teachers may assign work to be completed or may actively use the children's writing as a source for teaching one of the writing processes, such as revision.

ADAPTATIONS FROM MODELS

Though journals clearly serve a wide range of writing purposes, topics, and abilities, there may be times when a particular written form may be desirable. At such times, teachers may provide models for the children to work from. These models are often taken from poems or songs. Once the children have learned the original language, delete selected words, and brainstorm with the children the different words that could be substituted (like cloze sentences). This pattern is then printed on a chart or chalkboard, with a space for the child-selected word. The children can copy the displayed written words and insert their own words as they do so.

A caution relating to the use of frame sentences: Some children become dependent on that form of writing and limit their writing to them or their exploration to various forms of frames. Encouragement of these writers means accepting every attempt they make at writing independently and perhaps a short-term increase in taking dictation from them.

This model may consist of a single sentence or a series of sentences that are identical. These framing sentences form a pattern that the children are encouraged to repeat in their writing. McCracken and McCracken (1979) offer a variety of examples, such as the following in their book, *Reading, Writing, and Language:*

I play with _____ .
I play on _____ .

I can _____ .
I can't _____ .

I like _____ .
I don't like _____ .

POSTERS

Another form of communicating through writing is developed by encouraging the children to create posters based on topics, themes, or ideas. Advertisements for a community meal based on the folktale "Stone Soup," a wanted poster describing the physical characteristics and deeds of the wolf from "Little Red Ridinghood," or a labeled catalogue of items available for sale from the bakery of the "Little Red Hen" are example classroom uses of this type of written communication.

PART III
A MENU OF READING METHODS

It is accepted that beginning readers can be taught decoding skills and strategies effectively through a variety of different approaches. Some learners appear to benefit more than others from a particular approach. However, no one method works best with all learners all the time. Even the most effective learner tires of instruction that is lacking in variety or that is not flexible enough to accommodate individual factors that can surface on any given day at school. This text, in this and other chapters, presents what the authors believe is the best of what works, by offering an integrated language model for literacy instruction. Summaries of the following approaches, referred to by name, are presented as added information:

- Basal reader approach
- Language-experience approach
- Literature-based approach
- Whole-language approach

BASAL READER APPROACH

Most teachers in the primary grades use a basal reading series as the core of the reading program. The basal series determines the scope and sequence of the decoding skills to be taught and suggests an instructional approach for every lesson, usually in some detail.

Although different basal programs employ somewhat different approaches to instruction, most of the mainstream publishers of reading programs have become increasingly alike. There are some exceptions. A few have incorporated ideas consistent with a whole-language approach and a few still advocate a phonics approach, but publishers of basal

Have the students take a cooperative learning approach to reviewing the menu of reading methods. Working in teams, the students select a reading method and develop a presentation to the other teams outlining key concepts, rationale, research, and examples. The whole class conclusion to this project is a graph delineating the strengths and weaknesses of each of the methods in terms of teacher and student needs.

readers generally advocate a mix of deductive and inductive instruction, created from a series of parts rather than the whole of reading.

The instructional guides provided by the basal reading series usually consist of highly structured and finely detailed instructions for presenting and using the materials with the children. This degree of structure and detail has both advantages and disadvantages. The teacher's preparation time is reduced; instruction is more consistent across differing teachers and classes; and coverage of the entire range of skills and concepts is more likely to take place via direct instruction.

Unfortunately, such detailed and consistent format can also discourage the variety and flexibility necessary for keeping a classroom interesting on a day-to-day basis. The lack of alternative lesson formats or even alternative scenarios within a lesson is also a weakness. Typically, the same lesson plan format and instructional model is employed for all skills, all concepts, and all forms of literature.

Critics of basals often suggest that basals also do not encourage the incorporation of writing and oral language as effectively as they might. Supporters, however, indicate that basals have improved significantly over the recent past in incorporating high-quality literature, as well as oral language and writing activities. Further, it is the responsibility of the teacher to use the teacher's edition of the basal text wisely. The materials are intended to be directional (pointing the way) and not directive (defining the path) in character. Effective teachers can easily incorporate important elements of oral language and writing into the lessons when they perceive themselves as being the leaders and the materials as being supportive of their instructional objectives.

LANGUAGE-EXPERIENCE APPROACH (LEA)

Roach Van Allen, a reading and language arts educator, credits the label "language experience approach" to curriculum work done in the late 1950s and early 1960s in southern California, where researchers searched for the important early language experiences that support most significantly reading development in the young learner (Van Allen & Allen, 1970; Lee & Van Allen, 1963). The label "language-experience approach" (LEA) then came to be used to describe a school of thought for beginning reading instruction based on the techniques and strategies (a) that derive from the natural language environment of the child, and (b) that usually incorporate oral language, literature, and writing.

Van Allen outlines 20 different language experiences that are important to the beginning and developing reader:

1. *Sharing experiences*
2. *Discussing experiences*

3. *Listening to stories*
4. *Telling stories*
5. *Dictating words, sentences, and stories*
6. *Writing independently*
7. *Writing individual books*
8. *Conceptualizing relationships between speaking, writing, and reading*
9. *Expanding vocabulary*
10. *Reading a variety of symbols*
11. *Developing awareness of common vocabulary*
12. *Improving writing style and form*
13. *Studying words*
14. *Reading whole stories and books*
15. *Using a variety of resources*
16. *Comprehending what is read*
17. *Summarizing*
18. *Organizing ideas and information*
19. *Integrating and assimilating ideas*
20. *Reading critically*

R. Van Allen & C. Allen, *Language Experiences in Reading,* 1970

Although these elements are used in one fashion or another by most LEA supporters, the specifics of one LEA can differ considerably from another. For example, the LEA of Marlene and Bob McCracken (*Reading Is Only the Tiger's Tail; Stories, Songs and Poetry to Teach Reading and Writing,* et al.) is highly patterned and structured. Other approaches by other educators are often more open and less structured.

Here is a fairly typical LEA strategy:

1. The teacher provides a stimulus for discussion or introduces a topic that is of interest to and within the experience of the child.
2. A child then uses the teacher's account as a model and dictates a story to the teacher. The teacher records it on the board or another large surface exactly as it was dictated.
3. When completed, the teacher reads the story back to the child and asks for verification of its accuracy.
4. The child thinks of a title, and it is written above the story.
5. The story is transcribed onto paper (the original can be printed on newsprint on an easel initially, if desired).
6. The child illustrates the story and explains his or her illustration to the class.
7. The following day, the child reads the story alone again, underlining known words from step #6. Some words will have two lines under them at this point.
8. The child reads the story to the teacher. Words the child knows are then placed on individual cards, with the date and the story

indicated on the back of the cards. These become part of the child's "word bank."

9. The word bank is used for teaching a variety of phonics, structural analysis, and vocabulary building skills, such as the following:
   a. Sounds with short "a" are grouped; other sound-alike cards are grouped.
   b. Word-recognition contests are held.
   c. Words in the word bank are used in writing new stories.
   d. The child searches for his or her words in new stories.
   e. Words are alphabetized.
   f. The child draws pictures to go with words.
   g. Word cards are shared with other classmates.
10. Books (class big books and/or individual small books) are made from the children's stories.

Language experience approaches generally assume that the most effective way to teach beginning reading is to build from the language the child brings to the classroom. The children's language, oral and written, drives the instruction.

LITERATURE-BASED APPROACH

A literature-based reading program is derived from the use of children's literature as the medium from which reading instruction is given. Although many educators advocate trade books as the basic content of the reading program, with all reading instruction deriving from complete literary works, it is probably safe to say that most see literature as a significant supplement to a basal reading program or a program organized around some other basic materials. Some textbook publishers are developing their own literature collections as literature readers. These readers are supported with teacher's guides and are often correlated with a traditional basal text.

Literature-based approaches to reading instruction vary considerably in methodology. However, most include the following elements:

1. Initial instruction is in shared reading with big books, which contain traditional easy stories that many of the children already know by heart. The teacher reads aloud, with the children following as he or she points out the words being read. Usually, there is no attempt to isolate or break down any of the words or sentence elements in this initial reading; rather, the focus is on the rhythm and pattern of the story.

   Books with patterned sentences and stories, as well as other features that make them highly predictable, are important to the beginning reader. The repeated patterns and plots make the development of hypothesizing and predicting skills easier to acquire and master.

2. Although some authorities who advocate the literature-based approach see no need to dwell on instruction in phonics or in teaching sight-word vocabulary, many do recognize these as important aspects of reading instruction. Suggestions include using cloze techniques or using a pocket chart for identifying words taken from the text.

3. Children engage in writing activities, using the literature as models for the instruction. The children's stories are then published and shared with classmates. Sometimes, the writing is related to a theme developed from the literature and is used as a tool for the children to explore their thoughts and feelings.

4. Often, the children are encouraged to keep a journal of their thoughts and ideas as they read the literature selection. The teacher or other students may react to this writing by writing their ideas back to the student.

This approach to reading instruction has several advantages: Literature provides a powerful motivating force for engaging children in reading and the language, and language structures of literature are more natural than those typically found in reading primers. Children also gain a sense of story from literature, which forms a foundation for comprehension of fiction text.

Literature also provides an effective vehicle for communicating with parents of young children. The parents are more comfortable sharing a story with children than becoming involved in the technical and laborious task of teaching isolated skills. The relationship between a child and a parent can develop as a result of the shared literature, through the opportunities for oral interaction and enjoyment. Thus, the child learns not only to understand what is read, but also to enjoy it.

WHOLE-LANGUAGE APPROACH

Many educators support a whole-language approach to the teaching of reading, including the development of word-identification skills. In many ways, this approach is closely related to the language-experience and the literature-based approaches to reading instruction.

The basic underlying assumptions of the whole language approach are

1. The language of the child is the critical base for all reading instruction. Instruction methodologies should build from this language base and incorporate the language of the child in all facets of beginning reading instruction. It is like an LEA in this respect. Initial reading instruction is most effective when it focuses on the

child's language rather than a contrived language with controlled vocabulary, such as in the stories in the preprimers and primers of basal reading programs.

2. Language is used primarily for communication, and meaning is central to all language development. Therefore, reading skills should be taught in a meaningful language-using context for purposes that are significant to the child.

3. All of the language-consuming and -producing skills and processes (i.e., speaking, listening, reading, and writing) are interrelated. They are all important. Here, the whole-language approach probably differs somewhat from a literature-based approach, in that it would place a value on high-quality literature, but it would not give it any higher priority than the other language skills and processes in initial reading instruction.

4. Early writing development is not just encouraged by specifically incorporating it into reading instruction—Writing is given major emphasis. At least as much as any other approach, if not more than any other, the whole-language approach to reading uses writing as a dominant instructional component.

5. Instruction for individual skills and processes of reading are presented in relation to the context in which they can be discovered. Reading instruction is driven by the desire to have children derive meaning from print.

Summary of Reading Methods

Having examined the most salient features of several of the most easily identifiable approaches to reading, it is important to recognize that many features found in one may be found in others. Very few teachers actually teach reading or even specific reading skills strictly by one approach. Given that the majority of schools use basal programs, it is very likely that selected components and ideas from the approaches other than the basal are used in typical classroom reading instruction. All effective approaches to teaching reading share the following key features:

1. Word-identification skills should be taught in a classroom context that both values the language of the children and reflects a language-rich environment. Oral language activities are tied to nearly all of the reading instruction, and comprehension is the acknowledged purpose for learning word-identification skills.

2. Sound–symbol relationships are taught within the larger context of words, sentences, paragraphs, and stories.

3. Writing activities are an integrated and necessary part of the reading program. The children are involved daily in meaningful writing.
4. The teacher mixes and matches the materials and techniques selected for instruction, controlling the approaches and their role in a given lesson.

HIGHLIGHTS

1. Reading instruction in the primary grades takes three forms: instructional reading, practice reading, and pleasure reading. Each type of reading should be included in a balanced reading program.
2. Children learn sight words by experiencing them in meaningful contexts. The teacher facilitates this learning by providing the children with opportunities to participate in choral reading and guided writing activities.
3. Teachers can use either deductive or inductive strategies for presenting new vocabulary words before reading a selection. Deductive strategies are more efficient, and inductive ones encourage higher-level thinking.
4. Children use structural cuing to make sense of print. They use their knowledge of language structure and word and sentence patterns to predict and confirm what the print means.
5. Phonics instruction should take place only within the context of meaningful language. Sound–symbol relationships are more efficiently and effectively learned when the language is meaningful.
6. Two effective strategies for increasing comprehension are continuous questioning and culminating questioning. The teacher facilitates the children's knowledge of each process by modeling and demonstrating the behavior and by guiding and monitoring the children's practice of it.
7. The teacher uses a variety of grouping strategies to provide supported and independent reading opportunities. The students may read independently, with peers, in small groups, or in a large-group setting.
8. Teachers use a variety of strategies and materials selected from several approaches when developing an effective reading program. The teacher is seen as the driver of the program, actively making decisions that support the children's reading needs.

REINFORCEMENT ACTIVITIES

1. Select a fingerplay, poem, or song to use in teaching sight words. Select the sight word or words for instruction, and list the steps in the instruction.
2. Write a script for teaching a word skill or a phonics skill using a deductive instructional strategy. Repeat the process using an inductive strategy. Compare and contrast the strategies.
3. Discuss three ways you could provide opportunities for children to develop the visual and auditory skills that are prerequisites to reading acquisition.
4. Design a comprehension lesson using continuous and culminating questioning techniques. List the types of questions that would be asked, how they would be developed, and how they would be answered.
5. Select three different types of children's stories and create story maps from their plots. Analyze the pattern of each of these maps, and discuss how you would use this information for reading instruction.
6. Create a weekly reading schedule, using the different types of reading groupings with a variety of formats (i.e., instructional, supported, and pleasure).
7. Describe the type of reading approach you would select for classroom use. Compare it to the approaches described in this chapter.
8. Create a poster showing the most significant information about teaching beginning reading.

ADDITIONAL PROJECTS

1. Review several different basal texts at the same grade level. List the basic components of each program. Compare the components of the instruction reading lesson.
2. Visit teachers who teach from different basal texts. Compare their actual instruction to the instruction advocated in the teacher's edition. Discuss with the teacher the types of instructional decisions that are made before and during the reading lesson that may be different than those suggested in the text.
3. Listen to several different beginning readers talk about the stories they are reading. Listen to them read, and compare their strengths as readers.
4. Select stories found in a basal text and in several children's trade books. Compare these stories for length and complexity of sentence, sophistication of language, and type of vocabulary. Predict

which stories will hold the interest of the students. Test your prediction with students from a primary-grade classroom.

5. Design writing activities that would precede and follow a story from children's literature. Suggest how you might adapt these activities for students with differing abilities.

REFERENCES

Alvermann, D., Bridge, C., Schmitt, B., Searfoss, L., Winograd, P., & Bartram, B. (1989). *The Mouse in the House* (Teacher's. ed.). Lexington, MA: Heath.

Booth, J., Booth, D., Pauli, W., & Phenix, J. (1984). *Fly Away Home: Teacher's Resource Book.* Toronto, Canada: Holt, Rinehart and Winston.

Brown, M. (1952). *Where Have You Been?* New York: Scholastic Book Services.

Goodman, K. (1976). Behind the Eye: What happens in reading. In H. Singer & R. B. Ruddell (Eds.), *Theoretical Models and Processes of Reading.* Newark, DE: IRA.

Impressions (1984). Toronto, Canada: Holt, Rinehart and Winston of Canada.

Johnson, T., & Louis, D. (1987). *Literacy Through Literature.* Portsmouth, NH: Heinemann Educational Books.

Klein, M. (1988). *Teaching Reading Comprehension and Vocabulary.* Englewood Cliffs, NJ: Prentice Hall.

Lee, D., & Van Allen, R. (1963). *Learning to Read Through Experience.* New York: Meredith Publishing.

McCracken, M., & McCracken, R. (1979). *Reading, Writing and Language.* Winnipeg, Canada: Peguis Publishers.

McCracken, R., & McCracken, M. (1972). *Reading Is Only the Tiger's Tail.* San Rafael, CA: Leswing Press.

McCracken, R., & McCracken, M. (1986). *Stories, Songs and Poetry to Teach Reading and Writing.* Chicago: American Library Association.

Nash, P. (1983). *The Butterfly* (in the "See How It Grows" series). Cleveland, OH: Modern Curriculum Press.

Pepper, F. (Ed.). (1984). *Handbook of 20th Century Quotations.* London, England: Sphere Books, Ltd.

Van Allen, R., & Allen, C. (1970). *Language Experience in Reading.* Chicago, IL: Encyclopedia Britannica Press.

ADDITIONAL RESOURCES

Anderson, R., Anderson, C., Heibert, E., Scott, J., & Wilkinson, I. (1984). *A Nation of Readers: The Report of the Commission on Reading.* Washington, DC: National Institute of Education.

Applebee, A. (1978). *The Child's Concept of Story.* Chicago: University of Chicago Press.

Cambourne, B. (1988). *The Whole Story.* Sydney, Australia: Ashton Scholastic.

Darrow, H., & Howes, V. (1960). *Approaches to Individualized Reading.* New York: Appleton-Century-Crofts.

Goodman, K. (1986). *What's Whole in Whole Language.* Ontario, Canada: Scholastic Book Services.

Graves, M. (1985). *A Word Is a Word . . . Or Is It?* Ontario, Canada: Scholastic Book Services.

Holdaway, D. (1980). *Independence in Reading.* Sydney, Australia: Ashton Scholastic.

Johnson, T., & Louis, D. (1990). *Bringing It All Together.* Portsmouth, NH: Heinemann Educational Books.

Johnson, T., & Louis, D. (1987). *Literacy Through Literature.* Portsmouth, NH: Heinemann Educational Books.

Parsons, L. (1990). *Response Journals.* Ontario, Canada: Pembroke Publishers.

Weaver, C. (1988). *Reading Process and Practice.* Portsmouth, NH: Heinemann Educational Books.

PLANNING AND ORGANIZING INSTRUCTION FOR THE PRIMARY GRADES

There are only two qualities in the world, efficiency and inefficiency; and only two sorts of people, the efficient and inefficient.

George Bernard Shaw, *John Bull's Other Island,* **1904**

PREVIEW

Reading is a holistic process that depends on relationships such as those between reading and events, people, and things. In addition to these, there are relationships within the language itself, such as among linguistic elements. Initially, children's motivation to discover these relationships comes from their curiosity about the reading abilities they observe in adults. The sustaining motivation results from the intellectual satisfaction of mastery: gaining an ability, exercising the intellect, and becoming increasingly independent. Instruction activating the literacy process in the classroom draws from emotions and events experienced by the children outside the classroom.

This chapter presents systems and strategies for planning an instructional environment that encourages children's reading development. It is organized into two general sections covering the elements of effective instruction. These sections are "Organizing and Managing the Instructional Setting" and "Planning and Implementing the Instructional Process."

It is important for the students to keep in mind that children have been active learners before they walked through the classroom door. Equally important is the concept that what has been experienced previously serves as a foundation for the students' future learning. Using knowledge about children in creating the school learning environment will make that environment more effective.

FOCUS QUESTIONS

Think about the following questions as you read this chapter:

1. What elements does the teacher take into consideration when designing the classroom environment?

2. What types of organizational and management systems do teachers use to help them prepare for and provide instruction?
3. How does the teacher plan for the effective integration of the language arts?

ORGANIZING AND MANAGING THE INSTRUCTIONAL SETTING

Teaching is built on a foundation of organizational systems that can make living together in a classroom a pleasant, relaxing experience. Like most other people, teachers create schedules, routines, and systems for living and working in their environment; in particular, teachers develop organized systems for working with students at school. Every part of the classroom environment has some effect on the learning that takes place there. Careful planning and implementation of these systems creates a foundation for effective instruction.

Organizing the Environment

The thoughtful arrangement of classroom furniture and materials can significantly support the instruction by creating traffic patterns and work areas that increase the amount of time spent on tasks by diminishing interruptions and distractions. Each classroom comes with its own characteristics that may affect the room arrangement and the type of instruction provided. The unique placements of electrical outlets, bulletin boards, and closet doors can determine the placement of the listening center, the teacher's desk, and the way the classroom desks are arranged. Available classroom furniture can determine how the desks are arranged, where the children store their materials, and the types of centers that are created. All of these elements contribute to the environment, yet they are usually beyond the control of the teacher. Resourcefulness becomes the key element that the teacher can control to have the greatest effect on developing a positive, productive classroom environment.

Arranging the Furniture
The types of activities and instruction that make up the school day determine the types of spaces for which teachers need to plan. The room arrangement must allow for times when information is presented to the

Let the students measure samples of the paper sizes used at a particular grade level and then compare it to the table sizes recommended for a classroom. How many students can work at a 24" x 48" table using 12" x 18" paper and needing scissors, paste, and crayons? It is important for the students to realize that a table recommended to seat four children is actually suitable for only two children in certain circumstances.

class as a whole group. Will that be done when the children are in their desk chairs, or will they sit on the carpet as a group? It must allow for times when the children will be working in different areas of the room. Will these be designated learning centers, or will they be work spaces to which the children will take their work? How many students must be accommodated in each of the spaces available? Will the students keep their supplies with them, or will there be a central supply from which they will gather supplies as they are needed?

After assessing the needs, create a list of the priorities desired in the learning space. Such a list may look like this:

1. Large group seating area:

Clear vision of the chalkboard from all tables
Cluster seating for cooperative groupings
Near electrical outlet for record player
Informal story listening area
Chart rack
Calendar and attendance chart

2. Supplies and materials:

Port for shared pencils, crayons, scissors
Shared storage for gym shoes
Shelves for shared texts, paper, and materials

3. Individual work areas:

Library corner
Art center with easel
Listening center
Typewriter or computer table

4. Small-group work area:

Shelves for textbooks
Table and chairs
File cabinet
Optional: outlet, bulletin board

5. Other:

Bulletin board space for students
Display space for students' work
File for take-home or unfinished papers

With this list in mind, the teacher can make a diagram of the room and begin to play with configurations. The final plan meets the teacher's own valued criteria, creates a traffic flow pattern that minimizes the disruption of students, and provides easy access to centrally located supplies. Figures 5.1 and 5.2 illustrate a kindergarten and a primary-grade classroom, respectively.

Setting Up Individual Work Areas and Centers

Designating a space where either an individual child or two to four children can work away from the central activity of the large group challenges a teacher's creativity. Somewhat formal settings can be designated by a small table with chairs, a set of materials with instructions listed on a bulletin board or a table display, and a specific product or activity expected from the students. Less-formal work areas are created by using small carpet samples and pillows on the floor spaces between cabinets, behind room dividers or in classroom corners. In formal or informal centers, the instructional materials provided may be either structured or unstructured.

When creating an individual work space, promote a successful experience for the children by

1. Setting up the space away from a traffic area
2. Organizing the materials to be easily accessible and easily cleaned up
3. Having all the necessary materials at the center
4. Clearly designating the number of children who may use the center at one time
5. Using both pictures and words to list directions
6. Teaching the children a work routine

Planning the Daily Schedule

An important element of successful literacy experiences is a carefully organized daily schedule. A daily schedule maximizes the teacher's use of the time available in the school day for the selected instructional strategies and grouping configurations. Effective literacy instruction requires the flexibility to arrange instruction for a single daily time slot and for instruction that pervades the entire daily routine. Base decisions regarding instructional routines on consideration for the child's physical, emotional, social, and intellectual needs.

Physical

a. Amount of time sitting still
b. Amount of time moving
c. Large-muscle versus small-muscle exercise

Organizing supplies and materials goes beyond placing them in a space that is available to all without causing disruption as they are accessed. Visual cues such as consistent symbols for crayons, pencils, paste, and scissors will help them locate what they need while fostering the concept of symbolization. Having open containers that are safe and easy for small hands to carry will promote independence while facilitating instruction.

Use the classroom in which you meet with your students as a model for an elementary classroom, and have the students design a floor plan to meet their newly defined needs. What would they have to change (i.e., height of chalkboards, tables, sink, etc.)?

Figure 5.1   Diagram of a possible arrangement for a kindergarten classroom.

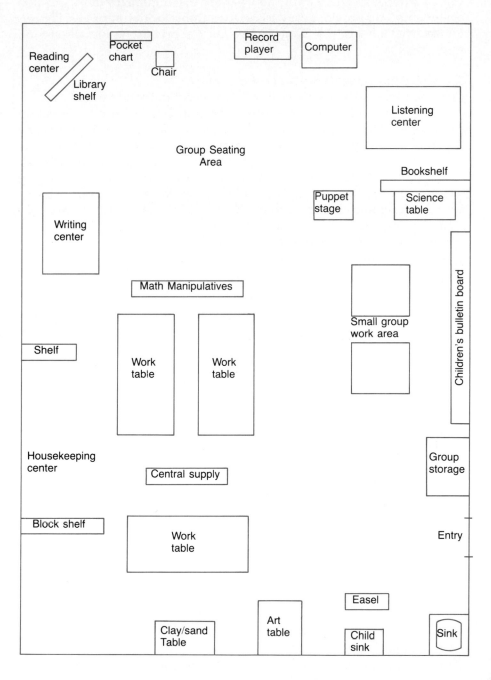

Figure 5.2 Diagram of a possible arrangement for a primary-grade classroom.

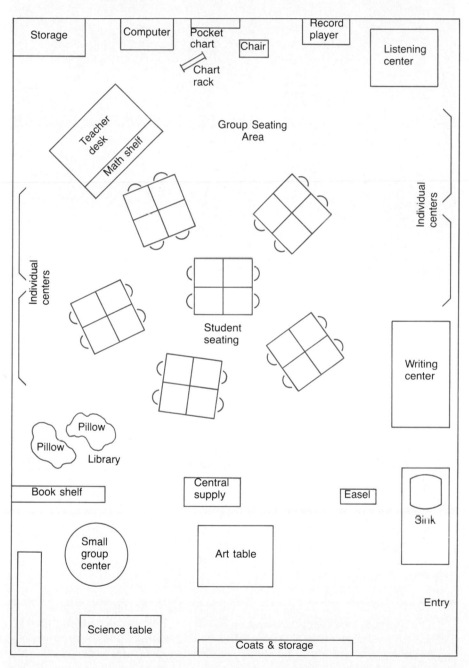

Desks grouped together in clusters like these allow for many different instructional approaches with children. Children can work together, in pairs, or individually.

Social

a. Amount of time working with peers
b. Amount of time working with teacher
c Amount of time working with other adults and older or younger students
d. Amount of time working independently

Emotional

a. Amount of self-directed exploration
b. Amount of teacher-directed instruction

Intellectual

a. Listening time versus talking time
b. Open-ended exploration versus structured instruction
c. Input versus practice

The Daily Routine

Building a sense of expectation and consistency, both in the daily routine and in the behavior that is appropriate for that routine, sets the ground-work for the other study skills that facilitate the child's learning.

The scheduled routine is the regularly repeated pattern of events within the school day. This daily routine is built from a series of subroutines, each with its own set of expected behavior patterns, which the child practices while engaged in a planned activity. It is necessary to provide instruction in each of these routines, usually combining the routine with an activity with which the children are already familiar. A daily routine offers the children an opportunity to plan for and organize anticipated events, as well as to have an opportunity to develop a mental set for the next activity. Children develop a sense of security through this feeling of preparedness and their prediction of events from the daily reference framework.

Flexibility within the Routine

Flexibility within the daily routine enables deviation from the regular schedule to occur without losing the integrity of the routine that the teacher normally uses. Once the routine has been taught, practiced, and mastered, changes can be made in the schedule, or activities may be deleted or added without undue distress.

Flexibility in the daily schedule provides an opportunity to take the time necessary to maximize the planned activity, thus increasing the options for enrichment, either in content or in process. The other positive attribute of flexibility is its relationship to developing continuity and integration with other curriculum content areas.

Flexibility in a reading lesson is created by extending the topic into language arts areas and connecting that topic with, for example, a science experience later in the day. Math could be moved to another time slot so that the topic-related content areas could be closely sequenced in the instructional day.

The following example demonstrates one way to adapt the regular daily schedule in order to create a block of time for an integrated language arts lesson.

Regular Schedule

Opening

Movement education

Reading/language arts (teacher input)

Related activity (guided practice)

Recess

Individual work time (independent practice)

Lunch

Story/rest

Math (teacher input)

Related activity (guided/independent practice)

One of the challenges of using centers with emergent readers is symbolically communicating the intent of the center. In other words, without depending on written communication, how can teachers pictorially or symbolically tell children how to use the materials available to achieve the instructional intent. Have the students work in partners to design directions for their peers, using symbols such as pictures, arrows, dotted lines, and so forth.

Each daily routine is composed of a set of shorter routines for each part of the students' day. To begin helping student teachers to develop their own classroom routines, have your students design and plan their routine for reading to their future students. Have your students begin this routine as the children enter the classroom or change activities and end it with directions for their next activity. In other words, show the transitions to and from the reading activity. Have your students write a sample dialogue for this routine and critique it with a team of other students.

Drama/music/art

Evaluation/dismissal

Flexible Schedule

Opening

Movement education

Math (teacher input)

Related activity (guided practice)

Recess

Integrated story/drama/music

Lunch

Review story

Extended art or writing project

Individual work time

Evaluation/dismissal

The students can help each other create a collection of transition activities by bringing to class three ideas that have been written and copied for each fellow student. These ideas should include teacher information, such as how much time it takes, whether any skills or knowledge needs to be pretaught, and what materials are required for the activity.

This change of schedule can induce overexcitement and fatigue in some children, to the point of disrupting their day. For this reason, it is very important that the plans for the day are clearly communicated with the group members and that they have an opportunity to receive answers to any questions they might have. It is also wise to have *filler activities* (which can expand or contract, to fill any length of time) available for the brief amounts of time (5–10 minutes), that may occur between activities. These transitional filler activities should be simple and routine. An example of one such transitional activity is to have children who have completed their work get a book and look at it alone or with a friend until the others have finished.

The Kindergarten Schedule

Ask students, "What are the advantages and disadvantages of the whole-day versus the half-day kindergarten? What are the long-term effects of the different schedules on student achievement? What social values are embedded in each of the schedules?"

In recent years, options to the traditional half-day kindergarten schedule have been created. The need for these options have been generated by the recognition of the importance of early education, the increased need for public childcare at an earlier age, and the economic considerations surrounding the allocations of funds earmarked for transportation and building use. In some school districts, children attend kindergarten every other day, alternating the Wednesday or Friday between the two classes. Some children attend kindergarten every day of the week but are dismissed earlier in the afternoon than the other primary children. Whatever the program configuration, careful planning of the daily schedule is necessary to facilitate the instruction while meeting the needs of the learners.

Full-Day Schedule
Opening
Child-centered
          and/or
Directed activity with follow-up
   activity (guided practice)
Individual work time
Recess
Snack
Child-centered or
 Directed activity
   with follow-up activity
Lunch
Story/rest
Individual work time
Music/P.E./art
Dismissal

Half-Day Schedule
Opening
Child-centered
          and/or
Directed activity with follow-up
   activity
Individual work time
Recess
Snack
Storytime
Directed activity
Music/P.E./art
Dismissal

Reading instruction occurs during the directed and follow-up activities, individual work time, and storytime. Children on the half-day schedule often receive a longer block of math instruction one day, rotated with a longer reading and language arts lesson the following day. The teacher also makes a greater effort to integrate the social studies and science objectives into the language arts instruction.

Grouping Primary Children for Instruction

In the implementation of the instructional plan, select one or more of several options for grouping the children that will facilitate the lesson. Intentionally use a variety of grouping strategies in order to offer students opportunities to learn a repertoire of group membership roles, to add freshness to the routine and to encourage children to explore different styles of learning.

Whole-Group Instruction

Whole-group instruction might bring to mind the picture of a traditional classroom. The teacher is at the front of the entire classroom group, giving information about a topic or demonstrating a concept. The children are quietly and passively attending to the teacher. This, however, is not the type of whole-group instruction that is advocated in this text. The effectiveness of whole-group instruction is significantly increased by developing the personal meaningfulness of the lesson for each student and by implementing techniques that increase student participation in the instruction. When children are encouraged to become actively involved in

Ask students, "How can a teacher tell whether a student is attending to a lesson? What things might a teacher do to keep students actively engaged in the instruction? How can a teacher monitor active engagement?"

the instruction, their attention to and participation in the instruction increases.

Interaction between the teacher and the students occurs through verbal and gestural signals, brief oral or written responses, and sharing such things as retelling poems, supplying missing words to songs, or predicting coming events. The efficiency of this large grouping makes it an attractive choice for giving input, such as directions or demonstrations; reading a story; choral reading from a chart or big book; singing and chanting; or modeling a new reading strategy.

It is also an advantage to have all the children involved at one time during many activities. One benefit is that reluctant participants receive peer support and encouragement to participate. Children who find it difficult to speak the language or read the words fluently can unobtrusively join in at any level of ability. Also, seeing peers successfully involved in an activity sends the message to all learners that the activity is within the realm of possibility for them. Peer modeling offers alternative possibilities for how they can begin succeeding.

Small-Group Instruction

Despite the numerous advantages of whole-class instruction, there are times when children need the increased personalized attention or specialized instruction that smaller groups provide. Teachers can work with children in groups of four to six members while the other students in the class work independently on assigned projects or in self-selected work areas.

The groups that are formed may be short- or long-term associations, and membership may have been designated by the teacher or by the children themselves. Small groups may be formed based on skill instruction, task assignment, common interests, or social needs. Monitor the group process closely to make sure the children are having positive opportunities to interact with other students and do not become strictly associated with only one group of students.

The following examples were taken from a teacher's edition of a primary reading series:

> Divide pupils into groups of four or five. Have them work together to find pictures of things they would find in a grocery store, a hardware store, and a toy store. Each picture should then be pasted on an index card. Have pupils use these pictures to play the "Shopping Game." The index cards are put face down on a table, and each pupil draws one card. Without looking at the picture on the card, each pupil in turn says, "I'm going shopping at the _____ store," specifying either the grocery, hardware, or toy store. If the drawn cards fits into the named category, the pupil may keep the card. If not, the card is put back on the table in a face-down position, and play proceeds to the next person. The game ends when all the cards have been awarded. The player holding the most cards wins the games.

(Sulzby, E., Hoffman, J., Niles, J., Shanahan, T., Teale, W., 1989)

Ask students, "How does a teacher plan for and encourage students who speak another language or come from environments that have deprived them of rich language experiences? What experiences might help these children maintain esteem in their learning ability while gaining academic achievement?"

Ask students, "What are the considerations a teacher makes in putting a group of children together to work on a project directed by the teacher? How would those considerations change if the group of children was expected to work independently?"

Peer Partners

Sometimes the teacher plans a lesson that requires children to work together on an activity that requires involvement in a specific social process (e.g., peer tutors, cooperative learning), as well as particular outcome. Examples of tasks and outcomes appropriate for a group of two children include creating a picture, mural, or diorama; organizing sequence cards; or playing a "Word Concentration" game.

Younger children prefer to work in groups of two on tasks that require a great deal of sharing and interaction because they are still developing the verbal communication skills necessary to maintain a conversation or discussion. They often have a lot to say and cannot hold it in their minds long enough for several people to take turns. They also are bridging from a very ego-centered emotional and social perspective. When together, the children are stretching their concepts of themselves and others in terms of these social and emotional understandings, as well as working intellectually with the instructional task. Limiting the group size for specific task work to a group of two is often the most effective in meeting the instructional goal, as well as fostering social and emotional growth.

Peer pairs can be used very effectively for writing activities such as this one:

> Recall with children that at first, Vanessa Mouse had a hard time getting to know her classmates. Suggest that each child get to know one classmate better by interviewing that person. Assign each child a partner, and suggest to children that they use the following questions in their interviews. Print these questions on the chalkboard:
>
> - How old are you?
> - How many brothers and sisters do you have?
> - What is your favorite food, color, TV show, movie, and sport?
> - Do you have a favorite book or story? What is it?
> - Do you have a hobby? What is it?
> - What are two things that you know how to do well?
>
> Direct children to make quick notes as each answer is given. After the interview, have children write a profile of the person they interviewed by answering the questions in complete sentences. Remind them to place the name of the classmate they interviewed at the top of the page. Display the profiles on the bulletin board so children can read about each other.

(Durr, W., Pikulsk, J., Bean, R., Cooper, J. David, Glaser, N., Greenlaw, M. Jean, et al., 1989)

Ask students, "How would you control the development of the peer partners? Considering the range of ability levels in the group, which children would you put together (i.e., high ability with low ability, low ability with low ability, etc.)? Why would you make these choices?"

Lucy McCormick Calkins (1986) describes a peer conferencing technique that can be used by partners once it is taught. The teacher models the technique by engaging in a demonstration lesson for the whole group. The steps of the conference are as follows:

1. The writer reads out loud.

2. Listeners respond, or if the piece is confusing, the listeners ask questions, then respond.
3. Listeners focus on the content, perhaps asking questions about it. The writer teaches them about the subject.
4. The focus shifts to the text. What will the writer do next, and how will he or she do it?

Younger children may find it difficult to differentiate between Steps 3 and 4. This could be initially introduced as a three-step process:

1. Listen
2. Question to understand
3. Question for the future

When children are working independently, it is helpful to design a poster outlining the expectations. Monitor the individual sets of partners while making general comments to the entire group reviewing the steps in the process.

Individualized Instruction

Many teachers use learning centers as a way of meeting the individual learning needs of their students. By developing a variety of work stations, they encourage exploration or practice of language arts concepts and skills. Either the children choose the centers based on their interests, or they are assigned to them. Students usually work at each center until they are ready to move to another. The teacher's role is to act as a resource person, moving about the centers, offering assistance, instruction, support, and guidance. This involves the teaching of a variety of instructional objectives, depending on the needs and interests of the children.

Another type of individualized instruction provides the children with a programmed learning system in which the children are given sequential tasks to complete while working independently in a booklet, on a computer, or in another medium of programmed instruction. The children work at their own rate and receive individualized instruction from you as it is needed.

Managing Classroom Groupings

Classroom teachers, in an effort to work with children according to perceived reading levels, often group them for instruction. Traditionally, this has been done through the use of three or four reading groups of six to eight children each. Teachers take turns giving smaller numbers of students more individualized instruction by rotating each group every 30–40 minutes.

A typical morning in a primary classroom using rotated reading groups (A, B, and C) might follow this schedule:

Children are generally eager to ask questions, but they often have not developed a concept of questioning. Ask your students, "What are some formal and informal instructional techniques a teacher uses in concept development? How will a teacher know whether a child understands how to control the use of different types of questions?"

Ask students, "Which type of individualized instruction do you think is the most beneficial to a student? When would you select each as the most appropriate use for a particular student or group of students?"

9:00–9:15	Opening: attendance, lunch count, calendar			
9:15–9:30	Organizing for instruction: assignments			
9:30–10:00	10:00–10:30	break	10:45–11:15	Activity
Group A	B	break	C	With the teacher
Group B	C	break	A	Writing/spelling (independent)
Group C	A	break	B	Reading assignment (independent)

11:15–11:30—evaluation   break
11:30—lunchtime

Use this schedule to more closely monitor skill development and support practice reading or project development.

The schedule presents some issues that require careful consideration in planning. First, the schedule limits the time the teacher can spend assisting the students. This influences the type of lessons or projects that are selected for instruction, in that they are often brief and simple. Second, because the teacher is unable to monitor the work that is being done independently by the students, either as a result of their group lesson or from the board, the instruction sometimes either is contrived to keep the kids busy or is forced to be of lower quality because of the lack of in-depth instruction or follow-up.

A third issue relates to the amount of time the children spend involved in the act of reading. It is possible that one third of the reading period could be spent in directed teacher instruction, one third in completing skill sheets, and one third in responding to assignments written on the board. The emphasis during reading instruction should be on preparing to read, reading, and thinking about (reviewing) what was read. Teachers must thoughtfully prepare for each group's work.

Alternatives to this grouping may assist in developing a literacy learning environment. Whole-group instruction can dominate the language arts schedule, with flexible small-group sessions created as they are needed. The children may work individually or in peer pairs on skill development, problem solving, or project development. The teacher may move around the room acting as a resource person, meeting with the groups, and monitoring the progress of the others.

Yet another grouping alternative is described in Figure 5.3, taken from *Learning to Read Naturally* (Jewell & Zintz, 1986). This plan groups the children by their reading level and provides both small-group and individual learning opportunities appropriate to those levels.

Alternate Ways of Managing Groups

Using a Theme for Organization One way to manage the classroom environment is to develop the instruction for all the children around a common topic of study or a literary theme. Give the same instruction to

The key to effective grouping of students for instruction is flexibility. In order to (a) avoid student labeling, (b) provide appropriate role models, (c) offer appropriate instruction, and (d) create opportunities for social growth, teachers must offer instruction that regroups students within each day and throughout the year. It is not harmful to have a student work within an ability group for a period of time. It *is* harmful, however, if the student always works in the same ability-level grouping every day in every subject area. Give the students the opportunity to discuss their personal experiences with groupings as early elementary students. Ask them, "Why were those groupings helpful? Harmful? How might that affect how you plan for instruction in your own classroom?"

Referring to the suggested grouping model by Jewell and Lintz, have students work in teams of four to list ways in which the teacher behavior could be different from that found in a classroom using traditional rotated reading groups.

9:00		WHOLE GROUP	SMALL GROUP AND INDIVIDUAL		
			P1	P2	P3
	9:00	Planning for day			
	9:15	Language Experience			
	9:45		Listening Center	Instruction Center	Writing Center
	10:05		Library Center	Writing Center	Study Center
	10:25		Discovery Center	Study Center	Library Center
10:45					
10:45	10:45	Movement Activity			
	11:00	Creative Activity			
	11:35	Sustained Silent Reading			
	11:45	Lunch			
	12:30	Story Listening			
12:45	1:00	Planning for afternoon			
1:00	1:20		Study Center	Library Center	Discovery Center
1:20	1:40		Instruction Center	Listening Center	Project Center
1:40	2:00		Writing Center	Study Center	Planning and
2:00	2:20		Project Center	Discovery Center	Instruction Center
2:20	2:30				
2:30		Closing the Day			

P1—Phase One Level
P2—Phase Two Level
P3—Phase Three Level
The legend for symbols on the schedule is as follows:
P1 represents Phase One Level children, those who are in the process of building a strong support system for entry into reading.
P2 represents Phase Two Level children, those who exhibit many emergent reading behaviors and are paying increasingly closer attention to specific features of print.
P3 represents Phase Three Level children, those who have developed sufficient competencies and insights about reading to be able to read some materials independently.

the whole group and then adjust the level of difficulty and/or create subgroups based on student interest. As they complete their work, the children have centers available to them for individual work.

A typical morning schedule for this type of environment is as follows:

9:00–9:15	Opening: attendance, lunch count, calendar
9:15–9:45	Whole group lesson
9:45–10:30	Differentiated follow-up work
10:30–10:45	Recess
10:45–11:30	Small group and individual work
11:30	Lunchtime

Figure 5.4 illustrates an alternative to this schedule, which is suggested by Brian Cambourne in his book *The Whole Story* (1988).

Assignment Charts for Children When the children are moving from center to center or are in transition in rotating groups, it is helpful for them to have a guide to their options. Several systems are available in managing this movement, but the most effective systems encourage the children to participate in taking that responsibility. Each of the charts described in Figures 5.5 through 5.7 are adaptable to a varying number of groups and to the types of centers or activities in which the children are to engage.

The first system for managing groups of children (Figures 5.5 and 5.6) is created by

1. Drawing and cutting a large circle from heavy paper
2. Drawing and cutting a smaller circle from heavy paper
3. Covering the circles with clear laminate
4. Attaching the centers of the two circles with a brad
5. Dividing the circles into wedges with lines, to make the number of wedges correspond to the number of groups
6. Printing the children's names in each of the wedges on the smaller wheel (using a water-soluble pen or a grease pencil)
7. Printing the group activities in the wedges on the larger wheel

Ask students, "How else might you manage groups without using charts? What are the advantages of one system over another?"

The children's names are printed on the sections of the smaller wheel with a water-soluble pen so that the groupings can be changed easily. Teach the children that the wedge with their name correlates to a section of the wheel that shows them where they are to work. When the wheel is moved, the children see that their names correlate with a new group activity.

Figure 5.7 illustrates a second system for managing groups of children. It follows the same organizational system, but it takes the form of a rectangle instead of a circle. This chart is created by

1. Cutting a large rectangle from heavy tagboard

Figure 5.4 **Alternative method of organizing classroom time, as suggested by Cambourne. Reproduced with permission from Ashton Scholastic, Auckland, New Zealand. Copyright 1988. All rights reserved.**

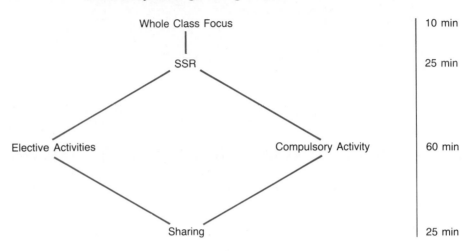

One Way of Organizing Time

Ask students, "How will you manage the movement of students in rotating groups if it takes one group longer than another to complete the work in their group? What options might you make available to students who complete work before other group members?"

This time line represents the first two hours of the school day. On the teacher's timetable it is represented by the label 'Language'. It can be seen from the figure above that the time has been organized by the teacher around four descriptive labels. These labels represent what the learners and teacher do during these periods of time:

(i) Whole Class Focus Time
(ii) Sustained Silent Reading Time
(iii) Activity Time—elective activity/compulsory activity
(iv) Sharing Time

2. Cutting a number of smaller rectangles from heavy tagboard, corresponding to the number of groups
3. Covering the rectangles with clear laminate
4. Gluing small pieces of Velcro on the backs of the small rectangles and on the corresponding spaces on the large rectangle
5. Printing the children's names on the smaller rectangles
6. Labeling the space above the small rectangles with the group activities

Using the children's pictures, with or without their names, is another way to designate their membership in a group. The pictures can be laminated and prepared for use on a chart by gluing a piece of Velcro on the back. The children could easily participate in forming the groups by attaching their own names to a chart's section.

Figure 5.5   Circular chart for managing three small groups for instruction.

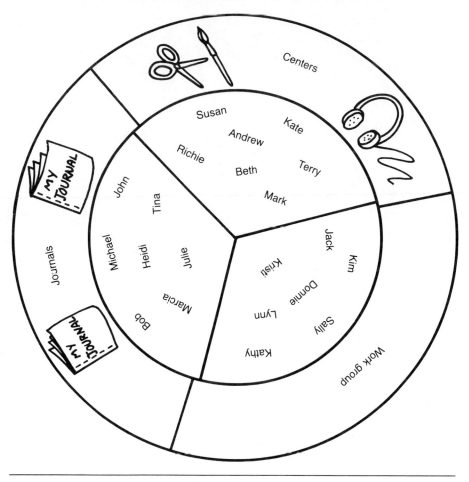

Teaching Work and Study Habits

Learning patterns of behavior occurs over long periods of time, with many opportunities to observe, model, practice, apply, and generalize. The daily work routine and approach to instruction provide the fundamental attitudes and behaviors necessary to further positive instruction in study skills. The daily routines and other aspects of classroom management provide a structure to facilitate instruction, and they provide the child with uniform information about systems for getting work done successfully at school.

Generally, school work habits are divided into two categories: group work skills and personal (individual) work skills. Group work skills relate

Figure 5.6   Circular chart for managing five small groups for instruction.

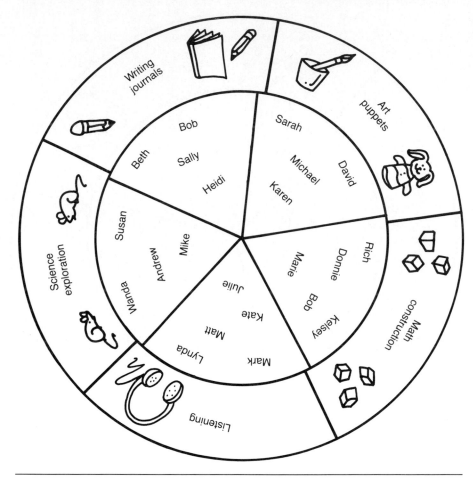

to those abilities that enable the child to function positively as a group member. Typical skills include

- Participating in a group activity
- Following directions when given in a group
- Attending to a group discussion
- Participating in a group discussion
- Following rules
- Attending to a task in a group setting
- Helping to clean up the group area

Personal or individual work skills are usually typified by the following:

Figure 5.7 Rectangular chart for managing small groups for instruction.

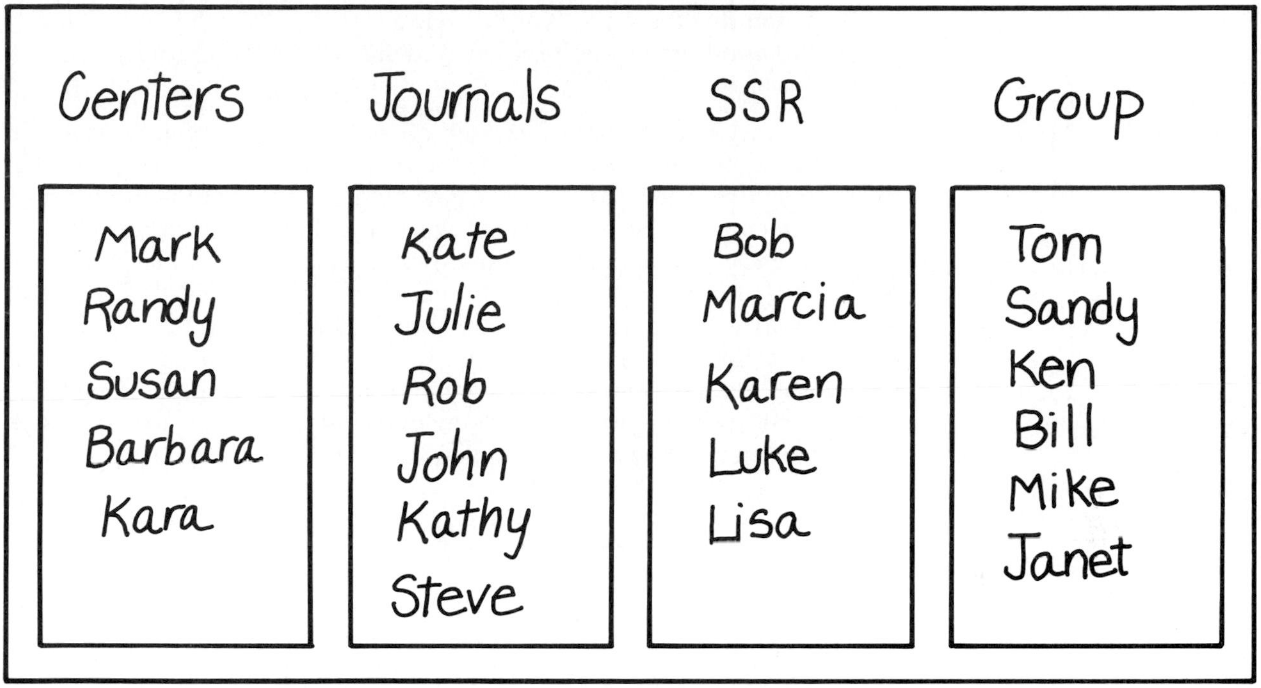

Centers	Journals	SSR	Group
Mark	Kate	Bob	Tom
Randy	Julie	Marcia	Sandy
Susan	Rob	Karen	Ken
Barbara	John	Luke	Bill
Kara	Kathy	Lisa	Mike
	Steve		Janet

- Cleaning up after oneself
- Taking care of personal belongings
- Working independently without distracting others
- Making choices
- Using time appropriately
- Attending to a task
- Finding solutions independently
- Initiating work

Assign the following task: "Write a letter to your students who are new to your classroom, outlining the group and individual work skills you expect them to use and explaining why these skills are important."

A basic work routine taught to the children at the beginning of the school year frees the teacher from continued student management and frequent interruption of the instruction. The children are trained to be independent, self-reliant workers with a system for solving problems and using their time responsibly.

The first step in training for responsibility is to teach the children a work pattern and then to systematically and consistently use it as a foundation for all other instruction. This typical work pattern has five steps:

1. Get a job.

2. Go to work.
3. Complete the work.
4. Clean up where you were working.
5. Get another job, and proceed with Steps 2 through 5 until signalled to stop.

Have students work in teams of four to six students to select an activity to teach their classmates, in which the goal of instruction is to teach a work routine. Have students keep in mind the use of specific key language they will want the children to learn and what they want that language to mean to the children.

Direct instruction relating to each of these steps is given, and many opportunities for guided and independent practice occur each day. During the first months of school, teachers spend a great deal of time monitoring and reinforcing this behavior. The implication of this work pattern is that the children are responsible for their own learning and that learning can continue without the teacher's presence. Not only does this free the teacher from constantly dominating the children's learning, but it also frees the children from viewing the teacher as the possessor of their learning ability. Learning this concept makes good sense in the long term as well, because we are encouraging the children to be independent lifelong learners rather than dependent classroom learners.

PLANNING AND IMPLEMENTING THE INSTRUCTIONAL PROCESSES

Planning for successful instruction requires the alignment of carefully selected instructional objectives with instructional processes that facilitate both the achievement of the objectives and the development of the children's social and emotional abilities.

As mentioned in the instructor's introduction to this chapter, many of your students received reading instruction that was segmented, with separate focus on listening, speaking, and writing, as well as on the separate content areas. First, on their own, and then, in partners, have the students define "integrated language arts." As a whole group, share those definitions, and create a definition on which the group can agree.

Designing instructional interludes requires (a) clear definition of the objective or purpose of the instruction, (b) analysis of that objective in terms of the level of readiness of the learners, and (c) development of a lesson that will achieve that objective. The purpose of the instructional design has two parts: the content and the method. The first part focuses on the question, "What is it the children need to learn?" The answer generally relates to the content area (e.g., language arts), and to the specific skill or concept (e.g., story character development, sound–symbol relationship). The second question, "How will I most effectively present the information of instruction?" deals with how to teach the objective in a way that most closely matches the way the children naturally learn.

Integrating the Language Arts

Integrating the language arts (reading, writing, speaking, and listening) requires a consistent instructional effort to develop the elements of each strand in relationship to the other. It involves an awareness of the interdependency of children's emerging skills and concepts in each strand. The

The needs of individual learners can most effectively be met when the classroom is well organized and there are learning centers that reflect worthy purposes and contain interesting material.

children are encouraged to use their strengths developed in one strand to promote or facilitate learning in another.

Planning for Integration

Integration requires awareness of the following:

- The objectives in each of the strands
- The developmental and academic levels of the children
- The strategies for linking, pairing, or combining instruction across the strands
- The available materials for facilitating instruction

Assessing the needs of the learners and identifying the educational objectives sets the foundation for any further planning. Once these have been established, lesson design and organization of material begins.

A central topic, a focus story, or a developed experience acts as a catalyst for the integration. From this catalyst, the teacher creates a network of related experiences in each of the language arts strands. Instruction is intentionally designed to develop the connections among strands by purposely linking, pairing, or combining learning opportunities from each of the language arts areas.

Linking The teacher first selects a central topic, then examines it for ways in which each of the language arts strands could be developed. The

Figure 5.8   Example of an integrated language arts lesson, linked via the theme, "pond life."

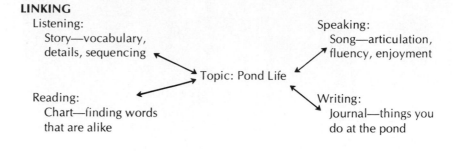

LINKING

Listening:
Story—vocabulary,
details, sequencing

Speaking:
Song—articulation,
fluency, enjoyment

Topic: Pond Life

Reading:
Chart—finding words
that are alike

Writing:
Journal—things you
do at the pond

strands are related to each other only through the content of the topic and not their interaction with each other.

Example: A topic such as "pond life" could lend itself to the following activities:

Listening: Story, *Where Mosquitoes Go When It Rains*

Speaking: Song, "Five Speckled Frogs"

Reading: Chart, "Mud, Mud, Mud"

Writing: Dictation, "A Visit to the Pond"

These activities all have to do with the topic. Introduce them as independent lessons not lessons that are the foundation for or extension of another. The integration (illustrated in Figure 5.8) exists through the development of all the language arts strands through individual activities. The activities all relate to a common topic, using a common vocabulary in varying genres.

Ask students, "Under what conditions would you select 'linking' versus 'pairing' for an integration strategy? What are the strengths or weaknesses of each in introducing a theme?"

Pairing A story, poem, or song often provides a focus for pairing two objectives from the language arts strands. The objectives in each of the strands are reciprocal, in that they mutually support the learning each activity is promoting. The activities may be related to each other sequentially, in that one activity must be completed as a first step to the next activity. For example, children might have to recall a sequence and create pictures before they can be sequenced as pages for a book.

Activities may also be related because the information and/or skills in one strand may form a foundation for success in the next strand, such as orally recalling the story sequence before the speaking parts in a drama are created. The language arts strands can be paired in a variety of configurations (i.e., reading–speaking, reading–listening, writing–listening, etc.). Figure 5.9 shows one way that this might be done.

Figure 5.9 **Example of an integrated language arts lesson. Strands are paired in relation to the story of the "Little Red Hen."**

PAIRING

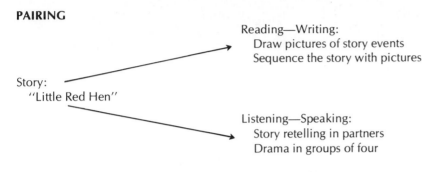

Story:
"Little Red Hen"

Reading—Writing:
Draw pictures of story events
Sequence the story with pictures

Listening—Speaking:
Story retelling in partners
Drama in groups of four

Combining Another approach to planning for integrating the language arts instruction begins by sequencing the events of a planned experience and then assigning objectives from the four language arts strands to those individual events. The order of the objectives relates to the natural order of the experience, although it is possible for the teacher to decide which language arts focus an event may take (e.g., directions may be given orally for a listening focus or given in pictures and print for a reading focus).

The linear sequencing of the strands helps to focus instruction during the experience. Other advantages of this type of planning include the assurance that objectives from each of the strands will be covered in instruction, and the increased possibility of discovering relationships in the instruction that may have been overlooked. The integration exists because the objectives of all the language arts areas are related to one experience. They may be happening in a simple sequence, as diagrammed in Figure 5.10, or in a complex sequence with many subsequences occurring simultaneously during the experience.

Ask students, "How does 'combining' differ from the other two suggested integration strategies? What types of instructional objectives are appropriate for this strategy? Give examples."

Providing Instruction

If each language arts strand within a lesson were to be fully developed, it would often not be possible to complete the instruction in the time provided. To adjust for this, select and emphasize particular strands of the instruction during different parts of the day or week, or choose to emphasize different strands in different lessons. Using the former system for organization, Monday and Tuesday could be spent teaching to objectives in listening and reading, Wednesday in writing activities, and Thursday and Friday working on speaking and reading by preparing to present a play. Any number of combinations or configurations could be developed, depending on the children's needs and the instructional goals.

Figure 5.10   Example of an integrated language arts lesson that combines the strands sequentially through a single learning experience.

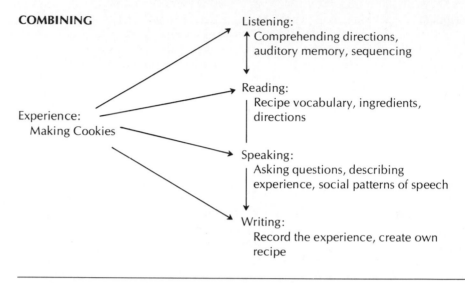

COMBINING

Experience:
Making Cookies

Listening:
Comprehending directions, auditory memory, sequencing

Reading:
Recipe vocabulary, ingredients, directions

Speaking:
Asking questions, describing experience, social patterns of speech

Writing:
Record the experience, create own recipe

Literary Themes and Content Units

The concept of integrating the language arts strands can be expanded to include other content areas, such as science, math, and social studies. Applying the strategies used for developing relationships in integrating the language arts strands, the teacher designs longer-term instruction based on literary themes or content units.

Literary Themes   *Literary themes* are investigations into human relationships and values. Such themes for primary-grade children focus on explorations of friendship, courage, helpfulness, growing up, and personal and group responsibility. Initiated from children's classics such as "The Little Red Hen," "The Three Bears," and "The Three Little Pigs," the theme development encourages the children to examine the meanings of cultural values, human behavior, and the different ways people relate to one another. The language arts theme provides an avenue for receiving, sharing, and analyzing the new information.

Content Themes   Units of study that relate to content areas, such as math, science, or social studies provide a wealth of topics for content themes. Broad topics such as transportation or the farm can be developed into integrated studies that last 2–3 weeks. Although topics such as cats, insects, or patterns can also generate this activity level, they usually last

Ask students, "What are the advantages of using literary themes as a central focus for reading instruction? Examine basal reading series for the quality of themes they have used in organizing the reading selections. Evaluate the extent to which these themes are developed through the suggested instruction."

Ask students, "Under what conditions might you use both a literary and a content theme in planning instruction? How could this benefit the students?"

Figure 5.11 Blank sample page used for planning a daily language arts lesson.

Language Arts Objective:			
Time:			
Reading W S P I			
Writing W S P I			
Listening W S P I			
Speaking W S P I			

fewer days. These themes are often initiated by events in the children's lives, such as a classmate's baby kitten or a jar of insects caught over the weekend. Recognize the value of this student-generated interest, and capitalize on it.

The Teacher's Plan Book

Plan the daily lessons by first selecting objectives for the instruction and then by developing lessons that help the children achieve those objectives. Organizing instruction goes beyond the lesson-to-lesson planning. Not only must the objectives of lessons within a day mutually support each other, but also the learning from day to day must have some continuity. Teachers use a variety of formats for planning reading or language arts instruction (e.g., see Figures 5.11 and 5.12). In Figures 5.13 and 5.14, the teacher uses the planning formats to create a balance of activities in both subject area and type of group work.

Figure 5.12   Filled-in sample page used for planning a daily language arts lesson.

Language Arts Objective: *recognizing and using questions; speaking, reading, writing*				
Time:	*9:15–9:45*	*9:45–10:30*	*10:45–11:00*	*11:00–11:20*
Reading ⓦ S Ⓟ Ⓘ			*Read to Students What's For Lunch*	*SSR*
Writing Ⓦ Ⓢ P Ⓘ		*Review Poem "Questions" Brainstorm small group Write Take-Off in journal*		
Listening ⓦ S P I	*Demonstration of Question/Answer Game move to*			
Speaking W S Ⓟ I	*Peer Practice Peer play the game*			

The teacher circles the symbols "W S P I," representing whole group, small group, peer partners, and individual instruction. This holistic planning offers the teacher an overview of the planned experiences, with the opportunity to look for areas to integrate or lessons that could be redesigned to support or reinforce other learning.

Many classroom activities provide experiences in more than one of the content areas. These integrated activities are represented by arrows connecting the boxes. It is also important to note that not all the subject areas need to be covered everyday. When using flexible blocks of time for planning, some days may have an instructional emphasis in only one content area. The goal is to generate a balance of instruction over the span of the school year.

Planning for instructional themes can be outlined for the school year by plotting them on a yearly calendar, such as the one in Figure 5.15. It is

Figure 5.13 Blank sample page used for planning weekly cross-curricular lessons.

Weekly Plan			
	Monday	*Tuesday*	*Wednesday*
Math W S P I			
Science W S P I			
Reading/L.A. W S P I			
Social Studies W S P I			
Music W S P I			
Art W S P I			
P.E. W S P I			

Figure 5.14   Filled-in sample page used for planning weekly cross-curricular lessons.

Weekly Plan *Living Things Unit:* *Theme: Frogs:*		*Attributes:* *1. look like* *2. sound like*	*3. eat* *4. live* *5. move*
March 16	*Monday*	*Tuesday*	*Wednesday*
Math W S P I	*number sequence on flannel board*	*number sequence game frogs in pond grouping in 10s*	*review Tues. record frogs in groups of 10*
Science W S P I	*walk to pond observe tadpoles*	*observe tadpoles in classroom*	*film: The Pond*
Reading/L.A. W S P I	*Chart:* *5 frogs* *make student books*	*Drama:* *Using frog puppets*	*Read:* *Frog & Toad are Friends* *Write in journals about friends*
Social Studies W S P I			*Friends at School*
Music W S P I	*Song:* *5 frogs*		
Art W S P I		*frog sack puppets*	*Create frogs from scraps for Pond bulletin board*
P.E. W S P I	*respond to song with motions*		

Figure 5.15   Sample calendar of instructional themes throughout a school year.

Sept.	**Oct.**	**Nov.**
1. school/safety 2. Myself/My Family	1. Fall Theme 2. Apples	1. Harvest 2. Mice
Dec.	**Jan.**	**Feb.**
1. Patterns 2. School Play & Program	1. Winter Theme 2. Bears	1. Friends 2. Mail
March	**April**	**May/June**
1. Spring Theme 2. Frogs	1. Community Helpers 2. Community Fair	1. Farm 2. Seeds & Plants

important to evaluate how these themes will flow from one to the other and how they relate to what else is going on in the children's environment. For example, if the teacher knows that there is a spring festival in the community or an anticipated school event related to a theme, then he or she may want to plan a theme that would use these activities to enhance the classroom experience.

HIGHLIGHTS

1. The teacher considers the developmental attributes of the learners in planning the daily schedule. In addition to the cognitive needs of the children, the teacher considers their social, emotional, and physical needs.

2. Before designing the classroom environment, the teacher evaluates the program design and the physical setting. A list of priorities for instructional areas facilitates appropriate furniture arrangement.

3. A daily routine creates a sense of consistency for children, which offers them an opportunity to plan and organize for anticipated events.

4. The teacher works with the children in a variety of groupings. The teacher increases instructional effectiveness by using whole group, small group, peer pairs, and individual strategies.

5. By linking, pairing, and combining the language arts strands, the teacher integrates instruction. This integration encourages the children to use strengths they have developed in one area to support the learning in another.

Have students work in teams of four to six to create a yearly plan for a selected grade level. Have them work as partners within the team to develop a general outline of language arts activities for a selected month.

REINFORCEMENT ACTIVITIES

1. Make a list of the types of equipment, materials, and furniture you would want in your primary classroom. Draw an outline of the classroom, and arrange it according to the considerations given in this chapter.
2. Discuss the value of each of the four instructional groupings. Plan a whole-group lesson. Plan the same lesson for a small group or peer pairs. Compare how the lessons differ.
3. Create a daily schedule for a classroom that begins at 9:00 A.M., has lunch at 12:00 to 12:45, and afternoon recess at 1:30. School dismisses at 2:30. Discuss your rationale for the schedule.
4. List three skills in each of the two categories of work habits, and discuss their value in supporting the children's instructional development.
5. Select and describe one of the integration models—linking, pairing, and combining. Discuss the value of these three in designing instruction.

ADDITIONAL PROJECTS

1. Select and construct one of the grouping management systems described in this chapter. Discuss how you will use it to facilitate your language arts/reading instruction.
2. Visit a kindergarten classroom, note the daily schedule, and observe the kinds of instruction that take place in each section of the schedule.
3. Visit a first- or second-grade classroom, and record the systems the teacher uses for scheduling, planning, and managing the instructional groupings.
4. Collect ideas for individual and small-group work centers. Categorize them, and put them into a file or notebook for your use.
5. Design an instructional theme using one of the models for integrating language arts and reading.

REFERENCES

Calkins, L. (1986). *The Art of Teaching Writing.* Portsmouth, NH: Heinemann Educational Books.

Cambourne, B. (1988). *The Whole Story: Natural Learning and the Acquisition of Literacy in the Classroom.* Sydney, Australia: Ashton Scholastic.

Durr, W., Pikulsk, J., Bean, R., Cooper, J. David, Glaser, N., Greenlaw, M. Jean, et al. (1989). *Houghton Mifflin Literary Readers: Book 2. Selection Plans and Instructional Support.* Boston, MA: Houghton Mifflin Company.

Jewel, M., & Zintz, M. (1986). *Learning to Read Naturally.* Dubuque, IA: Kendall/Hunt Publishing.

Kent, J. (1982). *The Caterpillar and the Polliwog.* Englewood Cliffs, NJ: Prentice Hall, Inc.

Scott, L.B., & Pavelko, V. (Bowmar Publishing/ASCAP). (1979). *Five Little Frogs* recorded on album *Singable Songs for the Very Young*, Raffi & Whiteley, K. Hollywood, CA: A & M Records, Inc.

Sulzby, E., Hoffman, J. Niles, J., Shanahan, T., Teale, W. (1989). *Up to the Sky* (Teacher's ed.). Oklahoma City, OK: McGraw-Hill School Division.

ADDITIONAL RESOURCES

Cummings, C. (1980). *Teaching Makes a Difference.* Snohomish, WA: Snohomish Publishing.

Good, T., & Brophy, J. (1984). *Looking in Classrooms.* New York: Harper & Row, Publishers.

Hunter, M. (1976). *Improved Instruction.* El Segundo, CA: TIP Publications.

Johnson, D., Johnson, R., Holubec, E., Roy, P. (1984). *Circles of Learning.* Alexandria, VA: Association for Supervision and Curriculum Development.

Schmuck, R., & Schmuck, P. (1971). *Group Process in the Classroom.* Dubuque, IA: Wm. C. Brown Publishers.

CHAPTER 6

THE ESSENTIAL ELEMENTS OF READING AND READING INSTRUCTION

The limits of my language stand for the limits of my world.
Ludwig Wittgenstein

PREVIEW

The majority of students can read by the time they complete the primary grades. By this time, most students have mastered most of what reading educators call the "foundation skills of reading." They can decode, comprehend, and apply their existing reading skills and procedures when they meet new and more challenging reading requirements. Many of these students not only have the necessary abilities to deal with most of what is required in their instructional settings, but they also often master even more demanding reading and writing situations.

This is not to say, however, that all students reach this level of achievement by the fourth grade. Some still have difficulty with both decoding and basic reading comprehension, and they may have limited reading vocabularies. Estimates vary, but it is safe to say that about 10–20% of students in any class may have such limited skills that they need more individualized attention than do other learners.

The upper elementary grades are critical for developing literacy. It is during these years that students are seriously introduced to the content (subject) areas of study. Social studies, science, math, and other areas are accorded specific blocks of instructional time. Typically, curriculum materials (including textbooks, a district curriculum guide, and a variety of other possible supplemental materials) are introduced during the intermediate years. In order to grasp the new load of concepts, students must learn *how* to learn the new content areas, which includes learning how to read the content-area texts.

Social studies, science, and mathematics each have different content and different structures of knowledge governing their mastery. Despite some similarities, these subject areas require different kinds of thinking, different perspectives, and different approaches to learning. Therefore, the structure and layout of these subjects' textbooks and other curricular materials differ across the three subjects, thereby requiring different approaches to reading.

Learners, too, are different during this period. According to developmental psychologists such as Jean Piaget, they are mastering the developmental tasks of the

You might want to examine briefly the format and text structure of an elementary social studies text and an elementary science text at this point.

162

"concrete operations" stage of reasoning, and in the later intermediate grades, many may move into the stage of "formal operations" reasoning. This transition from earlier preoperational thought impacts directly on their approaches to reading, writing, and talking.

FOCUS QUESTIONS

As you read this chapter, keep the following questions in mind:

1. What are some important characteristics of learners in the upper elementary grades that a teacher of reading should keep in mind?
2. What are the major indicators of reading ability that these students need to know?
3. What are the critical elements of reading that a teacher at these grades must focus on when teaching?

COGNITIVE DEVELOPMENT

Developmental Changes

Intermediate-grade students are more likely to approach reading and writing as logical acts than are children in kindergarten through second-grade years. During those early years, children often reason in nonlogical fashion—at least, according to adult standards of formal logic. They define cause–effect relationships, for example, in terms of wants, needs, or even guesses. Primary-grade children do make obvious cause–effect connections, but when challenged by more subtle relationships, they often revert to unrealistic reasons for events taking place or for occurrences that are out of the ordinary. For example, a boat can move across a lake simply because the boat "wants" to go across the lake. The rock is in the road because it does not "want" to move. The clouds float across the sky because the sun "pushes" them across.

By the intermediate grades, students move beyond believing that inanimate objects can consciously bring about results or actions simply because some inanimate force wants those results or actions. They also come to recognize that attention to physical, intellectual, and psychological attributes are prerequisites for comparison and contrast. For the teacher of reading, these developmental changes are quite important.

Ask students to find samples of first- and second-grade curriculum materials that purport to teach high-level thinking (e.g., cause–effect, inferring). Have students discuss appropriateness in view of what is known about the developmental level of the child.

Cause–effect relationships and comparison–contrast are two important categories of reading comprehension skills.

Understanding the "typical" intermediate-grade students' beliefs, ideas, and thought processes is important to instruction in literacy. Children from about 9 to 11 years of age have *concrete* orientations toward reality. This does not mean that they are unable or unwilling to deal with abstract ideas or topics, particularly those associated with emotional reactions or responses. It means instead that they are developing a cognitive understanding of reality that is more logical and reasonable according to conventional standards of formal logic. They are not as inclined to find idiosyncratic cause–effect relationships. When reasoning and searching for reasons for events, decisions, ideas, actions, and so on, they are more likely to consider realistic, probable, and logical alternatives.

Different Stories for Different Stages of Development

Stories derived from myth, fable, or fairy tale may still intrigue intermediate-grade students, but the students' interpretations of these stories differ significantly from the interpretations by their younger counterparts. Story characters' actions that are accepted as plausible by younger children will appear ludicrous or absurd to intermediate-age children. Animals do not talk. Giants do not walk the earth. Cars, trucks, and trains do not make decisions on their own and then proceed down the road or track according to some need or plan.

Also, the plausibility of animal characters lessens. Dogs and cats become pets. They remain very important, but they are not characters in the ongoing human dilemma in the same way that they could be just a few years before. Students in these grades prefer that animals function as animals in stories about humans. Notice that even in a classic such as *Lassie,* Lassie's role is empathetic because she remains believable as a normal animal, which makes her all the more admirable for *nearly* breaking those naturally imposed limitations that characterize animals.

Wordless picture books can still be fun, but their lack of text makes them different from other books.

Big picture books may have less appeal for these students. Their stories do not seem as realistic as stories with more print. It is important to note, however, that this does not mean that these students do not still enjoy big books and similar oral reading activities! Quite the contrary. Done well, oral readings of big books can be extremely effective and can be powerful assists to literacy instruction.

Some reading educators theorize that the reason that intermediate-grade students respond less warmly to poetry is attributable to the evolution of cognitive processing that is taking place during these years. In many instances, learners who earlier enjoyed poetry decide that it is not fun or even tolerable any more. Poetry's logic differs from what is more

---

Margin notes:

Have students share personal observations/experiences that reinforce this notion. What does this suggest about selection of topics, themes, and content for motivating young children to learn?

Discuss wordless picture books and big picture books here in light of what was said in earlier chapters in this book on teaching reading in the primary grades.

Ask students, "Is rejection of poetry by older boys a function of cognitive development or a function of cultural expectation?" Discuss the poetry of men and women in our society.

commonly perceived as logical in day-to-day life. Perhaps it is not the form or content of poetry so much as its internal logic that is difficult for young students to tolerate. While intermediate-grade learners are developing a conception of formal logic, poetry's conception of reality may be intolerable.

Students in this age range prefer a practical and personal orientation to their daily lives as well. Research has shown that girls, even in the primary grades, prefer personal topics for their writing. In addition, however, most students in Grades 3–5 enjoy stories and writing activities with wide-ranging orientations and subject matter. Nonetheless, girls prefer personal and family topics, and boys prefer adventure and fantasy-oriented themes in their reading and writing (Graves, 1975).

> Ask students, ''How would you explain sex differences in the writing performance of boys and girls through the grades? How can teachers improve the attitudes of both boys and girls toward writing as a personal expression of literacy?''

Differences in Instruction in Response to Developmental Differences

Book selection is not the only reason that intermediate-grade teachers must always be aware of the major developmental differences between their students and primary-grade students. These differences must guide instruction as well. Most basal reading programs focus on reading comprehension and reading vocabulary development through the intermediate grades. Study skills and literature concepts receive more attention. Also, many schools continue to have a separate block of instructional time for language arts and reading, and even for spelling and/or vocabulary instruction in some schools.

ESSENTIAL READING ABILITIES

Regardless of the organizational structure of reading instruction, certain indicators of reading ability are recognized as essential to all effective readers and are therefore seen as fundamental to a solid literacy program. Reading comprehension is the end result of many of these indicators, so in order to benefit from examining each indicator, *reading comprehension* must be defined, and general strategies for effective reading comprehension instruction must be reviewed.

Reading Comprehension

Klein (1988) defines *reading comprehension* as ''the act of using the knowledge and skills one possesses to process the information presented in the text'' (''text'' means any body of print a reader is supposed to read). Instruction in reading comprehension is defined as instruction that most directly assists the learner in:

> Ask students, ''Is reading comprehension simply thinking? If so, why so? If not, what is the relationship of thinking to the rest of the reading comprehension process? What do most authorities now say?''

1. *Developing the necessary skills for bringing to the reading act what the learner knows*
2. *Developing the skills necessary for processing the structures and meanings of language used in text*
3. *Refining the mental processing capacities used in the reading act*

Klein, 1985, page 11

Ask students, "How does self-monitoring enter into our other language processes (e.g., conversation and writing)? Ask students to recall personal examples of their use of "inner speech" (e.g., going over our notes before giving a report or speech, thinking ahead to what I am going to say in a debate or argument, talking to myself as I try to assemble a new appliance or toy).

This definition of reading comprehension instruction focuses on the reader, the text, and the interaction of the two. It indicates that the reader should approach the reading act as a process requiring the use of conscious strategies. By the third or fourth grade, learners competently use concrete reasoning in most situations. They have developed an inner-speech facility, which is necessary for self-monitoring of reading, and which is not accessible to most kindergarteners and many first graders. Thus, by the intermediate grades, teachers can use teaching techniques and strategies designed to teach learners how to be strategic readers. Their students are ready to learn how to self-monitor the reading act and to fine-tune its operation according to need, as dictated by complexity of text structure, content, and reading context.

In fact, students in the intermediate grades can master all of the important reading comprehension skills that any reader does. It is the sophistication of the skill and the subtlety and specificity of its application that develops from this point on in the education of the child.

Essential Indicators of Reading Ability

There are various theories about how learners acquire important abilities for reading. For example, some research denies the need for sequencing hierarchies of skills and subskills for instruction in reading, yet there is great concurrence that effective readers must develop several essential reading abilities. Before teachers of reading decide how best to develop these abilities, they must base their decisions on a thorough understanding of these abilities. The following abilities commonly serve as benchmarks for reading development by students and therefore represent goals for reading instruction through the elementary grades. Students should be able to do the following:

1. Paraphrase
2. Identify denotative and connotative meanings
3. Derive meanings through linguistic context
4. Identify secondary meanings when in context
5. Recognize irony
6. State the gist of a text passage
7. Identify the author's purpose or intent
8. Identify the mood of a text passage

9. Recognize valid inferences from a text passage
10. Distinguish reports from judgments
11. Discern the relative appropriateness of a text passage

Paraphrases

> Readers who comprehend text are able to restate the ideas presented in the text in their own words.

Although this may sound relatively easy, it is not necessarily so. Piaget notes that children through 10 years of age or so often have difficulty paraphrasing certain kinds of expressions, such as metaphors and figurative speech: "A penny saved is a penny earned," or "a bird in the hand is worth two in the bush." How can each of these expressions be paraphrased or restated? Another difficult expression is the "if–then" assertion. For example, "If you study, you will pass" can be logically paraphrased, "If you did not pass, you did not study." All "If–then" assertions can be paraphrased by reversing the positions of the antecedent and consequent clauses and negating each. Effective paraphrasing ability is developed over the years; it is not a skill that can be taught overnight.

Ask students to paraphrase famous sayings (e.g., a penny saved is a penny earned; a bird in the hand is worth two in the bush; a rose by any other name). Ask them, "How easy is it? Why are sayings such as proverbs or homilies often difficult to paraphrase?"

Denotations and Connotations

> Students must be able to identify both denotative and connotative meanings of words or phrases in context.

Words and phrases are used both denotatively and connotatively by speakers and writers. *Denotation* is the most likely literal or objective meaning of the expression being used. For example, "He is a real winner" can be used in sincere appreciation of or admiration for a star basketball player or winner of a spelling bee.

On the other hand, "He is a real winner" can be an expression putting down another or making fun of someone. Connotations are the suggested or implied meanings of words in use. Understanding connotation in its more refined uses requires knowledge of a wide range of figures of speech and a substantial background knowledge in a variety of subjects. Connotation may even require knowledge of literary allusions, historical achievements by predecessors, and general knowledge about the culture's social expectations. Connotative meanings are also important, to some extent, in appreciating humor. For example, a humorously titled country music song is "Some Men Leave Their Footprints on the Shifting Sands of Time, But I'll Just Leave the Mark of a Heel."

Ask students to supply examples of suggested connotations used in advertising.

Intentional use of connotation at a variety of levels is common in politics, law, literature, and other fields. Education in the language of intended and suggested meanings in speaking and text is a lifelong task.

Meanings Derived from Linguistic Context

> Effective readers must be able to reasonably guess a possible definition for a nonsense word if it is used in a proper linguistic context.

These words for which meanings are derived from context are often referred to as "nonce" words in the literature.

One of the most important comprehension skills readers must master is the ability to use the context of the text to infer a logical definition for an unknown word. Most readers do not rely on dictionaries to look up every new word in text they are reading. The use of the word in the sentence or paragraph is enough to give them a close approximation to the word's meaning. Contextual clues vary in type and quantity. Learners in the intermediate grades can be taught to employ many of these contextual aids while reading, to improve their comprehension.

Secondary Meanings

To what extent is a person's ability to utilize context in inferring meaning tied to the person's reasoning skills?

> Readers must know how to derive secondary meanings of words or phrases from their surrounding context.

Secondary meanings are those that are not directly stated but rather implied. This closely relates to connotative meanings, mentioned earlier. For example, an employee might say, "Sure, I'd be glad to comply with your directive and submit a request for approval for such activities before doing them again." If the employee were being dressed down for not complying with a regulation or policy of a business or institution, this statement could have a variety of secondary meanings. Notice, however, that secondary meanings in this statement are cued largely by pitch, stress, and juncture in speech and not in the vocabulary or the statement in print without the additional information. Therefore, contextual cues in the surrounding text are often critical in identifying secondary meanings in text.

Irony

Ask students to find examples of irony in poetry, on the sports page of a newspaper, and in a novel or short story. Discuss the differences across these literary forms.

> Effective readers must be able to recognize irony.

An event is *ironic* if its occurrence seems almost a deliberate attempt at being perverse by someone or something. It would be ironic, for example, if the greatest swimmer in the world should die by drowning. It might be considered ironic to purchase an expensive snowmobile while living in northern Wisconsin and to move to southern California within days after purchasing it.

Literary irony involves the use of words to convey an opposite, or at least different, meaning from the literal, denotative meaning of the word(s). Understanding irony either in text or in speech requires both background knowledge about a range of subjects and sensitivity to the nature of language and its use. Intermediate-grade students have both limited knowledge and limited sensitivity to the subtleties of language usage; they lack both sophistication in language use and the wide-ranging background often required for understanding irony. They can, however, appreciate the simple irony and humor in an ironic sequence of story or real-life events. Further, they should be able to understand simple satire and other more subtle meanings that authors may have. By the middle-school grades, learners become more sophisticated in their language knowledge and background, thus enabling them to deal with irony more maturely and knowledgeably.

Stating the Gist of a Text Passage

> Students must be able to state the general idea ("gist") of a passage of text.

Some would assert that the most important reading ability of all is the ability to articulate the *gist* (the main idea) of what a text passage contains. These are typically major questions on standardized tests, as well as on teacher-designed tests.

To state the main idea of a text passage is to summarize it.

Identifying the Author's Intent

> Effective readers can recognize the author's intention when writing a passage of text. Writers write text for a number of different purposes, including describing, explaining, persuading, and entertaining.

Upper-elementary grades students should be able to identify such purposes or intents. They should be able to discriminate between a descriptive essay and a persuasive argument, for example. They should be able to utilize knowledge about the author, the context, and the tone of the text to determine when what an author says on the surface does not correspond to the true intent of the text.

Although these intermediate-grade students lack the sophistication needed to comprehend author intent in demanding texts, they can develop this skill in a rudimentary form. Remember that it is the degree of sophistication and not the skill itself that evolves.

Moods in Text Passages

> Readers must learn how to identify the mood of any given text passage.

Ask students, "What is the relationship between the concepts of *mood* and *tone?*"

Some assessment data from the 1970s suggest that students, even in the middle grades, have difficulty identifying mood in poetry (e.g., the ability to tell the difference between a humorous poem and one not intended to be humorous). Variations or shifts in mood can be quite subtle, so even proficient and experienced readers may have difficulty distinguishing among different moods. However, much can be done throughout the grades to help learners make connections among content, context, and purpose of the text, to infer a reasonable guess regarding the mood of the text.

Implications and Inferences

> Effective readers must know how to identify implications made by the author or to derive valid inferences from a passage of text.

Many students untutored in formal logic tend to confuse truth and logical validity. You might point out here that in reasoning, there are three important sets of concepts: true/false, valid/invalid, sound/unsound. Reasoning is a logical process. That process itself can be valid (correctly implemented) or invalid (incorrectly implemented). We prefer to assume that the premises (the statements of information) being used in the reasoning process are true. However, the truth or falsity of the information does not affect the validity of the reasoning. That is why it is possible to have a valid argument with a false conclusion. Reasoning that employs a valid process and truthful premises results in a sound conclusion.

Reading, in many ways, is a guessing game—an ongoing educated projection or prediction of what the writer implies will take place next in the text. Good readers are constantly making predictions about what will occur next. However, in order to make such predictions, the proficient reader must infer implications from what has been read to assist in making logical predictions. Students who cannot infer reasonably have no data to use in making predictions. Their reading then becomes a wildly irrational guessing game.

This ability to infer and to use inferences for making predictions is a high-level thinking skill that can be the bread and butter of intermediate-grade reading instruction. Having moved beyond preoperational thought, these concrete-operation reasoners can be taught how to draw logical inferences and how to use such inferences as a basis for making predictions, which their younger friends cannot.

Reports Versus Judgments

> Competent readers can distinguish between reports and judgments.

This ability also requires the use of high-level thinking skills. This ability also closely relates to many of those described earlier. First, students must be able to distinguish between text designed to persuade them of something and text that simply describes something. They must then learn how to closely examine the persuasive text to see whether the author's persuasive argument depends on rhetoric and some sort of emotional appeal, or it is supported by reason and logic.

Ask students, "How can a newspaper be useful in demonstrating the difference between reports and judgments?"

Appropriateness of Text

> Students must learn how to determine the appropriateness of the text and its structure, in relation to its purpose and its context.

The concept of appropriateness is one that all literate individuals must strive to master. Appropriateness is not the same as correctness. In many senses, the concept of "correct versus incorrect" does not apply to any literacy act—speaking, writing, or reading. The appropriateness of the language, its structure, its form, and its content is determined by a number of factors, including the author's purpose, the subject, and the audience for the writing. Speech and writing never occur outside of a context. They are always shaped by the setting and associated factors, all of which the reader must consider when reading text.

The authors suggest that you repeatedly focus on the importance of the concept of "appropriateness" instead of the concept of "correctness" when it comes to language expression in either spoken or written text.

The Essential Elements of Literacy and Strategic Reading Instruction

Though the teacher of reading must know all 11 of the essential indicators of reading ability, simply knowing what they are does not spell out how to teach them. A teacher must know (a) their features and attributes, (b) their definitions, and (c) their importance for reading. However, though this is a necessary condition for teaching reading, it is not sufficient. Knowing about them does not ensure knowing how to teach children to acquire them for reading. These indicators represent benchmarks or goals that the teacher of reading should strive for rather than teaching methodologies that teachers should employ.

Ask students to hypothesize the characteristics of a strategic reader.

Effective teachers of reading want learners to develop strategies for applying the skills associated with the 11 indicator abilities needed by all effective readers. In other words, teachers seek to develop *strategic readers*. This requires the use of the teaching techniques that are most likely to ensure that learners will employ appropriate strategies for their reading. Such strategies enable students to approach reading in ways that help them to incorporate the necessary thinking skills, the appropriate background knowledge, and the critical contextual and linguistic features that are central to comprehension of text. Strategic readers are effective readers.

Key Features of Strategic Reading and of Strategic Reading Instruction

Simply put, strategic readers approach a reading task with a plan. They do not let the text dictate how they will read the text. They think about (a) the kind of text to be read, (b) the purpose of the reading, and (c) the way in which to actually do the reading.

In other words, when reading a story, a poem, a novel, a newspaper article, a book review, or a variety of other kinds of text, a strategic reader does not just pick up the text and start. A strategic reader begins the reading act by thinking about it. Strategic readers do the following:

1. Identify the purpose of the reading before starting to read
2. Identify the text's form or type before reading
3. Think about the general character and features of the text's form or type

   Example: Expository description—includes such examples as a front-page newspaper article; probably begins with a thesis or main idea sentence; is followed by ordered detail or support sentences; ends with a conclusion or restatement sentence
4. Project the author's probable purpose or purposes for writing the text
5. Select an overall plan of attack for the reading (e.g., skim, read excerpts selectively, read in detail and take notes)
6. During the reading, make ongoing predictions about what will occur next, based on (a) information obtained in earlier text, (b) prior experience and background knowledge, and (c) conclusions inferred from the foregoing Steps 1–5
7. Recapitulate the text after the reading, and formulate a summary or conclusion regarding the text

Ask students, "Is strategic reading more than high-level thinking? Or, is it simply that?"

The strategic reader must employ a number of important high-level thinking skills in each of the steps described here. In each step and throughout the application of reading strategies, the reader must do the following:

- Classify
- Sequence
- Establish whole–part relationships
- Compare and contrast
- Determine cause–effect
- Summarize
- Hypothesize or predict
- Infer
- Conclude

Some reading educators, in fact, assert that thinking and comprehension are so closely related that it is difficult to separate them as discrete skills or processes (e.g., work by Frank Smith, Kenneth Goodman, Jerry Harste and others). Regardless of professional posture on the definition of *reading* or on the selection of the most effective instructional approach. Most authorities agree on certain features of effective reading instruction:

1. Reading is a process that should be approached logically, employing applicable strategies. Students should be taught these strategies both directly and indirectly.
2. High-level thinking is the critical foundation of reading comprehension, and the important skills of high-level thinking should be taught both directly and indirectly to students.
3. It is important to teach self-monitoring, and its application should be included in the instructional program. In the upper elementary grades, learners can effectively develop self-monitoring as a conscious part of reading.
4. Reading instruction must continue across the curriculum at all grades. Social studies, science, math, and all other subject areas offer important text sources for developing effective readers. Remember that *the probability that a student will master the content and concepts of a subject is directly linked to the student's ability to read effectively!*
5. Because the cognitive tasks of writing and reading are closely linked, reading is most likely to be effective when this natural relationship is exploited to its fullest potential—using writing to generate reading comprehension, using text to generate writing, and using each to reinforce the other.

It is not enough simply to identify the instructional factors that are important for literacy development and instruction. Teachers of reading must also integrate these essential instructional elements to ensure that effective reading, writing, and speaking mastery occur.

What are those instructional elements? What must the effective teacher know about them and their use? The remainder of this chapter selectively examines the elements that are most critical for literacy instruc-

Are your students familiar with and able to employ one of the questioning taxonomies (e.g., Bloom or Sanders)? If not, this might be a good point at which to spend some time practicing application of the Sanders model.

tion and that come closest to representing what we (the authors) call "The Governing Principles of Effective Literacy Instruction." These principles relate to the following topics:

- Strategies related to questioning
- Strategies, techniques, and activities of reading instruction
- Suggestions for designing effective lessons
- Guidelines for facilitating the development of metacognition
- Guidelines for integrating the language arts

QUESTIONING

Of all the teaching tools available to the elementary teacher of literacy, the wise and judicious use of questions is perhaps the most beneficial. Reading instruction, in particular, turns on the ability of the teacher to use questions—primarily through oral language—to orchestrate learning in the classroom environment and to guide individual learning in the most productive direction.

Questions and questioning strategies are the stock and trade of the classroom teacher. This has been known for centuries. Yet, despite that long-standing knowledge, effective use of questioning for the development of reading does not always happen. In fact, in the late 1970s, Dolores Durkin's research indicated that teachers' use of questions in reading instruction left much to be desired (Durkin, 1978–1979).

Probe this distinction between instructional and monitoring questions, to be sure that your students understand it (i.e., monitor their understanding of it). Spend some time addressing what this means for the importance of the prereading stage of a reading lesson.

For example, all of the questions and question types available to the classroom teacher can be categorized into two groups: instructional questions and monitoring questions. *Instructional questions* are used by the teacher to specifically teach some aspect of reading. *Monitoring questions* are used by the teacher to find out whether the student understands what has been read. Most reading lesson questions are asked after the text has been read, so most of these questions are monitoring questions. Hence, most teachers neglect one of the most effective times for using questions, which is preceding or during the reading, and they underutilize the more valuable instructional questions in favor of postreading monitoring questions.

During the 1960s and 1970s, considerable time was devoted to the development and use of taxonomies of questions. The Bloom Taxonomy, the Barrett Taxonomy, the Sanders Taxonomy, and many others were developed to help teachers design and use questions at different cognitive levels. During that time, many assumed that too many low-level questions, such as memory- or fact-centered questions were being asked by teachers. Students were not being challenged enough by high-level questions requiring inference and logical analysis. Recent research (Hansen & Pearson, 1983) supports these early assumptions that teachers who focus their questioning on the higher levels do as well or better in teaching reading comprehension as do those who teach directly from basal questions—which tend to limit the taxonomic range—or from other sources.

This is not intended to imply that low-level questions are not important. They are very important in establishing a data base on which students can infer and perform the other cognitive tasks required in high-level questions. Thus, their relationship to the high-level questions is critical. Lower level questions should be designed to assist the learner formulating that data base.

Recent research suggests the need for questioning strategies that focus on overall lesson design of questions and questioning, from prereading through the actual text reading and during the postreading phase of the lesson (Armbruster, Anderson, et al., 1983; Cunningham & Tierney, 1984; Hansen & Pearson, 1983; Jones, 1985). When this is done, teachers use all kinds of questions.

Teachers of reading should keep in mind at all times a number of points about questions and question use. Figure 6.1 shows "a self-monitoring checklist for teachers." Teachers can use it to analyze their own instructional questions and questioning strategies. This checklist incorporates some of the key assumptions now made about effective use of questioning to develop strong readers.

Some students are likely to place memory-level questions in the same category with drill sheets! The authors suggest spending some time with examples that address the importance of memory-level questions in helping learners to infer sound conclusions from text.

From Strategies to Techniques to Activities

Effective teaching of any aspect of literacy requires the teacher to make important planning and teaching distinctions among three concepts: strategy, technique, and activity. These three terms are often used interchangeably in the literature and by practicing teachers. It is helpful, however, to attempt some distinctions among them.

In brief, a *strategy* is an overall plan for a particular lesson. In planning a lesson, the teacher needs to decide on an overall strategy, with techniques that are appropriate for implementing the strategy. A *technique* may be thought of as a "microstrategy": a combination of brief related *activities* that are usually designed to teach one particular skill, concept, or set of interrelated skills or concepts. Techniques include semantic mapping, direct instruction in vocabulary expansion or story grammar, sentence-combining as a tool for developing writing–reading connections, question insertion and advance organizers.

Activities include all the specific things that students do to learn, explore, or practice a skill or process being taught via a teaching technique. For example, a worksheet showing a story grammar map for students to complete while reading could be seen as an activity implementing a story grammar teaching technique, which fits into an overall strategy for teaching reading comprehension. Activities are specific applications or practice

The distinction between strategy and technique is intended to be a general conceptual one. Do not push too hard in arguing a distinction in all specific instances.

Note that some of the ideas and concepts referred to in this questioning checklist have not been covered yet in this text. They appear in later chapters. That should not be a significant problem, however, because most are defined or exemplified briefly here.

Figure 6.1   Attributes of effective questions and questioning for developing high-level thinking in learners: a self-monitoring checklist for teachers.

Directions: Rate your teaching by checking "yes" or "no" for each of the following criterion statements.

YES   *NO*

——— ———   1. **I try to use a questioning strategy rather than to ask questions as they come up or as they occur to me.**

(A *strategy* is a general overall questioning plan for the entire lesson where the teacher thinks through the prereading, reading, and postreading stages of the lesson with governing questions being thought out prior to the instruction.)

——— ———   2. **Questions that I ask after students have read the assigned text are tied to those I have asked prior to their reading of the text.**

(Teachers exploit the instructional power residing in questions that can be asked during the prereading stage of instruction. Remember that it is here where the teacher has the potential for exploiting the background knowledge students bring to the learning context. Questions asked at this time can help students establish the necessary mental benchmarks against which they can make predictions and draw inferences as they read.)

——— ———   3. **I am knowledgeable about different question taxonomies (e.g., the Bloom or the Sanders taxonomy), and I regularly use an appropriate one in examining suggested questions in all of my various textbooks and subjects and in my own question design.**

(Remember that there are various types of taxonomies, although most teachers think most often of Bloom or of Sanders.)

——— ———   4. **I self-monitor my questioning during class discussions and know approximately the proportion of high-level cognition questions I ask compared to the amount of low-level ones I ask.**

(Most authorities define *high-level questions* as those at the application level and higher—analysis, evaluation,

Figure 6.1 *(continued)*

and synthesis. Some prefer to include the interpretation level as well.)

_____ _____ 5. **I regularly ask students questions during the prereading stage of a lesson or assignment; these questions implicitly pressure them to make predictions or to hypothesize about what might take place in their reading of that text.**

(The prereading stage is the most useful for asking instructional questions. Questions that require learners to make educated guesses about what could occur given certain information provided in the text title or in other information from previous lessons can help provide excellent mental benchmarks against which to measure their reading.)

_____ _____ 6. **I regularly begin questioning with a high-level inferential question that requires students to infer a conclusion—usually a conclusion that can be stated in the form of a generalization or an instantiation of a generalization.**

(Remember that focusing students' initial thinking is important. Hypothesis, inferential, and suppositional questions typically require global thinking and searching for the gist. Other things being equal, it is more desirable to start with the bigger picture and move down to specifics, rather than the reverse.)

_____ _____ 7. **When I use low-level questions, such as memory or translation questions, they are chosen in order to require the student to use the necessary discriminating skills to determine the saliency and appropriateness of particular recall items.**

(Low-level questions are important! However, even more important is the ability to sift and winnow a myriad of details and facts to select only those relevant to important questions or problems guiding the reading.)

_____ _____ 8. **I use questions designed to help students establish analogies when the subject matter is new to them. For example, prior to students' reading of a text, I ask them questions designed to evoke thoughts about specific things that have happened to them that may be similar to important events or ideas in the text.**

Figure 6.1   *(continued)*

(It is reasonable to assume that all students do not have like background knowledge and experience that could be important for comprehension of the concepts and ideas in the lesson. Incorporating an analogy that will allow them to make a mental link with the familiar will help comprehension. Some authorities refer to this as helping students "bridge from the known to the unknown.")

9. **I use variety in the kinds of questioning strategies I employ, but I am consistent within a specific strategy so that students can anticipate the kinds of questions likely to follow from earlier ones.**

(Remember that strategies are essentially overall plans that provide the framework of the lesson. Features of a strategy should be consistent, regular, and quite predictable. Predictability is important for learners to be able to project what is to follow and to develop the necessary anticipatory mental set. Variety should be provided through activities and supportive techniques.)

10. **I regularly use *advance organizers* (which prepare students to organize the information that will be provided) and supporting questions in appropriate subjects.**

(Keep in mind that *advance organizers* can be in the form of outlines, summaries, graphics, and so on. The phrasing of questions in the appropriate language and form focusing on the advance organizer can help the learner establish that important overall picture of the lesson before he or she gets into it.)

11. **I provide a balance of oral advance organizer questions and written advance organizer questions.**

(Using written questions as guides to the reading or guides to the lesson is an effective alternative to the oral advance organizer. They provide variety, and they present an ongoing physical presence that students can keep in front of them throughout the lesson.)

12. **I use techniques that require the students to taxonomize their own questions; that is, I teach them a simplified taxonomy and how to use it.**

(An excellent metacognitive technique is to provide examples of fact questions and thought or opinion

Figure 6.1 *(continued)*

questions to students and then ask them to categorize questions on a text you provide. This should be followed by having them write examples of these two question types in relation to their text. This technique can be used as low as the primary grades. A more expanded taxonomy can be used in the upper grades.)

 13. **I regularly use glossing or inserted questions in texts students are required to read.**

(For example, choose nonfiction text [e.g., social studies or science texts] that can be duplicated as a handout. Type questions in the margin that interrupt the reading, requiring the reader to write out answers before continuing the reading. Notice how the opportunity to enter into the reading act and suggest predictions using proper questions can help the learner to think about his or her own thinking—a critical attribute of effective learners and thinkers.)

14. **I regularly use reciprocal questioning—both oral and written—in my teaching.**

(In *reciprocal questioning*, the teacher and the students reverse roles. For example, "Children, I want you to read these paragraphs in your social studies text, then I'm going to ask you three questions to see whether you understood what you read." After doing that, the teacher then indicates, "Now, boys and girls, we are going to read the next three paragraphs, and I want you to write down three questions you can ask me to see if I understood what I read." Students love it as an activity because they don't have to answer any questions!)

15. **I attempt to relate the questioning strategy and the questions I use to the objectives of the lesson. For example, if I am teaching a particular skill or set of skills, the proportion of questions I ask aimed at each skill relates to the importance of that skill in my objectives.**

(Although this sounds obvious and straightforward for most teaching, it is easy to get side-tracked and to forget that the quantity and quality of questions in the classroom should bear a relationship to the lesson objectives.)

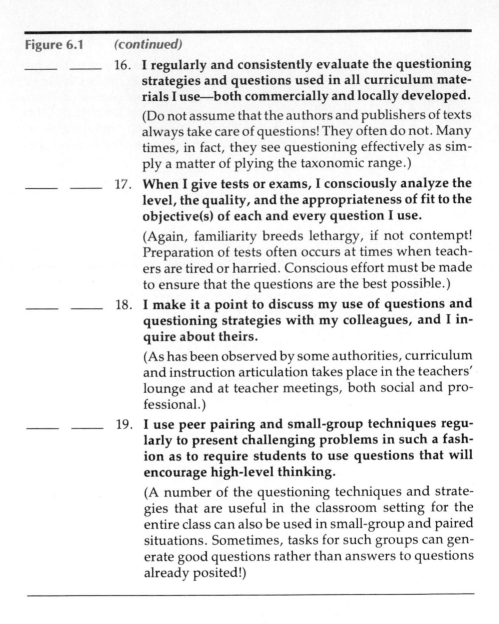

Figure 6.1   *(continued)*

_____ _____ 16. **I regularly and consistently evaluate the questioning strategies and questions used in all curriculum materials I use—both commercially and locally developed.**

(Do not assume that the authors and publishers of texts always take care of questions! They often do not. Many times, in fact, they see questioning effectively as simply a matter of plying the taxonomic range.)

_____ _____ 17. **When I give tests or exams, I consciously analyze the level, the quality, and the appropriateness of fit to the objective(s) of each and every question I use.**

(Again, familiarity breeds lethargy, if not contempt! Preparation of tests often occurs at times when teachers are tired or harried. Conscious effort must be made to ensure that the questions are the best possible.)

_____ _____ 18. **I make it a point to discuss my use of questions and questioning strategies with my colleagues, and I inquire about theirs.**

(As has been observed by some authorities, curriculum and instruction articulation takes place in the teachers' lounge and at teacher meetings, both social and professional.)

_____ _____ 19. **I use peer pairing and small-group techniques regularly to present challenging problems in such a fashion as to require students to use questions that will encourage high-level thinking.**

(A number of the questioning techniques and strategies that are useful in the classroom setting for the entire class can also be used in small-group and paired situations. Sometimes, tasks for such groups can generate good questions rather than answers to questions already posited!)

Ask students to suggest other similar or different strategies.

situations in which the learners engage in order to achieve the objectives being targeted by the overall strategy and the selected techniques.

Although strategies are commonly more global and informal in character, they can be fairly specific. For example, Klein (1988) describes three strategies as examples: the Predict–Test–Conclude Strategy, the Analogy–Fit–Infer Strategy, and the Summarize–Monitor–Summarize Strategy. Each is an overall plan for a lesson design to teach reading, although the plans could fit any of a number of content or concept areas.

Predict–Test–Conclude

The Predict–Test–Conclude strategy consists of the following steps:

1. During the prereading phase of the lesson, the teacher asks questions or uses techniques and activities that implicitly require the student to make predictions about outcomes likely to be read in text. For example, if the class is going to be reading a story entitled, "A Day at the Pond," the teacher might ask,

   "What do you think a story with this title will be about?"

   "What kind of characters will be in a story with such a title?"

   "Look at the pictures in the text, but do not read the text, and then write out three things that you think will happen in this story."

2. During the reading of the text, ask students to test their predictions. Note which predictions were correct or which were not. Ask them to think about why they were or were not on target.
3. Ask students to articulate the differences between what they predicted about the story and what the story was actually about. Ask them to explain where and why they went wrong in instances where their prereading predictions were off base.

This strategy is particularly effective in helping students become strategic readers. It helps them learn how to view reading as an active process during which the reader is constantly hypothesizing, predicting, and establishing predictions to bear in mind while reading the text.

Analogy–Fit–Infer

The Analogy–Fit–Infer strategy employs the following steps:

1. During the prereading phase, introduce a topic, problem, situation, experience, or object that is very similar to one that is central to the text to be read. For example, if the text is a social studies chapter dealing with the U.S. Supreme Court and its role in the U.S. federal government, and if the students have little prior knowledge or experience with the court, the teacher might search for an appropriate analogy that students could relate to.

   First, the teacher must determine the key concepts to be conveyed. In this example, it might be the following: An important role for the court is to ameliorate differences, to serve as arbiter in cases or instances where parties cannot agree. Sometimes the differences are between the U.S. President and the U.S. Congress. More often, they are decisive cases dealing with questions about how to apply the U.S. Constitution. To provide an analogy, the teacher might introduce the example of a brother and sister who have occasional differences of opinion with a discussion of how

Analogical thinking can be quite challenging to young learners, so student teachers should keep the analogies clean and simple in the early grade years. Remember also that analogies are simply comparisons of similar things, not identical things. All analogies break down at some point in their ability to compare or contrast all points or features of ideas or things.

such differences are resolved. "When discussion does not work in your family, Jimmy, and your sister and you cannot agree, who decides for you?" Next, discuss people and procedures involved in conflict resolution.

2. Students are instructed to keep the elements of the analogy in mind while reading the text, relating elements of the text to their counterparts in the analogy. For example, the family disagreement analogy includes a sister, a brother, and the parents. Assume that the text includes consideration of the U.S. President, the U.S. Congress, and the Supreme Court. Students can project relationships, using the prereading analogy as a structural guide for the reading and as the basis for making predictions.

3. After the text reading, ask students to verify their predicted analogical components and articulate specific ways the components are like each other.

This strategy is particularly effective when the subject of the reading is likely to be one where students have little or no background knowledge.

Summarize–Monitor–Summarize

The Summarize–Monitor–Summarize strategy is quite simple and straightforward:

1. The teacher presents a brief summary of the key ideas in the text to be read during the prereading phase. The summary can be provided as an outline, as a set of key idea statements, or as a brief paragraph. It can be presented in writing or orally.

2. Students use the summary as a guide during their reading.

3. Students are asked to summarize the text in their own words after the reading and are asked to explain differences between the teacher's summary and their own.

Ask students to think of how writing can be integrated into all reading instruction strategies.

In many instances, the third strategy is somewhat too teacher dominated and deductively organized. Its use would normally be reserved for topics that are extremely complex or in situations where the teacher wants to move rapidly through the topic of the lesson.

The preceding are only examples of a variety of strategies. To summarize strategies, techniques, and activities,

More detailed treatment of the differing needs of novice versus experienced teachers is covered in Chapter 8.

- Strategies are overall plans for lessons.
- Strategies incorporate techniques and activities.
- Strategies serve as models for thinking, which students can both observe and participate in.

Effective Lesson Design

With teaching experience, the practiced teacher needs less guidance than does the novice. The experienced teacher uses the lesson plan as a guide: It represents a probable scenario from which to deviate rather than a fixed and ordered process with little flexibility. In the early stages of teaching, however, it is important to have well-written, well-organized, and instructionally sound lesson plans in reading instruction.

Lesson plans can be designed to fit any of the different schools of thought about how literacy can best be developed. For example, a number of skills-based-program advocates argue that the lesson plan should be very tightly structured to ensure that all learning experiences focus on appropriately sequenced mastery of specific reading–writing–speaking skills. These advocates would usually suggest that these skills be taught by means of direct formal instruction, with students moving from (a) skill definition to (b) demonstrated uses to (c) guided initial experiences to (d) application of those experiences to (e) independent practice to (f) evaluation of mastery. Some programs still depend on the underlying assumption that a skills hierarchy exists and that the ordering of instruction is important, though this assumption has little empirical support (Athey, 1974; Rosenshine, 1980; White, 1973).

Lack of empirical support for a rigidly sequenced hierarchy does not mean, however, that authorities deny the importance of selected reading skills. For example, Rosenshine lists seven skills found most commonly in a number of respected sources: (1) locating details; (2) understanding words in context; (3) recognizing the sequence of events; (4) recognizing cause–effect relationships; (5) comparing and contrasting relevant attributes; (6) recognizing main idea, title, and/or topic; and (7) drawing conclusions and predicting outcomes (Rosenshine, 1980). Many of these have been listed earlier in this chapter as key reading indicators. Thus, though the hierarchical relationships of these elements are questioned, the importance of these skills as performance indicators of reading mastery is not.

Effective literacy instruction depends on lesson plans that have (a) a focus, with clearly stated objectives, (b) a strategy formulated to include appropriate techniques and well-described activities, (c) a method for monitoring or evaluating student progress, and (d) a basic guideline for the timing of events within the lesson. The chapter on reading comprehension in the intermediate grades provides more details about lesson plan design.

Developing Metacognitive Abilities

Thinking about thinking—Good readers, good writers, effective speakers, and logical thinkers all do that. They think about their own thinking. They

Ask students, "Is there a role for skills instruction in the reading program? What relationship is there between reading skills and reading processes? What is the relationship between reading instruction philosophy and reading instruction practice?"

Ask students, "How much time should be spent on direct instruction in metacognition? Should it all be addressed informally in role-playing activities or in language play?"

self-analyze and self-monitor. Following is an excellent example of megacognition based on personal experience:

> One of my favorite books is *The Name of the Rose* by Umberto Eco. It is an engrossing book set in 14th century Italy in a monastery where a series of strange incidents and, later, murders occur. The book is historically accurate, and the plot is very complex, with much detail about the religious turmoil of the period with a papacy in Rome and another at Avignon. There were numerous orders, cloisters, and complex belief systems associated with each.
>
> I was a history major and it was still a challenge to read this book. I dug into my personal library for old history texts that dealt with that period, realizing that background knowledge was critical.
>
> I remember reading and coming to the end of a paragraph. I stopped and said to myself, "Stop. You have just read this paragraph. You know the meanings of the individual words. You know the meanings of the sentences. And, yet, you have no idea what this paragraph means!"
>
> This was a typical reading situation for me. I self-monitored, constantly thinking about my own thinking.
>
> I am a self-monitoring reader: I maintain an ongoing questioning of my interpretation of what I read.

Unfortunately, it is easier to talk about using self-monitoring than it is to master the process. Students need to master the process. They must become conscious of what they already know. Remember, however, that research by developmental psychologists indicates that this ability to think about one's own thinking is a natural evolutionary development that cannot be hastened. However, the ability to consciously use this metacognitive ability is primarily a function of instruction from an effective teacher of reading.

Strategic readers have mastered the skill of self-monitoring. Strategic readers must be able to analyze their own thinking during the reading act while they are simultaneously analyzing the text being read (Bloome & Green, 1984; Garner, 1987; Palincsar & Brown, 1983; Paris, et al., 1982, 1983, 1984).

Garner (1987) recommends six guidelines for the classroom teacher to use to develop metacognitive (self-monitoring) facility in learners, which can be briefly summarized as follows:

1. Process orientation
2. Strategy analysis
3. Multisubject applications of strategies
4. Long-term use of strategies
5. Opportunities for practice of strategies
6. Opportunities for peer tutoring

Have students review recent issues of the *Reading Research Quarterly* for studies in metacognition and reading. Ask students what these studies have to say about metacognition and reading.

Guideline 1: Process Orientation

"Teachers must care about the processes involved in reading and studying, and [they] must be willing to devote instructional time to them."

Teachers must commit themselves to thinking about ways to capitalize on instructional opportunities for developing metacognitive skills in students. This can range from informal modeling to formal direct instruction that presents the actual steps in a reading task and then monitors students to see whether they employ them. Informal modeling may be simply a "Think-along" or "Read-along," as it is sometimes called: In this modeling, a reader reads a text orally with natural interruptions for articulating intruding thoughts as well as metacognitive applications that can be made during the reading. Students are thus allowed the opportunity to sort of look into another person's head, momentarily at least, to see how an efficient reader approaches the reading act.

Urge student teachers to remember to read different forms of text written for different purposes in their "read-alongs" or "think-alongs."

Guideline 2: Strategy Analysis

"Teachers must analyze the strategies to be taught."

This guideline fits naturally with the first. The teacher must do a task analysis of various reading acts and attempt to articulate step-by-step what goes on in his or her head during such reading. For example, what are the strategies used when reading "Rumplestiltskin" as opposed to reading a complex college textbook in chemistry.

Guideline 3: Multisubject Applications

"Teachers must present strategies as applicable to texts and tasks in more than one content domain."

Teachers must constantly look to various subjects—math, social studies, science, art, and so on—for useful texts to use to demonstrate or model a metacognitive technique or strategy.

Guideline 4: Long-Term Usage

> "Teachers must teach strategies over an entire year, not in just a single lesson or unit."

Remember the first guideline! The teacher must maintain an ongoing commitment to the importance and applicability of this important element of effective reading.

Guideline 5: Opportunities for Practice

> "Teachers must provide students with opportunities to practice strategies they have been taught."

Practice has an important place in literacy instruction. Though reading drill has certainly been overused, teachers should not generalize from that to assume that any and all practice situations are inappropriate and irrelevant. Such a belief would deprive students of an important component of any effective reading program. Though swimming, golfing, driving a car, and reading are all very different in nature, they all share at least one thing: increased practice results in increased skill. Practice is critical to becoming proficient in any undertaking.

Guideline 6: Opportunities for Peer Tutoring

> "Teachers must be prepared to let students teach each other about reading and studying processes."

Peer teaching cannot be underestimated as an instructional methodology. Modeling of thinking is an accepted contemporary teaching strategy. Adults should not, however, forget that their thinking processes may not match in every way with those of children. Cognitive development, experiences, and so on all play roles. Therefore, opportunities to learn from peers should be provided regularly.

Integration of Language Arts

Although it is possible to identify important discrete skills to be learned in reading, writing, speaking, and listening, reading and literacy educators have generally held that the reading teacher should capitalize on the

Ask students, "Is there a difference between 'integrated language arts' instruction and 'interrelated language arts' instruction?" Talk about how these two phrases are sometimes used interchangeably in the literature.

natural relationships among the various language arts domains (Graves, 1975; Harste, Woodward, & Burke, 1984; Johnson & Louis, 1985; Klein, 1985; McCracken & McCracken, 1986; Moffett & Wagner, 1976). The nature of written and oral text is generally similar. Even young children are tacitly encouraged in various ways to draw connections between print and speech. Longitudinal research has indicated a continuous strong correlation among the abilities of an individual to read, speak, and write (Loban, 1976).

It is important, however, to remember that one should not push these natural connections to the extreme. A substantial body of research suggests that traditional direct instruction in reading contributes little to the development of writing, although writing integrated into reading instruction seems to assist in the development of both (Stotsky, 1983).

The following should guide the design and development of instruction for effective integration of the language arts areas to improve reading:

- Integrate writing experiences with reading instruction.
- Build reading and writing skills via oral language experiences.
- Permeate all content-area instruction with language-arts instruction.
- Teach concepts, skills, and processes in equivalent measure.

> Make writing integral to the reading instruction, and also use it to supplement the instruction.

This important distinction is emphasized throughout this book. Ask students to keep it in mind as they read about reading strategies, techniques, and activities in the remainder of this book.

The following activities use writing to supplement the reading instruction:

- Ask children to write a poem about the topic they have just read in their reading lesson.
- Have students write a report on a related topic of interest after reading a unit on dinosaurs.
- Ask children to write follow-up letters to the editor of the local newspaper after they have read a selection about news writing in the basal reader.

These activities generally follow, or sometimes precede, the reading instruction.

To integrate writing into the instruction, the writing must occur at least occasionally during the reading process. For example, teaching children to write notes or comments in their journals during the act of reading integrates the writing into the reading. Other options for integration include (a) using texts that have written questions in the margins, which periodically interrupt the reading and require the reader to write answers to the questions, or (b) asking children to write one-sentence summaries for each paragraph in a nonfiction selection they are reading. These limited examples may have limited potential for application, but the important point is that writing activities should be offered that both supplement reading instruction and integrate into reading instruction.

> **Capitalize on oral language as the major integrating language arts skill for building reading and writing abilities.**

Remember that oral language represents the base of all language skills development. By focusing on oral language, the teacher accomplishes two important goals: (1) The student uses both thinking and language skills to further both cognitive abilities and oral language facility. (2) The student becomes aware of personal growth of knowledge and development of skills as a result of interactions with the teacher and with peers. At least some of the knowledge that aids in comprehension of text to be read can be generated in a prereading discussion. Oral language is the essential springboard to integration of the language arts and skills.

> **Recognize that all subject areas are learned and understood through integrated language arts instructional strategies and techniques.**

Students learn social studies, math, science, and all other subjects through the language vehicles of talking, reading, writing, and listening. In many senses, social studies cannot be taught without teaching reading comprehension and vocabulary. Further, reading comprehension and vocabulary cannot be taught without simultaneously teaching learners a great deal about some other content area (e.g., literature or social, biological, or physical science). The relationships among all school learnings are melded with the integrated language arts.

Metanalyses of research on writing instruction by George Hillocks, Jr., in 1984, suggests instruction in sentence-combining to be twice as effective as free-writing practice alone in improving writing ability in students. Balanced instruction is important.

> **Maintain balance in instruction among skills and processes and concepts.**

Integrated language arts instruction cannot be used as an excuse for not providing adequate instruction in the critical skills, processes, and concepts of various subjects. For example, virtually all educators would agree that mastery of cause–effect relationships is critical to effective reading. Further, most would agree that an ineffective way to develop this skill is by having students complete multiple pages of drill in workbooks. Nonetheless, practice and application of the skill must be incorporated somehow into the instruction. Somewhere between no direct instruction and rote drill lies an instructionally rich zone where introduction, application, and practice can be provided in a variety of contexts, with a variety of content.

Development of language arts skills and application of language arts processes are both necessary for literacy development. However, they function largely as learning tools for the learner to apply when mastering the generalizations, principles, and concepts that define the structure of knowledge in the various fields of learning represented in school subjects. Balance is important.

HIGHLIGHTS

1. Learners in the intermediate and middle-school grades are more cognitively advanced than their primary grades counterparts. Many of these cognitive developments have direct impact on the way students approach the reading act and thus on the kinds of teaching techniques and strategies teachers can use when teaching them how to read effectively.
2. Important reading indicators represent benchmarks that should govern the design and/or selection of appropriate instructional materials and methodologies for teaching children to read throughout the grades.
3. Strategic reading is an essential element of reading and reading instruction. Effective learners know how to approach the reading act by employing reading strategies.
4. Effective questions and effective questioning strategies and techniques determine in large measure the degree of success the teacher has in teaching children to read. Mastering the complexities and subtleties of effective questioning should be an ongoing goal of all teachers of reading.
5. Effective teachers of reading distinguish among strategies, techniques, and activities. Techniques and activities are fitted to the governing *teaching strategy*, which is the overall plan of instruction for a reading lesson.
6. Clear, concise, orderly, and tightly organized lesson plans are essential for effective reading instruction, especially in the beginning years of the new teacher. They provide the necessary guidance and direction for ensuring the likelihood of a successful lesson.
7. Ability to employ metacognitive skills in a conscious manner is a major attribute of an effective reader. Teaching students the rudiments of self-monitoring, or other conscious applications of some of their metacognitive abilities, is an important challenge for the teacher of reading.

8. Integrating the language arts in instruction is an effective means for developing good readers. Knowing how to integrate the language arts skills and processes naturally and meaningfully is a goal for the classroom teacher of reading.

REINFORCEMENT ACTIVITIES

Differences in student background are a factor for this activity. Ask students to consider their different coursework in developmental psychology.

It may be useful to pair students and ask them to react to each other's papers.

Ask for specific examples of teaching lessons or activities to exemplify applicability at given grade levels.

Discuss the answers in relation to this chapter's argument for a difference between *strategy* and *technique*.

Encourage some creativity in the responses to this activity.

Remember to be liberal in accepting student teachers' responses. Look for conceptualization rather than graphic detailed elaboration of differences.

Ask students to support their arguments with examples or illustrations of applicability.

1. Identify several distinguishing cognitive attributes of upper-elementary-grade students that have an impact on what reading content is used and how reading is taught to learners in this age range. Compare this content and these instructional approaches to one that might be used with primary-grade children.
2. Write your own definition of reading and reading instruction. Explain why you believe as you do.
3. Of the 11 reading indicators discussed in this chapter, indicate those that would be
   a. most difficult to teach to students in this grade range
   b. easiest to teach to students in this grade range
   Discuss the reasons for your choices with others in class.
4. What is meant by "strategic reading"? Why is it important?
5. Why is questioning so important for reading instruction? What are several important question-use characteristics of a classroom teacher who teaches reading well?
6. Explain the differences among strategies, techniques, and activities. Give an example of a strategy. Why is it important for a teacher of reading to know these differences?
7. Why is metacognition important to reading and to reading instruction?

ADDITIONAL PROJECTS

1. Visit a first-grade classroom, and note the behavior of the children, the kinds of materials the teacher uses for teaching reading, and the kinds of questions he or she asks the children. Observe, too, the kinds of tasks they are required to perform in the reading class.
   Do the same thing in a sixth-grade classroom.
   Discuss the major differences between the two classes in a small group discussion.
2. Obtain some examples of Piagetian measures or tests of concrete reasoning. Use the concrete tests (e.g., some vs. all, inclusion vs. exclusion) with both first graders and fourth graders. Notice the differences in performances between the two grades. Discuss the results with others in your class.

3. Invite a developmental psychologist to your class to discuss the important differences among primary-grade, intermediate-grade, and middle-school-level students, in terms of their implications for reading instruction.

4. Examine a number of contemporary reading text programs in use in the schools. Look especially for efforts by these programs to focus on strategic reading and the use of metacognitive or self-monitoring strategies or techniques in their teacher's editions or teacher's manuals.

5. Using one of the question taxonomies listed in the references section of this book, categorize questions used in several reading and social studies textbooks. Try to infer some generalizations about the question types used by the textbook authors. Discuss your findings in class.

REFERENCES

Armbruster, B., Anderson, T., et al. (1983). *What did you mean by that question? A taxonomy of American history questions* (Reading Education Report No. 308). Urbana IL: Center for the Study of Reading.

Athey, I. (1974). *Essential skills and skills hierarchies in reading comprehension and decoding instruction.* Paper presented at the Conference of the National Institute of Education, Washington, DC.

Bloome, D., & Green, J. (1984). Directions in the sociolinguistic study of reading. In P. D. Pearson et al. (Eds.), *Handbook of Reading Research.* New York: Longman.

Cunningham, J., & Tierney, R. (1984). Research of teaching reading comprehension. In P. D. Pearson et al. (Eds.), *Handbook of Reading Research.* New York: Longman.

Durkin, D. (1978–1979). What classroom observations reveal about reading comprehension instruction. *Reading Research Quarterly, 14,* 481–533.

Garner, R. (1987). *Metacognition and Reading Comprehension.* Norwood, NJ: Ablex.

Graves, D. (1975). An Examination of the Writing Processes of Seven Year Old Children. *Research in the Teaching of English, 9,* 227–241.

Hansen, J., & Pearson, P. D. (1983). An instructional study: Improving the inferential comprehension of fourth grade good and poor readers. *Journal of Educational Psychology, 75,* 821–829.

Harste, J., Woodward, V., & Burke, C. (1984). *Language Stories and Literacy Lessons.* Portsmouth, NH: Heinemann.

Johnson, T., & Louis, D. (1985). *Literacy through Literature.* Melbourne, Australia: Methuen.

Jones, B. F. (1985). Response instruction. In T. Harris & E. Cooper (Eds.), *Reading, Thinking and Concept Development.* New York: College Entrance Examination Board.

Klein, M. (1988). *Teaching Reading Comprehension and Vocabulary: A Guide for Teachers.* Englewood Cliffs, NJ: Prentice-Hall.

Klein, M. (1985). *The Development of Writing in Children: Pre-K through Grade 8.* Englewood Cliffs, NJ: Prentice-Hall.

Loban, W. (1976). *Language Development: Kindergarten through Grade 12.* Urbana, IL: National Council of Teachers of English.

McCracken, R., & McCracken, M. (1986). *Stories, Songs, and Poetry to Teach Reading and Writing.* Chicago: American Library Association.

Moffett, J., & Wagner, B. (1976). *Student-Centered Language Arts and Reading, K–13.* Boston: Houghton-Mifflin.

Palincsar, A. S., & Brown, A. L. (1983). *Reciprocal teaching of comprehension-monitoring activities* (Tech. Rep. No. 269). Urbana, IL: Center for the Study of Reading.

Paris, S., et al. (1984). The benefits of informed instruction for children's reading awareness and comprehension skills. *Child Development, 55,* 2083–2093.

Paris, S., et al. (1983). Becoming a strategic reader. *Contemporary Educational Psychology, 8,* 293–316.

Paris, S., et al. (1982). The development of cognitive skills during childhood. In B. W. Wolman (Ed.), *Handbook of Developmental Psychology* (pp. 333–349). Englewood Cliffs, NJ: Prentice-Hall.

Rosenshine, B. V. (1980). Skills hierarchies in reading comprehension. In R. J. Spiro, B. C. Bruce, & W. F. Brewer (Eds.), *Theoretical Issues in Reading Comprehension* (pp. 535–554). Hillsdale, NJ: Erlbaum.

Stotsky, S. (1983). Research on reading/writing relationships: A synthesis and suggested directions. *Language Arts, 60,* 627–642.

White, R. T. (1973). Research into learning hierarchies. *Review of Education Research,* 43, 361–375.

ADDITIONAL RESOURCES

Aulls, M. (1982). *Developing Readers in Today's Elementary Schools.* Boston: Allyn & Bacon.

Horowitz, R., & Samuels, S. J. (1987). *Comprehending Oral and Written Language.* New York: Academic Press.

Piaget, J. (1959). *The Language and Thought of the Child.* New York: The Humanities Press.

Sanders, N. (1966). *Classroom Questions: What Kinds?* New York: Harper Row.

CHAPTER 7

DEVELOPING READING COMPREHENSION IN THE ELEMENTARY GRADES

The right to know is like the right to live. It is fundamental and unconditional in its assumption that knowledge, like life, is a desireable thing.

G. B. Shaw, *Doctor's Dilemma*

PREVIEW

The primary responsibility of the teacher of reading in the intermediate and middle school grades is the same as that of teachers of reading throughout all of the grades: to develop perceptive, analytical, and sensitive comprehenders of written text—readers who are able both to understand a variety of texts and to respond appropriately.

It is clear that there will continue to be wide differences in reading ability through the grades, and teachers must be prepared to deal with many reading problems. Teachers' primary attention, however, should be on developing reading comprehension, reading vocabulary, and study skills, which are necessary for all developing readers.

This chapter focuses on teaching strategies, techniques, and activities that facilitate effective instruction in reading comprehension.

FOCUS QUESTIONS

As you read this chapter, keep the following questions in mind:

1. What does an effective reading lesson plan look like? Why is it important?
2. What and how does strategic reading develop, and what teaching techniques can facilitate its development?
3. What are some high-level thinking skills, and why are they important for reading?
4. How can teachers use writing and high-level thinking activities and experiences to facilitate the effective teaching of reading comprehension?

Teacher education programs vary enough that students in the reading methods course might not have had instruction in how to prepare a daily lesson plan. Therefore, the amount of time you wish to devote to this part of the chapter will depend on your students' backgrounds

193

FOUR KEY FEATURES OF A LESSON PLAN

The most important single step in the reading lesson is the design and development of an effective lesson plan. A variety of lesson plan formats are available for use, all of which contain four important components:

1. Statements of the lesson's objectives
2. Summary of the lesson strategy
3. Sequence of lesson events and their timing
4. Evaluation or monitoring

Statements of the Lesson's Objectives

A reading lesson's objective statements should be brief, succinct, specific, and limited in number—no more than two or three per lesson. It is commonly accepted today that most of these objective statements indicate some performance outcome. For example, ''The student will be able to . . . .'' (''SWBAT'') is common in objective statements.

For example, if the lesson were addressing cause–effect relationships, the following objective statements would be possible:

1. The student will be able to (SWBAT) recognize cause and effect.
2. SWBAT identify cause and effect relationships used in a story.
3. When given a statement of cause and effect, SWBAT tell which part of a sentence contains the cause and which part contains the effect.
4. SWBAT underline the cause part of a sentence in 8 out of 10 sentences.

Most contemporary reading teachers would probably suggest that the first objective statement is too general and vague, and that the fourth is probably unnecessarily too specific and mechanical. The second and third objectives seem more reasonable—not too detailed, yet adequately specific to allow an observer or the teacher to determine whether the learners are accomplishing the desired result.

- Choose important objectives relevant to the reading program and the needs of the learners.
- Articulate the objectives throughout the year so that learners benefit from any cumulative effect that some skills or concepts might provide.
- State the objectives clearly and with enough detail to ensure the teacher's ability to determine (after the instruction) whether the objective was achieved.

- Limit the number of the objective statements for individual lessons. Keep them in line with both the amount of instructional time available and the ability levels of the students.

Another consideration is the adopted reading program of the school district or the locally developed curriculum. Often, these will indicate the necessary skills and objectives to be addressed at each grade level, though there may be some variation as to how much discretion the individual classroom teacher has in determining objectives to be addressed throughout the year. If the district uses a commercially developed reading program with its own scope and sequence of skills and objectives, the teacher may be expected to be accountable for teaching to that scope and sequence. Such reading programs include teachers' editions and manuals with complete individual detailed lesson plans. In most school systems, however, there is considerable freedom allowed to individual teachers in the use of such manuals, and it is likely that the school district also uses a locally developed scope and sequence.

Regardless of whether teachers' manuals are used for reading instruction, individual teachers still must/can choose how to approach reading as it relates to lessons in the subject areas because reading programs typically assume a separate block of time for reading instruction. Also, to approach language arts/reading from an integrated orientation, teachers will need to design their own lesson plans.

> It is important that students be made aware that the degree of freedom they have regarding curriculum decisions will depend on the school district philosophy and policies. They must feel comfortable with those policies and philosophy in order to teach effectively.

Brief Description of the Overall Lesson Strategy

Usually, a paragraph or two describing the overall strategy of the lesson gives an overview of the lesson.

> *Example:* "During the prereading phase of the lesson, establish an analogy between a family disagreement and the division between England and the colonies leading to the American Revolution. Students will be asked to maintain the analogy through questions during reading and in the postreading discussion."

Some lesson-plan formats do not require this step, but the authors find it helpful for new teachers to write brief statements summarizing the main thrust of their lesson's approach.

Sequence of Teaching Events and Associated Timeline

Typically, this is done in outline form. This is the heart of the lesson plan governing the structure and procedure of the lesson. Though the outline must provide enough detail to know what is actually to take place, it is not necessary to have detailed narrative in this part of the plan.

The authors prefer to break this part of the plan into three phases—prereading, reading, and postreading. By doing this, it is easier to remember the importance of the prereading phase of instruction—a phase that is too often neglected during instruction.

Evaluation or Monitoring of Students' Progress

Each lesson plan should briefly describe how the teacher will evaluate or monitor the students' achievement of the lesson's objectives, in order to determine whether the lesson was successful. This further aids new teachers in determining which aspects of instruction were strong and which need improvement. This does not suggest a formal test to accompany each lesson. It simple means that teachers must articulate the way to determine the degree of success of this particular lesson.

THE TEACHER'S EDITION LESSON PLAN VERSUS THE TEACHER'S SELF-DESIGNED LESSON PLAN

As is generally well-known, commercially published reading programs dominate most school district reading programs in the United States. Most authorities would probably agree that the quality of these programs has improved markedly since the 1980s, especially during the late 1980s and early 1990s. The student texts have particularly improved. The artwork and graphics have improved, and the quality of the literature has improved. Where literary excerpts have been used, their removal from their context has been ameliorated by more adequate support narrative both before and after the excerpt, and the excerpting seems to be done more judiciously and appropriately.

Yet, there remains significant criticism of these programs. This criticism is often aimed at the teachers' editions or manuals accompanying the programs rather than at the student texts themselves. To illustrate the differences, following are two different lesson plans for teaching the same selection of text. The first is designed based on the preceding lesson plan model. The second is taken from a popular contemporary reading program. Compare the two.

Plan #1: The Teacher-Designed Lesson Plan

Example:
Selection Title: "Hearing Ear Dog" by Susan Meyers (1988)
Class: Fourth grade

A useful practice for the beginning teacher is to reserve a brief period of time at the end of the day (15 minutes or so is probably enough) to recapitulate the day's teaching: "How effective was I? What worked well? Why? What did not? Why?" Suggest to student teachers that jotting down brief notes to themselves during the course of the day can also be helpful because it is easy to forget particular incidents as the day progresses.

Objectives:

1. SWBAT identify cause–effect relationships in the text.
2. SWBAT predict outcomes using the story content.

Overall Plan:

Students will experience a simplified problem-solving model, moving from problem identification to prediction or hypothesis formulation to the testing of predictions and hypotheses to concluding. The use of cause–effect and prediction will be encouraged both indirectly and directly throughout the lesson.

Sequence of Teaching Events and Timeline

Approximate Time	*Event*
Prereading:	
3 minutes	Have students stuff sterile cotton into their ears and move around the room briefly. Teacher makes assorted noises during the movement.
7 minutes	Discuss the feeling of not hearing. "How did you feel?" "What would be some of the difficult things you would have to deal with every day if you couldn't hear? After looking at the title to this selection, guess what you think it will be about."
Reading:	
30 minutes	Have students read aloud. Prior to each reading, pose a question requiring them to make a prediction about the gist of the content they will be reading. After each student reads, ask the student to verify his or her initial prediction or to explain the causes for errors in the predictions made.

Evaluation (Follow-up) **(Postreading)**

Pair the students, and ask them to do additional research on hearing-ear dogs or the Society for the Prevention of Cruelty to Animals (SPCA) and its other activities. This project will be tied to their social studies unit on animals in America beginning tomorrow.

Plan #2: The Commercially Developed Lesson Plan

The lesson plan in Figure 7.1 (which continues for several pages) is from the basal program plus the publisher's supplemental information for teaching the text selection, "Hearing Ear Dog."

Alternative basal reading lesson plans might be introduced at this point, for comparison purposes. It is important that students be thoroughly familiar with a number of different basals and their approaches in order to more intelligently discuss their strengths and limitations. At a time when these materials are being criticized for a number of reasons, the intelligent critic or reviewer is one who knows fairly precisely what it is they do and do not do.

Remind students that it is also helpful to examine the student texts in basal series separately from the teachers' editions with the detailed lesson plans. In many instances, the student text is more like a children's literature anthology. With the cost of children's literature trade books being quite high, it may be difficult to purchase a variety of class sets of appropriate children's literature for use throughout the year. This is particularly true if these class sets cannot be shared throughout a large school district (e.g., the district is small, or few schools agree on the optimal choices of literature for the class sets).

Further, in addition to lesson plans, most teachers' editions in basal programs contain background information on authors, history, and science. They also often contain annotated bibliographies of children's literature that is related to a given theme or topic. This kind of information can be helpful even if the lesson plan and other structural elements of the program are rejected.

Figure 7.1   Lesson plan from *McGraw-Hill Reading* (Level L: "This We Wish"), a basal reader. The lesson plan relates to the story, "Hearing Ear Dog," by Susan Meyers. Reproduced with permission of McGraw-Hill Book Company. Copyright 1988. All rights reserved.

Introduction
Skills and Materials for Reading

"**Hearing Ear Dog,**" by Susan Meyers, Pupil pages 220–227

"**The Puzzle of the Sleeping Sharks,**" by Ann McGovern, Pupil pages 228–236

"**Fishes' Evening Song,**" a poem by Dahlov Ipcar, Pupil page 237

Lesson 1 Teaching the Strategy Builder, Teacher pages 290–292
Scientific Material   Objective: Recognize science selections as a kind of nonfiction.
Pupil pages 218–219
Workbook pages 83–84
Blackline Masters 000–000

Lesson 2 Introducing and Reading the First Selection, Teacher pages 293–298
Prior Knowledge Concept: How dogs and other pets help people
Understand selection vocabulary in context
Set a purpose for reading
Reading the selection: "Hearing Ear Dog"
Pupil pages 220–227
Workbook pages 85–86
Textmasters 000–000, Blackline Master 000

Lesson 3 Responding to, Extending, and Rereading the First Selection, Teacher page 299
Respond to the selection through writing, speaking, listening activities, including group activities
Relate selection content to Science
Reread the selection for a specific purpose
Apply understanding of Scientific Material
Workbook page 86

Lesson 4 Applying Skills: First Selection, Teacher page 300
Apply Charts and Graphs to the selection
Workbook page 87, Chart

Lesson 5 Introducing and Reading the Second Selection, Teacher pages 301–307
Prior Knowledge Concept: Wanting to solve a real-life mystery
Understand selection vocabulary in context
Set a purpose for reading
Reading the selections: "The Puzzle of the Sleeping Sharks" and "Fishes' Evening Song"
Pupil pages 228–237
Workbook pages 88–89
Textmasters 000–000
Blackline Master 000

Lesson 6 Responding to, Extending, and Rereading the Second Selection, Teacher page 308
Respond to the selection through writing, speaking, listening activities, including group activities
Relate selection content to Life Skills
Reread the selection for a specific purpose
Apply understanding of Scientific Material
Workbook page 89

288 Unit Opener

Lesson 7 Applying Skills: Second Selection, Teacher pages 309–310
Apply Specialized Vocabulary to the selection
Workbook page 90, Chart
Apply Diagrams to the selection
Workbook page 91, Chart

Lesson 8 Reteaching and Enriching Skills Applied in Unit 8, Teacher pages 311–312
Specialized Vocabulary, Skillmaster 000, Chart

Charts and Graphs, Skillmaster 000, Chart

Diagrams, Skillmaster 000, Chart

Lesson 9 Reviewing and Maintaining Vocabulary and Skills, Teacher pages 313–314
Review Unit Vocabulary, Charts 000–000

Review of Skills
Cause and Effect, Skillmaster 000, Chart
Author's Purpose, Skillmaster 000, Chart
Encyclopedia, Skillmaster 000, Chart

Maintenance of Skills
Synonyms/Antonyms, Chart

Mood, Chart

Inflected Forms, Skillmaster 000, Chart

Point of View, Skillmaster 000, Chart
*Skillmasters 00–00, available in the Teacher's Resource Book, are reproduced on Teacher's Edition pages 00–00 for your convenience.

Figure 7.1 *(continued)*

Summary of Selections

Hearing Ear Dog

by Susan Meyers

Summary This article explains how the Society for Prevention of Cruelty to Animals (SPCA) in San Francisco is training dogs to help deaf people. Linda Gunn, a trainer for the Hearing-Ear Dog Program chose to work with Penny, a stray dog who was brought to the animal shelter. Unlike seeing-eye dogs which are large and pure-bred, hearing-ear dogs are usually small, lively, and of mixed-breed. Hearing-ear dogs must hear very well, learn basic obedience commands such as sit, lie down, stay, and come, as well as follow hand signals. In addition, these dogs must learn special skills such as waking a person at the sound of an alarm, letting a person know a doorbell is ringing, a telephone is ringing, an oven timer is going off, and a baby is crying. After a dog is trained it usually is placed in the home of one of the many deaf people on the waiting list for a dog. But Penny did so well in her training that she was kept as a demonstration dog at the SPCA to help raise the money to train many more dogs to help deaf people.

Background Hearing-ear dogs also help their owners cross the street safely by walking in front of them if a car honks its horn. If a person is matched with a dog and the two do not get along well, another dog is assigned to the person. Massachusetts has passed a law permitting hearing-ear dogs the same privileges as seeing-eye dogs. If students want to learn more information about this program they may write to one of the following addresses:

The Hearing Ear Dog Program
c/o Bryant Hill Farm
76 Bryant Road
Jefferson, MA 01522

or

The National Hearing Dog Project
9725 E. Hampten
Denver, CO 80231

The Puzzle of the Sleeping Sharks

by Ann McGovern

Summary This article describes several adventures the Professor of Zoology at the University of Maryland, Eugenie Clark, goes on to study and learn if sharks really do sleep. On a trip to Mexico she observed big streamlined sharks in a sleeplike state. There in an underwater cave Eugenie noticed a little remora fish cleaning a shark —removing parasites from its body. She thought perhaps these caves were cleaning stations for the sharks. When Eugenie returned to the caves of Mexico the next summer, tests showed the water was different from the water in the open sea. She thought perhaps the water made the sharks groggy. In 1976, she went to Japan with her student, Anita George, and her stepfather. In underwater caves she observed sharks piled on top of each other seeming to be asleep. She observed two types of "sleeping sharks"—white tip requiem and white-tip reef sharks. More tests had to be done to find other reasons why these sharks were in a sleeplike state. Eugenie Clark is still at work doing underwater research.

Background In November 1986, Eugenie Clark co-authored another article in *National Geographic* about a new method of observing sharks at 2,000 feet underwater. She and Emory Kristof used Kristof's experimental technique combining fish bait, dim, green lights, and quietly lying in wait to observe the sharks at these depths. They used the submersible, *Pisces IV*, to make the dives. They would attach a can of bait to the mechanical arm of the submersible and have the green glow of a thallium iodide light shine on it and then just wait. They were able to observe and photograph sixgill sharks, which, according to Dr. Clark, was a rare opportunity. Previous to this method, bright lights would scare the sharks away. Although submersibles, thallium iodide lights, and baiting fish to cameras have been used before, Kristof was the first to combine these methods to bait the sharks to a submersible.

Author Ann McGovern lives in New York but travels around the world to go scuba diving and practice undersea photography; these concerns are reflected in such books as *Shark Lady*. Author of more than thirty-five titles, she won the Lucky Four Leaf Clover Award in 1972 for her work as a whole.

Figure 7.1   *(continued)*

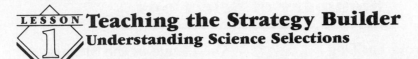

LESSON 1 Teaching the Strategy Builder
Understanding Science Selections

Objective: Recognize science selections as a kind of nonfiction.

Discussing Prior Knowledge

Have students read the title of the page and Starting with What You Know on pupil book page 218. Encourage students to discuss science questions they'd like to know the answers to. You might like to make a class list of science questions.

Presenting the Strategy

Have a volunteer read the section Thinking About Science. Ask students in what ways science writing is like other kinds of nonfiction writing. (It has a topic, main ideas, and features such as pictures and diagrams.) Ask students in what ways science writing is different from other kinds of non-fiction writing. (Science writing may have headings.) Ask students to discuss science selections they have read recently. Have them describe the topics, main ideas, and pictures or diagrams.

Modeling the Strategy

Copy and distribute Blackline Master 8-1 provided in the Teacher's Resource Book. The following text in regular type is what the students will read on the Master. The text in boldfaced type below provides teaching suggestions for how to model the skill.

What an Ocelot Is

An ocelot is a medium-sized cat. It is typically about 30 inches long, excluding the tail, and weighs up to 35 pounds. It has a yellow-brown coat with black spots, rings, and stripes.

Where and How the Ocelot Lives

The ocelot is found in Central and South America, and sometimes as far north as Texas. It lives in forests, preying on small animals. Man hunts the ocelot for its fur. **I know, by reading the headings, that the topic of this piece is the ocelot. The headings also point me to the main ideas—what the ocelot is and where and how it lives.**

Now have students read the paragraph under Before You Read on page 219. Emphasize the idea that science selections should be read slowly and carefully. Have students look again at the ocelot article. Ask them what questions they could make out of the headings. (What is an ocelot? Where and how does an ocelot live?)

Have students read the questions under As You Read. Students should not be expected to memorize all of these questions. The questions merely serve as a kind of guide for reading nonfiction in general and science writing in particular. You may want to make a classroom chart of the questions or have students do so. Encourage students to refer to these questions if they have trouble understanding a science selection.

Figure 7.1 *(continued)*

STRATEGY BUILDER

Hearing Ear Dog
and The Puzzle of
the Sleeping
Sharks

Understanding Science Selections

Starting with What You Know

Do you know why grass is green? Do you know how many moons each planet in our solar system has? Do you know what kind of an animal an ocelot is? Do you know how paper is made? You can find answers to these questions and more when you read about science. What other science questions can you think of that you would like to know the answers to?

Thinking About Science

Science selections present facts, explanations, and other interesting information about animals, plants, Earth, the universe, and outer space. Science selections are nonfiction. They have the same elements as all nonfiction.

Topic: This is what the selection is about, such as beavers or clouds.

Main Ideas: These are the important ideas you learn as you read about science topics.

Features: Nonfiction writing often has pictures and diagrams. A diagram is a picture that shows the parts of something. A science selection may also have **headings**. These are words in dark print that come before a paragraph. They tell you what you will learn as you read the next part of the selection.

Before You Read

Plan to read slowly and carefully. Read the title to find out what the topic is. Look at the pictures and think about what you will learn when you begin to read. Look at the headings. Turn each heading into a question if it is not already stated as one. For example, suppose the heading is *A Dog's Special Senses*. You can make a question that asks, "What special senses does a dog have?"

As You Read

Stop when you need to and summarize what you have read so far. If there are parts you don't understand, read them again. Ask yourself these questions as you read. The questions with a blue diamond are for all nonfiction. The questions with a red diamond are for science selections.

Topic: What is the selection about?
◆ What do I already know about this science topic?

Main Ideas: ◆ What are the important ideas in the selection?
◆ What are the important facts and ideas about the science topic?

Features: ◆ What information about the science topic do I learn from the pictures and diagrams?
◆ What answers am I finding to the questions I made from the science headings?

The next two selections in this book are science articles. Use the side notes to help you understand the facts and ideas in the following selection.

218   219

Guided Practice/Cooperative Learning

The practice activity is available on Blackline Master 8-2 in the Teacher's Resource Book. You may wish to reproduce the Master and distribute copies to students. Also, you may want to have students work in their cooperative learning groups to do this activity.

Independent Practice   Assign Workbook pages 83–84.

Name
Strategy Builder, pages 218-219
BLACKLINE MASTER 8-2
Understanding Science Selections

Read the following article. Look for the topic, main ideas, and features of a science selection. Write a sentence to answer each question after the story.

The History of Paper

Paper was probably invented by the Chinese, who made it from a mixture of bark and a plant called hemp. Papermaking was later introduced in Spain in about the year 1150. By the 1400s, when printing developed in Europe, paper mills had spread throughout Europe.

Summarize what you have read so far.

How Paper is Made

The main ingredient in paper is wood pulp. This is made by grinding the wood and then boiling it with chemicals. The pulp is then poured onto a wire screen. The water drains away and the fibers stick together. Rollers then dry, press, and smooth the sheets.

Turn the heading into a question.

1. What is the topic of this article?
   the history of paper

2. What questions can you make from the headings?
   What is the history of paper? How is paper made?

3. What special feature of science writing does this article have?
   headings

4. What are the main ideas of the article?
   The facts about the history of paper and how paper is made.

5. What is an important fact about the relationship between papermaking and printing in Europe?
   Printing developed 250 years after papermaking was introduced in Spain.

Blackline Master   **8-2**

Figure 7.1   *(continued)*

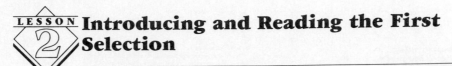

LESSON 2 Introducing and Reading the First Selection

Hearing Ear Dog

by Susan Meyers

Discussing Prior Knowledge

Begin a discussion with students about how dogs and other pets help people in everyday life. Help students bring out the following points about the ways dogs help people: they provide playmates and companionship; they fetch newspapers; they protect the house; they guide blind persons; and they walk children home from the bus stop. Have students draw conclusions about the attributes that certain animals have that allow them to be helpful in particular ways. For example: dogs are good at protecting homes because they generally have good hearing and sight and can bark to scare intruders; cats are good at catching mice because they have a keen sense of smell and can run fast; fish are good at helping people relax because they are graceful, pretty, and quiet; hamsters are good at providing companionship because they are fun to watch.

Write   Have students write a paragraph about a real or imaginary situation in which a pet helped someone they know. Have students save their paragraphs for use in Lesson 3.

Addressing Variations in Students' Backgrounds: Experiential

Many students may not be familiar with animal shelters or the work of the Society for the Prevention of Cruelty to Animals. Tell the students that the SPCA is an international organization that works to promote responsible treatment of animals. Explain that this organization maintains shelters and adoption services for lost or unwanted animals: The shelters feed and care for animals until owners can be found for them. Tell the students that in addition to the SPCA, other organizations operated by animal lovers have been established throughout the United States.

Ask the students to find the locations of animal shelters in their areas and to learn the names of the organizations operating them. Have them contact the shelters to find out more about the kinds of services they offer and the types of pets they have available for adoption. Refer also to the background information in the Unit Opener on page 289.

Introducing Vocabulary

demonstration **(T)** obedience **(T)** preferred **(T)** predict **(T)**

Untested words are listed under Text Analysis.

Definitions

demonstration—example, model
obedience—following orders; **predict**—tell beforehand;
preferred—liked better, chosen instead

Context Sentences

The following sentences are available on Blackline Master 8-3 in the Teacher's Resource Book. You may wish to copy and distribute this Master to students for use at this time.

1. Spanky was the <u>demonstration</u> dog that was used to show us how seeing eye dogs help people.
2. During <u>obedience</u> training, Spot learned to sit on command.
3. Since the puppy had large paws, Oscar could <u>predict</u> that it would grow to be a big dog.
4. Small dogs are often *preferred* by people who live in apartments.

Activity

Ask students to define as many of the new vocabulary words as they can. If students need help, use the definitions and context sentences, or have students look up the words in the Glossary. Next, ask students to name other words that have the same roots as the vocabulary words. Have volunteers record responses by drawing semantic maps on the board. Ask students to choose words from the maps and use the words in sentences. The maps might look like the ones that follow.

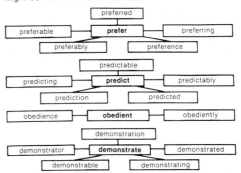

Finally, ask students to give a sentence using the vocabulary words.

Independent Practice   For additional vocabulary practice, assign Workbook page 85. Use Textmaster 31 for further practice.

Figure 7.1 *(continued)*

Helping Students with Limited English Proficiency

Use the following exercise to help the students become familiar with the Latin word part *pre*. Tell the students that *pre* is a Latin word part that is added to words and means *before*. Remind hispanic students that Spanish also uses the word part in words such as *predecir* (to predict), *prehistoria* (prehistory), and *prematuro* (premature).

Write the words *school, occupy, view, trial,* and *pay* on the board. Call for volunteers to add the word part *pre-* to the words and to tell the new meaning of each word. Then write the vocabulary words *predict* and *preferred* . Have the students find the origins and meanings of the word parts of these words in a dictionary.

Ask the students to take turns making predictions about the future. Then have them tell about the kinds of movies and television programs they prefer to watch.

Setting a Purpose

Review the previous discussion about the ways in which pets help people. Briefly review the vocabulary words that have been introduced. Then have students read the selection title and look at the illustrations in their books. Ask students to predict what questions will be answered by the article. (Possible questions: How are hearing ear dogs chosen? How are they trained? Who trains them? How does a person get a hearing ear dog? How do the dogs' owners learn to use the hearing ear dogs?)

> Note: Point out to students that the side notes with the next selection are included to help them apply the Strategy Builder as they read. Suggest to students that when they are reading the articles, they pause between paragraphs so they can read the side notes next to the text.

Selection Vocabulary

A. Read the story. Then write the word in dark print next to its definition.

Jerome was visiting an animal shelter with some students from his school. They watched a trainer and her dog show how a pet can be trained to do many things. This **demonstration** interested Jerome very much. He wanted to own and train a pet.

The dog trainer explained that it is important to train all dogs to behave well. **Obedience** training is the first thing a dog owner should do with a new pet.

Then Jerome walked around the shelter. He saw a spotted dog he liked. When he whistled, the dog perked up, wagged its tail, and started to bark. Jerome could **predict** that this dog would make a very good pet for himself and his family. After Jerome looked at other dogs, he came back to the spotted dog. He **preferred** the spotted dog to all the others.

liked better: **preferred**

doing what one is told to do: **obedience**

to know before something happens: **predict**

the act of showing how something is done: **demonstration**

B. Complete each sentence by writing one of the words in dark print from the story on the lines below.

1. The dog sat down, begged, and then rolled over during a **demonstration** with its trainer.
2. Whenever the trainer said the word "sit," the students could **predict** what the trained dog would do.
3. The trainer rewarded the dog with a hug, but the dog **preferred** a treat.
4. Maria knew that if her new puppy had lessons from a good dog trainer, he would not need any **obedience** training when he grew up.

To Do at Home Pretend that you are a dog trainer. Write a story about something funny that happens when you try to teach the dog a trick. Use at least two vocabulary words in your story. Then read your story to someone at home.

Workbook Page 85

294 LESSON 2 **Introducing and Reading**

PART TWO UNIT 8
Hearing Ear Dog

Figure 7.1 *(continued)*

Solutions sometimes come from the most unexpected sources. This article explains how some deaf people are being helped in a very unusual way!

HEARING EAR DOG

by Susan Meyers

How Penny Puts Her Ears To Work

You've heard of ears that wiggle. But have you ever heard of ears that bark? Many deaf people now have furry, barking, tail-wagging "ears." They are the lucky owners of hearing ear dogs.

220

For years, specially trained guide dogs have been helping blind people see. Now, dogs are also being trained to help deaf people hear. One of the most successful schools for hearing ear dogs is run by the Society for Prevention of Cruelty to Animals (SPCA) in San Francisco, California. That's where a bright-eyed little pup named Penny got her start.

Penny was a stray who was brought to the animal shelter at the San Francisco SPCA. She was hungry and dirty. Workers at the shelter fed her and gave her a bath. When no one came to claim her, the shelter put her up for adoption.

Penny was alert and friendly. She would have made a good pet. But Linda Gunn, a trainer for the Hearing Ear Dog Program, thought that Penny could be a good hearing ear dog.

Saving Strays

Most of the dogs trained for hearing work are strays like Penny. Trainers check dog-training centers and shelters every few days to find suitable dogs. They look for animals that seem alert. Small dogs are chosen

Linda found Penny at the San Francisco SPCA animal shelter. Most of the dogs trained for the hearing ear program were once strays.

221

Text Analysis

This selection includes pairs of sentences in which the second sentence begins with "But." Questions related to sentences them are identified as Text Analysis under Guided Reading.

The definition for each untested word listed here appears after the Guided Reading questions for the page on which the word appears.

alert   attachments   harness

Guided Reading
With Application of Strategy Builder

The following are options for using the Guided Reading questions.

1. Have students read the entire selection without asking the Guided Reading questions.
2. Have students read to the end of page 221 and ask them the Predicting question. After discussion have students read to the end of page 223 and ask them the next Predicting question. Use the same procedure for the Predicting question on page 225. Then have students read to the end of the selection.
3. Use all or some of the Guided Reading questions, perhaps focusing on the questions related to the Strategy Builder.

PART TWO UNIT 8
Hearing Ear Dog

Pages 220–221

How can you tell by looking at these pages that this might be a science selection? (The topic is about an animal aand the pages contain headings and a photograph.)   STRATEGY BUILDER/SCIENCE SELECTIONS

Do you think Penny will be a good hearing ear dog? (Answers will vary but most students will agree because she has the qualities for becoming a good hearing ear dog: small, alert, and friendly.)   PREDICTING

Text Analysis

Look at the first two sentences of the article. What purpose does the word *But* fill? (It joins the two sentences and sets up a contrast.)

Now look on page 221 at the sentences "She would have made a good pet. But Linda Gunn, a trainer for the Hearing Ear Dog Program, thought that Penny could be a good hearing ear dog." What purpose does the word *But* fill here? (It joins the two sentences and sets up a contrast.)

Figure 7.1 *(continued)*

because they're easy to care for in a small home. This is different from the way seeing eye dogs are chosen. Seeing eye dogs have to be large enough to wear a harness and guide a blind person.

Hearing ear dogs differ from seeing eye dogs in other ways, too. Many hearing ear dogs are **mixed breeds**: Each of the dog's parents is a different kind of dog. But **purebred** animals are preferred for seeing eye work. Each parent of a purebred is the same kind of dog. With purebreds, people can predict their size. Even a dog's personality matters. Calmness is important for seeing eye dogs. But bouncy, lively dogs do well at hearing work.

When Linda met Penny, the dog sniffed eagerly and wagged her tail. A medical exam showed that Penny was about a year old—a good age to start training. She was healthy. Her sense of hearing was excellent.

Dogs in general have good hearing. A dog can hear a noise 250 yards (229m) away that most people can't hear beyond 25 yards (23m). But some dogs hear better than others. It was important for Penny to hear very well. Soon she was going to learn to hear for two.

Penny Goes to School

The first step in training a hearing ear dog is basic obedience lessons. On command, dogs must learn to sit and lie down, stay, and come when called. They must also learn to follow hand signals because some deaf people have trouble speaking. Penny took to her lessons quickly. Soon she was ready to learn the special skills that would make her a hearing ear dog. The training takes about four months. In the San Francisco SPCA, dogs are trained in a homelike setting. An entire apartment has been set up. There is even a cat on hand to help the dogs get used to household pets.

222

Left: This graph compares the range of sound frequencies, in *hertz*, that humans and some animals can receive. The *hertz* is a unit used by scientists to measure frequency. One *hertz* equals one cycle, or vibration, per second. Many animals can receive frequencies that people cannot.

Right: Hearing ear dogs must learn to wake their owners when the alarm clock rings. Penny practiced this many times with her trainer, Linda.

223

Pages 222—223

How do the illustrations help you know that this is a science selection? (They include pictures and a graph that help explain ideas in the selection.)   STRATEGY BUILDER/SCIENCE SELECTIONS

What qualities did Penny have that made her a good candidate to be a hearing ear dog? (She was a healthy, mixed-breed, bouncy, lively, one-year-old with excellent hearing.)   MAIN IDEA & DETAILS/INFERENTIAL

- What did Penny do when Linda met her? (She sniffed eagerly and wagged her tail.)   LITERAL
- How old was Penny? (one-year-old)   LITERAL
- How good was Penny's sense of hearing? (excellent)   LITERAL

What does the author mean when she stated Penny was "going to learn to hear for two?" (She meant Penny's ability to hear would help a deaf person notice sounds.)   CRITICAL THINKING

What might Penny learn to enable her to be a hearing ear dog? (Answers will vary. Suggestions: waking people or alerting people to a phone or a door bell ringing) PREDICTING

Text Analysis

Find three pairs of sentences in which the second sentence begins with the word *But*. What role does *But* play in each case? ("Many hearing ear dogs are mixed breeds: Each of the dog's parents is a different kind of dog. But purebred animals are preferred for seeing eye work." "Calmness is important for seeing eye dogs. But bouncy, lively dogs do well at hearing work." "A dog can hear a noise 250 yards (229 m) away that most people can't hear beyond 25 yards (23 m). But some dogs hear better than others." The word "But" joins the sentences and sets up a contrast.)

alert—intelligent, sharp, wide-awake
harness—the straps and handle that a seeing eye dog wears to help guide its owner

Figure 7.1 *(continued)*

Many deaf people use hand signals to communicate. Hearing ear dogs like Penny are taught to understand hand sign language.

Penny's first lesson was waking her trainer when an alarm clock rang. Linda lay on the bed. She pushed a button that set off the clock. Penny came running. She jumped on the bed. Linda praised her and gave her a treat to eat.

Linda repeated this lesson until Penny learned to jump on the bed whenever the alarm rang. Sometimes Linda pretended to be sleeping. She made Penny work to wake her up. Then she gave the dog some food as a reward.

Penny also learned to tell Linda when the doorbell rang. She would run to the door, then to Linda and back to the door. She kept doing it until her trainer got up and answered the door.

224

Other sounds that Penny learned to answer were an oven timer going off, a baby crying, and a telephone ringing. Although completely deaf people can't use regular telephones, those with some hearing can use special phones that make sounds louder. There are also phones with typewriter attachments that deaf people can use to communicate.

Everyone in the program was pleased with Penny's progress. She was one of the best dogs they had ever trained. She liked people and she liked to work. Soon, it would be time to match her with a new owner.

A Surprise Ending

People who want hearing ear dogs apply to the SPCA. But there are always more people than dogs. The waiting list usually has 30 or 40 names on it. When a dog finishes its training, it goes to the first person on the list.

Training the new owner is important, too. The owner must learn what to expect of the dog and must learn how to keep up the dog's training. If not, the dog can forget all it has learned.

After taking a dog home, a new owner keeps in touch with the dog's trainer. If problems arise, the trainer helps solve them. Linda hears many success stories. Some dogs have saved lives by alerting their owners to fires or gas leaks.

At the San Francisco SPCA, dogs are given free to deaf people. But the cost is over $2,500 to train each dog. The SPCA raises that money.

As Penny finished her training, Linda and others in the program realized she was special. She was such an eager worker that everyone fell in love with her. They thought, why not keep her at the SPCA as a demonstration dog?

225

Pages 224–225

Why were the trainers pleased with Penny's progress? (She learned her lessons well; she liked people and liked to work.)   DRAWING CONCLUSIONS/INFERENTIAL

- How do you know Penny learned her lessons well? (The article states: "She was one of the best dogs they had ever trained.")   LITERAL
- Did Penny like people and her work? (Yes.)   LITERAL• Why was Penny almost ready to be matched with her new owner? (She had made good progress in learning her lessons.)   INFERENTIAL

If Penny had not learned her lessons well and you were one of her trainers, what would you have recommended? (Answers will vary. Suggestion: She would not have become a hearing ear dog, and would have been put up for adoption as a pet.)   EXPERIENTIAL

What question would you turn the heading "A Surprise Ending" into to help you know what to look for when you read the next section of the article? ("what is the surprise ending"?)   STRATEGY BUILDER/SCIENCE SELECTIONS

Why do you think there are always more people who want hearing ear dogs than there are dogs? (Answers will vary. Suggestion: It takes months to find and train each dog, and the training is costly.)   CRITICAL THINKING

What might happen if the dog's owner is not properly trained? (The dog might forget everything it learned.)   CAUSE-EFFECT/INFERENTIAL

- Why is it important that the owners be trained? (The owner must learn what to expect of the dog and how to keep up its training.)   LITERAL

What do you think will be the surprise ending? (Answers will vary. Suggestion: Penny will do something special.)   PREDICTING

Text Analysis

attachments—something fastened or connected to a machine to make it do a particular thing

Figure 7.1 *(continued)*

Now Penny's full-time home is at the SPCA. She greets reporters at the door and lets photographers take her picture. She goes to community meetings to show her skills. So even though Penny didn't go to live with a deaf person as most hearing ear dogs do, she has actually helped many deaf people. Penny helped the SPCA raise enough money to train many more dogs. She's become famous for spreading the word about the Hearing Ear Dog Program. Not a bad end for a hungry little stray pup!

Right: Most hearing ear dogs are given to deaf people after they have completed their training. But not Penny! She makes her home at the SPCA. She helps raise money to train other dogs, and she is always available to shake hands with people visiting the SPCA.

Reader's Response

I always knew that blind people could be helped by guide dogs, but I never imagined that a dog could help someone who is deaf.

How did you feel about the article?

226

After You Read

Thinking About What You Read

1. Why might people have come up with the idea that trained dogs could help deaf people?
2. How does the SPCA in San Francisco, California help animals as well as people?
3. Why are hearing ear dogs trained in a homelike setting?
4. Since Penny was so well trained, did the SPCA have a good reason to keep her? Why?

Thinking About How You Read

How did knowing the topic help you find important details?

Sharing and Listening

Tell what you think of this unusual solution for helping deaf people. Do you think a hearing ear dog would be very helpful to a deaf person? Why? Listen carefully as other people give their opinions.

Writing

List some ways not mentioned in the article that a hearing ear dog could help a deaf person. Think of how a deaf person might be helped by a hearing ear dog outside as well as in their home. For example, a hearing ear dog could tell someone when a tea kettle whistled in their kitchen, or when fire engine's siren sounded in the street.

227

Pages 226–227

What was the "Surprise Ending" for Penny? (The trainers kept her as a demonstration dog.) DRAWING CONCLUSIONS/INFERENTIAL

- What usually happens to hearing ear dogs once they finish their training? (They are assigned to new owners.) LITERAL
- How was Penny's fate different? (She was kept as a demonstration dog.) LITERAL

Do you think Penny will be happy as a demonstration dog? (Answers will vary. Suggestion: Yes, because she'll get a lot of attention and will be able to show her skills. Also, the people at the SPCA love her.) CRITICAL THINKING

Reader's Response

Answers will vary. Encourage students to cite examples from the article to support their ideas.

Discussing the Purpose

Have students recall the questions they predicted the article would answer. Ask students which of their questions from Setting a Purpose were answered and which were not.

After you Read

Thinking About What You Read

1. Answers will vary. Suggestion: Since dogs have been used so successfully to help people see, it makes sense that they could also help people hear.
2. The SPCA gives stray dogs homes and owners to care for them.
3. The dogs are trained in an apartment so that when they move to their new owner's apartments, the surroundings will seem familiar.
4. Answers will vary. Suggestion: Yes, Penny was the perfect demonstration dog. The people at the SPCA thought she would help convince others to help support the Hearing Ear Dog Program.

Thinking About How You Read Students may say that knowing the article was about specially trained dogs helped them look for descriptions of what the dogs could do.

Sharing and Listening Students may say that a hearing-ear dog would be very helpful because it can hear even more than a non-deaf human can.

Writing Students may describe a dog responding to the buzzer on a washing machine or dryer.

At this time, you may wish to do the activity and assign **Workbook page 86** under Applying the Strategy Builder on page 299. Use **Textmaster 32** for further practice.

PART TWO UNIT 8
Hearing Ear Dog

Figure 7.1 *(continued)*

Responding to, Extending, and Rereading the First Selection

LESSON 3

Cooperative Activity

Have students work in groups to compile a list of sounds that a dog might hear if it accompanied a fourth-grade student to school. Have one group of students list ten sounds that they can hear from their seats in the classroom. Have a second group take a "sound walk" to the gym and list ten sounds they hear on the way to the gym, at the gym, and on the way back to the classroom. Have a third group list ten sounds in the cafeteria. Allow groups time to share their lists.

Writing

Read aloud some of the paragraphs students wrote in Discussing Prior Knowledge in Lesson 2. Ask students to choose the paragraph about the pet they felt was the most helpful in a situation and write a few sentences explaining why they chose that pet.   EASY

Based on the information in the article, have students write a short story entitled "A Day in the Life of a Hearing Ear Dog." Students might write their stories either from a first-person or a third-person point of view.
AVERAGE>CHALLENGE

Speaking and Listening

Have students recall the theme of the unit: Solutions. Ask students to conduct a panel discussion on how animals help people with disabilities. Suggest that participants meet in advance to plan the discussion and assign specific topics, such as seeing eye dogs that help blind persons, hearing ear dogs that help deaf persons, and monkeys that are trained to help the paralyzed. Remind students that a panel is a give-and-take-situation and to follow good panel discussion procedures.   AVERAGE

Students can work in pairs to invent a series of hand signals that could be used to direct hearing ear dogs. Students may wish to invent signals for the following commands: sit, lie down, stay, come here, fetch, help. Allow students time to practice their signals and then to teach them to the class.   AVERAGE>CHALLENGE

Relating Reading to Science

Have students research the science of sound. Ask students to write reports on how we hear. In their reports, students should describe the path of sound waves. Encourage students to use visual aids in their reports.

Rereading and Reading

At this time, you may want to tell students to reread the selection or to read a library book suggested in the introduction to Part Two. Also, you may want to ask students to work on the projects they were assigned in the Part Two introduction.

Applying the Strategy Builder

Have students list the features of "Hearing Ear Dog" that help them to know that it is a science selection. Refer students to the Strategy Builder on Pupil pages 218–219 if they need to review the skill.

Independent Practice   Assign Workbook page 86 to check selection comprehension and to apply the Strategy Builder.

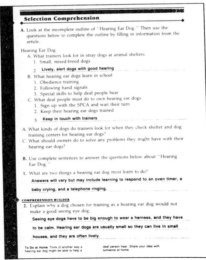

Workbook   **page 86**

Comparison and Contrast of the Two Plans

It becomes clear immediately that comparing the first and the second plans is somewhat like comparing apples and oranges. They seem to be two different creatures with two different purposes. Though both the teacher-designed lesson plan and the commercial basal reading lesson plan would look different if they were designed by different teachers or different publishers, the differences would still be about as substantial as those seen here. Following are some of the major differences between these two:

- In the teacher-designed plan, the objectives are very specific, and the content of the lesson plan is concise and quite brief. Some teacher-built lesson plans are longer than this one, but they would still be substantially less lengthy and detailed than the commercially developed plan in Figure 7.1.
- It is also probably safe to assume that teachers use a school district scope and sequence of reading objectives in designing their instructional plans.
- The timeline of the teacher-designed plan is obviously customized to suit whatever block of time is allotted in the curriculum at the school district where the plan was developed.
- The teacher-designed plan indicates a link between this lesson and work being done in social studies. This could be a prelude to an integrated unit between reading and social studies.
- The teacher-designed plan could easily allow integration of language arts and reading, permitting options for writing, reporting, and peer pairs and small-group work. Many options could grow from this lesson plan, which could be the first in a unit of integrated language arts and reading instruction.
- Perhaps the most obvious thing about the commercially developed plan is the quantity of information it has: summary of the reading selection; background information on the topic; additional resources; suggestions for cooperative learning; suggestions for prereading activities, including vocabulary activities and semantic mapping; specific ideas for modeling; questions to stimulate text analysis; follow-up discussion topics; and suggested extended activities to build from the lesson. It is a rich resource for the teacher.
- If the commercially developed plan were followed rigidly, it contains the kind of detail and guidance that many feel is too tight, too fixed. Whether it allows for enough flexibility or variation in student response could well be a moot point, for probably no lesson plan does that, teacher-built or otherwise.

Using the Advantages of Each Plan

A more realistic way to look at the two plans is to see how each can contribute in a significant way to the reading lesson. The authors of this text recommend the following:

> 1. For each reading lesson, the teacher should prepare an individual lesson plan that has a similar format to Plan #1.

The act of thinking through such a plan, with the attendant organization of teaching events, questioning strategies, and teaching techniques, will more likely ensure effective teaching of the lesson. Such a plan can help students to achieve the school reading program's objectives. The act of preparing the lesson plan (the process) is as important as the quality of the actual written plan (the product). The writing of the plan represents an important mental dress rehearsal for the actual instruction. Also, each school district's individual reading program, including its scope and sequence of reading objectives and their place in relation to other subjects, cannot be determined by someone outside the particular school program. Unless the district provides customized modifications of the commercially developed plans, each teacher must devise individual lesson plans.

> 2. The teacher-prepared lesson plan should be viewed as a first-choice scenario alternative, rather than as a fixed inflexible sequence of steps.

Life is seldom perfect. Be prepared to shift gears, to alter time segments or sequences. Even cut things short if all is not going well. There will be other opportunities for reaching these objectives.

> 3. Use the commercially developed lesson plan as a teaching resource.

Discuss the meaning of *direct instruction* with your students. Relatively sloppy use of this term has resulted in a perception by many that direct instruction is to be equated with basal reading programs or behavior modification or task analysis curriculum models or deductive teaching or behaviorist learning theory or some combination of these. Note that the authors of this text use *direct instruction* to mean the teacher-directed and -orchestrated strategies and techniques that are part of any effective curriculum and instruction model.

The commercially developed plan has a wealth of useful information that can be integrated into a teacher-designed lesson plan. This resource can save teachers a great deal of time. Remember that it is the intent of the publisher to make teaching easier, not harder. Publishers seldom prefer their teacher's editions to be viewed as directive so much as directional. Use the teacher's edition with the proper perspective: Allow it to do what it can do best—serve as a rich resource of ideas and background information.

DIRECT INSTRUCTION IN STRATEGIC READING BY MODELING

Students need direct instruction in the strategies used by effective readers. The teacher must plan to model the various strategies used when reading different kinds of text for different purposes under different conditions. The intent of such modeling should be reflected in the lesson plan and should be shared directly with the students prior to instruction. In short, be candid with students. For example, consider the following:

Point out the importance of modeling in teaching. Ask students for their observations of experienced teachers at work and how they use this technique.

"Boys and girls. I want to share with you a plan that I use when I read.

"Open your texts to the selection by Susan Meyers entitled 'Hearing Ear Dog.' Let's do this together.

"Before I read a story or an article or a book or anything, I do a number of things. You probably already know what they are, but if you don't, try to think about them as we do this.

"First, I look at the title. The title usually tells you a lot about what is going to be in the story. Jim, what are some things this title tells you about the story?

(Pause for response.)

"Second, I look at the pictures or charts or maps or photographs or other visual aids that are in the text. Let's look at those things in this story. What clues do they give you about the text, Sarah?

(Pause for response.)

"Third, I read the captions under the pictures or any notes that appear in the margins. Let's look at these. Jerry, did you get any more information about what might be in this text from that?

(Pause for response.)

"Fourth, I look at the headings and subheadings that break up the text. Let's look for those together. Let me know when you find them. Kareem, what do they say? What do they tell you about what is going to be following them in the text?

(Pause for response.)

"Fifth, I make a prediction about what the overall big idea of this selection is.

"Sixth, I look once more at the title and first heading and/or subheading. There is a beginning heading here that says, 'How Penny Puts Her Ears to Work.' I then make a prediction about how Penny puts her ears to work. What do I think she will do with her ears?

"Seventh, I begin reading, checking what I read against the prediction I have in my head about what Penny will do with her ears.

"Eighth, after I find out whether my first prediction was right, I make another one about what will happen next. And I keep doing that until I finish reading. So, I always have a prediction in my head about what will happen next.

"Finally, after I finish the reading, I think again about the main idea of the text and try to restate it."

Notice how the teacher here provides a direct model while instructing her students. Nothing is left for guesswork at this point. This overall strategy for reading is suited for all text types and genres.

Ample practice and application are required. Such modeling must be regularly reinforced, even for those who have mastered the procedures.

Note that question insertion or "glossing," as it is sometimes called, is not without critics. Some assert that interrupting the reading act is not good. Most, however, see it as a useful technique when used selectively, especially with nonfiction text.

Using Question Insertion to Teach Strategic Reading

Notice that the preceding instructional example is teacher-directed, with students using their individual texts to follow the teacher's lead. The preceding example is also orally focused, with the teacher leading the students through the steps orally. A variation of this can be used either in concert with it or separately for variation and flexibility in methodology; the variation uses "question glossing" or "question insertion" or "interrupted reading." The procedure may be called different names and may vary somewhat in format and operation. However, in practice, the intent is the same—insert questions into key parts of the text to be read; these questions should require the reader to articulate questions that model thinking during the reading. Readers are then usually asked to write out answers to the questions before proceeding to read the text.

Designing lessons that use inserted questions requires considerable skill and practice, beginning with selection of text that is appropriate for this use. Not all text necessarily works well with this technique.

A substantive body of research supports the efficacy of this procedure, at least as part of an overall approach to the teaching of reading (Frase, Patrick, & Schumer, 1970; Graves & Clark, 1981; Hershberger, 1964; McGaw & Grotelueschen, 1972; Rothkopf, 1966; Snowman & Cunningham, 1975; et al.).

Because the procedure does interrupt the reading and breaks the flow of the reading process, it has some disadvantages if overused or if used with inappropriate text (e.g., poetry may not be a desirable genre to use with this strategy). Nonetheless, its potential as an alternative teaching approach for inculcating the processes of strategic reading in the young learner warrants its incorporation into some lessons in the overall instructional plan. Figure 7.2 provides an example of text with inserted questions, demonstrating how it might be used with students. The examination of Figure 7.2 and other well-designed lessons with inserted questions reveals a number of characteristics to contemplate while designing lesson plans.

With older students, use of transparencies with an overhead projector allows for effective large-group instruction and minimizes the need to duplicate handouts.

1. Most of the questions should focus on hypothesizing or predicting (e.g., "What do you think this story will be about? What do you think will happen next? What do you predict Jan will do when she arrives at the beach?"). These kinds of questions require the reader to make predictions based on available information. In addition, they provide the reader with mental markers that can be used while reading the next part of the text. Remember that reading really is "an educated guessing game." Readers are always projecting and anticipating, bridging from the the known to the unknown with the aid of print and print adjuncts.

2. Read through the entire text before beginning to design the inserted questions. Determining the optimal locations for interrupting the reading with inserted questions is critical for an effective lesson. Questions must appear at logical places (e.g., where students have enough but not too many clues to the following events, or just before key information will be provided). Begin the questions at the very beginning of the text, before the student has read anything to require the student to begin making predictions even before any of the text has been read. This is an excellent way to help instill the habit of using text adjuncts to get an overview of the entire text before starting the reading.

3. After asking an inferential question, which requires the student to project or predict about coming events, follow up with specific data-acquisition questions that help the student to focus on the detailed information in the text that help him or her to validate or to reject a prediction with logical support from the text. Memory-based, fact-oriented, translation, and interpretation questions all have important roles to play—they provide information or data support for higher-level questions.

4. Be sure to include appropriate recapitulation or summary questions at the end of the text, and for longer texts, include such questions wherever appropriate in the middle of the text. These questions should pressure the student to mentally review the gist of what has been read.

5. Do not use too many questions. Probably no more than two or three questions per page of text is a useful general guideline, although the text content, of course, will dictate number, type, and location of the questions.

6. Nonfiction text—social studies, science, and so on—tend to lend themselves to this procedure more than does fiction, although fiction, too, can work well, depending on the story line. As a general rule, however, avoid using this procedure with poetry.

7. Do not always require students to write out their answers to questions. Instead, on occasion, ask them simply to use the questions as guides for their reading. Also, remember that to use the ques-

Figure 7.2 **Example of text with inserted questions (also called "glossing"). From:** *Science* **(5th grade): (1985) Lexington: Ginn/Silver Burdett, 214–215.**

WEATHERING CHANGES THE LAND

How does physical weathering occur?

If you view the earth while flying in a plane, you can see many features of its surface. You may see high mountains and rolling hills. You may see flat land, valleys, and cliffs. The surface of the earth is always changing. It is changed by natural processes. In time, flat land may become a mountain range. Hills and mountains may slowly be worn down. The land is worn down by weathering. **Weathering** is all the processes that break rock into smaller pieces. The processes of weathering can be put into two groups.

Photograph background **The mountain range is in Alaska; the rolling hills are in California, south of Big Sur; the rocky coasts in California, near Santa Cruz.**

214

GLANCE OVER THE FOUR PAGES LOOKING AT PICTURES, BOLD FACE WORDS AND CAPTIONS. ANSWER QUESTION ONE BEFORE READING THE SELECTION.

1. What do you think the main points of this selection will be?

_____

_____

_____

_____

READ THE PAGE.

2. Guess two ways rocks can be weathered or broken into smaller pieces.

_____

_____

_____

_____

Figure 7.2 *(continued)*

One kind of weathering is called physical weathering. **Physical weathering** is all the processes that break apart rock without changing its chemical makeup. This weathering causes rock to change its size and shape. The rock is broken into smaller pieces. But the pieces have the same makeup as the rock they came from. The only change they have gone through is a physical one.

The effect that the freezing and melting of water has on rock is a type of physical weathering. In some mountain regions the daytime temperatures are above the freezing point of water. Water seeps into cracks in rock. At night, temperatures drop below the freezing point. So the water turns to ice.

When water freezes, it expands. As the water in a crack expands, it pushes with great force against both sides of the crack. This causes the crack to become larger. The daily freezing and melting of water causes large rocks to break up into smaller pieces. This kind of physical weathering is called **frost action.**

STOP! – – – – – –→

3. Give a personal example of an experience you have had with physical weathering.

_____

_____

_____

_____

_____

CONTINUE TO READ.

_____

4. Do you think we have FROST ACTION in Portland? Why or why not?

_____

_____

_____

_____

_____

_____

_____

Ice on rock

Cliffs weathered by frost action

215

Although there is now considerable discussion of both expository and narrative text, students may still be confused or need additional practice in identifying the attributes of each. The front page of a newspaper is perhaps the best example of expository text. You might wish to use the newspaper as an example of most of the discourse modes.

The claim–support–conclusion model can be enhanced or reduced in complexity to meet the various developmental needs of children. Ask students to design some alternative ways to increase or decrease the complexity of this model.

Point out to students how writing and high-level thinking can be developed through this model.

tions as part of the modeling when conducting the class reading orally. This has the added advantage of not having to type and run off handouts for the students.

8. Do not overuse the strategy. Probably no more than once every 2 weeks is a useful guideline.
9. To avoid having repeatedly to design, type up, and duplicate handouts for each of these applications, maintain a file that can be built up and used over the years.

Using Expository Text Structure for Strategic Reading

Learners are introduced to increasing amounts of expository text, reports, news articles, and other descriptive expository text through all of the grades. Short pieces from the newspaper can be introduced effectively as a basic model of expository writing. The structure, in its ideal form, is simply

1. Claim sentence—also called a "thesis assertion," a "main idea sentence," or a "topic sentence"
2. Supporting detail statements that support or demonstrate the claim sentence
3. Conclusion or summary sentence, which restates the claim sentence in another way

Simplified models of the expository form can be created and taught structurally to students.

For example, consider the following passage:

Claim Sentence:	Our car is really in bad shape.
Support Sentences:	The bumpers are bent. The fenders are rusted out. The motor blew up last week.
Conclusion Sentence:	We sure can use a new one.

Notice that the conclusion sentence is similar in many respects to the claim sentence, and the support sentences all provide details that elaborate support for the claim.

Notice, also, that although this is a short paragraph, the same overall Claim–Support–Conclusion structure can hold for larger passages of text, as well. For example,

We really have a bad car. Last week, the family was planning to go on a trip to see our grandparents when Dad got home from work. We were packed and ready to go.

Dad walked in and suggested we have a family talk before we make the trip. We all knew that the car's body was rough. The bumpers had been bent out of shape when we bought it eight years earlier. The fenders were all rusty, and the two back ones looked like they were ready to fall off. We all remembered how the engine had blown up a couple of months back when we had driven out to get our Christmas tree.

"We agreed that it was probably not a good idea to take a long trip and that we needed to think about getting rid of the junker that we had."

A variety of approaches can be employed with this expository text structure:

- Choose or contrive passages of expository text that exhibit the structure in clear form, then scramble the sentences and ask students to reorder the text in the correct order.
- Provide students with a claim sentence and support sentences, and ask them to write a logical conclusion sentence.
- Provide students with support and conclusion sentences, and ask them to write a beginning claim sentence.
- Provide students with a claim sentence and a final conclusion sentence. Ask them to fill in appropriate support sentences in a logical order.
- Ask students to write expository text using the Claim–Support–Conclusion framework. A Skill-Development sheet could be created that provided blanks for a claim sentence, followed by blanks for writing support sentences (you can list numbers indicating the number of sentences they are to write), and blanks for a conclusion sentence.
- Ask students to find samples of expository text that exhibit the framework to share with the class.

All of these variations can be implemented as activities for individual students, for pairs, or for small groups.

Students not familiar with the story grammar research and its theoretical literature will probably need some additional explanation about the concept. For many students, *grammar* refers to "stuff in sentences." Grammars of constructs larger than or different from sentences requires, for some, a major revision of earlier thinking.

Using Story Grammar for Strategic Reading

Just as sentences have grammar (an orderly, predictable structure), stories, too, have "grammar" or structure. Certain structural elements appear in all stories at all levels. Although the sophistication or complexity of the story grammar will vary (e.g., many novels contain very complex plot and subplot and subsubplot relationships that are difficult to follow), the basic overall structure is essentially the same. Maurice Sendak's *Where the Wild Things Are* is built on the same basic story grammar elements as the Russian novelist Dostoyevsky's *Crime and Punishment*.

Although a variety of story grammars have been researched and described over the past several years, most are variations of one of the original grammars elaborated by Stein and Glenn (1979). Because the discussions of story grammars have tended to focus more upon their structural accuracy and integrity than on their instructional efficacy, more research is needed regarding their role in teaching reading. Nonetheless, research has shown that children who are proficient readers have more sensitive implicit knowledge of story grammars than do those who are poorer readers (Stein & Glenn, 1979; et al.). Also, Bowman (1981) found

This is a good time to discuss alternative story grammars that have been adjusted to consider the developmental level of the learners. For example, a very basic story grammar for kindergarteners has three components— beginning, middle, and end. Talk about how the elements and details of a story grammar can be simplified or elaborated further, according to level of learner.

that questioning strategies based on story structure had positive results in reading comprehension improvement for stories. Further, a variety of studies have found evidence supporting the idea of using a story map or other story structure to guide questioning (Beck, 1984; Gordon & Pearson, 1983; Singer & Donlan, 1982).

In short, there is enough positive evidence to warrant utilization of story grammar in a variety of ways during reading instruction in the elementary grades.

Key Elements of a Story Grammar

Following is a simplified description of the Stein and Glenn (1979) story grammar, along with an example of each element in a story:

1. *Setting.* Introduction of the protagonist (main character or "good" person); can contain information about physical, social, or temporal context in which the remainder of the story occurs

   Example: Once there was a big gray fish named Albert. He lived in a big icy pond near the edge of a forest. One day, Albert was swimming around the pond.

2. *Initiating Event.* An action, an internal event, or a natural occurrence that serves to initiate or to cause a response in the protagonist

   Example: Then he spotted a big juicy worm on top of the water. Albert knew how delicious worms tasted.

3. *Internal Response.* An emotion, thought, or motivating goal of the protagonist

   Example: He wanted to eat that one for his dinner. So he swam very close to the worm.

4. *Attempt.* An overt action to obtain the protagonist's goal

   Example: Then he bit into him. Suddenly, Albert was pulled through the water into a boat.

5. *Consequence.* An event, action, or end that marks the attainment or nonattainment of the protagonist's goal

   Example: He had been caught by a fisherman. Albert felt sad.

6. *Reaction.* An emotion, cognition, action, or result expressing the protagonist's feelings about her or his goal attainment or relating the broader consequential realm of the protagonist's goal attainment

   Example: He wished he had been more careful.

Using a story grammar model to teach strategic reading rests on the assumption that the instructional model puts learners through steps of the reading process in activities that replicate in one way or another the actual mental processes the reader goes through in reading the text. The following uses of story grammar attempt to do this to one degree or another.

Ask students to write three brief contrived simple stories exhibiting the basic story grammar elements, one each suitable for primary grades, intermediate grades, and middle-school grades. Compare and discuss them in class.

Have students design creative graphic story maps for different instructional uses.

Story Grammar as a Framework for Question Design

Story grammar can be used as the framework for designing questions to be used in teaching a story.

> *Example:* "Where does the story take place?" (*Setting*)
>
> "What is the first important thing that happens in this story?" (*Initiating event*)
>
> "What does the main character want to get?" (*Internal response*)
>
> "How does the main character go after her or his goal?" (*Attempt*)
>
> "Does the main character achieve the goal?" (*Consequence*)
>
> "How does the main character feel at the end of the story?" (*Reaction*)

When using these questions to guide discussion of the story, make sure students equate the questions with the appropriate elements of the story grammar.

Variations of this approach include using story-grammar-generated questions to provide study guides for students to use in reading text. Story-grammar-based questions can also be used with question-inserting approaches.

Story Mapping

Story mapping based on the story grammar concept has been proven effective with selected learners (note work by Beck, 1984, by Gordon & Pearson, 1983, and by Singer & Donlan, 1982). One way to use story mapping is by providing models to students to use as study guides or for developing outlines for their own creative stories.

Linear-Sequenced Story Maps A simple framed model is shown in Figure 7.3. Notice the slight variations between the story grammar outlined in this figure and the one described by Stein and Glenn (1979). Still other variations are possible, and story grammar can and should be adjusted to fit the grade level and ability of the students. For example, Figure 7.4 shows a story grammar frame cleverly designed to represent a main character in the story. Teachers can create other formats to use with story grammar frames based on favorite stories of children in the intermediate grades.

Ask students for additional ideas for using story maps in the elementary grades.

Reutzel's Use of Story Mapping An effective use of story grammar was described by Reutzel (1985). Reutzel's research with fifth-graders found reading comprehension improved significantly by incorporating story maps of various sorts into the reading instruction. He suggests different maps for different aspects of reading and for different forms of text (i.e., expository versus narrative, etc.). Figure 7.5 shows three different maps exemplifying portrayal of story grammar elements from different text types.

Figure 7.3   Simple example of a linear-sequenced story map (also called a "story grammar frame").

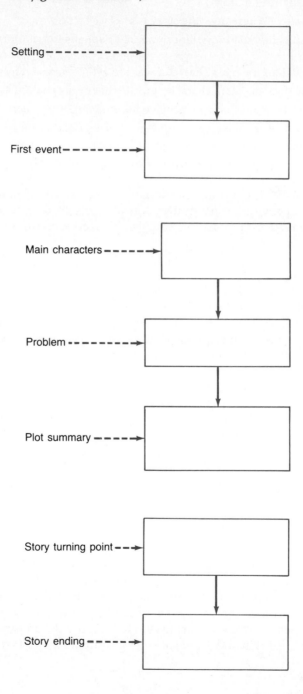

Figure 7.4   Variation of the linear-sequenced map (frame) of story grammar, which incidentally depicts the story's main character.

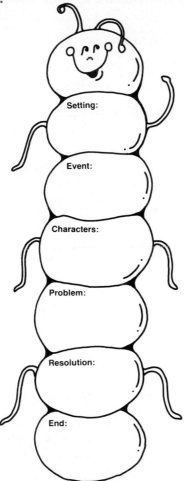

In Figure 7.5, Map 1 illustrates the main idea, with sequential details. Reutzel suggests the following steps for use of such a map:

1. Construct, in sequence, a summary list of the main idea, major events, and major characters in the story;
2. locate the main idea in the center of the map;
3. draw enough ties projecting out symmetrically from the center circle to accommodate the major events/characters on the summary list;

Figure 7.5   **Three alternative nonlinear maps of story grammar, taken from D. Ray Reutzel (1985, January), "Story Maps Improve Comprehension," *Reading Teacher*, pp. 400–404. Reprinted with permission of D. Ray Reutzel and the International Reading Association.**

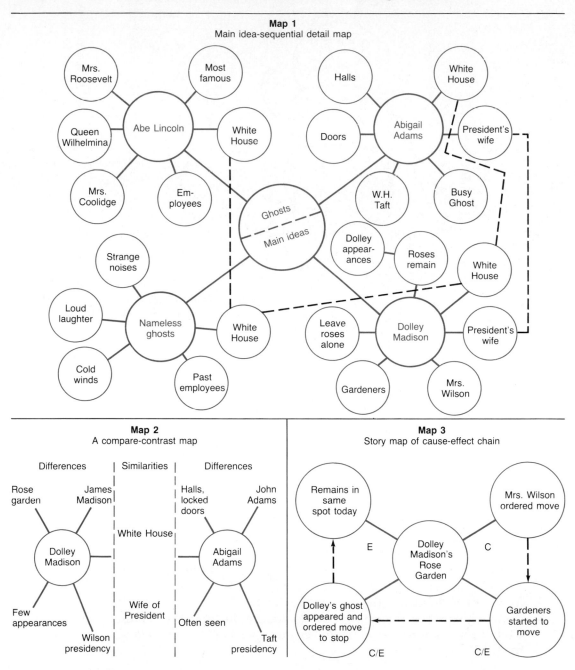

4. enter the major concepts or events in circles attached to these ties, including them in sequence clockwise around the center circle;

5. enter subevents and subconcepts in clockwise sequence around the circles containing major events or concepts in the story map.

Reutzel, 1985, page 400

Maps 2 and 3 are examples of how to use story grammar mapping to focus student attention on particular reading skills or concepts.

Various Uses for Story Maps As with the other procedures and techniques, there are a variety of possible uses for the story maps.

- Use the mapping technique during the prereading of the text as a means of tapping and/or expanding background knowledge for students prior to the text reading. Draw the map on the board, or use an overhead transparency, and have the students make predictions about the various things that might fit into the map. Of course, the final map produced during prereading will not match one that could be completed after the text had been read, because the prereading map is being constructed by conjecture.
- Prepare the map ahead of time, and provide it for students as a study guide in their reading of the text.
- Prepare a partial story map—leaving blank circles—and have students fill in the missing parts as they read the text, or use the map as a summarizing activity and fill in the missing parts together during a class discussion.
- Supply a map outline to students to complete as they read the text. Note that this, too, is a form of study guide.
- Have students prepare their own maps as a follow-up activity to the reading and as a summarizing or reviewing activity.

Remind students that nearly all teaching acts that involve teacher–student role reversals, with the learner being the teacher, are somewhat metacognitive in character. For example, having students prepare a test that covers a chapter they have just read in social studies implicitly forces them to review key concepts and ideas in the chapter. Also, when students "play teacher" and lead the class or a group in discussion of the role of the leading character in a short story, they must analyze that character as a teacher.

Summary of Direct-Instruction Procedures for Modeling Strategic Reading

The instructional approaches herein described as strategic reading models use the structure of the text as the basis for mental processing that takes place during the reading act. Readers impose what they know about the content, concept, and thinking when reading. However, the reader has little control over the form of the text structure. Readers take the structure and work from its most salient or critical features to structure a conceptualization of it.

These models, then, represent an attempt to formulate approaches to reading that incorporate the most important structural and content features of text by elaborating them as sequenced steps in the production and comprehension of text.

A very attractive benefit of these models is that they can work both for the comprehension of text and for the production of text. In other words, they can be used to teach students how to comprehend what they read, and they can be used as tools to teach students how to write text.

ADDITIONAL IDEAS FOR DEVELOPING SELF-MONITORING SKILLS

Question taxonomizing can be used throughout the grades in a similar fashion, simply by using a more complete or complex taxonomy. For example, in the intermediate grades, teachers might move to three or four levels of questions from the Sanders taxonomy.

The effective teacher of reading can use a number of teaching techniques to help learners develop the critical self-monitoring skills necessary for becoming good readers. Following are several that can be used in a variety of ways and in a variety of different contexts:

- Student-formulated questions
  - Reciprocal questioning
  - Question taxonomies
  - Story problems
- Student-formulated summaries

Teaching Students to Formulate Questions

Reciprocal Questioning
In brief, this technique requires the student to become the questioner, the designer, and the writer of questions for evoking comprehension. Here is one possible scenario using reciprocal questioning:

> "Boys and girls. I want each of us to read the first three paragraphs in this chapter on the life of the colonists in our social studies book. After we have read the paragraphs, I am going to ask you two questions to see whether you understood the paragraphs."
>
> After the children have read the paragraphs, ask them the two questions, and discuss the paragraphs using your questions as the discussion generators.
>
> "Now boys and girls, let's read the next three paragraphs in the chapter. This time, though, I want you to write out two questions that you can ask me to see whether I understood the main ideas in the paragraphs."

Notice what takes place here. In order for the children to think up two important questions that allow them to find out whether their teacher understood the text, they must think about what is important that could serve as answers to questions. In short, they have to think about their own thinking—engage in metacognition.

Question Taxonomizing

One of the most important skills teachers must develop is the ability to use various question taxonomies to design questions to use with students. Knowing the taxonomic levels of questions provides insight into the levels of cognition with which the students are being required to operate.

The "Question Taxonomizing Technique" is based on the same principles that teachers apply. It simply reverses roles so that students must use question taxonomies for generating questions. The following scenario illustrates the technique.

"Boys and girls, let's read this text aloud together:

> In 1492, Christopher Columbus sailed with his crews on three different ships—the Pinta, the Niña, and the Santa María—in search of the New World.
>
> After sailing westward for several weeks, they spotted land. They landed, probably some place in what is today called "Central America."
>
> After they established a small settlement, Columbus returned to Spain with some of his men. He was hoping to get more money from Queen Isabella in order to return to America and expand the settlement he had left there.

"Now, boys and girls, let's see if you can answer some questions I have about this text. When did Columbus sail for the New World? Jane? (Pause for response.) 1492—That's correct! How did you know? (Jane responds by saying something like—'You can point to it.' Or, 'It says so—right here.')

"Good. Now try this question. What were the names of Columbus's three ships? Jim? (Pause for response.) The Pinta, the Niña, and the Santa María. Correct! How did you know, Jim? (Jim responds with answers similar to Jane's.)

"Now let's answer this one. Do you think Columbus was frightened when he sailed in search of the New World?

"(Now there is a pause.) You can't see the answer to that one anywhere in the text, can you boys and girls? Or, can you? (At this point, the teacher generates some discussion with conjectures about the likelihood of Columbus being frightened, given what we know about the kind of ships and equipment they had in those days and the inadequate knowledge they had about world geography.)

"Boys and girls, questions like the first two where you can actually put your finger on the answer in the text are called 'fact' questions. Questions like the third one, where you cannot put your finger on the exact words in the text that answer the question, but you know from other information about the text what the answer probably is are called 'think' questions. Who can tell me why we call them that? (Children should offer ideas about how you have to think to come up with an answer.)

"Now let's read some more of this text to page 33, and here are three more questions. (Provide them with three more questions.) After you read the text, I want you to tell me which two of the questions are fact questions and which one is a think question.

Effective comprehension of reading is promoted by offering children many different opportunities to read in a variety of contexts. Both oral reading and silent reading need to be stressed.

Whether summarizing itself is a foundation skill is, to some extent, a moot point. It certainly is important and warrants attention by itself at given points in the curriculum.

"(After the children have completed this part of the assignment, move to the final part.)

"Now boys and girls I want you to finish reading this text. Then I want you to write three questions about it. Make two of your questions 'fact' questions and one a 'think' question."

As with the reciprocal questioning procedure, students must engage in metacognitive operations. They must think about some of the differences between levels of cognition and then use the text in structuring the correct types of question to meet the assigned task. Interestingly, children usually enjoy this procedure. They do not have to answer any questions! Quite a contrast to what they commonly must do in a reading lesson.

Writing Story Problems

Story problems have commonly been one of the most troublesome math tasks elementary children are asked to tackle. A metacognitively oriented technique that can be used is to reverse procedures.

Example: Boys and girls. Write a story problem that asks a question where $10 - 3 = 7$ is the correct answer.

Methods for Implementing Questioning Techniques

The techniques described here can be used in a variety of ways. Tasks can be assigned to individuals, to pairs of children, or to small groups of children. The question taxonomizing approach can be varied in several ways:

- Use a three- or four-level taxonomy instead of just a two-level taxonomy as described here.

- Assign children the task of preparing a test over an entire story or chapter.
- Have all children practice writing various questions at different levels, then have them exchange papers with their peers, who can try to categorize their questions.

Designing such techniques and activities calls for the teacher to think of role reversal. Any activity in which the students must challenge children to learn, just as teachers do, involves metacognition.

Teaching Students to Summarize

Perhaps the single most important ability that a student reader must be able to demonstrate is that of artfully summarizing the content of a passage or larger blocks of text. Summarizing requires use of almost all important foundation skills of thinking and comprehending—classifying, sequencing, comparing–contrasting, and determining cause–effect relationships. The reader must not only be able to eliminate nonimportant detail and generalizations, but must also be able to create new language that is consonant with the concepts elaborated in the original text, in other words, paraphrase.

Although mastering the ability to effectively summarize text is a skill that must be developed and refined throughout life, the basic strategies of summarizing are most effectively taught in the elementary grades. According to Brown and Day (1983), readers use a limited number of "macrorules" in creating passage summaries. They suggest that four of these macrorules lend themselves to direct instruction. In simplified form, these macrorules can be taught to elementary-grade students.

The four basic rules are

1. Deletion—eliminating unimportant information or information that is redundant
2. Superordination—grouping specifics or details in like groups and creating generalizations to describe them
3. Selection—picking important general statements to keep as key parts of the summary
4. Invention—generating specific topic sentences

Applying the rules to a selection of text would look like Figure 7.6.

Using the four summarizing rules, we can produce a summary of Figure 7.6 such as the following:

After years of controversy, Canadians announced that the Canada–United States free trade agreement is now law. Legal letters were exchanged with the Americans, and the law will be implemented on New Year's Day. Although liberal senators opposed the bill, they allowed the Conservatives to pass it. The Tory leadership in the Senate will act as watchdog on the deal.

Note that the reading instruction models presented here are not exhaustive. This is intended only as a selection of those the authors feel are most widely known and used. You may argue for others in addition to or in place of these. You might want to ask students to find additional models in the literature and compare them to those presented here.

Figure 7.6 Sample of text on which summarization rules and visual summarization techniques have been applied. Text taken from J. O'Neill (1988), p. A–1;4. Reproduced with permission. Copyright 1988. All rights reserved.

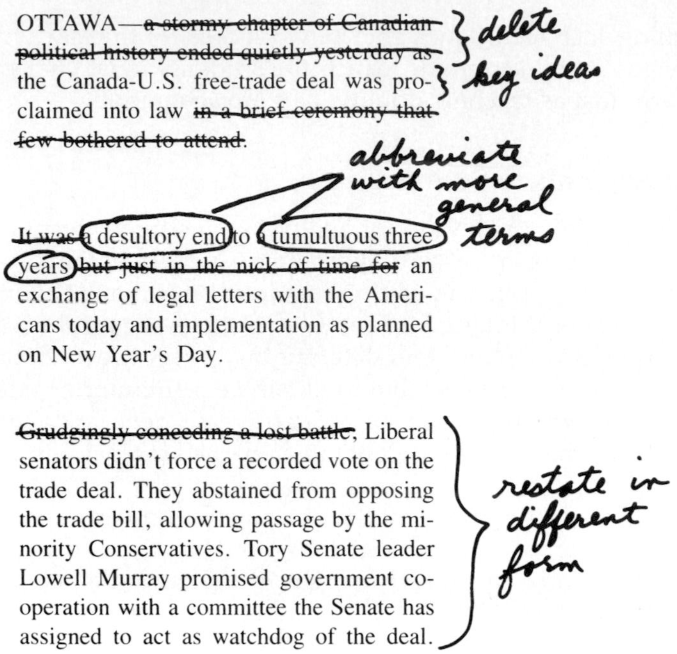

OTTAWA— ~~a stormy chapter of Canadian political history ended quietly yesterday as~~ the Canada-U.S. free-trade deal was proclaimed into law ~~in a brief ceremony that few bothered to attend.~~ *} delete* *} key ideas*

abbreviate with more general terms

~~It was~~ a desultory end to a tumultuous three years ~~but just in the nick of time for~~ an exchange of legal letters with the Americans today and implementation as planned on New Year's Day.

~~Grudgingly conceding a lost battle,~~ Liberal senators didn't force a recorded vote on the trade deal. They abstained from opposing the trade bill, allowing passage by the minority Conservatives. Tory Senate leader Lowell Murray promised government cooperation with a committee the Senate has assigned to act as watchdog of the deal. *} restate in different form*

Students should be given ample practice applying each of the steps, using a variety of text types and a variety of subjects.

Initial work with summarizing is best done with expository writing because this form is usually consistent in organization and structure. Also, use of summarizing should be used in reading instruction throughout the year, with application in various subject areas, especially social studies and science.

AN "ALPHABET SOUP" OF READING INSTRUCTION MODELS

various unusual ways to incorporate all of the instructional ideas they have learned into their approach to teaching.

Over the years, a number of models for reading comprehension instruction have been developed and used. These are often identified by abbreviations, acronyms, or, in some instances, simply the key letters from the phrase or other wording the developer used to name the model. Teachers should be familiar with all of these models, in order to effectively decide whether to use one or more of them in their teaching.

DRTA (Directed Reading–Thinking Activity)

Developed by Russell Stauffer (1969) originally for the primary grades, the DRTA has been used in a variety of modified forms with older children as well. It is a basic plan for directing children's reading in such a way that they are encouraged to think as they read and to make predictions about what will be occurring. One form of the DRTA is the following:

1. Identify a purpose for the reading (e.g., design a story map and encourage students to make predictions about what will be occurring); use the chapter title or story title as a prereading opening to ask students to make predictions using the title and/or graphic cues at the beginning of the selection.
2. Guide the reader initially through the material (e.g., skim the text prior to reading), encouraging students to use text adjuncts in making additional predictions.
3. Observe student behavior in reading (e.g., have them read in segments or blocks with question checks to monitor their progress). Individualize here as much as possible.
4. Discuss children's original predictions after reading (e.g., have students consider how the data or information in the text altered or supported their initial and ongoing predictions).

Notice the similarity to the inserted-questions procedure discussed earlier. When used in a simplified form, a kindergarten and first-grade teacher can use predictable books and predictable stories effectively with a version of the DRTA.

GRP (Guided Reading Procedure)

Manzo (1980) offers the GRP as an alternative approach to help readers develop comprehension and recall in a variety of content areas. The following steps are used:

1. Establish the primary purpose for the reading of a text with students. Have them read the first 250 or 500 words, trying to remember all that they can of the content. They are to close their books after silently reading the segment.
2. Students try to recall information, and the teacher records it on the chalkboard.
3. Have students reexamine the text and suggest additions or changes to be made on the chalkboard.
4. Have students make a semantic map or outline of the information. This can be done individually or as a cooperative learning small group or paired activity.
5. Ask questions that will help students to synthesize this information with previous knowledge they have about the subject.

6. Give a short test to check short-term recall.
7. Later give another test to check long-term recall.

Some research (Ankney & McClurg, 1981) suggests that GRP can be an effective approach for social studies, in particular.

PReP (Prereading Plan)

Designed by Langer (1981), PReP is intended as a prereading activity to ensure that the student's background knowledge is firmly established prior to the actual reading of the text. It consists of three stages:

1. Initiate prereading discussion with an *association question* (a question designed to stimulate cognitive associations with existing knowledge) for students. For example, "What do you think of when I mention the word *fishing*?" (if the students are reading a story about fishing). Follow through with discussion, writing student-generated ideas on the chalkboard.
2. Students explain why they made the associations they did. This is the justification stage of the prereading plan. During this stage, also work with students to create categories of associated terms and ideas. Complete this stage before proceeding with Stage 3.
3. Students reformulate their original conceptualizations of Stage 1. Help them to use the different categories to consider category relations that can be articulated as generalizations that are probably appropriate to the text.

Langer et al. contend that establishing a solid knowledge base during the prereading phase of instruction is more important than IQ and other variables in ensuring success of the reading lesson (Langer & Nicholich, 1981).

ReQuest (Reciprocal Questioning)

This is one version of reciprocal questioning (which was described earlier in this chapter). Developed by Manzo (1969) primarily for remedial readers, versions of his original model are now widely incorporated into metacognitively oriented models and plans for reading. In brief, ReQuest as elaborated by Manzo is as follows:

1. Students and teacher read a short segment of text silently.
2. The teacher closes his or her book and is questioned by students about the meaning of the text passage.
3. The teacher and students exchange roles, and the teacher asks students questions about the same passage of text.
4. Steps 1–3 are repeated with the next text segment.
5. Students are now asked to make predictions about what is likely to appear in the remainder of the text.

6. Students read the remainder of the text silently.
7. The teacher leads a follow-up discussion of the text.

QARs (Question–Answer Relationships)

Versions of the QARs have been proposed by a number of people in reading education over the years. Pearson and Johnson (1978) discussed two kinds of questions that the reader must attend to: "script-explicit" and "script-implicit" questions. Though their work relates closely to QARs, most educators probably associate Raphael (1982) with QARs as an instructional approach. The approach assumes that the two sources for questions—the text and the reader—lead to three different kinds of questions that the reader must address. "Right There" questions are usually literal, and their answer can be pointed to directly in the text. "Think and Search" questions require the reader to search the text for information and to generate relationships from that information. The think-and-search (textually implicit) and the right there (textually explicit) questions are clearly based on the text. "On My Own" questions, on the other hand, are based on the learner's schemata rather than on the text. The reader simply does educated conjecturing based on knowledge brought to the reading act. Vacca, Vacca, and Gove (1987) offer the following useful illustrations of the three types:

> TEXT: *Jimmy put some paper on a stool. With steady hands, he made the paper into a hat. The baby was looking at what he was doing. She didn't think about her toothache. He put the hat on his head. She smiled a little.*
>
> RIGHT THERE: *1. What did Jimmy put on the stool?*
>
> *Paper*
>
> THINK & SEARCH: *2. What is one thing you can do to make your mother or father happy?*
>
> *I would do something nice, like clean my room.*
>
> ON YOUR OWN: *3. What kind of boy do you think Jimmy is?*
>
> *kind, cares about the baby*
>
> **Vacca, Vacca, and Gove, 1987, p. 167**

When designing activities premised upon the QARs model, be sure to clarify the distinction between the think-and-search and the on-my-own question types; they can be confusing to intermediate grades students—or for that matter, to much older learners as well! The authors suggest starting with a simplified distinction such as that described in the question taxonomizing procedure described earlier in this chapter—Fact versus

Think questions. Textually implicit questions are very similar to schema-based questions.

The metacognitive facility of being able to read between the lines is important, and students must be engaged in some activities and procedures that require them to think about the different kinds of thinking that effective readers must do.

PIRL (Planned Inferential Reading Lesson)

PIRL, developed by Cunningham, Cunningham, and Arthur (1980), is basically a guided procedure for reading that requires students know about the differences between text-explicit and text-implicit questions. PIRL consists of two parts, but Part II is more advanced than most elementary students are likely to handle well, so it is not included here. Part I has four steps:

1. Prepare the statements. After personally reading the text to be assigned, the teacher lists several ideas that the students are to learn from the text. Two types of statements should be included (preferably in writing on the chalkboard): (1) statements that are explicit in the text, and (2) statements that are inferred—that are text-implicit.
2. Give directions. Have the students read each statement orally with the teacher. Tell the students that all of the statements are true and that their task is to determine which have been taken directly from the text (text-explicit) and which have been "inferred" from the text (text-implicit). (After students have some experience with this procedure, they might be asked to make predictions prior to the reading of the text regarding which statement belongs in which of the two categories.)
3. Read the text. Students read the text. Although students will probably do this individually in the initial stages, as students become more proficient, this can be done as a paired or small group activity, with students using copies of the statements while they read.
4. Discuss the statements. In reading follow-up, students are to read portions or segments of the text associated with the text-explicit statements and are to articulate those that are text-implicit, explaining their reasoning for saying that they are implicit rather than explicit.

PREP (Preview, Read, Examine, and Prompt)

Developed by Schmelzer, Christen, and Browning (1980), this is more accurately described as a model designed to develop study skills than it is a broader reading-comprehension model. Similar to many others, however, its benefits extend to comprehension generally. A four-step plan that is easy to implement, PREP looks like this:

- P: Preview. This is a simple prereading procedure. Have students look over the first page of text, skimming the text for subheadings, text adjuncts, and so on. Discuss the text with students, furnishing them with the purpose of the text and encouraging them to make predictions about what will be occurring in the text.
- R: Read. Students read the text. With older students, note-taking should be encouraged. Use simpler note-taking procedures for younger students.
- E: Examine. Have students write questions about the text—sometimes during the reading, sometimes after they have completed the reading. If students lack experience in writing questions, provide them with guides and examples such as "wh questions"—*what, who, when, where,* and *why* (and *how*).
- P: Prompt. Use a variety of techniques intended to help students remember what they have read. For example, have students recite orally the gist of what they have read; have them write a summary or outline of what they have read, and so on.

SLR (Simultaneous Listening and Reading)

This procedure simply asks students to read along with a tape recording or record of a text. The premise is that such activities will do a number of things—improve fluency, sense of rhythm, articulation, pronunciation, and phonics skills generally. The steps are as follows:

1. Students listen to recordings of various stories or text segments until they feel they can read a particular one fluently.
2. Students choose the text or text segment they wish to focus upon. The selection should be challenging but achievable for the individual student.
3. Students practice regularly, and if desired or possible, they should tape-record their own reading.
4. The teacher listens to students read every 3 or 4 days and offers suggestions for improvement.

It can take a month or more for students to become as proficient as they wish to when using this method. However, if used consistently, over time, students will reduce significantly the time required to perform the task proficiently (Chomsky, 1976).

SQ3R (Survey, Question, Read, Recite, and Review)

Developed by Robinson (1961), this is one of the older "alphabet soup" models. It, too, was designed originally as a study aid, yet it has implications for comprehension generally. Following are the five steps that students use in SQ3R:

1. Survey. Survey the text to be read, noting title, graphics, subheads and other text adjuncts.
2. Question. Write down a list of questions you expect to be answered when you read this text. Look to the heads and subheads for clues here.
3. Read. Read the text, taking brief notes as you read.
4. Recite. Try to answer your questions as you read the text. Do this without looking back at the text, if possible.
5. Review. Reread to verify your answers and to make sure that you have covered all the main points.

A version of the SQ3R was developed by Fay (1965), called the "SQRQCQ." Designed specifically for mathematics materials, it calls for the reader to survey, question, read, *question* (meaning that the reader makes a decision about the mathematical procedure to be invoked), *compute* (the student computes using the procedure determined in the previous step), and *question* (the student reexamines the computation and the answer to check for accuracy).

SSR (Sustained Silent Reading)

Hunt (1970) states the SSR concept succinctly:

1. Students select books or other texts they wish to read.
2. All students read silently for a fixed period of time.

Having children share a variety of reading and writing activities allows them to capitalize on the experiences of others as well as assist them in their own thinking.

3. The teacher reads also, and no interruptions are allowed.
4. Students are not required to answer questions about their reading or to give reports on the content.

Many school buildings identify a particular time in the day when all in the school take part in SSR.

During the 1980s, McCracken and McCracken (1978) have been most responsible for the ongoing interest in SSR. They offer some basic assumptions that the teacher must recognize about SSR:

1. Reading books is important.
2. Reading is something anyone can do.
3. Reading involves communicating with an author.
4. Children are capable of sustained thought.
5. Books are meant to be read in long passages.
6. Teachers believe that pupils are comprehending.
7. The teacher trusts the children to decide when something is well written.

Common Characteristics across Instructional Models

Although this chapter has provided only a selection of many different reading instructional models, this group is pretty representative. A few basic attributes surface as common to all or most of the models in this group.

1. Nearly all of these models attempt to capitalize on the relation between reading comprehension and thinking. Notice how prediction and inference are emphasized in many of them.
2. Metacognitive development is central to many of the models. Reading educators are attempting to design instructional approaches that help the learner think more about the mental processes of the reading act. The approaches range from direct efforts to focus on the steps of the reading process to more indirect approaches, such as question taxonomizing, which involve students with thinking about their own thinking.
3. Nearly all of the models call for multistep direct instruction. Students are led through the process a number of times.
4. Most of the models are amenable to use in a range of grades, ages, and content areas. In fact, many seem to emphasize application to content areas, so that they can be used to teach reading across the curriculum.
5. Although the models usually focus initially on performance of the students individually, many of them lend themselves to teaching

You might want to spend some time discussing with your students their concept of *writing*. Some may view writing in terms of products, such as poems, reports, stories, plays, and so forth. However, if they are to incorporate writing into their reading instruction effectively, they must view writing as a process; writing a word, phrase, statement, or question can be an effective way for obtaining daily writing. Further, and even more important, teachers should regularly look for opportunities to help children view reading as something to be done with pen or pencil in hand; this helps to reinforce the natural relationships that bind the two.

with paired or small-group activities. Cooperative learning potential is present in most of the models.

6. Many of the models offer the teacher opportunities to integrate writing into the reading instruction. For example, students can be asked to write answers in many situations instead of responding orally. The nice thing about this kind of writing opportunity is that students will be writing words and sentences as part of the ongoing reading instruction instead of using writing only as a supplement, as so often happens in lessons purporting to be making a reading–writing connection.

7. Finally, most of these models can be fitted into almost any kind of reading program, ranging from a basal reading program to a highly individualized or self-designed reading program. It is important, however, to remember not to overuse any one model. Because they all move the reader toward the same overall goals, variations can be made on each, and benefits from one model can carry over to another. If overused, any one of these models can become drill-like in nature and boring to the students. Remember to maintain balance and variety in using reading-instruction models.

BUILDING TEXT STRUCTURE KNOWLEDGE THROUGH READING AND THROUGH READING–WRITING CONNECTIONS

"Writing-as-supplement" to the reading act and "writing-as-integral" to the reading act are both important. However, their roles are different. These notions might be worth discussing before your students complete this section of the chapter.

Knowledge of different kinds of text and text structures is important for being an effective reader of different kinds of writing. Narrative, expository, descriptive, and persuasive purposes for writing within prose, poetry, and dramatic forms of writing all share many structural features. However, they also reflect some features unique to each. Poetry and plays are probably more visibly obvious in their distinction from other forms. Expository and narrative text, on the other hand, look similar on the surface. Closer examination, however, reveals some differences. This section of this chapter examines some of these differences and describes some techniques for helping students to become aware of them.

As mentioned previously, most of the strategies, techniques, activities, and instructional models that have been discussed so far in this chapter have potential for building writing into the reading instruction. There exists the same potential for incorporating writing into most of the instruction regarding the nature of text-structure differences. To facilitate the reading–writing connection, some of the ways writing can be used to build important reading skills are mentioned in this description of text-structure differences related to reading comprehension instruction.

Using Sentence-Combining for Narrative and Expository Text

Since the later 1960s, research has revealed that sentence-combining activities used systematically in the language arts program help improve sentence writing abilities (Mellon, 1969; O'Hare, 1973). Later research with sentence-combining suggests that selected kinds of sentence-combining activities improve sentence comprehension in reading (Combs, 1977; Stotsky, 1983). Sentence-combining offers a variety of uses, including uses in teaching both narrative and expository text structure. It also provides a number of additional benefits and attractions as an instructional tool.

For example, sentence-combining provides a means for teaching the structure of sentences by having students actually produce sentences in their writing. This seems far more effective than underlining parts of sentences, diagramming sentences, labeling parts of speech, and so on, and it allows the teaching of grammar without getting into the technical language of grammar. In addition, it provides an excellent way to integrate writing with the reading instruction. The following scenario shows how this can be done:

"Boys and Girls, I have been working on a story, and I would like to have you help me by offering suggestions about it. I have brought the first two paragraphs from my story for you to see. Some of my friends said that I need to rewrite it, but I'm not sure. What do you think? Here it is:

Dusk settled over the town. The dusk was murky. The town was small. Clouds scudded across the sky. The clouds were thick. The clouds were low. The river was swollen. Rain drenched the town. The mayor peered through his window. The town was frightened. The mayor was anxious. The window was smudged. The mayor peered up-river.

The dam protected the town. The dam was earthen. The dam was weakened. It was weakened by the rain. A flood seemed imminent. The flood would be dangerous. The mayor donned his slicker and boots. The slicker was for rain. The boots were rubber. He plodded out to his truck. It was a pickup truck. He wanted to look at the dam. The truck would get him closer to the dam. It would go to the dam. The dam was old.

Read the paragraphs orally to the children. Encourage the children to volunteer their opinions. After discussing the paragraphs briefly and leading the children to believe that they could probably improve the writing, pair them up or have them work individually rewriting the paragraphs. Point out to them that the gist of the content is to be preserved.

When the preceding text sample was used with fifth-graders, the students discovered that these were derived from the first two paragraphs of the next selection in their readers. We (the authors) had taken those first two paragraphs and rewritten them in short choppy sentences. Many of the children's rewritten versions were close to those of the originals in their books.

Ask students to keep in mind two important points as they study sentence-combining. One is that it is a more complex idea than simply putting a few short choppy sentences together. It requires considerable concentrated effort to design effective sentence-combining activities that fit naturally into the instruction and that are designed to meet specific reading and writing needs of learners.

Second, remember that this can be a very exciting and productive activity in which learners can engage. It can also be drill-like and boring if overused or used incorrectly. Nonetheless, the research is very solid in its support as an element of the reading program. You might encourage students to look to work by Bill Strong, Warren Combs, and others in sentence-combining.

Integrating reading and writing is important for both of these literacy acts. The classroom should provide ample opportunities for children to use both when the context calls for it.

This activity had incorporated writing into the reading lesson, and it had introduced the story content, providing a stimulus for excellent pre-reading discussions on the theme of the selection (which was about a historically famous flood).

This model can be used by simply pulling paragraphs from selections students will be reading and rewriting them as was done with these. It can be done with overhead transparencies or as handouts. The overhead has the advantage of allowing the teacher to hide most of the text with a paper, which can be gradually slid down to reveal more text. The children then gradually see the faults of the writing.

Another variation of this approach is to scan two or three pages of a selection of text to be read and find a key sentence—one that (a) has excellent description central to the theme of the text, (b) tells key information about the main character, or (c) contains an excellent statement of text's main idea. Once the sentence is selected, it can be noted and used for breaking it into short choppy sentences similar to those in the preceding example.

Ask students to combine the choppy sentences into one sentence. Then tell them that the choppy sentences were made from a single sentence much like the sentences they wrote, and that sentence can be found in their text between pages XX and XX (the pages surrounding the selected sentence, beginning with the first page of the story). Have students search for the sentence.

After they have located it, talk about the variations students have written as a whole class discussion or in small groups. Use this to lead into a prereading discussion that activates or builds on their background knowledge.

The potential for learning in such an activity is great: Students have an opportunity to develop sentence-writing skills; they get practice in skimming text for key ideas; and they receive an excellent preparation for reading the text.

Various sentence-combining experiences should be used throughout the language arts and reading programs. However, like any other excellent technique or activity, if overused, its value can be compromised. Use sentence-combining consistently throughout the year, but no more than once a week or so. Keep the sentence-combining experience relatively brief so that children will not view it as simply another workbook activity. Think creatively; this concept has a wide range of instructional uses in the reading and writing program.

Exploring Different Kinds of Text Structures

Readers must learn that different kinds of text exhibit different kinds of internal structures. The general text structure of expository text is the kind of writing that appears on the front page of newspapers. This is also the writing form that students are expected to employ when they write reports on various subjects.

Practice with Persuasive–Argumentative Expository Text

The general category of expository text has different subcategories that might vary somewhat in structure. The reportive or descriptive expository text found in newspapers purports to present information in a relatively objective form. Argumentative or persuasive expository text, on the other hand, is designed to persuade the reader of a position or a belief. Editorials in newspapers or attorneys' summations in trials are forms of expository text in which the primary purpose is persuasion. Among other distinctions, readers generally find more subjectively loaded verbs and adjectives in persuasive expository text. In addition, readers are likely to find more subordinating conjunctions and subordinate clauses—clauses beginning with "if," "since," "whenever," "although," "because," and so on.

Persuasive-exposition sentences tend to be more hypothetical in character. "If you believe that we should allow the new ferry landing to be built in our town, then you are implicitly supporting expansion of the tourist-oriented businesses in the south Bellingham area." Consider the grammatical and semantic complexity of sentences of this type. In many respects, argumentative exposition is the most difficult form of text to comprehend (National Assessment of Educational Progress—NAEP, 1977). It requires serious attention, and the elementary-grade classroom

A minor technical point: Some authorities treat expository writing and persuasive (argumentative) writing as separate discourse modes or writing genres. Others argue (no pun intended) that persuasive writing is simply a type of exposition (i.e., reportive or descriptive, explanatory, and persuasive discourse make up exposition). However, the trend that the authors of this text book have seen in many of the newer commercially published language arts and reading programs is to treat expository and persuasive writing as separate modes.

is an important place to begin serious instruction in comprehending this form of text.

The teacher should do the following:

- Search for samples of argumentative or persuasive text appropriate to the reading abilities of their students and use it as instructional text with students.
- Prepare contrived persuasive text to use with students.
- Look for flyers, brochures, and other advertising literature for things such as bicycles, skateboards, sports equipment aimed at this age of child, and use it as text samples with students. Examine the persuasive language. Question students about the logic of the arguments used in the literature.
- Have students write their own advertising brochures for any products they would like to sell. This can be done independently, in pairs, and as a small-group project.
- Have students prepare a class or school newspaper with a front page of reportive expository articles and an editorial page of persuasive articles. Use the paper as a class text for studying the different forms of expository writing.

Practice with Narrative Text

Narration is text that is usually a continuous string of text that is more subjective and personal in character than expository text, and it often is organized differently. Consider the following paragraph of narrative text:

> *On the half-decayed steps of the small old frame house on the edge of the ravine, a small nervous man stared down the road. The dust swirls in the distance hinted at the approach of a car on the gravel lane. The man seemed uneasy at the prospect of a long-overdue visit. He knew that the visit would be one he would remember for a long time.*

Claim sentence, topic sentence, or thesis sentence?

Support sentences?

Conclusion or summary sentence?

It is difficult to identify the same essential components of expository text in this kind of descriptive writing. Narrative writing tends to move in levels of abstraction from more to less specific or from less to more specific. In longer pieces of text than the preceding one, the movement goes back and forth in levels of abstraction.

Although narrative writing is normally found in stories, and that probably is the richest source of narrative text for students, narrative writing can also be found embedded in larger nonfiction text. For example, many biographies and autobiographies contain substantial passages of narrative text.

Narrative text is another area where some authorities disagree. Some, for example, think primarily or even only of fiction when thinking of narrative writing. Others, however, point to extended narrative that appears in biography or autobiography or extended subjective narrative embedded in nonfiction, such as history.

Some instructional materials encourage students to write narrative text in the same general manner that they do expository text (i.e., topic or thesis sentence, followed by detail or support and a summary sentence). Others, assert, however, that much, if not most, narrative writing—especially narrative paragraphs—appear without a topic or thesis sentence.

Given this situation, teachers of children need to consider closely the posture of the curriculum they are using and to be consistent in their instruction so that learners do not become more confused by what is, by its very nature, somewhat confusing to the experts!

The following can be done with elementary-grade students to help them develop an understanding of the structure of narrative text:

- Find short paragraphs similar to the preceding one about the nervous man, and contrast them with paragraphs that are more clearly expository in nature. Have students identify which are expository and which narrative. Ask them to explain or justify their choices.
- Provide students with models such as the following, and ask them to use the model to rewrite other narrative text you provide for them or which they find in their textbooks.

    1. The car approached slowly down the hill.
       2. Its shiny black finish glistened in the sun.
          3. A four-doored beauty, the Jaguar eased to the curb.
    1. The driver stepped out and looked down the street.
       2. He was looking for his passenger.

Number and indent the sentences to indicate their degree of specificity. A sentence with a higher number and a deeper indentation is more specific than the one that appears before it. This graphic method helps show how narrative text moves back and forth in its degree of specificity or generalization, as opposed to expository text, which tends to be more consistently structured around the claim–support–conclusion framework. Indenting and numbering of graphic models can be designed to be simple or quite complex, to match the level of instruction and ability levels of the students.

Teaching Text Cohesion

In addition to recognizing different types of text, students should be able to recognize some of the features of text that serve specific purposes for readers. For example, linguists and reading researchers have discovered some cohesive features of text (Halliday & Hasan, 1976). They have identified some of the internal grammatical and semantic features that appear in text to bind and hold it together. They refer to these features as "text cohesion factors."

Typically, these factors are *referential*—That is, the author uses words or phrases in text to refer to related ideas located elsewhere in the text. Pronouns are good examples of referential ties that help text to bind together ("cohere"). Developing readers must learn how pronouns serve to bind the text's structure and help it cohere. In fact, readers use various cohesive features to help mentally organize the text structure (Barnitz, 1979; Nash-Webber, 1977; Richek, 1977). Some of these features deserve closer examination here.

The most widely used and common of the cohesion features used in text are the anaphoric type: *Anaphora* are elements of text, words, or other

With renewed interest in the importance of writing and its development in children, researchers are turning again to measures of cohesion to assist in their consideration of text density, organization, and internal binding (note recent work by Elizabeth Sulsby, W. Teale, and others in emerging literacy).

Over the next few years, educators are likely to see some of these research measures and techniques moving into the teaching area, similar to what occurred with story grammar research, reconstructive memory studies, and semantic mapping. This might be one of several good places to discuss the importance of research and how it contributes to more effective curriculum and instruction!

grammatical constructs (such as phrases or clauses) that substitute for (and refer backward to) a preceding word or grammatical construct (i.e., a specific referent).

Halliday and Hasan (1976) identify four categories of anaphoric forms and types that the reader must master:

Anaphoric Forms and Types

1. *Referential cohesive ties.* These items in the language cannot be interpreted in their own right; instead, they make reference to something else for interpretation.

   Examples: Bill was proud of *his* new fishing rod and reel. His grandfather had given it to *him* for **his** birthday. (personal reference)

   Dad and I are going *fishing. This* will be our first trip this spring. (demonstrative reference)

   I'm going to use *worms* for my bait. Would you prefer *other* bait? (comparative reference)

2. *Substitution cohesive ties.* One of these items directly replaces another, even serving in the same syntactic capacity.

   Examples: This fishing *line* is not strong enough. I must get a heavier *one.* (nominal substitution)

   Shall I **put** the fish on the stringer? Please *do,* as soon as possible. (verbal substitution)

   Will we **catch lots of fish?** Dad says *so.* (clausal substitution)

3. *Ellipsis.* These items are omitted. Essentially, substitution and ellipsis are the same process, with ellipsis being a form of substitution in which the referent item is replaced by nothing.

   Example: Here are the *fish I caught.* Where are yours? [*fish*] (nominal ellipsis)

   Have you **been fishing?** Yes, I have. [*been fishing*] (verbal ellipsis)

   Who **taught you to cast so well?** Dad did. [*taught me to cast so well*] (clausal ellipsis)

4. *Lexical cohesion.* Cohesive effect achieved by the selection of vocabulary.

   Example: Bill fell into the *lake* while fishing. The *water* was very deep. (lexical reiteration)

   Bill baited the *hook* quickly. Then he dropped the *line* into the water. (lexical collocation—cohesiveness between items in some way associated with each other)

Pearson and Johnson (1978) recommend a somewhat different set of anaphoric relations (see Figure 7.7) that the teacher of reading should use as an instructional guide for developing students' knowledge and ability to use cohesive elements of text structure in reading comprehension.

Figure 7.7   **Table illustrating several kinds of anaphora, taken from** *Teaching Reading Comprehension,* **by P. David Pearson and Dale D. Johnson, copyright © 1978 by Holt, Rinehart and Winston, reprinted by permission of the publisher.**

Relation	Example	Possible Comprehension Probe
1. Pronouns: I, me, we, us, you, he, him, they, them.	Mary has a friend named John. *She* picks *him* up on the way to school. *They* walk home together too.	Who gets picked up? Who picks him up? Name the person who gets picked up.
2. Locative (location) pronouns: here, there.	The team climbed to the top of Mt. Everest. Only a few people have been *there*.	Where have only a few people been. Name the place where only a few people have been.
3. Deleted nouns: usually an adjective serves as the anaphora.	The students scheduled a meeting but only a *few* attended. Apparently *several* went to the beach. *Others* attended a dance in the gym. *Only the most serious* actually came to the meeting. (Notice that each adjective phrase or adjective refers to students.)	Who went to the beach? Who attended the dance in the gym? What does the word *others* refer to?
4. Arithmetic Anaphora	Mary and John entered the building. The *former* is tall and lovely. The *latter* is short and squatty. The *two* make an interesting couple.	Who is tall and lovely? Who makes an interesting couple?
5. Class inclusive anaphora: a superordinate word, substitutes for another word.	1. The dog barked a lot. The *animal* must have seen a prowler. 2. The lion entered the clearing. The *big cat* looked graceful as it surveyed its domain. 3. John was awakened by a siren. He thought the *noise* would never stop.	1. What animal must have seen a prowler? What does the word animal refer to? 2. What cat looked graceful? What does the word *cat* refer to? 3. What noise did John think would never stop?
6. Inclusive Anaphora: that, this, the idea, the problem, these reasons. Can refer back to an entire phrase, clause, or passage.	1. (After twenty pages discussing the causes of the Civil War.) For *these reasons,* the South seceded from the Union. 2. Someone was pounding on the door. *This* (or *it*) surprised Mary. 3. Crime is getting serious in Culver. The police have to do a better job with *this problem.* 4. "Do unto others as you would have them do unto you." *Such an idea* has been the basis of Christian theology for 2000 years.	1. Why did the South secede from the Union? 2. What surprised Mary? 3. What do the police have to do a better job with? 4. What has been the basis of Christian theology for 2000 years?

Figure 7.7 *(continued)*

Relation	Example	Possible Comprehension Probe
7. Deleted predicate adjective: so is, is not, is too (also). *as* is.	1. John is dependable. *So* is Henry. 2. John is dependable. Susan *is not*. 3. The lion was large but graceful. The tiger *was too*. 4. The lion, *as is* the tiger, is large but graceful.	1. Is Henry dependable? 2. Is Susan dependable? 3. Describe the tiger. 4. Describe the tiger.
8. Proverbs: *so* does, can, will, have, and so on (or), can, does, will *too* (or), can, does, will *not, as* did, can, will.	1. John went to school. So *did* Susan. 2. John went to school. Susan *did too*. 3. Henry will get an A. So *will* Theresa. 4. Amy can do a cartwheel. Matthew *cannot*. 5. Mom likes bologna. Dad *does not*. 6. John likes, *as does* Henry, potato chips.	1. What did Susan do? 2. What did Susan do too? 3. What will Theresa do? 4. Can Matthew do a cartwheel? What can't Matthew do? 5. Does Dad like bologna? 6. What does Henry like? Does Henry like potato chips?

Figure 7.8 shows how even something as simple as pronominal reference can be quite complex in just a short paragraph (circled words and arrows indicate pronouns and direction of reference).

Following are some suggested ideas for teaching text cohesion and its use to students:

Cloze technique has been offered in many different parts of this book for different purposes, as well as for similar purposes, adapted to learners with different abilities, including different developmental levels or school grades.

- Use cloze passages of text in which blank spaces have been intentionally substituted for words that are referents or words that refer to the referents. Here is an example in which pronouns are deleted.

  The cat moved slowly through the thick shrubs. _____ hid _____ approach toward the unsuspecting bird. _____ was perched on the edge of the bird bath, which was just beyond the _____ reach. _____ now started moving more quickly toward the bird bath. _____ was now very close.

  Notice that there are a number of instructional uses for the cloze technique and a variety of uses for referential ties in text.

- A technique similar to the cloze is the following, where students are provided the full text and are asked to identify the referents, the substituted forms (e.g., pronouns, which represent the referent), and their locations in the text. The students would be provided with the text sample and a blank table similar to the following one, which is filled in.

The last word ended in a long bleat, so like a sheep that Alice quite started (1).

Figure 7.8   **Sample of text on which pronominal anaphoric relations are graphically highlighted via circles and arrows.**

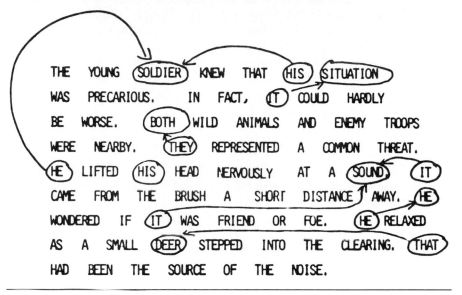

She looked at the Queen, who seemed to have suddenly wrapped herself up in wool (2). Alice rubbed her eyes, and looked again (3). She couldn't make out what had happened at all (4). Was she in a shop (5)? And was that really—was it really a sheep that was sitting on the other side of the counter (6)? Rub as she would, she could make nothing more of it (7).

Sentence number	Item being referred to	Cohesion Item (Pronoun or other word or words)
1	bleat	so
2	Alice (in #1)	She
	Queen	who; herself
3	Alice	her
4	Alice (in #3)	She
5	Alice (in #3)	she
6	sheep	that; it; that
7	Alice (in #3)	she; she
	sheep	it

Based on Halliday, M., & Hasan, R. (1976).
Cohesion in English. **London: Longman.**

- Another alternative is to provide students with handouts of sample texts (these should probably be typed and double-spaced in order for students to have room to complete their tasks). Ask students to circle the referents and their substitutes and to connect them with an arrow pointing in the direction of the reference. Excellent sources for text passages are the textbooks students are using in their various subjects. However, teachers can also make up their own text in order to focus instruction on particular types of referential ties.
- Reverse the role. Have students write short pieces of text using various cohesive devices. Have them exchange papers with their peers and use the circle/arrow technique to map out the references and the directions of reference in the peer-generated text.

Use both fiction and nonfiction text, and provide students with opportunities for developing a sense of cohesion in all of the major categories of cohesion and anaphora.

PART III
HIGH-LEVEL THINKING SKILLS (HLTS)

It is safe to say that although many reading educators see the role of high-level thinking in the reading act from different points of view, they all see high-level thinking skills (HLTS) as central to efficient and effective reading. Some have gone so far as to equate the two acts—comprehending and thinking (Smith, 1975). Contemporary focus on schema-based approaches to reading instruction also emphasize high-level thinking. Historically, institutions and agencies such as the National Assessment of Educational Progress (NAEP) have viewed inference and reasoning as important skills to be measured in their tests and assessment models (1977).

The various models, procedures, strategies, techniques, and activities considered so far in this chapter all require application of a variety of HLTS and other high-level processes. For example, almost all of the so-called alphabetic soup models required the use of prediction, inference, comparison–contrast, and so on. The models either attempt to help develop these skills, or they either explicitly or implicitly encourage students to apply them in the reading act.

Nonetheless, despite this apparently enthusiastic support for HLTS, direct instruction has not been aimed at HLTS per se but rather on their role in the larger factors of reading comprehension. The authors of this text agree with that basic instructional approach. Teaching HLTS in isolation or divorced from important reading content does not encourage the transfer or connection the learner should make between high-level thinking (HLT) and the reading process, though the ability to think at higher

During the mid-1980s, there was a major renewed interest in high-level thinking. Much of the push for that focus came from Association for Supervision & Curriculum Development (ASCD) and its publications, especially *Educational Leadership,* and Phi Delta Kappa and its primary publication, *Kappan.* Many articles and related materials were released by these two professional organizations throughout the 1980s. You might wish to have students research these and other resources and then discuss their findings.

Authorities on high-level thinking have positioned themselves into either one of two camps in terms of their fundamental approaches to HLTS instruction. The first believes that HLTS should be taught directly, as a separate identified curriculum in the schools, with a separate time slot and curriculum. The second asserts that HLTS should be integrated within the established curriculum. The latter position is endorsed by the authors of this text. We urge blending the learning of HLTS with their use and application so that students find a need and a value in HLTS. We suggest that you discuss the strengths and weaknesses of each position with your class.

cognitive levels must be viewed as central to the classroom teacher of reading.

In order to consciously employ teaching strategies and techniques that develop HLT and the ability to apply HLTS, the classroom teacher must understand just what HLT means. Therefore, this section first considers an operational definition of HLT that the teacher of reading in the elementary grades can find useful. Next, the various categories of thinking skills and their relation to each other are examined. After these are described, some performance-oriented objectives and guidelines for HLTS development are specified.

HLTS: DEFINITION AND OBJECTIVES

High-Level Thinking is the application of essential cognitive processes to hypothesize, predict, infer, and conclude in a reasoned and comprehensive fashion.

High-level thinkers possess all of the necessary inductive and deductive reasoning skills and a wide range of informal reasoning skills (e.g., analogical thinking and general problem-solving skills). In addition, they can do the following:

- They are astute observers. They know how to categorize information and to separate the salient or important from the less important or relevant.
- They know how to assess the context of the HLT need. That is, they see a problem and know what skills to apply and how to apply them. They can design an overall rational approach to any given learning or problem-solving situation.
- They are keen at detail recognition and can place detail, particulars, generalizations, principles, and concepts in relation to each other.

HLT FOUNDATION SKILLS

All HLTS require the utilization of basic cognitive foundation skills. These skills are central to all forms of thinking and reasoning in which the active reader must engage. These foundation skills require major emphasis in the primary grades. However, they should continue to be taught both directly and indirectly through the grades K–12. It is the degree of sophistication rather than a difference in specific skills and processes that separates the more mature learner from the beginner.

Notice that the authors suggest that HLT foundation skills precede and underpin the more commonly perceived HLTS—reasoning, inferring, deducting, and so forth. Whether teachers see classification, seriation, whole–part relationships, and so forth as fundamental to or simply parallel with the other HLTS may be unimportant. We simply find it more logical and conceptually satisfying to do it this way.

Six categories of foundation skills are found in all elementary reading programs and are necessary for mastery of more advanced HLTS:

Whole–part relations

Sequential relations

Comparative relations

Cause–effect relations

Classification

Summarization

For each individual category, following a brief description of the category is a short list of some supporting skills, to give some specific examples of skills that are important in the reading program, which have been derived from the HLT category. Next are listed some fairly precise example statements of objectives that classroom teachers can use when preparing daily lesson plans. These supporting skills and objective statements are intended only to serve as examples and are not intended to be either comprehensive in scope, adequate in depth, or even necessarily the best choices for many reading-instruction settings. They should, however, show quite graphically the way in which the larger concepts relate to the specifics that the classroom teacher must use.

Whole–Part Relations

> The ability to perceive the whole, the relevant parts, and the way they relate to each other and/or fit together

Supporting Skills

1. Ability to identify the main idea or grasp the gist
2. Ability to separate general from specific ideas
3. Ability to isolate and relate important individual parts

Examples

a. Grades K–2:

- The student will be able to (SWBAT) tell what simple stories are about after hearing them read or told orally
- SWBAT identify main characters in a story and tell why they are important
- SWBAT identify the important parts of a game, a farm set, or other model and tell why they are important
- SWBAT tell why inserted distractor details do not belong in a particular set or text

b. Grades 3–5:

- SWBAT summarize the main idea from both fiction and nonfiction text
- SWBAT identify both general and specific assertions in both oral and written form and tell which key words in those assertions cue the listener or reader
- SWBAT identify which particular statements support an argument and which do not
- SWBAT develop a simple argument, including a general claim and listing of supporting relevant details

Sequential Relations

The ability to take relevant detail for an idea, concept, or argument and sequence the detail in the most logical order

Supporting Skills

1. Ability to identify and use key words that assist in sequencing or ordering relevant information
2. Ability to identify major features of information being sequenced
3. Ability to order by various criteria (e.g., size, temporal position, shape, importance)
4. Ability to infer a simple conclusion from the ordered information

Examples

a. Grades K–2:

- SWBAT tell what information is being ordered
- SWBAT tell what criterion for ordering is being used
- SWBAT reach simple conclusions using ordered information

b. Grades 3–5:

- SWBAT identify key words (e.g., next, after, then) in text where ideas are ordered
- SWBAT use different methods of ordering information, according to purpose
- SWBAT reach conclusions with more complex arrays of information and ordering systems

Comparative Relations

> The ability to compare and to contrast both like and unlike objects, events, and ideas

Supporting Skills

1. Ability to tell what is being compared (or contrasted) and why
2. Ability to identify elements or features being compared (or contrasted)
3. Ability to articulate how elements are being compared (or contrasted)
4. Ability to reach a conclusion based on a comparison (or a contrast)

Examples

a. Grades K–2:

- SWBAT identify elements being compared in simple stories and in simple experiments
- SWBAT tell why there is a comparison
- SWBAT tell a result of a simple comparison

b. Grades 3–5:

- SWBAT identify elements being compared in several learning settings
- SWBAT make comparisons in both text and nontext settings
- SWBAT reach alternative conclusions for fixed comparisons

Cause–Effect Relations

> The ability to see causal connections among events, concepts, behaviors, and other elements in day-to-day life

Supporting Skills

1. Ability to identify a purpose for behaviors or events
2. Ability to identify and use key language reflecting cause and effect
3. Ability to identify and use antecedent–consequent assertions in logically reasoned arguments or in persuasive text of various kinds

Examples

a. Grades K–2:

- SWBAT identify things resulting from behavior or actions in stories or anecdotes
- SWBAT tell cause from effect in simple circumstances

b. Grades 3–5:

- SWBAT construct arguments leading from causal statements to a conclusion (effect)
- SWBAT tell why given arguments containing cause and effect statements are sound or are not sound

Classification

> The act of categorizing various elements, actions, objects, and ideas into different categories for different purposes

Supporting Skills

1. Ability to categorize according to different criteria
2. Ability to explain criteria used for given categories
3. Ability to identify features that bind a class of objects, things, events, and so on together
4. Ability to formulate a generalization about what is being categorized

Examples

a. Grades K–2:

- SWBAT group physical objects appropriately
- SWBAT tell why items or ideas belong in given groups
- SWBAT create simple classification categories and tell their logic

b. Grades 3–5:

- SWBAT identify different kinds of categories
- SWBAT justify placement of ideas into categories
- SWBAT explain the significance of some categories

Summarization

> The act of concisely abbreviating ideas such that all salient information is retained and critical relationships and/or causal connections are described

Supporting Skills

1. Ability to articulate the main idea of a concept, experiment, event, narrative, or other text
2. Ability to identify critical details and relationships
3. Ability to describe and/or infer an implied conclusion

Examples

a. Grades K–2:

- SWBAT articulate brief summaries of stories and events
- SWBAT tell why the story was interesting or not
- SWBAT retell in their own words occurrences or events experienced

b. Grades 3–5:

- SWBAT articulate summaries, including important details in logical order and with an appropriate conclusion
- SWBAT write summaries of both text and nontext experiences

These foundation skills represent the critical beginning for advanced comprehension development. Preschool children have already taken initial steps in incorporating these foundation skills into their daily thinking. However, it is during the school years when these skills should be directly built into the reading program, with particular application to reading comprehension. If this is done, the more advanced cognitive processes required in reading increasingly complex text are more likely to be mastered.

APPLIED HLTS: PROBLEM SOLVING

In many ways, problem-solving ability is an ability that requires the application of all HLTS. Problem solving also embodies important mental processes that help extend and refine the foundation skills. The more important of these processes are the following:

Perception	Ability to recognize main points and to distinguish the relevant from the irrelevant
Association	Ability to relate information (e.g., old to new, alike to alike, and similar to similar)
Self-monitor	Ability to monitor one's own thinking processes; ability to internally articulate a justification for various mental responses
Creative exploration	Ability to predict outcomes, to search for new and different connections and relationships among events, concepts, and ideas
Inference	Ability to select appropriate reasoning models, to relate hypotheses to evidence to reach a conclusion, and to assess the probability of a logical process being valid and sound

Effective problem solvers know about various kinds of problems and can skillfully work to solve them. Many problems are open-ended, with their resolution remaining problematic. Some problems are strictly dichotomous (i.e., either A or B must be chosen; it is either right or wrong; either something can or cannot be done, etc.). Some problems lend themselves to empirical investigation (e.g., Is fertilizer A better or worse than fertilizer B? This question can be tested, and the answer can be quantified in a variety of ways). Some problems are nonempirical and require subjective evaluations for their solution (e.g., Should we have capital punishment?).

Problem solvers should be able to identify a problem, articulate its nature, summarize its main features, and articulate its importance or role in a given situation. They should be able to map out a plan for attacking a problem and then proceed in a logical fashion in applying their plan.

Klein (1988) suggests a model for approaches to problem-solving instruction, modified for grade-level differences (see Figure 7.9). Notice that this is a fairly rigorous and formal outline of approaches to problem solving, certainly beyond the abilities of many elementary-grade students. However, the basic features of this model can easily be taught. At the least, having children think through the basic steps can help them develop the mental self-discipline that is ultimately necessary for being an effective reader of various sorts of texts. A simplified form of the model, such as the following outline, can be used as a basic instructional tool to walk students through the steps of problem solving:

You might wish to discuss the differences between the day-to-day ongoing kinds of problems people must face and the more substantial ones that occur less often. Ask students whether, from a problem-solving perspective, they are approached differently or similarly.

Also, ask students whether readers employ the same HLTS in comprehending text that they do in nontext kinds of situations. This textbook suggests that experiences with both informal and formal problem-solving procedures will serve the needs of both. Further, learners adept in various problem-solving approaches are better suited to address problems of any kind that appear in print, as well as any problems they encounter when considering how best to approach text as strategic readers.

Figure 7.9   Sophisticated model of steps in a problem-solving strategy, which can be simplified and used with elementary-school children. Taken from M. Klein (1988), *Teaching Reading Comprehension and Vocabulary: A Handbook for Teachers.* **Reproduced with permission of Prentice-Hall, Inc. Copyright 1988. All rights reserved.**

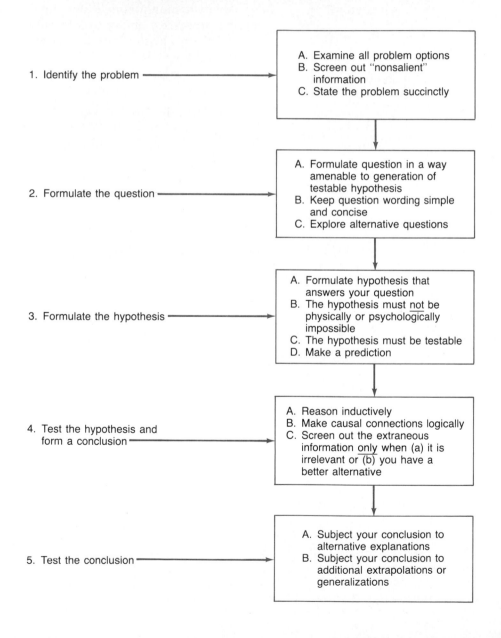

1. Identify the problem

A. Examine all problem options
B. Screen out "nonsalient" information
C. State the problem succinctly

2. Formulate the question

A. Formulate question in a way amenable to generation of testable hypothesis
B. Keep question wording simple and concise
C. Explore alternative questions

3. Formulate the hypothesis

A. Formulate hypothesis that answers your question
B. The hypothesis must not be physically or psychologically impossible
C. The hypothesis must be testable
D. Make a prediction

4. Test the hypothesis and form a conclusion

A. Reason inductively
B. Make causal connections logically
C. Screen out the extraneous information only when (a) it is irrelevant or (b) you have a better alternative

5. Test the conclusion

A. Subject your conclusion to alternative explanations
B. Subject your conclusion to additional extrapolations or generalizations

1. Find the problem. Write it out.
2. Think of a good question you can ask that will help you solve the problem.
3. Write out your best guess of what the final answer will be (hypothesis).
4. Tell the things you will do to try to answer your question (hypothesis testing).
5. How will you be sure the answer you finally decide on is the right one or the best one (conclusion testing)?

Children need to develop a problem-solving approach to reading text, not because they will necessarily run into text content that requires them to use the specific steps of the problem-solving procedure, but because knowing how to solve problems improves their reading comprehension. That is, knowing how to solve problems will help them to consciously apply questioning, hypothesizing, prediction/hypothesis testing, inferring, and concluding throughout their reading.

FORMAL REASONING: INDUCTIVE AND DEDUCTIVE REASONING

The ultimate refinement of HLT requires the mastery of inductive and deductive reasoning. The reasoner should be able to articulate the roles and relationships of the two reasoning processes. Although the nuances and complexities of these reasoning processes develop over the years, their foundations are established in the elementary-school years. The best opportunity for that development probably exists in the reading program.

Although students are not likely to run into text where the authors have used straightforward inductive or deductive logic, they should know the basics of each, for these two basic approaches to logical reasoning are used in various kinds of text in more general and informal ways.

Inductive and deductive reasoning are very much alike. Both are reasoning approaches that use given data or information to make an inference (or to draw a conclusion, as many reading programs put it). The primary differentiating feature of deductive reasoning is that the conclusion necessarily follows from the preceding information. To put it another way, if the premises of the argument or presentation are true, and if the principles of reasoning are logical, then the conclusion must follow.

Example:

1. If a car runs out of gas, it will stop.
2. The car runs out of gas.
3. Therefore, the car stops.

If numbers 1 and 2 are true, then number 3 *must* be true. For it to be false would be self-contradictory.

Some treat analogical reasoning as formal reasoning. Ask students, "What does *reasoning-by-analogy* mean? How can readers use it? How can teachers of reading use it?"

Confusion about the fundamental differences between inductive and deductive reasoning continues to present problems to many. Because both inductive and deductive reasoning work in concert in reading and writing processes, the authors of this textbook prefer to make the distinction between the two primarily on the basis that deduction involves a conclusion that is necessarily entailed by the premises that led to the conclusions this distinction appears to serve teachers well.

This is true of all deductive reasoning. (Note also that the reasoning proceeds from the general information in the first premise to specific information in the second and third premises.)

Inductive reasoning, on the other hand, always involves an extrapolation, or an "inductive leap," as it is sometimes called. There is always some chance that the information (premises) are true in inductive reasoning, but the conclusion still be wrong or false. This is because inductive reasoning proceeds from observations and specific information to a general conclusion or a generalization.

> *Example:* I might observe that it is cold today, and everyone I have seen is wearing a coat. I then infer or conclude that all the people I will see today will be wearing coats. Notice that there is a chance, albeit a small one, that I might see someone who is not wearing a coat.

There is a general rule in inductive reasoning that states, "The larger the inductive leap, the more powerful the conclusion, but the greater the probability that it is neither correct nor accurate. On the other hand, a greater probability of accuracy results from inductive reasoning with a relatively short or small inductive leap. However, the shorter the leap, the less useful or powerful the conclusion."

> *Examples:* No one really cares if I conclude that the sun will rise tomorrow because that has happened every day of my life, even though my conclusion is nearly 100% likely to be accurate.

> On the other hand, if I conclude that a particular virus has been identified as the cause of leukemia, I have reached a very powerful conclusion, but the probability of my being wrong is also much greater.

Inductive reasoning tends to move from particular data or observations or bits of information to a conclusion that generalizes to all similar situations. Most deductive reasoning moves from general premises to specific or particular instances or cases of application. However, notice that it is possible to reason inductively from general to general:

1. Some women I see wear dresses.
2. Some women I see wear slacks.
3. Therefore, all the women I see wear either dresses or slacks.

It is also possible to reason deductively, moving from particular to particular:

1. If Joe goes to the movie, he will not go to the basketball game.
2. Joe is going to the movie.
3. Therefore, Joe is not going to the basketball game.

This distinction is made quite well in a classic work by Stephen Toulmin (1969). *(The Uses of Argument).* Cambridge: Cambridge Univ. Press.

It is unlikely that elementary-grade readers will be reading text that employs formal logical syllogisms such as these. The logic used by most authors is much more informal. Even in argumentative or persuasive discourse where more formal reasoning is typically assumed, the logical structure is still quite informal. The author usually presents a thesis or an assertion (a claim), provides what he or she perceives to be convincing support or evidence, and then reaches a conclusion. The overall approach is often deductive in character, with the opening assertion used as a major premise, the supporting evidence as minor premises, and the conclusion *entailed* (i.e., logically determined) by the premises.

Internally, however, the text reflects inductive reasoning. The author usually relies on the supporting evidence in the body of the text to persuade the reader that the opening major premise is true.

> *Example:*
>
> *Our community is growing too fast. Our town had a population of less than 20,000 for more than 40 years, but in the past year alone, we have grown by 2,000 more people.*
>
> *Our tiny airport is now jammed with people, and the parking lot is always full. We have a new shopping mall built where we had a nice park before, and our schools are now overcrowded.*
>
> *At the same time, our ability to support important community services has declined. We don't have any more money. I think we should take some immediate steps to slow down our community's population growth.*

Notice how the author of this text relies on the individual examples of information as support. He then wants the reader to make the necessary inductive leap to conclude what he asserts in his opening assertion: "Our community is growing too fast." Inductive reasoning is embedded in an overall deductive outline or plan, which is what the reader must often comprehend.

Although the reasoning is less formal than that found in textbooks on logic, it is nevertheless there. The reader who is analytical must know when inductive reasoning is being employed and when deductive reasoning is being used. The reader can then focus on the legitimacy of the evidence, the soundness of the inductive leaps from support or data to major premises, and the validity of the conclusions reached.

> The authors feel that it is understanding of this recursive working relationship between deductive and inductive processes that determines readers' ability to comprehend and analyze persuasive text. The larger framework of the text is typically deductive; the supporting details within the framework are inferred inductively.

SOME TECHNIQUES FOR DEVELOPING HLTS IN READING

Making Inductive Inferences and Supporting Them

The following example illustrates a procedure that could be used with a variety of brief stories or text passages. Ask students to read the following brief story. In response to the questions that follow the story, they are to circle the "T" after the statements that are known to be true, to circle the "F" next to statements that are known to be false, or to circle the "?" when

Midwest Publications in Pacific Grove, California, publishes a wide range of HLTS curriculum materials designed for use in the elementary grades. Other small publishing houses are also moving into this arena (e.g., Perfection Form Company in Iowa). Remind students of the importance of these small publishing houses when seeking materials to incorporate into their reading program.

the reader cannot be sure whether the statement is true or false. Finally, readers are to circle the ''P'' if the statement is probably true, but the reader cannot be completely sure.

Billy Williamson will not be playing in Friday night's basketball game. The coach was not happy about it because Billy was a starter and one of Janesville's best players. Billy wasn't feeling well and couldn't decide whether to go to the game. It was going to be hard to face his teammates after the game was over.

1. Billy Williamson will not be playing in Friday night's basketball game. T F ? P
2. Billy Williamson was not playing because he was ill. T F ? P
3. Billy Williamson was not playing because he had been kicked off the team. T F ? P
4. The coach was worried about the outcome of the game. T F ? P
5. Billy's teammates were unhappy with him. T F ? P

This technique can be initiated in a couple of ways—having students work independently at first or pairing them and having them complete the task as a team. If they start by doing the task independently, have the students pair up to compare their responses. They should discuss their differences and find out how each used reasoning to determine the answers.

Discuss each of the items with the class:

- Notice that number 1 is the only one of the statements that is definitely true (assuming that the author is not intentionally lying in the first sentence of the story).
- Number 2 is either ''?'' or ''P.'' Some students might argue that the story says that he ''wasn't feeling well.'' Other students might argue that the ''?'' is the best answer because there is just not enough evidence to support concluding or inferring that he was ill. He could just as well have been ''not feeling well'' because he had been kicked off of the team, though other students might point out that there is no evidence suggesting his dismissal from the team.
- Number 3 is similar to number 2. The answer will be either ''?'' or ''P'' depending upon the inference of the reader. Have students try to justify their inference.
- Number 4 is more likely to generate the response ''P'' because most of us assume that coaches like to win, and Billy was a critical component. Ask students for other evidence in the story to support ''P'' as the best answer.
- Number 5, too, seems to call for ''P'' as a response, knowing how teammates must feel about losing one of their best starting players. Some students might argue, however, that if Billy had been kicked off the team, it provided an opportunity for them to function better as a team. Maybe Billy was a troublemaker.

Point out to your students the difference between answers directly provided in text (i.e., text-explicit) and those answers that require reading between the lines (i.e., text-implicit) or otherwise. Talk about the importance of inference in reading and the importance of examining both the text and the context carefully before reaching conclusions. Also, they must remember the importance of background knowledge. In this case, what students know about sports and how coaches and players approach athletic events help in making more logical inference.

Variations of this technique can be done by designing customized story versions, just as the authors of this text did with the example. Another possibility is to write a brief summary of a story that students will be reading and prepare statements like the ones used with the preceding example. Have students do the activity before they read the full text. Then tell them to use their activity as a study guide. As they read the actual text, they will get additional information and detail that will allow them to verify their original inferences or discover why they were wrong in their inductive leaps during the activity.

Using Reasoning-Centered Questions

The classroom teacher generally uses questions to guide or control students' thinking processes. When developing a lesson plan, one way to ensure effective instruction in HLTS is by couching the objectives statements in the language of HLT and then keying the questions to specific objectives. Notice how that is done in the following model in which a brief anecdote is used rather than a longer text, but the same general procedure can be used with text of any length.

This is a tightly structured direct instruction technique. Urge students to use such techniques and activities in balance with more informal strategies and techniques.

Developing HLT with Reasoning-Centered Questions, Using Anecdotes

Anecdote:	Billy's dog, Max, was not behaving as usual. Max was generally always friendly and eager to play. He especially liked the boys and girls who came to play with Billy. However, when Art came to see Billy, Max just lay very still. When Art tried to pet him, Max growled and snapped at him. Art thought that Max was just a mean dog after all.
Objectives:	1. To develop problem-identifying skills
	2. To develop skills in identifying necessary details related to probable causes
	3. To develop the ability to formulate reasonable hypotheses
	4. To develop hypothesis-testing skill
HLT Objectives-Centered Questions:	1. Do you think Art is right about Max? Tell why you do or do not think so. (Objectives 1 & 2)

2. What do you think might be some of the different things that could be wrong with Max? Tell why each one might be possible. (Objectives 2 & 3)

3. What do you think is the most likely problem with Max? Why do you think so? (Objectives 2 & 3)

4. How would you actually find out what is wrong with Max? (Objective 4)

5. If you are correct about Max's problem, what do you think Billy should do? (Objective 3)

HLT-Centered Follow-up Activity:

1. Have students make up an anecdote similar to the preceding one. Have them share their anecdotes with each other and discuss the likely problems and reasonable tests for each possible problem.

2. Provide another anecdote for students, and ask them to write questions that someone should be able to answer about the possible problem and how it might be solved.

Developing HLTS and reading comprehension go hand in hand. Successful reading comprehension cannot be achieved without the use of HLTS. Facility with HLTS, on the other hand, assists the reader greatly in reading critically and analytically. The teacher of reading in the elementary grades must see to it that instruction in reading incorporates HLTS and that both direct and indirect instruction in HLTS takes place, using text as the information base.

HIGHLIGHTS

1. Reading comprehension is the most important goal of any reading program, and instruction that fosters improved comprehension should be the most important goal of the reading teacher.

2. An effective lesson plan is critical for teaching reading comprehension. Its development requires the teacher to think through and to rehearse what is to be taught. Its presence represents a working guide for conducting the lesson.

3. The teachers' manuals or editions of basal reading programs have an important supporting role to play for the classroom teacher of reading. That role is primarily that of resource tool providing ideas that can enrich the background knowledge base of the teacher, as well as offer ideas for expanding and/or extending the lesson. Its role, however, should be directional and supportive rather than directive and limiting in nature.

4. Teaching learners how to become strategic readers is an important key to developing readers who are effective comprehenders of various kinds of texts. The teacher of reading should develop an array of modeling techniques and strategies for teaching students how to read strategically.

5. The ability to self-monitor is a critical skill necessary for becoming a strategic reader. Techniques and activities selected for use in the reading program should incorporate a number of research- and practice-based approaches to developing this important ability.

6. Direct instruction in reading comprehension should be a key part of any reading program throughout the grades. The classroom teacher should make use of a variety of direct-instruction reading models. Decisions regarding their use should be based on grade level, learner abilities, lesson purpose, lesson context, and the nature of the text to be read.

7. Effective readers know that different kinds of text reflect some differences in their internal structure (i.e., their overall organization; their use of cohesive, development, and transitional devices and techniques; their sentence types and structures; etc.). The reading program should reflect this fact and should include teaching strategies and techniques that are designed to develop readers sensitive to these features and able to comprehend text using them.

8. A high-quality reading program incorporates writing into its instructional approaches whenever possible and appropriate. The classroom teacher continually remains aware of the possibility for using writing as a direct aid in instructional design for students at all grades.

9. Both HLT and the application of HLTS in the reading act characterize the finest readers. Fine readers generate meaning by systematic use of basic HLTS. The teacher of reading must encourage the development of these skills and must incorporate their development and use in the design of instruction.

REINFORCEMENT ACTIVITIES

1. Describe the important parts of an effective reading lesson. Explain how and why each of the parts is important.

2. Is there any role for a teacher's manual or edition of a basal reading program? Why or why not?

3. What is meant by *strategic reading?* Give some examples of instruction premised on the importance of this concept.

You might want to emphasize the strengths and limitations of various lesson plan formats here.

At least half of American states (including the major purchasers—Texas, California, and Florida) have statewide textbook adoptions and use guidelines that often pressure publishers toward a cultural, political, religious, moral, and social neutrality. How does this fact bear on this question?

You might want students to demonstrate a lesson or activity designed to develop strategic readers.

Ask students how this relates to strategic readers.

Look for responses that may confuse the concept of direct instruction with a particular program or methodology.

Look for ability to articulate operational definitions of narrative and expository discourse.

Require students to link specific HLTS with specific reading skills (e.g., cause–effect, inference).

Allow flexibility in response to this question.

See whether students understand how the two forms of reasoning work together in most text.

Consider whether you want general guideline kinds of responses or specific instructional examples or both.

4. What is *self-monitoring*, and why is it important in reading? Give some examples of reader self-monitoring.
5. Briefly describe two or three direct reading instruction models. Tell the rationale for each and why you think each is or is not sound.
6. What is meant by *text structure*? Why is it important for the reader to be aware of this concept? Give some brief examples of text-structure differences. Describe one or two techniques for use in a lesson designed to enhance student awareness or ability in using text structure.
7. What are the HLTS, and why are they important for the reading program?
8. Describe a problem-solving model, and tell how it might be used to improve reading comprehension.
9. Define inductive and deductive reasoning. Tell how each plays a role in the reading act. Give your own views on how best to develop student abilities in these areas.
10. List what you think are the five most important things a teacher of reading in the elementary grades must do to teach reading comprehension well.

ADDITIONAL PROJECTS

1. Design and write a lesson plan intended for teaching some aspect of reading comprehension. Exchange it with a peer, and critique each other's lessons.
2. Visit some reading classes at different grade levels at which reading comprehension is being developed. Compare the instruction in terms of philosophy and approach. Discuss your observations in class.
3. Prepare a 5-day teaching unit for teaching reading comprehension for a selected grade level. Write all five of your lessons so that they are designed to teach students how to read strategically. Discuss your units with the whole class or in small groups.
4. Arrange to teach a lesson or two in reading comprehension in a local school. Discuss with the teacher how your lesson might focus on strategic reading, self-monitoring, or using writing to develop reading comprehension.
5. Review several new basal reading programs. Look especially at their philosophy regarding how best to develop reading comprehension. Compare their approaches with those suggested in this chapter. Discuss your findings with the whole class or in groups.

REFERENCES

Ankney, P., & McClurg, P. (1981). Testing Manzo's guided reading procedure. *The Reading Teacher, 34,* 681–685.

Barnitz, J. (1979). *Reading comprehension of pronoun–referent structures by children in grades two, four, and six* (Tech. Rep. No. 117). Urbana, IL: Center for the Study of Reading, University of Illinois.

Beck, I. L. (1984). Developing comprehension: The impact of the directed reading. In R. Anderson, J. Osborn, & R. Tierney (Eds.), *Learning to Read in American Schools: Basal Readers and Content Texts.* Hillsdale, NJ: Erlbaum.

Bowman, M.A. (1981). *The effect of story structure questioning upon the comprehension and metacognitive awareness of sixth grade students.* Unpublished doctoral dissertation, University of Maryland.

Brown, A. L., & Day, J. D. (1983). *Macrorules for summarizing texts: The development of expertise.* Unpublished manuscript, University of Illinois.

Chomsky, C. (1976). After decoding: What? *Language Arts, 53,* 288–296, 314

Combs, W. (1977). Sentence-combining aids reading comprehension. *Journal of Reading,* Oct., 18–24.

Cunningham, J., Cunningham, P., & Arthur, S. (1980). *Middle and Secondary School Reading,* New York: Longman.

Fay, L. (1965). Reading study skills: Math and science. In J. Firgurel (Ed.), *Reading and Inquiry.* Newark, DE: International Reading Association.

Frase, L. T., Patrick, E., & Schumer, H. (1970). Effect of question position and frequency upon learning from text under different levels of incentive. *Journal of Educational Psychology, 61,* 52–56.

Gordon, C., & Pearson, P. D. (1983). *Effects of instruction in metacomprehension abilities* (Tech. Rep. No. 269). Urbana, IL: Center for the Study of Reading, University of Illinois.

Graves, M. F., & Clark, D. L. (1981). The effect of adjunct questions on high school low achievers' reading comprehension. *Reading Improvement, 18,* 8–13.

Halliday, M. A. K., & Hasan, R. (1976). *Cohesion in English.* London: Longman.

Hershberger, W. (1964). Self-evaluational responding and typographical cueing: Techniques for programming self-instructional reading materials. *Journal of Educational Psychology, 55,* 288–296.

Hunt, L. C. (1970). Effect of self-selection, interest, and motivation upon independent, instructional, and frustrational levels. *The Reading Teacher, 24,* 146–151.

Klein, M. (1988). *Teaching Reading Comprehension and Vocabulary: A Guide for Teachers.* Englewood Cliffs: NJ: Prentice-Hall.

Langer, J. (1981). From theory to practice: A prereading plan. *Journal of Reading, 25,* 152–156.

Langer, J., & Nicholich, M. (1981). Prior knowledge and its relation to comprehension. *Journal of Reading Behavior, 13,* 373–379.

Manzo, A. (1969). ReQuest procedure. *Journal of Reading, 13,* 123–126.

Manzo, A. (1980). Three "universal" strategies in content area reading and languaging. *Journal of Reading, 24,* 147.

McCracken, R., & McCracken, M. (1978). Modeling is the key to sustained reading. *The Reading Teacher, 31,* 406–408.

McGaw, B., & Grotelueschen, A. (1972). Direction of the effect of questions in prose material. *Journal of Educational Psychology, 63,* 580–588.

Mellon, J. (1969). *Transformational sentence-combining: A method for enhancing the development of syntactic fluency in English composition* (Research Rep. No. 10). Urbana, IL: National Council of Teachers of English.

Meyers, S. (1988). Hearing ear dog. In E. Sulsby, J. Hoffman, et al. (Eds.), *McGraw-Hill Reading* (Level L: "This We Wish"). Oklahoma City, OK: McGraw-Hill.

Nash-Webber, B. (1977). *Anaphora: A cross-disciplinary survey* (Tech. Rep. No. 31). Urbana, IL: Center for the Study of Reading, University of Illinois.

National Assessment of Educational Progress. (1977). *National Assessment of Educational Progress Newsletter, 10* (5).

O'Hare, F. (1973). *Sentence-combining: Improving student writing without formal grammar instruction* (Research Rep. No. 15). Urbana, IL: National Council of Teachers of English.

O'Neill, J. (1988, December 31). Trade bill with U.S. is now law in Canada. *Seattle Post–Intelligencer,* p. A-1; 4.

Pearson, P. D., & Johnson, D. (1978). *Teaching Reading Comprehension.* New York: Holt, Rinehart and Winston.

Raphael, T. E. (1982). Question-answering strategies for children. *The Reading Teacher, 36,* 186–191.

Reutzel, R. (1985). Story maps improve comprehension. *The Reading Teacher,* Jan., 400–404.

Richek, M. (1977). Reading comprehension of anaphoric forms in varying linguistic contexts. *Reading Research Quarterly, 12,* 145–165.

Robinson, F. (1961). *Effective Study.* New York: Harper & Row.

Rothkopf, E. Z. (1966). Learning from written instructive materials: An exploration of the control of inspection behavior by test-like events. *American Educational Research Journal, 3,* 241–249.

Schmelzer, R., Christen, W., & Browning, W. (1980). *Reading and Secondary School Reading.* New York: Longman.

Singer, H., & Donlan, D. (1982). Active comprehension: Problem solving schema with question generation for comprehension of complex short stories. *Reading Research Quarterly, 17,* 166–186.

Smith, F. (1975). *Comprehension and Learning.* New York: Holt, Rinehart and Winston.

Snowman, J., & Cunningham, D. J. (1975). A comparison of pictorial and written adjunct aids in learning from text. *Journal of Educational Psychology, 67*, 307–311.

Stauffer, R. (1969). *Directing Reading Maturity as a Cognitive Process*. New York: Harper & Row.

Stein, N., & Glenn, C. (1979). An analysis of story comprehension in elementary school children. In R. O. Freedle (Ed.), *New Directions in Discourse Processing*. Norwood, NJ: Ablex.

Stotsky, S. (1983). Research on reading/writing relationships: A synthesis and suggested directions. *Language Arts, 60*, 627–642.

Vacca, Vacca, & Gove, (1987). *Reading & Learning to Read*. Boston: Little Brown & Co.

ADDITIONAL RESOURCES

Cooper, J. D. (1986). *Improving Reading Comprehension*. Boston: Houghton Mifflin.

Devine, T. (1986). *Teaching Reading Comprehension: From Theory to Practice*. Boston: Allyn & Bacon.

Estes, T., & Vaughan, J. (1986). *Reading and Reasoning Beyond the Primary Grades*. Boston: Allyn & Bacon.

Irwin, J. (1986). *Teaching Reading Comprehension Processes*. Englewood Cliffs, NJ: Prentice-Hall.

McNeil, J. (1987). *Reading Comprehension* (2nd ed.). Glenview, IL: Scott, Foresman.

CHAPTER 8

TEACHING READING VOCABULARY THROUGHOUT THE ELEMENTARY GRADES

I always wanted to write a book that ended with the word "mayonnaise."

Richard Brautigan, *In Watermelon Sugar,* 1969

This is a good point at which to spend a little time on the history of language, with consideration of the evolution of the English alphabet. You can also point out that Latin and Romance languages such as Italian and Spanish have played a significant role in contributing both morphemic bases and inflections to English, as well as semantic forms and categories. At the same time, however, English owes its grammar system to the Teutonic languages—primarily German—rather than to Latin.

PREVIEW

No one knows for sure how many words there are in the English language—perhaps partly, at least, because English speakers do not always agree on what a "word" is. It is estimated, however, that thousands of English words are not accessible to most people. Examination of the words that people actually use in their speaking and writing reveals substantially fewer than the possible number of vocabulary words. Most authorities agree that actual vocabulary of words mastered by learners in the elementary grades are just a few thousand (Chall, 1987; Lorge & Chall, 1963; Moe, 1974). The typical student adds only about 3,000 words per year through the grades (Nagy & Herman, 1987). Further, even for adults, typical discourse probably pulls from only about 10,000 words for about 90% of language use.

Most reading educators and classroom teachers agree that vocabulary acquisition and use are important for effective reading, writing, and speaking. Also, since the 1940s, research has documented that learners' knowledge of word meaning correlates strongly with their comprehension abilities (Davis, 1944; Thurston, 1946). Other research has connected reading vocabulary difficulty with reading comprehension scores (Chall, 1958; Wittrock, Marks, & Doctorow, 1975). Even in the 1920s and '30s, the Russian psychologist Lev Vygotsky asserted that the word was the locus of meaning and, therefore, central to all thought (Vygotsky, 1962).

Given educators' long-standing awareness that larger vocabularies relate to more effective reading, why do most readers (and nonreaders) have access to such a small proportion of the total number of English words? Countless answers can be offered. Certainly, no one needs a huge vocabulary in order to be literate. Also, elementary teachers have other major responsibilities and cannot devote large amounts of time to vocabulary instruction. Though many other reasons may be valid, one reason can be immediately dismissed as invalid: Vocabulary instruction is *not* neglected due to being ineffective. Quite the contrary—Effective vocabulary instruction directly increases the

You might want to discuss here the importance of vocabulary knowledge and word use in terms of social and career opportunities. Use of language in general and of words in particular dramatically affects people's responses to one another. Hence, this is a critical component of reading instruction.

reading vocabulary of students. This chapter is designed to assist you in designing instruction that effectively teaches your students to develop and improve their vocabulary.

FOCUS QUESTIONS

As you read this chapter, keep the following questions in mind:

1. What are some basic guidelines I should follow when I am teaching vocabulary?
2. Why is "word importance" critical for teachers, and how can I use a "word importance criterion"?
3. What are some effective strategies and techniques for teaching vocabulary in the reading program?

BENEFITS OF AND APPROACHES TO VOCABULARY INSTRUCTION

Although most teachers and other reading educators agree that vocabulary is important for the reading program, there continues to be some disagreement about how best to teach it. Some (Adams & Huggins, 1985; Becker, 1977) propose direct instruction for vocabulary-building. That is, segments of instructional time are allotted for specific focused attention to learning new vocabulary.

Others seem to favor vocabulary instruction based on a "language immersion" concept of vocabulary acquisition. According to this perspective, vocabulary is learned most effectively when the language arts program is based on (a) extensive oral and written language use in the classroom, (b) wide-ranging reading of high-quality literature and discussions focused on that literature, and (c) plentiful experiences with writing that derive both from the students' interests and from the literature, with primary attention to the writing's relevance for the learner (Michael, Zimmerman, & Guilford, 1951; Terman, 1918).

Discuss whether a teacher must choose only one approach to teaching vocabulary.

Still others seem to be somewhere in between the two extremes regarding vocabulary development. They (Beck, Perfetti, & McKeown, 1982; Johnson & Pearson, 1984; Stevens, 1982) suggest the importance of

- Providing a meaningful context for the new vocabulary

Learning new words in the reading class is secondary to learning how *to learn new words. Dictionaries are an important part of learning how to acquire and use new vocabulary.*

- Utilizing appropriately the students' prior experience when introducing new words
- Selecting and introducing vocabulary words that have important conceptual ties to critical ideas in the text to be read

Perhaps part of the reason for this division in thinking about how best to develop vocabulary derives from the different theories that drive instruction in vocabulary. Some endorse the *instrumental hypothesis*—the theory that words are *instrumental* in understanding text (i.e., they are used as instruments to reach the goal of comprehending text). They are primary in and of themselves as concept-identifiers. According to this hypothesis, if you know the meanings of each of the words in the text, you should be able to infer from those meanings to the meaning of the text itself.

Others endorse the *knowledge hypothesis*—the theory that vocabulary and comprehension primarily reflect a broader scope of more general knowledge that is organized and interrelated to form schemata. Thus, knowing how information fits into the scheme of things, so to speak, requires more information and knowledge than is embedded in individual words. From this perspective, the relations that hold among vocabulary, concepts, and accumulated knowledge meet in a given learning context to shape meaning of text.

It is our posture that **both** of these theories have some legitimacy and that instruction should derive from the thinking of both. What follows in this chapter reflects this posture and is based on the following basic assumptions or guidelines for vocabulary instruction.

The authors' decision to list six basic guidelines was entirely arbitrary; any number could have been suggested. You might ask students to generate additional ones as they work their way through this chapter, based on their readings, observations, and discussions.

Some Basic Guidelines for Vocabulary Instruction

1. Effective vocabulary learning requires both direct and indirect instruction. Instruction should include both specific focused step-by-step instructional strategies, with focus on high-priority vocabulary, and more informal immersion-based instruction through which the vocabulary is acquired via wider language-using contexts.
2. The classroom teacher must determine the importance of individual vocabulary items and must select a teaching approach based on the priority of the vocabulary. More time and direct instruction is allotted to critical vocabulary.
3. The primary goal of the teacher must be to teach learners how to learn new words.

> Learning new words is secondary to learning how to learn new words.

Instructional plans should include both—teaching learners new words and teaching learners how to learn new words.

4. Vocabulary development occurs most readily in a rich language-using environment where there students experience both high motivation and practical functional reasons for learning new words. Students are encouraged to use words in both language-consuming and language-producing domains. Natural interrelationships between reading and writing and speaking are developed and utilized.
5. Vocabulary acquisition and development through the upper elementary grades is most effective when it is appropriately *contextualized*—taught in contexts that are natural, functional, and of immediate interest and use. That means that the most effective vocabulary development takes place in lessons in content areas (e.g., social studies, science, mathematics, or literature) rather than within a discrete reading period. The linguistic and conceptual contexts of the content areas are more likely to be effective drivers of interest and relevant purpose than are instructional settings where new words are taught acontextually, even if the instructional model is one that is otherwise sound.
6. The higher-level thinking skills that are critical to comprehension and learning generally are also important to vocabulary development. Ability to infer; to detect specious logic or reasoning; to determine cause–effect relations; and to see whole-to-part, com-

parison/contrast, and analogical relationships are all important to vocabulary acquisition and development. They are central to the dominant goal, which is to teach learners how to learn new vocabulary.

SELECTING THE "DICTIONARY" TO WHICH TO TEACH NEW VOCABULARY

A cursory examination of basal reading programs reveals an importance attached to vocabulary instruction. Although their techniques and strategies may vary somewhat, they all include a vocabulary strand or component. Unfortunately, however, they are often not very helpful in determining the relative importance of individual new vocabulary to be taught. Of the mass of new words out there that educators would like students to learn, some are extremely important, some are fairly important, and some would be nice to know if only the time to teach them were available.

> *Example:* A contemporary reading program contains a short story in a fifth grade book with the word *finality*. "Her voice had a tone of finality to it." Suppose I suspect that most of my students do not know this word. On the other hand, I recognize that the word is not that central to the theme of the story or to an understanding of the nature of any important character or to the plot of the story. Should I be considering taking time for direct instruction of this new word?

> Now consider the word *ruination.* It appears in the same fifth grade volume. However, it is a favorite word used by a main character. He likes the word and uses it over and over. In fact, his use of this word provides some important insight into his personality and its place in the story. It seems more important than *finality* was to the gist of the earlier story. On the other hand, context clues are very helpful in this story, which my students can use to infer a meaning for *ruination.* And, even if they do not infer a reasonable meaning for the word, they can still handle the story, for the word is not that crucial.

> Finally, consider the word *immigrant.* It is used throughout a nonfiction history excerpt in this same book. The selection focuses on the nature and role of the immigrant to the United States in the nineteenth and twentieth centuries. Not only is it used throughout the narrative but it is also used in subheadings of the text. I also am aware of the fact that it represents an important concept that will reappear each year in some way in the social studies program through the rest of my students' grades. It is an important concept-bearing term. How should I teach this new word to my class?

Most of us would concur that of these three terms, *immigrant* is certainly most important; *ruination* is second in importance; and *finality* is least important of the three.

Having one or two popular basal programs available at class sessions can be helpful. Here, for example, you could readily show students examples of basal approaches to vocabulary instruction.

Figure 8.1   **The three mental dictionaries in which vocabulary words may be stored, indicating the direction in which words generally enter the dictionaries.**

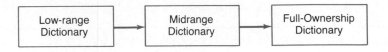

Ask students to identify examples of words that they have recently transferred into their full-ownership dictionaries.

Chapter 1 introduced, and Chapter 4 defined a good way to conceptualize the relative importance of new vocabulary for students—that is, in terms of three kinds of "mental dictionaries" that learners possess and must use in their language-using activities. Vocabulary that is of highest priority—students should be able to use the word in their speaking and writing as well as in their reading—belongs in their "full-ownership dictionary." They own the word and can use it at will.

They also have a "midrange dictionary" which includes words with meanings that can usually be inferred from context clues and other techniques when reading; the students are not, however, likely to use this word in their writing or speaking. If they do use the word when writing or speaking, they do it with less confidence than is comfortable. They may have the feeling that there is just a chance that they've used the word incorrectly.

Finally, students have a "low-range dictionary," which is where new words typically enter their vocabulary. These are words that are vaguely familiar, but students do not feel comfortable enough with them to attempt to use them. If they appear in text, students usually take a stab at guessing their meaning by using whatever textual clues they can find. However, they seldom go to a dictionary to double-check because they figure that their guess is probably close enough to get through the text passage.

The "dictionaries" model is intended to provide a graphic conceptual model for instructional purposes. It does not purport to be a detailed map of all mental processes involved in vocabulary development.

Normally, new vocabulary moves through the first two mental dictionaries before reaching the full-ownership one. However, if a new word is important, students might enter it directly into one of the two higher dictionaries, depending on its importance and the effectiveness of the instruction used to teach them the word. Words in the low and midrange dictionaries are constantly competing for movement into the full-ownership dictionary. That dictionary is more limited in size for most of us. Words there get constant reinforcement for being there because we draw on them for use on a fairly regular basis, whereas the other two dictionaries do not have that advantage. The movement of new terms through these dictionaries can be illustrated as shown in the left-to-right movement in Figure 8.1.

TEACHING TO THE FULL-OWNERSHIP DICTIONARY

Top-priority vocabulary warrants entry into the full-ownership dictionary. Research indicates that direct formal instruction is most effective for acquiring this vocabulary (Anderson & Freebody, 1977; Beck & McKeown, 1985; et al.). Direct formal instruction is taught step by step, with students knowledgeable about each of the steps and the steps' sequence; eventually it is hoped, students learn the steps well enough to apply them independently to add new vocabulary.

Five-Step Direct-Instruction Model

In Chapter 4, the authors introduced a five-step model for teaching sight vocabulary. Note that sight vocabulary is included in the full-ownership dictionary. The same five-step approach can be used for vocabulary instruction in the later elementary grades as well. The steps remain essentially the same. Remember that this model should be applied only to those words which meet either of two criteria:

1. The vocabulary provides essential information about a character in a story or about the plot of a story.

    Example: The word *pecuniary* is used often to describe the personality of Uriah Heap in the Dickens novel, *David Copperfield*. It can be viewed as being important enough for understanding of character in this novel to warrant direct instruction.

2. With nonfiction content-oriented text, in particular, high-priority words are important concept-bearing indicators.

    Example: Words such as *mercantilism* or *federalism* in social studies; words such as *continent, plateau, steppes, latitude,* and *longitude* in geography exemplify such vocabulary.

A complete description of that simple, but effective, five-step direct instruction model (Klein, 1988, pp. 71–73) was provided in Chapter 4, but the five steps were, briefly, the following:

1. Look at the Word; say the word
2. Tell the Meaning of the Word
3. Analyze the Word Structurally
4. Discuss the Word
5. Use the Word in Context

After this five-step model has been used, it is critical to have students engage in daily word-use maintenance activities over the next several days. Orchestrate the class environment and lessons in such a way that students will be encouraged to use the new word in both oral and written

Direct instruction has come to be used in a pejorative sense in recent years. It is often linked to particular programs or program types, such as those associated with programmed instruction or mastery learning or behavior modification. Our use of direct instruction is more generic and positive. The authors see direct instruction playing a positive role in all classes and in all teaching and learning philosophies.

A modified form of this model was also presented in the earlier section of this book, dealing with instruction in the primary grades.

Reinforce the idea that effective instruction requires *both* teaching strategies with predictable steps *and* teaching ideas and activities that are new and unusual, so that they are not always predictable. Learners need both familiarity and novelty: regularity and pattern for learning how to learn, and newness and creativity for maintaining motivation and excitement about the learning process. Direct instruction models represent the predictable side of learning. Emphasize the nature and order of the steps while student teachers learn about these models.

contexts. If maintenance activities are neglected, the fruits of the effective initial lesson may be lost.

Topic-Centered Model for Direct Instruction

This strategy is particularly effective in contexts where instructional content centers on themes, and the strategy can be implemented over a series of lessons. It works well in literature, social studies, science, and other content areas, as well as in a specific reading period if your school is organized in that fashion.

1. Choose a Theme

Select a relevant and appropriate theme that can be used as a curriculum organizer to extend over more than one lesson (e.g., over 2–5 days or longer). Choose relevant readings that can be tied to the theme.

> *Example:* You might cluster different literature genre (e.g., poetry, short stories, plays, and nonfiction) into a unit entitled "Follow the Yellow Brick Road," about the pursuit of dreams or new frontiers by adventuresome explorers and thinkers. Prepare students for the unit by designing appropriate activities and projects that will activate students' background knowledge. For example, have them do some research on people such as Jedediah Smith, a famous mountain man. Share findings in discussions prior to readings on the theme.

2. Select Theme-Related Words

After identifying a key term or phrase that defines the unit's theme, select a group of important vocabulary central to the theme and important to the various selected texts to be read. These words should be collocates of the broader identifier label. *Collocates* are words that are linked to the key term or phrase because they deal with the same topic. They represent a family of related words.

> *Example:* If you had a unit on law, you might anticipate words such as *justice, court, judicial, judge, jury, trial,* and so on to appear in the text.

Choose vocabulary words that are (a) central to the theme of the unit; (b) found abundantly in various texts to be read in the unit; (c) concept-bearing or otherwise telling in nature; and (d) likely to be needed and used over a period of several days, at least.

3. Introduce Theme-Related Words

Use a variety of techniques and activities to introduce the words to students. (Many of the techniques and activities described later in this chapter can be used in this step of this direct instruction model.) Think of ways to do this inductively (e.g., provide a list of related words, some of which the students already know, and ask them to infer some general features or characteristics they all have in common).

Remind students that theme- or topic-centered approaches to instruction remain the most popular way to organize concepts, skills, and processes for instruction in the primary grades. Learning centers are organized around themes or topics. Literature and social studies materials are presented in that way, and extended teaching units are often structured around a theme or topic.

A useful project to ask students to undertake here is to develop sample themes or topics for instruction at different grade levels. Discuss the differences between those that work well for the primary grades and those that would suit the upper grades.

Consider how semantic mapping or word networks could be used in this step.

Provide ample opportunity for students to discuss the word (or words) in context. During these discussions, frequently refer to the important role of the vocabulary throughout the unit.

4. Go Beyond the Text and the Classroom

Because the unit will extend over several days, this model provides an excellent opportunity to incorporate projects and assignments that move into alternative learning contexts.

Examples:

- Have students use notebooks throughout the unit of study. Ask them to record incidents of the new words they see or hear in other contexts (e.g., at home, in the newspaper, in other books or classes, on TV). Ask them to note where, when, and how each occurrence took place. Have teams or pairs compare notebooks for differences and similarities. Discuss notebook entries daily in class.
- Make thesaurus and dictionary assignments using the new words. Have contests and games using these reference tools.
- Have students conduct etymology searches. These word-history searches tied to the unit theme can be an excellent way to help the students fit the new vocabulary into the larger concepts important to the unit.

Point out the relationship of this step to the contemporary thinking about school restructuring (note April, 1990, Educational Leadership, for example). Ask students about the implications of these kinds of activities for redefining the role of the community and the home within the bounds of the enlarged community school.

5. Review All Words at the End of the Unit

It is essential that daily discussion of recent new words and periodic review of all new words introduced in the unit take place. Include writing and oral language activities and projects as part of the end-of-unit review.

6. Practice Maintaining New Vocabulary

As with any approach to teaching students to add vocabulary to the full-ownership dictionary, this step is critical. Ownership means that students can use the words whenever they need them. For them to gain this ability, the new words should be used throughout the unit and, at least, for several days following the unit's completion.

Ask students to generate ideas here for incorporating various subject areas, such as social studies.

TEACHING TO THE MIDRANGE DICTIONARY

The midrange dictionary benefits from direct instruction, just as does the full-ownership dictionary. However, briefer techniques and activities are appropriate for the midrange dictionary. Many of these techniques and activities fit into longer instruction models such as the five-step or theme-centered models just described. Effective midrange dictionary instruction can also use these techniques and activities in other instructional contexts or even independently of other contexts.

Most of these techniques and activities are geared to the following assumption:

Structural analysis skills are basically assumed here. However, there will always need to be review and/or reinforcement done. Many of the activities in the next section of text assist in developing structural analysis skills. Have students compare lists of different structural analysis skills, which are either identified by different reading authorities or presented in different reading programs.

> Effective vocabulary instruction should require the learner to use the two most important skills of vocabulary development: (1) the ability to use context and context clues and (2) the ability to infer reasonable pronunciation and meaning for new vocabulary.

The entire reading program should teach the ability to use context and the ability to apply the necessary thinking skills to infer a likely meaning for new words. These skills do not develop overnight, and they cannot be taught briefly, quickly, and easily. These skills develop with increasing sophistication through the grades when teachers of reading effectively design instruction that implicitly pressures learners to apply these skills.

By the time most children enter the intermediate grades, they have mastered the rudiments of these skills. What they need through the remaining grades is twofold: First, they need to practice using context and inference in both direct instructional lessons and in indirect learning contexts and projects. Second, they need to internalize the strategies effective readers use in applying context clues and making reasonable inferences.

Chapter 7, on reading comprehension, showed how to walk students through self-monitoring and other "thinking out loud" during the reading act. This procedure is one way to teach students how to acquire new vocabulary. Another technique is to explain to students what they are supposed to learn when they use specific techniques or activities with new vocabulary. The next two subsections describe each of these approaches.

Teaching Students to Infer Meaning of New Vocabulary from Context

- Select some sample text that students are expected to read, or write some text that includes a new word that the students should learn well enough to be able to infer a likely meaning from the surrounding context (i.e., a word for students' midrange dictionary).

    Example: "As the stranger approached the edge of the marsh, he hesitated. He listened carefully. He sensed more than he actually saw or heard some sort of presence. What was it? Who was here with him?

    "Hearing nothing, he slowly edged ahead along the marsh's border, peering nervously through the early morning mist that hovered in billowy drifts over the still water reeds. He could barely make out the outlines of a larger pond ahead, which shed its excess waters into the marsh.

    "Probing gently with his left foot, he felt the twig snap beneath his weight. Suddenly with a giant *cacophony* of sound, a flock of geese lifted in unison from the noisy pond waters."

Emphasize the importance once again of metacognitive development for facilitating what this textbook calls "self-monitoring" skills and processes for effective learning. Consider assigning outside reading, with responsibilities for reporting to classmates, on selected readings on metacognition. R. Garner's (1987) *Metacognition and Reading Comprehension* (Norwood, NJ: Ablex) is an excellent source, with many additional resources referenced. Ongoing research and writing in this area abounds in reports from the Center for the Study of Reading at the University of Illinois and, of course, articles published in journals such as *Reading Research Quarterly*.

- Prepare the text by copying it either onto a student handout or onto an overhead transparency that all students can read. Read the text aloud to the class, pausing to think aloud by sharing with the class what you are thinking while reading certain words. Pretend not to know the meaning of *cacophony* when reaching that word.
- Think aloud through the following specific steps:

1. "How is this word pronounced? The initial letter is probably hard 'c' because it is followed by the vowels 'a,' 'o,' or 'u.' I also know that almost every initial 'c' is hard. There are probably four syllables—ca-co-pho-ny." (The most likely problem is the 'o' in the 'pho' syllable—long or short?)
2. "The opening paragraphs create a very quiet mysterious setting. The man seems frightened or worried. He is really trying to be silent. Noise and sound, though, are in the paragraph where *cacophony* is used."
3. "A 'cacophony of sound.' Hmmmm. A 'bunch' of sounds? A 'strange' sound? A 'loud' sound? Heck, I'm not sure, but I think it must be something like a confusion of sounds or a lot of sound. That's close enough. It makes sense that way."

Now discuss the word with students. Ask them what they think it probably means. After discussing likely meanings and their reasons for guessing the meanings, have the class look up the word in the dictionary. Then reread the paragraph and talk about the clues in the text that helped us infer a close meaning.

Talk about whether our guessed meanings earlier were right or wrong. Were they close enough to keep the intended meaning that the author wanted?

- Review the following steps with students. "When you read a text containing a word you do not know the meaning of, do the following:

" 1. Look closely at the word. Look for syllable breaks. Try to sound it out.
" 2. Does it have a prefix or suffix? Think of what the prefix or suffix means.
" 3. Try to figure out the main idea or theme of the text.
" 4. Try to figure out the setting and mood of the text, if it is a work of fiction.
" 5. Reread the paragraph in which the new word occurs.
" 6. Think about the sentence it is in. Where does the word appear? What part of speech is it?
" 7. Examine the sentence that follows. Is there any new information there?
" 8. Substitute some words you think might fit in the place of the new word.

Have students in your reading methods class select samples of text to read aloud, and use the think-aloud steps to model their use.

Ask students to think of additional metacognitively oriented activities or teaching ideas they can use to teach vocabulary.

" 9.   Make up a new sentence with the substituted word. Does the sentence sound right?

"10.   Check your guess by using the dictionary."

Teaching the Use of Inference and Context for Acquiring New Vocabulary

Point out to your class how the following ideas for vocabulary development incorporate high-level thinking skills and processes and writing in one way or another. Ask them to think consistently in terms of how to incorporate high-level thinking and writing in all aspects of reading instruction.

- Present students with a series of sentences with decreasing level of abstraction in each, and ask them to infer a reasonable definition for a nonsense word used in the sentences. Show them the sentences in order and only one at a time.

  1. I really like *zuan* best because it tastes so good.
  2. I like *zuan* best when it is not cooked.
  3. *Zuan* really tastes great on hamburgers.
  4. My favorite kinds of *zuans* are the white juicy ones.

  What are zuans?

- Have your students make up a nonsense word for a new food. Ask them to write sentences like those in the *zuan* activity, with each sentence being more particular and specific in the kind and amount of information provided.

- Extend this idea by having your students write a paragraph using a nonsense word in context.

Using Cloze to Teach New Vocabulary

This textbook has used the cloze technique in several different places. Remind students that it is a long-standing technique for instruction that can be used for a number of skills and concepts.

Although the cloze technique was originally developed for purposes other than instructional ones, it possesses excellent features for teaching new vocabulary and the application of context clues in reading.[1] In addition to

[1]The cloze technique was developed years ago as a means for assessing the readability of text materials.It was then used also as an informal measure of learner reading ability. When used for this purpose, the technique requires the teacher to select a piece of text of at least 50 words in length. Next, one word, chosen randomly among the first 10 words of the passage is deleted. Then every "nth word" is deleted (usually every fifth word after the first deletion). A 15-space blank is inserted in every spot where a word has been deleted. The student is then asked to fill in each blank with the correct missing word. The following example is borrowed from Schwartz, with permission of the publisher:

"The _____ man peered _____ into the
       (funny, frightened)   (curiously, bravely)

smudged window. To the people he passed on the street, the man seemed

_____ . He walked with a _____ gait as he
    (normal, uneasy)   (typical, nervous)

listened _____ for something.
      (casually, hurriedly)

teaching context clues generally, the cloze technique is also useful for teaching the relationship between vocabulary choices and the author's purpose. Note the following use of the cloze, for example,

There are several _____ of print the child _____ already be familiar with _____

she first enters a _____ or kindergarten class. First, _____ is her name.

"Cindy _____ , Cindy Lou. My name _____ Cindy Lou, who are _____ ?"

Cindy Lou introduced herself _____ her preschool class with _____ simple

chant when she _____ in late November.

from Schwartz, E., *Encouraging Early Literacy,* 1988, page 62.

   Notice that the vocabulary item selected for the first blank of the two options dictates most of the remainder of the words that students can choose. It is possible to write this text reflecting with two totally different moods and/or purposes.

   As an informal test of student reading ability, cloze requires that the teacher start with the assumption that the text to be used with cloze is at the appropriate or desired reading level for the student(s). It is further assumed that the person being tested knows the source of the text and something about the theme or topic being addressed in the excerpt.

   If the learner can complete one-third of the blanks with the exact missing word, he or she is said to be reading the text with enough ability for guided instruction. If the learner can complete two-thirds of the blanks with the exact missing word, he or she is said to be reading the text well enough for independent reading.

   Although authorities disagree on the validity and/or usefulness of the cloze as an informal test, it is often used by classroom teachers, especially at the beginning of the year, as a technique to quickly assess students' overall reading ability.

   The cloze technique can also offer other uses for vocabulary development for the midrange dictionary with cloze. Regardless of the purpose for using cloze technique, it can be done as individual handouts for students or as a whole-class activity, using the overhead projector. For instructional purposes, passages of text can be clozed selectively—that is, you do not have to delete every fifth word; instead, you can selectively delete particular words you want students to practice using. The uses of cloze for vocabulary instruction are limitless; the following are just a few examples:

- Provide other passages of text to be clozed without providing alternative word choices. Ask students to create two different moods or purposes in the text by doing it one time with one set of vocabulary choices, then a second time, creating a different effect by choosing words with different connotations. Suggest that they might use a dictionary or thesaurus during this activity. With students in the upper intermediate grades and higher, it may be valuable to describe the technical differences between *denotation* (the word's common objective literal meaning) and the same word's *connotation* (implicit subjective meaning or meanings for the word).

- Have students create their own cloze passages or choose 50-word excerpts from one of their textbooks and use them with the cloze technique. Then have students exchange their cloze exercises with other students and complete the cloze activity. Pair students up to share their results.

- A more advanced version is to provide students with selected words to use in a text to be written. Have them write a passage leaving a blank for each of the new words.

Using New Vocabulary to Generalize Inferences

Provide students with lists of new vocabulary you want them to be able to read in context. Mix in some words that are already in their full-ownership dictionaries so that they will help the students to recognize word meanings in an appropriate context. Most of the new words will be collocates of the words the students already "own." Introduce the activity with the following or something similar:

> Boys and girls, they have just completed an archaeological dig in New England where the early colonists lived. They have found the remains of an early colonial village. However, the only thing really helpful is part of an old diary that has selected words that are readable. They are listed here. (Write the vocabulary words on the board.) Use these words to write some sentences about what life was probably like back in the early colonial days. For example, How did they make a living? What did they do for entertainment? What did they believe was important?

ax	hogshead	traps
baptism	indentured servant	squash
pewter	congregation	witch
pelt	flint	hunt
whipping post	pray	furs
keg	pillory	musket

Notice how such a vocabulary-building activity can be used during the prereading phase of a social studies lesson on life in the colonies. Any content area can be used similarly.

Example: science

These words were found in a science book. What do we know about animal and plant life?

red blood cells

nuclei

mitosis

Have students develop additional similar activities using social studies and science texts at various grade levels.

Using Mapping and Webbing Techniques

Semantic mapping (or "webbing") is widely espoused as an effective technique for teaching vocabulary as well as for improving reading comprehension generally. A semantic map, like a story map (described in Chapter 4), has many attractions. It graphically shows relationships in ways that appeal to and make sense to visual learners. Further, the specific advantages of semantic maps are unique: As the map or web grows and interrelates, students can see conceptual relationships and can develop a fuller understanding of word families and how they work. In addition, the process of doing the mapping provides excellent opportunities for activating students' existing background knowledge or for building new background for students during the prereading phase of the lesson.

Another key advantage of semantic mapping is its flexibility in adapting to student needs and abilities. It readily applies to very simple elaboration for lower grades or students having difficulties in reading. Yet it also can become quite complex and sophisticated. Its character is such that it works well in almost all content areas of the school curriculum.

The steps are simple:

1. Select a word that is important to the story theme or to the content area topic. Another option is to use the story or chapter title. Write the word or topic on the board, and circle it.
2. Ask students to guess or predict words that are likely to be found either in such a story or about the identified topic. As students volunteer words, write these on the board around the key word or title, and circle them as well. Use linear spokes to connect each of the circled words to the central title word or phrase at the hub.
3. As new words are volunteered, encourage students to tell why they think the words are important or are likely to be found in the text. Be careful here! One of the disadvantages of semantic mapping is the ease with which students can get off track and steer class discussion to irrelevant topics. Keep students and words on the topic, and discourage students from suggesting unlikely words for which they cannot offer a reasonable rationale.
4. After a number of words are generated, discuss ways that some words are related to some of the others. Look for subfamily word groups. Connect these to each other with more lines—perhaps

Semantic mapping is probably best known as a technique to be used during prereading. Remind students of additional uses (e.g., as a guide during reading, as a review or summarizing idea after the reading). Steer them to other resources on uses of semantic mapping and other related graphic techniques for teaching vocabulary. For example, a couple of useful resources are J. Heimlich & S. Pittelman (1986), *Semantic Mapping: Classroom Applications* (Newark, NJ: International Reading Association); and R. Marzano & J. Marzano (1988), *A Cluster Approach to Elementary Vocabulary Instruction* (Newark, NJ: International Reading Association).

dotted ones to distinguish them from the primary connector lines to the center.

A web or map can be as detailed and complex as is fruitful for learning, and the process can be expanded or contracted to fit almost any length of time.

Figures 8.2 and 8.3 show some examples of maps of differing degrees of complexity.

Using Feature Analysis Techniques

Point out to students that researchers and educators are not entirely sure which is more valuable in the use of graphics for learning: (a) the actual graphics themselves, (b) their production, (c) the discussion and thinking generated during their development, or (d) the interaction of some or all of these parts. It is, however, known that they work and that all of these aspects of their use contribute in some way to an effective instructional model. Therefore, appropriate time and attention should be given to the entire process.

Another graphic technique that is excellent for teaching students to identify salient features or defining characteristics of new words is through feature analysis charting.

In principle, feature analysis approaches derive from studies done by sociologists, anthropologists, and linguists during the 1960s and 1970s, when researchers were interested in children's acquisition of (a) the various features associated with concept-bearing words, (b) the kinds of features children acquired, and (c) the order in which children acquired those features. For example, *humans* can be analyzed in terms of several kinds of features: (a) physical features of a human (e.g., legs, arms, head), (b) behavioral features (e.g., eating, sleeping), and (c) emotional features (e.g., loving, caring, hurting, angering).

In short, using a feature analysis chart was a research tool and technique. Reading educators adapted it for teaching vocabulary. It works this way:

1. Create a chart such as Figure 8.4 on the board.
2. Ask students to help you identify features of the key concept word heading the chart (see Figure 8.5). Write the key features at the top of each column on the chart.
3. Ask students to volunteer types of vehicles, which you list in the far left column, labeled "vehicles" in Figure 8.6.
4. Now have students assist you in filling in the remaining squares in the rows and columns with a + (plus) or a – (minus) in each one. A + (plus) indicates that this is a positive feature for this particular vehicle. A – (minus) indicates that this particular vehicle does not have this feature.

Notice how our completed feature analysis chart reflects some interesting discussion opportunities for using our words on the chart and collocates of each. For example, Are trucks fast or not? Our students voted "no" but not without a strong argument for new trucks that are designed more for play than for work. Requiring students to describe such trucks, their features, and their purposes, as well as relationships among those elements provides excellent vocabulary building practice in oral language.

Figure 8.2 Very simple semantic map of "boating."

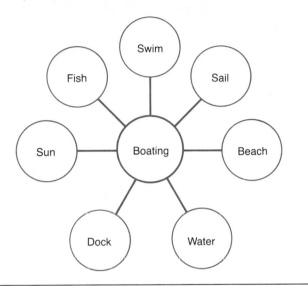

Discuss the similarities between semantic mapping and story mapping for both reading comprehension and instruction in writing.

Figure 8.3 Somewhat complex semantic map of "school."

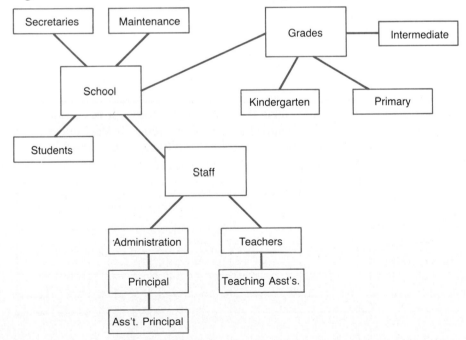

Ask students to explore the literature for examples of different types of semantic maps. Consider duplicating copies of these maps for all students in the class, for a teacher resource manual. (Be sure to obtain permission from the publisher, indicating that these are just for your class's use.)

Figure 8.4   Sample chart showing the first step in feature analysis—labeling the concept word to be analyzed.

Vehicles					

Figure 8.5   Sample chart showing the second step in feature analysis—labeling the features to be analyzed in relation to the concept word.

Vehicles	4 wheels	Fast	Cargo Carriers	Sporty	Slow

Figure 8.6   Sample chart showing the third and fourth steps in feature analysis—naming specific items that exemplify the concept word, then noting whether the items have (or demonstrate) each feature.

Vehicles	4 wheels	Fast	Riders	Cargo	For Work
Cars	+	+	+	+	+
Trucks	+	−	+	+	+
Motorcycles	−	+	+	−	−
Tractors	−	−	−	−	+

Any vehicle or feature might lead to discussion. For example, motorcycle police officers might offer another springboard for discussion about which vehicles are used for work and which for play.

Think about how the feature analysis chart can be used in various content areas to focus on important concepts. Alternative uses include having small groups complete charts (xerographically reproduced as handouts with blank spaces throughout or with only the head concept word topping the far left column), and comparing their charts with other groups.

Have students generate sample feature analysis charts for different grade-level examples.

TEACHING NEW VOCABULARY TO THE LOW-RANGE DICTIONARY

As was mentioned in the opening of this chapter, vocabulary is built in a few different ways. For example, direct instruction can use predictable-model strategies to effectively teach to the full-ownership dictionary. A number of other techniques and activities can be incorporated into content area instruction, to immerse students in a meaningful language-using environment, which may help move new words into their midrange dictionaries. In addition, research indicates that an ongoing language- and literature-rich environment is necessary for sustained vocabulary growth and development. If students have learned how to learn new words, and they have been provided with a rich language setting, and they have been imbued with their teachers' love and respect for literature and learning, then their vocabulary grows—sometimes, even in spite of their teachers!

This language-rich and language-loving environment is what teaching to the low-range dictionary is about. Anything that contributes to a rich language-using environment qualifies as a technique or activity for teaching vocabulary to be entered into this dictionary. The following few examples may help you to discover and invent many others throughout your teaching career.

Point out that for most people, the most important part of the lifetime vocabulary comes from immersion in language as a lifelong activity—talking, listening, reading, and writing it. Therefore, the need for a rich language-using environment in the classroom cannot be overemphasized!

Resources such as the "Sniglets" books and books by Richard Lederer (e.g., *Anguished English* (1987), and *Get Thee to A Punnery* (1988), NJ: Dell Publishing Co.) offer delightful language play ideas. Kornei Chukovsky's (1968), *From Two to Five* (Berkeley: University of California Press) offers excellent language examples by young children, which reveal the humorous convolutions language can take in the young experimenter. Also, the works of Willard Espy entertain as well as inform.

Language Play

Example: Making Up New Words that We Need!

"Boys and Girls—Have you ever thought about the new words we need in our language? Just think for a minute about some of our needs. For example, what are some of the best times of the school day? Sure, recess and lunch. But think about the very best time: the time between when school is dismissed in the afternoon and dinner time. That is a time so important that we need a word to name it. Can you think of a good name for that time?

"Here is another example. When you use a dust pan and sweep the dust into it with a broom, what happens when you lift the dust pan? There's a line, right? You put the pan down, sweep that line of dust in and what happens when you lift the pan? Right! Another line of dust. You can't get rid of it. We all live with it. That line of dust needs a name. What would be a good name?''

*Example:*Making Up New Group Names

''Boys and Girls—Think about the words we have to name groups of animals or things. We call a bunch of elephants a ''herd.'' We call a bunch of fish a ''school.'' We call a bunch of lions a ''pride.'' We call a bunch of geese a ''gaggle.'' What might we call a bunch of quilters? (a patch?) What would be a good name for a bunch of accountants? (a sum of accountants?) What would we call a bunch of slugs? (a slime?)

Children love new-word-naming activities. Notice that many children also learn words such as ''pride'' and ''gaggle'' in the process of playing with the language to create new words.

Etymology (Word History)

Word etymology and dialects both represent activities in vocabulary that are interesting, informative, and fun. They represent excellent motivating examples, which help teachers get children ''hooked'' on language.

Exploring word history is a fascinating way to learn how words change, how they are developed, and how language is constantly changing to add or modify new words. This is also an excellent technique for getting students into serious use of dictionaries, including some of the more substantial dictionaries such as the *Oxford English Dictionary*.

Words usually change over time in one or more of several ways, which we can discover in the dictionary. Find some words that have changed by becoming more

- General—The word *manuscript* once meant only a hand-written copy but now means any kind of copy prior to final book form. What other words have become more general in meaning over the years?
- Specialized—The word *starve* once meant ''to die''—by any means. *Starve* now means specifically to die from lack of food. What other words now have a more specialized meaning than they did earlier?

Dialect Study Projects

Point out the importance of dialect study as another opportunity for children to be accepting and open to people from different cultures and subcultures. Dialect study can reinforce the important notion that language is neither correct nor incorrect but rather is appropriate or inappropriate to different locations, contexts, purposes, and subjects.

People in different parts of the country speak differently. For example, regional sound systems vary, and different regions even have different terms for the same thing. In southern Illinois, for example, the words *form* and *farm* are pronounced the same. Also, the words *pore, pour,* and *poor* are all pronounced the same. However, people in Wisconsin would not likely pronounce *pore* the same as *poor*. Is one pronunciation ''right'' and the other ''wrong''? Of course not.

Also, in southern Illinois, people fish with ''fish worms,'' while in Wisconsin they use ''angle worms.'' People in Tennessee use a ''skillet,'' while people in Michigan would more likely use a ''frying pan''; people in Kentucky carry water in a ''bucket,'' while New Yorkers are more likely to use a "pail." We often use completely different words to name the same thing in different parts of the country. Is one word "wrong" and the other "right"? Of course not.

Dialect study projects and activities offer children an opportunity to learn new vocabulary and different phonological principles, as well as an appreciation for the unique societal differences that language can reflect. Here are a few:

- Have one (or more) of your students read part of a story for an audiotape. Send the tape with a copy of the text to a class in a different part of the country. (Usually, one of your students will have relatives or friends in a part of the country where you could identify the school and even the specific class in the school.) Remember to select a location that is likely to have a different dialect than the one in your region of the country. Send along a letter to the teacher, and ask if he or she would have one (or more) of his or her students record a reading of the same text and mail the tape back for your students to hear.

  Compare the tapes in class when it has been returned. Discuss the differences with your students. Point out to them the particular sound differences and vocabulary differences that might appear.

  If there is enough interest, this project can expand to multiple tapes sent to major dialect regions throughout the nation.
- Have students make a dialect map of the United States. Draw in the main dialect boundaries, and locate vocabulary differences that exist across the country.
- Select children's literature examples (trade books) where regional dialects are reflected in the dialogue and other narrative of the story or book. Ask children to identify and describe some of the dialectical features that are different from those in their own dialect.

The examples of techniques and activities presented here barely touch on the range and variety possible. Reviewing and reading the professional literature, along with publications from commercial companies, will ensure an ongoing file of creative and interesting things children can do with language to enhance their vocabulary and help expand their low-range dictionaries.

HIGHLIGHTS

1. Vocabulary development requires both direct instruction and a rich language-using environment that incorporates literature and other texts that are meaningful, important, and interesting to the children.

2. The effective teacher of reading makes decisions about the relative importance of specific new vocabulary before deciding on an instructional approach. The selection of one of the three mental dictionaries when learning new words can help in determining the most appropriate instructional strategy or technique.
3. The effective teacher of reading strives constantly for strategies and techniques that help learners learn how to learn new vocabulary. The specific new words learned are secondary in importance to the mastery of how new words can be learned.
4. Vocabulary instruction should be taught within the context of appropriate content areas and purposes. Vocabulary taught in isolation, devoid of context and purpose important to the student, is largely wasted instruction.
5. A wide range of instructional approaches can be used for developing vocabulary. These approaches range from tightly ordered direct-instruction models with fixed steps to informal language-play activities. They all add to the richness of the literacy experience, as well as to the specific development and growth of vocabulary. The effective teacher knows how each plays a role, what that role is, and when it is appropriate.

REINFORCEMENT ACTIVITIES

1. What is the best way to teach new vocabulary to students?
2. What is meant by a "dictionaries approach to teaching vocabulary"?
3. Explain the significance of "Children learn new words, and children learn how to learn new words."
4. Briefly describe the steps of the direct-instruction models presented in this chapter. How do they fit into the larger picture of vocabulary instruction?
5. Describe the physical character of a classroom designed to assist in vocabulary development.

ADDITIONAL PROJECTS

1. Observe an intermediate-grade class in which the teacher is using a direct-instruction approach to vocabulary. Compare the lesson with those presented in this chapter.
2. Work with a partner to prepare a lesson in vocabulary instruction, using one or more of the ideas presented in this chapter. Teach it to the rest of your class, with your colleagues role-playing as students.

Of course, there is no one correct answer to this question. Students should be able to articulate responses that require contextualization according to circumstances of the lesson, lesson objectives, and so forth.

Look for responses to this question, which point out significance for deciding how to teach in given teaching situations.

Students should include some discussion of metacognition, self-monitoring, and so forth, for children's learning how to learn new words.

Students should incorporate explanation of direct instruction—its strengths and limitations in teaching vocabulary.

Students might want to refer to the other chapters in this text, which discuss classroom organization and its place in instruction. Also, they should include information indicating their knowledge of the relationship of classroom organization to philosophy or teaching beliefs.

3. Review a selection of curriculum materials designed for elementary-grade vocabulary instruction. Compare them with those presented here. Discuss their similarities and their differences.

4. Read an article in *The Reading Teacher* or another professional journal on teaching vocabulary in the elementary grades. Share the article with fellow students in a class discussion.

REFERENCES

Adams, M. M., & Huggins, A. W. F. (1985). *The growth of children's sight vocabulary: A quick test with educational and theoretical implications* (Tech. Rep. No. 330). Urbana, IL: University of Illinois, Center for the Study of Reading.

Anderson, R., & Freebody, P. (1977). *Vocabulary knowledge and reading* (Tech. Rep. No. 11). Urbana, IL: University of Illinois, Center for the Study of Reading.

Beck, I. L., & McKeown, M. (1985). Teaching vocabulary: Making the instruction fit the goal. *Educational Perspectives, 23,* 11–15.

Beck, I. L., Perfetti, C., & McKeown, M. (1982). Effects of long-term vocabulary instruction on lexical access and reading comprehension. *Journal of Educational Psychology, 74,* 506–521.

Becker, W. C. (1977). Teaching reading and language to the disadvantaged—What we have learned from field research. *Harvard Educational Review, 47,* 518–543.

Chall, J. (1958). *Readability: An appraisal of research and application.* Columbus, OH: Ohio State University, Bureau of Educational Research.

Chall, J. (1987). Two vocabularies for reading: Recognition and meaning. In M. McKeown & M. Curtis (Eds.), *The Nature of Vocabulary Acquisition.* Hillsdale, NJ: Erlbaum.

Davis, F. B. (1944). Fundamental factors of comprehension in reading. *Psychometrika, 9,* 185–197.

Johnson, D., & Pearson, P. D. (1984). *Teaching Reading Vocabulary.* New York: Holt, Rinehart and Winston.

Klein, M. (1988). *Teaching Reading Comprehension and Vocabulary: A Handbook for Teachers.* Englewood Cliffs, NJ: Prentice-Hall.

Lorge, I., & Chall, J. (1963). Estimating the size of vocabularies of children and adults: An analysis of methodological issues. *Journal of Experimental Education, 32,* 147–157.

Michael, W. B., Zimmerman, W. S., & Guilford, J. F. (1951). An investigation of the nature of the spatial relations and visualization factors in two high school samples. *Education and Psychology Measurement, 11,* 561–577.

Moe, A. (1974). *A comparative study of vocabulary diversity: The speaking vocabularies of selected first-grade primers, and the vocabularies of selected first-grade trade books.* Paper presented at the annual meeting of the American Educational Research Association, Chicago. (ERIC Document Reproduction Service No. ED 090 520).

Nagy, W., & Herman, P. (1987). In M. McKeown & M. Curtis (Eds.), *The Nature of Vocabulary Acquisition.* Hillsdale, NJ: Erlbaum.

Schwartz, E. (1988). *Encouraging Early Literacy* (p. 62). Portsmouth, NJ: Heinemann.

Stevens, K. C. (1982). Can we improve reading by teaching background information? *Journal of Reading, 25,* 326–329.

Terman, L. M. (1918). Vocabulary test as a measure of intelligence. *Journal of Educational Psychology, 9,* 452–466.

Thurston, L. (1946). A note of a reanalysis of Davis' reading tests. *Psychometrika, 11,* 185–188.

Vygotsky, L. (1962). *Thought and Language.* Cambridge, MA: MIT Press.

Wittrock, M. D., Marks, C., & Doctorow, M. (1975). Reading as a generative process. *Journal of Educational Psychology, 67,* 481–489.

ADDITIONAL RESOURCES

Devine, T.(1986). *Teaching Reading Comprehension: From Theory to Practice.* Boston: Allyn & Bacon.

Dickson, P. (1982). *Words.* New York: Delacorte Press.

Espy, W. (1975). *Words at Play.* New York: Clarkson Potter.

Farb, P. (1975). *Word Play.* New York: Knopf.

William Nagy's (1988) *Teaching Vocabulary to Improve Reading Comprehension* (Newark, DE: International Reading Association) is a very useful professional resource students may wish to acquire. D. Johnson and P. D. Pearson's (1984) *Teaching Reading Vocabulary* (2nd ed.) (New York: Holt, Rinehart and Winston) remains a useful teaching resource also.

CHAPTER 9

TEACHING STUDY SKILLS THROUGHOUT THE ELEMENTARY GRADES

Do not on any account attempt to write on both sides of the paper at the same time.
W. C. Sellar & R. J. Yeatman, *1066 and all that, 1930*

PREVIEW

One of the important areas of reading instruction is the teaching of study skills. Yet, it is often neglected. Perhaps this is because each educator thinks that it is being taught elsewhere. Perhaps it is because teachers think that these skills are being learned implicitly in the context of other content areas being taught. Perhaps it is because educators cannot quite agree about what constitutes study skills. Perhaps there are other reasons.

The authors of this text, however, believe that study skills are important enough to warrant (a) specific attention and instruction and (b) incidental or implicit inclusion in the various content areas studied in the elementary grades. Elementary-grade instruction in study skills is important for the following reasons:

1. Mastery of effective and efficient study skills is important for learning in all content areas of the curriculum.
2. Learning how to learn and how to access new information are the cornerstones of all lifelong knowledge. These two abilities form the core of study skills. Those students who know how to study, how to learn, and how to use the tools of and for learning are most likely to continue developing their knowledge and their literacy throughout their lives.
3. Given its crucial role in a person's lifelong learning, the earlier these skills are acquired, the better. Therefore, it is both appropriate and desirable to provide instruction in this area throughout the elementary grades.

Although these skills are acquired by many students with little direct instruction, most continue to need attention to this area of skill development. They depend on guidance and instruction to become as proficient as possible in the use of study skills.

Ask students to recall their elementary and secondary school years: "were you taught study skills? When? Where? How? Do you feel that the instruction was helpful to you? Have you observed any instruction in study skills in your practical or field experiences in teacher education?"

288

FOCUS QUESTIONS

As you read this chapter, keep the following questions in mind:

1. What are the important study skills, and why are they important?
2. What is the difference between "study skills" and "study tools"?
3. Should study skills be part of the reading program or part of the content curriculum areas?
4. What are some of the best ways to teach both study skills and the use of study tools?

INTRODUCTION AND DEFINITIONS

Perhaps part of the difficulty in addressing study skills adequately is an inability to conceptualize the area precisely yet inclusively enough to satisfy everyone. Examination of some reading methods texts reveals study skills included in the reading comprehension processes and skills domain.[1] When others think of study skills, they think of ability to use the library or library resources.

This text defines *study skills* as "those skills necessary for acquiring critical information from a variety of text and media sources for differing purposes and uses." In other words, a person who has mastered study skills knows how to review and read different kinds of texts and knows what information is important for the task at hand. The individual can also function similarly with nonprint media. Furthermore, the individual knows how to retrieve essential information and cast it into a form and a format that makes it usable for the purpose necessary. For example, the skillful student knows that notes must be different when they serve different purposes. Notes for personal use during an individual informal presentation differ in form and format from notes used when preparing a research project that will require substantial time and study.

If students need only to get the gist of a short story, skillful students know to skim it for key ideas and only the detail that is necessary to flesh out the general information. On the other hand, if they are going to have a comprehensive examination over a chapter in a physics text, they must study it quite differently.

Ask students whether they believe that study skills are just sort of self-taught for most people. Ask them how learner ability level affects the answer to this question, if it affects it at all.

Have students hypothesize what they predict to be the differences between the study skills and the study tools that are suggested in this chapter. Ask them whether this is a useful distinction.

The point made in this footnote is important. Examination of a variety of reading methods texts suggests that those skills typically associated with study also make sense as comprehension skills. We have attempted not to duplicate such ideas as SQ3R, but it could be worthwhile to discuss this arbitrary distinction at this point.

[1]Note. In this book, many of the direct-instruction models mentioned in Chapter 7, on reading comprehension (e.g., SQ3R), are also important study skill instruction models.

Ask students whether there are particular study skills that are necessary or useful unique to individual study tools.

Ask students, "Is this reflected in the scope and sequence of typical basal programs?"

In many senses, the content areas might be viewed as the primary instruction and learning context for teaching and learning study skills. Social studies and science in particular tend to have heavy narrative density. Further, they usually have textbooks formatted in ways that lend themselves to instruction in study skills (e.g., subheads, subtitles, marginal notes, altered font sizes, and use of graphics).

Emphasize the importance of this idea. The heart of effective study lies in the ability to self-analyze thinking about and comprehending text.

Study tools are the resources students must be able to use in order to apply their study skills. These tools include standard library resources, such as dictionaries, thesauruses, the card catalogue, and various other reference works.

Most students have acquired basic knowledge about study tools by the time they complete the primary grades. They know, for example, that the table of contents of any book is in the front of the book and lists the main categories of information or topics to be found in the book. They know what a dictionary is, and they know its commonly perceived general purpose (i.e., to find meanings for words). They know about other basic reference works, such as encyclopedias, although they have usually done little or nothing with them.

Study skills should be addressed throughout the grades, beginning in kindergarten, and instruction in the use of study tools should also be done throughout the grades; however, the first substantial opportunity for direct in-depth instruction comes during the intermediate grades.

BASIC ASSUMPTIONS

This textbook's treatment of study skills and study tools operates from the following assumptions, many of which are reflected in the content of the rest of this book:

1. Study skills can and should be taught through all grades, K–12.
2. Study skills instruction should be seen as a broad encompassing area that warrants both direct focused instruction and indirect inclusion in other areas. For example, study skills instruction should be a part of social studies, science, math, and all other content areas. Further, much of the content of reading comprehension is designed to further study-skill abilities (e.g., how to summarize, paraphrase, infer conclusions from text).
3. The heart of study skills, as well as of reading comprehension, is the ability to self-monitor one's reading; as well as the ability to select and apply particular appropriate reading strategies in a given reading task. For many reasons, an ongoing top priority in the reading program must be to teach students to be self-monitors who know when and how to apply various reading strategies.
4. Knowledge about study tools is important but still secondary to mastery of study skills.
5. Study skills are most effectively taught in contexts that are important and meaningful to the learner. This means that their integration within the content areas is important.

THE IMPORTANT STUDY SKILLS

The following study skills are important for focused instruction:

- Establishing a mental set (framework) for studying
- Adjusting reading rate for different reading tasks, reading types, and reading purposes
- Previewing text
- Skimming
- Note-taking
- Outlining
- Interpreting graphic information (charts, graphs, etc.)
- Portraying ideas graphically (clustering, mapping, charting)
- Assessing relative importance of information
- Summarizing

Ask students, "What are other skills that might be included here?" Note the earlier marginal comments in this chapter.

Establishing a Mental Set for Studying

Clearly, students must spend time studying if they are to learn. However, effective studying is not just a function of the amount of time spent on the process. Many students—including college students—believe that if enough time is spent studying, learning will take place. ("I don't understand why I did so poorly on the test. I spent five and a half hours studying!") Thus, time spent in study is a necessary but not a sufficient condition for learning.

Quality study time can occur only when the learner has established the appropriate study-related *mental set* (i.e., a mental framework that prepares the student to select and organize the information obtained through study). Before students even begin studying for any particular purpose, they need to prepare mentally by following these important steps:

1. *Determine why the studying is important.* If the learner is not convinced that the studying is justifiable, the effort will likely be ineffective. If students do not believe in the value of the effort, then the effort will have no worth. Help your students understand why a particular assignment or study task warrants their attention.
2. *Determine specifically what is to be accomplished during the study session.* Before beginning the study session, decide what is to be achieved in the effort. Ask students to write this out by completing the following sentence: "I will be able to _____ ." or, "I will know about _____ ."
3. *Design a plan of study for each important study project.* Teach your students to use a model outline such as the following to get them

This is a good spot to discuss Instructional Theory into Practice (ITIP) (M. Hunter's model for instruction) because it emphasizes the importance of the mental set for learning. Many learners, including college and university students, believe that learning is entirely a function of time on task. That is, if I spend 2 hours of reading my history lesson, that translates into 2 hours of learning. Observe students who interrupt their study with constant glances at their watches, for example. It might be wise here to discuss the importance of "quality" time and how to teach that concept to children and older learners as well.

Ask students to design alternative simple plans of study that can be used. Talk about the extent to which the actual writing of such a plan can be helpful to learners with inefficient study skills.

in the habit of thinking through each of the steps to be taken while studying.

a. These are the things I should know/be able to do after I have finished studying: (List them)

b. These are the resources (books, papers, references, etc.) I will need for my study (do not forget human resources if you will be working with peers): (List them)

c. This is the time that I need to do the study: (Indicate an amount)

d. This is where I will do my study: (Indicate a place)

e. This is what I expect to result from my study: (e.g., receive a good grade)

Students need to formally work through this plan of study in order to internalize the process.

4. *Complete all steps of the plan of study.*

Taking the time to work through these steps will help ensure that learners begin their study with a study-related mental set appropriate to their task.

> Effective study relies on the learner's belief that it is important enough to warrant the learner's time and that study requires more than just logging time.

Adjusting Reading Rate for Different Reading Tasks, Types, and Purposes

Many students in the elementary grades have yet to learn that effective readers adjust their reading rate according to the nature of the text and the requirements of the reading task. Here are some things teachers can do at these grade levels to help students learn this important skill.

Consider bringing a specialized or technical piece of text to class (e.g., an advertisement for a motorcycle performance data or a selection from an advanced chemistry or physics or calculus text). Discuss the way that adult university students respond to different kinds of text. Talk also about personal importance. Some might choose to read particular authors more slowly than necessary for satisfactory comprehension in order to savor the beauty or wonder of the text (e.g., the writing of William Styron). Ask students, "What are some of the factors employed by efficient readers when deciding reading rate? What are the implications of this information for teaching reading rate adjustment to elementary school children?"

- During prereading periods in different content areas, talk your way through the text to be read with the class. Point out headings, subheadings, and text adjuncts (margin notes, graphs, charts, etc.), and discuss their importance.

- Get in the habit of providing written *advance organizers* for your students. These are study guides of various kinds that students can use in their reading, which help them to prepare for organizing the information they will be reading. You can use a list of important questions for them to think about as they read. You can provide a topic or sentence outline of the reading. You can provide a story map or content cluster graph of the key ideas and concepts in the text to be read.

- Have students role-play being the teacher and preparing sample advance organizers for an assignment in their social studies text. Pair students up, and have them compare and contrast the advance organizers they designed. Alternatively, you can assign the task as a joint task for pairs of students to prepare their advance organizers together.

- Contrive different hypothetical study assignments, and have students work their way through a different plan of study for each. For example, ask students to prepare for a research project on the life of Benjamin Franklin, and to compare that to studying a chapter in their science textbook in preparation for a chapter review test. Assign students to small groups after completing each of these two plans of study, and have them share their plans with each other. Discuss in class the differences in approaches to study for each of these assignments.

- Provide students with the following three types of text:
  a. A three-paragraph sample of expository text—Be sure that each paragraph has a topic sentence and clear support sentences
  b. A three-paragraph sample of narrative text—perhaps select three paragraphs that describe a character or a setting for a story
  c. A social studies content textbook—Use one that provides headings, subheadings, marginal notes, and so forth.

Have students work individually or in pairs to list the differences in the way these different kinds of text are written. For example, their lists might include some observations such as the following: Text sample a does not have subheads. The b text sample is not true and did not really take place.

Ask your students to design short tests for each of the texts. Tell them to include questions that will get at the most important ideas or information in each of the texts. Ask them to compare their tests in small groups. Talk about some of the similarities and differences in their tests.

- Provide students with an article from the front page of a newspaper. Also, provide them with an important passage of text from their science book. Talk about the differences in these two kinds of writing and the differences in the ways that most people read a newspaper as opposed to a textbook.

Previewing Text

Elementary-grade students tend to be impatient to get things done. If they have to read an assignment, they want to do it right away and be done with it. However, an important key to effective study is taking the time at the beginning of the study to get an overview. That is one of the goals of establishing a study-related mental set. Once learners are considering a

Here is an example of a handout or worksheet that is tied to instruction. Remind students to be careful not to assume that all handouts are automatically skill-and-drill. They may miss some excellent teaching opportunities if they do not consider use of various things, such as study guides, and so forth, simply because they are sheets of paper.

If possible, keep some sample copies of elementary content area texts available. They often need to be pulled out for examination at a moment's notice when discussion warrants.

Remind students of the importance of the prereading phase of the reading lesson. Although this has been mentioned in the book in other places, it deserves repeating.

text, they need to think about its content, structure, and organization wholistically before beginning to read specific passages.

The reading teacher can help by engaging students in necessary discussion and activities to activate students' existing background knowledge or to develop some new background knowledge to serve as a base for the study. However, independent study requires that the student be able to do some of this independently.

Provide students with direction in using the following questions and statements as guides during the preview phase of text study:

Ask students whether other questions are important here.

1. What is the general topic being addressed during this study session?
2. What are some of the things I already know about this? (Write down some of these as statements.)
3. What are some questions I should keep in my mind when I read this text? (Write these down.)
4. Glance through the entire text. Write down the key words you see that catch your attention. Try to make up sentences using each of them.
5. Skim through the text a second time, this time more slowly and thoroughly. Write a short paragraph describing your guess as to the gist of this text. Remember that this is just a guess!

Practice in formally working through these steps a number of times until they are internalized will yield high dividends for your students in terms of their quality of study.

Skimming

Ask students, "Is skimming reading? What is 'speed reading'?" It is helpful, the authors feel, to view skimming and reading in the normal sense as two different operations. If for no other reason, it can help students approach the skimming act with a different point of view than that employed when reading complex and dense text.

Skimming is actually a key part of previewing a text. However, it is important enough to warrant separate attention, for it is the key to effective study through the years. Effective skimming saves time, provides important key information and allows the individual to devote more time and energy to other important areas of study.

Skimming is not a skill that is easily taught in a few brief steps or in a few lessons. Teachers can identify features and some key things involved in skimming and can offer guidelines. However, the real teacher of effective skimming is time, text, and practice. Further, although readers can utilize skimming with any form of text, it is much more effective and easy to use with variations of expository text than it is with narrative. Expository text has more predictable and useful summarizing characteristics. For example, most paragraphs in exposition open with a topic or main idea sentence. This is followed by support or detail sentences for the main idea. Many expository passages also end with a conclusion or summary sentence.

Much of the expository text students are expected to read (i.e., social studies, science, math and other content texts) also incorporate text adjuncts in a logical and predictable fashion. Side notes, headings and subheadings, outlines, inserted questions, charts, graphs, and so forth are all easy to locate and glance over. Similarly, readers of newspapers can skim the front page by simply glancing over the headlines and skimming the opening sentence of each article, or, if they seek a bit more detail, they can skim over the opening sentence of each paragraph in a given article.

Unfortunately, narrative text is seldom quite this neat, orderly, and logical. As noted earlier, narrative text often does not have opening topic or main idea sentences for paragraphs. In stories, dialogue is interspersed with the author's descriptive or explanatory narrative, and it is not always easy to separate the important from the incidental information. In narratives that include graphic arts, even though there are photographs or artwork of various kinds, it is often used randomly and not always tied to key ideas in the story.

Therefore, one of the keys to successful skimming is in knowing the basic differences in text structure between expository and narrative text.

Assist your learners in becoming effective skimmers by teaching them these guidelines:

1. Make sure all of the preceding study-skill processes in this section of this chapter are being implemented. Skimming is one technique that fits into the study skills, but it is only important in relation to the many other steps that students must incorporate into their study behaviors.
2. At every opportunity, point out important structural and content differences between various genres and text forms. Discuss with students how the unique features of each text type and format can be used effectively in skimming.
3. Spend ample time during the preview phase of study and during the prereading phase of any lesson in helping your students activate and build their background knowledge. Take all opportunities available to teach students how to activate their own background knowledge in preparation for study. Point out the importance of this initial step in developing a necessary overall sense of what the reading will be about.
4. Design activities for skimming in content area study so this important study skill will be seen contextually rather than in isolation.

Note-taking and Outlining

There are several important reasons for note-taking and outlining. Perhaps one of the most important reasons for note-taking and outlining is

---

Bring handouts of narrative and expository text from various sources. Search for narrative text that differs from other narrative text in many ways, to point out the kinds of differences in structure and meaning that the reader must attend to.

Ask students to generate some additional guidelines that could help.

Formal outlining per se is seldom used by professional writers, yet many students leave high school English classes believing that it represents the main part of the writing act. Discuss the strengths and limitations of outlining for the efficient writer.

Knowing how and when to use various study skills is an important mark of an effective reader. The reading program should include instruction in all study skills that the learner uses in reading.

that literate learners learn content through writing and learn to write by writing. The act of engaging in writing directly assists cognitive development. Further, writing serves as a bridge to move print information into the writer's personal schema (Klein, 1985; Vygotsky, 1962, 1978).

Most learners consider both note-taking and outlining to be highly personalized literacy acts. For example, my notes from a lecture or from a book would be of limited value to another. My outlining is spare, and I use my own system of indenting, capitalizing, underlining, circling, using asterisks, and so on to indicate idea relationships and relative importance. They would be of little use to anyone else.

Nonetheless, it is a good idea to teach children certain basics about note-taking and outlining that hold regardless of personal style. These should be taught in the intermediate grades and then reinforced with students through the remainder of their school years as they personalize their own system so that they have something that they will continue to use during study.

Following are some useful techniques and activities for teaching these important basic skills.

- Provide practical examples of outlined text. Select a unit or chapter from one of the students' content subjects, and prepare an outline of it. Design a series of modified cloze outlines with some of the information provided but blank lines left to be completed by students. For example, note the example of text in Figure 9.1; the following outline could be completed by students, based on their reading of the text.

Figure 9.1   **Sample of expository text that can be used to teach students to touline texts. Taken directly from M. Klein, L. Matteoni, F. Sucher, K. Welch (1986).** *Copper Sky* **(Economy Reading Series; p. 217). Oklahoma City, OK: McGraw-Hill. Reproduced with permission of McGraw-Hill Book Company, School Division. Copyright 1986. All rights reserved.**

zzzzzZZZZZZZZZ

Everyone needs sleep. In laboratory experiments, people deprived of sleep have difficulty thinking and controlling their tempers. In other experiments, scientists have made some interesting discoveries about what happens during sleep.

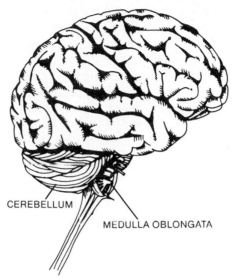

CEREBELLUM

MEDULLA OBLONGATA

Brain Activity   The human body experiences several changes during sleep. Some body muscles relax, because the *cerebellum,* the area of the brain that controls muscle coordination, becomes less active. The part of the brain called the *medulla oblongata* remains active. This area controls involuntary functions such as heartbeat, breathing, coughing, swallowing, and digestion. However, even these processes slow down during sleep.

Body Changes   If a sleeping person stayed in the same position all night, all of the muscles would not have a chance to relax. Therefore, without fully realizing it, a person will change position at least a dozen times during a period of sleep. Also, the body grows cooler, so it is necessary to wear loose, warm clothing or have other sufficient covering.

Sleep
  I. Everyone needs sleep
     A. Without sleep, thinking and temper control are difficult
     B. _____

Have students design similar models with actual elementary curriculum materials.

II. The body experiences changes during sleep
    A. The cerebellum becomes less active
    B. The medulla oblongata _____

III _____
    A. A person changes position many times during sleep
    B. The body grows cooler during sleep

You should design a number of different outlines, with increasing degrees of difficulty. Adjust them to the level of your students. After they have considerable practice completing increasingly blank and/or complex outlines that have basically been framed for them, they will be able to frame out their own more readily.

As a variation, after students can do some simple outlining, ask them to design some modified cloze outlines, which they can share with peers. Have students exchange their modified cloze outlines and complete one another's. Ask students to discuss their completed outlines with the designers.

■ Use the same technique with note-taking. Provide an example of text to students, with accompanying notes you have taken. Discuss your notes with students in class. How did you decide which points to write? How does your note-taking system work for you? What are some unique features of your notes that might not work for others?

■ Use the same text for both outlining and note-taking practice. After students have done both, have them use the outline and notes to write a brief report on the topic addressed in the text.

■ Ask students to keep a notebook for one of their subjects. Periodically discuss the notebook with them (as you might do their journals).

■ Provide students with 5- x 7-inch notecards, and design different approaches to note-taking using the notecards. The following are examples:

    a. Use one notecard for each one, two, or three paragraphs.

    b. Label a main idea at the top of each notecard, and make only notes related to that heading on that card.

    c. Provide xerographically reproduced notecards to students. Scramble the card order. Then provide the students with the text for which the notes were made. Have the students reorder the notecards according to the order of the information in the text.

    d. Have students take notes on a short story and then notes on a front-page newspaper article. Compare the notes, and discuss in class which was easier to do and how the note-taking techniques of the students differed for the two forms of text.

Minimize the use of note-taking and outlining instruction outside of a content-oriented context. Most content-related instruction offers ample

Ask students to compare their notes with one another, from courses they are currently taking. Ask them, "How are they alike? How do they differ? When can children be taught note-taking in the elementary grades?"

opportunities for using these skills in context. Therefore, in the techniques and activities for teaching study skills, always try to use text that students are actually studying and need to learn. The value of these skills lies in their ability to help students to gain access to and to store information for later use.

Mapping, Clustering, and Other Graphics

Earlier chapters discussed the value of using techniques such as semantic mapping (Chapter 8) and story grammar mapping (Chapter 4) for purposes of visually enhancing concepts and other content. These graphic techniques are also useful for study skills development. They represent effective ways to outline ideas so that their relationships are more visually observable. This is especially true when students are familiar with a few different graphic clustering systems. Examine the examples in Figures 9.2 through 9.5.

Compare Figure 9.2 with the way that the same information would look if just the terms were listed or if the components of a school system were written in sentences. If students were asked to write a report describing the various components of the school, preparing a cluster map like the one in Figure 9.2 could be helpful as an initial outline.

The teacher should prepare a variety of cluster maps, either with limited information or—for more practiced students—with only blank spaces with various lines. Figure 9.3 shows a map on which only identifiers were used.

A key part of instruction with mapping and clustering graphics is the discussion and sharing that occurs with them. If not used as part of the specific reading lesson with opportunities for oral sharing, these techniques and activities can easily become drill—rote in character. Use them selectively and as part of whole-class, small group, or paired discussion.

Branching charts are also helpful for seeing relationships. Notice that they are used within the clustering map in Figure 9.3. However, they can be used alone to display increasing and decreasing levels of abstraction or specificity between and within concepts. Figure 9.4 shows a branching chart that illustrates some of the rather complex concepts, components, and interrelationships of language. Figure 9.5 shows that the complexity of branching trees or charts can vary dramatically. A simple branching tree, for example, can be useful for teaching a variety of concepts.

Graphic presentation of information provides a useful adjunct to study at any time during the instructional process. Preparing any chart or cluster map prior to the reading of a text can be a useful way to guide study through the text to be read. Also, developing a map during and/or after the reading of text represents an excellent way to review and retain key information that has been studied.

Discuss the variety of uses for mapping and clustering. Discuss the importance of considering different learning styles (e.g., visual vs. print). How do graphics assist in conceptualization of ideas and relationships among ideas? Have students construct maps of elementary social studies and science texts. Discuss the role of mapping as a review process.

Emphasize the need to be a pack rat as an elementary teacher. In fact, students should already be collecting ideas and resources to use in the classroom. The popular, colorful plastic milk carton cases make excellent files. Manila file folders fit neatly in them. Discuss with students some other storage and organizing ideas.

This is a very important point for beginning teachers. Semantic mapping is a good example of an excellent teaching technique that can be overused. Some teachers attest to that happening in their classrooms with journal writing. Ask students what can be done to keep these excellent teaching techniques alive and working.

Ask students, "What other graphic techniques can be added?"

Figure 9.2 Sample cluster map that shows components of a school system.

EXAMPLE #1

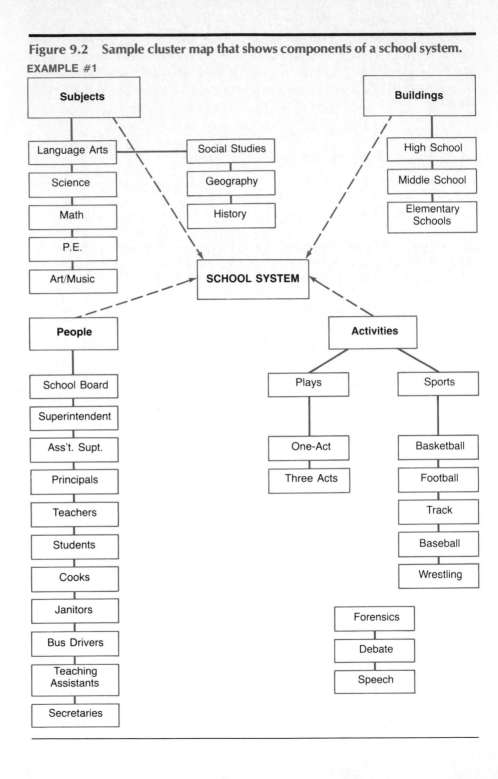

Figure 9.3 **Sample cluster map showing only key identifiers and relationships, with blanks for students to fill in.**

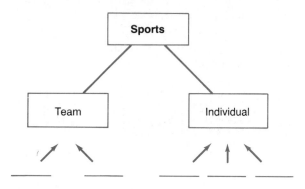

Figure 9.4 **Sample branching chart showing moderately complex interrelationships within language.**

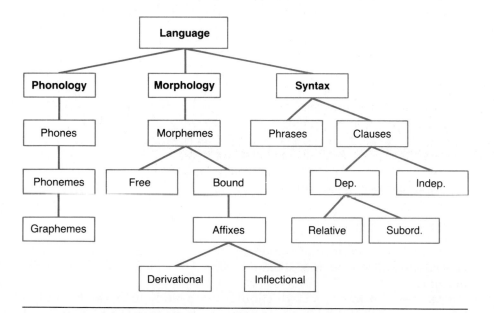

Figure 9.5   Sample branching charts showing somewhat simple interrelationships among elements.

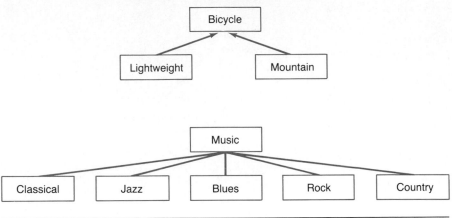

Other Study Skills

Prioritizing information according to its relative importance for the task was a key feature of many of the other skills described in this chapter. A related skill, summarizing, was described in Chapter 7, on reading comprehension.

STUDY TOOLS

Effective study requires the use of learning tools. The most important for the elementary grades student are the following:

Charts, tables, and graphs

Maps, globes, and atlases

Dictionaries and thesauruses

Encyclopedia

The card catalog

In the later intermediate grades, you may want to introduce certain specialized indexes, such as *Readers' Guide to Periodical Literature* and *Books in Print*.

However, before any instruction in these study tools can be undertaken successfully, children must know the basic format and purpose of most nonfiction books. For example, children must know the location and purpose of a book's table of contents, index, glossary, appendix, and preface. They also must know the answers to the following questions:

Discuss additions to expand this list.

Ask students when these concepts regarding the use of study tools and references should be taught in the elementary grades.

How do you use a table of contents or an index?

Why are glossaries sometimes included?

What do you use an appendix for?

Graphics and visual aids, such as charts, maps, and graphs, are more specialized study tools that are used only in some of the many types of text. They are very important, however, and warrant special attention and study.

The following guidelines for instruction in study tool use and application should be followed:

1. Include direct instruction in all of these study tools throughout the school year, according to the scope and sequence of study tools taught in your school district curriculum.
2. Be sure your students understand the study tool basics (i.e., book components and uses) before you devote instructional time to the more specialized tools listed here.
3. Include some brief direct instruction in study tools each week.
4. Capitalize on opportunities to incorporate study tools into your instruction in all subjects and in all areas of direct instruction in reading (e.g., using the dictionary in various vocabulary instruction lessons).
5. Design instruction so that use of study tools is critical to the objectives of the lesson, and students perceive that mastery of their use is important.

Charts, Tables, and Graphs

For students in the intermediate and middle grades, charts, tables, and graphs are often studied for the first time. Because their methods for presenting or displaying data may be new to students, teachers must provide many examples of different types appropriate to the levels of students. Tables (shown in Figure 9.6) have no pictorial representation.

Graphs and charts can appear in a multitude of display forms and formats. Intermediate-grade students should not be expected to master all of these; however, by the middle grades, they should be able to recognize and use all of the graph formats shown in Figure 9.7. Notice, too, that it is relatively easy to limit the kinds and amounts of information to be presented, as well as the format type.

Figure 9.8 shows the major skill areas and an approximate grade K–6 sequence of steps through the tables and graphs for use as a guideline for instructional decision-making.

Following are some ideas for teaching these important skills:

Have students bring examples of graphs and charts of various kinds. Discuss the range of complexity of these graphic presentations of information.

Figure 9.6   **Samples of tables used to display information. Taken directly from H. M. Hartoonian (Ed.).** *Skill Development in the K–6 Social Studies Program* **(p. 131). Madison, WI: Wisconsin Department of Public Instruction. Reproduced with permission of the Wisconsin Department of Public Instruction.**

Spelling Tests

	1	2	3	4	5
Dora	85	63	94	72	91
Jane	96	78	84	92	80
Tom	72	53	68	65	72
Bob	81	69	74	83	63
Jack	67	73	83	78	82
Ruth	73	66	56	66	74

Per Cent of Students Absent Each Day One Week from Four Junior High Schools in Altown

School	Mon.	Tues.	Wed.	Thurs.	Fri.
A	3	2	1	2	4
B	4	7	3	5	6
C	2	4	1	3	2
D	3	8	4	4	6

Speeds in m.p.h. of Four Airplanes at Six Different Points in a Cross-Country Race

Plane	1	2	3	4	5	6
W	530	530	520	540	550	540
X	550	570	600	560	580	590
Y	470	490	510	500	510	520
Z	560	570	580	590	580	600

Weather Report—January

City	Number of Days	
	Cloudy	**Clear**
Buffalo	22	2
Chicago	15	10
Cincinnati	16	10
Duluth	12	9
Kansas City	13	11

- Ask pairs of students to use one of the tables in the Figure 9.6 to generate as many sentences as they can, summarizing important information that can be inferred from the data provided.
- Find some simple tables and/or graphs in the newspaper (e.g., *U.S.A. Today*) or some other information source. Discuss the information that can be inferred from the table or graph.
- Present students with numerical data. Have them make graphs from the information. This can be done in independent work or as a paired activity. Discuss students' graphs in class, and talk about the differences in the way the information looks in the charts as opposed to numerical listings.

Challenge students to think of as many different visual display methods as possible for one set of data.

Figure 9.7 **Samples of several kinds of graphs. Taken directly from H. M. Hartoonian (Ed.).** *Skill Development in the K–6 Social Studies Program* **(p. 131). Madison, WI: Wisconsin Department of Public Instruction. Reproduced with permission of the Wisconsin Department of Public Instruction.**

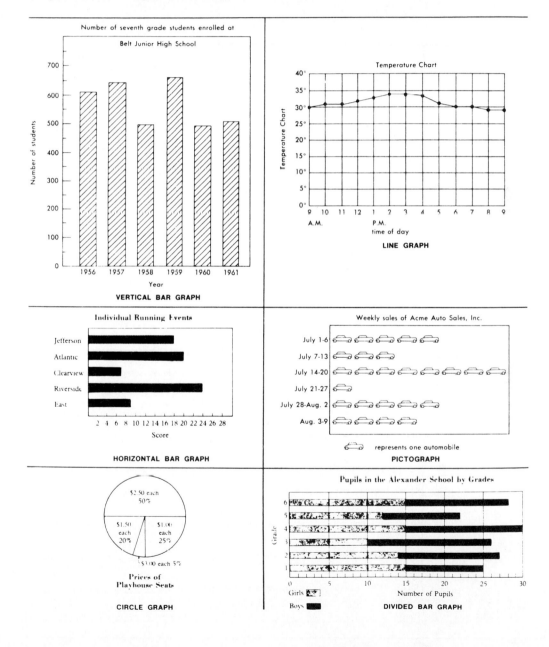

Figure 9.8   Table showing the sequential steps suggested for "accurate interpretation and construction of tables and graphs." Taken directly from H.M. Hartoonian (Ed.). *Skill Development in the K–6 Social Studies Program* (p. 131). Madison, WI: Wisconsin Department of Public Instruction. Reproduced with permission of the Wisconsin Department of Public Instruction.

MAJOR SKILL AREA	TABLES	GRAPHS
ABILITY TO IDENTIFY THE PURPOSE OR TOPIC OR A TABLE OR GRAPH.	1. Locates the title of the table. 2. Identifies the purpose or topic of the table.	1. Locates the title of the graph. 2. Identifies the topic or purpose of the graph through use of the title.
ABILITY TO INTERPRET INFORMATION PRESENTED IN A TABLE OR GRAPH.	3. Locates the vertical columns of the table. 4. Identifies the units used in each vertical column of the table. 5. Locates the horizontal rows of the table. 6. Identifies the units used in each horizontal row of the table. 7. Finds specific facts through proper use of the table columns and rows. 8. Interprets the table to find the most, least, largest, smallest, etc.	3. Locates the vertical axis of the graph. 4. Identifies the units used in the vertical axis of the graph. 5. Locates the horizontal axis of the graph. 6. Identifies the units used in the horizontal axis of the graph. 7. Finds specific facts through proper use of the graph's horizontal and vertical axes. 8. Interprets the graph to find the most, least, largest, smallest, etc.
ABILITY TO DRAW CONCLUSIONS FROM INFORMATION PRESENTED IN A TABLE OR GRAPH.	9. Forms generalizations based on data given in the table. 10. Predicts trends or tendencies that go beyond data given in the table.	9. Forms generalizations based on data given in the graph. 10. Predicts trends or tendencies that go beyond data given in the graph.
ABILITY TO TRANSLATE RAW DATA INTO SIMPLE TABLES OR GRAPHS.	11. Recognizes a table as a method of presenting quantitative data. 12. Recognizes data suitable for table (tabular) presentation. 13. Selects appropriate units for use in presenting data. 14. Translates data into the selected units in order to construct a table. 15. Constructs a table from appropriate raw data.	11. Recognizes a graph as a method of presenting quantitative data. 12. Recognizes data suitable for graphic presentation. 13. Selects appropriate symbolic units for use in presenting data. 14. Translates data into the selected symbolic units in order to construct a graph. 15. Constructs a graph from appropriate raw data.

Maps and Globes

Map and globe skills are important for social studies and for day-to-day life in society. Instructionally, they also represent an excellent opportunity to both develop and use high-level thinking skills. Classifying, seeing part:whole relations, and inferring are among the important thinking skills involved in using maps and globes.

Typical of the kinds of skills and suggested abilities associated with these skills for the elementary grades are shown in Figure 9.9, from the curriculum publication, *Skill Development in the K–6 Social Studies Program* (Hartoonian) of the Wisconsin Department of Public Instruction. The abilities elaborated in the grade column in each of the charts in Figure 9.9 suggest ideas for activities and techniques for teaching map and globe skills.

Here are some other ideas that have worked well with learners:

- Draw fictitious maps of various kinds, make xerographic copies, and ask students to use the maps to answer various questions. Figures 9.10 and 9.11 show how this might be done. Vary this activity by using it sometimes as an individual assignment with students working independently and other times making it a paired or small group project.

Compare different curriculum guides developed by the various state education agencies. Note how information is presented about curriculum through the use of visuals.

Map and globe skills are critical to learning in social studies and for knowledge about our own world. Children should have both reading and hands-on experiences with maps and globes.

Figure 9.9 **Chart of map and globe skills for grades 3–5. Taken directly from H. M. Hartoonian (Ed.),** *Skill Development in the K–6 Social Studies Program* **(p. 131). Madison, WI: Wisconsin Department of Public Instruction. Reproduced with permission of the Wisconsin Department of Public Instruction.**

MAP AND GLOBE SKILLS CHART: GRADE THREE

MAJOR SKILL AREA	EXPLANATION	Grade Three	
DIRECTION	Ability to orient maps and globes. Use of cardinal and inbetween directions.	1. Locates continents, islands, and lakes on the globe or world map with reference to the equator (e.g. north of it or south of it). 2. Shows on a world map or globe that the prime meridian divides the earth into an eastern and western hemisphere. Identify which is which. 3. Uses the north arrow on a map as a direction finder.	4. Locates on a globe and world map the inbetween directions (NE, SE, NW, SW) 5. Constructs a simple school or neighborhood map which is properly oriented to a direction. 6. Tells the cardinal direction of one place from another.
SCALE	Ability to recognize the scale of a map and to compute distances.	1. Expresses time as related to distance: relative time it takes traveling from home to school, to the fire station, to the store, etc. 2. **Recognizes the similarity** between an area first introduced on a globe and the same area shown on a map. 3. Recognizes that cities, states, countries, continents are different sizes.	4. Makes simple large scale maps of a familiar area, classroom, neighborhood, etc. 5. Explains that a globe is a model of earth, but sometimes a map can be more useful than a globe because it can show details and can be folded.
LOCATION	Ability to locate major features, both cultural and natural, in the world. Use of latitude, longtitude, and/or grid systems to identify specific locations.	1. Construct a simple school map locating specific places on it. 2. Locates and identifies the three big oceans: Atlantic, Pacific and Indian. 3. Locates Lake Michigan on a globe or world map.	4. Locates rivers on a map and globe. 5. Calls the earth's largest land areas continents, and the earth's largest water areas oceans. 6. Locates and distinguishes between states and cities on a map of the United States.
SYMBOLS	Ability to correctly interpret dots, lines, lettering, and color on maps, globes, and legends.	1. Interprets legend and identifies capital cities on a population map. 2. Makes maps of simple familiar areas and uses symbols to represent desks, houses etc.	3. Interprets basic map symbols.
COMPARISON AND INFERENCE	Ability to use information to make an intelligent hypothesis which cannot be proved from information on the map itself. Comparison of two or more maps to see relationships, draw conclusions, and form generalizations.	1. Infers from a map or maps why cities are located where they are. 2. Compares symbols on one map to those on another.	

Figure 9.9 *(continued)*

MAP AND GLOBE SKILLS CHART: GRADE FOUR

MAJOR SKILL AREA	EXPLANATION	Grade Four	
DIRECTION	Ability to orient maps and globes. Use of cardinal and inbetween directions.	1. Locates countries, cities, and lakes on a globe or world map with reference to the prime meridian (e.g. east of it or west of it). 2. Locates continents, islands, etc. on globe or world map with reference to whether they are in the eastern or western hemisphere.	3. Orients all maps correctly to the north. 4. Designates specific areas of a country, state or city by accurately using the cardinal and/or inbetween directions. 5. Follow highways on a road map, north-south and east-west. 6. Tells the direction on one place from another.
SCALE	Ability to recognize the scale of a map and to compute distances.	1. Identifies the scale of miles on a map. 2. Estimates, under the guidance of a teacher, distance between places by using the scale of miles on a map. 3. Recognizes that a globe shows a distance, size, and shape more accurately.	4. Recognizes the same map area when drawn to different scale. 5. Understands that large-scale maps show more detail than small-scale maps.
LOCATION	Ability to locate major features, both cultural and natural, in the world. Use of latitude, longtitude, and/or grid systems to identify specific locations.	1. Locates the Arctic and Antarctic Circles, Tropic of Cancer, Tropic of Capricorn and the Equator on a world map or globe. 2. Locates mountains and/or mountain ranges on a map or globe. 3. Defines and locates peninsulas on a map or globe.	4. Locates and distinguishes between continents and countries on a world map or a globe. 5. Defines and locates Temperate and Torrid Zones on a world map or globe. 6. Locates the continents of North and South America on a world map or globe.
SYMBOLS	Ability to correctly interpret dots, lines, lettering, and color on maps, globes, and legends.	1. Reads the titles of particular maps. 2. Interprets map legend for a particular purpose (e.g. the amount of rainfall at a given location, the population of cities, etc.)	3. Identifies and distinguishes between county, state, and national boundary lines. 4. Locates and identifies highways on various maps.
COMPARISON AND INFERENCE	Ability to use information to make an intelligent hypothesis which cannot be proved from information on the map itself. Comparison of two or more maps to see relationships, draw conclusions, and form generalizations.	1. Recognizes that there are many kinds of maps for many uses, and selects the best map for the purpose at hand. 2. Identifies an occupation that requires the use of maps. 3. Understands that the only true representation of the earth is a globe.	4. Realizes that Northern and Southern Hemisphere seasons are opposite. 5. Correlates temperature with latitude and elevation. 6. Translates geographic data into simple bar graphs.

Figure 9.9   *(continued)*

MAP AND GLOBE SKILLS CHART: GRADE FIVE

MAJOR SKILL AREA	EXPLANATION	Grade Five	
DIRECTION	Ability to orient maps and globes. Use of cardinal and inbetween directions.	1. Indicates on a world map a country located in each of the four hemispheres. 2. Shows on a map that lines of latitude run east and west. 3. Shows on a map that lines of longtitude run north and south. 4. Selects two cities on a map and correctly indicates which cardinal or inbetween direction must be followed to get from one city to another.	5. Select places want to visit and locate region of country, state and city they are in. 6. Knowing where N,S,E,W are outside of school bldg., be able to figure out where bldg. or streets are relative to where you are (i.e. if I'm walking south away from school, grocery store is N,S,E,W from me, etc.)
SCALE	Ability to recognize the scale of a map and to compute distances.	1. Estimates distance between places by using the scale of miles on a map. 2. Recognizes that different maps have different scales. 3. Knows that one degree of latitude equals about 70 miles. 4. Explains that lines of latitude are parallel and are sometimes called parallels.	5. Explains that lines of longitude are also called meridians. 6. Realizes that all flat maps distort part of earth they show the larger the surf surface area, the greater the distortion.
LOCATION	Ability to locate major features, both cultural and natural, in the world. Use of latitude, longtitude, and/or grid systems to identify specific locations.	1. Locates and identifies on a globe or world map lines of latitude (parallel) 2. Locates places in the low, middle and high latitudes. 3. Explains that a degree of latitude can be divided into sixty minutes. 4. Locates and identifies on a globe or world map lines of longitude (meridian) 5. Locates and identifies Great Circles on a globe or world map.	6. Identifies time zones of the United States and relates them to longitude. 7. Defines and locates on a map bays, gulfs, and deltas. 8. Locates the continents of Africa and Australia on a world map or globe. 9. Locates and distinguishes between natural-cultural features presented on a map. (e.g. mountains, rivers, cities, highways, etc.)
SYMBOLS	Ability to correctly interpret dots, lines, lettering, and color on maps, globes, and legends.	1. Uses a map legend to identify map title, scale of miles, and symbol meaning. 2. Correctly interprets a land use map, a rainfall map, and a natural vegetation map.	3. Develops the habit of interpreting the map legend before trying to read the map.
COMPARISON AND INFERENCE	Ability to use information to make an intelligent hypothesis which cannot be proved from information on the map itself. Comparison of two or more maps to see relationships, draw conclusions, and form generalizations.	1. Determines from an elevation map the direction in which rivers flow. 2. Interprets a map legend and describes a specific area shown on the map. 3. Compares maps published on different dates and notes differences in population, industries, etc. 4. Translates information derived from maps and globes into bar graphs. 5. Infers from a visual or verbal description of a specific area, where that area might be located on a world map or globe.	6. Explains that the Tropic of Cancer and the Tropic of Capricorn are boundaries for the northern and southern most positions of the sun's vertical rays on the earth. 7. Identifies the approximate elevation of specific cities located on a relief map. 8. Uses the title and general content of a map to determine its purpose. 9. Explains how specific occupations utilize maps. 10. Understands that flat map projections distort the earth's features.

Figure 9.10   Sample worksheet showing the use of maps. Taken directly from M. Klein, G. Lamb, and K. Welch, Teacher's Edition of *Reading Workbook C* of *Think and Write,* © Copyright 1987 by Silver, Burdett & Ginn. Used with permission.

Maps can tell you directions for getting from place to place. There are four main directions: **north, south, east,** and **west.** The direction sign on a map is called a **compass rose.**

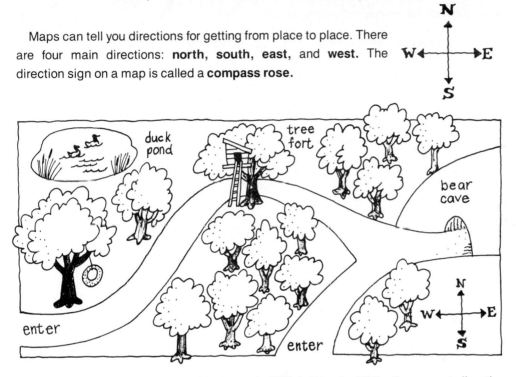

A. Use the map to tell where things are in Willy's Woods. Write the correct direction names.

 NOTICE   Sometimes you need to name two directions to give exact locations: **southwest, southeast, northwest, northeast.**

1. You can enter Willy's Woods on the _____ side.

2. There is another entrance to Willy's Woods on the _____ side.

3. The bear cave is on the _____ side.

4. The tree fort is on the _____ side.

5. The tire swing is on the _____ side.

6. The duck pond is in the _____ corner of the woods.

Figure 9.11   Alternative sample worksheet on map use. Taken directly from M. Klein, G. Lamb, and K. Welch, Teacher's Edition of *Reading Workbook D* of *Think and Write*, © copyright 1987, by Silver, Burdett & Ginn. Used with permission.

Directions and **details** are important in reading a map.

A. Study this map. Then answer the questions.

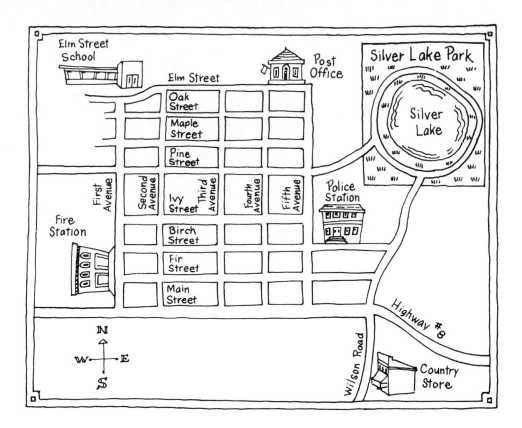

1. Is the Elm Street School on the north or south side of Elm Street? _____

2. What two roads go to Silver Lake Park? _____

3. What direction is Silver Lake Park from the Country Store on Wilson Road? _____

4. What direction is the Post Office from the Country Store? _____

5. What direction is the Police Station from the Fire Station? _____

6. What direction is Elm Street School from the Post Office? _____

- Have students create maps and write questions for the maps, modeled after those in the earlier examples.
- Have students determine which states they would fly over if they left Chicago and flew to Japan. (Teach them to use a piece of string to make a fairly straight line between the two points.)
- Bring actual maps of your city or state to class, and design questions that require students to use the various elements of a map. For example, require them to use the accompanying tables to determine distances between various local landmarks or between various cities on the municipal or state maps, respectively.
- Make copies of national weather maps that appear daily in newspapers, and ask students to use the temperature bands and the color or shading codes to predict the temperature and weather conditions in different parts of the country.
- Prepare an outline map of the United States or another country that students are studying in social studies. Ask them to draw in selected important geographical features (e.g., Mississippi River, Ohio River, Rocky Mountains, Great Lakes). Have students compare their maps in small groups or in pairs.

Ask students to generate additional map-using activities.

Dictionary and Thesaurus: Tools for Word Usage

The **dictionary** is a very complex and often mystifying study tool. It contains a wealth of information beyond word meanings. Even many teachers are unaware that dictionaries are compiled by field linguists who collect thousands and thousands of language samples from people in all walks of life. They then use these samples to find the relative importance of words according to use. Hence, they are not *prescriptive* (i.e., prescribing what words people should use and how they should use them) but *descriptive* (i.e., describing the words people do use and how they do use them) tools. They do not set the standards of language use so much as describe the language that people actually use.

In the elementary grades, students should be introduced to some of the various uses of the dictionary. The following are appropriate at some point in this grade range:

- Different meanings listed for the same word are usually presented in order from the most common literal use to more specialized uses. (Note that this does not necessarily equate with the most important use to the least important!)
- Dictionaries help in knowing how to pronounce words in the most commonly accepted way. Students should know how to use the basic symbols for sound designation and emphasis (e.g., accent marks of primary, secondary, and tertiary emphasis) in order to be able to pronounce words they have not heard before.

Ask students to visit commercial bookstores and their university bookstore. List and describe the number of different resources found in the "Language Reference" section. Most university undergraduate students will find language reference materials they did not know existed.

Ask students to examine an Oxford Unabridged Dictionary: "What information does it contain? How do abridged dictionaries differ from unabridged ones?" Also, have them examine some of the specially designed dictionaries that publishers have produced that are intended to be grade-level appropriate for elementary children.

- Dictionaries show how to *syllabicate* (i.e., divide words into syllables).
- Dictionaries can assist in ascertaining correct and preferred spellings for words.
- Some dictionaries can provide information about the history of a word.

The **thesaurus** is a very helpful tool that can be taught in conjunction with the dictionary. It is also helpful in teaching such technical terms as *antonym, synonym, homophone, homograph,* and *homonym.*

Following are some suggested techniques and activities for teaching the use of both the dictionary and the thesaurus as study tools.

- Have students do word searches for selected key words in a text. Ask them to determine which of the definitions provided is most appropriate for the text. Discuss why the alternative definitions are less so.
- Select words students are not likely to know how to pronounce. After you have instructed them in use of the basic symbol system used in their dictionaries, ask them to look up these words and determine how to pronounce them. Discuss the pronunciations in class.
- Have students indicate points of syllabication for words in a text they are to read. After they have done this, ask them to check their predictions by using the dictionary. Discuss their results.
- Provide students with short passages of text with various adjectives and verbs highlighted. Ask them to use a thesaurus to find better and more expressive words to substitute for these words in the text.
- Have students use the thesaurus when editing various writings that they have done. Discuss why they chose certain words for certain writings.

Encyclopedias

Discuss whether students still consider encyclopedias to be valuable study tools. Explore ways in which encyclopedia formats may be changing in the electronic age.

The encyclopedia is usually the first reference work that elementary children use as a study tool. Because its subject organization and narrative format are pretty clear cut, they can be a useful study tool for introducing students to the concept of research and for showing them how to do it in their school library or resource center.

It is important to remember, however, that there can be considerable difference in difficulty level of encyclopedias. The *Encyclopedia Britannica,* for example, is likely to be too detailed and difficult for many elementary-grade students. An encyclopedia such as *World Book* is less difficult and detailed and is probably a more appropriate beginning resource for some.

After you have carefully demonstrated the nature of the encyclopedia and how it is organized, provide ample practice in its use for your students. Following are some ideas:

- Have students gather additional information about some famous person in history that they have just studied in social studies or science. Ask them to use the encyclopedia and to take notes on the person. Ask them to present informally to the class what they have learned, using their notes.
- Ask students to write brief research papers about a topic they will be studying soon. Use the project as a means of building background knowledge for your students.
- After students have some practice in using reference sources such as the encyclopedia, give them a more demanding task by formulating a question they need to research in order to answer.

  Examples: "Why is bituminous coal (soft coal) less desirable as a fossil fuel for industry?" "Who invented the first automobile? Tell us something about the person."

Card Catalog

The card catalog uses a fairly simple and straightforward system, yet it continues to confuse many learners. The most effective instruction for use of this study skill is to teach its use in a meaningful context in which students have an important reason for knowing how to use it. Here are some ideas that will help you make this instruction productive:

Ask students, "How modern are contemporary elementary school libraries and learning resource centers? How are computers being used, or are they?"

- Provide ample examples. Xerographically reproduce sample card catalog cards for both title and author listings. Explain the placement and role of all the information on the card.
- Provide 3- x 5-inch notecards to students and ask them to prepare card entries for some of their books.
- Ask the learning resource teacher (or librarian) to walk your class through the card catalog in your school and to explain its use.
- Assign paired research projects that require students to use the card catalog and other reference tools.

SUMMARY: OTHER RESOURCES FOR LEARNERS

The study skills and study tools addressed in this chapter only represent basic ones. In some situations, you should be prepared to expand the list of skills and tools to be covered. For example, the computer should be viewed as an important study tool that students should be able to use. Its study skill role will be dictated, to some extent, by the amount and kind of equipment and software the school has. Become familiar with the computer situation in your individual school district as soon as possible, and review the software resources to see which are appropriate and available for your classes.

HIGHLIGHTS

1. Study skills and study tools are both important for the reading program. *Study skills* are those skills important for the reader in order to acquire critical information from different kinds of texts, for different purposes. *Study tools* are the various resources that a literate person must be able to use in acquiring important information.
2. Establishing a study-related mental set and developing a study plan for study are two important steps in the development and use of study skills.
3. Many of the skills and abilities important for effective study are the same as those typically treated as comprehension skills (e.g., self-monitoring, adjusting reading rate, summarizing, paraphrasing).
4. Effective use of graphics and other text adjuncts should be taught as part of the study skills development component in a reading program.
5. Study skills mastery and mastery of study tools are best achieved by teaching them in contexts important to the learners. Subject-matter content and projects can be used to provide a realistic need for study, which increases students' motivation to learn them.

Expect students to talk about lifelong needs for the individual.

Pay more attention to student logic and justification than to the actual skills argued for.

Have groups summarize their critiques for the whole class.

Check the student teachers' questions according to appropriateness for children's cognitive level, as well as for content.

Note how many of these employ graphics or other visuals.

REINFORCEMENT ACTIVITIES

1. Why are study skills important for the reading program?
2. Describe the study skills that are most important. Discuss in class which are the most critical and why.
3. Prepare a lesson plan designed to teach study skills. Share the plan with students in a small group. Discuss the plans and how they might be improved.
4. Prepare a test that you could give to fourth-graders to find out whether they know how to use important basic study skills and/or study tools. Compare your test with those prepared by your colleagues.
5. Briefly describe additional activities you might use to teach important study skills. Explain to the class how you would conduct the lesson.

ADDITIONAL PROJECTS

1. Interview an elementary school teacher to find out how he or she teaches study skills and how important this teacher thinks these skills are. Share the key findings of your interview with your classmates.

2. Visit an elementary school library or resource center. Talk with the director or librarian to find out what kind of curriculum or instruction their school has regarding the use of study skills and study or reference tools.

3. Design a short lesson for teaching a study skill. Teach it to a small group of children in a cooperating school. Ask some of your colleagues to observe the lesson. Discuss the lesson with them after it is completed.

4. Examine a number of basal reading or language arts programs (K–8), and compare their scope and sequence of study skills. Discuss the appropriateness of their grade-level skill assignments in class.

5. Examine curriculum guides prepared by state education agencies. Summarize for others in your class the relative value that they appear to place on study skills and study tools.

REFERENCES

Hartoonian, H. M. (Ed.). *Skill Development in the K–6 Social Studies Program.* Madison, WI: Wisconsin Department of Public Instruction.

Klein, M. (1985). *The Development of Writing in Children: Pre-K Through Grade 8.* Englewood Cliffs, NJ: Prentice-Hall.

Klein, M., Lamb, G., & Welch, K. (1987). *Think & Write: A Reading Workbook.* Boston: Ginn & Co.

Vygotsky, L. (1962). *Thought and Language.* Cambridge: MIT Press.

Vygotsky, L. (1978). *Mind in Society.* Cambridge: Harvard University Press.

ADDITIONAL RESOURCES

Bragstad, B., & Stumpf, S. (1982). *A Guidebook for Teaching Study Skills and Motivation.* Boston: Allyn & Bacon.

Christen, W., Searfoss, L., & Bean, T. (1984). *Study Skills Scope and Sequence Chart: K thru 12.* Dubuque: Kendall/Hunt.

Devine, T. (1981). *Teaching Study Skills.* Boston: Allyn & Bacon.

Graham, K. G., & Robinson, H. A. (1984). *Study Skills Handbook: A Guide for All Teachers.* Newark, NJ: International Reading Association.

MONITORING AND ORGANIZING FOR READING INSTRUCTION AND LEARNING THROUGHOUT THE GRADES

Conductors must give unmistakable and suggestive signals to the orchestra—not choreography to the audience.
George Szell, *Newsweek,* 1963

Prior to reading this chapter, discuss the term *monitoring* and its various ramifications for reading assessment and instruction.

PREVIEW

Effective teaching of reading requires a teacher who knows how to monitor students learning to read and how to organize the classroom for effective reading instruction.

Conceptions of reading and of how the learners' reading ability can be assessed and monitored have changed dramatically since the early 1980s. This chapter focuses on the kind of reading assessment that is designed to be most useful in helping the classroom teacher to teach reading effectively to children. Also, knowing how to structure the classroom learning environment and how to vary the instructional settings and groupings used in teaching reading are important for the teacher of reading. This chapter examines some selected grouping models and offers suggestions for their use in the elementary grades.

FOCUS QUESTIONS

As you read this chapter, keep the following important questions in mind:

1. What is an "Assessment Portfolio," and what role does it play in the reading program?
2. Why is reading ability diagnosis important, and how can I do it in a reasonable and workable way with a class full of children?
3. What are some ways to group for reading instruction?

PART I
SOME PROBLEMS WITH THE MEASUREMENT OF READING ABILITY

DIFFICULTIES AND TRENDS IN THE MEASUREMENT OF READING ABILITY

Measurement of reading performance or ability in learners remains very controversial. Educators often disagree on what it is, why it is done, and what is to be done with the information acquired thereby. In addition to these major disagreements, there are disagreements regarding the meanings of important terms in measurement: *assessment, diagnosis, evaluation.*

Over the years, the standardized test has been the most commonly recognized measure of student performance in reading. The tests are objective (e.g., multiple choice) and are usually broken down into subtests that purport to measure mastery of skills and subskills in decoding, vocabulary, comprehension, and other areas typically associated with reading. The test-taker is generally presented with samples of text and asked to select a correct answer from the multiple options provided.

These tests are standardized, in the sense that they have been developed over many years and used with various populations. Results have been *normed* (i.e., levels of acceptable performance based on average scores derived over the nation and over time are established and used as benchmarks against which individual children's performance is measured).

Recently, these tests have come under considerable attack from many educators (*Educational Leadership,* 1989; Farr & Carey, 1986; Flood & Lapp, 1989):

- Standardized tests are *acontextual* (e.g., the passages of text used to test comprehension or vocabulary, for example, often have little relationship to the interests or background knowledge of the test-taker. Hence, scores are of questionable value.
- Standardized tests are premised on the assumption that reading mastery is largely a function of the sequenced acquisition of skills and subskills, a notion that is now largely rejected within the reading education profession.
- Standardized test scores are culturally, socially, and/or economically biased in favor of particular population groups more likely to have experienced the kinds of things assumed as necessary background knowledge for the tests.

Ask students to address the problems of assessing reading abilities, based on their own personal experiences as students in reading classes or in classes heavily dependent on reading ability.

Most undergraduate students will have had little experience with the technicalities of standardized and criterion-referenced testing at this point in their teacher education. You may wish to spend some time on basic concepts and terminology and consider out-of-class projects examining various tests and test types.

- Standardized test scores are often used only for political or publicity purposes to show the public how well or how poorly given schools or given school districts are doing. Few of the data are used by classroom teachers for diagnostic or application purposes in reading instruction.
- Evaluation of the test data, even when analyzed and summarized by the testing company, is not easy and often seems added on to an already enormous amount of paper reporting responsibilities faced by the classroom teacher.

Others, however, contend that the standardized test has an important role to play in helping schools monitor their students' reading performance and thus helping districts in making policy and determining curriculum, even if the direct classroom use is not always there.

Some suggest that a criterion-referenced test is the best option for testing because the students' performance is measured against particular objectives of the reading program and not against some nationally normed score. Most basal reading programs include such tests, which are designed to test selected important objectives and skills in their scope and sequence. The format and content of criterion-referenced tests are quite similar to those of standardized tests. However, these tests are custom-built for a particular reading program, so they purport to be more accurate and fairer indicators of actual reading development in students.

School districts vary in how they use such tests—from not at all to total evaluation of program and reading performance in students.

The matter is further complicated since United States national assessments began at the end of the 1960s. The original purposes of the first national assessments were altruistic. Voters, tax-payers, schools, and school districts wanted a general picture of how they were doing in relation to the rest of the nation in terms of education. Also, educators saw a chance to influence legislation at the national and state levels to provide schools with necessary resources and funding, at least partly derived from information provided in the assessments.

Since its implementation, however, educators have given mixed reviews to these assessments. Also, data from these assessments seldom reach the classroom where the teacher of reading works with learners. Teachers' and learners' particular individual needs are different from those targeted by these assessments.

SOME CHANGES IN THE MEASUREMENT OF READING ABILITY

Some important changes have taken place, and others are still occurring, which offer the classroom reading teacher practical assistance. Educators

---

Almost all states now conduct statewide reading and writing assessments. For example, with the publication of this text, the state of Illinois has just completed a writing assessment model for use in that state's assessment program. Most state education agencies have information available on their literacy assessment program. It could be helpful to obtain some of these and discuss their relationship to classroom assessment.

Assessment issues are addressed regularly in professional journals such as *The Reading Teacher*. Ask students to review those that are usually nontechnical in nature and to discuss them in class.

are reconceptualizing reading assessment in a number of ways, based on more contemporary views of the reading process (*Educational Leadership*, 1989). New assessment models for state and national use are offering ideas for considering performance only in light of what the individual learner brings to the act in background knowledge and attitude. Further, newer assessment models are attempting to provide a context that is relevant for the test-taker.

Perhaps the most important new direction in reading assessment, however, is the trend toward an assessment portfolio for use by the classroom teacher.

PART II
USE OF THE READING ASSESSMENT PORTFOLIO

OVERVIEW

An *assessment portfolio* is a collection of literacy performance measures and indicators that a teacher accumulates and maintains for each child. Common elements found in a typical assessment portfolio are the following:

- Norm-referenced and criterion-referenced scores from tests used in the school system
- Informal measures (e.g., cloze test scores and informal reading inventory [IRI] scores)
- Writing samples
- Teacher grades and evaluations of reading and writing
- Student learning contracts and self-assessments
- Samples of reading materials used for instruction with this student

Uses for the assessment portfolio include the following:

- To provide a developmental picture of the child's literacy growth across the school year
- To provide a diagnostic tool for individualizing reading instruction for each student in a class
- To provide a data base for conferencing with students regarding their reading
- To provide a data base for discussing children's progress with their parents
- To provide a reading performance information base for school administrators and supervisors

Ask students, "Are there other roles? How important are the ones listed here?"

HOW TO SET UP AND USE AN ASSESSMENT PORTFOLIO

You might want to point out the variations that exist in different school districts and, often, in different schools within those districts. For example, some schools using basals adhere to the criterion-referenced tests accompanying the program as the basis for their assessment program. Others rely only on standardized tests of one sort or another. Yet others rely on the individual assessments designed by the school site staff or by the individual classroom teacher.

Take the following steps:

1. At the beginning of the school year, share with students, parents, and administrators your plan for the portfolio. Successful use of the information will, at least partly, depend on all parties knowing what it is and how it will help them.

   Begin by explaining to your students the importance of this information for their reading development. Discuss the portfolio in the context of an instructional assist rather than in terms of a collection of tests to see how well or how poorly they are doing.

2. Initially, label at least one file folder for each student, and designate an assessment portfolio file drawer. Eventually, each student will have several file folders, one for each component of the portfolio. However, this segregation is not essential at the very beginning of the school year.

3. Develop a yearlong plan for use of the portfolio. Include as much of the following as you can, with information you have available:

   a. Dates, times, and places for individual conferences with students. These regularly scheduled conferences do not preclude those additional meetings you have with students based on need or schedule changes.

   b. Dates, times, and places for meetings with parents and an agenda outline of possible things to discuss with them. Some of these times should also include students.

   c. Regular dates and times for meeting with supervisors and/or the building principal, to discuss student progress.

HOW TO GENERATE ASSESSMENT PORTFOLIO DATA

Norm-Referenced and Criterion-Referenced Test Data

A useful activity might be to develop some contrived test score data on a fictitious classroom and ask students to discuss the reading profile that might be inferred from the data and the strengths and limitations of any inferences they make.

Test data from school-administered standardized tests may be the first data you have in the fall if tests were given the previous spring. If you are using a basal reading program with accompanying assessment criterion-referenced tests, you will be developing data from these tests fairly early in the year if your district requires their substantive use. If you have a choice, however, you may prefer to use only a selection of the tests provided. Many of the reading programs provide assessment tests that are far more detailed in number and individual test volume than most teachers need.

If the tests are optional, examine the tests for your grade level, and decide how valuable the information will be to you. Plan to use them selectively, based on the skills and objectives you want tested and the amount of time you choose to use for this kind of testing.

Informal Measures

Ongoing Teacher Monitoring

The most important and useful informal measures of reading and writing performance used by classroom teachers are those obtained through on-going personal monitoring of student behavior and literacy performance. There is no set body of information you can study or memorize that will enable you to do this, but you will learn it nonetheless, as a result of (a) your education and training, (b) your knowledge of the reading and writing processes, (c) your sensitivity to language and its use, (d) your knowledge of child development and literacy acquisition and growth, and (e) your experience with children and your maturity as a professional. Some of this you already have as you begin teaching. Much of the ability to maintain an ongoing personal monitoring of children in acts of literacy will come. Count on it.

Ask students to visit elementary classrooms and observe student performance informally. Have them discuss their observations with the classroom teacher and compare their conclusions with the teacher and among themselves.

Initially, however, you can help its development by consciously observing children as they (a) read silently, (b) write, and (c) engage in using oral language.

Observe Children as They Read Silently Do they read word by word? Do they need to point to individual words with their fingers as they read? How often can you see physical eye movements—That is, how much print do they appear to be taking in with a single glance before moving their eyes to new groups of print? What is their attention span—For example, do they tire or bore with the reading act more quickly than their peers? When children have free time, do they elect to read? What kinds of materials do these children prefer to read when allowed free choice? What kinds of facial expressions occur during their reading (e.g., any smiling, frowning, or signs of emotional involvement with the text)?

Observe Children as They Write Do they seem comfortable with writing materials? Are these children eager to write? Indifferent? Fearful? Resentful? How do the children approach the writing act (e.g., do they begin immediately to produce narrative? make notes? outline?)? Do the children adjust their approach to the writing act according to the subject, audience, and/or purpose of the writing? How do the children respond to feedback from others? How do they feel about sharing the writing? While writing, do the children generate bursts of syntax or ideas between pauses, or do they seem to struggle with one word at a time? Do these children opt to write in their free time or on their own? Do they voluntarily find ways to tie reading and writing together?

Observe Children Engaged in Oral Language Use Do the children seem to look forward to talking, especially about their reading and writing? How well do these children function in different conversational contexts (i.e., in pairs [dialogue], in speaking to multiple others informally [monologue], in formal presentations to large groups [soliloquy])? Pay attention to children's syntax when they speak. For example, do the children overrely on generalities such as pronominal reference or do they specify and elaborate with details in clauses and embedded phrases? How logical are the arguments or persuasive language presentations? How well organized are the children's thoughts when speaking? What kind of vocabulary do the children use? Is the vocabulary and syntax adjusted to the audience and purpose of the talk?

As you observe the children throughout the day in these various literacy contexts, make mental notes. As soon as convenient, jot down notes and put them in the portfolios. Periodically, go through your notes that have been collected over time in the portfolio; organize, consolidate, and synthesize the notes so that they can be used for reference in conferencing with various audiences throughout the year.

Informal Reading Inventory (IRI)

An IRI is an individually administered reading test. It is designed to take a short time and give a quick general picture of the child's reading ability. If time is taken to do a more detailed analysis of the oral reading by the learner, additional diagnostic information can be obtained. Many educators and reading researchers suggest that the ability to administer the IRI is one of the more important skills a reading teacher must have (Johns, 1985). Information gathered from an IRI can be useful for general monitoring purposes, for adjusting teaching in large-group contexts, and for placing students into small groups for specialized reading instruction focus.

Although IRIs are available commercially, they can be easily constructed and custom designed for your teaching situation because you can use the actual text that your students are expected to be able to read.

To construct an IRI, follow these steps:

1. Choose a representative passage of text you think the student should be able to read. Duplicate a 100- to 200-word section of the passage. This can be chosen from a basal reading series, a trade book, or a content-area textbook. If you use a passage of text from any of these sources, you may wish to check the readability of the

Point out the range of IRIs that are out there—ranging from brief, very simplified inventories to extremely comprehensive, complex ones. Discuss the advantages and disadvantages of each.

Discuss what the advent of computers means for doing things such as readability checks. You also might wish to point out that states that have "state textbook adoption policies" typically require a grade range in basal text readabilities, which are often two grade levels above and below the grade level of focus. Learner verification reports should be available from the commercial publishers for each of their basal reading programs. Ask for copies from sales representatives.

passage in order to more accurately estimate the reading level. Basal reading programs have all been "readabilitied." However, because they try to include text within a grade range that might run two grades or more above and below the actual grade level for which the text is intended, you will still need to check the readability to get a feel for the particular text passage you are using. Although there are a number of different readability formulas available for use, most of them rely heavily on sentence length and the number of polysyllabic words in the text to determine grade-level difficulty. One of the more commonly used is the Fry graph. It is presented in Figure 10.1. The Fog Index is an acceptable alternative readability measure if you prefer. It is presented here, following the directions for the Fry graph.

2. Prepare five or more comprehension questions for the text passage. Remember to write questions that require the student to determine cause–effect or other relationships (e.g., part:whole, compare–contrast) and/or to infer the main idea. Try to avoid questions that require short "yes/no" kinds of answers or answers that are too long and convoluted. Although you can include memory-level questions, limit them, and tie them to information that is critical to inferring a key idea or a main theme of the text.

Two Versions Of IRI   Two different IRI versions are considered here. The first, the simplified IRI, is the shorter of the two and is designed to provide more general information and an overall reading ability picture for the teacher. Although it can provide some specific information about the student's reading vocabulary knowledge and reading comprehension abilities, it is relatively weak as a diagnostic tool.

A second version, the full IRI, includes a more detailed analysis of oral reading miscues for diagnostic purposes.

Simplified IRI   To administer the IRI, follow these steps:

1. Establish a positive comfortable environment. Choose a quiet pleasant place, if possible, at which to administer the IRI.
2. Explain to the student the purpose and nature of the IRI. Make sure the student knows everything that is going to take place, what he or she is expected to do, and what you will be doing during the IRI.
3. Orally provide a context for the passage of text to be read (e.g., tell what it is taken from, the main idea of the general content and thesis of the larger text from which the passage is taken).
4. Have the student read the passage silently.
5. Orally ask the student the questions. Provide prompts and additional information as required to assist the student.

Requiring students in reading methods classes to administer one or more IRIs is an excellent way to provide a practical experience with instructional implications for the prospective teacher while she or he does not have to worry about the complexities of managing a large number of students.

Figure 10.1   **The Fry graph for checking the readability of a given text passage. Fry, E.B. (1968). A readability formula that saves time. *Journal of Reading*, 11, 513–516, 575–578.**

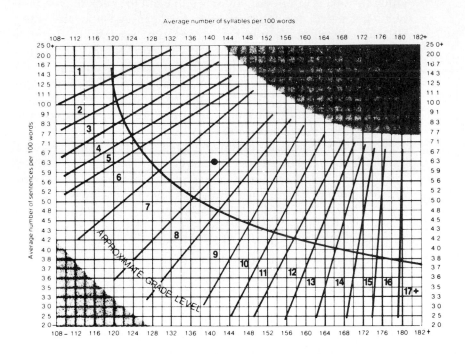

Directions for Using the Fry Readability Graph

1. Select three one-hundred word passages from near the beginning, middle and end of the book. Skip all proper nouns.
2. Count the total number of sentences in each hundred-word passage (estimating to the nearest tenth of a sentence). Average these three numbers.
3. Count the total number of syllables in each hundred-word sample. There is a syllable for each vowel sound; for example: cat (1), blackbird (2), continental (4). Don't be fooled by word size; for example: polio (3), through (1). Endings such as -y, -ed, -el, -le, usually make a syllable, for example: ready (2), bottle (2). It may be convenient to count every syllable over one in each word and add 100. Average the total number of syllables for the three samples.
4. Plot on the graph the average number of sentences per hundred words and the average number of syllables per hundred words. Most plot points fall near the heavy curved line. Perpendicular lines mark off approximate grade level areas.

Example

	Sentences/100 Words	Syllables/100 Words
100 word sample, page 5	9.1	122
100 word sample, page 89	8.5	140
100 word sample, page 160	7.0	129
	3) 24.6	3) 391
Average	8.2	130

Plotting these averages on the graph, we find they fall in the fifth-grade area; thus the book is about the fifth-grade difficulty level. If great variability is encountered either in sentence length or in the syllable count for the three selections, then randomly select several more passages, and average them in before plotting.

Fog Index

The Fog index is a measuring technique that finds the approximate grade level of the vocabulary in the book. To find the readability of a book,

1. Select any 100-word section in the book. Count the number of sentences in the 100-word group. Stop the sentence count with the sentence that ends nearest the 100 word count. Divide the total number of words in the passage by the number of sentences. This gives the average sentence length of the passage.
2. Count the number of words of three syllables or more per 100 words. Do not count the following words: if capitalized (i.e., proper nouns), if they are combinations of short easy words (such as *butterfly* and *bookkeeper*), or if they are verb forms that are made of three syllables (such as *created*).
3. Add the two factors: the average sentence length plus the number of words of 3 syllables.
    Multiply the sum by 0.4.
    The result is the approximate reading grade level of the material.

Note: The Fog index indicates reading level, not intelligence level.

Example

    Hans Brinker by Mary Mapes Dodge
        6 sentences in 100 words: average number of words per sentence 16.6.
        Number of 3 or more syllable words: 5.
        Total of 2 factors: 21.6.
        Multiply by 0.4; result is 8.6 reading grade level.

    The Grapes of Wrath by John Steinbeck
        8 sentences in 100 words: average number of words per sentence 12.2.
        Number of 3 or more syllable words: 0.
        Total of 2 factors: 12.2.
        Multiply by 0.4; result is 4.8 reading grade level.

Table 10.1 Betts's Criteria for Determining Reading Levels

Reading level	Behavioral characteristics commonly observed	Word recognition	Comprehension
Independent	Reads easily; comprehends fully; displays confidence; shows high interest	99 percent accuracy, or 1 error per 100 words	90 percent or greater accuracy
Instructional	Reads somewhat smoothly, occasionally word-by-word; understands and is challenged but not overwhelmed by the material; may seek help	95 percent accuracy, or 5 errors per 100 words	75 to 89 percent accuracy
Frustration	Often refuses to read or continue reading; lacks expression during oral reading; moves lips or points during silent reading. Lacks understanding of material	90 percent accuracy or less: 10 or more miscues per 100 words	Less than 50 percent accuracy
Capacity	Understands and is able to discuss material		75 percent accuracy or better

6. Make written and/or mental notes about student strengths and weaknesses in answering the questions.

Full IRI

1. Follow Steps 1–3 from the simplified IRI.
2. Have the student read the passage orally. During the reading, note the student's reading *miscues*,[1] such as mispronunciations, omissions, and substitutes for words. (Note the guide for analyzing oral reading miscues to follow in Table 10.1.)
3. Determine the student's reading level with a criteria set such as the Betts criteria (1946) (see Table 10.1).
4. Prepare a written diagnosis and a proposed plan for improving student reading in areas where there is need.

[1]K. Goodman (1973) asserts that the term *reading error* is negatively loaded and inappropriate as a description of reading behavior. Even very proficient readers make so-called errors by leaving out words or substituting similar words when they read. However, these miscues are minor and do not detract from the intended meaning of the text. It is only the more serious miscues, which detract from text understanding, that are important. Teachers need to be able to distinguish between minor miscues and major miscues.

Perhaps a bit of history of miscue analysis would be valuable here. Goodman's initial work that received public attention dates back to the 1970s. His work and the work of Frank Smith coincided to some extent, and both appeared at a time when management-by-objectives and applications of systems approaches were being espoused for reading instruction.

Doing an Oral Reading Analysis for a Full IRI There are a number of different systems for noting, categorizing, and interpreting oral reading miscues. One of the best known was developed by Goodman and Burke (1972). Their system is designed to answer four important questions:

1. Does the miscue change the meaning of the text? For example, a reader might substitute *big* for *large* or *little* for *small* without dramatically affecting the meaning of the text. However, substituting *quick* for *slow* or *trial* for *timber* would more likely be unacceptable miscues.
2. Does the miscue sound like language should? Substituting an article such as *the* for a verb such as *running* or using a preposition such as *of* in place of the noun *girl* would result in ungrammatical language. Hence, they would be unacceptable.
3. Do the miscue and the text word look and sound alike? For example, *familiar* and *family* look a lot alike. *Contempt* and *condemn* look similar also. *In* and *remember* do not.
4. Was an attempt made to self-correct the miscue? It is quite natural for any reader to stumble briefly while reading orally. Most of us will self-correct our brief stumble if it is important to the meaning of the text. Otherwise, we often must continue on with our reading of the text.

Discuss ways to simplify further the miscue analysis model presented here.

A useful oral reading analysis system should include examination of (a) syntactic miscues (grammar factors), (b) semantic miscues (word/vocabulary factors), and (c) graphophonemic miscues (letter–sound correspondence factors). Further, because the reading is being done orally, the teacher cannot make extensive notes and needs a shorthand or coding system in order to record the miscues.

The system presented in Figures 10.2 and 10.3 is a simplified modification of the earlier miscue analysis system of Goodman and Burke (1972).

As the student reads, the teacher makes the appropriate notations on a copy of the text being read, using a code such as the following:

- A circled *c* = self-corrected by the reader
- A line through a word or word group, with a different word or word group written over the original = new word or word group is substituted for the words ruled out in the original text
- A circled word = omitted in the reading
- An encircled *uc* = remains uncorrected by the reader

Using this system, the notated text and summarizing chart enable you both to categorize miscue by type and quantify miscue types by number. These are only a starting point for evaluation, however. As the teacher, you must make professional qualitative judgments about the relative seriousness of the miscues. Using the four questions of Goodman and Burke as criteria, you must decide whether the miscues are minor and,

Figure 10.2 A sample miscue worksheet, for use with the miscue chart, based on the miscue model by K. Goodman, Y. Goodman, and C. Burke among others.

```
                   MISCUE WORKSHEET

        The Name of the Tree


               Once upon a time, in a faraway country,
                        ① music              ② tree
        there grew a beautiful magic tree full of ripe,
                             ③
        golden fruit.  There was (enough) fruit to feed all

        the people in the country.  But the people could
                          ④ a        ⑤ that
        not get the fruit from the tree, for they did not

        know the tree's name.  And until someone said the
     ① JK 2.music's
           1.music
          magic name, the fruit would not fall down from the
                                    Ⓐ 2.no matter ⑥
                                      1.no matter
        tree, and no one could pick it, no matter how hard
     ⑦ you ⑧ put ⑨
        he pulled.
          2.So the people stood
     ⑩ C 1.So the people pushed
               So the people stood under the tree and looked
                             ⑪ any
        up at the beautiful, ripe fruit they could not eat.
              ⑫ the      ⑬ Let's use sense
        At last, a wise man said, "Let us send someone to
                             Ⓤ Ⓙ 2.choose
        the King of the next country.  He will (surely) know
                                         ① music.
        the name of the tree because he knows magic."
                              ⑭ that's different
               "Yes!" the people cried.  And they decided to
        2.sent cats to the king.
     ⑮ 1.sent cats
        send Cat to the King. 2.say
                        ⑯ JK 1.say cats ⑰
               "I will go," (said) Cat (bravely,) and he set out

        to the place where the King of the next country

        lived.  He ran almost all the way.
```

Figure 10.3   Sample miscue chart, for use with the miscue worksheet, based on the miscue model by K. Goodman, Y. Goodman, and C. Burke among others.

Story	Student's Name						
# of Miscues	Text	Student	Sound Graphic	Gram-matical	Mean-ing	Self Corr	Repeated Miscues
1							
2							
3							
4							
5							
6							
7							
8							
9							
10							
11							
12							
13							
14							
15							
16							
17							
18							
19							
20							
21							
22							
23							
24							
25							
	Total of +'s						

therefore, not worthy of focused attention or whether they are serious enough to warrant your instructional attention. In addition to the four question guidelines, look for patterns and regularities in the students' miscue.

Also, administration of the full version of the IRI requires practice to ensure accuracy and valid data. Further, the IRI needs to be repeated over time, especially for students with reading difficulties, in order to monitor their progress and to determine appropriate instructional steps.

The Cloze Procedure

The *cloze procedure* is an easily designed and administered informal measure of reading. Developed initially by Wilson Taylor (1953), cloze was intended to be used to determine the readability of given text for learners. It was converted over the years to measure instead the reading ability of the reader, assuming that the text is important enough and appropriate for reading by the reader. Cloze has also come to be used as an instructional tool for teaching the use of context clues, for development of reading vocabulary, and for other concepts and skills, such as distinguishing between denotation and connotation in word use. (Note the discussion in Chapter 8 on reading vocabulary.)

The cloze procedure became quite controversial in the late 1960s and 1970s when state assessment of reading became popular. The cloze procedure was offered as one model for assessing reading performance by some reading authorities. This generated considerable discussion about its validity in such a role.

Cloze Procedure Construction The cloze passage can be constructed by doing the following:

1. Select a reading passage that is at least 60 words long and preferably even somewhat longer.
2. Leave the first sentence intact, and then choose a number randomly between 1 and 10, and delete the word.
3. Thereafter, delete every fifth word, and type in a 15-space blank line for each word deleted.

Cloze Procedure Administration Administration of the cloze procedure should be done as follows:

1. Indicate to students the purpose of the cloze procedure and what will be done with the data provided by it.
2. Tell students that they are not to use their books or any other materials while doing the cloze procedure.
3. Provide background information about the passage of text the students will be using: where it is from, what it is about, what kind of information preceded and what will follow it, what kind of text it is and what its purpose is. If the text is nonfiction content-area text (e.g., social studies), type the chapter title, adjuncts, heading, subheadings or whatever text adjunct information in the original that will help the students to see a context for the passage.
4. Allow as much time as students need to complete the cloze procedure.

Cloze Procedure Scoring and Interpretation   Score by doing the following:

a. Count as correct only exact correct words supplied by the students. Do not count synonyms even though they function satisfactorily in the text.

b. Compute the percentage of correct words for each student.

c. Record the percentage scores with the text passage, the text source, and the date of test administration, and file that record in the portfolio.

Interpret the score by using these guidelines:

- Independent Reading Level—A score of 65% or higher indicates that the student reads well enough to read this material independently.

- Instructional Reading Level—A score of 33% to 64% indicates that the student reads this text well enough to use it during instruction. It may be challenging, but doable.

- Frustration Reading Level—A score of less than 33% suggests that the material is too difficult for the student to comprehend effectively enough. The student will need substantially more reading instruction before this level of text can be read well enough for instructional purposes.

Writing Samples

The assessment portfolio should also include writing samples by students.

Compiling Writing Samples   One sample for each month of school is a good general rule of thumb. Also, expository writing samples should be predominant. Expository text enables teachers to make judgments about students' organization, syntax, and other important writing skills more objectively than is possible with narrative text or creative writing of various kinds. Thus, the teacher will be able to articulate the condition and development of the writing more easily with students and parents.

Scoring Writing Samples   Writing samples should include three types of evaluation: (1) holistic, (2) feature-analytic, and (3) syntactic.

Holistic Evaluation   You should give the writing sample an overall numerical score using a 1–4 scale: 1 for low, 4 for high, 2–3 for average. Write important comments about strengths and needs in the writing. When assigning the number score, consider the time of year, the grade level, and the hypothetically "typical" paper that an "average" student might produce as your benchmark.

Feature-Analysis Evaluation   Feature analysis requires you to identify specific features of the writing on which you wish to focus (e.g., organi-

Decisions about how many writing samples and what kinds of writing samples to include in an assessment portfolio should be made only after considering a number of factors, particularly, "What information do I want?" Perhaps expository, narrative, poetic, and dramatic writing samples should be maintained for a more comprehensive picture. However, portfolios can demand a great deal of teacher time and effort in a class of 25 to 35 children if a number of information types are also included.

Ask students to examine a variety of analytic scales and compare them for content and usefulness.

Table 10.2   Analytic Scale

Name _____ Date _____

	Low		Middle		High
I. General qualities					
A. Organization	2	4	6	8	10
B. Cohesion	2	4	6	8	10
C. Voice	2	4	6	8	10
D. Development	2	4	6	8	10
II. Specific qualities					
A. Grammar	2	4	6	8	10
B. Usage	2	4	6	8	10
C. Punctuation	2	4	6	8	10
D. Spelling	2	4	6	8	10
E. Vocabulary choice	2	4	6	8	10

Total _____

zation, thesis development, main idea statement, use of transition devices, support of main idea with relevant detail). A numerical scoring system should be developed similar to that used for the holistic scoring. Table 10.2 shows a sample analytic scale chart.

Focused feedback is a method of focusing attention on particular features of a student's writing over time in order to concentrate instruction where it is most needed. An assessment portfolio that includes feature analysis allows you to do this more effectively. It also provides some insight into text areas where students are more likely to have reading difficulties. Patterns in writing performance and in IRI results can be helpful in diagnosing and designing compensatory instruction.

T-Unit (Syntactic) Analysis T-unit stands for terminal unit and was introduced as a measure of syntactic complexity by Kellogg Hunt (1965). A T-unit is any independent clause and embedded or attached dependent clauses (relative and/or subordinate clauses). Hunt computed the number of words-per-T-unit (WPTU) at different grade levels. His techniques have been used enough over the years to establish WPTU averages at various grade levels. These can serve as general indicators of students' syntactic complexity generation abilities.

Following are computation guidelines and benchmark WPTUs you can use at various grade levels:

T-Unit Count Rules

1. A T-unit is an independent clause *plus* all attached or embedded dependent clauses (i.e., relative clauses and/or subordinate clauses). Relative clauses are introduced by relative pronouns (e.g., who, which and that—"John is the boy *who left the game.*"). Subordinate clauses are introduced by subordinating conjunctions (e.g., if, after, before, because, since—"John left the game *because he was ill.*"). Hence, the sentence "John, who is my cousin, left the game because he was ill" consists of an independent clause ("John left the game"), an embedded relative clause ("who is my cousin"), and an attached subordinate clause ("because he was ill"). The sentence consists of one T-unit. "John is my friend, and John left the game, and John was ill" consists of three independent clauses conjoined by the coordinating conjunction *and.* Therefore, it contains three T-units.

2. Sentence fragments with single words missing are counted as T-units with the missing word supplied. An example would be "The boy (*left*) the game." If you cannot make the fragment into a sentence with only one word—"A man (had) (hit) the ball"— then the entire fragment is just deleted from computation, and the words are not counted.

3. Contractions are counted as two words in computation.

4. Unintelligible word strings or ungrammatical units that do not reflect meaning are discarded.

5. To compute WPTU,
   a. Select an expository writing sample by a student. (Do not use narrative writing that contains dialogue or other forms of creative writing.)
   b. Count the number of T-units in the sample.
   c. Count the total number of words in the sample, following the preceding guidelines.
   d. Divide the number of T-units into the total number of words in the sample to arrive at the WPTU. Carry the division into the tenths.

	4th grade	8th grade	12th grade
Hunt-based norms for WPTU—	8.60	11.50	14.40

Point out that the WPTU figures for 12th graders are likely to be higher than those for adults who are not involved in careers or activities requiring writing. Hunt's figures for adults (not included here) were obtained by analyzing published articles in upper-scale magazines and journals. Hence, they probably are not realistic measures of typical adult writing.

Compute WPTUs in each of the writing samples from each student over the year, and collect the analyzed samples in their assessment portfolios. These are excellent quantification measures to show progress in the grammatical complexity of student writing.

Student Self-Assessments

Student Learning Contracts Perhaps the most important component in the assessment portfolio, as far as learning is concerned, is the component for which individual students are responsible. Throughout this book, the authors have emphasized the importance of learners developing self-monitoring abilities, self-analysis skills, and skills in self-criticism (and self-appreciation) regarding literacy behaviors. Conscious attention to personal responsibilities in developing and maintaining the assessment portfolio is another important way that students can learn critical self-monitoring skills. The following form could be adapted to your students' needs and abilities, to aid students in setting objectives, to aid in self-monitoring.

Hello! My name is _____

Today is _____

What I will do today:

Reading:

Writing:

Social studies:

Other:

Teacher Signature: _____

Figure 10.4 illustrates an alternative or a complement, which can be used for reflective self-monitoring at the end of the school day.

A valuable part of self-evaluation is the *student learning contract*. This is a written contract negotiated between the student and the teacher. It indicates what both perceive to be reasonable goals and objectives for the student in reading and reading-related areas. The contract represents an opportunity for task-oriented student–teacher conferences. The contracts can be used as part of your regular conferencing with students, using the assessment portfolio data.

Figure 10.4   Sample self-monitoring worksheet, used for periodic student self-evaluation.

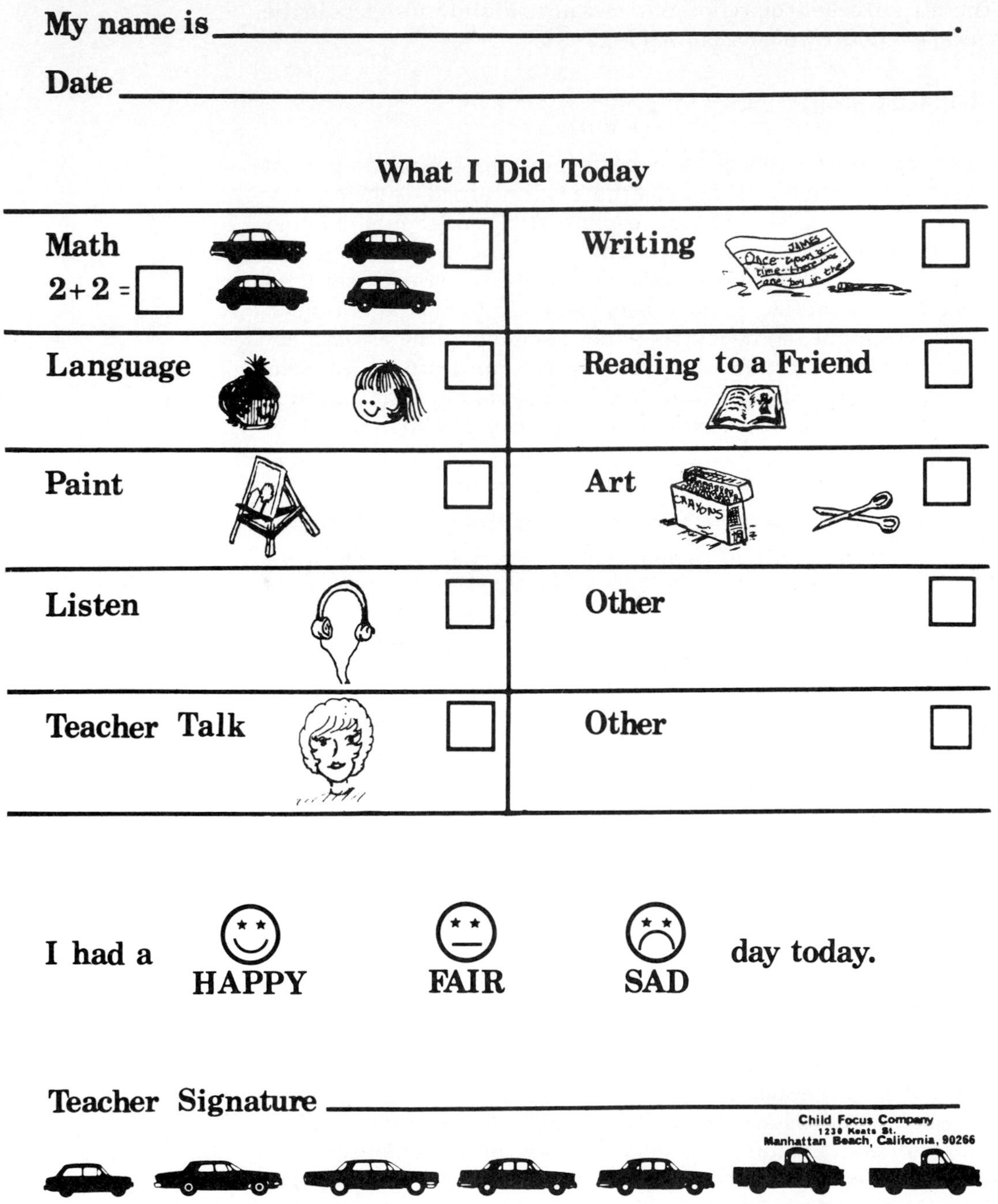

My name is _____ .

Date _____

What I Did Today

Math 2+2 = ☐		☐	**Writing**	☐
Language	☐	**Reading to a Friend**	☐
Paint	☐	**Art**	☐
Listen	☐	**Other**	☐
Teacher Talk	☐	**Other**	☐

I had a   **HAPPY**   **FAIR**   **SAD**   day today.

Teacher Signature _____

Child Focus Company
1238 Keats St.
Manhattan Beach, California, 90266

Figures 10.5 and 10.6 show examples of learning contracts you may wish to consider. You may prefer to design your own or to modify one of these. The important thing is to have something that can be a concrete representation of student–teacher articulation.

Have students search for various kinds of learning contracts in commercially developed materials.

Student Free Reading Log Students should maintain a reading log of their independent voluntary or free reading. Prepare a model form that you can duplicate, making multiple copies for each student. The form can be as simple as a listing of books with author, title, and date reading was completed. More detailed forms call for book review information (e.g., rate the quality of the book, write a brief summary of the book plot, identify the strengths and/or weaknesses). Because this represents reading that is not required of students, you probably should keep this element as brief and easy to do as possible. The following example offers a form you can modify to suit your and your students' needs.

Reading

My name is _____

Today is _____

A story I want to read today is _____

How did you like the story? _____

Tell about the story:

_____

_____

_____

Please draw a picture about someone or something in your story.

What would you like to read next?

_____

Self-Assessment Progress Forms Student self-assessment of learning progress can be effective as a part of the assessment portfolio (Wixson, et al., 1984). The format of this progress report can vary. You can design a simple form with questions or guideline statements the student can self-assess with. Figure 10.7 shows a format that could be used even with young children. With older children, you can simply ask students periodically to write brief self-assessments of their learning. They should indicate the areas where they perceive themselves to be strong and where they need to improve. In conferences, plans for improving weaknesses can be articulated and structured into the learning contract to make it an ongoing

Spend some time discussing why self-assessment is important for learning and how children can be encouraged to become objective self-assessors.

Figure 10.5   Sample learning contract that can be used for student–teacher conferences.

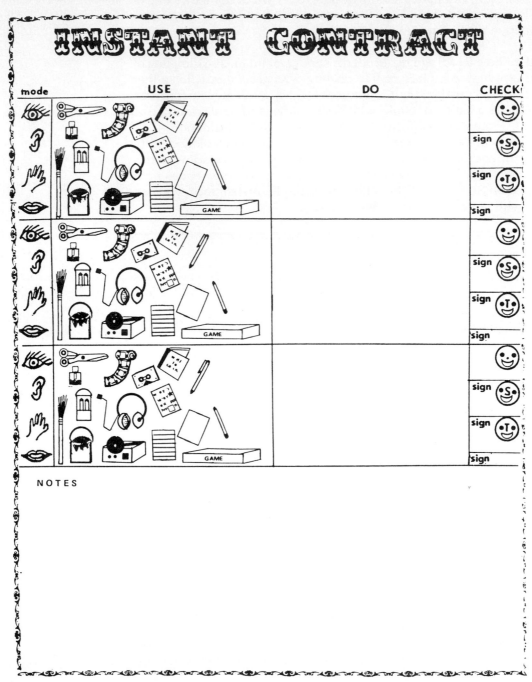

Figure 10.6   Sample learning contract, emphasizing reading and writing, for use in student–teacher conferences and assessment portfolios.

My name is _____.

Reading & Writing Contract

	Mon.	Tues.	Wed.	Thurs.	Fri.
Text Reading					
Scholastic Reading					
Partner Reading					
S.R.A. Reading					
Library Center Reading					
Listening Post (stories)					
Picture Book Report					
Writing (puppet stories)					
Word Dictionary (notebook)					

Choose 3 activities each day. When you finish the 3 activities, put an X in the 3 boxes.

Child Focus Company
1236 Keats St.
Manhattan Beach, California, 90266

Figure 10.7   This sample self-assessment can be used by very young children, who may either color in the represented achievement or mark an "x" over the appropriate square. This idea can also be adapted to take the form of a graph; if a graph is used, each child should have her or his own graph record.

I know these colors:	Red	Orange	Yellow	Green	Blue	Purple
I know these shapes:	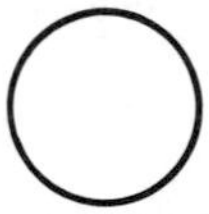 ○	□	 ▭	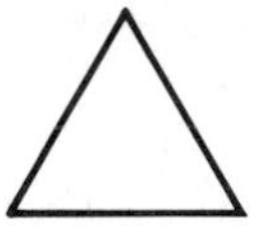 △	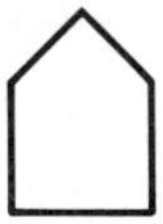 ⬠	 ◇
I can count to:	5	10	20	30	50	100
I know my:	Full name	Address	Telephone number	Mother's name	Father's name	Number of family members

living document for structuring individual approaches and plans to learning.

Sample Reading Materials

This component of the assessment portfolio should be custom developed by the teacher. Also consider including examples of activities, description of their scope and sequence, and other instructional guidelines that might be helpful in conferencing with parents and school supervisors. This component of the portfolio will probably change as you move into using new materials and resources.

PART III
CLASSROOM GROUPING MODELS FOR READING INSTRUCTION

Even a cursory examination of approaches to grouping for instruction that have been endorsed over the years reveals lack of consensus. Educators have gone through periods of time when individualizing instruction by designing self-paced instructional materials was popular (e.g., in the

1960s). Programmed reading and language arts materials theoretically allowed for students to progress at their own pace. Critics often pointed to the lack of interaction and opportunities for peer learning to occur in such environments.

During the 1970s, there was more interest in establishing small reading groups, based on need. Diagnostic tests structured into the management-by-objectives reading program design encouraged teachers to use grouping to help students in specified skill need areas (Otto et al., 1984).

It is probably safe to assert, however, that today's education community has moved back toward whole-class instruction, with small-group cooperative learning options structured within the whole-class instruction model. The small groups are more often mixed groups, and their orientation is not so much remediation as it was in earlier years.

A teacher of reading today must be prepared to teach to the whole class effectively. However, she or he must also be knowledgeable about techniques and strategies for grouping in various ways and for different purposes. Remember that grouping can be helpful if just for the sake of variety. Chapter 4 mentioned, and Chapter 5 elaborated on strategies for managing different kinds of instructional groupings, focusing particularly on groupings for primary-grade children. The following section considers some additional instructional options.

Have students examine some of the objectives-based approaches to reading instruction (e.g., Wisconsin Design for Reading Skill Development). Compare them to approaches being advocated today.

PLANNING AND INITIATING INSTRUCTION

As students mature and become more independent in the management of their own learning within the classroom setting, the configurations for providing instruction, and the options for organizing and scheduling them, expands. Not only does the teacher consider the length of time the students are able to work on their own, but also the way in which the students might work together to achieve an objective. Different types of groupings, different ways of combining the types of groupings, and different objectives for applying the use of particular groupings are some of the instructional considerations.

Ask students, "What other factors should be considered?"

CONSIDERATIONS FOR INSTRUCTIONAL GROUPINGS

The teacher uses a bank of knowledge about the students in order to select student grouping arrangements. (Chapter 5 mentioned several important considerations.) Data from five main areas are crucial in appropriately selecting the grouping that is best.

Ask students to examine the literature advocating teaching to modalities (e.g., work by Dunn, Carbo, Barbe, & McCarthy). Discuss the importance of considering the sensory modalities when teaching reading.

1. *Familiarity with the content.* Once you have selected the content and the materials to be used for instruction, an assessment of the students' level of knowledge is made.
2. *Modality for learning.* You must consider the importance of auditory, visual, and tactile learners when determining groupings.
3. *Perspective for the learning.* Do the students need a perspective of the whole project, or can they operate from small pieces of the project, building toward the whole?
4. *Process for the learning.* Have the students had opportunities for learning to work independently? Have they worked together cooperatively? How do they respond to direct instruction? Does this content and the students' previous knowledge make this a good lesson for which to design small discussion groups or individual projects?
5. *Materials available for instruction.* Sometimes, the deciding factor in selecting a lesson design is the number and type of materials or key resources to which you have access. If the key resource for introducing an instructional set is a filmstrip, video, or motion picture, you may elect to use it with the entire group of children because in the typical classroom, an audio sound track would disrupt other groups of learners. However, if you have access to video equipment that could be used in a small, nearby room with a parent volunteer, you may select to use the resource with a small-group configuration. If the best way to practice guided reading is for each student to have a copy of the selection, and there are only six copies

Effective reading groups and paired learning must be a part of effective reading instruction. The classroom using these approaches must be well organized and monitored.

and no overhead projector equipment, then you should plan on working with students in small groups. If each child has a copy of the selection, partner groupings can be used.

Based on the content of the intended instruction, the availability of materials, and the level and type of expertise of the learner, the teacher selects one or more instructional groupings.

A Menu for Grouping for Reading Instruction

As mentioned in Chapter 5, the traditional types of groupings—large groups or whole classes, small groups, and rotating small groups, and individuals—continue to be popular choices for providing reading instruction. However, in recent years, teachers have begun exploring new ways to adapt these configurations to meet the needs of a broader range of learners and to integrate other learnings into reading instruction. Cooperative learning groups are an example of a formalized grouping structure that is organized to teach a content skill while developing social interaction skills.

Have students examine the cooperative learning literature (e.g., Johnson & Johnson). Discuss its role in developing literacy in the elementary grades.

Individualized Instruction

In an effort to personalize the instruction of reading for each student, individualized reading programs were developed. Each child reads independently selections of his or her choice. The teacher creates individual instructional objectives for each student and uses the students' selected text as the foundation for providing that instruction. The goals of this type of instruction are

1. To allow for individual pacing of instruction
2. To encourage students to read by setting their own purposes
3. To foster independence in learning
4. To meet the students' instructional needs through the use of individualized objectives.

You can prepare for this type of instruction by collecting a wide variety of frequently selected trade books, magazines, catalogues, and so forth at various reading and interest levels and by displaying the reading materials in an attractive, easy-to-access manner. Instruction is facilitated by preparing cards containing a summary of the book, questions designed to enhance instruction of particular skills or strategies, and suggestions for possible projects.

Instruction is managed by creating systems for the students so they can effectively select and read the materials available. The materials can

Point out the strengths and limitations of children's literature based on using trade books. Ask students, "How might high-quality literature be incorporated into your individualized instruction approaches?"

be arranged into a library, with materials on similar topics together, or they can be arranged by theme or reading level. The students also need adequate time to become familiar with the texts they are reviewing for selection.

Reading time can be arranged in several ways. Most commonly, all the students read their individual selections during a designated classroom reading period. This provides the children with an uninterrupted reading time and allows you a specified time to account for each student's reading.

As the students are reading, you move about the group listening to individuals read, answering questions, and carrying on reading conferences. Reading conferences, which are held on a regular or flexible schedule, are a time for the teacher and student to work closely together on reading goals. You can listen to the student read to assess strategies and skills, discuss topics related to the selection, or help the student plan projects related to the text. Through this conference, you are able to create and recreate the instructional objectives with the student. The process is individually tailored to the student's needs and carried out with materials of his or her interest.

The recording of data related to the reading instruction can also be a part of the reading conference. The students can keep track of their progress through a series of charts and reporting cards. These daily or weekly accounts can help students recognize the progress they are making toward their reading goals and can help you to evaluate their progress and adjust the instruction, as needed.

Advise student teachers to keep mental notes, and record these in writing as soon as possible for maintenance in student folders.

Small-Group Instruction

Working with small groups of learners can be a very effective way of personalizing instruction. In groups of three to eight students, you can take the time to listen to individual student responses and to more closely monitor and adjust the instructional needs of students. Small-group instruction is also a way to increase positive social interactions among students. Systems such as cooperative learning can develop group work skills and problem-solving abilities during reading instruction.

Small-Group Membership

Note again the cooperative learning literature for grouping and instruction ideas.

Small-group membership can be determined through student or teacher selection. Students may form groups by working on topics of mutual interest, projects related to a story or theme, or strategies or skills they want to develop. You can create groups in response to students' instructional needs in skill, strategy, or content areas. You can also create groups based on student interests or by selecting students who work productively together in a small-group setting. Sometimes, groups are randomly selected, but this option is rarely your first choice unless the grouping is short term and the task is very specific and directly guided.

Variety can be added to grouping procedures by having students share with you the responsibility for control of group selection and by using a variety of group membership criteria. For example, sometimes, a student may be designated as a member of a small group because the teacher has requested that student to receive specific skill instruction. At other times, a student may decide to become part of a group that is studying a topic of shared interest or working on a common goal.

Scheduling Small-Group Work

Sometimes, groups may rotate, and you may work with each of the groups either within a reading period or some scheduled time within a few days. As you work with one of the groups, the others continue their work without your assistance. Chapter 5 suggested strategies and tentative considerations for scheduling small groups. You can keep track of group progress and needs by using the recording sheet shown in Figures 10.8 and 10.9.

Some Basic Guidelines for Small-Group Operation

Effective use of the grouping techniques described here require the teacher to keep in mind a few basic guidelines:

1. Be sure that learners know exactly what they are expected to accomplish during their time in the group. Clearly state goals or objectives to be achieved.
2. Be sure that learners know exactly what tasks or activities they will engage in during the group operation.
3. Appoint a chair or group leader responsible for coordinating activities while you are monitoring other groups. Rotate leadership roles and do not rely on the same people indefinitely.
4. Appoint a secretary or scribe to be responsible for note-taking when this is appropriate for the purposes of the group. Often, such a role will not be necessary for the objectives of the group.
5. Mix group memberships according to needs, objectives, and purposes for the grouping.
6. Vary the grouping techniques and approaches throughout the year. Work toward custom-designing the grouping approach to accomplish reading objectives.

Large-Group Instruction

Use large-group instruction for creating a mental set or otherwise preparing for introducing small-group instruction, for reviewing previously presented information, for sharing new information, and for demonstrating a strategy. One effective model includes the following elements:

Learning centers can be used throughout the grades, although many think of them as being used mostly in the primary grades. Remind students that learning center variations can work throughout all the grades.

Figure 10.8   Sample blank recording sheet that is used to facilitate the management of small groups for instruction.

Lesson		Time: _____ Date: _____

Lesson   Time: _____ Date: _____

Students Goal _____	Students Goal _____
_____ _____ _____ _____ _____	_____ _____ _____ _____ _____
Students Goal _____	Students Goal _____
_____ _____ _____ _____ _____	_____ _____ _____ _____ _____
Students Goal _____	Students Goal _____
_____ _____ _____ _____ _____	_____ _____ _____ _____ _____

Discipline problems often occur when physical movement from one place to another is involved. Developing and using simple orderly procedures to make the process efficient can reduce such problems dramatically.

1. Provide a connection between the information about which the students already have knowledge and the content of the instruction. This helps the students bring what they already know to support the learning of something new. A clear definition of the objective is presented, and the steps for instruction are outlined.
2. Demonstrate what the learning is and how it is used, in a way that makes it valuable to the students. Present the concept or skill in a

Figure 10.9 Sample filled-in recording sheet that is used to facilitate the management of small groups for instruction.

Lesson: Projects from trade books **Time:** 1:10 p.m **Date** 2/23	
Mike Shelly Linda John Sid **Poster** 1. Brainstormed list of ideas for poster. 2. Ready for decision making process. * maybe need more research into complexity of ideas first.	Sally *Josie Jason Peter Lee 1. still deciding which project to work on. 2. Sit with group and work on selecting an option and develope a process for getting work done. * Josie absent
Leslie Margo Jerry Ross Tom **Poem** 1. Shared the poems they had selected. 2. work in partners to practice reading with meaning. * Tom work with Leslie + Margo	Jack Nancy Pamela Bob Teri **Reading** 1. Working on completing the reading of their selection. 2. Move along by getting Mrs. Olson to read pgs. 47-60 to them.
Susan Kate Rich Beth Mark **Newscast** 1. Each have taken a part for newscast. 2. Suggest they take dictation for each other in recording 1st drafts.	Kathy Kim Lynn Kelsey **Play** 1. Decided on puppet play. 2. writing script with selected characters. Well organized! X check for materials

way that the students can observe it occurring in a meaningful context.

3. Apply the new learning in order to clarity and practice the instruction. The student is given opportunities for guided and independent practice of the new learning.

4. Extend the learning beyond the context in which it was taught. Encourage students to generalize their learning so that it is useful to them in making meaning out of new situations.

In order to make this type of instruction meaningful to a wide variety of learners and to monitor the students' understanding of the instruction, be careful to design the instruction to actively involve the students. Encourage the students to use comprehension strategies such as questioning, paraphrasing, and summarizing, as well as other techniques that check for students' understanding and foster their participation.

To facilitate the implementation of the instructional plan, it is important to develop an environment that clearly defines and encourages behavioral and instructional standards. Rules are few and clearly displayed. Teach the rules to the students, and consistently encourage the students to use them as a basis for functioning as a group. A classroom schedule should be developed, and the daily routine followed regularly so that students are able to pace their time and have a sense of security about what is to come next in their day. Changes to the schedule are tolerated but are clearly exceptions.

Learning Centers

Ask students to think of other center types and configurations that are workable at grades K–8.

As a variation that combines individual and small-group instruction, learning centers offer another configuration for providing instruction. Learning centers are usually stations or microcosms of instruction that you create in the classroom. Each has a well-defined instructional objective and a procedure for students to follow. The objectives and instructions are clearly stated in language the students can read and understand, and these are posted in the learning center work area. The materials necessary for completing the task are close at hand, and explicit directions are given for seeking assistance, for task completion, and for transitional activities to pursue once the learning center task has been completed.

Preparation of Learning Centers

Ask students to suggest some other configuration possibilities.

Before beginning the use of centers, teach the students how to get to the learning center, what to do when they are there, how to record or store their work, and what to do when they are finished. Usually, the rules for working in centers are very similar to those used in the normal classroom routine:

1. Help others to learn.

> Work without disturbing others.
>
> Make positive, encouraging statements to others.
>
> Share your knowledge and skill when appropriate.
>
> Take care of the materials.
>
> Clean up after yourself.

2. Help yourself to learn.

> Attend to your work.
>
> Organize your materials.
>
> Ask questions when you need information.
>
> Talk yourself through complicated situations.

The purpose for using centers is to offer a variety of ways for students to engage in an activity that encourages them to explore, practice, apply, or extend their learning.

In preparation for developing centers, ask three questions:

1. What is it that the students are to learn about or learn how to do?
2. How can they best learn the information or the skill?
3. How can students communicate their understanding or ability to use this learning?

From the answers to these questions, you can develop methods and materials to meet the diverse needs of a variety of learners.

You can use work stations for follow-up work after large-group instruction, as independent work for those students not involved in teacher-directed small-group work, or as a whole-class independent work time. Projects can be developed that focus on the same objectives but support the students' varying learning styles and learning abilities. Centers organized around comprehension strategies (e.g., summarizing) may take several different forms, such as creating representative sculptures, drawings, diagrams, posters, songs, dances, or poems.

Strategies for Implementation of Learning Centers

Teachers have several ways of using centers in creating their menus of instructional offerings. Depending on the goal of their instruction, each option can be a valuable help in supporting students' learning. Three strategies for preparing instructional centers are (1) instructional skill-, strategy-, or content-centered approaches, (2) theme-centered approaches, and (3) text-centered approaches.

Expect students to address the difference between assessment for district use in choosing curriculum or setting curriculum policy and classroom teacher use for daily instruction and communication.

Centers can be created around several individual unrelated topics, each center focusing on an isolated skill, strategy, or content area.

Example: The teacher works with a group of 15 students. Together, they are reading a novel, stopping to analyze and discuss the development of the main and supporting characters. Around the periphery of the room are several work stations or centers that are unrelated to the novel in content and in focus skill. These centers are developed around any of the following:

Set of spelling words

Dictionary skill

Punctuation skill

Main idea strategy

Worksheet of riddles

Poem pattern

Word processing

Study skill worksheet

Students are working at these centers individually or in pairs. The teacher has encouraged the students to work in a center of their choice. During the week that these centers are available, the students are responsible for completing work from four different centers.

Centers can be developed based on the theme the students are exploring during classtime. This theme forms the foundation for the development of each of the experiences the students will have.

Example: The theme in Mr. Johns's class is "courage," and the students have read stories, both factual and fictional, that have helped them begin to define courageous people and deeds. Mr. Johns's classroom is divided into four main work areas, and subareas are defined within each. Some examples within each of the areas are the following:

Writing
1. Write a story about a character who chooses to do a courageous deed. Include why it was courageous and why the character decided to do it.
2. Write a summary of a television news report of a courageous person or deed.
3. In writing, try to convince someone that you are the most courageous person he or she has ever met.

Reading

1. Read a collection of poems written about courageous people, animals, deeds, or feelings.
2. Read a collection of magazine and newspaper articles about courageous people or deeds. Think about what made these acts courageous, and discuss it with a parent or teacher.

Oral Language

1. Make a tape recording of sound effects to go with a story we have read about courage.
2. Write a speech as if you were being given a medal for doing a courageous deed.

Arts

1. Depict the elements of courage in a collage or poster.
2. Select a story about courage, and create a diagram of the events that led to the courageous act. Use the materials to show the emotions of the characters and the importance of each event.

Texts can be used as the connecting factor in developing centers for student use.

Example: Ms. Trumble's class is reading a trade book. Each student has a copy of the book and, although the students follow Ms. Trumble's daily lesson through the story, they are free to read on if they wish. Some days, the reading period is longer than others, depending on the amount the students need to read in order to have a meaningful discussion. When the reading is completed, the students are responsible for work from at least one of the centers that is related to that reading. The following are examples of these centers:

Produce a newscast based on today's reading.

Plan a birthday party for your favorite character.

Design a board game using the story setting and events.

Construct a diorama of a story event.

Research the history of this country.

Collect recipes that you would give to the villain.

Keep a journal of your thoughts about the story.

Make a list of new words you find in the story.

If you prefer to make these centers somewhat generic, they can be used for several different selections. This has the potential of giving students more opportunities to experience a wider variety of options and also adds the possibility for comparison among selections when using one of the options (e.g., How do the recipes you collected for this villain differ from those you collected previously?).

Figure 10.10   An option for coordinating reading instruction: (1) Teacher provides large-group instruction; (2) students share and plan in small groups; (3) students carry out the plan individually.

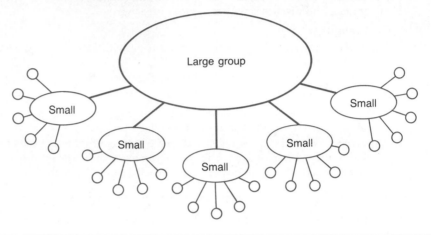

COORDINATING THE OPTIONS

Require students to articulate the strengths and weaknesses of *both*.

As the preceding menu of options for grouping children for reading instruction has shown, the strategies for grouping for instruction are not necessarily used in isolation. In fact, most often you will use a combination of two or more options in creating the lesson. Figures 10.10 through 10.14 show some of the lesson configurations used in a typical reading lesson. Tailor selected configurations to respond to your instructional goals, the needs of the learners, and the available materials.

HIGHLIGHTS

1. The teacher of reading should maintain an assessment portfolio for each child in the classroom.
2. The assessment portfolio is designed to serve a number of purposes, all of which are intended to further the reading growth and development of children.
3. The assessment portfolio should contain data acquired from both formal and informal measures and should also reflect substantial input from the child.
4. Regular use and maintenance of the assessment portfolio throughout the school year are critical to its utility.

Figure 10.11 **A second option for coordinating reading instruction: (1) Teacher provides large-group instruction; (2) teacher organizes students to work in (a) small groups with the teacher, or (b) individually and independently.**

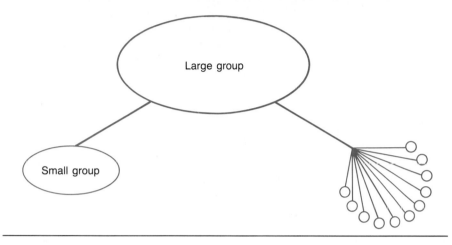

Figure 10.12 **A third option for coordinating reading instruction: (1) Teacher provides a large-group instructional experience; (2) students work individually on exploration or on a problem; (3) students work in pairs to solve the problem or to edit their work.**

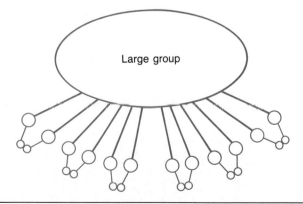

Figure 10.13   **A fourth option for coordinating reading instruction: (1) Teacher presents a problem to small groups of students; (2) small-group members report to the large group; (3) teacher provides instruction.**

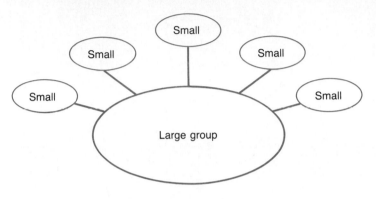

Figure 10.14   **A fifth option for coordinating reading instruction: (1) Teacher offers an exploration experience to small groups of students; (2) small-group members share their experiences with the large group; (3) teacher provides instruction; (4) students work individually on a problem.**

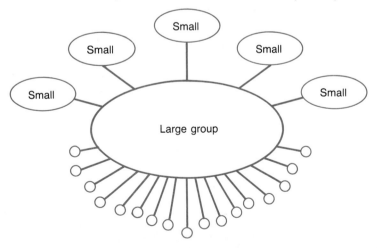

5. Although whole-class instruction is probably the most dominant instructional model in use, small-group instruction should be integrated into the reading program.
6. Effective use of group instruction depends on clear purposes and well-organized classroom procedures.

Ask students to provide a rationale for each component.

REINFORCEMENT ACTIVITIES

1. What is an assessment portfolio, and what is its role?
2. Explain the difference between formal and informal measures of reading performance.
3. Identify each of the following, and tell how each is used in the assessment portfolio:
   a. Criterion-referenced tests
   b. IRI
   c. Cloze procedures
   d. T-unit analyses
4. Explain the role of grouping for reading instruction.
5. Describe one grouping technique for reading instruction.

Answers can tend to be quite general. Pressure your students to provide specific examples of their general observations or assertions about grouping.

Allow for variations in answers.

Encourage students to remember to utilize the publications division of state education agencies, which are usually responsible for developing state assessment. They often have a variety of publications, including actual assessment samples.

ADDITIONAL PROJECTS

1. Visit an elementary classroom that uses small groups in a reading class. Talk with the teacher about his or her use of grouping and other classroom organization techniques.
2. Interview an elementary school principal or other administrator or supervisor, and find out how they approach reading performance measurement and monitoring in their school.
3. Prepare a sample student assessment portfolio. Compare your model with that of others in your class.
4. Review the cooperative learning model of Johnson and Johnson or others. Discuss its use in reading instruction.

REFERENCES

Betts, E. A. (1946). *Foundations of Reading Instruction*. New York: American Book.

(1989, April). *Educational Leadership*.

Farr, R., & Carey, R. F. (1986). *Reading: What Can Be Measured?* (2nd ed). Newark: International Reading Association.

Flood, J., & Lapp, D. (1989). Reporting reading progress: A comparison portfolio for parents. *The Reading Teacher, 42,* 508–514.

Goodman, Y. (1973). *Miscue Analysis: Application to Reading Instruction*. Urbana, IL: National Council of Teachers of English.

Goodman, Y., & Burke, C. (1972). *Reading Miscue Inventory Manual: Procedure for Diagnosis and Evaluation*. New York: Macmillan.

Hunt, K. (1965). *Grammatical Structures Written at Three Grade Levels*. Urbana, IL: National Council of Teachers of English.

Johns, J. (1985). *Basic Reading Inventory* (3rd ed). Dubuque, IA: Kendall-Hunt.

Johnson, D., et al. (1984). *Circles of Learning*. Alexandria, VA: ASCD.

Otto, W., et al. (1984). Managing instruction. In P. D. Pearson et al. (Eds.), *Handbook of Reading Research*. New York: Longman.

Taylor, W. (1953). Cloze procedures: A new tool for measuring readability. *Journalism Quarterly, 30,* 415–433.

Wixson, K., et al. (1984). An interview for assessing students' perceptions of classroom reading tasks. *The Reading Teacher, 37,* 346–352.

ADDITIONAL RESOURCES

Moffett, J., & Wagner, B. J. (1983). *Student-Centered Language Arts and Reading, K–13*. Boston: Houghton Mifflin.

Routman, R. (1988). *Transitions From Literature to Literacy*. Portsmouth, NH: Heinemann.

Smith, C., & Dahl, K. (1984). *Teaching Reading and Writing Together: the Classroom Connection*. New York: Teachers College Press.

CHAPTER 11

READING AND THE
MIDDLE-SCHOOL LEARNER

Eth: *It's time he was taught you are now an adult.*
Ron: *Exactly what I told him, Eth. I said quite firmly, I said,*
      "Look, Dad. You got to realize I am now a grown-up
      adult with all an adult's desires and capabilities."
Eth: *When did you tell him that?*
Ron: *When he was peeling the silver paper off my Easter Egg.*

F. Muir and D. Norden, *The Glums,*
London Weekend Television, 1978

PREVIEW

The reading needs of young adolescents differ from those of primary and intermediate-grade children, due to a number of factors:

- The developmental characteristics of early adolescence
- The knowledge, skills, attitudes and experiences that adolescents have gained
- The learning demands made of adolescents in a middle-school setting
- Societal demands imposed on adolescents

This chapter is designed to provide an opportunity to examine these factors and their implications for reading instruction in the middle school.

FOCUS QUESTIONS

As you read this chapter, keep the following questions in mind:

1. What are some important developmental differences between middle-school learners and children in the earlier elementary grades?
2. How are learning demands for students in the middle grades different from those in the earlier grades?
3. What are some general instructional approaches that a middle school teacher should use?

DEVELOPMENTAL CHARACTERISTICS OF MIDDLE-SCHOOL LEARNERS

Ask students to recall their years in junior high school or in middle school: "What are the kinds of things that stand out? Do they relate to learning content, or do they have to do with adolescence, peer pressures, and so forth? What does this say to a prospective middle-school teacher?"

As young children enter the middle grades, they begin to perceive themselves and to be perceived by others in terms of the adults they are becoming rather than the children they were. Writer and researcher Joan Lipsitz captures the essence of this unique developmental period:

Early adolescence is a time during which life-changing growth occurs. It is a time when young people begin to define themselves as social beings with a sense of commitment to their personal futures and their society. It is a time to begin considering how to function on one's own. It is a time too for establishing a firm sense of racial identity and for sorting through feelings about sexual identity. It is a time when the capacity for hypothetical abstract thought begins to develop. Physically, it is a time of the most rapid growth and change in the entire [remembered] human experience. It is, in other words, a critical time of development that can determine the quality of one's future.

J. Lipsitz, 1981, page 2

Physical Development

Consider bringing a developmental psychologist to class to discuss the nature of the middle-school learner.

Numerous physical changes are occurring in early adolescence that affect not only young people's appearance but also their behavior and attitudes. Both boys and girls enter a growth spurt during this period, which can lead to a dramatic increase in strength, height, weight, and bone growth. Because bones tend to grow faster than muscles and tendons, children often lack coordination, have bad posture, or are susceptible to injury. Metabolism rates also change significantly, causing them to fluctuate between hyperactivity and listlessness (Buan & Olson, 1988).

As children enter puberty, sexual changes are also occurring that affect students' physical appearance, social interests, and perceptions of self. The fact that these physical changes occur at varying rates among children can cause them special concerns. Constantly comparing themselves with others, they can feel weird and abnormal if they do not approach the ideal of physical and social maturity simultaneously with their classmates. Concerns about physical changes and appearance consume a considerable portion of adolescents' time and attention. Adults must be sensitive to these concerns, must provide opportunities for discussing them, and must offer lots of reassurance that their experiences are a normal part of development.

Intellectual Development

Intellectually, young adolescents are increasingly able to engage in abstract thought and hypothetical reasoning. However, their expanding intellectual capabilities still require a great deal of structured instructional support from teachers if they are to develop fully. Most middle-schoolers need continued direct instruction in such reasoning skills as inferring, generalizing, and hypothesizing, especially when asked to apply them to the more complex text found at this level. New concepts must be carefully taught, using a variety of examples and as many concrete experiences as possible. Teachers should also be alert to the fact that differences in prior knowledge, skills, and experiences, as well as differences in intellectual maturation, can be as significant with this age group as their physical differences. Careful assessments of student knowledge and capabilities, with the subsequent adjustment of lessons to the appropriate level of difficulty, should occur on a regular basis. Broad assumptions about what students know and are able to do should be carefully avoided.

Social–Emotional Development

Young adolescents' growing capacities to think abstractly underlie many of the social–emotional changes that are also occurring at this time. Their ability to think about their own thinking (metacognition) and to begin to see the world through multiple perspectives (decentration) may have positive implications for learning, but they can also complicate their emotional and social life. Middle-schoolers frequently become intensely introspective and preoccupied with inner thoughts, feelings, and concerns about what others think of them. Everything they do, think, and say can take on tremendous importance. They may often feel that everyone is watching them, that they are always center stage. At other times, they can feel very alone and isolated, so unusual and so special that no one else in the world can possibly understand them. These perceptions, and their attendant emotions, can create extreme self-consciousness, egocentrism, inability to put events into perspective, and reckless disregard for the effects of destructive behavior. They sincerely believe that what happens to others could not possibly happen to them. What they feel could not possibly be felt by others. The following example shows how seriously adolescents consider peer evaluations of them:

Ask students what the developmental characteristics of middle-school learners implies in regard to their developing skills and abilities in metacognition.

Episode 1—From the Serious to the Silly: Peer Relations and Egocentricity

I have a conference with three girls in the hall. Two are about ready to fight; the other is trying to prevent the fight by seeking my assistance. I try to get to the cause of the problem. The cause, I am told, is eyeball-rolling. One girl rolled her eyes at the other, a sure sign of disrespect, an indication of a desire for combat. The eyeball-rolling, the perpetrator explained, was the result of being told by a classmate, who told another classmate, who told her friend, that the other girl didn't like her. The victim exclaims that she never said that. I suggest to the victim of the eyeball-rolling that she might check her sources before jumping to conclusions and that even if the girl had said that, it was not the end of the world. We discussed alternatives ways to handle the problem. Both girls agreed to let the conflict drop, and I assured them that I would be "on the lookout" for any more eyeball-rolling, understanding more fully after our conversation the seriousness of its implications. All three girls laughed and went happily on their way. As silly as this incident may sound, it is an example of both the seriousness with which early adolescents view their status with peers and their egocentricity. Every real and perceived social slight is accorded great personal significance.

Ask students about the implications of adolescent identity development in regard to teaching ideas such as cooperative learning.

Young adolescents are also struggling self-consciously to establish their own identities and to become less dependent on adults. They begin to consciously try to determine their own values and beliefs and frequently question the perceptions, values, and authority of teachers and parents. Peer groups frequently become a source of affirmation and support for adolescents as they struggle with their identity issues. These same peer groups may also impose considerable pressure on adolescents to conform to group standards and norms. When these norms are destructive, peer pressure can be a dangerous force for these children who so often desperately seek acceptance. Drug use, sexual precociousness, and gang involvement are all examples of the destructive types of activities students can become involved in as a result of negative peer pressure. The following example illustrates this destructive potential:

Episode 2—The Search for Identity: For Some Early Adolescents, a Dangerous Journey

I meet with counselors to discuss how we can help an eighth-grader who is afraid to go home. His mother, addicted to crack cocaine, has recently been evicted from their home and has now moved in with the dealers who supply her with the drug. Many of her relatives and associates are involved in gang activity. In seventh grade, John could have been described as a typically charming, tender, immature middle-school boy. Although experiencing difficulties and uncertainties at home related to his mother's drug involvement, he did not exhibit negative acting-out behaviors at school.

This year, we observed a change in John. He began hanging out with a group of boys who were exhibiting gang-related behaviors. His friendliness began to be replaced by sullenness. You could see him experimenting with his new image although it often made a very poor fit with his natural inclination to reach out positively toward others. Luckily for John, he retained enough trust in the counselor to ask for help and had other family members who were able to give it. Unfortunately, not all middle-schoolers in his situation, or equally difficult ones, do. For these children, the search for identity can be a dangerous one.

As young children grow and mature, their social and emotional needs also change. The classroom teacher must consider these factors in making reading instruction for these boys and girls more appropriate to their age.

While early adolescents' interest in social interaction and peer group acceptance can cause problems in the classroom, it can also be channeled productively to support academic learning. Cooperative learning strategies, for example, allow teachers to direct students' interests in social interaction toward productive academic work. These structured group activities provide an excellent example of how developmental needs can be met rather than ignored or suppressed through the selection of appropriate learning strategies.

Diversity in Developmental Characteristics

Because each young person operates on his or her own developmental time clock, the most obvious and startling characteristic of the middle-school student population is its great diversity. Even one grade-level classroom may have children who (a) range in size from 4 feet to 6 feet, (b) have interests that vary from He-Man to the causes of injustice, and (c) engage in social activities from fort-building to sexual intimacy. Not only are there vast differences among children, but often, within the individual child, developmental changes occur at different rates. A young adolescent's intellectual and social maturity, for example, may lag well behind her or his physical maturity. One assumption that teachers should

Discuss how significant these problems can be during the critical years of adolescence.

not make at the middle-school level is that big bodies indicate social and emotional maturity. This assumption is usually not supported by reality!

To illustrate the wide diversity that exists, compare the example in Episode 2 with the following episode:

Episode 3—The Search for Identity: For Some Adolescents, a Smooth Untroubled Process

One of our most charming and self-contained eighth-graders asks me to give her a ride home. Her "stupid, selfish sister" had forgotten to make arrangements for her transportation. In the car, we talk about her next year in high school. A student with a 4.0 grade-point average and an energetic basketball player, she wants to become a doctor. She will be attending a technical high school across town in the hopes of getting an education that will adequately prepare her for her future goals. Already planning to organize a study group with friends from her church, she's entering this new period in her life with anticipation and confidence. Her large, loving family supports and nurtures her dreams.

OTHER LEARNER CHARACTERISTICS: PRIOR KNOWLEDGE, SKILLS, AND ATTITUDES

Just as children come to the middle school with a wide range of developmental characteristics, they also come with substantial differences in general world knowledge, experiences, skills, attitudes, and interests. As was mentioned earlier in the text, these unique characteristics of the learner have a significant impact on the reading process. If a good match is not made between the learner, the task, the text, and the strategies required to achieve the task, then failure or inadequate performance will most likely result.

To create a good match in the variables that affect the reading process, teachers must know their students. An understanding of the developmental characteristics of this age group will provide teachers with that information. Consideration of the aforementioned other factors that affect learner characteristics provides another. By the time students reach middle school, the effects of both family and school experiences on their prior knowledge, skills, attitudes, and interests may be seen. While children who come from families who have been able to nurture their intellectual, emotional, and social development may continue to maintain a distinct advantage in relation to school learning and adjustment, the benefits of effective primary programs can be seen in all learners.

The effective-schools research of the 1970s demonstrated that low socioeconomic status and other factors generally associated with underachievement do not have to be the primary determinant of student performance. However, because family background and experiences exert a significant influence on what children bring to the school, and because most primary programs, unfortunately, do not reach the standards of excellence highlighted in the effective-school research, children continue to arrive at the middle school with very unequal preparation for learning.

Two middle schools in a large urban school district provide examples of the distinct differences in learner characteristics that can be found in the schools and their effects on performance and the learning environment. In the first school, 70% of the students come from families who qualify for free or reduced lunches under federal guidelines. To qualify for this subsidy, a family of four must earn less than $15,000 per year. Many parents work at low-skilled jobs and earn little more than the minimum wage; even two wage-earners (or one wage-earner with two full-time jobs) would barely earn that much in a year. It is not uncommon for these families to have no health insurance and to have difficulty providing the basic needs of housing, clothing, food, and health care for themselves and their children.

To compound the serious difficulties these families face, two thirds have at least one family member who has problems with alcohol or other drug abuse. Many of their children require counseling because of emotional problems associated with living in drug-affected families, and they are often underachievers in the classroom. Thirty-five to forty percent of the student population as a whole qualify for Chapter I federal assistance to needy students, performing 2 or more years below grade level on school district basic skills achievement tests. Parental expectations for the educational achievement of their children are often low, with many expressing concern that their children will not make it through high school. College or postsecondary training is remote and an occasional dream, not an expected outcome. Low self-esteem, emotional stress, difficulty adjusting to behavioral norms, and a lack of experience and exposure to the world outside their immediate community are common characteristics of these students.

In the second school, most students come from affluent or middle-income homes. Parents typically are professionals or work in other well-paying jobs that require advanced technical training. Books, travel, and a wide array of educational and cultural experiences are a common part of students' everyday lives. Parents expect their children not only to graduate from high school but also to go on to college, and more often than not, not just any college but the best one. Ninety-two percent of the students who attend this school perform at or well above the school district average on basic skills achievement tests. While some students in this school experience emotional problems requiring counseling services, their numbers are smaller and the problems tend to be different from those in the first school. Typical concerns are peer and parental pressure related to competition for social status and grades, as well as loneliness caused by

Ask students, "How does the teacher–parent relationship change from the early elementary-grade years to the middle-school years? What are some things the middle-school teacher can do to keep communication channels open with parents?"

When student populations vary significantly between schools in the same community, problems can emerge. Ask students, "What are some of these problems? How can these be ameliorated?"

parents who are often preoccupied with their own careers and their own social status issues.

As might be imagined, meeting the needs of these very different student populations require, in many ways, different responses from school staff. In the first school, substantial resources must be allocated to meeting the emotional as well as academic needs of students. Counseling, administrative, and teaching staff must work in concert to provide the counseling, discipline, and educational support these children so desperately require. Teachers must carefully build background knowledge, continue a strong focus on basic skill instruction, and build confidence and self-esteem while maintaining strict behavioral limits and discipline. Counselors and administrators must provide constant and consistent support for both teachers and students, and they must do everything possible to assist teachers and students in their efforts to teach and to learn. Most important, everyone must deliver one consistent and powerful message to both the parents and children of this community, and that is their faith in these children's potential and their belief in the children's ability to succeed.

In the second school, staff may have to work equally hard to meet the very high and often demanding academic expectations of both parents and children. They may have to work even harder to get parents to attend to the affective and developmental needs of their children. For example, they may need to accept that their child may not be able or interested in attending a prestigious university or to accept that what their child needs right now is more time and attention from them, not more preplanned and structured educational enrichment activities after school.

In their own way, children from affluent homes may be as culturally isolated as children from impoverished ones. Children of European heritage, in particular, may have very limited exposure in their daily lives to people from different social classes and ethnic backgrounds. Teachers must be sensitive to this potential isolation and provide substantive opportunities for their students to learn about the rich and varied contributions and experiences of all cultural and socioeconomic groups.

In the two schools used here as examples of the differences in student characteristics that can be caused by social class, both groups were of predominantly Western European heritage, the same heritage that for the most part shapes the values, traditions, and perspective of our public schools and curriculum materials. What of the children who come from families shaped by different cultural traditions? Since the early 1970s, educators and the communities they serve have shown increasing concern for the difficulties children face when they make the transition from the culture of the home to the culture of the school, where orientations toward time, achievement, competition, and interpersonal relations may be very different.

Discuss the differences in support staff availability between the middle-school years and the earlier elementary grades. Ask how this affects the classroom teacher.

There has also been increased recognition of the lack of inclusion and frequent distortion in content materials of the experiences and contributions of different cultural groups to both national and global heritage. Native Americans, African-Americans, Hispanic-Americans, and Asian-Americans, for example, have spoken forcefully for changes in curriculum materials and teacher training to correct these omissions, distortions, and insensitivities to cultural differences found in society at large and reflected in public schools. The same issues have been raised and argued effectively for women in all ethnic groups. While educators and publishers have made progress in these areas over time, few would argue that educators and others have met the goals of cultural and sexual equity and sensitivity in the schools. Many children, unfortunately, continue to see little of themselves reflected in the images, history, literature, and teaching staff they encounter in the classroom.

Social class and cultural differences play an important role in children's comfort with the expectations of the school, their ability to trust and relate to staff, and their interest in and acceptance of both the content and the instructional methodology. Teachers must be both well informed about these differences and sensitive to their implications for the academic and affective needs of their students.

Ask students, "What can be done to help children from culturally diverse populations learn to read?" Discuss this question from the standpoint of instruction and from the standpoint of curriculum.

Learning demands begin to change as students near the middle grades. They are required to attend to subject content in more depth and, often, methods of instruction change.

LEARNING DEMANDS OF THE MIDDLE SCHOOL

Students in the middle school often encounter two important changes in the learning environment: (1) increased focus on content or subject matter, and (2) more reliance on lecture or other teacher-directed instructional formats than on student-centered ones.

Although elementary-grade students are introduced to subjects such as social studies, science, and mathematics at the beginning of the primary grades, they receive far more emphasis in the middle-school grades. In fact, it is reasonable to assert that most reading instruction in the middle grades is done in the context of reading in the content areas. Some middle schools have no reading classes other than remedial or developmental reading. In many schools, language arts or English classes focus on the concepts and applications of language and reading knowledge more than on instruction in language and reading.

The middle-grade teacher then is expected to incorporate reading instruction largely within the context of instruction in particular subject areas. This is why most of our attention to reading comprehension in this text has been oriented toward its application to knowledge.

In contrast, most primary-school teachers are expected to teach all subject areas within the confines of one classroom. Because of the demands placed on the primary teachers to build the foundations of literacy in reading, writing, and mathematics, most of their time and attention is directed to these areas. While districts expend considerable energy developing curriculum for the sciences and the social studies for young children, it is the rare primary teacher who has the time necessary to teach them consistently and well.

In addition to reading textbooks, a common way for middle-school students to learn content is through classroom lecture. Unless the teacher has an extraordinary gift for delivering that content in story form, it places demands on the listener similar to those of reading expository text. Students must be able to (a) distinguish main ideas from supporting details, (b) comprehend complex cause and effect relations, and (c) grasp unfamiliar and often technical vocabulary. Certainly, effective middle school teachers use a variety of additional strategies to both deliver content and make it meaningful, but the fact remains they are expected to deliver a lot of it, and this expectation places new and difficult demands on middle school students. Episode 4 describes one teacher's creative response to teaching physics.

Episode 4—An Active "Hands-On" Curriculum Maximizes Student Involvement and Ties Abstract Concepts to Concrete Experiences

For days, I've been noticing students carrying strange wooden constructions to science. One has a little toy car attached with a straight pin

---

Point out the organizational diversity that exists among middle schools. Departmentalization, for example, begins in some schools at the sixth-grade level, while at others, it is barely visible anywhere in the middle grades. Engage students in a discussion of the advantages and/or disadvantages of departmentalization by subject matter in the middle school.

Ask students whether there should be separate reading classes in the middle grades.

Ask students, "How pervasive is the lecture method of teaching in the middle grades?" Have your students visit local middle schools and discuss the matter with classroom teachers.

projecting from its bumper. Another has a tiny plastic He-Man tied to a lever with a pin in his boot. Still another has what appears to be a plastic attachment from his mother's vacuum cleaner coiled in a spiral and directed at a balloon. Speaking of balloons, I've seen a number of them in the hall and have been assured by students of their intent to use them in science experiments, not in balloon fights. What's up? At 10:00 A.M. I get a call from the science teacher to come and observe "The Great Balloon Popper Experiments."

When I arrive in class, an intensely serious seventh-grader is positioning his toy car with a needle projectile at the top of his spiral. The project requires students to design an apparatus that uses three simple machines to pop a balloon. Most children's inventions perform successfully. Those that fail are reconstructed, applying the scientific principles involved. All children are able to explain how their inventions work using these principles. No one is off task, bored, or restless. They are all very proud of their accomplishments.

Students are also expected to respond to what they read and hear in new ways. They are asked more frequently to interpret and evaluate information, to make inferences and formulate conclusions, and to support both with evidence and well-reasoned arguments orally and in writing. They are also expected to write summaries and research reports using longer and more difficult research materials. Each of these types of responses, whether oral or written, require a thorough understanding of the content presented, the ability to think about that content in increasingly complex ways, and the ability to organize and communicate their thoughts to others, typically in expository forms. Without direct instruction, frequent opportunities for application, and clear feedback from teachers on both the thinking processes and the response or communication form required, most students have difficulty with these tasks.

> Talk about this shift from the narrative mode of writing to expository writing in many schools. Ask about the implications of this shift for the middle-school teacher.

These new and more complex learning demands, and young adolescents' need for support in their efforts to meet them, create unique problems at the middle level for both students and teachers. Unlike the primary teacher in the self-contained classroom, middle-school teachers of content subjects might not be familiar with the literacy needs of their students, or they might not be trained regarding how to structure lessons and assignments to accommodate the range of skills they may encounter in any one classroom. Their ability to cope with these differences may also be inhibited by (a) the large numbers of students they teach each day (sometimes as many as 180), and (b) their perception that literacy instruction robs time from content teaching. Episode 5 shows a way in which one teacher designed instruction to overcome some of the difficulties of teaching inexperienced and unskilled middle-school learners.

> Discuss the implications for the classroom teacher when your expertise in one or two subject areas is more important in your career than being responsible for all subjects. For example, ask students whether this means that teachers are less sensitive to students as learners and are more concerned with content knowledge.

Episode 5—Involvement in the Writing Process: A Way to Meet Both the Emotional and Social Needs of Young Adolescents

On the way back to the office from the science lab, I drop in on a sixth-grade Chapter I Humanities Class. Most of the children in the class began the year by performing at least 2 and sometimes 3 years below grade level in reading and language. Many come from troubled families and may be struggling emotionally with the effects of parental alcohol and other drug abuse, family violence, and poverty. Their self-esteem and ability to cope with the academic, social, and behavioral demands of the school are, as you might imagine, severely impaired. I provide you this background so that you can truly appreciate the following classroom observation.

Children are organized at tables in clusters of four. All are busy working on their individual writing projects. Some are giving constructive feedback to each other on their works in progress, others are intensely engrossed in their revisions, still others are conferencing with the teachers about writing problems and achievements.

I sit next to one boy, who is finishing a five-page final draft of a murder story. Although alarmingly violent, the story has sound structure and flow, and he has made good use of descriptive language. We have an opportunity to talk about what experiences inspired his story. He shares concerns with family conflicts and elements of a movie he saw on TV. Both are interwoven in his story. Through daily involvement in the writing process, this child and others have gained confidence in their ability to communicate, have learned to integrate and apply an array of language and thinking skills, and have discovered a needed outlet for expressing often troubling experiences and feelings.

Although the middle-school movement has continually emphasized the needs for schools at this level to focus on the development of programs specifically designed to meet the developmental needs of young adolescents, there is still a great deal of uncertainty on the part of many middle-school teachers regarding how this translates into practice in the area of intellectual and skill development and content learning in the classroom.

FACTORS AFFECTING MIDDLE-SCHOOL LEARNERS

To facilitate an understanding of how to teach middle-school learners, it may help to clarify several assumptions about the middle-school learner:

1. Middle-school learners are in the midst of a critical developmental period in their lives, which affects them physically, intellectually, socially, and emotionally. They may be socially and emotionally preoccupied with establishing a sense of personal identity and gaining acceptance from peers. Although maturing intellectually, they still require considerable support and guidance in their efforts

to comprehend abstractions and to exercise high-level thinking skills.

2. Variations in students' changing developmental characteristics; prior knowledge, skills, and experiences; and present attitudes increase rather than decrease in the middle school. Some young people come to the classroom ready and willing to learn; others do not. Cultural experiences can significantly affect students' attitudes toward learning, their comfort with the culture of the school, and their trust in teachers.

3. Demographic data indicate that increasing numbers of students suffer from the effects of poverty, neglect, abuse, and alcohol and other drug problems—factors that can significantly affect emotional adjustment and school performance.

4. Achievement data indicate that many students will perform adequately on basic skills tasks, but they will have difficulty with high-order thinking skills, and they may possess inadequate background knowledge in literature, social studies, and science.

5. Middle-school teachers across subject areas may not provide the strategy instruction students need in order to comprehend the greater quantities of complex and abstract content presented in academic classes.

6. Without improved reading instruction at the middle level and beyond, many young people will not possess the skills necessary to complete postsecondary vocational or academic education or to compete successfully in the job market.

Ask students to list other points.

MIDDLE-SCHOOL LEARNERS' READING NEEDS

The reading needs of young people become increasingly complex as they make the transition to the middle school. Two factors require from both students and teachers a larger, more sophisticated repertoire of teaching and learning strategies: the demands for content learning and the diversity of learner characteristics within the student population. These strategies must enhance all students' abilities to comprehend and assimilate information and to cope with expository and narrative reading, writing, and listening forms. The following learner needs (related to literacy instruction) can provide teachers with relevant guidelines for the selection, development, and sequencing of instructional methods and activities to improve student competencies in these areas:

1. Reading and other communication arts strategies that are applicable across disciplines whenever possible

Have your students share this list with practicing middle-school teachers, to find out whether practicing teachers concur and whether additional points should be added.

2. Strategy instruction that can be taught and practiced in the context of content instruction
3. Assistance in developing comprehensive reading plans that help them learn when and why to use strategies, as well as how to integrate them
4. Strategies that help them to recall, comprehend, relate, and organize information that will allow them to build needed background knowledge
5. Assistance with development of a larger repertoire of reading response strategies (e.g., descriptive, comparison and contrast, argumentation)
6. Scaffolded instruction that supports their efforts to learn and apply high-level thinking skills (e.g., complex inferencing, generalizations)
7. Strategies and content that accommodate their wide range of cognitive levels, skills, background knowledge, affective needs, and cultural experiences
8. Ways to relate new content to prior knowledge and personal experiences
9. Activities that encourage their active involvement and participation (e.g., cooperative learning)
10. Exposure to narrative and expository content that fosters increased understanding of multicultural perspectives
11. Opportunities to read for different purposes and knowledge of how to adjust reading strategies to match those purposes

IMPLICATIONS OF LEARNERS' NEEDS FOR TEACHERS OF READING

Literacy instruction at the middle grades should be (1) holistic, (2) interactive, and (3) transferable in practical ways.

Invite a middle-school teacher to visit class and discuss these implications with your students.

1. Holistic—The reading teacher in the middle grades should do the following:
    a. Develop an overall general plan of instruction for the entire school year with the understanding that change is likely
    b. Place all important reading skills, processes, and concepts in a meaningful communication context in which students can see the practical application potential
2. Interactive—The teacher should do the following:
    a. Help learners see the important relationships among knowledge about the text; about their own experiences, abilities, and learning styles, and about the context

    b. Capitalize on the potential of cooperative learning, conferencing, feedback systems, and personal interaction

3. Transferable and practical—The teacher should do the following:

    a. Assist students in seeing the value of methods for using critical reading skills and processes in all content areas

    b. Assist students in seeing the application of reading skills and processes in all aspects of their daily lives outside the classroom

Episode 6—Lunch Duty: Are You Sure You Want to Work in a Middle School?

When the bell rings, 500 active, noisy young people converge on cafeteria and activity areas. We adults are ready, dutifully holding watch at our stations on the playground, in the gym, cafeteria, library, and halls. By carefully positioning ourselves, we are hoping to be able to visually monitor every nook and cranny in which these irrepressible, not altogether trustworthy children may lurk. Our job—to stop running, jumping, poking, pushing, name-calling, fighting, littering, truancy, and, on occasion, drug use. We tell them to stop doing many of these things at least 100 times each lunch period. They sincerely promise to oblige, and they do—until they round the corner out of sight of the enforcer, or get distracted by a friend whose attention they want to draw, or are captured by some inner bodily urge before their minds can "kick into gear," with promises and obligations temporarily forgotten.

Our most difficult and hopeless task is to keep them from clustering for lengthy periods of time at their lockers, the repository of all things special and personal to middle-school students—stashes of food, pictures of their favorite rock video stars and friends, mirrors, hair spray, and deodorant. Lockers also serve many important functions for 11- to 14-year-olds other than a private place to stash stuff. You can bang on them, hide behind them, crawl in them, and hang out at them. They are a wonderful place to take care of your personal grooming, almost like your own personal dressing room. You can comb your hair, put on your deodorant, even change your clothes. If you're a beginning sixth-grader, they serve as an intellectual challenge. It may take you 2 months and lots of help from teachers, custodians, and administrators to figure out their intricate complexities.

Five minutes until the bell rings—The student management specialist is carrying an eighth-grader who may have broken his kneecap when he tripped while playing touch football. Well, you might think, it's not uncommon for children to get hurt playing football. You need to know, however, that middle-schoolers can and do get hurt while sitting in their chairs in classrooms, while walking down unobstructed halls, or while standing and talking to friends. We go through several pounds of ice and band-aids each day ministering to their various cuts, bumps, and bruises.

The bell rings, and most children and adults have survived intact. We've achieved our goal for this break period.

HIGHLIGHTS

1. Middle-school students are significantly different developmentally than their younger counterparts. This has direct impact on how teachers of reading instruct them.
2. Young adolescents are more sophisticated than students in the earlier grades. They can reason more hypothetically and can deal with more abstract ideas and concepts.
3. Middle-school students must deal in a more concentrated and detailed way with content-area subjects than they did in their earlier years, and they are expected to bring more personal experience and more substantial background knowledge to the learning situation than are younger students.
4. Teachers of reading in the middle grades must be prepared to focus most of their reading instruction on critical reading comprehension, reading vocabulary, and study skills within the context of subject matter in content areas.
5. Although young adolescent students are generally more sophisticated than their younger friends in school, the range of abilities within these learners is very wide, thus challenging the middle-school teacher to search for ways to individualize learning and instruction as much as possible.

REINFORCEMENT ACTIVITIES

Look for attention to all areas—physical, cognitive, emotion, and so forth.

Expect some attention to the role of academic subjects.

Consider asking your students to generate some of their own episodes, based on their personal experiences as middle-school students and/or their observations of students in middle schools.

Point out the need to find both advantages and disadvantages.

1. What are some key developmental differences between middle-school students and children in the earlier elementary grades?
2. Describe some of the typical differences in learning requirements facing middle-schoolers as opposed to those for children in the earlier grades.
3. Identify some specific characteristics of middle-school learners depicted in the episodes presented in this chapter.
4. Think of the advantages and/or disadvantages of teaching reading to middle-school learners in separate classes in reading, as opposed to teaching the same skills and processes within the various subject areas that middle-school learners study.

ADDITIONAL PROJECTS

1. Visit a middle school, and observe middle-school students both in classrooms and in out-of-class contexts. Compare their behavior, comportment, attitudes, and so forth with those of younger learners.

2. Interview a middle-school reading teacher or reading coordinator. Gather information about how the nature of the middle-school learner affects how reading instruction takes place.

3. Examine various textbooks in content areas that middle-school students are expected to use. Check them for readability, vocabulary, and content difficulty, compared to texts for the earlier grades and for high-school students.

4. Read one or more adolescent novels that are popular with middle-school students. Discuss these in class, and relate their content to the developmental level of young adolescents.

REFERENCES

Buan, C., & Olson, T. (1988). *An Oregon Guide to Middle Level Schooling: Issues, Options, and Resources.* Portland, OR: Northwest Regional Educational Laboratory.

Lipsitz, J. (1981). *Early adolescence: Social psychological issues.* Paper presented in March at the annual conference of the Association for Supervision and Curriculum Development, St. Louis, MO.

CHAPTER 12

TEACHING THE NOVEL IN THE MIDDLE GRADES

Every novel should have a beginning, a muddle, and an end.
Peter DeVries

PREVIEW

Chapter 7, on reading comprehension in the elementary grades, examined a number of different techniques and strategies for teaching the comprehension of different kinds of text. It explored approaches to expository text, and it mentioned approaches to narrative text, including the use of story grammar, especially for teaching the comprehension of short stories. While expository text and short stories continue to be read in the middle grades, instructional time shifts increasingly to the novel. Indeed, for most adults, reading of fiction is almost entirely focused on the novel.

Middle-schoolers, who often resent reading any kind of expository text, will become very engrossed with a paperback novel that has adolescence-related content. The novel, therefore, represents an excellent opportunity for the teacher of middle-schoolers to develop a number of important reading skills.

In this chapter, the more sophisticated aspects of story elements taught at the middle-school level are described, along with recommendations for incorporating these elements into instructional techniques and strategies. During the year, most teachers will find it necessary to spend some time focusing lessons directly on these story elements and on related skills. A recommended approach is to begin the year with a simple review of these elements, followed by more focused instruction related to their application in particular stories and novels throughout the year.

This chapter also includes a model for teaching students how to read novels, which incorporates important information obtained from contemporary research and practice, in regard to the reading process.

FOCUS QUESTIONS

As you read this chapter, please keep the following questions in mind:

1. How are the elements of the story grammar more sophisticated and complex in relation to the novel than those story grammars described earlier in the book?

2. What are some effective techniques or strategies for teaching the various elements of story grammar with the novel as the content?
3. What are some important factors to keep in mind when selecting a novel for middle-grade students?
4. What are the key components of a "guided-response" model for teaching a novel?

INSTRUCTIONAL SCAFFOLDING

A reading-instruction strategy now advocated by a number of reading authorities, e.g., Ogle, et al. (1986), is *scaffolding*. The concept is based on the idea of beginning instruction with substantial direction and support and then gradually reducing that support as the student progresses through the learning and becomes more self-directed and self-sustaining in the learning. Thus, the approach works much as a temporary scaffolding does for construction workers building a new home or remodeling an older one. Temporary scaffolds are built around the building, some to support parts of the construction itself, some to provide support and safety for the workers doing the construction. As the work progresses and the building becomes substantial enough to support itself or parts of itself, the scaffolding is removed.

Students' learning can be seen in the same way. The teacher scaffolds instruction by *supporting* student attempts to use a particular reading strategy or set of strategies. The teacher also provides scaffolding through consistent *modeling,* as the need dictates. The teacher is also *adjusting* this support, according to the learning characteristics of the student, the nature of the material to be read, and the nature of the application tasks to be performed by the learner. The teacher must be *monitoring* student progress throughout the strategy in order to decide how much support must continue to be given and how much can be withdrawn.

The teacher can structure the lesson so that the support remains relatively constant, but the task demands increase gradually for the student. Another alternative approach is to keep the difficulty level of the tasks relatively constant, but after offering substantial support to introduce the lesson, the teacher can gradually reduce the level of support. In either case, the amount of scaffolding relative to the task demands decreases as the lesson progresses.

Teacher support may be offered in a variety of ways—verbally, in writing, through the use of graphics and other visual aids, and so forth.

Discuss the relationship between text type (i.e., expository and narrative) and teaching strategies. Also, consider the general perception that most writing experiences and the majority of reading experiences in the early elementary reading program are of the narrative text type. When students begin middle school, however, focus shifts to expository text and to extended narrative text (novels and novelettes). Ask students what this suggests to the middle-school teacher.

Remind students of the importance of this motivation.

Discuss, from an instructional point of view, how the complexity of story grammars increases through the grades.

Ask students to use the *scaffolding* idea in developing some short lessons that focus on language arts or reading skills or processes (e.g., topic sentences or cause–effect relationships), to provide them practice with increasingly shifting responsibilities onto the shoulders of the learner.

Spend some time providing additional examples and asking students to give examples using the support–model–adjust–monitor components of scaffolded instruction.

Regardless of the support type, however, it is important to keep in mind that gradual reduction of support is the key. When teaching reading, teachers are constantly monitoring student progress and considering how support can be adjusted upward or downward in response to students' needs.

Story Elements at the Middle-School Level

The elements of story grammar and their role in reading instruction have been treated earlier in this book. However, the level of sophistication increases when these elements are taught at the middle-school level. Most middle-school learners have developed a basic knowledge or, at least, a sense of awareness of the story grammar elements. Within the context of a novel, the story elements encompass subcomponents and interact with each other in increasingly complex ways. Stories are not clear-cut, straight forward plots in simple settings. Characters are not just right or wrong, good or bad. The hero and the villain are not as clearly delineated as they are in shorter and easier stories.

Story elements are incorporated into instructional designs for reading in order to help students to develop more insight into stories, which offers two key benefits:

> *Select two or three popular adolescent novels with which to demonstrate the complexity of literary elements and their interrelationships.*

1. It gives students sophisticated tools for comprehending stories and for appreciating the role of these elements in literature.

   Example: How does the *setting* affect the main *character* in *The Red Badge of Courage* by Stephen Crane? (This novel is set during the Civil War, and the main character is caught up in examining his own courage and sense of responsibility—heavily shaped by where he is and the time and place of the novel.)

2. It enables students to peer into the author's craft as a writer so that students can apply in their own writing some of these important elements during the writing process.

> *Emphasize this point. The purpose of instruction in the story elements that follow is to provide solid understanding of how they work together to build a novel or story that is whole.*

Thus, the primary focus of instruction is the use of story elements as tools and not as ends in themselves. The following text describes ways in which the key story elements (setting, plot, character, and theme) can facilitate the design of strategies for helping middle-school students to develop their comprehension and appreciation of narrative text.

Story Elements: Understanding the Role of "Setting"

At the middle-school level, students can explore the social, cultural, and historical nature of setting, as well as the simpler physical and temporal aspects. Young adolescents can learn to distinguish between the uses of setting as a backdrop for a story and its use as an integral component that significantly influences the plot, characters, and/or theme of the work. In fact, they should read literature in which setting serves various roles:

as antagonist

as symbol

as establisher of mood

as character shaper

as instrumental to plot

In the novel, more often than not, the setting plays a dominant role throughout the entire story. It certainly plays a more significant role than in many of the stories children read in the elementary grades. Students also should be led to examine setting through direct description, implicit description, character dialogue, character actions, and any other ways in which authors incorporate setting into their stories.

> Ask students to bring examples of middle-school-appropriate literature to class, within each of which these various roles of setting are demonstrated.

Instructional Objectives in Regard to Setting

Students should learn to do the following in relation to setting:

- Identify details that describe the setting
- Infer generalizations about the setting and its role, based on both explicit detail and implicit and indirect information
- Articulate the role of social and cultural conventions, as well as the role of the historical period for the novel
- Interrelate the setting with the other story elements in shaping the character of the story
- Provide examples of evidence for theories regarding the role of setting, derived from the text itself

> Ask students, "What would be some useful performance indicators that would demonstrate middle-schoolers' mastery of these abilities?"

Sample Questions about a Particular Novel's Setting

- What are some details the author uses to reveal the setting and its role in this story?
- How is the setting used in this story (e.g., as antagonist, as a way to establish a mood, as a key to the plot)? Give some examples to support your opinion.
- Is the setting critical to this story, or is it only a background?
- Could this story take place in a different time or in a different location? Explain your reasoning.

Sample Activities for Developing an Understanding of Setting and Its Role

1. Select magazine pictures, photographs, and/or art prints that show distinctive settings. Ask students to generate descriptive words

Figure 12.1   Settings as a mirror of character: branching map of the *Magnum, P.I.*

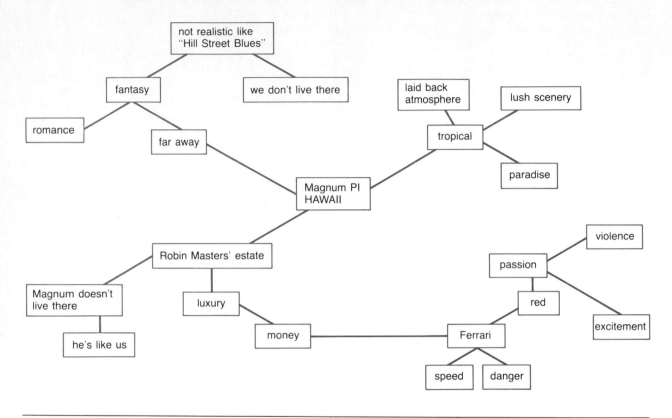

and phrases for the settings and to identify clues related to its time and place. Have them identify and explain any clues in the pictures that relate to social or cultural understandings. Conclude the lesson by having students (a) write a description of the setting and (b) suggest the synopsis of a story that could be derived from the setting or that could be integral to it.

2. To introduce the idea that setting can illuminate character, have students complete activities such as the following:

    a. Select a popular TV show. Discuss the setting and what it reveals about an important character. Complete a graphic map with the main character in the center and objects from the environment radiating out from the center. Around each object, list character qualities or characteristics that the object represents. Figure 12.1, showing a branching map of *Magnum, PI*, illustrates how this might be done.

Figure 12.2   Interpretation of settings-chart used in an activity to personalize the meaning of settings.

Column 1	Column 2	Column 3	Column 4	Column 5
Items in or around my home (a brief description)	What I think these items say about me to others.	What these items do say about me to others. Response 1	What these items do say about me to others. Response 2	What these items do say about me to others. Response 3
1. Shade garden filled with camellias, ferns and cymbidiums.	1. Plants are my companions and my hobby.	1. Very romantic garden. Likes a place to go to feel "civilized."	1. You like to get next to nature.	1. The kind of plants you like convey a mood—something about tranquility.
2. Heavy, graceful wrought iron candelabra chandelier over dining area. Candles are the only light in the room.	2. Quiet dining is pleasant and candlelight brings peaceful moments.	2. Very elegant and refined.	2. A person who appreciates craftsmanship and history of people.	2. Like the shade garden, this space says, "Slow down. Relax. Enjoy."
3. Oak étagère filled with cut crystal, silver pieces, and our stereo tape player and tunes.	3. The past is important and music is my passion.	3. Likes to conceal modern things with old, graceful things.	3. A person who likes elegant things.	3. Your objects are like works of art to be appreciated over time.
4. Three stair step redwood decks down the hill behind our home.	4. Outdoors is vital and intriguing. I spend much time outside.	4. Luxury. Three decks. That's a lot of room for sunning.	4. You like to get outside.	4. Can't get a reading on this. Are they in the sun? Perhaps they show the more extroverted side of you.

b. Have students use a chart similar to the one in Figure 12.2. In column 1 of the chart, students should list several objects from their homes that have special meaning for them. Have them list in the second column what they think these items would say about them to others. Ask other students to respond to the same items without looking at each other's responses. Discuss the inferences made—their similarities and differences.

c. Pair students and have them look in each other's lockers and list what they see. What do the objects in the lockers and the condition of the objects reveal about the student? Have the pairs write a descriptive essay about each other using that information. This activity could also be done by individuals about themselves.

3. Have students listen to a radio mystery and list the words and sounds that created a mysterious or frightening mood. (There are wonderful cassette tapes now of some of the old classic radio mystery programs, e.g., "Suspense," "The Green Hornet," "The Adventures of Sherlock Holmes.")

4. Have students describe or draw in large or small groups the images created in their minds when a teacher reads aloud. What were their similarities and differences? How did the students' personal images of the setting affect their perception of the characters or their predictions about what was going to happen in the story?

5. Have students do the following:
   a. Describe a setting for a favorite TV show.
   b. Select a picture of a setting, and write a story using that setting.
   c. Describe a setting that reveals clues about a character.
   d. Describe a setting to create a mood (e.g., mysterious, peaceful, exciting, humorous).
   e. Describe a science fiction setting.

Have students generate additional ideas to add to this list.

When the setting is integral to a story because it creates a mood, illuminates a character, or drives the plot, it should become a key part of the overall strategy for teaching the work. If students have not had previous experiences that are important to the concept of setting as it was used by the author of the novel being read, some introductory activities should be used prior to reading the novel. Specifically, the introductory activities should relate to the way setting is being used in the particular story being used. For example, if the author uses setting to illuminate character, the activities in Item 2 of the preceding list might be used as an introduction to the story (i.e., the activities using the TV character, the objects from the student's home, or the student's locker).

Story Elements: Understanding the Role of Plot

Definition

Suggest the complexity of these ideas in plot. Have students bring literature examples to class, ranging from simple, limited plots to complex ones. Ask them to point out specific differences in each of their examples.

The *plot* comprises the overall structure of the story. It is the organizational structure of the narrative form and includes the following elements:

Exposition: The introduction to the main characters, settings, and situations in the story

Conflict: The problem(s) between the opposing forces in the story—the protagonist and the antagonist. There are several types of conflict: person against self (an internal conflict), person against person, person against society, and person against nature or some other impersonal force

Inciting force: An action or event that triggers the conflict

Rising action: The actions or events that result from the conflict and build toward the climax of the story

Crisis: The turning point at which the climax becomes most intense

Climax: The point of greatest interest and involvement in the story when the outcome of the conflict can be predicted

Falling action: The events that happen after the conflict peaks and that lead to the conclusion of the story

Denouement or resolution: The final outcome of the story

Plot Sequence

Generally, the events of the story occur in chronological order, but authors can change this sequence through flashbacks. *Flashbacks* allow the author to describe past events that may explain a character's actions in the present. *Foreshadowing,* another technique related to plot development, is used when the author wants to provide clues or hints to what will happen in the future. This technique helps build suspense and advances the plot.

Sample Questions about a Particular Novel's Plot

1. What is the sequence of events that lead to the climax in this story?
2. What is the conflict(s) in this story?
3. Are the characters and events in this story believable? If so, why? If not, why not?
4. How would the events in this story change if it were moved to another location or another historical period?
5. Are foreshadowing or flashbacks used in this story? If so, give examples. Explain how they are used.
6. Is the ending believable? Would you write a different ending? If so, describe it. Explain your reasons for writing a different one.

Ask students to suggest other useful questions.

Sample Activities for Developing a Concept of Plot and Its Role

1. Complete a "Plot Chart," such as the one in Figure 12.3, for your favorite movie, TV show, or novel. Use your plot chart to write a plot summary.
2. Identify the story elements in a front-page newspaper article. Write a short story with the information from the article.
3. After reading a portion of a short story or novel, predict how it will end, and write your own ending.
4. Write a flashback scene that would explain your behavior during some important event in your life. Share your scene with other students.
5. Identify the story elements in a wordless picture book. Write the text to the story.

Story Elements: Understanding the Role of Character

Discuss the intricacies of character and of character development. Use literature examples to contrast simple and complex characterization in stories and novels. Another useful technique for helping learners understand character and characterization is by having them write from two different perspectives. One perspective is to assume a third-person stance in describing the behavior of a given character in a particular context or situation in a story. Then have the student assume the identity of the character and write a description of what is happening to him or her in the situation.

Ask your student teachers, "How important is it for students to like or to admire characters in text? Why is it important to be able to move back and forth from empathizing with a character to stepping outside the character and analyzing his or her behavior from other perspectives?"

Well-defined lifelike characters are central to good novels and to all short stories. The author usually presents the key characters as evolving persons who develop through the story. In other words, the key characters do not have fixed personalities that do not change; instead, the characters live, grow, and change as various story elements affect them. Understanding this evolving nature of characters in the novel or the extended story is important to comprehending the theme and central plot of the work.

Though at least one (and usually more) of the key characters in a novel must develop and change, not all characters in a novel are so richly drawn, multidimensional, or dynamic. Novelists use various kinds of characters to serve various purposes within the context of the story.

Types of Characters

Flat Characters: Flat characters are not fully developed in the story and usually demonstrate just one aspect of their personalities. This type of character is used by authors to flesh out the scene and make the setting believable, to advance the plot, and/or to show how the main character relates to others.

Round Characters: Rounded characters are fully developed by the author, who reveals many aspects of their personalities to the reader. Enough information is provided about these types of characters that the reader is able to anticipate what they might do and how they might react.

Figure 12.3 Plot chart that can be used for summarizing any plot.

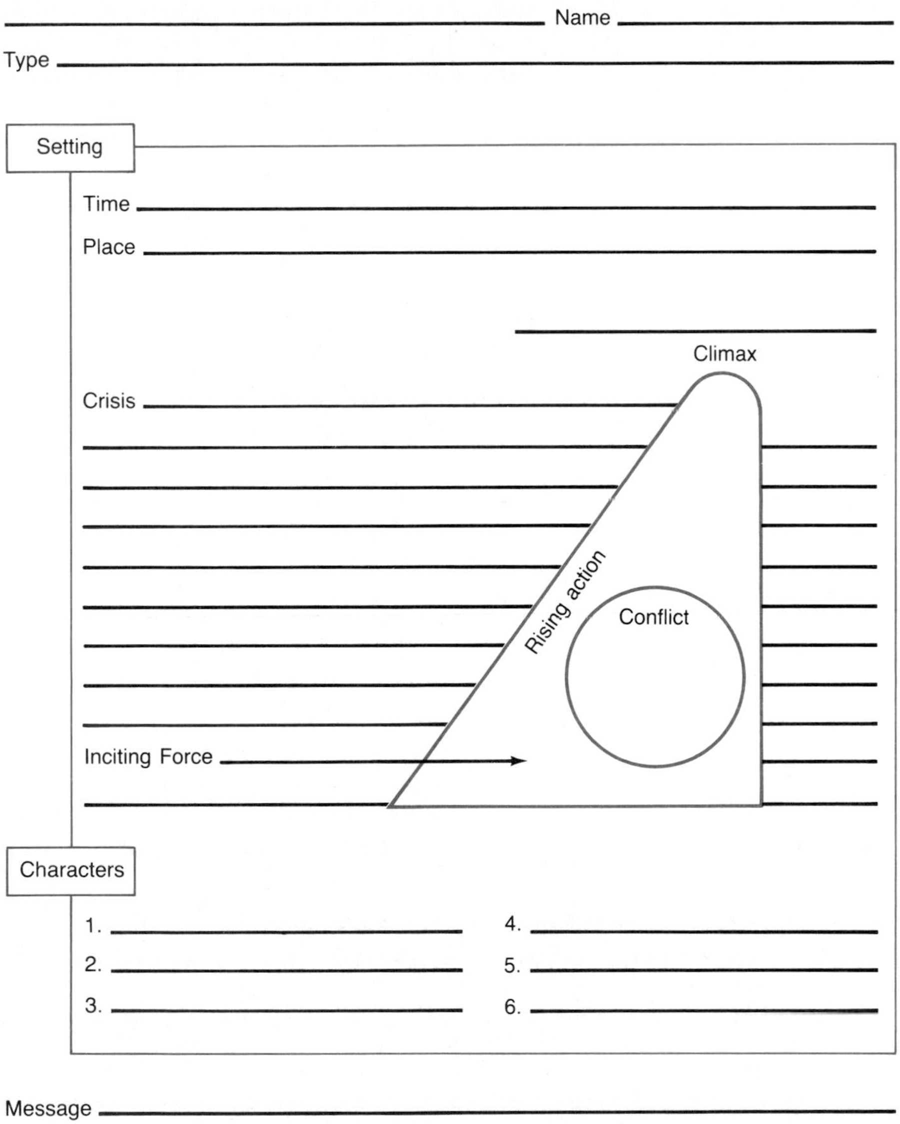

Name _____

Type _____

Setting

Time _____

Place _____

_____

Climax

Crisis _____

_____

_____

_____

Rising action

Conflict

_____

_____

Inciting Force _____→

_____

Characters

1. _____   4. _____

2. _____   5. _____

3. _____   6. _____

Message _____

Other Character Types: The stereotype, the foil, and the observer
and other character types used by the au-
thor for different purposes. The *stereotype*,
who has a few traits of a class or group, may

perform an easily understood role (e.g., the stereotyped villain or hero). The *foil* provides a contrast to the main character and in that way reveals many of the main character's traits. The *observer* is the character who watches the plot unfold. The reader sees and hears through the observer, who often presents the author's perspective. All of these character types may be static and may have personalities and values that do not change during the course of the story. Others will be dynamic and change in some important way as a result of their experiences in the story.

Main Characters: The main characters in the story are the protagonist and the antagonist. The *protagonist* is the leading character in the story, and the *antagonist* is his or her adversary.

Ways in Which Characters Are Revealed

Students must learn how to use information provided by the author to infer important characteristics of key characters in the story, as well as to recognize the kinds of characters being described. Sometimes, the characters are described directly by the author. At other times, however, the author provides clues to character qualities (a) through the words and thoughts of the character, (b) through the character's actions, (c) through the reactions and descriptions by other characters, and (d) through descriptions of the character's appearance or surroundings.

Instructional Objectives in Regard to Character

Middle-school learners should develop the following critical skills in character understanding:

- Ability to identify key characters' beliefs, values, attitudes, needs, and goals that are directly stated or described by the author or that can be inferred based on information provided about characters' actions, words, thoughts, appearance, surroundings, or effects on other characters
- Ability to articulate reasonable justification for assertions about characters and their personalities and roles in a given story
- Ability to compare and contrast characters and their various features and tell how their interactions shape the story.

Character Qualities

Clearly, a goal for students is to use the information provided by authors about the characters' beliefs, goals, attitudes, and attributes, in order to make inferences that explain the characters' actions in the story. Middle-school students will need assistance in developing strategies that will help them to collect evidence from the story and to connect that evidence with what they already know about human behavior, both to generate the inferences and to support them.

One of the difficulties middle-school students have with this task is the generation of terms that describe character beliefs, attitudes, and attributes and understanding those terms well enough to determine whether they adequately describe the character. Thus, an additional objective may be to develop a broad vocabulary of descriptors, including denotative and connotative meanings for these terms.

> *Example:* The term *courageous* may be used to describe a character, but what does courage mean? How do students determine whether a character's actions are truly courageous or simply foolhardy. To make these distinctions, students have to fully comprehend the attributes of the term *courage* and be able to identify examples that do or do not show the attribute. Prereading activities should be included that will make this job easier for students. Also helpful would be the technique developed by Kahn, Walker, and Johannessen (1984), described in the sample activities related to an understanding of character.

Vocabulary enrichment activities should be included, which will enable students to explore the many subtleties and nuances of meaning encompassed by terms used to describe characters. These always have more meaning when studied in relation to a particular character or characters. In addition, several other questions may help students to develop deeper understandings of the story characters.

Sample Questions for Developing an Understanding of a Particular Character

1. What beliefs, values, traits, attitudes, needs, and goals does this character have? Provide evidence from this story.
2. How does this character change in this story? What events cause that change? Provide evidence from this story.
3. Have you had similar experiences to those that this character had in this story? If so, did you react in the same way? Why? Why not? If you haven't had similar experiences, please imagine yourself in the character's situation. Would you react the same way? Explain why or why not.
4. What did you learn from this story that you can apply to your own life?

Ask students to identify examples of each of these character types in stories and novels appropriate for middle-schoolers.

5. Compare this character with one other character in the story. How were they the same? How were they different? What were the effects of these differences on the relationships these characters had with other characters in the story and on the outcome of events in the story?

6. What qualities do you have in common with this character? Have these qualities affected your life in any ways that are similar to their effects on this character?

7. Identify a stereotyped character in the story. Why is this character a stereotype? How do people differ in real life?

Have students generate some additional questions.

Sample Activities for Developing an Understanding of Character

1. Have students make inferences about the characteristics of individuals shown in paintings or in photographs. Have them list the visual clues and their own past experiences with people or characters in novels or TV shows that helped them make those inferences. A more interesting and elaborate version of this activity would be to have students complete the task in small groups, sharing their inferences and the reasons for them until they come to consensus. Group conclusions could then be shared with the whole class, and comparisons could be made. This would give students an opportunity to understand that inferences are based on a variety of data, some of which come from the text (the photos or paintings in this case) and some of which come from personal experiences. They could also see how very different conclusions can be drawn from what seems on the surface to be similar data.

2. Have students describe the characteristics of their favorite TV personalities and how these characteristics affect the plot of the story. They should use examples.

Ask students how creative interpretation or improvisation activities might be used in implementing the second sample activity.

3. Kahn, Walker, and Johannessen (1984) suggest a technique that chains a series of steps to help students develop an understanding of character. Students are asked to make a choice between two different interpretations of a major character (e.g., "Is Character X a good parent or a bad one?"). At the conclusion of these activities (or steps in this process), students are asked to write a persuasive essay applying the same question to another character. In the essay, they are to support their conclusion with evidence from the story and present an explanation that connects the evidence to their conclusion. (When planning instruction, it may be helpful to recall the comments related to "Character Qualities," earlier in this section.)

   a. Activity 1: Students individually read two or three different scenarios the teacher has prepared, describing parents in action, and ranks the parents from best to worst. Students then meet in small groups and attempt to reach agreement on a group ranking. The teacher orchestrates the interactions in a way that requires students to articulate specific qualities of a "good" parent. These qualities are then listed by the group.

b. Activity 2: The teacher presents two statements about a parent: (1) a conclusion about the worth of the parent, and (2) a specific example that gives supporting evidence of that worth assignment. Students discuss the difference in the nature of the two statements—conclusion and support statements. Students then use a main character in a text they are reading, to make a conclusion statement regarding the character's worth and a series of statements of support, citing specific actions or other examples to justify the conclusion.

c. Activity 3: Students are provided three or four pieces of evidence from their text, which can support a claim of either positive or negative worth of a character. They choose a claim and write an explanation of how each piece of evidence supports the claim they have selected. These are discussed in small groups and in the class as a whole.

d. Activity 4: Students are asked to now choose a different character and work their way through Activities 3 and 4, to generate an argument for the worth or importance of the new character.

Story Elements: Understanding Theme

The *theme* of a novel or other narrative is its central point or key idea: the statement of the whole—what it exemplifies or illustrates. Themes in novels are seldom simple or easy to identify in a few words. However, the ability to identify and articulate the theme of an extended narrative work is typically considered the mark of a good reader.

Discuss the difference between *theme* and *moral* in literature.

Some examples of simple themes in narrative could be "Live and let live." "Appearances can deceive." "The value of people cannot be easily identified until they are observed during a time of trauma." However, trying to capture a theme's essence in one or two sentences can lead to oversimplification. For example, the theme of *David Copperfield* could be identified as, "Money cannot buy happiness." The theme of the great Russian novel *Crime and Punishment* could be labeled, "Crime does not pay." However, both of these novels demand more elaboration if their respective themes are to be identified honestly.

In the middle grades, the main purpose of raising questions about theme is to make students think about the gist of the text and to try to articulate it in a reasonable and telling fashion. Students should have opportunities to discuss the work and to discover its theme through discussion with others as much as through the individual reading of the work.

Sample Questions for Generating Discussions about Themes in Particular Stories

- What lessons has the main character (or characters) learned in this story? How do these lessons apply to people outside the story?
- What idea or attitude toward life do the characters and actions demonstrate in this novel?
- What words, ideas, or actions seem to be repeated in the story? Why are they repeated? What does the repetition indicate?
- What emotions do you feel about this story? Why does the author want you to think and feel the way you do?

Some Activities for Developing a Concept of Theme and Its Role

1. Present students with brief fables that are famous for containing specific morals lessons (e.g., "A penny saved is a penny earned."). Have students write their own moral lessons for each work. (Note: For students having difficulty with the concept of theme, you might begin by presenting them with three or four different fables, with each of the morals separated from its fable. Ask them to join the appropriate moral with the appropriate fable. Thus, the students would not have to generate the moral or theme themselves in this initial stage.)

2. Have students read stories from earlier grade levels of your school system's reading program (e.g., third or fourth grade), and ask them to write one- or two-sentence themes for the stories. In small groups, have students share their theme statements and discuss which ones they would choose as group statements of the themes.

3. Have the class identify a TV show that the majority like and watch. Agree on a particular show for viewing by all of the class. Ask each student to write a brief statement of theme for the show. Have them bring their statements to class for sharing. Discuss the show and why particular statements appear to be more salient than others.

4. Choose three or four different short stories that have differing degrees of theme complexity. Have students read them, then rank order the stories in terms of their complexity of theme. Pair them and ask the pairs of students to write theme statements for each of the stories. Ask them to share their theme statements with others in class. Discuss the differences among the statements prepared by different pairs of students.

SELECTING A NOVEL FOR WHOLE-GROUP STUDY

Before introducing the framework selected by the authors to guide your selection and integration of skills, strategies, and activities for a particular work, it may help to consider criteria for selecting literature to use for whole-group study. A number of criteria can be used when choosing a literary work—poem, short story, play, novel, and so forth—for use in your classroom. (See Chapter 13, on children's literature, for an example.) However, when it really comes down to it, there are just three questions the teacher of the middle-school grades must really consider. Careful consideration of these questions during the selection process will help to prepare for planning and presenting the literature you choose. While these particular questions were specifically written to guide novel selection, they may be used with other genres as well.

1. Is the novel one you personally enjoy and will enjoy sharing with your students?

   The enthusiasm, interest, and insight you bring to the sharing of a novel will have a significant impact on the students' receptivity to the novel. If you enjoy a particular work, you will be more likely to spend the time required developing activities that will help students to appreciate it too. Your delivery and interest in student responses to the author's craft and insights into the human condition will invite involvement.

2. How will your students respond to the work?

   What experiences have your students had that will help them relate to the characters and events in the story? Will these connections be obvious to students, or will they need substantial support from you to make them? What background knowledge—literary, cultural, and/or historical—will your students bring to the text? What background knowledge will you need to build to make the novel comprehensible and meaningful?

3. Will the novel help you share or illustrate important ideas, information, or strategies with your students and/or simply enhance their enjoyment of reading because it is a good story?

   There are many legitimate reasons for sharing a particular novel, but you should be clear about what your purposes are so that you can develop activities and questions that will help you and your students achieve those goals.

This might be a good point at which to discuss the problems of controversial topics and censorship in the middle grades. Guidelines developed by the American Library Association (ALA) and the National Council of Teachers of English (NCTE) can be helpful. You might also ask students to inquire into local school policies regarding complaints about instructional materials and whether they have written guidelines for handling such matters.

Examples: If you have chosen a novel for its sheer entertainment value, you may wish to do no more than simply read it aloud, letting the students enjoy it in a relaxed and casual manner.

- If you have chosen one in order to develop background knowledge about a historical period, you should develop activities that highlight (a) the important understandings about that period, including key events; (b) the cultural and social context of the story's characters and events; and (c) the ways in which the historical, cultural, and social contexts influenced the development of those characters and those events.
- If you have chosen a novel because of the insights it provides on the human condition, you must clarify for yourself what those insights are in order to develop activities that will provide students with opportunities to grasp those understandings and relate them to their own personal experiences.
- With many of the novels you share, you may wish to highlight the author's craft, such as the devices she or he uses to build suspense, or the author's use of descriptive writing to establish the mood or to define the characters. Sharing this type of information can help students with their own writing, and it can be fun and interesting to explore how the author achieved certain narrative effects.

For many novels, you will have a combination of many of these purposes. The important thing to remember is to be clear about your own purposes and to develop questions and activities to support those purposes. In addition to your purposes, students should also always be encouraged to develop purposes of their own, even with novels you carefully selected and developed activities for in advance. Good readers intuitively do this, and it has been demonstrated to enhance both their comprehension and their enjoyment of reading. You can help students develop this skill by giving them an opportunity to establish their own prereading questions and by providing frequent opportunities for students to search for answers to those questions and to make connections between the characters' experiences and their own.

A MODEL FOR INTEGRATING AND APPLYING READING STRATEGIES

The Complexities of Integration

One of the most difficult tasks for the literature teacher is to design a set of questions and activities that will support students in their efforts to understand (a) the key story elements and their interrelationships, and (b) the numerous major concepts and generalizations presented in narrative text. Before deciding how to integrate these understandings into a balanced program of instruction, the educator must consider the learner's perspective. Consider for a moment what this complex integration of literary knowledge, reading process skills, and general world knowledge and experience requires of the reader. It may help to consider some of the readers' abilities in terms of questions that students might ask themselves (or that teachers might encourage students to ask themselves):

1. The ability to make connections between the text and other personal and literary experiences

   - How do the main characters' experiences compare and contrast with my own?
   - How do the social and cultural norms portrayed in the book compare and contrast with those I see around me?
   - How would I respond in similar circumstances?
   - What does this novel have in common with other novels on the same theme, by the same author, or written in the same period? How does this novel differ?

2. The ability to identify story elements and their interrelationships

   - How does the social–cultural context affect the beliefs and attitudes of the characters?
   - What does the setting reveal about the characters?
   - What techniques does the author use to build suspense?

3. The ability to make complex inferences about these interrelationships across long stretches of text

   - How do the physical setting, the cultural context, and the events of the story interact to cause changes in the characters' behaviors and values?

4. The ability to make judgments about different aspects of the work and to explain and support those judgments with evidence from the text, from personal experience, and from general world knowledge

   - In what ways are the two main characters in the novel alike, and in what ways do they differ? Who was the most courageous? What evidence from the text and from my own experience supports my opinion?

5. The ability to infer generalizations about the world outside the work from the fabric of the work as a whole

   - What is the author's message about human nature or the human condition?
   - How do my own views differ from those of the author?

As you might imagine, these are very difficult tasks for middle-school students who are just beginning to think abstractly and whose literary and life experiences are still limited. Nevertheless, with careful support and

Remind students that these are important guidelines to use when choosing any instructional model for teaching the novel.

guidance from skilled and caring teachers, most middle-schoolers are willing and able to reach this level of sophistication in the reading process, and the rewards of helping them do so are well worth the effort.

Criteria for an Instructional Model for Teaching a Novel

Although the same elements of story grammar that underpin a short story are fundamental to a novel, the novel still is a special form of literature. It is much longer, more complex in structure and content, and more demanding in patience than other forms of literature. An effective approach to teaching a novel must include strategies that meet several instructional criteria:

1. Activities must be developed and sequenced that will help students to activate necessary background knowledge and reading strategies for this particular form of narrative.
2. Instruction must encourage students to use strategic reading appropriate to the text and to their own reading needs.
3. Developmentally appropriate lessons must enable students to internalize strategic information so that learners will not only know how to use the approach in dealing with this text but will be able to generalize its applicability to reading of *all* novels.
4. Instruction on the novel must also address students' needs in their daily lives, in other subjects, and in reading across the range of reading genres.

The Key Criterion of Instruction on Novels: Students' Understanding and Enjoyment

Teachers often assume that the questions and activities chosen and designed for adolescent literature are as easy for students as they are for adults. Adults, however, bring a wealth of knowledge and experience to the questions and activities that young people do not have. As a result, teachers frequently do not provide enough support or structure in activities or questions, to ensure that students will achieve success.

Student responses to literature and to the literary experience are critical to their deriving any value from the experience. If middle-schoolers do not like a selection of literature, the chance for improving their reading comprehension or their appreciation for high-quality literature will be minimal. Students must feel a personal reason for reading the work. In attempting to help students interpret and analyze a literary work, teachers often destroy students' interest in and motivation for the reading.

The long-range goal of narrative instruction in the middle-school grades is to establish a positive attitude toward reading that will sustain the learner through a lifetime of reading. In order to achieve this goal,

Learners face much more complex reading demands in the middle grades. It is in these grades that stories, novels, and nonfiction texts utilize more detailed vocabulary and heavier concept load.

students must know how to interpret a novel. They must be able to analyze its structure, interpret its content, and respond to its intent. The reader must actively engage with the text, must become part of what is going on in the story.

A MODEL FOR EXPLORING THE NOVEL: *GOING AFTER CACCIATO*

The following model was used by a middle-school principal with her teachers, to model an approach to teaching the novel to middle-school students. The novel, *Going After Cacciato* by Tim O'Brien (1989), is not a novel you would likely teach to middle-school students. An adult novel is more appropriate as a model for teachers and prospective teachers because it enables them to experience the same feelings and responses their students will have when reading a novel at their own developmental level. This novel was chosen because it reflects all of the complexities that are likely to be encountered when using any novel with middle-school students. Though this model was implemented with adults, it shows how a

A technique to consider using here, if time allows, is to divide the class into teams of three or four students and to have each team prepare a brief teaching unit. This unit would be used to teach the rest of the class, using a novel that is appropriate for undergraduate college student interests.

teacher might orchestrate the teaching of a developmentally appropriate novel to middle-school students.

Going After Cacciato: Scenario for Teaching a Novel

Choosing the Novel

Going After Cacciato is a complex novel that describes the difficult psychological conflicts experienced by a young soldier during the Viet Nam War. It provides a special challenge to the reader because of the author's interweaving of reality and fantasy to portray one of the major conflicts of the story: to flee or to fight. In the novel, one of the characters (Cacciato) chooses simply to walk away from the fear and confusion of battle and head for Paris, 8600 miles away. His squad decides to follow him and bring him back. During this fantastic and surreal journey, through flashbacks, and through the recollections of the main character of the story, Private Paul Berlin, the reader is given insights into the minds of the soldiers. Readers observe the soldiers' daily fears, their confusion about the war, and their extreme inner conflicts in facing the decisions they are forced to make about death and survival, courage and cowardice, honor and dishonor, duty and obligation.

I chose to use this particular novel with my staff for several reasons. One, it intrigued me. Initially, I had strong negative emotional reactions to the confusion and moral indecisiveness of the main character. On the other hand, I was strongly attracted to the moral and philosophical clarity of another character, Lieutenant Martin, who was described in detail only once in the story but who provided a stark, psychological contrast to the other soldiers. Second, I was enthralled by the author's use of language— his ability to capture so clearly in certain passages the beauty and horror of the physical setting and the inner doubts and conflicts of the characters. These passages were so beautifully written and so compelling in their insights that they simply invited the reader to share them with a friend.

Choosing the Focus for Instruction

As I began preparation for the staff development sessions, I went back to one of these captivating passages, a chapter in the book that described the soldiers on a long, hot, arduous march to do battle. For Private Paul Berlin, it was his first battle. In this chapter, which comes well into the middle of the book, the author provides a stark contrast between the physical and mental numbness of the soldiers and the apparent philosophical clarity and purpose of young Lieutenant Martin. It also sets the stage for the conflict that occurs between Martin and Berlin.

As I reread the chapter, I tried to determine what it was that intrigued me about it. I came to the conclusion that it was the contrast in these two characters' experience and point-of-view and the conflict that eventually

Point out to students how the personal narrative is a dominant instructional model used in teaching the writing process now (e.g., journals and classroom book publishing). In addition, the idea of history-as-story and oral history or history-as-narrative are endorsed as a legitimate way both to document history and to learn about it. You might ask students to maintain a journal of their own efforts to teach a story or novel in a practicum or student teaching experience.

Talk about how decision making in teaching is always dictated, to some extent, by the way instruction evolves (i.e., how students respond, what they do or do not know, what you were or were not prepared for, etc.).

developed from these differences. At this point, I decided on a general focus of character development for the activities I would share with the staff. I still was not sure where I was going with it.

In contrasting Berlin and Martin, I began with this chapter, listing characteristics of each that I inferred from the reading. What became apparent immediately was that while the author had given the reader a great deal of information about Lieutenant Martin's beliefs and values, and some strong indications of the types of actions he would take in battle, he gave very little information about Private Berlin. Who was this man? What was his background? What did he believe in? Where was he going?

To find the answers to these questions, I searched through the novel looking for clues the author had given. It was during this search that I became aware of the significant development of this character over time, his past history, his characteristics, his inner conflicts and moral dilemmas. I also became increasingly attached to him and began to realize that his struggle to clarify his own beliefs, to grapple with moral choices, to face himself and his frightening predicament, were not unlike those we all face at different points in our lives.

In Paul Berlin's case, because of his involvement in a war, a morally ambiguous and confusing one for most participants, this struggle is telescoped in time with extreme and lasting physical and psychological consequences. It is this telescoping of time and events and the life-and-death consequences of decisions that make war novels dramatic and interesting. As with Paul Berlin, there is really no place to hide. The characters must act, and it is in their actions and their reflections on those actions that the author and the reader have the opportunity to explore some of the fundamental questions about what it means to be human.

What began in my planning with a return to the chapter in the book that captured my attention and an initial decision to focus on the comparison of two characters in the story, led, with further exploration, to the decision to focus on the development of the main character as he struggled to resolve his inner conflicts caused by his participation in the war. While there may have been many other points of focus I could have chosen, the inner conflicts Berlin had to face and his struggle for resolution seemed to me to be the most powerful and universal.

Monitoring Reactions and Thoughts in
Order to Develop Instruction

From this point forward, I became immersed in the task of trying to understand this character. What experiences had shaped his early life? How did they lead to his participation in the war? What were his inner conflicts? How did they affect his actions in different situations? How would he resolve his conflicts? How did his experiences in the war change him? I also began asking myself questions. Why did I respond so negatively to this character at first and so positively to Martin? What caused

Point out that in teaching a literary selection, the teacher is not so much teaching something that he or she already knows, but rather teaching something that he or she is still in the process of learning. All readers learn something new about a book when it is reread and/or discussed with others. Literature seems to take on a life of its own, which is greater than the original writer may have intended it to be. Realizing this can help beginning teachers be more receptive and open to various interpretations of a work.

those feelings to change? Why do I like war novels anyway? What do these different responses reveal about me? What experiences have I had that are similar?

Through these and other questions, I carefully monitored my own reactions and strategies as I read in the hope of discovering information that will help me develop appropriate activities. In the reading of this novel, I made several interesting observations that I thought I could use:

Talk about the importance of these things when one is choosing a selection of literature for use in the classroom.

- I immediately began to connect the characters' experiences to my own. These connections evolved and became clearer with repeated readings to answer my questions about the character.
- I had to be persistent in searching for information on Berlin that was revealed in bits and pieces throughout the book. It helped to have a framework for analyzing a character (e.g., beliefs, attitudes, values, cultural setting, goals, actions, thoughts). These categories helped me to sort and synthesize information and to monitor changes.
- I brought a lot of literary as well as world knowledge to the reading that probably affected my interpretation of the work. I had been a young adult during much of this war. I had watched it on daily newsreels, argued about it, and had friends who participated in it. I had also read several other war novels, including many on Viet Nam, and I had seen a variety of films on the subject.

I used these observations, ideas from contemporary theory on literary response, and knowledge of text structures and literature elements to design a set of questions and activities. My goal for these questions and activities was to support the readers' understanding of the main character and his development as he participated in and reflected on the events in the story. I also placed special emphasis on the design of activities that would help readers connect the characters' experiences to their own lives.

Because my time with staff was limited, I had them read only the sections of the text that were particularly relevant to understanding the main character. Although this decision was one of practical mechanics at the time, the excerpts greatly simplified the reader's task of searching for information. It allowed me to guide their analysis in a way that was supportive and helpful. Using relevant excerpts is also a good way to simplify the evidence search for younger students, who often become overwhelmed by this task.

The next section includes the specific activities I designed, as well as a brief identification and discussion of each. The graphic organizers that I designed to accompany the activities are mentioned, but they are not included herein. I have also continued to include the personal observations I made while writing and teaching them.

Going After Cacciato: Questions and Activities

When attempting to make complex inferences with longer texts such as novels, one of the areas of special support that middle-school students need is a system for collecting and organizing evidence. Most of the activities described in this section include charts or forms of graphic organizers as aids to data collection and review. As was mentioned earlier, graphic organizers can improve comprehension by helping students select, organize, and visualize relevant information and the relationships that tie that information together. While there are many prestructured graphic organizers for students and teachers to choose from, it's also possible to design your own to more specifically fit a particular task. Both teachers and students, as they acquire skills in this area, should be encouraged to do so.

Activity 1: Assessing, Sharing, and Building on Prior Knowledge (Engaging and Connecting)

Context-Building Prereading Activity Describe the setting, characters, plot, and conflicts you would expect to encounter in a novel on the Viet Nam War. Descriptions can be recorded in words or phrases on a "Viet Nam War Story Chart." List the sources of your predictions. Discuss and explain.

Rationale and Objectives of This Activity In this activity, I had participants work in small groups to complete a "Viet Nam War Story Chart." The purposes of the activity were threefold. First, it gave me, the instructor, an opportunity to assess participants' prior knowledge and/or experiences related to the Viet Nam War. In this case, I had already predicted that they would bring considerable knowledge and experience to the reading because of the age of the group. Most were young adults during this period in U.S. history. Second, it gave participants an opportunity to recall prior knowledge and created an anticipatory set for subsequent readings and activities. Third, because this activity was done in group discussion with other people, it also provided an opportunity to build additional prior knowledge through the sharing of information and to build awareness of the similarities and dissimilarities of knowledge and perceptions readers bring to a story.

As we progressed through the readings, it became apparent that the differences in knowledge and experiences and the values and beliefs that evolved as a result had a significant impact on the readers' interpretation and evaluation of the text. To give just a few examples, some participants were antiwar activists, others were from military families who strongly supported and participated in the war, others had friends who were injured or died in the conflict, and still another was Vietnamese and lived in Viet Nam at the time, and she offered her perceptions from that perspective. A few were too young to remember this period in U.S. history and only knew of the war in terms of what they had studied in school or seen at the movies.

Important Points to Remember A few points are important to consider in designing this stage of instruction.

1. Design activities that allow you to assess students' prior knowledge. While your assumptions about what students already know may be fairly accurate, you may also be in for some surprises. Use this information to plan or adapt subsequent activities. For example, if the participants in the workshop had been less knowledgeable, I would have developed some additional prereading activities, such as watching a film about the war, sharing news clips, or presenting a lecture to provide an overview that would build prior knowledge.

2. Keep in mind that while you are assessing prior knowledge, you can also be building it. Activities that take advantage of cooperative learning in small groups can provide a less threatening format for sharing information and many more opportunities for students to interact.

3. Prereading activities are an important aid to comprehension and should not be neglected or relegated to a couple of casual introductory questions. They can help you assess and build prior knowledge and create a sense of anticipation and interest in the reading when done well. Do not skimp on this area of your planning!

Ask students what other points should be considered as well.

Activity 2: Developing Personal Prereading Questions (Connecting)

Personalizing Prereading Activity What kinds of questions might you want answered from a novel of this kind? List them, and share them with your group.

In Activity 2, I have participants construct their own prereading questions and share them with their group. Research has shown that good readers often do this naturally and it helps both to motivate and to focus their reading. I strongly suggest getting into the habit of doing this with your own reading and with the books you share with children. This is an exercise that can offer considerable insight into the reading process and also provide ideas for areas of focus for the activities you develop for your students. I have included mine for the novel *Going After Cacciato*. Notice how many of the themes or issues that are included in the questions later surface in the activities.

Sample Personal Prereading Questions

1. How do people behave when faced with extreme conditions where life-and-death choices must be made?
2. What beliefs, values, fears, and attitudes motivate those choices?
3. How would I behave under these circumstances? Are my values clear? Would I have the courage to act on these values in those circumstances?
4. How do behavior and the motivations for behavior under extreme circumstances differ from those experienced under more normal circumstances?
5. What kinds of experiences might I have in normal life that are similar to these peak experiences and that may require similar personal resources?
6. Why do these peak or extreme kinds of experiences appeal to people?
7. What can I learn from how people behave in these unusual circumstances that can help me lead a better life—a more ethical life?

> Ask students, "What prereading questions would you use with another novel (e.g., *The Light in the Forest*)?"

Important Points to Remember

1. Give students an opportunity to develop personal prereading questions to help motivate and focus their reading.
2. Writing your own can provide insight into the reading process and can help themes to surface for subsequent activities.

Activity 3: Comparing and Identifying with Characters (Connecting)

Read "The Way It Mostly Was" (O'Brien, 1989, pp. 194–204). Which character, Berlin or Martin, do you identify with the most? Explain why. (Do you have similar attitudes, values, beliefs? Have you had similar experiences, etc.?)

> Ask students, "What are some ways in which to get into the minds of literary characters?" Note the earlier suggestions about writing *inside* a character (i.e., from that character's point of view) and from writing *outside* the character (i.e., as others see him or her).

Rationale and Objectives of This Activity In this activity, I begin to focus the reader's attention on the important ideas I've chosen to explore in this novel: the evaluation of the main character, Private Paul Berlin, as he faces the physical, emotional, and ethical challenges of his involvement and actions as a soldier. In this and several subsequent activities, I focus on the comparison between Berlin and Lieutenant Martin because Martin's character, his belief system, his values, and his actions are such a contrast to Berlin's and the other soldiers and because of the conflict that develops between them. This conflict symbolizes much of the conflict in views that surrounded the Viet Nam War and leads to a significant event in the novel that influences the development of the main character. I also had several other purposes in developing this activity.

Because my time with staff was limited in this workshop, I decided from the beginning to use excerpts from the novel, rather than the entire text, to develop the activities. Although initially this was a practical decision, the insights I gained from focusing on the excerpts have some important implications for instruction:

First, it forced me to concentrate on a limited number of significant ideas that could be taken from the many possible ones presented in the text. Second, it freed me from thinking that you have to move through a novel in sequence from beginning to end to cover it, a very common approach in literature classes at this level. Quite often, when teachers make plans to study a novel with their whole class, their approach is to develop a set of questions for each chapter. As you can see from these activities, there are alternatives that can allow you to narrow your focus for group study. Later or concurrently on their own, students can read the whole text in total from beginning to end. With this novel, the excerpts were so interesting that the majority of staff purchased the novel and read it in its entirety.

Whether you choose to study the text from chapter to chapter or change the sequence or scope of your study, I strongly recommend that you select at least some sections to read aloud. There is something very special about a shared oral reading. With this novel, I hoped that sharing this chapter with my staff would be as moving an experience for them as it was for me. It did, in fact, have the effect of stimulating intense involvement and interest in the story and a deep respect and appreciation for the author's use of language. Reading this section aloud intensified this effect by slowing down the delivery of the language and allowing all of us to hear and experience the imagery associated with it at the same time.

You will also notice that this activity, as well as Activities 1 and 2, asks participants to react to the question from a personal point of view. We run the risk of losing the interest of students when we deal with the novel on a level that is too abstract for them to grasp, and we impede comprehension by not helping them link the text with their own prior knowledge and experience.

Important Points to Remember

1. When possible, choose a segment of the text to read aloud that fits with the major ideas you plan to develop and that will motivate and involve students. Feel free not to begin with the first chapter if it suits your purposes and will not ultimately spoil students' interest in reading the entire text.
2. Develop activities that will engage the interest of your students (a) by helping them connect the text to their own personal experi-

---

Discuss further the potential offered by exploring a novel in ways other than in exact page sequence.

Ask students to suggest additional important considerations.

ences, attitudes, and beliefs, and (b) by eliciting some type of emotional as well as intellectual reaction.

Activity 4: Collecting Evidence, Making Inferences, Comparing (Describing and Interpreting)

Do you find you need more information on Paul Berlin? Read "Who Was Paul Berlin" (O'Brien, 1989, pp. 101, 102, 218, 219, 271). Use data from these pages and from "The Way It Mostly Was" to complete your "Character Comparison Chart." Use excerpts to support your judgments.

Rationale and Objectives of This Activity In this activity, the reader reviews additional excerpts, to collect more information on the main character and to begin to make some generalizations about him and the contrasting character, Lieutenant Martin. The graphic organizer of a "Character Comparison Chart" helps the reader categorize and compare character actions, characteristics, beliefs, values, and goals. The categories are helpful for two reasons: (1) They help the reader know what to look for, and (2) they make the comparison easier by grouping similar information visually side by side.

In addition to the graphic organizer, readers are given a list of descriptors for values and characteristics, to help them formulate their generalizations about characteristics, values, beliefs, and goals. Both young people and adults can have difficulty coming up with adequate descriptive words for both values and characteristics. These lists can be very helpful for jogging students' memories and expanding their vocabularies, especially when the author has not been explicit in the descriptions and expects the reader to infer these qualities. Another problem may surface even with the use of these lists, and that is the lack of reader clarity on the meaning of the terms. The activities earlier in this chapter that focused on the concept of a "good parent" addressed this need. You may need to develop similar activities, especially if the ambiguously understood quality is central to the understanding of the character.

Important Points to Remember

1. Carefully constructed graphic organizers can help students collect, organize, and perceive relationships in relevant data. After teachers have introduced and modeled the use of these organizers, students often internalize the process and develop their own.
2. Help students expand their capacities to analyze and communicate character qualities by providing lists of descriptive words and phrases.
3. Make sure that students understand these terms and can cite both examples and exceptions. If necessary, develop activities to improve student comprehension of key vocabulary.

Activity 5: Comparing and Predicting (Interpreting)

Ask students to suggest some other ways in which writing could be used in a unit such as this.

Using the information you've collected so far, write a rough draft comparing Paul Berlin and Sidney Martin. Include in your essay the behavior, characteristics, values, and feelings that you feel distinguish the two characters. Support your judgments with evidence from the novel. What predictions can you make about each man's behavior and inner feelings as they participate in this battle and in other operations in the days or weeks to come? What conflicts may arise within themselves and with each other? What changes can you predict may occur in their personal value systems, their behavior, their attitudes toward war? List these ideas at the end of your rough draft.

Rationale and Objectives of This Activity At this point, I ask the readers to stop and synthesize what they learned about each character, using the evidence and initial generalizations collected and formed in Activity 4. The comparison chart from the activity was designed to help students to organize their writing and provide evidence for their generalizations. They are also asked to use this information as the basis for making predictions about the external and internal conflicts that surface in the text. An adequate understanding of these conflicts is essential to the idea of main character development.

Important Points to Remember

1. Writing activities, both formal and informal, are integral components of literature instruction. They can help students to organize and clarify their thoughts about the work, as was done in this case, or it can help them to connect the work to their own experiences.
2. When students are asked to respond in writing in more formal structured forms, such as this character comparison, earlier activities should help prepare them to do so. These prewriting activities enhance student thinking and writing. When left out of the instructional sequence, both can suffer.

Activity 6: Using the Social Setting or Context to Understand Characters (Interpreting)

The social setting or context in which a character finds her- or himself often reflects or influences the character's behavior, attitudes, and values. An analysis of that setting can provide further insight into the character. Read "The Soldiers War" (O'Brien, 1989, pp. 62–64, 176, 214–215, 320–321), and complete a chart comparing the soldiers' perceptions of war with Sidney Martin's perceptions. Does this give you any additional insights into Berlin and Martin? Does it change or confirm your predictions? If so, rewrite your rough draft to include this new information. Edit your draft, and write your final draft.

In this activity, readers have an opportunity to revise their initial hypothesis about the characters by taking a look at the social context in which they function. (See the "Important Point to Remember" following Activity 8.)

Activity 7: Exploring Events Leading to Internal Conflicts (Describing and Interpreting)

Read "The Result" (O'Brien, 1989, p. 194). Does it confirm your prediction of the conflict Berlin and Martin might have? Does this act fit with what you know about Berlin? What inner conflict will his participation in this event cause Berlin? What was his motive?

Activity 8: Exploring Internal Conflicts Coming to the Surface (Describing and Interpreting)

Read "The Question" (pp. 310–314). At this point in the story, Berlin's inner conflicts begin to surface and become more clearly articulated. What are they? What does he see as the cause(s)? Use a "Conflict Chart" to help you.

Rationale and Objectives of These Activities These two activities (7 and 8) ask readers to collect information that reveals the internal and external conflicts of the main character. As he summons the courage to face these conflicts and makes an effort to resolve them, we see his character evolve.

Important Point to Remember (Activities 6, 7, and 8) Good readers make predictions and formulate hypotheses about the elements of a story as they read. They constantly revise and reformulate initial interpretations and judgments. Activities and/or questions can and should support this process.

Activity 9: Summarizing and Judging the Conclusions of the Character (Interpreting and Judging)

Read "His Answer" (O'Brien, 1989, pp. 376–378). How does Berlin come to some kind of resolution of his inner conflict? Summarize it. Would his answer satisfy you? Why or why not?

Rationale and Objectives of This Activity In this activity, the reader is asked to identify, summarize, and judge the conclusions of the main character regarding his reasons for serving in the war. As readers, we have struggled with him as he painfully grappled for an answer. Now we have a chance to consider his answer and to reflect on its potential adequacy for us if we had been in his position. In judging his conclusion, we have to draw on our own beliefs and values. It is hoped, however, that we

Ask students, "How deep can the external–internal conflict idea be explored with middle-school students? Can you think of adolescent literature that is particularly good for dealing with this matter?"

approach this task with the added sensitivity and insight the novel provides into the difficulty of the question.

Important Point to Remember The process of judging a character's actions involves as much self-exploration as it does the exploration of the character. It gives the reader the opportunity to evaluate her or his own underlying assumptions and the beliefs on which they are based. In some instances, these beliefs may be clarified, enhanced, or changed by the reading experience.

Activity 10: Using What You Have Learned to Analyze a Character (Describing, Connecting, and Interpreting)

Ask students how writing could be used here.

When reading this novel, as with most good literature, readers have an opportunity to learn more about themselves—about what it means to be human. In Going After Cacciato, *we meet a character, not unlike many of us at this age, who comes into direct confrontation with himself—his fears, his values, his beliefs—and finds that he cannot run. What can we learn from the evolution of Paul Berlin's character about our own development as emotional, social, and moral beings. To help with this analysis complete a timeline for Paul Berlin. Use words and phrases to describe his emotional, social, and moral experience at each point in time.*

Activity 11: Using What You've Learned to Analyze Yourself (Describing, Connecting, and Interpreting)

Remind students that, although these questions and ideas can be important in teaching literature, they often can also allow you to stray into irrelevant areas of concern, too.

Can you identify a series of events or an event that forced you to reassess or clarify your behavior and beliefs or values? What insights did you acquire into your own character? What changes, if any, did these insights cause you to make? Create a personal timeline like the one you made for Paul Berlin. Use descriptive words and phrases to describe the event, your behavior (actions), your feelings, and your values/beliefs at each point in time. Highlight the changes you have listed. Use the information on the chart and the insights you acquired from exploring the evolution of Berlin's character to write a one- or two-page essay describing the evolution of your own character that were caused by this series of events.

Rationale and Objectives of This Activity In these activities, readers are asked to pull together all the data they have collected and the interpretations they have made of the main character, Paul Berlin. The timeline was used to help the reader identify Paul's emotional, social, and moral development at different points in the novel. In this final activity, the readers must connect Paul's development with their own. It became clear to me when reading the novel that although Paul's experiences were extreme, most of us have had experiences in our lives that were significant enough to force us to face ourselves and clarify or reassess our beliefs, values, and actions. Like Paul, we have bumbled into tough situations that forced us to make some hard choices for which we were not prepared. Because this is a universal experience and was central to the novel, I chose to develop it as the culminating and major understanding to which all of the activities would lead. It also provided the readers with an opportunity to reflect on what they had learned and to use that information to gain a better understanding of themselves.

Important Points to Remember

1. In general, questions and activities developed for a novel or short story should lead to a major understanding or generalization revealed by the story.
2. Final activities should focus on pulling previous learnings related to that generalization together and then helping the reader reflect on them and connect them to their own lives. For young people, an opportunity to reflect on what they have learned can reinforce the primary value of reading—its potential for giving them useful and interesting information, enlarging their world view, and stretching their understanding of themselves.

As I review these activities again, I see many things I could have done differently. For example, my prereading activities could have focused on the moral conflicts the main character would face in the form of an anticipation–reaction guide. Concepts such as duty, honor, and obligation could have been explored to prepare students for their encounters with them later. This self-questioning and the recurring feelings that your activities could be better are normal experiences in the planning and evaluation process. Do not be intimidated by them. Good teachers have the courage to explore and experiment with new ideas and strategies, and they constantly evaluate and revise what they do.

After teaching any extended unit, debriefing is important in order optimally to learn from experiences. Information gathered at this time allows fine tuning of teaching strategies and techniques.

HIGHLIGHTS

1. The story elements that serve as the foundation for the novel are also fundamental to all other stories. In the novel, however, those elements become much more complex and interrelated.
2. The middle-school years represent the first important opportunity for developing the concept of the novel with learners. Young adolescents are particularly receptive to adolescent novels that focus on issues important to them at this time in their lives.
3. The middle-school teacher must develop a range of techniques and activities designed to help middle-schoolers understand the nature and role of story elements in a novel.

4. To ensure success in teaching the novel for students of all ability levels in the middle grades, provide scaffolding strategies that help learners to explore the novel.

REINFORCEMENT ACTIVITIES

Ask students to provide specific examples of scaffolding.

1. What is meant by "scaffolding" instruction in reading?
2. Why is the novel of particular importance in the middle grades?
3. What are some specific techniques and activities that are appropriate for middle-school students, and why are they appropriate?
4. Do you think you would have enjoyed the series of lessons used by the author in teaching *Going After Cacciato*? Explain why you feel as you do.
5. Do you think that the techniques employed in that teaching unit would work with a middle-school-level novel? Explain why or why not.

Expect students to address the matter of opportunity to consider ideas in depth, to have greater personal involvement, and to sustain motivation.

Remind students of the importance of considering developmental appropriateness.

Push students for explanation.

Ask students to identify and describe the modifications that might be necessary.

ADDITIONAL PROJECTS

1. Review several of the newer novels for the middle-school level learner. Discuss some of their basic characteristics in class.
2. Interview some middle-school teachers and/or reading coordinators. Ask them what the most popular novels seem to be with their students, and inquire about those chosen for whole-class instruction.
3. Prepare a teaching unit for an adolescent-appropriate novel, using the approach elaborated in this chapter.

REFERENCES

Jones, B. F., Palincsar, A., et al. (1987). *Strategic Teaching and Learning: Cognitive Instruction in the Content Areas*. Alexandria, VA: Association for Symposium and Curriculum Development.

Kahn, E., Walker, C., & Johannessen, L. (1984). *Writing about Literature* (pp. 35–51). Urbana, IL: ERIC Clearinghouse on Reading & Communications Skills.

O'Brien, T. (1989). *Going After Cacciato*. New York: Doubleday & Co.

Ogle, D., Palincsar, A., Jones, B. F., Carr, E., & Ransom, K. (1986). *Teaching Reading as Thinking*. Alexandria, VA: Association for Symposium and Curriculum Development.

CHAPTER 13

THE FOUNDATIONS OF CHILDREN'S LITERATURE

Darlene Michener

*The single most important activity for building
knowledge required for eventual success in reading
is reading aloud to children.*

Report by the Commission on Reading, 1985

You may wish to share an example of an old first-grade readability-based basal reader, or to read parts of *More Fun with Dick and Jane* (1986, by Marc Gregory Gallant, Penguin Books), which is a spoof on the old Dick and Jane basal series. Compare that with current literature-based preprimers (such as *Beginning to Read A* by Houghton-Mifflin Company Publishers' 1989 Reading–Language Arts program).

PREVIEW

Children's literature is becoming an increasingly important component of the reading program. No longer do good teachers limit their students to the stereotypic Dick-and-Jane type of basal readers, with their readability formulas and sequenced sets of isolated skills. No longer do good teachers spend up to 70% of their reading class time having their students master coloring and pasting (completing approximately 1000 worksheets per year) at the expense of having their students master and fall in love with reading and writing (Anderson, Hiebert, Scott, Wilkinson, & the Commission on Reading, 1985). No longer do good teachers follow reading programs that spend most of their time pretesting and posttesting students over endless lists of isolated subskills, seldom giving students the chance to enjoy reading good stories! Instead, based on research data about how children acquire literacy, about the reading process itself, and about environmental influences and classroom practices, good teachers are finally incorporating a rich variety of high-quality children's literature into their reading, as well as their language arts, programs.

It is true that when the full variety of reading-instructional methods are analyzed (Bond and Dykstra, 1967), almost any method a teacher uses will work if the teacher really believes in it and in the students. However, closer scrutiny of those programs reveals that although they may all teach children to decode written symbols adequately, students seldom seem to attain high-level comprehension with many of those approaches. Furthermore, most approaches fail when it comes to instilling in children the will and desire to be lifelong readers! Educators and researchers agree that a literature-rich approach to developing literacy will not only produce students who can read and write but also will produce students who continue to be readers and writers

409

Figure 13.1   Quality children's literature gives students a better understanding of the way written language operates.

Share with your students information about the U.S. Department of Education Commission on Reading report, *Becoming a Nation of Readers* (Anderson et al., 1985). Point out the marginal notes that summarize the document and make it very easy to peruse for highlights and/or to locate sections they may want to read in greater depth. Point out also that students may wish to look over the references listed in that document, for help in locating journal articles on certain aspects of reading research.

Locate (or ask students to locate) the Bond and Dykstra 1967 results and share them with the class.

(e.g., Anderson et al., 1985; California State Department of Education, 1987) (Figure 13.1).

Falling in love with reading and writing develops from high-quality children's literature that offers many intrinsic values, such as the development of a joy for reading and a greater appreciation for the power of words and language (Huck, 1979). It gives children a better understanding of the way in which written language operates (as opposed to the less formal spoken language children regularly hear). It helps children internalize important reading awarenesses (metacognition), such as the idea that using the same reading rate may not be appropriate for all types of written material. "The lilting language of literature that falls softly on our ear lingers in the mind; it appears in our speech and writing" (Cullinan, 1987, p. 6). Making children's literature an integral part of the reading program will not only help your students to develop literacy skills, but it also will encourage your students to continue to be literate (Figure 13.2). "Then they will want to read and you will have succeeded twice!" (p. 13).

This chapter (a) introduces you to the role of children's literature in the curriculum, (b) explains the language and content of children's literature, and (c) guides you through using children's literature in your reading program.

Figure 13.2   Including high-quality literature in the reading program encourages enjoyment of reading and promotes literacy skills.

FOCUS QUESTIONS

As you read this chapter, think about the following questions:

1. Why is children's literature important?
2. What types of children's literature selections are available?
3. How can children's literature be incorporated into my reading program and across my curriculum?
4. Which books will I want to use with my students?

THE ROLE OF CHILDREN'S LITERATURE

Literary Experiences

Ask students to help you generate a list on the board of some other factors in determining how well children read. This may also be a good time to point out to your students why standardized test scores do not show the whole picture and therefore should not be used as the sole basis of evaluating reading progress/placement.

An earlier chapter in this textbook discussed the premise that learning to read involves cognitive development, perceptual development, and language development. A multitude of other factors also determine how well a person reads. Among those factors are the person's physical well-being, self-concept, experiential background, amount of practice, ability to use a variety of decoding strategies and reading speeds, and motivation. Exposure to a wide variety of children's literature introduces students to many new and exciting words. It arms them with a "storehouse of images and story patterns" (Cullinan, 1987, p. 6), familiarizes them with various writing styles and sentence structures, and increases their background of experiences—which is imperative to a deeper understanding of what students take from the reading experience (Rosenblatt, 1978). Literature offers students a deeper understanding of themselves as well, and a vicarious understanding of other people, places, and things. Great literature motivates students to stick with reading and to want to read more.

The success of a literature program, however, depends a great deal on the teacher's ability to plan and organize. A literature-based classroom environment that facilitates learning includes the following:

You may wish to break your students into small groups. Allow each group to select two or three of these components and brainstorm how they might design and/or implement them in their own teaching.

- A classroom library with access to many books (approximately 2.5 per student minimum at all times)—Good resources for books include garage sales, secondhand book stores, and student paperback book clubs
- A rotating selection of books covering the range of topics, styles, and (if applicable) languages of the students—Seasonal books and multiple copies of popular books should also be included
- Stimulating classroom library displays—These stimulate students' interest in new books
- Classtime each day for independent reading—sustained silent reading (SSR) for older students, book browsing and quiet reading for younger students
- Advertisements for reading other selections—Book sharing, reading aloud, and book talks are all useful
- Units organized by author, illustrator, subject, and genre themes— Some newer reading textbook series already do this (for example: Cooper, J. D., et al. *Houghton Mifflin Reading/Language Arts*, 1989)
- A variety of activities for selections shared with the entire class, either by the teacher reading aloud or through independent read-

ing—Commercially prepared booklet units are available, or you can design your own

- A writing center with a variety of writing papers and writing instruments—if possible, also include a computer armed with simple word processing software (such as FrEdWriter, a public domain word processing program)
- A publishing center with art and book binding materials for students to use
- A comfortable, quiet area for self-selected silent reading during planned reading time or during breaks in the daily curriculum

Teachers may also choose to select student class librarians, which serves two purposes: (1) It saves valuable teacher time, and (2) it helps selected students to develop independence and responsibility. This student job assignment includes the responsibility for arranging and rotating the books, checking the books in and out of the class library, assigning fines (i.e., additional tasks or jobs) for overdue or lost books, and creating attractive classroom library displays.

Literature as a Springboard to Literacy

"The meaning constructed from the same text can vary greatly among people because of differences in the knowledge they possess" (Anderson et al., 1985, p. 9). Chapter 1 of this text presented a text passage that was very confusing until the context, "laundry," was added. That passage exemplifies the importance of background knowledge for effective comprehension of printed material. In fact, David Wiekart, a leading early childhood education researcher, found that building a wide experiential background not only affects students' reading abilities, but their entire lives as well. To name a couple of examples, Wiekart's longitudinal research comparing individuals who encountered Head Start preschool experiences to similar individuals who had not had such background experiences discovered (a) a 1 1/2-year advantage on eighth-grade achievement tests; (b) an average of 53% fewer teenage pregnancies for girls by age 19; and (c) that 38% of the Head Start individuals received some kind of post-secondary training compared to 21% of the non-Head Start individuals (Ranbom, 1983). While early and regular exposure to a variety of children's literature cannot alone give students the same advantages, it can offer many vicarious opportunities to expand their background knowledge about language and about the world.

At the same time, readers must be able to decode words quickly and accurately so that this process can coordinate fluidly with the process of constructing meaning from the text (Anderson et al., 1985, p. 11). In order

Locate the "laundry" example in Chapter 1, and refer to it here, or read part of a children's book or poem and discuss what it might mean to different students in your methods class.

Locate (or ask students to locate) the Weikart article, and share the entire article with the class.

to do so, students must be armed with a variety of decoding strategies, such as the following:

- Building an extensive sight vocabulary is a good start, and exposure to a variety of children's literature increases sight vocabulary better than flash cards or drills, and even better than looking up new words in a dictionary (Taylor, 1976).
- The ability to use a variety of context clues is the most efficient way to recognize an unknown word. When students read for pleasure and enjoyment, reading to the end of the sentence, using picture clues and content information to figure out an unknown word is more likely to occur because this is a low-pressure situation and intelligent guessing (using context clues) is usually sufficient to understand new words without interrupting the flow of the information.
- Although phonics alone is a slow, tedious, often frustrating process for figuring out unknown words, when combined with context clues, phonics becomes another way of figuring out an unknown word.
- Structural analysis of the word is the next recourse a student might use.
- As a last resort, looking up the unknown word in a dictionary or the glossary (which may be necessary only in a few cases, such as with informational books) could apply.

Read a predictable children's book aloud to the group, leaving out some words, which they can supply through the context clues of the selection.

Teachers who always supply students with the unknown word are merely making the students unnecessarily dependent on others.

Correspondingly, exposure to reading may be a factor as important as, or more important than, writing practice or formal writing instruction itself for growth in students' written composition skills (DeVries, 1970; Stotsky, 1983). Similarly, sharing children's literature orally with students can be an important teaching tool for all students, especially students who have not grown up with English as their primary language. A study conducted in the Fiji Islands involving over 380 children, for example, discovered that reading selections aloud in English to non-English-speaking children helped those 10- and 11-year-old children to learn English twice as fast as their control group counterparts (Elley & Mangubhai, 1983). Reading aloud to limited English proficient (LEP) students also helps these students acquire standard English without losing their native dialects (Strickland, 1971). In any event, questions asked after children have read a story on their own ultimately (a) improve comprehension, (b) aid in recollection of thoughts and facts, and (c) review and reinforce concepts.

Figure 13.3   Students enjoy books that are presented in a variety of formats.

THE LANGUAGE AND CONTENT OF CHILDREN'S LITERATURE

Book Formats

A variety of book formats can be found among children's literature selections (Figure 13.3). Many of these should be included in both classroom and school libraries. The formats include

Wordless picture books

Picture books

Short or long novels

Riddle and other word-play books

"Choose-a-path" books

Touch and feel books

Books with unusual page formats

Bring in, or ask students to bring in, a variety of book formats to share in class (such as wordless picture books, choose-a-path books, and big books).

Books with cassette or record accompaniment

Big books (described in Chapter 3) for fun and shared reading

Literature Genres

A good reading program also includes a balance of different genres of children's literature selections. Children's literature experts vary slightly on genre classifications, but the most common follow here.

- *Folklore, tall tales and fairy tales:* These also include legends, customs, superstitions, games, songs, old tales, and verses. *Tall tales* are usually regional in setting and dialect, with exaggerated sizes and events. Fairy tales often include magic and witches, giants, elves, and other imaginary beings. Because this literature has been passed down through oral language tradition, there may be many versions of the same tales, with no single author identified. Fairy tales also contain universal themes (e.g., you will find versions of Cinderella in African, Japanese, and American literature, to name a few). Characterization is stereotypic, plots are repetitive (events generally happen in "threes" or "sevens"), and good always wins over evil.

  Examples: *Strega Nona; Oh, A-Hunting We Will Go.*

- *Fables and myths: Fables* are single-incident-plot stories with a moral lesson. Myths present explanations regarding otherwise inexplicable events or circumstances (such as the origin of the earth), regarding natural phenomena (such as the color or shape or behavior of an animal), and/or regarding the relationship between humans and gods.

  Examples: *Tikki, Tikki, Tembo; Fables* by Arnold Lobel.

- *Fantasy: Fantasy* includes imaginary stories that generally personify toys, animals, and inanimate objects. Fantasies differ from folklore in that they generally have a single author and have not been passed down through oral tradition. Science fiction stories also fall under this genre.

  Examples: *Charlotte's Web; The Lion, The Witch, and the Wardrobe.*

- *Historical fiction:* These are stories that could have happened in the past but probably did not. These books usually strive to be historically accurate and reflect the language and values of the period even though several of the events and characters are changed to make the story more appealing.

  Examples: *Little House in the Big Woods; Ben and Me.*

- *Realistic fiction:* Realistic fiction contains stories that could happen but are probably not true. Realistic fiction themes include humor, family, mystery, romance, and adventure!

    Examples: *Alexander and the Terrible, Horrible, No Good, Very Bad Day; Ramona the Pest.*

- *Information books:* Information books are factually accurate (at least at the time of their publication) and are intended to teach or to inform others. Concept(s) and format should be developmentally appropriate, and glossaries and indexes are especially helpful in these books.

    Example: *Encyclopedia Brown's Record Book of Weird and Wonderful Facts.*

- *Poetry:* Poetry is available in anthologies or in single works (as in some picture books). The forms of poetry include narrative, limericks, haiku, cinquain, tanka, ballads, sonnets, free verse, and others. Poetry is characterized by its pleasing use of language and can include several of the following: metaphors, similes, personification, rhyme, rhythm, alliteration, assonance, and onomatopoeia.

    Examples: *Where the Sidewalk Ends; The Random House Book of Poetry.*

- *Biography:* These are stories about actual men and women written by other people. *Autobiography* is different only in that it is written from a first-person point of view by the person who lived it. Facts should be authentic and verifiable.

    Example: *And Then What Happened Paul Revere?*

> If you have asked students to bring in their favorite children's book to share in the read-around group activity listed at the end of the chapter, ask students to categorize those selections by genre.

Literary Aspects of Literature

An awareness of the literary aspects of literature is helpful to students in two basic ways (Figure 13.4). (1) For students to fully comprehend a literature selection, they must understand plot, setting, point of view, and so on. (2) As students begin to think of themselves as authors, they can begin to gain insights into the writing tools that professional authors use. However, "well-written materials will not do the job alone. Teachers must instruct students in strategies for extracting and organizing critical information from text" (Anderson et al., 1985, p. 71). Important literary aspects to investigate with elementary-school students include the four key elements of story grammar (plot, character, setting, and theme), as well as three others (i.e., style, point of view, and climax).

> If you are reading a children's literature selection aloud to your methods class weekly, choose one of those recently read and discuss its plot, setting, and so forth.

- *Plot:* The pattern of action in the story that involves the resolution of one or more conflicts—Events should be logical and credible. Although flashbacks and foreshadowing techniques are sometimes used, plots at the elementary-school level generally progress chronologically.

Figure 13.4   Students must have opportunities to become aware of the literary aspects of literature.

- *Character:* What the people and animals in the story are like—Characters are revealed to the reader in several ways, such as through what the character says, does, thinks, and so on. Good authors show readers what a character is like rather than just telling readers what a character is like.
- *Setting:* When and where the story takes place—The setting affects all of the other literary elements in the story. A good setting is believable and appeals to several of the reader's senses.
- *Theme:* The author's purpose or the main idea on which the story is based—It is the message the author is trying to convey to the readers.
- *Style:* The way the author uses words—The book's style can be presented as a mystery, an adventure, a drama, and so forth; style determines the mood, tone, and atmosphere of the work.
- *Point of View:* One or more perspectives from which the story is told, such as a first-person narrative told by the protagonist or an all-knowing third person telling the story—A stimulating high-level thinking activity for students is to try telling or rewriting the story from another character's point of view.
- *Climax:* The high point of the story—This is usually the place in the story where the main character has to make a critical decision.

Figure 13.5 Children need a wide range of quality literature available from which they can freely select.

USING CHILDREN'S LITERATURE IN THE READING PROGRAM

Selecting Literature

Selection Based on Literary Criteria

Once you recognize some of the benefits of becoming knowledgeable about children's literature and of incorporating it into your reading program, the next step is to select the literature you want to use (Figure 13.5). Most school districts, and most teachers use a reading series that is based on literature selections a publisher has chosen for students at each grade level. If you have an opportunity to serve on the selection committee at your school or school district, you have the chance to ensure that the series chosen incorporates excellent literature and uses it appropriately. You may even be in a position to design or tailor a literature-based reading and/or language arts program from scratch. In any event, you should know how to evaluate a literature-based reading program.

You might have fun with your class evaluating *Dick and Jane* or some other skills-based, readability-formula-written basal series according to these guidelines.

Evaluating Elementary School Literature-Based Reading (and Integrated Reading/Language Arts) Textbooks and Materials for Their Use of Children's Literature

- Are entire selections by original authors and illustrators an integral part of the series?
- Does the series incorporate high-quality children's literature selections to represent various genres and literature types? How many of the following does it include?

poetry	contemporary fiction
picture books	fables
riddle books	informational selections
short stories	fairy tales
novels	myths
plays	diaries
choose-a-path selections	legends
biography	tall tales
historical fiction	

- Are there selections with predictable story patterns (repetition, rhyme, and rhythm)?
- Are there selections related to diverse students' personal lives and cultural backgrounds?
- If excerpts are used, are children referred to the original works to be found in class, school, or community libraries?
- Does the series use readability formulas and worksheets to turn high-quality children's literature into basal reading selections?
- Are the literature selections organized around themes or merely a hodgepodge of unrelated stories?
- Is the series actually the publisher's old basals with some children's literature selections sprinkled in?
- Are the reading/language arts skills taught as they relate to the selections? (Or are skills taught according to some type of hierarchy unrelated to the selections?)
- Are reading, writing, listening, and speaking all taught in the context of the literature selections?
- Is new vocabulary taught in context?
- Are students ever allowed just to enjoy the literature selections (in part or in full)?

In addition to being able to evaluate a literature-based reading program or series, you must know how to select suitable individual literary works, either to supplement the series or to formulate an alternative literature-based program.

Hints for Choosing High-Quality Children's Literature The primary consideration in choosing literature selections is quality. The following list describes some important considerations for choosing children's literature for your reading program:

Evaluate writing:	Fictional books should include well-developed plot, characterization, setting, and theme. Nonfiction books should include clear and accurate writing. Poetry should include language that is both beautiful and expressive.
Evaluate content:	Good literature avoids stereotyping with respect to gender, cultural background, handicaps, religious beliefs, or other perceived differences.
Evaluate subject matter:	Age-level appropriateness of subject matter is essential both to children's understanding and to avoidance of censorship dilemmas.
Evaluate illustrations:	A variety of artistic formats and styles appeal to children and young adults. Use caution with anthologies, and carefully screen reading materials for adaptations in the stories and/or the illustrations.
Consider awards:	Caution should be used with reference to lists of award-winning titles. For example, two excellent American Library Association Awards are given by adults to adults (Caldecott Medals are given to illustrators for what adults feel are distinguished picture books; Newbery Medals are for story content), and therefore they may not always reflect children's interests. Children's Choice Awards, on the other hand, are voted on by children for books that are of interest to them; however, quality of writing and/or illustrations may not always be a factor in these selections.

Ask students to apply these guidelines to their favorite (or least favorite) literature selection in class or for homework and share their results in class (or in a one-paragraph summary).

Selection Based on Student Interests and Inclinations

After considering quality, next consideration in choosing appropriate literature for your program is interest. Several factors are associated with student interests. Primarily, their parents' educational level, family size, and social status, and the family's interests and hobbies all significantly affect reading interests (Spache, 1978). Differences in interests, to some extent, also seem to parallel gender differences. For example, third-through fifth-grade boys seem to be more interested than girls in adventure, tall tales, history, geography, travel, how-to, sports, and science (Summers & Likasevich, 1983). Girls, on the other hand, seem to prefer fairy tales, biography, romance, mystery, and books about other children and animals. Horse stories appeal to both boys and girls in third grade, but they seem to become a passion with girls by fourth or fifth grade (Huck & Kuhn, 1968).

With respect to poetry, most elementary-school children appear to enjoy limericks and narrative poems but do not like free verse or haiku (Donoghue, 1985). Primary-grade children generally prefer contemporary, easily understood poems about familiar, enjoyable experiences and animals (Fisher & Natarella, 1979), as well as humorous poems and poems with strong rhythm and rhyme (such as Ogden Nash's "The Adventures of Isabel" and Shel Silverstein's poetry). Primary-grade children least prefer free verse, limericks with figurative language, poems with subtle humor, and poems with metaphorical language. Perhaps this can be explained by the semantic and syntactic maturity of students in these early grades. Moreover, younger children prefer traditional poetry, while older students seem to prefer modern poetry.

Selection by Students

While information concerning general preferences is helpful, it is not foolproof. Further, it would be difficult for any teacher to find any single literature selection that would interest every student at any given moment. Caution must be taken to avoid replacing a forced basal reading program with a forced literature-selection reading program. Therefore, it is essential that a high-quality literature-based reading program also include some self-selection of materials by students to meet individual interests, needs, and personalities. Two ways to do this are (1) through small cooperative learning groups that use student-selected books by the same author, on the same theme, or in the same genre; and (2) during sustained silent reading (SSR) time or through other individualized reading programs.

Responding to Student-Selected Literature Unfortunately, student-selected literature poses another problem. How does a teacher provide instructional guidance for stories that the teacher may not have had the opportunity to read . . . yet? First and foremost, be honest with students. Explain that you have not read all 50,000-plus children's books in print . . . but you're working on them! Then use some general questions that can be used with almost any literature selection. Use the following ones or brainstorm several of your own.

You may wish to have your reading methods class students verify this information by having them ask young children they know to choose their favorite poem or story from two that your students read to them. You may wish to graph the results on the board for a metanalysis of their data and a discussion on the individuality of each child and/or each classroom full of children. (Point out that there really is no one child or one class that perfectly fits any mold!)

Point out to your students some local reading incentive programs, such as summer reading programs by local libraries or the free-pizza program sponsored by a national pizza restaurant chain.

Questions That Respond to Student-Selected Literature

Plot: What happened in the story? Describe the main problem in the story. How was it solved? How might you solve the problem if it were you?

Characterization: Who are the main characters? What would you describe as their best/worst qualities? How did either of those qualities affect the way the plot progressed? How would the story have changed if the author omitted one of the characters? Give two examples.

Setting: Where does this story take place? How would you describe the way it looks? When does the story take place? How do you think the story would have been different if it happened at a different time (today or in the past)? What are the most essential elements about the setting of the story?

Theme: What was the author trying to tell us by writing this story? Do you feel the author has a valid point? Why or why not?

Style: Do you think this could be a true story? Why or why not? Can you think of another story format the author could have used to communicate the theme? What conclusions might people draw about the author after reading this story? Find some information about the author, and see if those conclusions would be accurate.

Point of view: Would the story have been different if one of the other characters told it? How? Rewrite one scene in the story from another character's point of view.

Climax: What was the high point in the story? Can you describe that part in one word? Explain the connection between that part of the story and the beginning/ending of the story. If you were the author, what alternative solution could you pose?

> Your students may want to try out some of these generic questions on books shared in the read-around activity.

Annotated Sampling of High-Quality Children's Literature

The preceding discussion may have helped you to decide what kinds of literature selections you should consider. While only you can best select specific children's literature for your students and your curriculum, the following annotated bibliography of high-quality books for children may help you to get started. The listing contains a variety of choices, both classics and contemporary favorites.

For Reading Aloud to Students, for Prereading, and for Beginning Reading

Wordless Picture Books. Excellent for prereading and writing skills!

Ah-Choo—Mercer Mayer. Dial Books, 1976. A book about what happens when an elephant has to sneeze.

Bobo's Dream—Martha Alexander. Houghton Mifflin Company, 1970. A dog that dreams he saves a boy's football just as the boy earlier saved the dog's bone.

Deep in the Forest—Brinton Turkle. Houghton Mifflin Company, 1989. Reverse adaptation of Goldilocks and the Three Bears . . . a baby bear cub in a people cottage.

You may wish to have students go to the library and examine two or three of these resources. (Or perhaps your librarian may gather these for you and allow you to borrow them for one class meeting.)

Sequential and Repetitive Stories. For beginning readers and English as a second language (ESL) students.

The Day Jimmy's Boa Ate the Wash—Trinka H. Noble. Dial Books, 1980. A field trip to a farm and the string of logical events that occur.

Don't Forget the Bacon—Pat Hutchins. Puffin, 1978. A memorized shopping list that changes time and again during a child's trip to the market.

Good-Night Owl!—Pat Hutchins. Macmillan, 1971. All day long, forest animal sounds keep owl awake; when night falls, it's owl's turn.

If You Give a Mouse a Cookie—Laura Joffe Numeroff. Scholastic, 1985. A book capitalizing on logical sequences: If a person gives a mouse a cookie, the mouse will probably want some milk, then a straw for his milk, and so on.

It Could Always Be Worse—Margot Zemach. Farrar, 1976. Folktale about a noisy crowded house and how a rabbi helps a villager gladly accept his surroundings.

The Napping House—Audrey Wood. Harcourt Brace Jovanovich, 1984. Even the illustrations in this book are predictable as every character in the story piles on the bed and then flies back off.

Nobody Listens to Andrew—Elizabeth Guilfoile. Follett, 1957. A boy tries to tell everyone something important, but nobody has time to listen!

Oh, A-Hunting We Will Go—John Langstaff. Houghton Mifflin Company, 1989. Illustrated version of this traditional song.

One Fine Day—Nonny Hogrogian. Macmillan, 1971. A series of events begins after a fox drinks milk from an old woman's pail.

The Runaway Bunny—Margaret Wise Brown. Harper Junior Books, 1942. Each time the little bunny threatens to run away from home, the mother rabbit counters with how she will come and find him.

Tikki Tikki Tembo—Arlene Mosel. Scholastic, 1972. Chinese legend about why firstborn sons no longer have long names.

Whose Mouse Are You?—Robert Kraus. Macmillan, 1970. A heroic mouse tells how he could save his family.

Predictable Rhyme, Rhythm. Good pattern selections for early readers and writers.

Brown Bear, Brown Bear, What Do You See?—Bill Martin, Jr. Holt, 1983. Few words per page end in a rhyme to answer, "What do you see?"

The Cat in the Hat—Dr. Seuss. Random House, 1957. An easy-to-read rhyming story about some fantastic adventures on a rainy day.

Figure 13.6 Literature can serve as a marvelous springboard for all of the language arts. Reading, writing, talking, and listening all develop from literature.

Green Eggs and Ham—Dr. Seuss. Random House, 1960. An easy-to-read rhyming story about convincing a character to try green eggs and ham.

The Little Engine That Could—Watty Piper. Putnam, 1984. A little train accomplishes an enormous task by thinking positively.

Millions of Cats—Wanda Ga'g. Coward, 1928. An old man goes to find a cat for his lonely wife and brings back many, many cats.

The Real Mother Goose—Blanche Fisher Wright. Rand McNally and Company, 1944. Classic collection of traditional nursery rhymes.

Books with an Interesting Format. Especially popular for reluctant and less-able readers.

Picture Books

I Know an Old Lady—Rose Bonne. Child's Play International, 1973. Traditional song with nontraditional illustrations and pages.

The Jolly Postman—Janet and Allan Ahlberg. Little, Brown, 1986. Written partly in rhyme, every other page is an envelope.

The Very Busy Spider—Eric Carle. Putnam, 1984. A spider builds a web, which is embossed on the pages.

The Very Hungry Caterpillar—Eric Carle. Putnam, 1981. Life cycle of a caterpillar who eats through the pages.

Where's Spot—Eric Hill. Putnam, 1980. A mother dog looks for her lost puppy. The reader lifts the flaps on the pages as the story is read.

Riddle Books

Ten Copycats in a Boat and Other Riddles—Alvin Schwartz. Harper and Row, 1980. A collection of funny riddles.

Picture Books with Few Words

Animals Should Definitely Not Wear Clothing—Judy Barrett. Atheneum, 1970. A book about what might happen if animals did wear clothes.

What Next Baby Bear—Jill Murphy. Dial Books for Young Readers, 1984. Fantasy adventures about a baby bear.

Where the Wild Things Are—Maurice Sendak. Scholastic, 1963. A boy misbehaves and dreams he becomes king of all the wild things.

For Refining and Practicing Reading Skills[1]

Picture Books

Alexander and the Terrible, Horrible, No Good Very Bad Day—Judith Viorst. Atheneum, 1972. When nothing goes right one day, Alexander thinks of moving to Australia.

Amelia Bedelia—Peggy Parrish. Harper Junior Books, 1963. Amelia Bedelia does everything literally.

Bedtime for Frances—Russell Hoban. Harper, 1960. All the excuses an animal child comes up with to get out of going to bed.

Corduroy—Don Freeman. Puffin, 1976. A teddy bear who is finally bought and loved.

I'll Fix Anthony—Judith Viorst. Atheneum, 1969. A child thinks that when he's six, he'll do everything better than his older brother.

Ira Sleeps Over—Bernard Waber. Houghton Mifflin, 1975. A child decides whether to take his teddy bear to a sleepover.

Leo the Late Bloomer—Robert Kraus. Crowell, 1971. It's OK that Leo cannot read, write, and talk as early as other children. He will do these things when he is ready to.

Mike Mulligan and His Steam Shovel—Virginia Lee Burton. Houghton Mifflin, 1943. An outdated steam shovel and how it once again becomes useful.

Miss Nelson Has a Field Day—Harry Allard. Scholastic, 1985. "Coach Swamp" straightens out an out-of-line football team.

Miss Nelson Is Missing—Harry Allard. Houghton Mifflin, 1977. Kids misbehave and get a mean substitute named "Miss Viola Swamp."

My Mama Says There Aren't Any Zombies, Ghosts, Vampires, Creatures, Demons, Monsters, Fiends, Goblins, or Things—Judith Viorst. Atheneum, 1974. Sometimes, even mamas make mistakes.

Space Case—Edward (James) Marshall. Scholastic, 1980. A robot from outer space visits just in time for Halloween.

Stone Soup—Marcia Brown. Scribner, 1947. A hungry soldier tricks a villager into feeding him.

Strega Nona—Tomie de Paola. Prentice-Hall, 1975. Big Anthony uses part of a magic spell to make spaghetti, but he can't stop making it.

Sylvester and the Magic Pebble—William Steig. Simon and Schuster, 1969. A donkey turns himself into a rock with a magic pebble.

A Tale of Peter Rabbit—Beatrix Potter. Fredrick Warne & Co., 1902. Peter Rabbit doesn't listen to his mother and gets into trouble.

The Whingdingdilly—Bill Peet. Houghton Mifflin, 1982. Story of a dog who wants attention and the trouble he gets into.

William's Doll—Charlotte Zolotow. Harper, 1985. William's grandmother knows that little boys can play with dolls too.

[1]Most selections in these sections are also appropriate as read-aloud selections of high-quality children's literature.

Yummers!—James Marshall. Houghton Mifflin, 1973. A pig eats too much and decides her stomachache is caused by all the walking she did.

Poetry

The Night Before Christmas—Clement Moore. Holiday House, 1980. Illustrated (Tomie DePaola) version of the traditional poem.

The Random House Book of Poetry—Jack Prelutsky. Random House, 1983. Arnold Lobel illustrations of children's favorite poems.

Short Novels with an Interesting Format

Pick-a-Path (Scholastic) and *Choose Your Own Adventure* (Bantam Books) book series. Books that give the reader an option of turning to different places in the book to continue the story.

For Continued Reading[1]

Picture Books

Gila Monsters Meet You at the Airport—Marjorie Weinman Sharr. Penguin Books, 1980. Illustrates the humor in stereotypes.

Moja Means One—Muriel Feelings. Dial Books for Young Readers, 1971. Swahili counting book, which teaches also words and facts of the culture.

Piggybook—Anthony Brown. Alfred A. Knopf, 1986. What happens to the family when mother decides to stop doing everything herself.

Poetry

A Light in the Attic—Shel Silverstein. Harper Junior Books, 1981. Collection of humorous poems for children.

The New Kid on the Block—Jack Prelutsky. Greenwillow, 1984. Contains over 100 humorous poems.

Where the Sidewalk Ends—Shel Silverstein. Harper and Row, 1974. Collection of Silverstein poems that children love!

Shorter Novels

And Then What Happened Paul Revere?—Jean Fritz. Coward, 1973. Historically accurate humorous account of Paul Revere's ride.

Bunnicula: A Rabbit Tale of Mystery—Deborah and James Howe. Atheneum, 1980. A dog and cat suspect that a bunny is really dracula!

Chocolate Fever—Robert K. Smith. Dell, 1972. A boy eats too much chocolate and gets chocolate freckles all over his body.

The Courage of Sarah Noble—Alice Dalgliesh. Scribner and Sons, 1954. Historical fiction about a girl who stays with Native Americans.

Dear Mr. Henshaw—Beverly Cleary. Dell, 1983. A fatherless child writes a series of letters to an author.

Encyclopedia Brown Sets the Pace—Donald J. Sobol. Four Winds Press, 1982. Ten mysteries in this Encyclopedia Brown edition.

The Hundred Dresses—Eleanor Estes. Harcourt Brace Jovanovich, 1944. A deaf girl dreamed of having a wardrobe full of dresses.

Sideways Stories from Wayside School—Louis Sachar. Avon, 1978. Stories about the kids from a typical, yet strange school!

---

[1]Most selections in these sections are also appropriate as read-aloud selections of high-quality children's literature.

Figure 13.7   *Charlotte's Web,* by E. B. White, has long inspired children and teachers in pursuit of literary delights.

Novels

Bridge to Terabithia—Katherine Paterson. Crowell, 1977. One friend drowns in their imaginary kingdom; the other is left to cope.

Caddie Woodlawn—Carol R. Brink. Macmillan, 1973. Historical fiction of a tomboy growing up in Wisconsin territory.

Charlotte's Web—E. B. White. Harper Junior Books, 1952. A spider saves her friend's life by writing messages in her web! (See Figure 13.7.)

The Diary of a Young Girl—Anne Frank. Doubleday, 1952. Jewish girl's account of her days in hiding during Nazi occupation.

The Enormous Egg—Oliver Butterworth. Little Brown, 1956. A boy finds an unusual egg in the henhouse, which hatches into a dinosaur!

The Great Gilly Hopkins—Katherine Paterson. Crowell, 1978. A foster child finally finds much-needed love in one foster home.

The Hobbit—J. R. R. Tolkien. Houghton Mifflin, 1984. Dwarfs, goblins, dragons, and humans have many adventures in this fantasy land.

Indian in the Cupboard—Lynne Reid Banks. Doubleday, 1980. A boy who magically makes a small plastic Indian (Native American) come to life.

Island of the Blue Dolphins—Scott O'Dell. Houghton Mifflin, 1960. Story based on historical information about a girl who spent 18 years stranded on an island off the coast of California.

James and the Giant Peach—Roald Dahl. Knopf, 1961. Adventure story about a boy and the giant insects he befriends.

The Lion, the Witch and the Wardrobe—C. S. Lewis. Macmillan, 1950. Some children enter a strange world through an old wardrobe.

Little House in the Big Woods—Laura Ingalls Wilder. Harper Junior Books, 1953. The original of the series about pioneer days.

The Phantom Tollbooth—Norton Juster. Random House, 1961. A book full of puns with numbers and letters.

Ramona the Pest—Beverly Cleary. Morrow, 1968. This book in Cleary's series tells of Ramona's kindergarten experiences.

Where the Red Fern Grows—Wilson Rawls. Doubleday, 1961. The boyhood memories of a boy and his dogs.

A Wrinkle in Time—Madeleine L'Engle. Dell, 1962. Newbery Award-winning fantasy about three young children and a magical stranger.

Additional Resources for Locating High-Quality Children's Literature

You may wish to consult the following additional resources for locating particular children's literature books. New books are being printed all the time, and even more new books are written every day. Do not feel compelled to choose only selections named in any specific list.

The ALAN Review. Assembly on Literature for Adolescents, National Council of Teachers of English, 1111 Kenyon Rd., Urbana, IL 61801 (for adolescent literature).

Annotated Recommended Readings in Literature Kindergarten Through Grade Eight. (1988) Sacramento: California State Department of Education.

Best Books for Children. (Annual catalog). New York: Bowker.

The Bookfinder: A Guide to Children's Literature About the Needs and Problems of Youth Aged 2–15. Sharon S. Dreyer (Ed.; 1981). Circle Pines, MN: American Guidance Service (split-page format for topics and annotations).

Books in Spanish for Children and Young Adults: An Annotated Guide (Series 4). Isabel Schon (1987). Metuchen, NJ: Scarecrow Press.

Children's Books in Print. (Annual index). New York: Bowker.

For Reading Out Loud. Margaret Mary Kimmel and Elizabeth Segel (1983). New York: Delacorte Press.

Horn Book Magazine. The Horn Book, Inc., Park Square Building, 31 St. James Ave., Boston, MA 02116.

Notable Children's Books. (1986) Chicago, IL: American Library Association.

The Read Aloud Handbook (2nd ed.). Jim Trelease (1985). New York: Penguin Books.

School Library Journal. R. R. Bowker Company, 249 W. 17th St., New York 10011.

Bring in as many of these as you can locate. (Your librarian may be able to locate these for you ahead of time.) You can then share parts of (or overviews of) some of these in class or you might prefer to have your students choose one or two to read in class and highlight in class and "show 'n tell" for the other students.

I also suggest taking a good children's literature course, attending reading and language arts organization conferences (such as International Reading Association; National Council of Teachers of English; and their local branches), and asking librarians, colleagues, and young children.

Sharing Children's Literature with Students

Most kindergarten and first-grade teachers regularly read aloud to their students. However, as students begin to master the basics of reading on their own, most teachers somehow stop reading to their students. If they do share literature with their students, they often expect their students to read to them.

In a 1967 article, Root asked teachers why they did not read aloud to their students. One teacher answered that learning was serious and that we could not afford to let children have any pleasure while learning.

Figure 13.8　Students of any age and reading ability benefit greatly when adults read high-quality literature aloud.

Another said that the school's job was to teach children to read, not to read to them. This was followed by a response saying that children read to themselves, and that teachers knew that they did because teachers require book reports. One teacher even said that she did not read aloud to her students because children cannot learn anything worthwhile from being read to.

First of all, reading high-quality children's literature aloud to students exposes students to a wealth of written material that they may not read on their own, due either to lack of skills or lack of inspiration (Figure 13-8). Reading aloud to students has been shown to relate positively to reading achievement (Cohen, 1966; Raftery, 1974), as well as to increases in the quality and quantity of selections children choose to read on their own (Porter, 1969). Having been read aloud to is one factor common to *all* early readers (Durkin, 1974). It exposes students to many prereading understandings and builds background experiences they can later draw from when decoding words (Pearson, 1981; Rosenblatt, 1978). Further, recent studies show that reading aloud to students helps them to become better writers (Michener, 1989).

The November, 1988, *Reading Teacher* journal has a fun quiz ("Test Your Reading Aloud IQ," pp. 118–122) on the benefits of reading aloud to children. You may wish to obtain a copy of it and give the "Reading Aloud IQ" quiz in class.

Though teachers do not need a doctorate in reading aloud before they can read good stories to their students, they should consider paying attention to the following (Michener, 1986).

- *Formalities*—Is there a traditional time of day for this? Have you introduced the story, given the title, and identified the author or other recognizable features of the book?
- *Your presentation of the reading*—Are you enthusiastic? Are you conveying appropriate emotions through your voice and body language? Is the book being held appropriately? Have you briefly previewed the selection for appropriateness?
- *Your voice*—Is your voice projecting to all students? Are you varying the volume, speed, and pitch as called for by the story? Are you using subordination for quotes and continuity for poetry?
- *Your audience*—Did you allow a few moments for the students to settle down? Can all students see and hear comfortably? Can you maintain eye contact and observe each student during the reading of the selection?

Storytelling is a related form of literature exposure. Predictable stories and fairy tales are especially good for this. Remember that language is the basis for all four language arts communication components: reading, writing, listening, and speaking (see Chapter 2, "Early Literacy Acquisition and Development"). Storytelling gives students experience with high-quality literature using a less formal oral language approach. Storytelling by the teacher improves students' reading ability, self-concept, creativity, and empathy, and it increases their library usage and interest in literature (Ziegler, 1971).

Storytelling can be shared with or without props and can include

Providing or showing concrete objects as they appear in the story

Physical and verbal stimulation (singing, music, dance)

Related fingerplays or body gestures and movements

Flannelboard activities

Student choral participation in repetitive portions of a story

Puppetry

Vividly colorful large pictures

Food

Chalk talks

String stories

Cut-as-you-tell stories

Flip charts

Roll (or scroll) stories

Students can choose a story to memorize and tell (with or without props) to a young child or in class.

There was one response in the Root (1967) article that reiterates what many teachers still feel today: reading aloud may be nice, but we have textbooks to cover. This "cover the curriculum" philosophy is one that keeps many teachers away from sharing quality children's literature with their students. Calkins (1986) says that the "cover the curriculum" philosophy should be replaced with an "uncover the curriculum" philosophy; rather than rushing to superficially attend to each and every item on the curriculum outline, teachers should selectively spend more time on some items in order to gain a more in-depth understanding of the most important concepts and ideas. An "uncovering" of some topics of the curriculum would, therefore, afford teachers the necessary time to work with quality literature selections that enhance and clarify the understanding of those important concepts and ideas.

U.S. society now faces several literacy crises: Not only are many adults *illiterate*, but also a high percentage of adults are *semiliterate* (those who can decode but not understand what they read) and, perhaps worse, a high percentage are aliterate (those who can decode and understand what they read, but who choose not to read) (Alexander, 1987). It is hoped that the current move toward literature-based reading and language arts textbooks and materials will allow teachers to both cover the curriculum and include high-quality children's literature in that curriculum. Teachers should, however, ensure that literature-based reading/language arts textbooks and materials remain high in quality and build, rather than destroy, a love of reading and writing in students.

FOLLOW THROUGH: INCORPORATING LITERATURE ACROSS THE CURRICULUM

If the goal in teaching reading is to develop literate individuals, then elementary-school students must be shown the practical applications of literacy throughout all phases of their daily curriculum. Most educators agree that the four components of language arts (reading, writing, listening, and speaking) are closely interrelated. All four of these components should therefore be integrated throughout the school day across all areas of the curriculum (Goodman, 1986). Often, however, teachers are unsure of how to do this.

This section gives some generic suggestions for integrating children's literature across the curriculum. The suggestions are called "generic" because they can be applied to (or easily adjusted to fit) almost any children's literature selection. Further, these suggestions can often lead to a brainstorm of other new ideas by the teacher. Choose and adjust these ideas to fit particular books, and use these ideas as stimuli for developing your own ideas.

Figure 13.9 Literature-related computer software can provide a useful adjunct to the reading program, both for students and for teachers.

Reading

- Hold small-group discussions before, during, and after the literature selection. Address topics and questions such as the following: What are similar events in students' lives? How can students explain unusual events in the story? How might characters look or act in other situations?
- Play trivia games modeled after a variety of TV game shows, to offer interesting alternatives to traditional comprehension-checking strategies.
- Allow students to find and compare two or more versions of the same literature selection (including TV or videotape versions).
- Encourage older students to read stories to lower-grade students.
- Read similar stories or stories by the same author as a follow-up activity.

You can choose a book you have recently read in class or a story with which your students are all familiar. Ask students to work in small groups to develop ideas for incorporating this book across the curriculum. Assign one curricular area (e.g., math) to each group. Record the ideas they share, and duplicate the ideas for all students in your reading methods class.

Other Language Arts

- Have students write telegrams to one of the main characters, warning of an upcoming catastrophe.
- Make up crossword or word-search puzzles with key words from the literature selection. Students can work your puzzle or create their own. Some computer programs can help teachers do this (Figure 13.9).
- Brainstorm new endings for stories.
- Hold debates about the pros and cons of certain events in literature selections.
- To enhance listening skills, let students tell circle stories (one child starts, another adds on, etc.), collectively making up different versions or additional chapters of a selection you read aloud to the class.
- Encourage students to pantomime parts of the selections.
- Write stories for wordless picture books.
- Write letters to pen pals (or to authors) about literature selections.
- Publish a class newspaper about the children's literature selections shared in class. Student assignments might include
  a. Advertisements
  b. Articles about other versions of the selection
  c. Book reviews
  d. Cartoons or caricatures of characters
  e. Headlines, captions, and pictures
  f. "Dear Abby" kinds of questions and answers from characters
  g. Lost-and-found ads for the characters
  h. Situations-wanted ads for characters
- Rewrite the story from a character's point of view (different from the viewpoint shown in the story) or as a different literature genre (such as a mystery).
- Ask students to act out high-action parts of selections by following these steps:
  a. Discussing the story in detail
  b. Breaking the selection into acts
  c. Determining the sequence of the action, the setting, and the characters
  d. Casting the characters
  e. Playing the scene
  f. Discussing how the scene went
  g. Repeating it with a new cast or trying it with puppets!
- Design bumper stickers or slogans related to selections.
- Broadcast book reviews over the school public address (PA) system.

Math

- Create a barter system similar to one used in pioneer stories.
- Follow recipes (e.g., Stone Soup), and include attention to measuring, fractions, time, and so on.
- Subtract years to compare dates of historical events to stories in current times.
- Have children create word problems with the numbers of characters or the times of story events as clues.
- Help students write a class "Choose-a-Path Adventure Story" with alternate series of events and various endings. Children will have to figure out correct ways to number the pages for the various routes readers can follow. (The *Super Storytree* computer program [Brackett, 1989] can help students do this.)

Social Studies

- Encourage a volunteer to dress up like a character and tell the character's life story.
- Create a mural or a diorama of the life and times of a character.
- Make a relief map of places in the literature selections.
- Evaluate the selection for hidden bias.
- Have students search through a newspaper for facts, for scavenger hunt locations, or to find coupons to help the literature characters save money.
- Find literature that relates to students' cultural heritages.
- Conduct a mock interview of one of the characters.
- Make timelines of events in the selections, as well as related historical events that affected the story.
- Role-play characters and events from the stories.
- Design travel brochures for places in the stories.
- Hold mock trials for characters.
- Take field trips to historic sites in local stories.

Science

- Review a story of a scientific event as a person who lives 100 years from now (or 100 years ago) might.
- Weave cloth or make paper just as the characters did.
- Do a scientific experiment associated with a literature selection.
- Hypothesize about how a modern invention might have changed a historical literature selection.
- Classify important events or articles in a literature selection.
- Create shadow puppet show of the story, using various lighting effects.

- Follow directions given in informational books.
- Investigate habitat and care of animals or plants from literature selections.

Art, Music, and Physical Education

- Design sets and costumes or caricature T-shirts!
- Sculpt a character, a place, or an event out of clay, soap, papier-mâché, or plaster of Paris.
- Make mobiles of characters, places, or events.
- Design a rebus book of the selection.
- Make a three-dimensional collage of people, events, or places.
- Draw original illustrations for the story, using chalk, mosaic, crayon relief.
- Make a story roll (scroll) of the literature selection events.
- Students can draw pictures of the selection while reading it.
- Students can find appropriate background music and/or sound effects to accompany the selection.
- Encourage students to design make-up and/or perform dances from the culture described in the selection.

Read *The Jolly Postman* in class.

An Example of Integrating Children's Literature Across the Curriculum: *The Jolly Postman*

Reading
- Read related literature
- Individual/cooperative groups (report to rest of class)
  - "Three Little Pigs"
  - "Goldilocks and the Three Bears"
  - "Hansel and Gretel"
  - Compare/contrast versions
- Discuss reality/fantasy
- Rhyming words (poetry)
- Book reviews
- Design trivia games (comprehension)
  - Cooperative groups
- Riddles

Language arts
- Write letters
  - Proofread
  - Pen pals in England
- Skits, plays for other classes
  - Pantomime
- Write a sequel

- - New characters
  - Cooperative learning groups
  - Editing marks/skills
- Travel brochures
- Bumper stickers
- Pop-up books of adventures
- British dialect
- Write a commercial
  - Dress up like characters
  - Videotape to show to other classes
- Postcards
- Writing invitations—handwriting
- Vocabulary words—spelling

Math
- Time difference (England/U.S.) (clocks)
- Weigh packages/envelopes
  - Estimate weights (metric/standard)
  - Figure out correct postage (money system comparisons)
  - Rate of exchange
- Measure packages
  - Chart/graph measurements
- Flow chart of events
- Design a board game using dice

Social studies
- Career education
  - Trip to post office
  - Guest speaker (postal worker or lawyer)
- Civic education
  - Legal rights
  - Law suits
  - Court system
- Geography/history/culture (England)
  - Geographical location
  - Climate
  - Flag
  - Government
  - U.S./England historical ties
  - Customs (Tea Party)

Science
- Frog powder recipe experiments
  - Hypothesize what will happen
- Design magic spells

- Classify types of animals in spells
- Bears
  - Hibernation
- Research a newt
  - What does it eat?

Art, music, drama and P.E.
- Design stamps
- Make a diorama
- Travel posters
- Mobiles
- Slides
- Story rolls (scrolls)
- Library displays
- Puppets
- Role-play characters
- Costumes
- Sets
- Background music
- Sound effects (e.g., doorbell)
- Scavenger hunt to characters' homes
- Obstacle course to deliver mail

PARENT INVOLVEMENT

Parents are teachers too, and children's literature is an ideal way to involve parents in their children's literacy development. Although many parents begin reading aloud to their preschoolers, when those preschoolers begin reading on their own, parents feel compelled to stop reading to their children and to begin listening to their children read to them. However, it is at that very time that children should be read to often by their parents and teachers—to be relieved from the struggle of early decoding, and to be reminded of the joy, excitement, and beautiful flow of the language in high-quality children's literature selections.

Encourage parents to lend their support and to become involved in the educational program by (a) continuing to read aloud to their children throughout the grades, (b) helping their children with homework, and (c) modeling their own interest in reading, thereby helping their children to develop lifelong reading habits. Parents do not really need intense training in the selection of high-quality children's books. It seems that most parents instinctively know what books fall within their children's "zone of proximal learning" (the difficulty level of learning material ranging from slightly below to slightly above that level for which the child is most ready to understand at any given time in the child's development). Thus, a library card or a simple booklist is usually sufficient. The incidental learning is the most important benefit of parents sharing reading with their children, especially with economically deprived children and children for whom reading may not be considered important. One cautionary note may be helpful, however: Advise parents that when their children are reading to and with them, they should feel free to ignore most of their children's reading mistakes unless the mistake disrupts the meaning of the text.

Sometimes community readers, friends, and other school staff may become involved in sharing literature with some children. Another important benefit of having parents and other community members involved in sharing good children's literature with the children is that such involvement may help to avoid censorship dilemmas over isolated words or sections of literature selections the children may bring home.

A different parent-involvement issue that teachers should recognize is what David Elkind refers to as the "Superbaby Syndrome" (1981). Some parents feel that if their children can begin to read earlier than everyone else, this will somehow give their children a head start over other children. As a result, some parents begin to push their children into developmentally inappropriate decoding activities. Unfortunately, this often leads to frustration in both the parent and the child because the child is unable to perform at that developmentally inappropriate level. A more deleterious consequence is the potential for creating a low self-concept in the child, which is one of the factors that affects how well a person ultimately reads. It is also likely that eventually these parents and their children will both think of reading time at home as punishment, based on the frustration level they have endured.

Children's literature can be a tremendous asset to a child's literacy development if used appropriately. "Parents should read to preschool children and informally teach them about reading and writing. Parents should support school-aged children's continued growth as readers" (Anderson et al., 1985). Developing a parent communication network at your school or in your classroom can help parents feel that they are important components in their children's education. After all, they are.

HIGHLIGHTS

1. Children's literature plays an important role in the educational curriculum. It helps students to develop background knowledge for reading, it exposes them to a wealth of written language models, and it teaches students that reading and writing can be fun and interesting.
2. Children's literature comes to a variety of book formats and writing styles.

3. Discovering the ways in which authors use a variety of literary aspects (e.g., story-grammar elements) in children's literature selections is an important aid to children's reading and writing success.

4. Selecting appropriate children's literature is essential to an effective reading program. Literary quality, student interests, and students' self-selection of literature should be considered.

5. A variety of literature is available for all ages. Teachers should also consider the objectives of the lesson and the reading-ability levels of the students when choosing specific titles.

6. Reading aloud to students and storytelling are effective ways of sharing literature in the classroom throughout the grades.

7. Follow-through literature activities are also important to literature-based reading programs; these activities should include all four language arts components and should expand the literature across the curriculum.

REINFORCEMENT ACTIVITIES

1. Evaluate a children's literature unit available from a publisher or school district. Does it enhance or destroy the spirit of the children's literature selection? (For example, does it ask children to find all the nouns on page 13 of *Charlotte's Web* or does it ask children to write a reaction to page 13 of *Charlotte's Web* being sure to include appropriate nouns as they write?)

2. Describe how *you* will arrange and manage *your* classroom for one typical day's reading period using a reading approach built around quality children's literature selections. Be sure to list representative reading activities, note general room arrangements, scheduling pattern, and groupings (if any).

3. Imagine that you have the opportunity to design your own literature-based reading textbook series. Describe what you will design. How will you teach reading, writing, listening, and speaking? What materials will your series include (workbooks, teacher's manuals, kits, software, etc.)?

4. Read an article about using children's literature in the reading program and give a personal reaction to it.

5. List several factors (as discussed in earlier chapters) that affect learning to read and write. List one or two specific children's literature books that might be either directly or indirectly helpful for each of those factors.

6. Gather a collection of children's literature books with unusual or interesting formats (such as *The Very Hungry Caterpillar* and *I Know*

an Old Lady, which were listed in the chapter). How many different types of book formats were located?

ADDITIONAL PROJECTS

1. Bring your favorite children's literature selection to the next class meeting. Break up into small groups so that each can share information about the selection and, following good read aloud techniques, read-aloud one section of the literature selection to the rest of the group.
2. Choose one picture book and read it aloud to a young child. Note the child's reactions to the way you read and to literary aspects of the story.
3. Choose a poem for choral reading and arrange it into parts for individual voices, small group voices, and entire class.
4. Design a university-wide or school district-wide read-aloud day where individuals from the community and others come in and read quality children's books aloud to classes of elementary school students. Readers can include parents, dentists, secretaries, police officers, children's book authors, high school students, college professors, etc.
5. Observe a classroom teacher using children's literature across the curriculum. Note interesting insights into how this is done.
6. Talk to a school librarian about censorship. Has he or she ever run into difficulty with a parent or parents about a particular children's literature selection in their school collection?
7. Try your hand at authorship! Working individually or in small groups, write a "picture book" about a current social issue and research submission procedures and possible appropriate publishers.

In your methods class, generate plans for parent involvement in a hypothetical schoolwide literature festival. Be sure to discuss (1) which types of community members you might invite to read-aloud to children at the school; (2) whether to include storytelling; (3) whether to include read aloud stories the children have written; (4) how you might expand the festival by allowing students to write a new story afterward and then publishing their stories in a school storybook for each student; and (5) other ideas they might have about the festival and/or logistics of coordinating one.

REFERENCES

Alexander, F. (1987). "California Reading Initiative." In B. E. Cullinan (Ed.), *Children's Literature in the Reading Program*. Newark, DE: International Reading Association.

Anderson, R. C., Hiebert, E. H., Scott, J. A., Wilkinson, I. A. G., and the Commission on Reading (1985). *Becoming a Nation of Readers*. Washington, DC: U.S. Department of Education (National Institute of Education).

Bond, G., & Dykstra, R. (1967). The cooperative research program in first grade reading instruction. *Reading Research Quarterly, 2*, 1–142.

Brackett, G. (1989). *Super Storytree*. New York: Scholastic Software.

California State Department of Education. (1987). *English–Language Arts Framework for California Public Schools*. Sacramento: Author.

Calkins, L. M. (1986). *The Art of Teaching Writing*. Portsmouth, NH: Heinemann Educational Books.

Cohen, D. (1966). Effect of a special program in literature on vocabulary and reading achievement of second grade children in special service schools (Doctoral dissertation, New York University, 1966). *Dissertation Abstracts International, 27*, 4162A. (ERIC Document Reproduction Service No. ED 010 602).

Cooper, J. D., et al. (1989). *Houghton Mifflin Reading/Language Arts K-8 Program*. Boston: Houghton Mifflin Company.

Cullinan, B. E. (Ed). (1987). *Children's Literature in the Reading Program*. Newark, DE: International Reading Association.

DeVries, T. (1970). Reading, writing frequency and expository writing. *Reading Improvement, 7,* 18–19, 23.

Donoghue, M. R. (1985). *The Child and the Language Arts* (4th ed.). Dubuque, IA: Wm. C. Brown.

Durkin, D. (1974). A six-year study of children who learned to read in school at the age of four. *Reading Research Quarterly, 75,* 9–61.

Elkind, D. (1981). *The Hurried Child*. Reading, MA: Addison-Wesley.

Elley, W. B., & Mangubhai, F. (1983). The impact of reading on second language learning. *Reading Research Quarterly, 19*(1), 53–67.

Fisher, C., & Natarella, M. (1979). Of cabbage and kings: Or what kinds of poetry young children like. *Language Arts, 56,* 380–385.

Goodman, K. (1986). *What's Whole in Whole Language?* Portsmouth, NH: Heinemann Educational Books.

Huck, C. S. (1979). Literature for all reasons. *Language Arts, 56*(4), 354-355.

Huck, C., & Kuhn, D. (1968). *Children's Literature in the Elementary School* (2nd ed.). New York: Holt, Rinehart and Winston.

Michener, D. (1986). Reading aloud to students: Remediation or foundation. In M. P. Douglass, *Claremont Reading Conference Fiftieth Yearbook* (pp. 365–375). Claremont, CA: The Claremont Reading Conference Center for Developmental Studies.

Michener, D. (1989). Reading aloud to students and written composition skills: assessing their relationship. *English Quarterly, 21*(4), 212–223.

Pearson, P. D. (1981). A decade of research in reading comprehension. In V. Froese & S. Straw, *Research in the Language Arts: Language and Schooling* (p. 259). Baltimore: University Park Press.

Porter, J. (1969). Effect of a program of reading aloud to middle grade children in the inner city (Doctoral dissertation, Ohio State University, 1969). (University Microfilm No. 70-14, 084).

Raftery, E. J. (1974). The effect of a quality literature program conducted by elementary education majors on the reading achievement of second grade students (Doctoral dissertation, New York University, 1974). *Dissertation Abstracts International, 35,* 2830A.

Ranbom, S. (1983). Preschool study (Weikart, D.) finds long-term gains. *Education Week,* September 7, 1983, pp. 5, 24.

Roots, S. L. (1967). What's wrong with reading aloud? *Elementary English, 12,* 929–932.

Rosenblatt, L. (1978). *The Reader the Text the Poem*. Carbondale: Southern Illinois University Press.

Spache, G. D. (1978). *Good Reading for Poor Readers* (10th ed.). Champaign, IL: Garrard Publishing.

Stotsky, S. (1983). Research on reading/writing relationships: A synthesis and suggested directions. *Language Arts, 60*(5), 627–642.

Strickland, D. S. (1971). The effects of a special literature program on the oral language expression of linguistically different, Negro kindergarten children. *Dissertation Abstracts International, 32,* 1406A. (University Microfilm No. 71-28, 560).

Summers, E. G., & Likasevich, A. (1983). Reading preferences of intermediate grade children in relation to sex, community, and maturation (grade level). *Reading Research Quarterly, 18,* 347–360.

Taylor, M. (1976). A study of the effects of presenting literature to first grade students by means of five visual–verbal presentation modes. (Doctoral dissertation, University of Southern California, 1976). *Dissertation Abstracts International, 32,* 1393A.

Ziegler, E. M. (1971). A study of the effects of creative dramatics on the progress in the use of the library, reading interests, reading achievement, self-concept, creativity, and empathy of fourth and fifth grade children. *Dissertation Abstracts International, 31,* 6482A, Temple University, 71-10, 843.

ADDITIONAL RESOURCES

California State Department of Education. (1987). *Handbook for Planning an Effective Literature Program*. Sacramento, CA: Author.

Hansen, J. (1987). *When Writers Read*. Portsmouth, NH: Heinemann Educational Books.

Michener, D. (1988). Test Your Reading Aloud I.Q. *The Reading Teacher, 42*(2), 118–122.

Sutherland, Z., Monson, D. L., & Arbuthnot, M. H. (1981). *Children and Books* (6th ed.) Glenview, IL: Scott Foresman and Company.

CHAPTER 14

TEACHING READING TO THE STUDENT WITH READING DIFFICULTIES

MARIE EATON

"When I use a word," Humpty Dumpty said, "it means just what I choose it to mean—neither more nor less." "The question is," said Alice, "whether you can make words mean so many different things." "The question is," said Humpty Dumpty, "which is to be the master—that's all."

Lewis Carroll, *Through the Looking Glass*

Language used to describe learners with different kinds of learning problems has changed over the years. It continues to change, and, to make matters more difficult, it often varies from state to state and from agency to agency. Student teachers need to be aware of the various terms used to describe populations of learners with various kinds of physical, emotional, and cognitive disabilities, as well as other kinds of learning disabilities.

PREVIEW

Every teacher is challenged by students who do not seem to learn the basic skills as easily as the other children. They may be baffled by the alphabet and letter sounds and do not seem to be able to make words mean anything, much less master them. They have trouble understanding or remembering much of what they read. They have trouble finding their place on the page and avoid any free-reading activity. Older students may have difficulty reading their texts in social studies or science. If you have had some previous experience with this kind of child, or if you are a careful observer, then you may recognize the difficulty that the child is having. If not, you might assume that the child is stubborn, careless, inattentive, or lazy.

Children who fail to learn to read or write adequately become increasingly handicapped as they progress through school. These are the children who may be held back a grade, may fail classes in high school, and may finally drop out. Often, their increasing academic difficulties result in classroom behavior problems. Their lack of ability in interpreting written language severely limits their choice of occupation, and an established pattern of failure may persist into their adult years.

These children often have labels such as "learning disabled," "underachievers," "remedial readers," or "mildly retarded," or they may simply be the children who seem to struggle with your reading assignments day after day. If you are a teacher who has worked with younger children, you may find that these children use language and reading skills in ways that remind you of those younger readers.

Although your district or school may have given these students different labels, in practice, their learning characteristics are more similar than they are different (Epps, Ysseldyke, and McGue, 1984). Most underachieving students, regardless of the labels they are given, have common patterns of delay in the development of their reading and writing skills and considerable overlap in the characteristics that discriminate them from your other students. The label they are given (and your stereotypes about children with those labels) may actually distract you from the most important questions—what can we do to help them? The task that faces you is to find the most effective strategies to teach them to read and write to the best of their ability.

Some of these children may work with a special teacher during the reading period, or they may visit a resource room for extra help in reading. Many of these children, however, will spend all or most of their time in your classroom and will work with the other children in reading-related activities during the day.

The number of children identified as having some type of reading disability seems to be increasing. The rapid increase in the identification of these students may give the impression that there is an epidemic of dyslexia, learning disabilities, or other causes internal to the child. However, this increase in referral must be examined in the social context in which it occurs. As Sleeter (1984) asserts, there has been an increase in standards for reading achievement in the past few decades. American society has increasingly higher expectations for literacy. The increase in reading failures may actually reflect an increase in standards, rather than a change in the ability of the children in the system.

Dyslexia has always been a controversial topic. It has been referred to as a disease, a disability, and a fiction (i.e., a specious label used to disguise another kind of learning problem). Have student teachers examine contemporary literature on this topic.

That no single approach is uniformly effective holds true, of course, not only for learning disabled students but for all students.

This differentiation is important. Too frequently, the *child's* disability is cited as the cause for the reading failure; instead, perhaps the *curriculum* and the *instructional methods* have failed to meet the child's needs. The learning environment is an interaction among these three variables. Educators cannot alter the learning characteristics of the child, but we can adapt the curriculum and the instructional methods to ensure the greatest possible growth for each individual learner.

Many of the strategies discussed in the other chapters in this text will be as useful for the troubled learner as for the child who avidly comes to reading. The common characteristic of all exceptional children, however, is that they are not able to reach their full potential without assistance beyond the normal classroom routine. Some additional guidelines and strategies have proved successful in helping troubled learners become more effective readers. One of the important things for teachers to remember, however, is that no *single* approach to the teaching of reading will accommodate the individual differences in these readers. To be successful in working with these children, teachers must possess a thorough understanding of the reading process and the component skills that reading comprises, a philosophy of reading that permits flexibility in choice of methods, and skills in assessment so that the learner's current instructional needs can be matched with methods and materials (Schloss & Sedlak, 1986).

The remainder of this chapter discusses the characteristics of the student with reading difficulties, the characteristics of effective learning environments, and the characteristics of effective curricula.

FOCUS QUESTIONS

As you read this chapter, think about the following "advance organizer" questions:

1. What do I know about the differences in the ways these children learn language and reading skills when compared to normal readers?
2. How does this knowledge help me to develop effective learning environments, including adaptations in instructional strategies and curriculum?
3. What is the difference between instructional strategies and learning strategies?

CHARACTERISTICS OF THE STUDENT WITH READING DIFFICULTIES

Although the children in your classes may have been given a variety of labels (learning disabled, mildly mentally retarded, emotionally disturbed, remedial reader, etc.), most of these children share common characteristics that cause them difficulty in the learning environment. The labels serve primarily as a means for districts and programs to access federal and state funding for the additional support services required. When it finally comes down to the teacher making instructional or treatment decisions for the child, the label is not very relevant. You will need to carefully assess the child's individual learning characteristics and plan instruction to meet those needs.

As these common characteristics are discussed, however, remember that although these characteristics may contribute to the difficulty these children have in learning to read, they should not be used as an excuse for reading failure. Educators have the ability to alter both the learning environment and the curricula to help children with these characteristics become effective, strategic readers.

Limited, Delayed, or Different Language Experiences

Some of the children identified as poor readers come to school with limited reading and writing experiences. They may come from environments where literacy is not modeled or valued. Language and vocabulary development may be delayed, or they may have undeveloped language experiences from which to draw. Other students have rich language experiences, but in languages or dialects other than the standard English typically spoken in classrooms. The mismatch between their spoken language and the instructional language may cause them difficulty.

Remind students that most children entering school have production vocabularies of 5000 to 8000 words and comprehension vocabularies nearly twice that. However, even at the kindergarten level, there will be major language ability differences in a typical heterogeneous class. If students have not studied developmental psycholinguistics, a brief overview of oral language development from preschool through the elementary grades would be appropriate.

Some of these children may have delays in language that parallel developmental delays in other areas. Their language skills may simply be lagging a few years behind their normal peers.

Inconsistent Learning Profiles

These children often have holes or gaps in their development of language and reading skills. You will not be able to assume that the child does not know any of the second-grade skills just because she or he scores at the first-grade level on a reading test. These children's learning is often inconsistent, and you will need to become skilled at assessment and observation to learn which reading and comprehension skills are causing the students the most difficulty and which they have mastered.

Difficulty Following Directions

Many reading tasks require that the child follow written directions; this is a complicated task for the child with reading difficulties. According to Cohen and de Bettincourt (1988), the most common directions use about 15 key words and phrases, and the child's difficulty in decoding them often results in incomplete or incorrectly done work. There are a few simple strategies that you can use to help the child become more successful in following written directions:

Ask students for some other ideas you can use to develop these abilities.

- *Use picture directions:* Simple rebus symbols for the key words can help the child follow the directions independently.
- *Underline or highlight key words:* If the significant words in the directions are underlined or emphasized in some other way, the child's attention is focused on the important features.
- *Record directions:* Tape-recorded directions can simplify the child's task.
- *Assign a buddy:* A peer can be assigned to read the directions to the reading-disabled child and can be available to answer questions about procedure.
- *Rewrite directions:* Commercial materials often have verbose and confusing directions. If these directions are rewritten in simpler language, including only the significant information, the child will be more likely to be able to work independently.

The importance and optimal teaching of visual discrimination skills and abilities have been controversial issues for many years. Authorities still disagree. Have students review research work by experts such as Jay Samuels, as well as theoretical work by such theorists as Frank Smith. Discuss their areas of agreement and disagreement on these issues as they relate to reading and reading instruction.

These children may also have difficulty following directions during group lessons or chalkboard work. They may have difficulty maintaining attention, or they may have difficulty following a directional sequence. If you keep your directions simple, present them clearly, and ask the child to paraphrase the directions to check for understanding, you will encourage more successful independent behavior from your students.

Difficulty in Discrimination

These children frequently fail to notice the distinctions between configurations of words and letters and may confuse "b" for "d" or "was" for "saw." Although these reversal and transposition errors are common with these students, they are not actually seeing the letters backward, but most likely have not yet learned to discriminate the distinguishing feature of direction, as it relates to discrimination of letters or words (Moyer & Newcomer, 1977; Smith & Lovitt, 1973).

Direct and explicit instructions that focus on the directional differences with both immediate and delayed practice have proved effective strategies for increasing the child's ability to use directionality as a strategy for discriminating letters and words. Moyer and Newcomer (1977) suggest that teachers use a three-stage instructional strategy:

1. Explicitly discuss the difference in direction of the words or letters. This discussion should include practice in matching letters or words.
2. Build visualization and use of the strategy by flashing letters or words. The child is encouraged to verbalize the discriminating feature (e.g., "It must be a 'b' because the circle pointed to the right." or "The word started with 's'. The word must be 'saw.' "), and then circle the appropriate letter or word.
3. Provide extended practice of the discrimination strategy in context, to ensure mastery.

Throughout this process, the practice should focus on those letters and words the child has actually confused. Practice with geometric shapes, designs, or objects is not likely to transfer to the confused letters or words (Smith, 1981).

Inefficient Learning Patterns

Many of these children require more demonstrations of the tools and strategies successful readers use to make sense of printed material. They are less able to intuit strategies from observation of effective readers, and they require overt and explicit instruction in skills that other readers just seem to learn effortlessly. They may need to have concepts presented in a variety of ways before they grasp the idea. They must have more opportunities to practice literacy skills than the children who come to literacy easily.

These children may need more repetition and practice than other students in order to master some of the skills you are trying to teach. Do not, however, forget to answer the question "Memory for what?" and "In what context?" (Rhodes & Dudley-Marling, 1988). Most persons have difficulty with isolated memory tasks that seem unrelated to daily life.

Ask students, "How important is practice? How should practice be built into teaching plans?"

Ask students the following: "What is the contemporary posture on the concept of *readiness*? What does it mean? Is the issue moot (i.e., a straw man of sorts) because an effective teacher determines where individual learners are and then proceeds to build from there regardless of what this building or instructing is called?" Discuss this thoroughly—especially from the standpoint of the concept of *reading readiness*.

Ask students to suggest some effective techniques for maintaining learner attention.

These children do not have an across-the-board memory problem. They can remember how to turn on the T.V. and how to play baseball according to the rules. However, they often have not developed the strategies for organizing and remembering academic material.

These children typically make slower progress in learning reading skills. Their teachers may need to continue to work on readiness skills, such a developing oral language skills, listening comprehension and decoding, well into the elementary grades (Hallahan & Kauffman, 1982).

Attention Deficits

Some of these children have difficulty maintaining attention and concentrating on a task for a sustained period. They may show a deficit in selective attention and may have difficulty filtering out extraneous noise or visual stimuli in order to focus selectively on a task (Hallahan & Kauffman, 1976). This problem with selective attention can cause academic difficulties. The ability to select and concentrate on the relevant aspects of a task are essential to any kind of academic work. This difficulty may result in the kinds of impulsive, random responses observed in these children.

Research on metacognition cited earlier in this book suggests that self-monitoring and verbal rehearsal strategies can be effective ways to increase the child's ability to stay focused on tasks. Most of these strategies include some kind of prompt to the child (e.g., a bell, a tone, or a teacher signal), which cues the child to ask self-monitoring questions like, "Am I doing what I am supposed to be doing?" "Am I getting the correct answers?" "Am I paying attention?" The child keeps track of how successfully he or she is paying attention by marking a "yes" or "no" box on a sheet of paper tacked to the corner of the desk. This strategy often results in improved attention during academic tasks.

Although attentional difficulties often seem to be characteristics of these children, you should consider that everyone gets antsy when asked to listen to incomprehensible information or to work on tasks far beyond present abilities. The squirminess you see in students may be most easily remediated by making sure that they are working on tasks and in materials that are actually appropriate to their instructional level.

Lack of a Variety of Successful Learning Strategies

Discuss the idea of different learning modalities as it relates to the learning strategies of learning disabled populations.

Students with learning problems are frequently unable to generate appropriate learning strategies without help. They are often passive and inactive in the learning process and are frequently unaware of how to structure their own thinking when engaging in decoding or comprehension tasks. These students often are unable to use prediction or knowledge of the content to assist in comprehension of written material. They tend to rely on attempting to decipher a passage on a word-by-word basis.

In addition to the need for more practice to gain the tools and skills needed to construct meaning from text, these students also need instruction in the *executive function* (metacognition; self-monitoring) used by children to regulate their own learning. These children not only require *more time* to learn, but they also do not effectively use the time they are given.

Some of these children may not lack strategies (i.e., they are not "strategy deficient"; they have indeed developed several strategies for organizing material), but they may lack strategy flexibility. That is, they may be unable to determine when to use which strategies (Gerber, 1983). For example, unlike effective readers, who shift the speed and strategies used in reading different kinds of text, these students often approach all reading tasks in the same manner. Although these students are often disorganized random learners, they can become more successful if they are taught various strategies for organizing learning situations, for self-regulating their attention to the learning task, and for selecting the reading strategies that match the text/task demands (Gerber, 1988; Palincsar & Brown, 1984). When these students are given models for appropriate use of learning strategies and given guided practice (with feedback) in using them, they are able to become more strategic learners. (Chapter 7, on reading comprehension, describes ways in which to provide this.)

Specific learning strategies that can improve the child's ability to read effectively are discussed later in this chapter; however, teaching children strategies for organizing their learning during independent work can make your job as a teacher much simpler. Cohen and de Bettincourt (1988) suggest a simple strategy called a "job card." The card, which can be used with any independent learning task, cues the child to answer the following questions:

1. What do I need?
2. Where is it?
3. Where should I work?
4. How much time do I have?
5. What do I do with myself and my work when I'm done?

Although it takes some time initially to teach the child how to use the job card effectively, it will save you a great deal of time in the long run.

Teacher Dependency

These children are often highly teacher dependent and demand a great deal of assistance from the teacher, even on tasks that are within their instructional range. They may be afraid to work independently because

It is important to remember that the development of metacognitive skills is important for all learners. The task of teaching self-monitoring to these learner populations is more challenging, however. Have students examine literature dealing with this issue, and discuss it in class.

Group and paired learning experiences are excellent for all grades and all learners. Many of these grouping arrangements allow for peer tutoring and many other learning approaches.

Ask students how cooperative learning might relate to independent work and to peer tutoring.

they cannot match the strategy to the task or because they are afraid of making errors.

Although the goal in classrooms is to teach students to work independently, you will need to develop a support system for these students, which encourages independent work while providing strategies for gaining assistance, particularly when new skills are being introduced and practiced. One particularly successful strategy for providing immediate help and preventing frustration is peer tutoring, which is described later in this chapter.

CHARACTERISTICS OF EFFECTIVE LEARNING ENVIRONMENTS

As indicated earlier, it is not only the characteristics of the learner, but also the interactions among the learner, the instructional environment, and the curricula that make it difficult for these children to succeed. In order to become more effective teachers of the slow learner, teachers need to carefully examine the structure of the regular classroom environment to make sure not to perpetuate or exacerbate the problems for the student through the classroom and instructional organization.

Those who have examined learning environments that have proved to be most effective for the child with reading difficulties have agreed on some common instructional and organizational characteristics that promote greater achievement for these students:

- Consultation and support for the classroom teacher
- Clearly stated expectations for students
- Careful and frequent assessment of student performance
- Reading activities founded on basic skills
- Development of fluency, as well as accuracy
- Instruction in reading comprehension
- Provision of sufficient practice
- Active involvement and engagement in learning
- Appropriate combinations of classroom groupings for instruction
- Instruction in strategies for learning
- Use of flexible models of instruction

Consultation and Support for the Classroom Teacher

Your school should have a consultant or specialist on staff who can provide extra support and assistance in planning and implementing the most appropriate programs for these learners. As mentioned previously, each district makes decisions about how the exceptional child can best receive services. The child who has severe reading difficulties may leave the class for a period or two each day to get extra assistance in reading from a resource teacher, but the emphasis is on maintaining the child in the regular classroom whenever possible. When the child remains in the regular classroom for all or part of the reading work, it is important that you communicate frequently with the specialist about the instructional strategies, materials, and assessment procedures you have chosen for this child.

If the consultant is not making frequent visits to your classroom, you may want to develop a routine way to communicate about the troubled readers in your classroom. For example, you may want to meet each Monday morning before school for coffee and discussion of your plans for the week.

Discuss federal and state laws now affecting the staffing of specialists in schools and the kinds of roles they are to serve. It is helpful for beginning teachers to be knowledgeable about such laws for a variety of reasons.

Clearly Stated Expectations for Students

Children who have learning difficulties usually respond best to predictable learning environments. They are able to work independently most effectively when the rules are clearly stated, the conventions are predictable, the instructions are clear and unambiguous, and explanations are free of extra, irrelevant details (Ringler & Weber, 1984).

The expectations for academic work also need to be clearly understood by both you and the student. Each time you begin a lesson with your students, you must assess the purpose of the lesson. If your focus is to

As mentioned previously, predictable learning environments help all learners.

derive meaning from the material or to express meaning, then a detailed focus on text rules or errors can actually detract from the child's ability to gain meaning from the language. If, however, the goal is to provide some practice in using strategies or skills, then your feedback to the students should follow that focus.

Careful and Frequent Assessment of Student Performance

Ask students how these assessment needs fit with the concept of the *student assessment portfolio*.

In order to be certain that the child is receiving instruction appropriate to his or her current level of functioning, careful and frequent assessment of performance is necessary. These children will not be performing at expected achievement levels and probably not even at the levels reflected by their achievement test scores. Just because the child has been promoted to your fourth-grade class does not mean that he or she is ready to handle all the materials you will be using in your reading activities.

A careful assessment of current skill development and reading ability will allow you to tailor the activities and instructional strategies to the child's needs. Also, carefully matching the child's skills to the instructional materials allows you and the child to build from successful experiences instead of continuing failure. Two types of assessment are crucial for teachers to use: (1) assessment for instructional planning and (2) assessment to monitor student performance. In order for the assessment process to tell you either of these things, you will need to develop ways to observe how your students work in the curriculum in your classroom.

Achievement tests or other commercially constructed assessment tools will tell you little that will help you either in planning instructional strategies or in determining the content of instruction (Eaton & Lovitt, 1972). Instead, frequent measures of the student performance taken directly from reading tasks that you use in the classroom will help you monitor the success of your choices of materials and instructional strategies.

This kind of assessment is usually referred to as "curriculum-based assessment" (Howell & Morehead, 1987). If you can provide success experiences and help children to monitor their own improvement through curriculum-based measures, you can help these learners view themselves as children who *can* learn to read and construct meaning from written language. Many kinds of assessment strategies can be used to help you assess the student's current performance levels in oral reading and in reading comprehension.

Oral Reading

The IRI can also help in assessing oral reading.

A number of tests can be used to analyze the child's specific reading skills. *Teacher-made word-recognition tests* can give both an idea of the student's sight-word vocabulary and clues to the kinds of word-attack skills the child uses to figure out difficult words. These words can be presented on flash cards or on lists. These lists should be presented in both a timed and an untimed setting. During the timed session, the teacher or tutor records those words that are not immediately recognized by the child (a hesitation of 1 second or more) as "errors" and asks the child to move on to the next word. During the untimed session, the child is given the opportunity to reexamine those words and use any analysis skills available to decipher the word, and the tutor or teacher carefully records the student's responses.

When the data from these two sessions are combined, the teacher is able to track those words that the child does not know, those words the child recognizes immediately, and the kinds of analysis skills the child used to attack difficult words. When the errors are reviewed, patterns should emerge that can then guide the instructional procedure and the selection of materials. These oral reading errors and miscues can give clues about the strategies and the rules that children use to make sense of text, and they should guide the choice of instructional procedures (Goodman, 1973).

Reading in Context

Although it is instructive to test for skills both within text and independently, do not forget that *the real test*, however, *is the students' use of effective reading strategies within the context of meaningful material.* Frequent opportunities for children to read orally either with you or with a peer will give you a more accurate indication of their ability to construct meaning from the written page. During these sessions, *reading rate, cues and miscues,* and *reading comprehension* should be assessed. A timed sample of oral reading will provide you with reading rate measures and will give you a clearer picture of the child's ability to read fluently. Usually a 1-minute sample of oral reading is sufficient to track fluency. During this sample, you should also notice the kinds of errors the child makes, to provide you with information about ineffective strategies the child may be using. Finally, some measure of comprehension, including both literal and inferential measures, will provide information on the child's ability to gain the meaning of the text.

Frequent measures of this kind will ensure (a) that you have placed your students in curriculum that is matched to their instructional level and (b) that you have selected instructional strategies that are helping the student make appropriate progress.

Reading Activities Founded on Basic Skills

Chall (1989) recommends emphasis on decoding as a beginning reading method to build the ability to recognize words in context and develop fluency. This does not mean phonics drills in isolation, to the exclusion of

Any miscue analysis model used here must be simple enough and easy enough to administer, or the teacher will probably not bother or will be so bogged down with testing/assessing that teaching will suffer.

Let students know that in spite of the differences that hold across various reading instruction theories and practices, few will disagree with the assertion that effective readers must master decoding skills. The issue of *how* these skills should and can be taught most effectively is the heart of the differences that exist in different approaches to reading instruction.

reading for meaning practice. Dykstra (1974, p. 397) summarized the research on code-emphasis instruction by saying that "early systematic instruction in phonics provides the child with the skills to become an independent reader at an earlier age than is likely if phonics instruction is delayed or less systematic."

If your low-achieving reader lacks the strategies for decoding, and too many words are missed or omitted in context, or if the recognition is too slow, then it is difficult to perceive the words and phrases as having meaning. Without efficient decoding strategies, the resemblance to oral language becomes so remote that the intended meaning cannot be apprehended.

Development of Fluency, as Well as Accuracy

As mentioned, *fluency* refers to the learner's comfort with literacy acts and *not* necessarily to the learner's ability to perform them well. Many writing authorities assert, for example, that writing can be taught only after the learner has some fluency (i.e., can put words on paper even though they are not well written).

A lack of fluency in both reading and writing are common characteristics of these students. They read word by word, often in a choppy, staccato manner or in a stumbling monotone. Writing, if they write at all, is also extremely slow and disfluent.

Skilled readers and writers have the ability to process text smoothly and efficiently. They are able to concentrate on the content of the text they are reading or writing.

In early stages of reading and writing, the elemental skills simply require sufficient practice until enough automaticity is attained to allow for cognitive attention to the other tasks, such as comprehension in reading or composition in writing. Failure to develop proficiency in these fundamental tool skills works to the increasing disadvantage of the slow learner. As they tackle increasingly complex cognitive tasks, their deficiencies in both knowledge and skill become an increasing burden.

Other children may be afraid to take risks in the process of reading or writing. They may have developed beliefs that being correct is more important than being fluent.

> One 12-year-old student, Paul, had worked hard from September to January and had successfully mastered many reading strategies and had progressed from primer level material to third- or fourth-grade text. He was still extremely slow in his reading, however, paying laborious attention to each word as he read. His teacher discussed his slow reading with him before reading one day, mentioning that although she was proud of his improvement, she wished he could read more smoothly. She asked if he thought he could read a little faster. He replied, "Sure I can!" and proceeded to double his reading speed from 30 to 60 words per minute without any increase in miscues. Clearly, Paul had gotten the message that accurate decoding was the most important part of reading. Once the teacher clarified her expectations, Paul was able to show his abilities.

Reading Fluency

Reading fluency can be developed through a number of instructional strategies. Prereading, assisted reading, repeated reading, and sustained silent reading are commonly used.

Prereading Strategies Having children read silently prior to reading aloud is a common instructional strategy. Although this strategy does help the deficient reader become more familiar with the text, because they do not typically possess effective strategies for deriving meaning from context, this exercise may often be fruitless for them. Lovitt, Eaton, Kirkwood, and Pelander (1971) found that prereading strategies that allow the student to access the text accurately result in more fluent reading during the reading session. Some of the strategies that were successful in increasing both accuracy and fluency during the reading sessions included: (1) listening to the story on a tape, (2) listening to the teacher or a peer read the selection, and (3) prereading the story aloud to a teacher or peer who can provide assistance with difficult words.

Activating and building background knowledge may be more challenging for the disabled learner but is probably even more important than it is for other readers.

Assisted Reading Rhodes and Dudley-Marling (1988) suggest using assisted reading as a strategy for building fluency. In this procedure, the teacher and the student read a familiar story together. The teacher paces the story, reading smoothly and evenly, dropping her voice if the student is in control of the text and raising her voice if the student hesitates. The goal is to experience fluent reading through the entire text. Assisted reading can also be accomplished by the student reading along with a recording of the text.

Repeated Reading Strategies O'Shea and O'Shea (1988) found that a repeated reading strategy enabled students to develop fast and accurate word recognition. In this strategy, the student chooses a story or passage to read and reread to develop fluency. As fluency increases, the student is more likely to focus attention on the context of materials rather than on the individual words. Students may be assigned in pairs and may work together through a passage to develop skills in word recognition and passage meaning. If the reader is especially nonfluent, it may be helpful to select highly predictable materials to practice. Once students experience fluent reading, they begin to understand that reading is like spoken language, and they can transfer this fluency to a wider range of materials.

Although a repeated reading strategy may seem overly repetitious to some teachers, children respond positively to the opportunity to read a favorite book again and again. They are very proud when they can read a book or story as well as any other child in the class.

Consider sustained silent
writing (SSW) as a partner for
SSR.

Sustained Silent Reading Fluency is usually developed first orally so that the student and teacher can monitor progress. However, most adult reading is done silently, and practicing silent reading is one of the best ways to develop fluency. Many classrooms use sustained silent reading (SSR) practice as a method for increasing fluency. For the reading disabled child, strategies for gaining assistance with troublesome words or passages should be available so that SSR practice can be used productively.

Writing Fluency

Like reading fluency, writing fluency is developed best by providing many opportunities to write in which the emphasis is not on the precise use of the conventions of writing, but on the expression of ideas. Most of the strategies for developing the writing skills discussed in this book, such as journal writing or written conversation, will also be helpful with the slower or disfluent child. The major difference for you will be the need for extra encouragement for these children to continue to write even though the process is difficult for them. Frequent opportunities in which assistance is available when they feel stuck will improve their ability to commit ideas to paper with greater ease.

In the beginning, you may wish to transcribe their ideas to help them develop the feeling for their own words in print and to reinforce their understanding of writing as a way to convey meaning. Graves (1983) suggests a prewriting conference with students in which you take time to explore the student's topic choice. You record the key words and phrases the student uses in discussing the topic and leave the notes with the student to use during the writing session.

Sometimes, spelling or handwriting skills are so impaired for students that they become a barrier to writing. Extra practice with these skills can help the student become more proficient during the writing time. You can use the child's writing to find words or letter forms that seem to consistently cause trouble and target them for extra practice in a peer tutoring session. This is also a teaching context where computers can play a more effective role. Changes in the area of computers and computer-assisted instruction are taking place very rapidly now.

Instruction in Reading Comprehension

Discuss once more the
concept of direct instruction
as it has been used in this
book.

Teachers rarely teach or model reading comprehension strategies or performance (Schenkat, 1988), yet troubled readers are often deficient in this area. Research on comprehension indicates that it is a skill that is more frequently assessed than it is taught. Although teachers frequently ask questions of students after a passage is read, the types of questions are frequently literal or recall questions. Some studies indicate that as much as 75 to 95% of questions asked at both the elementary and secondary level may fall in this category (Schloss & Sedlak, 1986). Additionally, less than

1% of the time spent in reading instruction focuses on the development of comprehension skills (Durkin, 1978). Finally, the research on wait time indicates that teachers typically do not allow students enough time after a question has been asked to develop their answers. Slower students are given even less time than brighter students (Lucking, 1975).

Teachers who work effectively with these slower readers provide instruction that models and develops both literal and inferential comprehension skills and fosters the development of critical reading comprehension skills. Asking students to read a story and to answer questions either orally or on worksheets is *not* teaching comprehension. Teaching requires explanation, demonstration, and clarification.

Direct Explanation

One strategy for teaching comprehension skills is for the teacher to model ways to monitor their comprehension and to solve comprehension problems. In the direct explanation strategy, the invisible reasoning processes used by strategic readers are made visible through teacher modeling (Duffy, Roehler, & Herrmann, 1988).

Herrmann (1988) described a planning and implementation process that could be used in developing a direct explanation lesson. When *planning* the lesson, the teacher should do the following:

1. Decide which reasoning process to emphasize and when students would need to use it.
2. Decide how the reasoning process works. For example, when using prediction, readers must use their prior knowledge to guess what might happen.
3. Collect text examples that can be used when explaining and modeling this reasoning process.
4. Decide how to introduce the lesson, including a description of the process, why it is important, and when it should be used.
5. Decide what to say and do while modeling the process.
6. Assess the text for opportunities to practice the reasoning process.
7. Anticipate problems, and decide how to provide different and varied examples.

According to Herrmann, when *implementing* the lesson, the teacher should do the following.

1. Activate the student's prior knowledge of the topic by discussing the title, pictures, and other clues.

    T: Today we're going to read a story about a vacation. How many of you took a vacation last summer? (Students answer). Look at the picture of the girl in our story. What is she doing? (Students answer). That's right, she's playing on the beach. Let's read the title of the story together.

2. Introduce the reasoning process that will be taught.

> T: I want you to know something about this story. There are some hard words in it that might give you trouble. I am going to teach you how to figure out hard words like these so that when you read the story, you will be able to figure them out.

3. Think aloud to model the reasoning process.

> T: Okay, I'm going to pretend I don't know this hard word in this sentence. Hmmm. I don't know this word. I'll skip it and keep going and see if I can guess the word.

4. Think aloud how to repair a comprehension breakdown.

> T: Not knowing that word makes it hard for me to read this sentence, but I can figure out what it might be. Let me read the sentence again. What could that hard word be. It says that she is sitting under something. I've been at the beach before. What kinds of things are on the beach? I know that some people sit under umbrellas at the beach. Maybe this word is "umbrella." Let's see if that fits. "Sally sat under the umbrella to keep out of the hot sun." That makes sense.

5. Check whether students understood the reasoning strategy you used.

> T: Now I want you to tell me what I did when I got stumped by a hard word.
> S: You read the sentence again.
> T: That's right, but I also did something else. What else was I thinking about when I read the sentence again?
> S: You thought about when you were at the beach before.

6. Provide opportunities for them to practice using the process.

Herrmann's strategies are similar to those described by Carnine and Gersten (1988) as part of the direct-instruction approach in teaching reading comprehension. The direct-instruction approach includes explicit training in comprehension strategies, which includes modeling and extensive practice, coupled with immediate feedback. The modeling allows the student to observe overtly the strategies that successful readers use to organize and make sense from written text. Some explicit skills taught in this program include the following:

1. Drawing inferences in the context of distracting information

2. Using knowledge of story grammar to assist in comprehension
3. Detecting faulty arguments
4. Learning vocabulary from context

For each of these skills, Carnine and his associates have developed explicit instructional procedures and tasks, which include the following steps (Carnine & Gersten, 1988):

1. Instruction on or modeling of the explicit strategy
2. Student mastery of each step achieved through practice
3. Corrective feedback for student errors
4. Gradual withdrawal of teacher assistance
5. Systematic practice with extensive range of examples
6. Cumulative review
7. Teaching formats that anticipate errors and provide strategies for correct responses

Rose, Cundick, and Higbie (1983) describe a similar process, which they term "think aloud." To use this process, students read short passages in a small-group setting and "think aloud" about what they understand and how they understand it. In this setting, the students are taught to use the comprehension strategies, such as visual imagery, mnemonic devices, prediction, prior knowledge, rereading, and reading ahead to construct the meaning from the text. The other students comment on whether they have used similar strategies as they read silently. Notice that the focus of this session is *not* comprehension of the content of the text, but *the process* the student is using to comprehend.

> Ask students what other metacognitive techniques might fit within the direct instruction plan offered here.

Reciprocal Teaching

Reciprocal teaching is a strategy to help the student understand how to study and learn from text. The teacher's role is to show students how to use the skills of generating questions, summarizing, predicting, and clarifying to improve their comprehension of written material (Palincsar & Brown, 1984). In this strategy, the teacher reads a passage aloud, stops and "thinks aloud" about the predictions the child might make about possible content, the kinds of questions the students should be asking about the passage (e.g., "Is this really true?" "What might happen next?"), makes summary statements about segments of text, and models how to clarify confusing passages. The teacher then encourages discussion about these questions and explains and clarifies the importance of the questions. Students finally practice developing questions on their own.. Palincsar and Brown (1984) found that the modeling and practice of these kinds of self-monitoring skills produced considerable improvement in the comprehension skills.

> Ask students how other instructional models offered in this book work with these learning populations.

Although the strategies are similar, this process differs somewhat from direct explanation. In reciprocal teaching, the teacher models the strategy, but does not verbalize the mental processes used when figuring out how to apply the strategy. For example, in reciprocal teaching, the teacher might model a summary statement and then ask students to state a different summary statement in their own words. In direct explanation, the teacher would also model the clues used to derive the summary statement initially. Both these strategies have been used successfully to help poor readers become more strategic.

Question Modeling

The kinds of questions the teacher asks can also influence the development of more sophisticated comprehension skills. Frequently, teachers ask for recall of small details (e.g., "What color was Tony's dog?"). Questions of this nature frequently focus on inconsequential details and distract the student from concentrating on the main idea of the passage or story line. Questions that integrate story parts are more likely to enhance comprehension (e.g., "Why was Tony's dog barking?"). Questions beginning with "Why" or "How do you know" are more likely to be inferential in nature. Using these kinds of questions in combination with feedback and expanded explanations are the principal ways of teaching the more sophisticated comprehension skills.

Ask students to model question strategies and techniques that would be used with the learning disabled, and compare them with those used to teach the same comprehension skills, processes, and/or concepts to normal learners.

During the discussion, the teacher should not only confirm the student's correct response, but also help the student identify what component of the response made it correct. For example, if the teacher asks a question like "How do you know what season it is in the story?" the student may reply "It's winter." Further discussion with the student should be elicited, to determine the supporting details the student has used to come to that answer. By asking "How do you know?" the teacher may find that the student has successfully noticed the author's descriptions of woolen coats and cold winds. This kind of discussion not only confirms the student's successful strategy, but also models the strategy more explicitly for other students.

Active Participation

Schewel and Waddell (1986) discussed two additional strategies that are useful in helping readers develop the specific skills for effective reading comprehension. These strategies help shift students from passive to active roles in the reading process.

Self-questioning In this strategy, the student is encouraged to increase awareness of textual elements. The strategy is a four-step sequence in which the student is asked to

1. Identify the main idea of a paragraph and underline it
2. Develop and write questions related to the main idea
3. Check answers with the teacher's model

4. Review questions and answers

Look Back In this strategy, questions about the passage are interspersed within the text, requiring that the student look back at the material. The student is asked to

1. Pause in the middle of the passage
2. Ask themselves general questions about the material
3. Recognize and acknowledge answers that they do not know
4. Look back over materials for answers to their unanswered questions

In order for students to use these strategies effectively the teacher must *teach* them by modeling, explanation, and clarification.

Story Grammar Training

Like Carnine and his associates, Short and Ryan (1984) found that when students were specifically trained to pay attention to the story schemata, they were able to comprehend new material as effectively as those readers considered more proficient. Less-skilled readers seem to be able to use story schemata to aid their comprehension, but apparently in the absence of training, they fail to use their knowledge of the structure of stories spontaneously. Specific training in story grammar teaches students through modeling and practice to pay attention to four questions as they read (Carnine & Kinder, 1985):

The use of visual aids and graphics with story mapping and semantic mapping can be particularly effective with these learners.

1. Who is the story about? (addresses character, theme, and plot)
2. What does he or she want to do? (addresses the initiating problem that the plot must resolve)
3. What happens when he or she tries to do it? (addresses the attempts at resolving the plot's problem)
4. What happens in the end? (resolution of the plot)

(Refer to Chapters 7 and 13 for more information on teaching story grammar to elementary and middle-school students, respectively.)

Marginal Notes, Graphic Organizers, and Study Frames

Reading comprehension for older students who are reading content material in science and social studies can be improved if either a study frame or marginal notes are provided in advance, which can guide the student to focus on the most important information in the text. A graphic organizer or a framed outline presents 10–12 of the main ideas of a chapter in a logical sequence in a study guide. This outline furnishes a structure with which students can identify the main ideas of the chapter. The major topics are identified, but some important points are left blank for the student to fill in. This kind of guide can provide the student with assistance in seeing

Suggest that students prepare study frames, story maps, word webs, advance organizer questions and outlines, and so forth in advance and that they file these aids according to their intended use. Over a period of a few years of teaching, this material will be modified to become more finely tuned to their own and their students needs and will save a lot of preparation time.

the relationship between the structure of the text and the information therein (Rhodes & Dudley-Marling, 1988).

Provision of Sufficient Practice

Scheduled reading periods do not always provide sufficient active practice on reading skills necessary for low-achieving students. Practice improves reading, but low-achieving students typically spend less that 5 minutes a day in active reading practice (Schenkat, 1988). One of the characteristics of children who are considered poor readers is that they often require *more* time and practice to ensure acquisition rates equivalent to their normally achieving peers (Gettinger & Lyon, 1983). Because of their difficulty in attaining mastery of skills in the time allocated by teachers in regular classroom, the achievement pattern for slow-learning children becomes a spiral in which the insufficient time to learn on earlier occasions results in an even greater need for learning time later on (Gerber, 1988). In order to increase the achievement level of these students, you will need to find ways to increase the amount of practice students get on each strategy or skill you are teaching.

> To become successful readers, these students must have frequent practice in using language and print and opportunities to see others using language.

Active Involvement and Engagement in Learning

Create a print environment! Books, writing and reading centers, vibrant print-oriented bulletin boards and walls all convey an attitude toward reading and writing that is contagious.

Even when more time for practice is provided, the low-achieving student is not always actively engaged in learning. When others are reading or working on worksheets, the slower student has difficulty following along and often drifts. Effective instructional settings for these students include organizational structures that require active participation, such as choral responses, peer tutoring groups, collaborative learning groups, and immediate or frequent feedback of corrective strategies.

The effective-schools literature has been examining allocated time versus engaged time and the effects of these on students' achievement. According to Rosenshine and Berliner (1977), academic engaged time is the time that a student spends in academically relevant material at an appropriate level of difficulty.

In the middle grades, unsupervised seatwork occupies more than half the allocated time (Calfree & Hoover, 1976). Because it is unsupervised, there is little to ensure that it is also engaged time. Direct teacher instruction, peer tutoring, or peer working groups in which students are accountable for their responses are usually more effective in increasing the engaged time, particularly for students who have difficulty maintaining active involvement while working independently.

Appropriate Combination of Whole-Group, Small-Group, and Individualized Instruction

Whole-Class Instruction

These children often get lost in classrooms where the majority of the instruction takes place in large groups. In successful classrooms, the teacher tailors the size of the group to the instructional goal. Appropriate whole-class activities might include common new learning, in which a skill or concept is introduced to the whole class, such as the use of a table of contents and indexes or the discussion of word meanings or current events. Even though not all students will learn the concept or skill at the same rate, all will benefit from the whole-group instruction.

Individualized Instruction

Appropriate individualized reading activities include individual recreational reading and individual skills practice. You must not assume that all the children in the class have the same deficits. Careful assessment of current reading abilities will highlight some areas of particular weakness for each child. These skills or concepts may need extra individualized practice to reach fluency. This can be done in individual conference sessions with you or by cross-age or peer tutors.

Peer Tutoring

In peer tutoring, the child is paired with another student who has mastered the skill or concept. In these dyads, the more proficient students assist those who have not yet mastered skills. This strategy allows the child to get the extra *guided* practice without taking undue teacher time.

Peer tutoring has many advantages. Students are able to get more practice on the concepts and skills that are at their appropriate instructional level, and the amount of active learning time is increased. Extensive research in peer tutoring indicates that when the tutoring sessions are well constructed and monitored, student achievement is increased for both the tutor and the tutee. Jenkins and Jenkins (1988) identified the following essential elements of successful peer tutoring programs.

Lesson Formats Tutoring lessons should be highly structured and carefully prepared by the teacher. This lesson format should stay the same from day to day so that both the tutor and the tutee can learn and predict the format.

Content of Instruction The lessons should provide the opportunity for extra instruction practice, repetition, or clarification of skills or concepts presented in the classroom. The tutoring sessions should match the demands of the independent work the student will have to do. For example, a student who is tutored in social studies content should practice answering in the same format in which he or she will be tested finally (e.g., short answer, multiple choice, true–false).

Mastery Learning Select skills to be practiced in the peer tutoring session that are of sufficient importance to be mastered. The tutoring sessions should provide enough practice that the student is able to master the skill or content.

Frequency and Duration of Sessions Tutoring sessions seem to be most effective when they occur daily and have individual sessions of under 30 minutes. Schedule sessions that fit your own classroom programming.

Tutor Training To be successful, tutors need to be trained in appropriate interpersonal and instructional behaviors that will result in a satisfying and successful experience for both the tutor and the tutee. These behaviors include

- Giving clear directions
- Confirming correct responses
- Correcting errors appropriately
- Encouraging without overprompting

This training should match the instructional format you have selected. If you provide specific instructions on how to organize the tutoring sessions, and if the tutors and tutees are given explicit directions on gathering materials, recording student answers, and gaining assistance, the sessions will run smoothly.

Class Climate and Active Supervision Interact each day with each dyad. The tutor should be encouraged to establish high expectations while maintaining respect for the learner. You should model the kinds of positive interactions you want the tutors to demonstrate. Personal attention from you will keep your tutors motivated.

Tracking Progress Establish procedures for the tutor to maintain daily records of performance data on the skill or content that is being practiced. These data will help you adjust the materials or the practice strategies to achieve greater learning. Often, a visual display, such as a chart of performance, can provide both the tutor and the tutee with clear feedback about progress. For example, in an oral reading practice session, the tutor might track the number of errors made, jot down what the child read, the number of questions the child was able to answer, and take a timed sample to get some fluency data. The teacher, in reviewing the tutor's notes, might notice a pattern in the errors, which could guide the tutoring session for the next day.

Small-Group Instruction

You can also provide individualized reading within a group. If you use a "round robin" reading format (with each child taking a turn to read a passage aloud) in your reading groups, you can tailor the kinds of feedback you provide as each child reads. This individualized feedback can focus the child's attention on the skills that currently are being emphasized in his or her instructional program.

Oral reading by students requires a risk-free (in terms of self-concept) learning environment.

Instruction in Strategies for Learning

In Chapter 6, the characteristics of strategic readers were discussed. Two characteristics of the troubled readers are (1) the development of ineffective strategies or simply the lack of development of critical strategies for understanding written material, and (2) the inability to match a given strategy to the instructional task at hand.

In contrast to skilled readers, less-skilled readers lack knowledge about the purpose of reading, lack the sensitivity to behave strategically, and fail to evaluate the appropriateness of the strategies they choose to use (Short & Ryan, 1984). The development of reading awareness is an important cognitive attainment because it distinguishes beginning and advanced reading levels. Skilled readers often engage in deliberate activities that require careful thinking, flexible strategies, and periodic self-monitoring. Over the years, this kind of awareness has been referred to by terms such as "reflective thinking" and, most recently, "metacognition" (Scott, 1984). Enhancing awareness of the purposes of reading and providing systematic strategies may enable less-skilled readers to surmount obstacles to efficient reading.

Current research indicates that students can develop effective strategies. The research focuses on the development of specific strategies for learning. *Learning strategies* are techniques, principles, or rules that enable a student to learn, to solve problems, and to complete tasks independently (Deshler & Schumaker, 1986). The overall intent of learning-strategies instruction is to teach students skills that will allow them not only to meet immediate requirements successfully, but also to generalize these skills to other situations and settings over time. Many of these strategies involve metacognitive tactics, which are designed to increase the student's awareness of the *thinking* process uses in reading. These approaches have been developed to increase the repertoire of effective and explicit problem-solving strategies for these learners.

Emphasize metacognitive abilities once more.

There is a difference between *instructional strategies* (what the teacher does to convey information) and *learning strategies* (what the learner does to gain information). Many of the suggestions already discussed in this chapter involve instructional strategies that are designed to improve the student's learning strategies. The effective reader has a variety of strategies that can be used flexibly to meet the requirements of the text.

Strategies for Discerning Meaning

Finding and Using Cues   All written language is not only a collection of words and sounds, but also a complex, sociopsycholinguistic combination of sounds, syntax, semantics, and context in order to create meaning (Harste & Burke, 1978). Most readers use a variety of problem-solving strategies to find the meaning in passages and to make decisions about the author's intent. These strategies attend to the following cues (Rhodes & Dudley-Marling, 1988):

Pragmatic cues:	What the reader expects from the context
Semantic cues:	Knowledge shared by the reader and writer about the topic
Syntactic cues:	Morphological and word-ordering rules, "-s" for plural nouns, "-ed" for past-tense verbs, "-ing" for participles and gerunds
Graphophonemic cues:	Letter–sound relationships, knowledge of legal and illegal letter combinations

Discuss the importance of developing high-level thinking skills with all *learners.*

Predicting, Confirming, and Integrating Meanings   In addition, the effective reader uses the skills of predicting, confirming, and integrating to derive meaning from printed material. *Predicting* involves anticipating what the author will say (the next event in the story) and what kind of word will come next in the sentence (the language construction) or what letters will be used to complete a word. Readers use a knowledge of language and events to help us read.

The skill of *confirming* involves asking the question "Does what I have just read make sense?" If the text does not make sense, the proficient reader may continue reading in search of more cues, go back to see if there were some missed cues prior or they may look for outside help. Both predicting and confirming provide a continual check for comprehension.

Integrating involves the reader in putting together what the reader knows with what the author intends. Children who are not proficient readers often lack these skills. They frequently rely heavily on a single word-attack strategy and give up when this strategy fails.

The correction strategy described next is a good example of an instructional strategy that results in more effective learning strategies for the reader.

Personal responsibility and self-reliance are two critical elements for all learners. Students who are effective readers and are good writers reflect these attributes.

Correction Strategies Eaton and Hansen (1978) developed a correction strategy to help deficient readers develop a wider range of reading strategies. The following corrective sequence is a top-down sequence and provides cues to the deficient reader to use the aforementioned skills (i.e., predicting, confirming, and integrating):

Notice how this set of strategies is simple, straightforward, and easy for limited focus. Ask students to think of other strategies they can design, which reflect the same attributes.

Try another way: The first correction strategy cues the student that a word had been misread. The student is encouraged to select another strategy to read the word.

Finish and guess: The second correction strategy cues the student to use the skills of predicting and confirming. The student is encouraged to use both language expectancies and any knowledge of the story context to read the word.

Break into parts: The third correction strategy encourages students to use the morphological components of words to decode. Students are guided to find the roots of words and to work toward decoding from the meaning-bearing element of the words.

Locate sounds: The fourth correction strategy encourages students to use their knowledge of the grapheme–phoneme relationships to decode the word. The teacher helps the student isolate the troubling sound or combination and asks, "What sound does _____ make?"

Provide the word: If the previous strategies have not been successful, the teacher provides the correct word to the student.

Eaton and Hansen found that when they used this correction hierarchy in oral reading practice sessions, their students began to develop a wider range of options for deriving meaning from text. After a few weeks of practice, the students began independently to use the skills of predicting and confirming as their initial decoding strategies.

The self-monitoring ability mentioned in early chapters is a critical element of the strategic reader often missing from the troubled reader. While the normal reader often develops this executive function without explicit instruction from the teacher, the reading-disabled student may need specific, overt instruction in self-monitoring. Gerber (1988) described a successful strategy in which students were taught (and prompted) to ask specific questions during three academic tasks designed to regulate the quality of performance. When students asked themselves questions such as, "Will I be able to answer the questions?" or "Am I checking my capitals and punctuation?" during reading comprehension and expository writing tasks, respectively, their performance was significantly improved.

Use of Flexible Models of Instruction

Remind students that *flexibility* means the ability to adjust teaching in midstream. Point out that much of the "effective schooling" research indicated that effective teachers teach from "scenarios" more than fixed detailed lesson plans. They begin a lesson with an understanding that it can go in more than one direction. This is not to suggest that beginning teachers not have a well-detailed lesson plan! Obviously, they should. However, experience will provide increased comfort with the scenarios concept and will allow them to teach with greater flexibility.

Teachers have often developed a philosophy of teaching reading, which relies heavily on one model. They may have adopted a language-experience-based reading approach, or they may rely heavily on a code-based program. The slow-learning students in your class may not be learning successfully with the model you have chosen. The effective teacher of the slow-learning child has developed instructional flexibility and is able to tailor the instructional activities to respond to the demonstrated needs of the learner.

> Teachers who lack instructional flexibility often do more of the same when their students are not succeeding. Successful instructional environments are those in which teachers have a variety of instructional strategies and adjust their teaching based on the student's performance.

Further, it is reasonable to assume that the same instructional approach cannot be used consistently with each individual learner. Children will at times need flexibility, freedom, and self-directed study time. At other times, the same child will be open to a tightly structured, direct-instruction model.

Since the mid-1980s, the direct-skills-instruction models for use with special learners have yielded to more holistic approaches. Influenced by leaders in language experience and by whole language advocates, more of the contemporary approaches to reading instruction for the special learner reflect a broader language-in-use perspective (Clay, 1988). Certainly, most experts in reading today agree that instructional models that are solely skills-based, teaching phonics and skills in isolation from other reading activities, are not effective teaching practices (Chall, 1989). Programs that focus the child's attention on the skills and elements of the text, without simultaneously developing strategies for reading, are seen as undesirable.

Instructional approaches with the special learner, as with all learners, must view the act of reading as an interactive process (Ringler & Weber, 1984). Both reading and writing skills, according to authorities, can be successfully learned in context (Rhodes & Dudley-Marling, 1988). However, although experts advocate developing skills in the context of meaningful reading and writing activities, they also recognize that instruction for these students is most successful when it is part of a planned sequence, which includes direct explanation and instruction on skills and strategies used in successful reading and many opportunities for the children to practice each skill and use it successfully.

Harris and Sipay (1980) summarize the characteristics of effective reading instruction as follows:

Teaching is more likely to be effective when

1) *The teacher plans, assigns and supervises learning activities.*
2) *Reading is scheduled for enough instructional time to accomplish mastery of the program's objectives.*
3) *The pace of instruction is adjusted to differences in the learning rates of groups and individuals.*
4) *Instructional material is easy enough to allow pupils to concentrate on new words or ideas, develop fluency and enjoy reading.*
5) *Classroom conditions prevail that are conducive to concentration and sustained attention.*
6) *Teachers maintain order while showing warm interest in the children, and are generous with praise for [students'] efforts.*
7) *The proportion of lesson time spent in academic engaged activity is high.*
8) *Teachers are optimistic about the learning potentialities of their pupils and do not allow their perceptions of individual differences to influence their behavior so as to affect the morale of some pupils adversely.*

Can your students think of other items to add to Harris and Sipay's list?

Characteristics of Other Special Student Populations and Appropriate Learning Environments

Visually Impaired

This final section of this chapter is not intended to be a definitive treatment of any of these additional special learner populations; rather, it is only a brief overview. The authors strongly suggest that additional readings and projects be assigned in the reading methods class in these areas, so that students will have an opportunity to study these in greater depth.

The visually impaired include children who are legally blind and those who are partially sighted. Eighty-two percent of people who are legally blind have some vision and are often able to read print materials with the assistance of large-print books or magnifying devices (Willis, 1976). Visual impairment does not affect the child's language development or the potential for developing good reading comprehension skills. However, you should be aware of several characteristics regarding learning and regarding classroom organization, to help these children most effectively:

1. A consistent physical environment in the classroom will help this child. If you make new seating arrangements or introduce new learning centers, be sure to introduce the changes to the visually impaired child.
2. When new concepts or vocabulary are introduced, use any of the nonvisual senses you can to augment the instruction.
3. Provide a rich listening environment. Books and stories on cassette tapes in a listening center can be particularly enriching for these children. You can also get taped books on specific topics through your local library or by contacting

Recordings for the Blind
214 East Fifty-Eighth Street
New York, NY 10022

Hearing Impaired

If hearing-impaired children have been placed in your classroom, you will also probably be working with a specialist who can help you develop appropriate activities for these student. Depending on the degree of hearing loss, many of these children can compensate through the use of amplification devices, speech-reading, and sign language. The most important learning characteristic for you to remember is that these children are extremely dependent on visual cues. You will need to be particularly aware of how you use facial expression, lip movements, and written information to cue the student. Positioning of these children in the classroom can make a big difference to their ability to track the instructional activities occurring. If you stand with your back to the student or with your back against a brightly lit window when you are giving instructions, you will make it more difficult for the student to use visual cues.

Additional learning characteristics that you should consider include the following:

1. Extra noise in the classroom can be distracting to hearing-impaired children with amplification devices. These devices amplify *all* sound, not just your voice or the other important sounds.

2. Hearing-impaired children may be delayed in areas of language development, depending on the severity of their loss and the age of onset. Because reading and listening comprehension are so dependent on language development, children with significant language delays may have difficulties in developing comprehension skills.

3. Orally presented instructions and learning tasks require intense concentration for hearing-impaired children. They may become fatigued if these kinds of tasks are not interspersed with some that do not require the same level of attention.

4. Because these children have difficulty distinguishing sounds, they will respond best to programs that emphasize more sight-word instruction, paired with the development of strong contextual analysis skills to aid decoding.

5. Because of their reliance on visual cues, these children succeed best in classrooms that use visual aids, such as overhead projectors, to communicate new concepts.

English as a Second Language (ESL) or Limited English Proficient (LEP)

The number of nonnative speakers in this country is increasing. Many of these children are limited-English-speaking students who have not yet developed fluency with the English language. They come from a wide variety of linguistic and cultural backgrounds. You will not be able to prepare for all the different languages and linguistic characteristics you might encounter in your teaching career. (One principal in a small rural school in Kennewick, Washington reported that over 14 different languages were spoken in his school.) Nonetheless, recognizing several learning and organizational characteristics will help you work most effectively with these children:

1. Encourage talking between your limited-English students and your other students. Structure cooperative learning or peer-tutoring activities to facilitate the development and practice of oral language skills.

2. Focus on meaning and communication, and do not accentuate pronunciation or grammatical errors initially.
3. Choose materials that are culturally appropriate, and demonstrate respect for the cultural and linguistic heritages of your students.

Gifted

This chapter has focused on the student who is not able to handle written materials as easily as most children. However, you will also have children who have already developed reading skills beyond those of most of the rest of your students. These children can also pose a challenge for you.

Although these students may appear to be doing well in reading and language arts areas, you may need to use the same skills of observation and monitoring that you have developed for the reading-disabled child, to help you develop the best possible learning environment for these students. For example, these students often master the basic skills of reading and writing early and can use them in creative products and understanding the complexities of other subject areas. However, these children are often so facile with language that the teacher assumes that they have mastered skills in language and reading that they have not. They can race through book after book, absorbing only the basic plot line and never noticing the details the author used to create depth in the character.

Just like the disabled learner, these students respond well to direct instruction in the skills of reading and language arts. The clearest difference between these students and the others discussed in this chapter is the amount of *time* and *practice* required to develop the skills and to transfer them to other learning situations.

The key considerations in working with the student who is talented in language-related subjects are (a) careful assessment of the skills and strategies the student has already mastered, and (b) flexibility in altering the curriculum and assignments to both extend current skills and develop those not yet mastered. For example, a student who is already able to see the story grammar of a passage and can easily identify the character and plot may be ready to ask the more complex questions of how point of view was developed by the author. These students also thrive in classrooms where the teacher is able to cross curricular boundaries within assignments and allow the student to use their skills to pursue universal questions as they are presented in literature, social sciences, and sciences.

This kind of flexibility means that you as a teacher will need to develop ways to extend your current activities and assignments to allow these students to stretch themselves. This does not mean creating an entirely new curriculum, but rather finding the logical places where students can develop at the outer edges of their abilities.

Maker (1982) suggests that altering the content, the process, or the product in regular curriculum can provide challenges for the advanced student. For example, if you are doing a unit on fables or myths with all your students, you could alter the *content* by allowing the advanced student to study fables from additional cultures beyond those typically featured in your unit. *Process* might be changed by encouraging the student to compare and contrast the fables from the Pacific Rim countries with those from Europe. *Product* adaptations might allow the more advanced students to substitute the regular assignment of paraphrasing a fable with a student-initiated project, such as writing a book of riddles about characters in fables or myths, or identifying a current moral issue and writing a modern fable (Gallagher, 1985).

These kinds of assignments should not be given in addition to the regular assignment, but rather as an alternative for students who clearly have mastered the skills and concepts you hope to develop through the regular assignment. Gifted students need to explore the same concepts and content as the rest of the students, but in more depth and with greater complexity and sophistication. In addition, they can move into new content and knowledge. Both are important.

HIGHLIGHTS

1. No one instructional approach meets the needs of all special learners. Their diversity in ability, interests, and personal needs requires flexibility in choice and use of various instructional models for developing reading.
2. Continually assessing and monitoring learners' reading growth will enable the teacher to select and apply different teaching strategies and techniques more effectively with special learners.
3. As with all readers, comprehension is the key goal of reading instruction for special learners. Comprehension is developed most effectively for all learners in a language-rich, motivating environment where language for functional purposes dominates the classroom.
4. There should be both direct and indirect instruction in reading strategies for special learners.

REINFORCEMENT ACTIVITIES

1. Describe some of the key characteristics of special learners.
2. How are special learners and other learners different? How are they similar?

3. What are some important guidelines the teacher of learning should keep in mind when making decisions about teaching the special learner?
4. Describe how you would go about designing a lesson plan to meet the identified learning needs of a special learner.

Have students particularly note the ways in which direct instruction fits in different instructional settings.

Behavior modification and various time-on-task models are popular in many special education programs. Ask students where such approaches fit in a reading program.

With your students, discuss different mainstreaming models with which you are familiar.

ADDITIONAL PROJECTS

1. Visit a learning resource center or other instructional component of a school, which is designed for special learners. Observe the teaching strategies and techniques used by the resource teacher. Compare them with those used in other instructional settings.
2. Arrange a visit with a special education teacher. Ask the teacher about his or her philosophy or theory about the best way to teach reading to special learners.
3. Arrange a visit with a curriculum coordinator or director of instruction in a school district, and find out how *mainstreaming* (i.e., integration of students with specialized needs into the mainstream of the school population) works in their school.

REFERENCES

Calfree, R., & Hoover, K. (1976). Reading and mathematics observation system: Description and analysis of time expenditures. In F. J. McDonald (Ed.), *Beginning Teacher Evaluation Study: Phase II*. Princeton, NJ: Educational Testing Service.

Camp, B., et al. (1977). Think Aloud: A program for developing self-control in young aggressive boys. *Journal of Abnormal Child Psychology, 5*, 157–169.

Carnine, D., & Gersten, R. (1988). Direct instruction in reading comprehension. In E. Meyen, G. Vergason, & R. Whelan (Eds.), *Effective Instructional Strategies for Exceptional Children* (pp. 65–79). Denver: Love Publishing.

Carnine, D., & Kinder, D. (1985). Teaching low-performing students to apply generative and schema strategies to narrative and expository material. *Remedial and Special Education, 6*, 20–30.

Chall, J. (1989). Learning to read: The great debate 20 years later. *Phi Delta Kappan, 70*, 521–538.

Clay, M. (1988). *The Early Detection of Reading Difficulties* (3rd ed.). Portsmouth, NH: Heinemann.

Cohen, S., & de Bettincourt, L. (1988). Teaching children to be independent learners: A step-by-step strategy. In E. Meyen, G. Vergason, & R. Whelan (Eds.), *Effective Instructional Strategies for Exceptional Children* (pp. 319–334). Denver: Love Publishing.

Deshler, D., & Schumaker, J. (1986). Learning strategies: An instructional alternative for low-achieving adolescents. *Exceptional Children, 53*, 583–590.

Duffy, G., Roehler, L., & Herrmann, B. (1988). Modeling mental processes helps poor readers become strategic readers. *The Reading Teacher, 41*, 762–767.

Durkin, D. (1978). What classroom observations reveal about reading comprehension. *Reading Research Quarterly, 14*, 481–533.

Dykstra, R. (1974). Phonics and beginning reading instruction. In C. Walcutt, J. Lamport, & G. McCracken, *Teaching Reading: A Phonics/Linguistic Approach to Developmental Reading*. New York: Macmillan.

Eaton, M., & Hansen, C. (1978). Reading. In N. G. Haring, T. C. Lovitt, M. Eaton, & C. Hansen (Eds.), *The Fourth R: Research in the Classroom*. Columbus, OH: Merrill.

Eaton, M., & Lovitt, T. (1972). Achievement tests vs. direct daily measurement. In G. Semb (Ed.), *Behavior Analysis and Education* (pp. 78–87). Lawrence, KS: University of Kansas Press.

Epps, D., Ysseldyke, J., & McGue, M. (1984). I know one when I see one—Differentiating LD and non-LD students. *Learning Disabilities Quarterly, 7*, 89–101.

Gallagher, J. (1985). *Teaching the Gifted Child*. Newton, MA: Allyn & Bacon.

Gerber, M. (1983). Learning disabilities and cognitive strategies: A case for training or constraining problem solving? *Journal of Learning Disabilities, 16*, 255–260.

Gerber, M. (1988). Cognitive–behavioral training. In E. Meyen, G. Vergason, & R. Whelan (Eds.), *Effective Instructional Strategies for Exceptional Children* (pp. 45–64). Denver: Love Publishing.

Gettinger, M., & Lyon, M. (1983). Predictors of the discrepancy between time needed and time spent in learning among boys exhibiting behavior problems. *Journal of Educational Psychology, 75*, 491–499.

Goodman, K. (1973). *Miscue Analysis: Applications to Reading Instruction.* Urbana, IL: National Council of Teachers of English.

Graves, D. (1983). *Writing: Teachers and Children at Work.* Portsmouth, NH: Heinemann.

Hallahan, D., & Kauffman, J. (1982). *Exceptional Children* (2nd ed.). Englewood Cliffs, NJ: Prentice-Hall.

Harris, A., & Sipay, E. (1980). *How to Increase Reading Ability: A Guide to Developmental and Remedial Methods.* New York: Longman.

Harste, J., & Burke, C. (1978). Toward a socio-psycholinguistic model of reading comprehension. *Viewpoints in Teaching and Learning, 54*, 9–34.

Herrmann, B. (1988). Two approaches for helping poor readers become more strategic. *The Reading Teacher, 41*, 24–28.

Howell, K., & Morehead, M. (1987). *Curriculum-Based Evaluation for Special and Remedial Education.* Columbus, OH: Merrill.

Jenkins, J., & Jenkins, L. (1988). Peer tutoring in elementary and secondary programs. In E. Meyen, G. Vergason, & R. Whelan (Eds.), *Effective Instructional Strategies for Exceptional Children* (pp. 335–354). Denver: Love Publishing.

Lovitt, T., et al. (1971). Effects of various reinforcement contingencies on oral reading rate. In E. Ramp & B. Hopkins (Eds.), *A New Direction for Education: Behavior Analysis.* Lawrence, KS: University of Kansas Press.

Lucking, R. (1975). *Comprehension and a model for questioning.* (ERIC Document Reproduction Service No. 110 988).

Maker, J. (1982). *Curriculum Development for the Gifted.* Rockville, MD: Aspen Systems.

Moyer, S., & Newcomer, P. (1977). Reversals in reading: Diagnosis and remediation. *Exceptional Children, 43*, 425–429.

O'Shea, L., & O'Shea, D. (1988). Using repeated reading. *Teaching Exceptional Children, 20*, 26–29.

Palincsar, A., & Brown, A. (1984). Reciprocal teaching of comprehension-fostering and comprehension-monitoring activities. *Cognition and Instruction, 1*, 171–175.

Rhodes, L., & Dudley-Marling, C. (1988). *Readers and Writers with a Difference: A Holistic Approach to Teaching Learning Disabled and Remedial Students.* Portsmouth, NH: Heinemann.

Ringler, L., & Weber, C. (1984). *A Language–Thinking Approach to Reading.* New York: Harcourt Brace Jovanovich.

Rose, M., Cundick, B., & Higbie, K. (1983). Visual rehearsal and visual imagery: Mnemonic aids for learning disabled children. *Journal of Learning Disabilities, 16*, 352–354.

Rosenshine, B., & Berliner, D. (1977). *Academic engaged time: Content covered and direct instruction.* Paper presented at the annual meeting of the American Educational Research Association.

Schenkat, R. (1988). The promise of restructuring special education. *Education Week, 8*, 36.

Schewel, R., & Waddell, J. (1986). Metacognitive skills: Practical strategies. *Academic Therapy, 22*, 19–25.

Schloss, P., & Sedlak, R. (1986). *Instructional Methods for Students with Learning and Behavior Problems.* Newton, MA: Allyn & Bacon.

Scott, G. P. (1984). The benefits of informed instruction for children's reading awareness and comprehension skills. *Child Development, 55*, 2083–2093.

Short, E., & Ryan, E. (1984). Metacognitive differences between skilled and less skilled readers: Remediating deficits through story grammar and attribution training. *Journal of Educational Psychology, 76*, 225–235.

Sleeter, C. (1984). *Why is there learning disabilities? A critical analysis of the birth of the field in its social context.* Paper presented at the annual meeting of the American Educational Research Association, Chicago, IL.

Smith, D. (1981). *Teaching the Learning Disabled.* Englewood Cliffs, NJ: Prentice-Hall.

Smith, D., & Lovitt, T. (1973). The educational diagnosis and remediation of written b and d reversal problems: A case study. *Journal of Learning Disabilities, 6*, 356–363.

Willis, D. (1976). *A study of the relationship between visual acuity, reading mode, and school systems for blind students.* Louisville, KY: American Printing House for the Blind.

APPENDIX A

LINGUISTICS TERMINOLOGY OFTEN USED IN READING INSTRUCTION

The following terms are used in many basal reading programs that contain instructional strands or components focusing on teaching decoding as a foundation skill in reading instruction.

consonants—Consonants are all of the sounds in the language represented by letters and letter combinations other than vowels (a, e, i, o, and u). They are described by some linguists and reading authorities in further technical detail as "stops" (p, t, c [when having the /k/ sound], d, and g [as in "gorilla"]); "affricates" (ch and j [or the same sound for the letter g]); "fricatives" (f, v, and th); "sibilants" (s, z, sh, and medial s [or the /s/ sound]); "nasals" (m, n, and ng); "laterals" (l); and "semivowels" (r, w, y, and h).

consonant blends—Certain consonant letters appear together so often and behave in the same way that they are referred to as "blends" or "clusters." Common initial or beginning consonant blends are bl, cl, dr, fl, gl, pl, sl, sm, and tr. Common final position consonant blends include ft, lt, nk, sk, and st.

consonant digraphs—Consonant digraphs are similar to consonant blends. That is, they are consonant letters which appear together so often that their appearance as paired letters is predictable. The primary difference between consonant blends and consonant digraphs is that consonant digraphs are pronounced as one sound—neither letter alone signifies even a part of the sound—whereas one can note features of two different sounds in a blend. Some of the more common consonant digraphs are ch, sh, th, ph, and ng.

decoding—*Decoding* refers to the ability to see sound–symbol relationships in words and apply this knowledge in the act of reading. Hence, decoding instruction teaches learners how to decode these relationships in printed words. Note also the definitions for *phonics* and for *word attack* in this appendix.

grapheme—The term *grapheme* is used by many reading educators to denote a specific letter or letter combination as a symbol for a phoneme, as opposed to the actual sound the letter or letter combination it represents. It is important to remember that there are many more meaningful sounds in the English language than there are letters used to represent them. Many sounds in words, therefore, are represented by letter combinations (e.g., consonant or vowel digraphs).

morpheme—A *morpheme* is the smallest unit of sounds (or combination of letters) that can communicate meaning in the language. A morpheme can be *free* (able to stand alone as a word, e.g., "bad"), or it can be *bound* (must be attached to other word parts, e.g., "pre-" or "un-"). A morpheme can even be a single letter (e.g., the "-s" in "cars" communicates meaning— i.e., more than one car).

phoneme—A *phoneme* is a single unit of sound used in the language to produce words. Some individual letters represent phonemes in English (e.g., the letter "a"). Some letters also must work in combinations to represent single units of sounds in the English language (e.g., "th"). Also, note the various blends and digraphs. Although English has only 26 letters in its alphabet, it has over 40 important phonemes represented by those 26 letters.

In order to identify the sound or phoneme represented by a letter or letter combination, many basal reading programs and reading texts place the letters in slanted bars if they refer to the phoneme (e.g., /th/) instead of to the letters.

phonics—The term *phonics* is often used by different people to mean differ- ent things. For some, *phonics* means the content of sound–symbol relation- ships necessary for the beginning reader to master in order to be able to decode words. For others, phonics means a particular method of teaching decoding skills, requiring students to focus specifically on studying graph- eme–phoneme relationships. Authorities often disagree as to whether one method of this type of instruction is better than another or whether one method is actually a phonics approach, while another is not. Finally, for many laypersons, *phonics* means simply whether some direct instruction is being used to teach decoding and/or word attack skills in the reading program.

phonograms—Some authorities assert that certain letter clusters or patterns appear often enough to generate word families. For example, "ad" in words such as *bad, mad, sad, rad,* and so forth, is called a "phonogram." Others include "ed," "at," "ine," and "ike."

schwa—The *schwa* is actually a short vowel sound. Its most common location is in unaccented (unstressed) syllables of polysyllabic words. For example, the schwa sound is the "uh" sound in words such as *focus, woman, handily,* and *victim*. Many reading authorities argue that teaching the schwa as a separate sound category in beginning reading is not only unnecessary but also generally confusing and often frustrating for beginning readers. However, it still receives special attention in the teachers' editions of many basal reading programs.

suprasegmental phonemes—*Suprasegmental phonemes* are those phonemes in the language that carry or impart meaning in ways other than through letters. Note that the various consonants and vowels and subtypes of each are represented by letters and are referred to by linguists as "segmental phonemes"—they "segment" the language by breaking it up into predictable letter patterns and pattern combinations. Suprasegmental phonemes, however, are voice-actuated or -controlled units of meaning. Three of these are suprasegmental phonemes important for language meaning: (1) *pitch,* the relative tonal height at which a phoneme is uttered; *stress,* the relative loudness with which it is uttered; and *juncture,* the relative length of pauses between words, clauses, and sentences. Their role is obviously more important in oral language than in written. However, many reading experts argue that more attention to them would help students to be both better readers and better writers.

syllables—A *syllable* is a single vowel or a combination of letters containing a vowel that is pronounced as a single unit. Therefore, the number of syllables in a word corresponds to the number of vowel sounds in the word.

syllable patterns—Syllables in the English language contain stress points, which are called "accents." Examination of many multisyllabic words reveals some generalizations about their behavior:

1. If the first vowel is long and precedes two consonants, the first syllable is stressed (e.g., *library*).
2. If a word has two syllables and the second contains a long vowel, the second syllable is stressed (e.g., *proceed*).
3. If the first vowel is short and precedes two consonants, the first syllable is stressed (e.g., *mystery*).
4. If the final syllable contains "le," it is not stressed (e.g., *bottle*).

Here are the most common syllable patterns (C = consonant; V = vowel; lowercase letters signify those exact letters):

BASIC SYLLABLE PATTERNS

I.	Long vowel patterns	CV	go, me, be
		CVe	mate, date, rate
		CVVC	real, pain, moat
II.	Short vowel patterns	VC	in, is, at
		CVC	can, met, lot
III.	Final "r" pattern	CVr	mar, car, bar
IV.	Final "e" pattern	CVCCe	judge, rinse, mince

Remember that different reading authorities have different numbers of patterns, so a basal reading program may present fewer or more than the preceding four.

syntax—*Syntax* refers to the phrasal and clausal structure of sentences. Frequently, the term *grammar* is used when referring to a sentence's syntax.

unvoiced and *voiced*—The phoneme /th/ illustrates the difference between *unvoiced* and *voiced* phonemes in the English language: The initial sound in "that" illustrates the voiced phoneme /th/, and the initial sound in "think" is unvoiced. Unvoiced sounds often produce a short sharp burst of air (if you place a tissue in front of your mouth while speaking the word, you should see the tissue flutter). Voiced words, such as "that," produce less of an air burst, but if you place your fingertips gently over your throat, you will feel the vibrations caused by voicing the sound.

Although many basal reading programs devote some time to teaching voiced and unvoiced sound distinctions to beginning readers, most reading authorities indicate that such instruction is not necessary.

vowels—Vowels are the sounds represented in the English language by the letters a, e, i, o, and u. Linguists categorize vowels by the location of their production in the mouth (i.e., tongue position in relation to cheeks, jaws, and lips). Hence, they would describe the vowel sound of /i/ in *big* as being "high up front," while /au/ in *caught* is "low back." Most reading authorities, however, are satisfied with simply classifying vowels as long and short (e.g., long ā as in *mate* and short ă as in *mat*).

vowel digraphs—*Vowel digraphs* are two consecutive vowel letters representing only one single vowel sound or phoneme, rather than a combination of both as in a diphthong. For example /oa/ in *moan*, /ie/ in *shield*, /ai/ in *bait*, and /ee/ in *beet*.

vowel diphthongs—*Vowel diphthongs* are two vowel letters contained in one syllable in which both of the vowel sounds represented by the letters have a distinctive sound, but the two sounds are combined so closely that it produces a single sound (e.g., the /oi/ combination in *boil*). Examples of other common vowel diphthongs are /ay/ in *say*, /oy/ in *boy*, /aw/ in *saw*, and /ou/ in *house*. (Notice that /ou/ in *house* is a diphthong, but /ou/ in the word *enough* is a digraph.)

word attack—Most reading educators use this term to indicate approaches to teaching structural components, patterns, and applications in individual words (e.g., prefixes, suffixes, inflections, derivational endings, syllabication). Sometimes, this is taught as part of the plan for vocabulary development in reading instruction. Sometimes, it is taught as part of the decoding component of instruction—Some reading authorities prefer to think of word-attack skills as being fundamental to vocabulary instruction. Some use *word attack* to mean the same thing as decoding, but most educators prefer to delineate the two concepts.

QUESTION TAXONOMIES

Most of the various question taxonomies owe their genesis to the work of Benjamin Bloom (1956), whose taxonomy of questions (developed in the 1950s) focused on the cognitive levels of different kinds of questions. A somewhat less cumbersome taxonomy, which also focuses on cognitive levels, is that of Norris Sanders (1966). It is elaborated more fully in his book, *Classroom Questions: What Kinds?*

The following synopsis includes basic assumptive statements, sample questions, and descriptions of the conditions under which the question categorization took place.

SYNOPSIS OF A TAXONOMY OF QUESTIONS

Underlying Ideas

1. All thinking can be classified into seven categories: memory, translation, interpretation, application, analysis, synthesis, and evaluation.
2. These categories of questions fit all subjects in elementary school.
3. Every category of questions has easy questions appropriate for young students or exceptional learners. Every category also has other questions that are challenging enough for advanced students.
4. The definitions of the seven kinds of questions overlap somewhat so that equally knowledgeable experts often differ on the best classification of a certain question. This need not bother classroom teachers.
5. By knowing the definitions of the kinds of questions, a teacher can make certain that students use appropriate thinking levels when reading various texts.

Note that for each question, one or more conditions should be confirmed.

Memory Questions

A memory question asks students to recall or to recognize ideas presented to them previously through reading or listening. Memory questions can require the student to recall a single fact or a much more involved idea.

Examples of Memory Questions
1. *Conditions:* The students have read that Washington, D.C. is the capital of the United States.
   Question: What is the name of the capital of the United States?
2. *Conditions:* The teacher has given the definitions of "solid," "liquid," and "gas." Examples were displayed illustrating each.
   Question: What is the definition of a solid? What is the definition of a liquid? What is the definition of a gas?
3. *Conditions:* The students have learned which products are manufactured in their community.
   Question: Check each of the following that are manufactured in our community: _____ cement _____ aluminum _____ automobiles.
4. *Conditions:* The students have been drilled on their multiplication tables.
   Question: Solve these problems:

   $$\begin{array}{ccc} 5 & 2 & 6 \\ \underline{\times 4} & \underline{\times 6} & \underline{\times 7} \end{array}$$

5. *Conditions:* The students have studied a list of spelling words. The teacher reads the list as the students write their responses to the question.
   Question: Spell these words correctly: animal, snowman, right, funny, mouse.

Translation Questions

In translation, the student is presented an idea and then is asked to restate the same idea in a different way.

Examples of Translation Questions
1. *Conditions:* The student has read a paragraph in the textbook.
   Question: Now tell me *in your own words* what you read.
2. *Conditions:* The teacher has explained how a store owner buys food from farmers and sells it to families in the neighborhood.
   Question: The teacher assigns students to play the roles of store owner, farmers, and family members. In a sociodrama, the students are to act out the roles that the teacher explained to them.
3. *Conditions:* Students have read the story *The Ant and the Grasshopper*.
   Question: Tell what happened in the story.
4. *Conditions:* The teacher displays a picture of men cutting wheat with a scythe.
   Question: Tell what you see in the picture.

5. *Conditions:* The teacher demonstrates the operation of a siphon.
   Question: Draw a picture of the siphon you were shown.

Interpretation Questions

The question asks the students to *compare* and/or *contrast* two or more ideas or to *use* an idea that they studied previously to solve a problem that is new to them. The idea may be in the form of a skill, definition, law, rule, or generalization. The student does not have to figure out which idea is to be used in interpretation because the question or the classroom context tells this. The question can be in short-answer or discussion form. Usually, the answer is quite objective. In other words, there is usually a right answer, which the teacher expects students to reason out.

Examples of Interpretation Questions

1. *Conditions:* The students have studied the generalization that warm air rises.
   Question: If you place a thermometer on the top shelf of a refrigerator and another on the bottom shelf, which would show the lowest temperature?
   Another question on a test the next day: Why don't grocery stores put frozen food onto refrigerated shelves, such as those used for the canned goods, instead of storing them in containers that are open on the top but closed on the sides?

2. *Conditions:* The students have studied temperature, rainfall, and topography maps of the United States. They may use these maps in answering the question. In addition, they are given a dot map showing where cotton is grown in the United States.
   Question: In what range of temperature, rainfall, and topography is cotton grown in the United States?

3. *Conditions:* The students have seen a film on the customs related to marriage and bringing up a family in an African society.
   Question: In what ways are the marriage and family customs in the movie similar to those in our society, and in what ways are they different?

4. *Conditions:* The teacher has explained the generalizations that the amount of money people earn depends on such things as the following: (1) Jobs that require more training or education usually pay more than jobs that require less training or education; (2) Jobs that require talents that few people have usually pay more than jobs that require talents that most people have.
   Question: Which do you think earns most in each pair? Tell why in each case.
   A. A teacher or a window washer _____ .
   B. An engineer who designs highways or a truck driver _____ .
   C. A house painter or a star baseball player _____ .

5. *Conditions:* The teacher has taught students the definitions of *rectangle* and *triangle.* (The students know their colors.)

Question: Color all rectangles red and all triangles green. Do not color any other shapes.

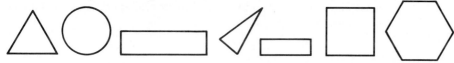

Application Questions

Application questions are similar to interpretation questions, in that both kinds of questions require students to *use* ideas learned previously when solving new problems. However, in an interpretation question, the students are specifically told to show that they can use a specific idea to solve a particular problem. Application goes one step further. In an application question, the students must show that they can use an idea when the problem demands it, even when they are not told to do so. In other words, application calls for appropriately transferring learned skills and concepts to new situations.

Examples of Application Questions

1. *Conditions:* In language arts class, the teacher has taught students how to use an index and a table of contents. Later, in a social-studies class, the students all have social studies textbooks.
   Question: Look in your social studies textbook to find the page that tells about Booker T. Washington. (The question would have been interpretation if asked this way: Use the index to find the page in your social studies textbook that tells about Booker T. Washington.)

2. *Conditions:* The students have been taught to write complete sentences. Some time later, the class takes a trip to a dairy.
   Question: Write a letter to Mr. Jones thanking him for showing us the dairy. (The teacher expects that students will write complete sentences. The same question would have called for interpretation if the teacher had added, "Be sure to write complete sentences.")

3. *Conditions:* A class has studied the main regions of the United States. This included consideration of climate, topography, crops, population, vegetation, manufacturing, and agriculture. At the end of the year, the teacher displays a half dozen big landscape pictures.
   Question: Study each picture carefully and then name a state in which you think the picture might have been taken. Give as many reasons as you can why you think the location of the picture might be in the state you name.

4. *Conditions:* The students have learned subtraction. In science class, the students were studying the hatching of eggs.
   Question: We put the eggs in the incubator on March 4. The first chick hatched on March 25. How many days did it take the first egg to hatch?

5. *Conditions:* The students have studied the concepts of *specialization* and *division of labor* in their social studies class. The class is going to make 10 identical Christmas window decorations. Each involves about six steps of cutting and folding and pasting.

Question: How might we organize ourselves to make these decorations most easily? (The question would be interpretation if asked this way: How can we use division of labor and specialization to make those decorations?)

Analysis Questions

Analysis questions require the student to consciously apply a rule of higher-level thinking, e.g., deductive or inductive reasoning. Analysis questions include formal problem-solving techniques. They are intended to get at the kind of thinking being used in a particular context or event.

Examples of Analysis Questions

1. *Conditions:* Students have been studying inductive reasoning.
   Question: What is wrong with the following statements? "I have seen three different redheaded people angry this week. Boy, redheads sure are temperamental."
2. *Conditions:* Students have been studying cause-effect relationships.
   Question: Which of the following statements shows cause and effect? Tell why the other does not.
   A. She is a doctor because she wishes to serve humanity.
   B. He isn't in school because I just saw him up town.
3. *Conditions:* Students have studied the differences and similarities in deductive and inductive reasoning.
   Question: In this mystery story, the author creates a detective who uses both deductive and inductive reasoning. Find examples of each and justify your choices.

Synthesis Questions

These questions ask the student to create something. The product to be created may be a physical object, a communication, a plan of operations, or a set of abstract relations. In other kinds of thinking, there may also be products but the distinctive thing about synthesis is the great freedom students have in deciding what is to be created and how it is to be created. A synthesis question never has one correct response. There are always many good answers that students may work out.

Examples of Synthesis Questions

1. *Conditions:* The students have read a story called "Indian Bill." One student said he did not like the way the story turned out. The teacher then assigned this synthesis question:
   Question: Write a different ending to the story of "Indian Bill."
2. *Conditions:* A kindergarten class is preparing a Christmas program. The students learn songs and then act out parts of the song. For example, the students crouch and waddle during a duck song. The children learned a new song about an old car that rattles and shakes.

Question: Think of something we can do that would show how the car might look.

3. *Conditions:* The students are studying poetry in language and astronomy in science.

   Question: Write a poem about a star.

4. *Conditions:* The teacher plays the cat music, the duck music, and the wolf music from *Peter and the Wolf* but does not play the part of the record that gives the story.

   Question: Tell what each of these three musical selections makes you think of. (After responding, the students can listen to the record and see what the composer had in mind. Though discovery of the single "correct" response is not synthesis thinking, it probably makes the lesson more interesting. The synthesis thinking is the students' diverse responses to the original question.)

5. *Conditions:* Students have been studying artifacts as part of a cultural anthropology unit in social studies. A box is to be inserted into the cornerstone of a new school. The students in a class are in charge of filling the box with things that show what it is like to go to school during that time.

   Question: What do you think should go into the box?

6. *Conditions:* A teacher suggests that a visit to a local factory would help the class understand more about manufacturing. The teacher says that the class can plan the field trip.

   Question: What must we do to organize the field trip?

Evaluation Questions

The students are asked to make a *value judgment* (rating of something as being good or bad, right or wrong, or perhaps beautiful or ugly) of some product, communication, event, or situation. Part of the answer always requires the students to tell what considerations led them to make the judgment. A value judgment is never provable. The best that can be done is to present good supporting evidence.

Examples of Evaluation Questions

1. *Conditions:* Students in a school are putting on a science fair. The sixth-graders have been asked to write an article for the city newspaper telling about the fair and inviting the public to attend. The teacher selects 10 of the best articles and runs off enough ditto copies for each student without including the names of the student authors.

   Question: Choose the article that you think should go into the newspaper. Write a paragraph telling why you think it is the best one. (Note—The original writing of the news articles is a good example of synthesis.)

2. *Conditions:* The students are studying how to use the library.

   Question: Suppose a boy took a library book home and left it on the floor of the living room. His little brother found the book and tore out some pages. Do you think either boy should be punished? Tell why.

3. *Conditions:* The teacher displays five very different pictures.
   Question: Which do you think is the prettiest? Tell why you chose the one you did.
4. *Conditions:* The students have studied the colonial period of United States history.
   Question: Did the colonists do the right thing when they threw the tea overboard at the Boston Tea Party? Tell why you believe as you do.
5. *Conditions:* The students have read a story about two brothers. One is a good athlete but a poor student. The other is a good student but clumsy and weak.
   Question: Which of these brothers would you rather be? Tell why.

PRACTICE IN CLASSIFYING QUESTIONS

Which of the categories in the taxonomy of questions is illustrated by each of the following?

1. A student in a home economics class is given rolls baked by seven students from another class and asked to select the best rolls.
2. Water would boil at the lowest temperature: (a) in the Netherlands, (b) in Wisconsin, (c) in Bolivia.
3. What, if anything, is wrong with these statements?
   BILL: I would never vote for Democrats. They got us into war under Wilson, Roosevelt, and Truman.
   JOHN: Yes, but what about the Republicans? There was an economic depression under Hoover and a recession under Eisenhower.
4. What were the causes of the Great Depression?
5. Write an ending for the story "The Lady and the Tiger."
6. In the following list, circle the numbers that are prime numbers: 2, 4, 7, 9, 11, 42, 52, 57
7. (Class is shown a political cartoon.) Write a paragraph or two that will present the argument shown here.
8. Prepare a scale drawing of the floor plan of your home.
9. (The class is shown a picture of a crowd walking on a sidewalk in a large city.) Is this a group?
10. What is the distance between the pitcher's mound and home plate on a baseball diamond?

SAMPLE QUESTION TAXONOMY TAILORED TO SOCIAL STUDIES

The following question taxonomy was designed for use in social studies. Notice how the category types differ from those in the Sanders taxonomy in some ways, but they overlap in others. Each question type (identified by roman numeral) is followed by several sample questions.

I. Identification
   Who is it?
   What is it?
   Where did it take place?
   Can you define . . . ?

II. Descriptive
   What happened?
   What are they doing?
   What is going on?
   How many different kinds
      are there?
   How long is it?
   What did it look like?

III. Comparative
   How are they different
      from each other?
   How are they similar?

IV. Historical
   When did it get started?
   How did it get started?
   Has it changed from the
      way it used to be?
   What have they found to
      be true in the past?
   Which came first?
   What is their chronological
      order?

V. Cause and Effect
   What caused him or her to
      behave that way?
   Why did it turn out that
      way?
   How could the situation
      have turned out differ-
      ently?
   If _____ had hap-
      pened, what might have
      been the effect?

VI. Prediction
   What is going to happen
      next?
   How will it end?

From what you know of
   the situation, how might
   it change _____
   years from now?

VII. Creative
   What would happen if I . . . ?
   What would you do if . . . ?
   How can we show . . . ?
   How could we organize . . . ?
   Can you develop a new way?

VIII. Research
   How can we find out?
   Where can we locate re-
      sources?
   Are these observations reli-
      able?
   Where did you get your in-
      formation?
   Which are facts and which
      are opinions?
   What reason or evidence
      can you give?

IX. Value Inquiry
   Which way is best?
   Is that a good way for
      things to end?
   What was the author's pur-
      pose, bias, or prejudice?
   For what reason would
      you favor . . . ?

X. Relevance or Application
   How does this apply to
      you?
   How does this idea or gen-
      eralization apply to
      other situations?
   What can we do to apply
      or implement our conclu-
      sions?
   How can we use these ma-
      terials?

THE LANGUAGE OF QUESTIONS

Descriptions Versus Explanations

A very important feature of questions is their unique language and the subtle (sometimes) differences that can be found in similar but not synonymous words. For example, consider the following two questions that you might ask about a selection of text.

1. Describe what happened on the ship in this story.
2. Explain what happened on the ship in this story.

Describe and *explain* are two entirely different terms, which require the learner to respond differently. The two should not be confused. Descriptions simply provide a narrative account of an event, concept, idea, or thing, either objectively or subjectively. An *explanation*, on the other hand, provides justification or logical (or at least causal) reasons for events to occur or things or ideas to develop.

In most instances, a description question would probably be an interpretation-level question in the Sanders taxonomy. If you ask students to explain something, however, you are probably looking for analysis-level thinking. Explanation questions require answers that are usually "attributional" in nature. The answer goes beyond description and goes on to identify attributes or characteristics that can justify or rationalize; cause and effect are often tied into explanatory answers.

> *Example:* A teacher asks a student, "Why does a kangaroo jump so well?" (The question requires an explanatory answer. Depending on what information is found in the text, various explanatory answers are possible.)
>
> "A kangaroo is able to jump well because of its unusual skeletal and muscular design."
>
> "Cause it has these funny back legs that are really strong."
>
> "Because the muscles are different from those of other animals."

Explanations are either good or bad, depending on the relevance and/or depth of the reasons the learner infers from the text. The student response determines which kind of question should follow—often asking students to provide additional factual or memory-level information, although the follow-up questions could be interpretation-level if the student apparently knew the necessary facts but did not see their relationship to each other.

Question Words and Question Categories

Unfortunately, there is no easy formula that allows us to generalize question's category based on specific key question words we commonly use in designing questions. For example, the word *how* can be used in a synthesis-level question (e.g., "How would you write a different ending for this story?"), but it can also be used as a key question word in a memory-level question (e.g., "How did Joe go to town?" where the text explicitly indicates Joe's mode of transportation).

Some basics about some of the commonly used question words can be generalized, but most of these can have exceptions:

1. *When* and *where* are often used to introduce lower-level questions—memory or recall questions.
2. *How* is often used in interpretation-level questions.
3. *Describe* is often used in interpretation-level questions, but it is also used quite often in memory-level questions, depending on the kind of explicit information provided in the text that is being read.
4. *Explain* often calls for analysis-level thinking.
5. *What* is often used for memory-level questions, but when used in conjunction with words and phrases asking for personal opinion or feelings, it functions at the evaluation level. For example, "What did the boy use to start the fire?" is a memory-level question, but "What do you think the boy should have done when he discovered that he was lost?" is an evaluation question.
6. *Compare* and/or *contrast* are usually interpretation-level questions.
7. *Summarize* is usually found in interpretation-level questions.
8. *Why* is commonly used at the interpretation level.
9. *Predict* is often used with analysis-level questions.

Remember to use the preceding only as a general guide. Knowing the taxonomies of cognitive-level questions will not assure that you will be a good teacher, but it is a necessary condition for being an effective teacher of reading.

BASIC GUIDELINES FOR USING A QUESTION TAXONOMY

Some Dos

- Do use a taxonomy such as Sanders's as a basic tool for assessing the kind and quality of questions used in curriculum materials developed and published for the elementary grades.
- Do use a taxonomy as a guide for designing and using questions in your daily lesson plans and for test design.
- Do use a taxonomy to informally monitor your use of questions in the classroom on a regular basis—at least once a week.
- Do develop your questions strategically with your questions tied closely to your lesson objectives as much as possible.

- Do focus most of your efforts in reading classes on higher-level questions that require students to think inferentially.
- Do use lower-level questions, but use them judiciously. Use memory- or recall-level questions that focus the student's attention upon facts, details, events, and ideas that can be clustered together as support data for a larger inference or conclusion.
- Do put your students into activities that require them to become question taxonomizers, to think consciously and directly about the fundamental differences among a number of different kinds of question. Have them try being the teacher.

Some Don'ts

- Don't assume that simply using the full taxonomic range of question levels will ensure the most effective teaching and learning for students. Questioning must be fitted into a strategy for the overall lesson. Sometimes, that will call for specialized use of question types and levels.
- Don't assume that all memory- or recall-level questions are bad. Students need to have facts and events they can utilize in developing support for larger inferences. Use these questions appropriately and wisely.
- Don't assume that just because published curriculum materials use a variety of question levels that their questioning is well done. It is certainly possible to ask some very stupid and/or inappropriate higher-level questions! Check to see how well the questions address the key ideas in the text and how well they are tied to the text lesson's objectives.
- Don't assume that effective questioning is all there is to effective teaching, even though it is very important. Consider your questioning within the larger overall context of teaching, which also includes factors such as the appropriateness of the objectives, the students' interest in the content, and classroom rapport. Each factor plays a critical role in effective teaching.

REFERENCES

Bloom, B. (Ed.). (1956). *Taxonomy of Educational Objectives: Handbook I. Cognitive Domain.* New York: David McKay.
Sanders, N. (1966). *Classroom Questions: What Kinds?* New York: Harper & Row.

ADDITIONAL RESOURCES

Armbruster, B., Anderson, T., et al. (1983). *What did you mean by that question? A taxonomy of American history questions* (Reading Education Report No. 308). Urbana, IL: Center for the Study of Reading.
Costa, A. (Ed.). (1985). *Developing Minds: A Resource Book for Teaching Thinking.* Alexandria, VA: Association for Supervision and Curriculum Development.

Jones, B. F. (Ed.). (1987). *Strategic Teaching and Learning*. Alexandria, VA: Association for Supervision and Curriculum Development.

Krathwohl, D., Bloom, B., & Masia, B. (1964). *Taxonomy of Educational Objectives: Handbook II. Affective Domain*. New York: David McKay.

Stiggins, R., Rubel, E., Quellmalz, E. (1986). *Measuring Thinking Skills in the Classroom*. Washington, DC: National Education Association.

NOTE: A number of other resources on the development of questioning are available through the Association for Supervision and Curriculum Development (ASCD), Phi Delta Kappa (PDK), the National Education Association (NEA), and a variety of other professional organizations, such as the International Reading Association (IRA) and the National Council of Teachers of English (NCTE).

INDEX

Acontextual tests, 319

Activities, for reading instruction, 175, 180

Adams, M. M., 266

Adolescent. *See* Middle school, student in

Advance organizers, 292

Alexander, F., 432

Aliteracy, 2, 3, 432

Allen, C., 122, 123

American Library Association Awards, 421

Analogy-fit-infer strategy, for reading instruction, 180, 181–182

Analysis questions, 484

Anaphora, 241–246

Anderson, R. C., 6, 271, 409, 410, 413, 417, 439

Anderson, T., 175

Ankney, P., 230

Antagonist, 386

Apples (Peterson), 60

Application questions, 483–484

Apprentice reader, teaching and mentoring of, 88–127

Armbruster, B., 175

Art, reading and, 436

Arthur, S., 232

Artistic value, of book illustrations, 48

Assessment, of reading ability. *See* Reading assessment

Assimilation, 10–11

Athey, I., 183

Au, K., 30

Auditory sensory modality, learning through, 70

Author's intent, 169–170

Barnitz, J., 241

Barrett Taxonomy, of questions, 174

Basal reader approach, to reading, 121–122

Bean, R., 141

Beck, I. L., 218, 219, 266, 271

Becker, W. C., 266

Becoming a Nation of Readers (Anderson, Hiebert, Scott and Wilkinson), 6

Betts, E. A., 329

Betts's criteria, for determining reading levels, 329

Bloom Taxonomy, of questions, 174

Bloom, Benjamin, 480

Bloome, D., 6, 184

Bond, G., 8, 12, 409

Books:
  big, 50–52
  for children. *See* Children's literature
  class, 53–54
  constructing, 52–58
    self-made, 57–58
  formats of, in children's literature, 415–416
  group big, 54–56
  individual small, 56–57
  for reading aloud, 48, 50–52

Books in Print, 302

Bottom-up reading model, 13–14

Bowman, M. A., 217

Bransford, J. D., 11, 16

Brown, A. L., 184, 227, 449, 459

Brown, Margaret Wise, 48, 94

Browning, W., 232

Bruner, J., 36

Buan, C., 360
Burke, C. L., 12, 30, 187, 330, 331, 332, 466
Butterfly, The (Nash), 114–115

Caldecott Medals, 421
California State Department of Education, 410
Calkins, Lucy McCormick, 30, 141, 432
Cambourne, Brian, 145, 146
Card catalog, as study tool, 315
Carey, R. F., 319
Carle, Eric, 48
Carnine, D., 458, 459, 461
Cazden, C., 22
Chall, J., 14, 265, 453, 469
Character, as story element, 384–389
Charts, for reading instruction, 58–64
Child-centered instruction, 38–40
Children, early literacy development in, 20–31
Children, learning patterns of, 36–38
Children, reading aloud to, 47–49, 50–52
Children's Choice Awards, 421
Children's literature:
    language and content of, 415–418
    list of recommended, 423–429
    literary aspects of, 417–418
    resources for locating, 429
    role of, 412–414
    selection of, 419–423
Chomsky, C., 233
Christen, W., 232
Claim-support-conclusion structure, in expository text, 216–217
Clark, D. L., 212
Classroom configuration:
    for kindergarten, 131–134
    for primary grades, 110–113, 131–133, 135
Classroom Questions: What Kinds? (Sanders), 480
Clay, M., 77, 469

Cloze technique, 63
    for reading assessment, 333–334
    for vocabulary instruction, 276–278
Cognitive development, in intermediate-grade students, 163–165
Cohen, D., 430
Cohen, S., 446, 449
Cohesion in English (Halliday and Hasan), 245
Collocate, 272
Combs, W., 237
Commission on Reading, 409
Composition. *See* Writing
Comprehension development:
    in reading, 64–69, 89, 103–106, 165–166
    for reading difficulty students, 456–462
Concepts, integrated approaches to, 41–42
Connotation, 167–168, 278
Consonant, 476
Consonant blend, 476
Consonant digraph, 476
Content themes, 154–155
Context:
    in language learning, 42–43
    for reading, 12
    vocabulary acquisition in, 268, 274–276
Contract, student learning, 337, 339, 340–341
Conversation, early experiences with, 29–30
Cooper, J. David, 141, 412
Copper Sky (Klein, Matteoni, Sucher and Welch), 297
Corduroy (Freeman), 48
Crime and Punishment (Dostoyevsky), 217, 389
Cullinan, B. E., 410, 412
Cultural diversity, in middle school, 364–367, 371
Cultural literacy, 3
Cundick, B., 459
Cunningham, D. J., 212
Cunningham, J., 175, 232
Cunningham, P., 232

Daily schedule:
    for kindergarten, 138–139
    for primary grades, 133, 136–138,
        144
Dale, P., 22, 23
David Copperfield (Dickens), 389
Davis, F. B., 265
Day, J. D., 227
de Bettincourt, L., 446, 449
Decoding, 64, 101–102, 476
Deductive model, of direct reading
        instruction, 96, 101–102, 103
Denotation, 167, 278
Department of Education, U. S., 2
Descriptive study tool, 313
Deshler, D., 465
Developmental characteristics, in
        middle school students,
        360–364
Developmental psycholinguistics, 4,
        21–22
DeVries, T., 414
Dialect study projects, for vocabulary
        acquisition, 284–285
Dictation, in kindergarten, 82–84
Dictionary:
    full ownership, 95, 270, 271–273
    low-range, 95, 270, 283–285
    midrange, 95, 270, 273–283
    as study tool, 313–314
    types of mental, 270. *See also*
        Vocabulary
Direct instruction, 40–41
    inductive model of, 101, 102–103
    modeling in, 40
    five-step model of, 95–97, 271–272
    for reading, 49–76
    teacher and, 40–41
    topic-centered, 272–273
Directed reading-thinking activity
        (DRTA), 229
Doctorow, M., 265
Donlan, D., 218, 219
Donoghue, M. R., 422
Dostoyevsky, Fyodor, 217
Dudley-Marling, C., 447, 455, 462,
        466, 469
Duffy, G., 457
Durkin, D., 430, 457

Durr, W., 141
Dykstra, R., 8, 12, 409, 454

Eaton, M., 452, 455, 467, 468
Educational Leadership, 319, 321
Effective schooling research, 12
Elementary grades:
    reading in, 193–260
    study skills in, 288–316
    vocabulary in, 265–285
Elkind, David, 439
Elley, W. B., 414
Encouraging Early Literacy (Schwartz),
        277
Encyclopedia Britannica, 314
Encyclopedias, as study tools,
        314–315
English as a Second Language (ESL)
        students, reading instruction
        for, 471–472
Environment, language
        development and, 23–24
Epps, D., 444
Etymology, for vocabulary
        acquisition, 284
Evaluation questions, 485–486
Expository text:
    persuasive-argumentative, 239–240
    sentence-combining for, 237–239
    in strategic reading instruction,
        216–217

Farr, R., 319
Fay, L., 234
Feature-analysis evaluation, of
        writing samples, 334–335
Fein, G., 39
Fillion, B., 24
First Grade Studies (Bond and
        Dykstra), 8, 12
Fisher, C., 422
Five Little Pigs, The, 68
Five-step direct-instruction model:
    for reading, 95–97
    for vocabulary acquisition, 271–272
Flashbacks, in plot, 383
Flood, J., 319

Fog index, for reading assessment, 325, 328
Foil, as story character, 386
Foreshadowing, in plot, 383
Frase, L. T., 212
Free reading log, student, 339
Freebody, P., 271
Freeman, Don, 48
Fry graph, for reading assessment, 325, 326–327
Full ownership dictionary, 95, 270
    five-step direct-instruction model for, 271–272
    topic-centered direct-instruction model for, 272–273
Furniture, classroom arrangement of, 131–133, 134–135

Gallagher, J., 473
Garner, R., 7, 184
Genre, in children's literature, 416–417
Gerber, M., 449, 462, 468
Gersten, R., 458, 459
Gettinger, M., 462
Gifted students, reading instruction for, 472–473
Gingerbread Man, The, 70
Glaser, N., 141
Glenn, C., 217, 218
Glossing, in strategic reading instruction, 212–216
Going After Cacciato (O'Brien), 395–407
Goodman, Kenneth, 109, 173, 329n, 331, 432, 453
Goodman, Y., 330, 331, 332
Goodnight Moon (Brown), 48
Gordon, C., 218, 219
"Governing Principles of Effective Literacy Instruction, The," 174
Grammar, story, 29, 217–223
Grammar system, 22
Grapheme, 92, 477
Graphophonemic system, text and, 9–10
Graves, D., 30, 187
Graves, M. F., 212

Green, J., 6, 184
Greenlaw, M. Jean, 141
Grotelueschen, A., 212
Grouping:
    in primary grades, 139–147, 148, 149
    for reading in elementary grades, 342–356
        individualized, 345–348
        large-groups, 347–348, 350, 354–356
        learning centers, 350–353
        small-groups, 346–347, 348, 349, 354–356
    types of, 345–356
Guided reading procedure (BRP), 229–230
Guilford, J. F., 266

Hallahan, D., 448
Halliday, M. A. K., 24, 241, 242, 245
Hansen, C., 467, 468
Hansen, J., 174
Harris, A., 469
Harste, Jerry, 12, 27, 30, 173, 187, 466
Hartoonian, H. M., 304, 305, 306, 307
Hasan, R., 241, 242, 245
Head Start, 413
Hearing Ear Dog (Meyers), 196, 197, 198–208
Hearing impaired students, reading instruction for, 470–471
Hearing, learning through, 70
Herman, P., 265
Herrmann, B., 457, 458
Hershberger, W., 212
Hickman, J., 12
Hiebert, E. H., 6, 409
Higbie, K., 459
High-level thinking skills (HLTS):
    defined, 247
    formal reasoning and, 255–257
    foundation skills for, 247–252
    problem solving and, 252–255
    reading and, 257–260
    vocabulary acquisition and, 268–269

Hoffman, J., 140
Holdaway, D., 12, 28
Holistic evaluation, of writing samples, 334
Horowitz, R., 26, 30
Houghton Mifflin Reading/Language Arts (Cooper), 412
Howell, K., 452
Huck, C. S., 410, 422
Huggins, A. W. F., 266
Humpty Dumpty, 72–74
Hunt, Kellogg, 335
Hunt, L. C., 234

Illiteracy, 2, 432
Independent reading, 113–119
Individualized instruction:
    in elementary grades, 345–346
    for reading difficulty students, 463
Inductive model, of direct reading instruction, 96, 101, 102–103
Inferences, in text passages, 170
Informal reading inventory (IRI):
    full, 329–333
    for reading assessment, 324–333
    simplified, 325, 329
Instruction:
    child-centered, 38–40
    direct. *See* Direct instruction
    in primary grades,
        classroom setting for, 131–150
        grouping for, 139–147, 148, 149
        planning and implementing, 150–159
    in strategic reading, 171–174, 211–224
    literacy and, 41
    models, for reading, 95–97, 228–236, 271–273
    modes of, 70–76
    predictable language for, 70–76
    questions for. *See* Questioning
    readiness for, 35
    strategies for, 466
    for student with reading difficulties, 450–469

Instructional reading, in primary grades, 89–106
Instructive teaching, 40
Instrumental hypothesis, of vocabulary, 267
Integrated independent reading, 118–119
Intellectual development, in middle school students, 360–361
Intermediate grades:
    cognitive development in, 163–165
    reading instruction in, 162–189, 228–236
International Reading Association, 429
Interpretation questions, 482–483
Ira Sleeps Over (Waber), 48
Irony, 168–169
    literary, 169
Itsy Bitsy Spider, 75

Jewell, M., 143
Johannessen, L., 388
Johnson, Dale, 231, 242, 243, 266
Johnson, M. K., 11, 16
Johnson, T., 106, 108, 187
Jolly Postman, The, 436–438
Jones, B. F., 175
Journals, writing of, 119–120

Kahn, E., 388
Kauffman, J., 448
Kindergarten:
    creating instructional environment in, 38–41
    daily schedule for, 138–139
    high-level thinking skills in, 247–252
    historical perspective on, 34
    learning patterns of children in, 36–38
    literacy instruction in, 34–86
Kinesthetic, sense for learning, 70
Klein, M., 4, 20, 22, 24, 27, 30, 95, 165, 166, 180, 187, 253, 254, 296, 297, 311, 312

Knowledge hypothesis, of
    vocabulary, 267
Kraus, R., 66
Kuhn, D., 422

Lamb, G., 311, 312
Langer, J., 230
Language. *See also* Oral language
    concrete versus abstract use of, 26
    functional use of, 22
    grammar system for, 22
    how children learn, 42
    idea-oriented uses of, 24
    predictable, for instruction, 70–76
    social uses of, 24–26
    strategies for learning, 42–47
    systems of, 9–10
Language arts. *See also* Reading;
        Writing
    incorporating across curriculum,
        432–438
    integration of, 150–153, 154, 155
        in intermediate grades, 186–189
Language-experience approach
        (LEA), to reading, 15,
        122–124, 125
Language Experiences in Reading (Van
        Allen and Allen), 123
Language literacy, 4
Language play, for vocabulary
        acquisition, 283–284
Language structures, integrated
        approaches to, 41– 42
Lapp, D., 319
Large-group instruction:
    in elementary grades, 347–348,
        350, 354–356
    of students with reading
        difficulties, 463
Learning centers, for reading
        instruction:
    in elementary grades, 350–353
    in kindergarten, 39
Learning contract, student, 337, 339,
        340–341
Learning strategies, 466
Learning to Read Naturally (Jewell and
        Zintz), 143

Learning to Read: The Great Debate
        (Chall), 14
Lee, D., 122
Lesson plan:
    key features of, 194–196
    for language arts instruction,
        155–159
    for reading instruction, 183
    teacher's edition versus
        self-designed, 196–210
Levin, J. R., 14
Library corner, 117
Likasevich, A., 422
Limited English Proficient (LEP)
        students:
    reading aloud to, 414
    reading instruction for, 471–472
Linguistic context, meaning derived
        from, 168
Linguistics, structural. *See* Structural
        linguistics
Lipsitz, Joan, 360
Literacy:
    cultural, 3
    defined, 2–3
    early development in, 20–31, 35–38
    foundations for, 41–49
    instruction for, 121–127
    in kindergarten, 34–86
    in language, 4
    literature and, 413–414
Literacy through Language (Johnson
        and Louis), 106
Literary irony, 169
Literary themes, 154
Literature:
    -based apprach, to reading,
        124–125
    for children. *See* Children's
        literature
    incorporating across curriculum,
        432–438
Loban, W., 4, 187
Log, student free reading, 339
Lorge, I., 265
Louis, D., 106, 108, 187
Lovitt, T., 447, 452, 455
Low-range dictionary, 95, 270,
        283–285

Lucking, R., 457
Luria, A., 27
Lynch, P., 70
Lyon, M., 462

Magnum, P.I., 380
Make Way for Ducklings (McCloskey), 48
Maker, J., 473
Management-by-objectives (MBO) curriculum system, 14
Mangubhai, F., 414
Manzo, A., 229, 230
Map reading, as study tool, 307–313
Mapping:
    semantic. *See* Semantic mapping
    story. *See* Story mapping
Marks, C., 265
Mason, J., 30
Materials:
    structured, 39
    unstructured, 39
Math, reading and, 435
Matteoni, L., 297
McCaig, G., 38
McCloskey, Robert, 48
McClurg, P., 230
McCracken, Marlene, 120, 123, 187, 235
McCracken, Robert, 120, 123, 187, 235
McGaw, B., 212
McGraw-Hill Reading—Level L: "This We Wish," 198
McGue, M., 444
McKeown, M., 266, 271
Meaning:
    development of, in language, 24–26
    secondary, 168
    strategies for discerning, 466–468
Mellon, J., 237
Memory questions, 481
Metacognitive abilities, developing, 183–186
Metalinguistic awareness, 27
Meyers, Susan, 196, 198–208
Michael, W. B., 266

Michener, D., 430, 431
Middle school:
    learning demands of, 368–370
    reading in, 368, 371–373
    student in,
        attitudes of, 364–367, 371
        developmental characteristics of, 360–364, 370
        prior knowledge of, 364–367, 371
        skills of, 364–367, 371
    teaching novels in, 376–407
Midrange dictionary, 95, 270, 273–274
    cloze technique and, 276–278
    feature analysis techniques and, 280, 282–283
    inferences and, 278–279
    meaning from context and, 274–276
    semantic mapping and, 279–280, 281
Miscues, in reading, 329–332
Modeling:
    in direct instruction, 40
    in strategic reading instruction, 211–224
Moe, A., 265
Moffett, J., 187
Monitoring questions, 174
Moods, in text passages, 170
Morehead, M., 452
Morpheme, 96, 477
Mosenthal, P., 4
Mother Goose, 71, 73
Moyer, S., 447
Music, reading and, 436

Nagy, W., 265
Narrative text, 240–241
    sentence-combining for, 237–239
Nash, Ogden, 422
Nash, P., 114
Nash-Webber, B., 241
Natarella, M., 422
National Assessment of Educational Progress (NAEP), 16, 239, 246
National Council of Teachers of English, 429
Newbery Medals, 421

Newcomer, P., 447
Nicholich, M., 230
Niles, J., 140
Normed standardized tests, 319
Novel(s):
    instructional model for 392–407
    selection of, for whole-group
        study, 391–392
    story grammar in, 378–390
    teaching of, in middle school,
        376–407

O'Brien, Tim, 395, 401, 403, 404,
    405
Observer, as story character, 386
Office of Education, U.S., 2
Ogle, D., 377
O'Hare, F., 237
Olson, T., 360
O'Neill, J., 228
Oral language:
    early development of, 22–24
    functions of, 24–26
O'Shea, D., 455
O'Shea, L., 455
Oxford English Dictionary, 284

Palincsar, A. S., 184, 449, 459
Paraphrase, 167
Parents, involvement of, in
    children's education, 438–439
Paris, S., 184
Patrick, E., 212
Pearson, P. David, 174, 218, 219,
    231, 242, 243, 266, 430
Peck, J., 38
Peer dialogue, in language learning,
    46–47
Peer partners, for primary children,
    141–142
Peer tutoring, of students with
    reading difficulties, 463–465
Perfetti, C., 266
Peterson, Susan, 60, 67
Phoneme:
    defined, 92, 477
    suprasegmental, 478

    unvoiced, 479
    voiced, 479
Phonics, 98–101, 477
Phonogram, 477
Physical development, in middle
    school students, 360
Physical education, reading and, 436
Piaget, Jean, 10, 15–16, 23, 25, 162
Pikulsk, J., 141
Plan book. See Lesson plan
Planned inferential reading lesson
    (PIRL), 232
Plot, as story element, 382–384, 385
Porter, J., 430
Posters, writing and, 121
Predict-test-conclude strategy, for
    reading instruction, 180, 181
Predictable language, for instruction,
    70–76
Predicting, meaning, 466
Prereading plan (PReP), 230
Prescriptive study tool, 313
Preview, read, examine, and prompt
    (PREP) reading instruction
    model, 232–233
Primary grades:
    classroom setting for, 131–150
    grouping for, 139–147, 148, 149
    high-level thinking skills in,
        247–252
    planning and implementing
        instruction in, 150–159
    reading instruction in, 89–119,
        121–127, 140, 143, 150–159,
        228–236
Print:
    developing concepts of, 76–79
    early awareness of, 27–28
Protagonist, 386
Psycholinguistics, developmental.
    See Developmental
    psycholinguistics
Psycholinguistics, reading
    instruction and, 15

Question-answer relationships
    (QARs), 231–232
Question cards, 106

Questioning:
    instructional, 174
    language of, 488–489
    methods of, 226–227
    monitoring, 174
    for reading comprehension, 65–66,
        104–105
    for reading instruction, 174–189
        strategic, 212–216
    reciprocal, 224, 230–231
    self-monitoring checklist for,
        176–180
    taxonomies for, 174, 225–226,
        480–490
        classifying, 486
        for social studies, 486–487
        synopsis of, 480–486
        using, 489–490

Raftery, E. J., 430
Rain, 69, 71
Ronbom, S., 413
Raphael, T. E., 231
Reader:
    apprentice, teaching and
        mentoring of, 88–127
    schemata of, 10–11
Readers' Guide to Periodical Literature,
    302
Readiness program, for instruction,
    35
Reading. *See also* Language arts
    ability in, 165–171
    across curriculum, 433
    aloud,
        to children, 47–49
        to large groups, 50–52
        to LEP students, 414
        to middle school students,
            429–432
        by parents, 438–439
    arguments for, 410
    assessment of. *See* Reading
        assessment
    cloze technique of, 63
    cognitive development and,
        163–165

comprehension in. *See* Reading
    comprehension
defined, 5–7
difficulties with. *See* Reading
    difficulty students
direct instruction for, 49–76
    five-step models of, 95–97
early print awareness and, 27–28
early experiences with, 28–29
in elementary grades, 193–260,
    342–356
errors in, 329n
essential elements of, 162–189
grouping models for, 342–356
high-level thinking skills (HLTS)
    and, 257–260
independent, 113–119
individual practice, 112–113
instruction models for, 228–236
integrated independent, 118–119
in intermediate grades, 162–189
in kindergarten, 35–85
miscues in, 329–332
methods of teaching, 121–127
in middle school, 368, 371–373,
    376–407
oral language and, 24, 30
in primary grades, 89–119,
    121–127, 140, 143, 150–159,
    228–236
process of, 6, 7–9, 12–15
psycholinguistic elements of, 9–12
rate of, as study skill, 292–293
scaffolding for instruction of,
    377–378
in small groups, 140, 142–143, 144,
    147, 148, 149, 456
strategic. *See* Strategic reading
strategies of, 7
student log of, 339
supported practice, 106–113
sustained silent (SSR), 117,
    234–235, 456
writing and, 119–121, 334–337
Reading assessment, 318–342
    cloze procedure for, 333–334
    informal reading inventory (IRI)
        for, 324–333
    portfolio for, 321–342

of reading difficulty students, 452–453
sample reading materials for, 342
student self-assessment for, 337–342
teacher monitoring for, 323–324
test data for, 322–323
trends in, 319–321
writing samples for, 334–337
Reading comprehension, 64–69, 89, 103–106
defined, 165–166
questioning for, 65–66, 104–105
retelling in, 67–68
Reading difficulty students:
active involvement by, 462
characteristics of, 445–450
comprehension of, 456–462
fluency of, 454–456
grouping of, 463–465
instruction of, 450–469
flexible models for, 468–469
learning strategies for, 465–468
practice time for, 462
Reading Is Only the Tiger's Tail (McCracken and McCracken), 123
Reading Systems (Scott Foresman), 14
Reading, Writing, and Language (McCracken and McCracken), 120
Reasoning, formal, 255–257
Reciprocal questioning (ReQuest), 224, 230–231
Reciprocal teaching, 459–460
Recordings for the Blind, 470
Representation, concept of, 37
Retelling, in reading comprehension, 67–68
Reutzel, D. Ray, 219, 221–223
Rhodes, L., 447, 455, 462, 466, 469
Rich, M. D., 14
Richek, M., 241
Ride a Cockhorse to Banbury Cross, 67
"Right to Read" movement, 2
Ringler, L., 451, 469
Rivkin, M., 39
Robinson, R., 233

Roehler, L., 457
Rose, M., 459
Rosenblatt, L., 412, 430
Rosenshine, B. V., 6, 183
Rothkopf, E. Z., 212
Ryan, E., 461, 465

Samuels, S. J., 26, 30
Sanders, Norris, 480
Sanders Taxonomy, of questions, 174
Sapp, M., 38
Scaffolding, for reading instruction, 377–378
Schema(ta), 10–11, 12–13
Schenkat, R., 456, 462
Schewel, R., 460
Schloss, P., 444, 456
Schmelzer, R., 232
Schumaker, J., 465
Schumer, H., 212
Schwa, 477–478
Schwartz, E., 277
Science, reading and, 435–436
Scott, G. P., 465
Scott, J. A., 6, 409
Scott-Foresman, 14
Secondary meanings, 168
Sedlak, R., 444, 456
See How it Grows (Nash), 114
Self-assessment, for reading ability, 337–342
Self-monitoring skills, 184–186, 224–228
Semantic mapping, for vocabulary acquisition, 279–280, 281
Semantic system, text and, 9
Semiliteracy, 432
Sendak, Maurice, 217
Sentence-combining, writing and, 237–239
Setting, as story element, 378–382
Shanahan, T., 140
Short, E., 461–465
Sight word, 90, 91–92
Sight-word vocabulary:
developing, 90–91
teaching, 92–95
Silverstein, Shel, 422

Simultaneous listening and reading (SLR), 233
Singer, H., 218, 219
Sipay, E., 469
Skill Development in the K–6 Social Studies Program (Hartoonian), 304, 305, 306, 307
Skimming, as study skill, 294–295
Sleeter, C., 444
Small groups:
    in elementary grades, 346–347, 348, 349, 354–356
    for primary children, 140, 142–143, 144, 147, 148, 149
    for reading difficulty students, 465
Smith, D., 447
Smith, F., 24, 173, 246
Snowman, J., 212
Social studies:
    question taxonomy for, 486–487
    reading and, 435
Social-emotional development, in middle school students, 361–363
Sociograms, 106
Spache, G. D., 422
Special student populations, reading instruction for, 443–473
Standardized tests, 319–320
Stauffer, Russell, 229
Steig, William, 48
Stein, N., 217, 218
Stereotype, as story character, 385–386
Stevens, K. C., 266
Stories, Songs and Poetry to Teach Reading and Writing (McCracken and McCracken), 123
Story grammar, 29
    character in, 384–389
    key elements of, 218
    in novels, 378–390
    plot in, 382–384, 385
    setting in, 378–382
    in strategic reading instruction, 217–223
    theme in, 389–390

Story mapping, 105–106
    linear-sequenced, 219, 220–221
    Reutzel's use of, 219, 221–223
    uses of, 223
Story problems, 226
Storybox: Hands-on Reading-Writing for Young Children (Peterson), 67
Stotsky, S., 187, 237, 414
Strategic reading, 171–174
    expository text in, 216–217
    glossing in, 212–216
    modeling in, 211–224
    questioning for, 212–216
    story grammar in, 217–223
Strategies, for reading instruction, 175, 180–182
Strickland, D. S., 414
Structural cuing, for reading instruction, 97–98
Structural linguistics, reading and, 13
Structured materials, in kindergarten, 39
Stuart, V., 30
Student free reading log, 339
Student learning contract, 337, 339, 340–341
Study skill(s):
    basic assumptions about, 290
    defined, 289
    in elementary grades, 288–316
    graphics as, 299–302
    important, 291
    mental set and, 291–292
    note-taking as, 295–299
    outlining as, 295–299
    previewing text as, 293–294
    in primary grades, 147–150
    reading rate and, 292–293
    skimming as, 294–295
Study tool(s), 302–303, 315–316
    card catalog as, 315
    charts, tables, and graphs as, 303–306
    defined, 290
    dictionary as, 313–314
    encyclopedias as, 314–315
    maps and globes as, 307–313
    thesaurus as, 314

Sucher, F., 297
Sulsby, E., 26, 30, 140
Summarize-monitor-summarize strategy, for reading instruction, 180, 182
Summarizing, 227–228
Summers, E. G., 422
"Superbaby Syndrome," 439
Supported practice reading, 106–113
Survey, questions, read, question, compute, question (SQRQCQ) mathematical instruction model, 234
Survey, question, read, recite, and review (SQ3R) reading instruction model, 233–234
Sustained silent reading (SSR), 117, 234–235, 456
Swain, M., 24
Syllable, 478
syllable pattern, 478–479
Sylvester and the Magic Pebble (Steig), 48
Symbol, 28, 37
Syntax, 64
    defined, 9, 479
    system of, 9
Synthesis questions, 484–485

T unit (syntactic) analysis, of writing samples, 335–337
Tactile-kinesthetic sense, for learning, 70
Tamor, L., 4
Taylor, D., 28
Taylor, M., 414
Taylor, Wilson, 333
Teacher:
    context of reading and, 12
    dependency on, by reading difficulty students, 449–450
    direct instruction and, 40–41
    importance of, in reading instruction, 7, 8
    interaction with child by, 43–46, 71
    plan book of. *See* Lesson plan
    skills needed by, in reading instruction, 8–9

Teaching, reciprocal, 459–460
Teaching Reading Comprehension (Pearson and Johnson), 243
Teaching Reading Comprehension and Vocabulary: A Handbook for Teachers (Klein), 254
Teale, W., 26, 30, 140
Terman, L. M., 266
Terminal unit. *See* T unit
Test(s):
    reading assessment, data for, 322–323
    standardized, 319–320
Text:
    language systems and, 9–10
    reading models and, 12–13
Text structure:
    cohesion of, 241–246
    sentence-combining and, 237–239
    types of, 239–241
Theme, as story element, 389–390
Thesaurus, as study tool, 314
Think and Write: Book C (Klein, Lamb and Welch), 311
Think and Write: Book D (Klein, Lamb and Welch), 312
Thinking, high-level skills in, 246–260
Thorndike, E. L., 5
Three Bears, The, 69
Three Billy Goats Gruff, The, 68
Thurston, L., 265
Tierney, R., 175
Top-down reading model, 14–15
Topic-centered direct-instruction model, for vocabulary acquisition, 272–273
Tough, J., 24, 25, 37
Translation questions, 481–482

U.S.A. Today, 304
Unstructured materials, in kindergarten, 39

Value judgment, 485
Van Allen, Roach, 122, 123
Very Hungry Caterpillar, The (Carle), 48

Viet Nam War, teaching about, 395–407
Visually impaired students, reading instruction for, 470
Vocabulary. *See also* Dictionary, types of mental
  average size of, 265
  early development of, 23
  instruction of, 266–267, 268
    in elementary grades, 265–285
  integrated approaches to new, 41–42
  sight-word, 13, 90–91, 92–95
Vowel, 479
Vowel digraph, 479
Vowel diphthong, 479
Vygotsky, Lev, 9, 10, 265, 296

Waber, Bernard, 48
Waddell, J., 460
Wagner, B., 187
Walker, C., 388
Walmsley, S., 4
Webbing. *See* Semantic mapping
Weber, C., 451, 469
Welch, K., 297, 311, 312
Where Have You Been? (Brown), 94
Where the Wild Things Are (Sendak), 217
White, R. T., 183
Who Stole the Cookies from the Cookie Jar?, 66
Whole-language approach, to reading, 15, 125–126
Whole Story, The (Cambourne), 145
Whose Mouse Are You? (Kraus), 66
Wiekart, David, 413
Wilkinson, I. A., 6, 409

Willis, D., 470
Wittrock, M. D., 265
Wixson, K., 339
Woodward, V., 30, 187
Word acquisition, 89, 90–103
Word attack, 479
Word history, 284
Words-per-T-unit (WPTU), 335–337
Work habits, teaching of, 147–150
World Book Encyclopedia, 314
Writing. *See also* Language arts
  in daily living, 80–81
  early experiences with, 30–31
  encouraging, 79–85
  instruction of, in kindergarten, 76–85
  as integrative activity, 119
  involving children in, 79
  of journals, 119–120
  from models, 120
  oral language and, 24, 30
  with peer partners, 141–142
  for planning, organizing and recording, 80
  posters and, 121
  print concepts and, 27–28, 76–79
  reading and, 119–121
  for reading difficulty students, 456
  samples of, for reading assessment, 334–337
  sentence-combining for, 237–239

Ysseldyke, J., 444

Ziegler, E. M., 431
Zimmerman, W. S., 266
Zintz, M., 143